To Redraf

—JG

CONTENTS

PREFACE

Welcome to the fourth edition of *Managing Behavior in Organizations*. Its diminutive size (at least relative to traditional, full-featured texts in this field) and paperback format suggest that it is not intended to be an in-depth account of the field of organizational behavior (OB, as it's called). Instead of covering every surface of the field's terrain, this book may be considered a tour of the scientific and practical highlights of OB housed in a succinct package. It gets "right to the point" by focusing on essential concepts and practices that students *really* must know. Fortunately, the thousands of students to whom I have taught this material over the years have done a fine job (albeit sometimes with painful bluntness) of letting me know precisely what is wheat and what is chaff. It was with an eye toward answering their proverbial question, "What's the most important stuff?" that I wrote this book.

For Whom Is This Book Intended?

This book is aimed squarely at readers who have no special background or training in the social sciences. It is designed to be read by students taking their first class in management or organizational behavior. Specifically, these readers include:

- Undergraduate students (in both two-year and four-year colleges)
- MBA students, and those in related masters-level programs
- Practicing managers and executives in corporate training programs

Because this book is a stand-alone guide to the essentials of OB, in previous editions it has been supplemented by additional materials such as cases, exercises, and readings that reflect instructors' particular approach to teaching OB. In fact, rather than attempting to be an all-inclusive package that dictates precisely what and how to teach, this book offers instructors the ultimate in flexibility. Whether an instructor is teaching OB using the case method, an experiential approach, a seminar format, distance learning, or a traditional series of lectures, students must recognize, understand, and appreciate the essentials of OB as a practical and scientific field. Regardless of the mode of delivery (and previous editions have been used in all these ways), it is necessary to understand the basics of the field. And this, in a nutshell, is what this book offers.

A Balanced Approach to Research, Theory and Practice

Many textbooks take a particularly narrow approach to whatever field they are describing. In the field of OB, some texts focus primarily on research and theory whereas others focus primarily on managerial practice. In my opinion, these skewed orientations are misleading and do readers a disservice insofar as they fail to reflect the true nature of the field of OB. By its very nature, OB is a deliberate blend of the scientific and the practical—an applied science in the truest sense. And, this carefully balanced orientation is reflected in this book. Accordingly, I have prepared this book such that readers will come away with a firm understanding of *what* should be done (and what currently is being done) to improve the functioning of organizations and the satisfaction of people who work in them, as well as the research and theory that accounts for *why* these practices are effective.

Although examples of this balanced approach to theory and practice may be found throughout this book, a few illustrations of this approach are in order. Take Chapter 6, on motivation. Here, my treatment of the various classic theories of motivation is framed in terms of the central practical question: How do you motivate employees? The same may be said for Chapter 12 on creativity and culture. Here, readers come away with not only a basic understanding of the concepts of culture and creativity, but also the very practical matter of how to promote a culture in which creativity abounds. Virtually every chapter captures this dual allegiance to theory and practice.

Because OB is a field predicated on sound scientific research, I used the occasion of revising this book as an opportunity to highlight specific examples of the research that OB scholars conduct. This edition of the book now contains many more accounts of OB research than its predecessors did. In each such instance, I describe the question the researchers were attempting to answer, how they went about finding the answer, and what the findings reveal about the question they raised. A graph (the "talking graphics" to which I refer below) highlights and explains the findings in a manner that ties them back to the question of interest. By stripping away all the technical details, my descriptions of contemporary OB research are designed to be not only informative, but interesting as well. These accounts of OB research are designed to give students a good idea of *how* scientists come to understand behavior in organizations. I believe that it is important to describe some scientific studies not only as an end in themselves, but to emphasize the key point that there is a sound scientific basis for the useful advice offered by OB practitioners.

Mission: Keeping Abreast of the Shifting Landscape

Keeping up with the ever-changing world of organizations is a full-time job. I know, because it's mine. As a researcher, consultant, educator, and author, I spend my working hours probing into the world of organizational behavior, which at cocktail parties I have been known to define as the field that explains "what makes people tick" on the job. In the three decades I have studied, taught, and written in this field, my standard cocktail party line has not changed (much to the chagrin of my wife), although the field surely has. Several of the topics we regarded as central while I watched the Watergate hearings have faded into the background as others have gained prominence. Research findings I took for granted when my hair covered my ears like headphones are seen in a new light today, when I consider myself lucky to have hair at all. And, those organizations in which I applied my knowledge while wearing my best double-knit polyester slacks have undergone dramatic transformations—if, unlike those pants, they even still exist. Such core issues as what people do, how and why they do it, and even where they do it, cannot be understood from the lava lamp mentality of the 1970s.

NEW TOPICS COVERED

Importantly, to truly understand the world of organizations today, we must seriously consider changes in organizational theory and practice that were made in only the three years since the previous edition of this book was published. Taken together, sweeping changes in the economy, Internet technology, and the world's new political realities have revolutionized the functioning of organizations and the ways people work within them. Any reasonable effort to characterize the world of OB must reflect these rapid advances. Indeed, keeping abreast of such changes is both the challenge and the joy of writing textbooks in this field. Finding a sufficiently stable terrain about which to write amidst an ever-shifting landscape is my ongoing mission in revising this book. It was with an eye toward chronicling the most current thinking about the state of the field of OB that I prepared this book. As a result, it contains topics that are completely new to this edition as well as material that was presented in different contexts or with different emphases in earlier editions.

These changes are not merely cosmetic, but reflect my objective—to present the most recent knowledge about the field of organizational behavior in a way that describes the field of OB as it is studied and practiced today. Specifically, here are just a few of the topics that are new to the fourth edition of this book:

- Virtual enterprise (Chapter 1)
- Repatriation (Chapter 1)
- Interpersonal and informational justice (Chapter 2)
- Fair process effect (Chapter 2)
- Laws governing ethics (Chapter 2)
- Cognitive moral development (Chapter 2)
- Ethics programs (Chapter 2)
- Virtuous circle (Chapter 2)
- 360° feedback (Chapter 3)
- Team halo effect (Chapter 3)
- Self-monitoring (Chapter 3)

- Acute, chronic, and episodic stressors (Chapter 4)
- Bodily responses to stressors (Chapter 4)
- Steady-state, linear, spiral, and transitory career types (Chapter 4)
- Holland's theory of vocational choice (Chapter 4)
- Unfolding model of voluntary turnover (Chapter 5)
- Electronic meeting systems (Chapter 10)
- Computer-assisted communication (Chapter 10)
- Group decision support systems (Chapter 10)
- Leadership development (Chapter 12)
- Action learning (Chapter 11)
- Exposure to creative coworkers (Chapter 12)
- Competing values framework (Chapter 12)
- Hierarchy, market, clan, and adhocracy organizational cultures (Chapter 12)
- Vertically integrated organizations (Chapter 13)
- Centralization and interactional justice (Chapter 13)
- Online competitive intelligence (Chapter 14)
- Issue selling (Chapter 14)
- Openness to organizational change (Chapter 14)

These additions reflect growing interest in these topics in recent years. They were guided by informal feedback from professors and students using the previous edition of this book, formal feedback by reviewers, as well as my own assessment of what's happening in the field of OB. I resisted the temptation to include the latest fads. To have done otherwise would have triggered a departure from my mission of focusing on the essentials—in addition to dating the book prematurely and diminishing its usefulness for readers. As such, changes in content were made only where warranted.

NEW AND NEWLY ORGANIZED CHAPTERS

Completely new to the fourth edition of this book is a chapter on "Organizational Justice, Ethics, and Corporate Social Responsibility" (Chapter 2). This new chapter summarizes the rapidly growing research and conceptual advances in the field of organizational justice that have dominated the field of OB in recent years. It also highlights the growing concerns about matters of business ethics and corporate social responsibility that have captured headlines in recent years. Integrating these themes in a single chapter highlights their importance in today's organizations.

The book also includes two chapters whose content has been reorganized so as to streamline and/or highlight content more appropriately. One of these is Chapter 3, "Individual Processes: Personality, Emotions, Perception, and Learning." This new combination of topics covers individual processes in organizations more logically and thoroughly than before. Likewise, a new combination of material may be found in Chapter 4, "Coping with Organizational

Life: Stress and Careers." Combining these two important topics into a single chapter now highlights the interconnections between them and has permitted more thorough coverage.

Pedagogical Features

In addition to changes in coverage, I also added and enhanced the pedagogical features in this book. These upgrades have been included with an eye toward making the task of learning OB easier and more effective than ever before.

INTEGRATIVE CASE

Completely new to this book is an integrative case. Entitled, "The *Columbia* Space Shuttle Disaster: Organizational Behavior as a Matter of Life and Death," it illustrates how various OB concepts are applicable in a complex organizational setting and how they are interrelated. To make these connections explicit, appropriate cross-references are included that tie the case material back to the relevant portions of the text. Insofar as the in-chapter examples, of necessity, focus on individual issues, I believe it is important to rely on an integrative case to show how various OB concepts can be used in conjunction with one another. After all, the world is not as highly compartmentalized as the chapter divisions of a textbook tend to suggest.

Looking at the August 2003 report of the *Columbia* Accident Investigation Board, I believe this case illustrates something more—namely, how misapplying or ignoring various OB principles can lead to tragic consequences. Given that many of the causes of the *Columbia* accident are OB-related, I think that pointing these out is a responsible thing to do insofar as what we learn from the past may help to avoid more tragedies in the future.

CHAPTER-OPENING CASE: "MAKING THE CASE FOR . . ."

Unlike most other brief OB texts, this book includes a chapter-opening case that introduces and leads into the material. It is entitled, ***Making the Case for . . .*** , and is designed to do precisely what the name implies—describe a real organizational case that foreshadows and suggests the importance of the material in each chapter. Although such cases are more commonly found in full-featured OB texts than in brief ones, I added them here because they play the vital pedagogical function of establishing the relevance of the topic. And, insofar as the true importance of OB may be found in the insight it provides into real organizational situations, these cases play a critical role in conveying the nature of the field.

In my quest to keep the book as current as possible, the majority of these cases are new to this edition of the book. These reflect a broad range of organizations, such as the ancient soy sauce maker, Kikkoman (Chapter 1), the nonprofit organization Amnesty International UK (Chapter 6), the small high-tech startup Sendo (Chapter 7), and the venerable corporate giants Procter & Gamble (Chapter 14) and Lockheed Martin (Chapter 9). They also profile such key personalities as New York City's former mayor Rudolph Giuliani (Chapter 11), and the late retailing genius Sam Walton (Chapter 8). And, of course, they also cover news events ranging from stories that have rocked the financial world, such as the Enron scandal (Chapter 10), to those that have interested only fans of professional football, such as the instant replay rule (Chapter 2).

HIGHLY DIVERSE COMPANY EXAMPLES

In this book, it is not only the chapter-opening cases, but organizational examples peppered throughout that reflect the varied nature of today's organizations. Some references are made to giant multinational corporations, whereas others chronicle small, entrepreneurial-based businesses. Some of the organizations portrayed are government agencies, some are nonprofits, and still others are for-profit companies in the private sector. And, of course, some examples illustrate the dynamics of today's fast-paced Internet-based businesses (dot-coms, as they are known)—while not forgetting the traditional brick-and-mortar businesses. This diversity in company examples is quite intentional. I want to illustrate that OB principles and practices are relevant to all types of organizations, not just some. And, insofar as students are likely to work at a wide variety of organizations, I think it was important for them to be able to relate to some of the examples, and to learn about the others.

HIGHLIGHTING ORGANIZATIONAL PRACTICES

Two different features in each chapter reflect my commitment to capturing the interplay between the theoretical and the practical sides of OB. First, each chapter contains a special boxed section entitled, ***Winning Practices***. These sections call readers' attention to current organizational practices that illustrate one or more key OB concepts from each chapter. They provide close-up examples of specific ways in which organizations have been using OB principles to improve a wide variety of different aspects of organizational functioning.

Second, within each chapter about a half-dozen special "callouts" also identify examples of real organizational practices illustrating OB concepts in action. Cumulatively, these paint a picture of OB as a field whose principles are highly relevant to managers and leaders in today's organizations.

ENHANCED TABLES AND ILLUSTRATIONS

This book is more richly illustrated and full of descriptive tables than its predecessors—and most other brief books in this field. I have incorporated these features into this edition because I am convinced that material presented in these formats helps many students understand and remember ideas that otherwise get camouflaged in the body of the text. Over the years, my students have always expressed their appreciation for interesting figures and tables, so I have gone out of my way to ensure that the ones in this book are as useful as possible.

Especially noteworthy is the addition of figures using "***talking graphics***" throughout this book. These are graphs summarizing the findings of recent OB research in a manner that highlights the key conclusions to be drawn from them. By reinforcing the points made in both the figure captions and the body of the text itself, these diagrams are a useful tool for helping the findings of OB research "pop out" before the reader, thus greatly facilitating interpretation. Of course, more visually-oriented learners will find these especially beneficial.

RETURN OF POPULAR PEDAGOGICAL FEATURES

Back by popular demand are several of the most popular pedagogical features from the previous edition of this book. These features, found in each chapter, are as follows:

- *Learning Objectives.* At the beginning of each chapter, readers are provided a list of six specific things they should be able to do after reading that chapter. These all begin with action words such as "define," "describe," "identify," and "distinguish." Special notes in the margins point to the places in the text where readers can find material bearing on each of the learning objectives.

- *Three Good Reasons Why You Should Care About* . . . . Understandably, today's busy students may be prone to challenge the relevance of material, asking what value it has to them. Assuming that students are most receptive to learning about topics that have some recognizable benefits to themselves, these sections begin each chapter by indicating precisely why readers should care about the topic at hand.

- *You Be the Consultant.* These brief sections describe a hypothetical organizational problem and then challenge readers to draw on the material to find ways of solving it.

I also have retained in each chapter the two skills-based exercises that were so popular in earlier editions of this book. These are as follows:

- *Self-Assessment Exercise.* These exercises are designed to provide readers insight into key aspects of their own individual attitudes and/or behavior relevant to the material covered.

- *Group Exercise.* These are hands-on experiences requiring the joint efforts of small groups of students to help illustrate thinking about key phenomena described in the text.

These exercises can be an important part of students' learning experiences. They not only expose students to some of the phenomena described in the text on a first-hand basis, but they also stimulate critical thinking about those phenomena. And not unimportantly, they also are fun.

Teaching and Learning Aids

This book is accompanied by a very helpful set of materials to aid both students and instructors. These teaching aids and learning aids were prepared especially for this book.

FOR STUDENTS

Students reading this book will benefit greatly by using several special features.

- *Learning Objectives*: Each chapter includes six specific learning objectives. These are things students should be able to do (e.g., key concepts to recognize and understand) after reading each chapter. Readers should find these useful both *before* studying a chapter, by cluing them to things to look for while reading, and *after* studying a chapter, by providing a checklist of key points covered.

- *Interactive Study Guide*: The book's Companion Website, www.prenhall.com/greenberg, also includes a set of test questions based on the material appearing in each chapter. The questions are of three different types: multiple-choice, true-false, and essay. To make these effective as a study aid, feedback on these tests is provided instantly. Also, to stimulate thinking about each question, helpful "hints" are also a mouse-click away. The *Interactive Study Guide* was prepared by Sharon A. Taylor.

FOR INSTRUCTORS

Available to professors adopting this book is a complete set of instructional aids consisting of the following items:

- *Instructor's Manual with Test Item File (print version)*: Each chapter of the *Instructor's Manual* includes a chapter synopsis, lecture outline, and suggested answers to end-of-chapter questions. The Test Item File provides 25 multiple-choice questions, 25 true-false questions, and 5–7 short answer/essay questions based on the material in each chapter.

- *Prentice Hall Test Manager*: A comprehensive suite of software tools for testing and assessment is included in the *Test Manager* package. To facilitate the process of creating exams, this package includes all the questions from the printed version of the *Test Item File*.

- *PowerPoint Electronic Transparencies*: More than 100 full color slides are available both on CD-rom, and from the password-protected Instructor's section of this book's Web site: www.prenhall.com/greenberg. The slides were prepared by Courtney Hunt at Northern Illinois University.

Instructors requesting any of these materials should contact their local Prentice Hall sales representative.

Acknowledgments

In closing, I wish to acknowledge the many talented and hard-working individuals whose efforts have made this book possible. To begin, I thank my colleagues who have provided valuable suggestions and comments in response to various drafts of this and earlier editions of this book. These include:

- Richard Grover, *University of Southern Maine*
- Jeffrey Miles, *University of the Pacific*

- Michael Buckley, *University of Oklahoma*
- Suzyn Ornstein, *Suffolk University*
- Fabia Fernandes, *Boise State University*
- Pal A. Fadil, *Valdosta University*
- William A. Walker, *University of Houston*
- Henry Moon, *University of Maryland*
- Raymond T. LaManna, *New York Medical College*
- Charles Albano, *Farleigh Dickinson University*
- Leonard Glick, *Northeastern University*

Second, I wish to thank the editorial, production, and marketing teams at Prentice Hall. My editors, Jennifer Glennon and Christine V. Genneken, provided the steadfast support, along with the "gentle reminders," required to bring this book to fruition. Their contributions to shaping the form, tone, and direction of this book were immeasurable. I am indebted as well to Marcela Boos for guiding this book through the production process, copyeditor Donna Mulder, designer Michael Fruhbeis, and Jennifer Welsch at BookMasters, Inc. Their tireless efforts (not to mention their tolerance for my bouts of impatience) transformed my ramblings into the beautiful book you have before you. Shannon Moore and Anke Braun also must be acknowledged for their insightful marketing advice that helped me make key decisions at various stages of this project. Finally, my efforts to acknowledge the dedicated folks at Prentice Hall would not be complete without also thanking Jeff Shelstad. His leadership of the best management and organizational behavior publishing group in the business has been inspirational. I am truly indebted to these kind professionals for lending their talents to this project.

Finally, I wish to acknowledge my many colleagues and students at the Fisher College of Business who somehow always can tell from my demeanor when I am writing a book. I shudder to think what the cues may be, but I thank them for sheltering me from this information. Most notably, I am grateful to my most recent research and teaching assistants, Ed Tomlinson, Kyra Sutton, and Marie-Élène Roberge, for gathering much of the material that helped me prepare this book. And, as always, I wish to thank the family of the late Irving Abramowitz for their generous endowment to The Ohio State University, which provided invaluable support while I was preparing this book.

Jerald Greenberg
Columbus, Ohio

Managing Behavior in Organizations

Chapter **One**

LEARNING OBJECTIVES

After reading this chapter, you will be able to:

1. **DEFINE** organizational behavior (OB).

2. **DESCRIBE** the major characteristics of the field of OB.

3. **DISTINGUISH** between the Theory X and Theory Y philosophies of management.

4. **IDENTIFY** the fundamental assumptions of the field of OB.

5. **DESCRIBE** the historical roots of the field of OB.

6. **CHARACTERIZE** the nature of the field of OB today.

The Field of Organizational Behavior

Making the Case for...
Organizational Behavior

There's No Business Like Shoyu Business

How many companies can you think of that have been in continuous operation since 1630? Pass? Okay, then, how about companies that have manufacturing plants in both urban Tokyo and rural Wisconsin? Not getting any easier? Here's the final hint: It manufactures the world's oldest condiment from fermented soy beans and wheat. Give up? It's Kikkoman—one of Japan's oldest and largest companies known worldwide for its soy sauce (called *shoyu* in Japanese).

Kikkoman soy sauce holds a commanding 50 percent share of the market in North America and 30 percent in Japan for Oriental bottle sauces. To meet worldwide demand (selling in 100 countries around the world), production has increased tenfold in the past 20 years. In 2003 alone, Kikkoman produced and sold over 120 million gallons of the ebony-colored liquid. That's really an enormous quantity when you consider that soy sauce isn't gulped like a soft drink but sprinkled sparingly onto foods to help bring out their natural flavors. Another fact that makes this statistic so impressive is that Kikkoman makes its soy sauce using a method dating back to the seventeenth century, requiring several months of brewing time before it is ready.

Although it relies on traditional, natural ingredients (including a proprietary microorganism to create a culture called *koji*) instead of chemical substitutes used by competitors, Kikkoman is far from ancient in its manufacturing processes. In 2002 its state-of-the-art manufacturing plant in Walworth, Wisconsin, was recognized as one of the few in the world to meet critical environmental management standards that reduce the use of natural resources, increase the use of recycling, and maintain a safe working environment. High tech production is nothing new to Kikkoman. For Kikkoman, advanced technology extends beyond the soy sauce business. The company is regarded as a world leader in genetic engineering, biotechnology, and biochemistry. In fact, using cell-fusion technology, Kikkoman has developed an entirely new species of citrus fruit—hardly what you'd think of from a company pushing 400 years old.

Actually, there are several ways in which Kikkoman is unusual. To begin, its founder is a woman, which is incredibly rare for the 1600s. Also, unlike most Japanese companies, which produce goods that originated in the United States (such as autos and electronic goods), Kikkoman has turned its uniquely Japanese product into a staple found in kitchens around the world. Still, the company adheres to the strongly held Japanese tradition of being loyal to employees, an ideal that most Western companies have abandoned. In fact, Kikkoman's commitment to treating individual workers like family permeates all aspects of the company's operations. Interestingly, it was Kikkoman's adherence to the honored Asian traditions of harmony and loyalty that made it an attractive partner for U.S.-based companies, such as Del Monte, whose products the company distributes throughout Asia. Today, in large part because of such partnerships, Kikkoman is considered one of the key players in the world of international business. As the ancient Japanese saying goes, "A frog in the well does not know the ocean." Clearly, Kikkoman has long left the well and continues to explore many different oceans.

Despite its international reach, Kikkoman is faithful to the countries in which it does business. In the United States, for example, Kikkoman management at the

GOOD REASONS why you should care about...

Organizational Behavior

You should care about organizational behavior because:

1. Understanding the dynamics of behavior in organizations is essential to achieving personal success as a manager, regardless of your area of specialization.

2. Principles of organizational behavior are involved in making people both productive and happy on their jobs.

3. To achieve success in today's rapidly changing environment, organizations must successfully address a wide variety of OB issues.

Wisconsin plant has been a generous contributor to the local community not only in terms of expanding its tax base but also in making contributions to everything from 4-H projects to college scholarships for high school students. The same goes for doing business with local suppliers. Aiding local economies, Kikkoman plants in the United States in California and Wisconsin and in Singapore, Taiwan, the Netherlands, and China procure most of the nonspecialized ingredients (e.g., soy, wheat, salt, and water) and equipment needed to make soy sauce from local sources.

It's safe to say that few organizations have enjoyed Kikkoman's level of success. A key to the company's longevity lies in its special ingredients—not just koji but also people. Clearly, the company's consideration for employees and the community makes Kikkoman more than just another big player in the global arena. Behind it all lies a management team whose members recognize the importance of the human side of work. There can be no organizations without people, of course. So, no matter how sophisticated a company's equipment may be or how healthy its bottom line, people problems can bring an organization down very quickly. By the same token, organizations in which people work happily and effectively can benefit greatly. Hence, it makes sense to realize that the human side of work is critical to the effective functioning—and basic existence—of organizations. It is this people-centered orientation that is taken in the field of *organizational behavior*—the topic of this book.

This chapter will introduce you to the field of organizational behavior—its characteristics, its history, and the tools it uses to learn about the behavior of people in organizations. We will begin by formally defining the field, describing exactly what it is and what it seeks to accomplish. Following this, we will summarize the history of the field of organizational behavior, tracing its roots from its origins to its emergence as a modern science. Finally, we will outline the methods scientists use to learn about the behavior of people in organizations.

What Is Organizational Behavior and Why Does It Matter?

Before going any further, it is necessary for you to understand exactly what we mean by organizational behavior and why it is important to learn about it.

learning
objective

Organizational Behavior: A Definition

As I have been alluding, the field of **organizational behavior** (or, **OB**, as it is commonly called) deals with human behavior in organizations. Formally defined, organizational behavior is the multidisciplinary field that seeks knowledge of behavior in organizational settings by systematically studying individual, group, and organizational processes.[1] This knowledge is used both by scientists interested in understanding human behavior and by practitioners interested in enhancing organizational effectiveness and individual well-being. In this book I will highlight these dual purposes, focusing both on explaining the nature of this scientific knowledge as well as how it has been—or may be—used for practical purposes. This dual focus is fundamental to the field of organizational behavior because it is considered an applied science.

Having formally defined the field of OB, we now are ready to examine more closely some of its core characteristics.

Characteristics of the Field of OB

learning objective

Our definition of OB highlights four central characteristics of the field. First, OB is firmly grounded in the scientific method. Second, OB studies individuals, groups, and organizations. Third, OB is interdisciplinary in nature. And, fourth, OB is used as the basis for enhancing organizational effectiveness and individual well-being. We will now take a closer look at each of these key characteristics of the field.

OB applies the scientific method to practical managerial problems.   Our definition of OB refers to seeking knowledge and to studying behavioral processes. Although it is neither as sophisticated as the study of physics or chemistry nor as mature as these disciplines, the orientation of the field of OB is still scientific in nature. Thus, like other scientific fields, OB seeks to develop a base of knowledge by using an empirical, research-based approach. That is, it is based on systematic observation and measurement of the phenomena of interest.[2] For an overview of some of the research techniques used in the field of organizational behavior, see Table 1.1.

Why is it so important to learn about behavior in organizational settings? To social scientists, learning about human behavior on the job—"what makes people tick" in organizations, so to speak—is valuable for its own sake. After all, scientists are interested in the generation of knowledge—in this case, insight into the effects of organizations on people and the effects of people on organizations. This is not to say, however, that such knowledge has no value outside of scientific circles. Far from it! OB specialists also apply knowledge from scientific studies, putting it to practical use. As they seek to improve organizational functioning and the quality of life of people working in organizations, they rely heavily on knowledge derived from OB research. Thus, there are both scientific and applied sides to the field of OB—facets that not only coexist but that complement each other as well. (Because we have all experienced OB phenomena, it sometimes seems commonsensical, leading us to wonder sometimes why the scientific approach is necessary. However, as you will see in the **Group Exercise** on pages 30–31, our common sense is not always a reliable guide to the complexities of human behavior at work.)

OB focuses on three levels of analysis: Individuals, groups, and organizations.   To best appreciate behavior in organizations, OB specialists cannot focus exclusively on individuals acting alone. After all, in organizational settings people frequently work together in groups and teams. Furthermore, people—alone and in groups—both influence and are influenced by their work environments. Considering this, it should not be surprising to learn that the field of OB focuses on three distinct levels of analysis—individuals, groups, and organizations.

The field of OB recognizes that all three levels of analysis must be considered to fully comprehend the complex dynamics of behavior in organizations. Careful attention to all three levels of analysis is a central theme in modern OB and will be fully

Table 1.1	Research Methods Used in OB: A Summary

The field of OB is based on knowledge derived from scientific research. The major techniques used to conduct this research are summarized here.

Research Method	*Description*	*Comments*
Survey research	Questionnaires are developed and administered to people to measure how they feel about various aspects of themselves, their jobs, and their organizations. Responses to some questionnaires are compared to others, or to actual behaviors, to see how various concepts are interrelated.	This technique is the most popular one used in the field of OB.
Experimental research	Behavior is carefully studied—either in a controlled setting (a lab) or in an actual company (the field)—to see how a particular variable that is systematically varied affects other aspects of behavior.	This technique makes it possible to learn about cause–effect relationships.
Naturalistic observation	A nonempirical technique in which a scientist systematically records various events and behaviors observed in a work setting.	This technique is subject to the biases of the observer.
Case study	A thorough description of a series of events that occurred in a particular organization.	Findings from case studies may not be generalizable to other organizations.

reflected throughout this text. For example, we will be describing how OB specialists are concerned with individual perceptions, attitudes, and motives. We also will be describing how people communicate with each other and coordinate their activities between themselves in work groups. Finally, we will examine organizations as a whole—the way they are structured and operate in their environments and the effects of their operations on the individuals and groups within them.

OB is multidisciplinary in nature.   When you consider the broad range of issues and approaches taken by the field of OB, it is easy to appreciate the fact that the field is multidisciplinary in nature. By this, I mean that it draws on a wide variety of social science disciplines. Rather than studying a topic from only one particular perspective, the field of OB is likely to consider a wide variety of approaches. These range from the highly individual-oriented approach of psychology, through the more group-oriented approach of sociology, to issues in organizational quality studied by management scientists.

For a summary of some of the key fields from which the field of OB draws, see Table 1.2. If, as you read this book, you recognize some particular theory or approach as familiar, chances are good that you already learned something about it in another class. What makes OB so special is that it combines these various orientations together into a single—very broad and very exciting—field.

OB seeks to improve organizational effectiveness and the quality of life at work.   In the early part of the twentieth century, as railroads opened up the western portion of the United States and the nation's population rapidly grew (it doubled from 1880 to 1920!), the demand for manufactured products was great. New manufacturing plants were built, attracting waves of new immigrants in search of a living wage and laborers lured off farms by the employment prospects factory work offered. These men and women found that factories were gigantic, noisy, hot, and highly regimented—in short, brutal places in which to work. Bosses demanded more and more of their employees and treated them like disposable machines, replacing those who quit or who died from accidents with others who waited outside the factory gates.

Clearly, the managers of a century ago held very negative views of employees. They assumed that people were basically lazy and irresponsible, and they treated workers with disrespect. This very negativistic approach, which has been with us for many years, reflects the traditional view of management called the **Theory X** orientation. This philosophy of management assumes that people are basically lazy,

learning
objective

Table 1.2	The Multidisciplinary Roots of OB

Specialists in OB derive knowledge from a wide variety of social science disciplines to create a unique multidisciplinary field. Some of the most important parent disciplines are listed here, along with some of the OB topics to which they are related (and the chapters in this book in which they are discussed).

Discipline	*Relevant OB Topics*
Psychology	Perception and learning (Chapter 3); personality, emotion (Chapter 3), stress (Chapter 4); attitudes (Chapter 5); motivation (Chapter 6); decision making (Chapter 10)
Sociology	Group dynamics (Chapter 9); socialization (Chapter 9); communication (Chapter 8)
Anthropology	Leadership (Chapter 11); organizational culture (Chapter 12)
Political science	Interpersonal conflict (Chapter 7); organizational power (Chapter 11)
Economics	Negotiation (Chapter 7); decision making (Chapter 10); organizational power (Chapter 11)
Management science	Technology (Chapter 13); organizational quality and change (Chapter 14)

dislike work, need direction, and will only work hard when they are pushed into performing.

Today, however, if you asked corporate officials to describe their views of human nature, you'd probably find some more optimistic beliefs. Although some of today's managers still think that people are basically lazy, many others would disagree, arguing that it's not that simple. They would claim that most individuals are just as capable of working hard as they are of "goofing off." If employees are recognized for their efforts (such as by being fairly paid) and are given an opportunity to succeed (such as by being well trained), they may be expected to work very hard without being pushed. Thus, employees may put forth a great deal of effort simply because they want to. Management's job, then, is to create those conditions that make people want to perform as desired.

The approach that assumes that people are not intrinsically lazy but that they are willing to work hard when the right conditions prevail is known as the **Theory Y** orientation. This philosophy assumes that people have a psychological need to work and seek achievement and responsibility. In contrast to the Theory X philosophy of management, which essentially demonstrates distrust for people on the job, the Theory Y approach is strongly associated with improving the quality of people's work lives (for a summary of the differences, see Figure 1.1).

The Theory Y perspective prevails within the field of organizational behavior today. It assumes that people are highly responsive to their work environments and

Figure 1.1   Theory X Versus Theory Y: A Summary

The traditional *Theory X* orientation toward people is far more negativistic than the contemporary *Theory Y* approach, which is widely accepted today. Some of the key differences between these management philosophies are summarized here.

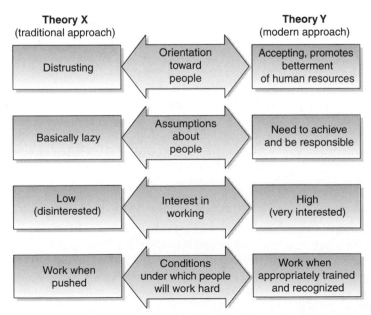

that the ways they are treated will influence the ways they will act. In fact, OB scientists are very interested in learning exactly what conditions will lead people to behave most positively—that is, what makes work both productive for organizations and enjoyable for the people working in them. (Do your own assumptions about people at work more closely match a Theory X or Theory Y perspective? To find out, complete the **Self-Assessment Exercise** on pages 28–29.)

After reading this section, you may find yourself wondering about productivity and profitability. After all, the primary reason why businesses exist is to make a profit. What does all this talk about people have to do with the bottom line? The answer is simple. Yes, OB is concerned about the profit of organizations. In fact, making organizations more profitable is one of the field's key objectives. However, the way it goes about doing this is different than in other areas of business. OB doesn't deal with the design of machines used in manufacturing; it doesn't address a company's accounting and marketing procedures; and it has nothing to say about the pricing strategies that help sell products and services. Instead, OB seeks to make organizations more profitable by addressing the treatment of people and the way work is done. As you read this book, you will see exactly how vital this mission is and how the field goes about meeting it.

Why Does OB Matter?

Rather than keep you in suspense, however, I will give you a preview of things to come by showing you the importance of just a few of the ways in which the field of OB matters to people and companies. With this in mind, I pose a question that asks you to draw on your personal experiences: Have you ever had a job where people didn't get along, nobody knew what to do, everyone goofed off, and your boss was—well, putting it politely—unpleasant? I can't imagine that you liked working in that company at all. Now, think of another position in which everyone was friendly, knowledgeable, hardworking, and pleasant. Obviously, that's more to your liking. In such a situation you are likely to be interested in going to work, doing your best, and taking pride in what you do. At the heart of these differences are all issues that are of great concern to OB scientists and practitioners—and, as a result, they are the ones that will be covered in this book.

"Okay," you may be asking, "in some companies things are nice and smooth, but in others, relationships are rocky—does it really matter?" As you will see throughout this book, the answer is a resounding *yes*! For now, here are just a few highlights of specific ways in which OB matters to people and the organizations in which they work.

- Companies whose managers accurately appraise the work of their subordinates enjoy lower costs and higher productivity than those that handle their appraisals less accurately.[3]
- People who are satisfied with the way they are treated on the job are generally more pleasant to their coworkers and bosses and are less likely to quit than those who are dissatisfied with the way others treat them.[4]
- People who are carefully trained to work together in teams tend to be happier and more productive than those who are simply thrown together without any definite organizational support.[5]

- Employees who believe they have been treated unfairly on the job are more likely to steal from their employers and to reject the policies of their organizations than those who believe they have been fairly treated.[6]

- People who are mistreated by their supervisors on the job experience more mental and physical illnesses than those who are treated with kindness, dignity, and respect.[7]

- Organizations that treat employees well with respect to pay and benefits, opportunities, job security, friendliness, fairness, and pride in company are, on average, twice as profitable as the Standard & Poor's 500 companies.[8]

- Companies that offer good employee benefits and that have friendly conditions are more profitable than those that are less people oriented.[9]

By now, you might be asking yourself: Why, if OB is so important, is there no one person in charge of it an organization? After all, companies tend to have officials who are responsible for other basic areas such as finance, accounting, marketing, and production. Why not OB? If you've never heard of a vice president of OB or a manager of organizational behavior, it's because organizations do not have any such formal posts. So then, back to the question: Who is responsible for organizational behavior? In a sense, the answer is everyone! Although OB is a separate area of study, it cuts across all areas of organizational functioning. Managers in all departments have to know how to motivate their employees, how to keep people satisfied with their jobs, how to communicate fairly, how to make teams function effectively, and how to design jobs most effectively. In short, dealing with people at work is everybody's responsibility on the job. So, no matter what job you do in a company, knowing something about OB is sure to help you do it better. This is precisely why it's vitally important for you to know the material in this book.

4
learning
objective

What Are the Field's Fundamental Assumptions?

All fields are guided by a set of basic assumptions, and OB is no exception. I am referring to the fundamental ideas that are widely accepted by everyone who does scientific research on OB or who puts into practice the things we learn from those studies. For you to get the most out of this book, it is essential for you to understand the two central tenets of the field of OB that I now will describe.

OB Recognizes the Dynamic Nature of Organizations

Thus far, our characterization of the field of OB has focused more on behavior than on organizations. Nonetheless, it is important to point out that both OB scientists and practitioners do pay a great deal of attention to the nature of organizations themselves. Under what conditions will organizations change? How are organizations structured? How do organizations interact with their environments? Questions such as these are of major interest to specialists in OB. But, before we can consider them (as we will do in Chapters 13 and 14), we must first clarify exactly what we mean by an organization.

Formally, we define an **organization** as a structured social system consisting of groups and individuals working together to meet some agreed-upon objectives. In other words, organizations consist of structured social units, such as individuals and/or work groups, who strive to attain a common goal. Typically, we think of making a profit as the primary goal of an organization—and indeed, for most business organizations, it is. However, different organizations may be guided by different goals. For example, charitable organizations may focus on the objective of helping people in need, political parties may be interested in electing candidates with certain ideas, and religious organizations may strive to save souls. Regardless of the specific goals sought, the structured social units working together toward them may be considered organizations.

In studying organizations, OB scientists recognize that organizations are not static but are actually dynamic and ever-changing entities. In other words, they recognize that organizations are **open systems**—that is, self-sustaining systems that use energy to transform resources from the environment (such as raw materials) into some form of output (e.g., a finished product).[10] Figure 1.2 summarizes some of the key properties of open systems.

As this diagram makes clear, organizations receive input from their environments and continuously transform it into output. This output gets transformed back to input, and the cyclical operation continues. Consider, for example, how organizations may tap the human resources of the community by hiring and training people to do jobs. These individuals may work to provide a product in exchange for wages.

Figure 1.2   Organizations as Open Systems

The *open systems* approach is characteristic of modern-day thinking in the field of OB. It assumes that organizations are self-sustaining—that is, that they transform inputs to outputs in a continuous fashion.

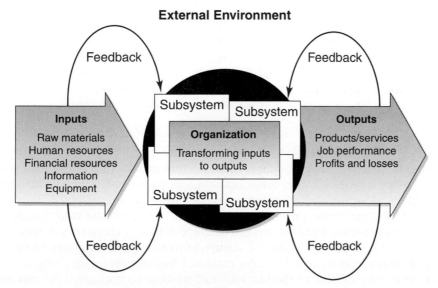

(Source: Based on suggestions by Katz and Kahn, 1978; see Note 10.)

They then spend these wages, putting money back into the community and allowing more people to afford the company's products. This, in turn, creates the need for still more employees, and so on. If you think about it this way, it's easy to realize that organizations are dynamic and constantly changing.

The dynamic nature of organizations can be likened to the operations of the human body. As people breathe, they take in oxygen and transform it into carbon dioxide. This, in turn, sustains the life of green plants that emit oxygen for people to breathe. The continuous nature of the open system characterizes not only human life but the existence of organizations as well.

OB Assumes There Is No "One Best" Approach

What's the most effective way to motivate people? What style of leadership works best? Should groups of individuals be used to make important organizational decisions? Although these questions are quite reasonable, there is a basic problem with all of them. Namely, they all assume that there is a simple, unitary answer—that is, one best way to motivate, to lead, and to make decisions.

Specialists in the field of OB today agree that there is no one best approach when it comes to such complex phenomena. To assume otherwise is not only overly simplistic and naive but, as you will see, also grossly inaccurate. When it comes to studying human behavior in organizations, there are no simple answers. Instead, OB scholars embrace a **contingency approach**—an orientation that recognizes that behavior in work settings is the complex result of many interacting forces. This orientation is a hallmark of modern OB. Consider, for example, how an individual's personal characteristics (e.g., personal attitudes and beliefs) in conjunction with situational factors (e.g., an organization's climate, relations between coworkers) may all work together when it comes to influencing how a particular individual is likely to behave on the job.

Explaining OB phenomena often requires saying, "it depends." As our knowledge of work-related behavior becomes increasingly complex, it is difficult to give "straight answers." Rather, it is usually necessary to say that people will do certain things "under some conditions" or "when all other factors are equal." Such phrases provide a clear indication that the contingency approach is being used. In other words, a certain behavior occurs "contingent upon" the existence of certain conditions.

OB Responds to Advances in Technology

Since the industrial revolution, people had performed carefully prescribed sets of tasks—known as *jobs*—within large networks of people who answered to those above them—hierarchical arrangements known as *organizations*. This picture, although highly simplistic, does a good job of characterizing the working arrangements that most people had during much of the twentieth century. However, today, in the twenty-first century, the essential nature of jobs and organizations as we have known them is changing, and the major catalyst is rapidly advancing computer technology, especially the use of the Internet and wireless technology.[11] As you might imagine, this state of affairs has important implications for organizations—and, hence, the field of OB.

After all, as more work is shifted to digital brains, some work that was once performed by human brains becomes obsolete. At the same time, new opportunities arise as people scurry to find their footing amidst the shifting terrain of the high-tech revolution. The implications of this for OB are considerable. We will now consider some of the most prominent trends in the world of work that have been identified in recent years. These involve how work is organized and performed, as well as the need for flexibility.

Leaner organizations: Downsizing and outsourcing.   Technology has made it possible for fewer people to do more work than ever before. **Automation**, the process of replacing people with machines, is not new, of course; it has gone on, slowly and steadily, for centuries. Unlike the gradual process of automation, advances in information technology are occurring so rapidly today that the very nature of work is changing as fast as we can keep up. With this, many jobs are disappearing, leaving organizations (at least the most successful ones!) smaller than before.[12] Product manufacturing also has been informated. At GE's Faunc Automation plant in Charlottesville, Virginia, for example, circuitboards are now manufactured by half as many employees as required before informating the facility.[13] But it is not only blue-collar, manual-labor jobs that are eliminated but white-collar, mental-labor jobs as well. In many places, middle managers are no longer needed to make decisions that can now be made by computers. It's little wonder that middle managers, while only 10 percent of the workforce, comprise 20 percent of recent layoffs.

Indeed, organizations have been rapidly reducing the number of employees needed to operate effectively—a process known as **downsizing**.[14] Typically, this involves more than just laying off people in a move to save money. It is directed at adjusting the number of employees needed to work in newly designed organizations and is, therefore, also known as **rightsizing**.[15] Whatever you call it, the bottom line is clear: Many organizations need fewer people to operate today than in the past—sometimes far fewer. The statistics tell a sobering tale. From January 1997 through December 1999, 3.3 million American workers found their jobs eliminated.[16] Since 2000, the most job losses have occurred in Internet-based ("dot-com") companies, retail stores, the auto industry, and the media (e.g., publishing and advertising). Downsizings are not a unique manifestation of current economic trends. During the past decade, some degree of downsizing has occurred in about half of all companies—especially in the middle management and supervisory ranks (to see who's most likely and least likely to get laid off, see Table 1.3).[17] Experts agree that rapid changes in technology have been largely responsible for much of this.

Another way organizations are restructuring is by completely eliminating those departments that focus on noncore sectors of the business (i.e., tasks that are peripheral to the organization) and hiring outside firms to perform these functions instead—a practice known as **outsourcing**.[18] By outsourcing secondary activities an organization can focus on what it does best, its key capability—what is known as its **core competency**. Companies like ServiceMaster, which provides janitorial services, and ADP, which provides payroll processing services, make it possible for their client organizations to concentrate on the business functions most central to their

Table 1.3	Are You Likely to Become a Victim of Downsizing?

Based on prevailing patterns of downsizing, some people are more vulnerable to getting laid off, whereas others are generally safer. Here are some rough guidelines for assessing your own vulnerability to downsizing.

You Are Vulnerable to Getting Laid Off if . . .	*You Are More Immune from Layoffs if . . .*
You are paid over $150,000.	You have a good relationship with your boss.
You are inflexible and unwilling to transfer to a new job or to another city.	You have a midrange salary.
	You generate revenue for the company.
You work in retail, automotive, or manufacturing businesses.	You have expertise in a technical field.
You are a top executive of a division that is not performing up to expectations.	You have demonstrated willingness to work long hours whenever necessary.
You lack computer skills.	You are willing to relocate to another city or to transfer to another position in the company.
You do not have good leadership skills.	

(Source: Based on suggestions by McGinn & Naughton, 2001; see Note 17.)

missions. So, for example, by outsourcing its maintenance work or its payroll processing, a manufacturing company may grow smaller and focus its resources on what it does best—manufacturing.

Some critics fear that outsourcing represents a "hollowing out" of companies—a reduction of functions that weakens organizations by making them more dependent on others.[19] Others counter that outsourcing makes sense when the work that is outsourced is not highly critical to competitive success (e.g., janitorial services) or when it is so highly critical that it only can succeed by seeking outside assistance.[20] For example, it is widespread practice for companies selling personal computers today to outsource the manufacturing of various components (e.g., hard drives, CD-ROMs, and chips) to other companies.[21] Although this practice may sound atypical compared to what occurs in most manufacturing companies, it isn't. In fact, one industry analyst has estimated that 30 percent of the largest American industrial firms outsource over half their manufacturing.[22]

The virtual corporation: A network of temporary organizations.   As more companies are outsourcing various organizational functions and are paring down to their core competencies, they might not be able to perform all the tasks required to complete a project. However, they can certainly perform their own highly specialized part of it very well. Now, if you put together several organizations whose competencies complement each other and have them work together on a special project, you'd have a very strong group of collaborators. This is the idea behind an organizational arrangement that is growing in popularity—the **virtual corporation**. A virtual corporation is a highly flexible, temporary organization formed by a group of companies that join forces to exploit a specific opportunity.[23]

For example, various companies often come together to work on special projects in the entertainment industry (e.g., to produce a motion picture) and in the field of construction (e.g., to build a shopping center). After all, technologies are changing so rapidly and skills are becoming so specialized these days that no one company can do everything by itself. And so, firms join forces temporarily to form virtual corporations—not permanent organizations, but temporary ones without their own offices or organization charts. Although virtual corporations are not yet common, experts expect them to grow in popularity in the years ahead.[24] As one consultant put it, "It's not just a good idea; it's inevitable."[25]

Telecommuting: Going to work without leaving home.   In recent years, the practice of **telecommuting** (also known as **teleworking**) has been growing in popularity. This is the practice of using communications technology to enable work to be performed from remote locations, such as the home. Telecommuting—which is used at such companies as JCPenney and Pacific Bell—makes it possible for employees to avoid the hassle of daily commuting.[26] It also allows companies to comply with governmental regulations (e.g., the Federal Clean Air Act of 1990) requiring them to reduce the number of trips made by their employees.

Statistics indicate that telecommuting is in full swing today. In fact, as of 2001, 28.8 million American workers (one in five) engaged in some form of telework, representing a 17 percent increase from 2000. Not surprisingly, according to an official of the International Teleworkers Association and Council, "Telework has evolved beyond the pioneering telecommuters of the '80s" and "it appears to be entering the mainstream of today's workforce."[27]

The typical telecommuter works at least one full day away from the traditional office—most work from the road or from home, with smaller numbers working at special telework centers (offices in different locations that teleworkers from different companies can rent as needed) or satellite offices (small facilities operated by the company for use by its own employees). Most teleworkers use some combination of these facilities. Most teleworkers are employees of very small companies (that cannot afford permanent facilities) or very large companies (that easily can afford having some employees work off-site).

Given its technological advantage, it's probably not too surprising that IBM has been one of the first companies to use telecommuting. Although IBM's Midwest division is headquartered in Chicago, few of its 4,000 employees (including salespeople and customer service technicians) show up more than once or twice a week. Instead, they have "gone mobile," using the company's ThinkPad computers, fax-modems, e-mail, and cellular phones to do their work from remote locations. In just a few years, the company has slashed its real estate space by 55 percent, cut the number of fixed computer terminals required, and does a better job of satisfying its customers' needs. And, at the same time, telecommuting has done well for IBM employees themselves: 83 percent report not wanting to return to a traditional office environment.

Reports from companies such as Great Plains Software, Traveler's Insurance Co., US West Communications, and the NPD Group have all reported similar benefits with respect to savings in office expenses, gains in productivity, and satisfaction among employees.[28] Most telecommuters like the arrangement, reporting that it

Figure 1.3 Adapting to Telecommuting

Jobs in which people engage in telecommuting often have to be adjusted in one way or another. Here are some of the major considerations.

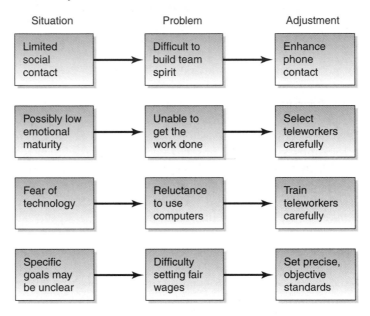

gives them the kind of flexibility they need to balance work and family matters. Not surprisingly, the vast majority of telecommuters are highly committed to their employers and plan on staying at their companies.

Despite these benefits, as you might imagine, telecommuting is not for everyone; it also has its limitations.[29] It works best on jobs that require concentration, have well-defined beginning and end points, are easily portable, call for minimal amounts of special equipment, and can be done with little supervision.[30] Fortunately, at least some aspects of most sales and professional jobs meet these standards. Even so, making telecommuting work requires careful adjustments in the way work is done. For a closer look at these considerations, see Figure 1.3.

OB Takes a Global Perspective

To fully understand behavior in organizations we must appreciate the fact that today's organizations operate within an economic system that is truly international in scope.[31] The nations of the world are not isolated from one another economically; what happens in one country affects other countries. For example, when terrorists struck the United States on September 11, 2001, it sent ripples throughout the economic markets of the world for many months. This tendency for the world's countries to be influenced by one another is known as **globalization**—the process of

Figure 1.4   Adjusting to Foreign Culture: The General Stages

People's adjustment to new cultures generally follows the U-shaped curve illustrated here. After an initial period of excitement, *culture shock* often sets in. Then, after this period of adjustment (about six months), the more time spent in the new culture, the better it is accepted.

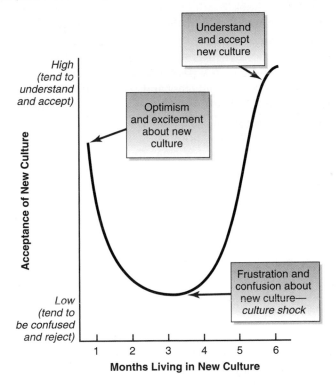

interconnecting the world's people with respect to the cultural, economic, political, technological, and environmental aspects of their lives.[32]

While working abroad, people are exposed to different **cultures**—the set of values, customs, and beliefs that people have in common with other members of a social unit (e.g., a nation).[33] And, when people are faced with new cultures, it is not unusual for them to become confused and disoriented—a phenomenon known as **culture shock**.[34] People also experience culture shock when they return to their native culture after spending time away from it—a process of readjustment known as **repatriation**. In general, the phenomenon of culture shock results from people's recognition of the fact that others may be different from them in ways that they had never imagined, and this takes some getting used to.

Scientists have observed that the process of adjusting to a foreign culture generally follows a U-shaped curve (see Figure 1.4).[35] That is, at first, people are optimistic and excited about learning a new culture. This usually lasts about a month or so. Then, for the next several months, they become frustrated and confused as they struggle to learn the new culture (i.e., culture shock occurs). Finally, after about six months, people adjust to their new culture and become more accepting of it and satisfied with it. These observations imply that feelings of culture shock are inevitable. Although some degree of frustration may be expected when you first enter a new country, the more time you spend learning its ways, the better you will come to understand and accept it.[36]

In general, culture shock results from the tendency for people to be highly *parochial* in their assumptions about others, taking a narrow view of the world by believing that there is one best way of doing things. They also tend to be highly *ethnocentric*, believing that their way of doing things is the best way. For example, many Americans tend to be highly parochial by speaking only English (whereas most Europeans speak several languages) and ethnocentric by believing that everyone else in the world should learn their language. Such narrow and biased views about the management of people in organizations may severely limit our understanding about behavior in organizations.

With today's global economy, it is clear that an American-oriented approach may be highly misleading when it comes to understanding the practices that work best in various countries. In fact, there may be many possible ways to manage effectively, and these will depend greatly on the individual culture in which people live. Thus, understanding the behavior of people at work requires carefully appreciating the cultural context within which they operate. For example, whereas American cultural norms suggest that it would not be inappropriate for an employee to question his or her superior, it would be taboo for a worker in Japan to do the same thing. Thus, today's organizational scholars are becoming increasingly sensitive to the ways in which culture influences organizational behavior.

OB Embraces the Trend Toward Diversity

A broad range of people from both sexes, different races, ethnic groups, nationalities, and ages can be found throughout U.S. organizations, and as summarized in Figure 1.5, their proportions have been changing.[37] Modern organizations have taken steps to accommodate—and capitalize on—growing levels of diversity within the workforce. This trend takes several forms, all of which have important implications for the field of OB.

More women are in the workforce than ever before.   In the 1950s, the "typical American family" was characterized by a man who went to work and his wife who stayed at home and watched the children. Although this profile still may be found, it is far from typical. In fact, over half of all women are employed outside the home, and just under half of all people in the workplace (46.2 percent) are women—and these figures have continued to rise steadily over the years.[38] This trend stems from not only economic necessity but also from the growing social acceptance of women working outside the home. As women, who traditionally have worked inside the home, have moved to working outside the home, companies have found it beneficial—or even necessary, in some cases—to make accommodations that help make this possible. (For a look at some of the most popular practices in this regard, see the accompanying **Winning Practices** section.)

Winning **Practices**

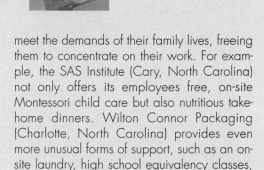

Employee Support Policies

With increasing frequency, companies are taking proactive steps to help employees meet their personal needs and family obligations. In so doing, they make it possible for employees to satisfy the demands imposed by their nonwork lives. And this allows companies to draw on the talents of a diverse group of prospective employees who otherwise might not be able to lend their talents to the organization. Three practices have proven especially useful in this regard.

- **Child-care facilities.** These are sites at or near company locations where parents can leave their children while they are working. America West, for example, believes so strongly in the importance of providing child care that it offers these services 24 hours a day. The company even maintained these benefits while it was going through bankruptcy proceedings in 1991.[39]

- **Elder-care facilities.** Just as companies are making facilities available to employees for taking care of their children, they are, with increasing frequency, making facilities available for the care of their elderly relatives, such as parents and grandparents.[40] For example, Lancaster Laboratories (in Lancaster, Pennsylvania) provides a place where its employees can bring adult family members who are in need of care during working hours.[41] The *St. Petersburg Times* advises its employees about ways to help meet the problems of elderly family members.[42] Such practices are designed in large part to help avoid some of the challenges confronted by multigenerational families—that is, those in which children live together with their parents and grandparents. As such arrangements become increasingly commonplace in the next few decades, we can expect elder-care facilities to grow in popularity.

- **Personal support policies.** These are widely varied practices that help employees

meet the demands of their family lives, freeing them to concentrate on their work. For example, the SAS Institute (Cary, North Carolina) not only offers its employees free, on-site Montessori child care but also nutritious take-home dinners. Wilton Connor Packaging (Charlotte, North Carolina) provides even more unusual forms of support, such as an on-site laundry, high school equivalency classes, door-to-door transportation, and a children's clothing swap center.[43]

Although these practices may be expensive, the organizations that use them generally are convinced that they are in several respects wise investments. First, they help retain highly valued employees—not only keeping them from competitors but also saving the costs of having to replace them. In fact, officials at AT&T found that the average cost of letting new parents take up to a year of unpaid parental leave was only 32 percent of an employee's annual salary, compared with the 150 percent cost of replacing that person permanently.[44]

Second, by alleviating the distractions of having to worry about nonwork issues, employees are freed to concentrate on their jobs and to be their most creative. Research has found that people who use the support systems their employers provide are not only more active in team problem-solving activities but also are almost twice as likely to submit useful suggestions for improvement. Commenting on such findings, Ellen Galinsky, copresident of the Families & Work Institute, said, "There's a cost to *not* providing work and family assistance."[45] A third benefit—and an important one at that—is that such policies help attract the most qualified human resources, giving companies that use them a competitive edge over those that do not.[46]

Figure 1.5   Women and Minorities in the Workplace: Their Numbers Are Rising

Statistics have shown that the relative percentage of white non-Hispanics in the U.S. workforce, although currently highest, is dropping. However, the relative percentage of women, African Americans, Hispanics, and Asians is rising. As this trend continues, the term *minority* group will lose its meaning.

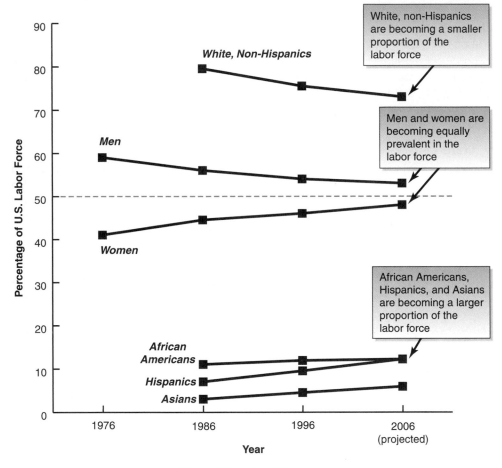

(Source: Based on data reported by Lerman and Schmidt, 2002; see Note 37.)

Racial and ethnic diversity is reality.   Just as yesterday's workers were primarily males, they also were primarily white. However, just as growing numbers of women have made men less of a majority, so too has an influx of people from different racial and ethnic groups made white people a smaller majority. Specifically, although white non-Hispanic workers are currently the dominant group, their proportion dropped from 79.8 percent in 1986 to 75.3 percent in 1996, and is expected to drop still further to 72.7 percent by 2006.[47] At the same time, there will be increases in the numbers of African Americans, Hispanics, and Asians in the workforce (see Figure 1.5)—in large part due to liberal immigration policies. Beginning in 1990, members of minority groups entered the workforce at a greater rate than the majority, thereby making them even more prevalent. In fact, it is estimated that by 2050, racial and ethnic minorities will comprise 47 percent of the U.S. population, making obsolete the current term *minority*.[48]

People are living—and working—longer than ever before.   In the years after World War II the peacetime economy flourished in the United States. With it, came a large increase in population as soldiers returned from war and began families. The generation of children born during this period is widely referred to as the **baby boom generation**. Today, the first of these baby boomers are turning 55 and are considered "older workers" by labor economists. And, only a few years from now, the number of older people in the workplace will swell dramatically. Living in a period in which retirement is no longer automatic at age 65, aged baby boomers will comprise a growing part of the population in the years to come. In fact, people over 85 years old are already the fastest-growing segment of the U.S. population.[49] Clearly, this trend has profound implications on the traditional patterns of work and retirement that have developed over the years.

Implications for OB.   That more women, people of color, and older workers are in the workforce than ever before is not merely an idle sociological curiosity. It also has important implications for OB—ones that we will examine more closely in this book. After all, the more people differ from each other, the more challenges they are likely to face when interacting with one another. How these interactions play out is likely to be seen on the job in important ways. For example, as we will describe, differences in age, gender, and ethnic group membership are likely to bring with them differences in communication style that must be addressed for organizations to function effectively (see Chapter 8). It also is the case that people at different stages of their lives are likely to be motivated by different things (see Chapter 6) and to be satisfied with different aspects of their jobs (see Chapter 5). And, as workers adjust to a wider variety of people in the workplace, issues about their norms and values (see Chapter 9) are likely to come up, as well as their willingness to accept others who are different from themselves (see Chapter 5). This can have important implications for potential stress and conflict in the workplace (see Chapters 4 and 7) and their career choices (see Chapter 4), which may be expected to influence their capacity to work effectively as members of the same work teams (see Chapter 9).

OB Then and Now: A Capsule History of the Field

5
learning
objective

The importance of understanding the behavior of people at work has not always been as recognized as it is today. In fact, it was not until the early part of the twentieth century that the idea first developed, and it was only during the last few decades that it gained widespread acceptance. Now, in the twenty-first century, it is clear that the field has blossomed and matured. So that we can appreciate how the field of OB got to where it is today, we will now briefly outline its history and describe some of the most influential forces in its development.

Scientific Management: The Roots of Organizational Behavior

The earliest attempts to study behavior in organizations came out of a desire by industrial efficiency experts to improve worker productivity. Their central question was straightforward: What could be done to get people do more work in less time? It's not particularly surprising that attempts to answer this question were made at the turn of the twentieth century. After all, this was a period of rapid industrialization and technological change in the United States. As engineers attempted to make machines more efficient, it was a natural extension of their efforts to work on the human side of the equation—making people more productive too. Given this history, it should not be too surprising that the earliest people we now credit for their contributions to OB were actually industrial engineers.

Frederick Winslow Taylor worked most of his life in steel mills, starting as a laborer and working his way up to the position of chief engineer. In the 1880s, while a foreman at Philadelphia's Midvale Steel Company, Taylor became aware of some of the inefficient practices of the employees.[50] Noticing, for example, that laborers wasted movements when shifting pig iron, Taylor studied the individual components of this task and identified a set of the most efficient motions needed to perform it. A few years later, while at Pittsburgh's Bethlehem Steel, Taylor similarly redesigned the job of loading and unloading railcars so these tasks too could be done as efficiently as possible. On the heels of these experiences, Taylor published his groundbreaking book, *Scientific Management*. In this work, he argued that the objective of management is "to secure the maximum prosperity for the employer, coupled with the maximum prosperity of each employee."[51]

Beyond identifying ways in which manual-labor jobs can be performed more efficiently, Taylor's **scientific management** approach was unique in its focus on the role of employees as individuals. Specifically, this approach emphasizes the importance of designing jobs as efficiently as possible. Taylor advocated two ideas that hardly seem special today but were quite new at the beginning of the twentieth century. First, he recommended that employees be carefully selected and trained to perform their jobs. Second, he believed that increasing workers' wages would raise their motivation and make them more productive. Although this idea is unsophisticated by today's standards—and not completely accurate (as we will see in Chapter 6)—Taylor may be credited with recognizing the important role of motivation in job performance.

It was contributions such as these that stimulated further study of behavior in organizations and created an intellectual climate that eventually paved the way for the development of the field of OB. Acknowledging these contributions, management theorist Peter Drucker has described Taylor as "the first man in history who did not take work for granted, but who looked at it and studied it."[52]

The publication of *Scientific Management* stimulated several other scientists to pick up on and expand Taylor's ideas. Among the most strongly influenced were the industrial psychologists Frank and Lillian Gilbreth. This husband-and-wife team pioneered an approach known as **time-and-motion study**, a type of applied research designed to classify and streamline the individual movements needed to perform jobs with the intent of finding "the one best way" to perform them. Although this approach appears to be highly mechanical and dehumanizing, the Gilbreths, parents of 12 children, practiced "Taylorism" with a human face in their personal lives. (If this sounds at all familiar, it may be because you recall the classic film *Cheaper by the Dozen*, which tells the story of how the Gilbreths applied the principles of scientific management to their own rather large household.)

The Human Relations Movement and the Hawthorne Studies

Although scientific management did a good job of highlighting the importance of the efficient performance of work, it did not go far enough in directing our attention to the wide variety of factors that might influence work behavior. In fact, many experts rejected Taylorism, favoring instead an approach that focused on employees' own views and emphasized respect for individuals. At the forefront of this orientation was Elton W. Mayo, an organizational scientist and consultant widely regarded as the founder of what is called the **human relations movement**. This management philosophy rejects the primarily economic orientation of scientific management and focuses instead on the noneconomic, social factors operating in the workplace. Mayo and other proponents of the human relations movement recognized that task performance was greatly influenced by the social conditions that existed in organizations—that is, the way employees were treated by management and the relationships they had with each other. For a comparison between scientific management and the human relations movement, see Table 1.4.

In 1927 a series of studies was begun at Western Electric's Hawthorne Works outside Chicago. The researchers were interested in determining several things, including the effects of illumination on work productivity. In other words, how brightly or dimly lit should the work environment be for people to produce at their maximum level? Two groups of female employees took part in the study. One group, the control room condition, did their jobs without any changes in lighting; the other group, the test room condition, worked while the lighting was systematically varied, sometimes getting brighter and sometimes getting dimmer. The results were puzzling: Productivity increased in both locations. Just as surprising, there was no clear connection between illumination and performance. In fact, output in the test room remained high even when the level of illumination was so low that workers could barely see what they were doing!

In another study conducted at the company's Bank Wiring Room, male members of various work groups were observed during regular working conditions and were interviewed at length after work. In this investigation, no attempts were made to alter the work environment. What Mayo found here also was surprising. Namely, instead of improving their performance, employees deliberately restricted their

Table 1.4	Scientific Management Versus the Human Relations Movement: A Summary

Although both are early approaches to the study of behavior in organizations, *scientific management* and the *human relations movement* are different in several key ways summarized here.

Scientific Management	*Human Relations Movement*
Emphasis on human efficiency on the job	Emphasis on social conditions in organizations
Sought to improve productivity by minimizing wasted movements	Sought to improve productivity by developing good working relationships
Major proponent was Frederick Winslow Taylor	Major proponent was Elton Mayo

output. Not only did the researchers actually see the men stopping work long before quitting time, but also in interviews the men admitted that they easily could have done more if they desired.

Why did this occur? Eventually, Mayo and his associates recognized that the answer resided in the fact that organizations are social systems. How effectively people worked depended, in great part, not only on the physical aspects of the working conditions experienced but also on the social conditions encountered. In the Hawthorne studies, Mayo noted, productivity rose simply because people responded favorably to the special attention they received. Knowing they were being studied made them feel special and motivated them to do their best. Hence, it was these social factors more than the physical factors that had such profound effects on job performance.

The same explanation applied in the Bank Wiring Room study as well. Here the employees feared that, because they were being studied, the company would eventually raise the amount of work they were expected to do. So to guard against the imposition of unreasonable standards (and, hopefully, to keep their jobs!), the men agreed among themselves to keep output low. In other words, informal rules (known as norms) were established about what constituted acceptable levels of job performance (a topic we will discuss more thoroughly in Chapter 9). These social forces at work in this setting proved to be much more potent determinants of job performance than the physical factors studied.

This conclusion, based on the surprising findings of the Hawthorne studies, is important because it ushered in a whole new way of thinking about behavior at work. It suggests that to understand behavior on the job, we must fully appreciate people's attitudes and the processes they use to communicate with each other. This way of thinking, so fundamental to modern OB, may be traced back to Elton Mayo's pioneering Hawthorne studies. Although the research was flawed in some important ways (e.g., conditions in the study rooms were not carefully controlled), what they revealed about the importance of human needs, attitudes, motives, and relationships in the workplace was quite influential and novel for its time.

Classical Organizational Theory

During the same time that proponents of scientific management got people to begin thinking about the interrelationships between workers and their jobs, another approach to managing people emerged. This perspective, known as **classical organizational theory**, focused on the efficient structuring of organizations. This is in contrast, of course, to scientific management, which sought to effectively organize the work of individuals.

Although several different theorists are identified with organizational theory, two of the best known are Henri Fayol and Max Weber. Fayol was a French industrialist who attributed his managerial success to various principles he developed. Among these are the following:

- A division of labor should be used because it allows people to specialize, doing only what they do best.
- Managers should have authority over their subordinates, the right to order them to do what's necessary for the organization.

- Lines of authority should be uninterrupted; that is, a clear chain of command should connect top management to the lowest-level employees.
- There should exist a clearly defined unity of command, such that employees receive directions from only one other person so as to avoid confusion.
- Subordinates should be allowed to formulate and implement their own plans.

Although many of these principles are still well accepted today, it is widely recognized that they should not always be applied in exactly the same way. For example, whereas some organizations thrive on being structured according to a unity of command, others require that some employees take directions from several different superiors. We will have more to say about this subject when we discuss various types of organizational designs in Chapter 13. For now, suffice it to say that current organizational theorists owe a debt of gratitude to Fayol for his pioneering and far-reaching ideas.

Probably the best-known classical organizational theorist is the German sociologist Max Weber. Among other things, Weber proposed a form of organizational structure well-known today—the **bureaucracy**. Weber's idea was that the bureaucracy is the one best way to efficiently organize work in all organizations—much as proponents of scientific management searched for the ideal way to perform a job. The elements of an ideal bureaucracy are summarized in Table 1.5.

When you think about bureaucracies, negative images probably come to mind of lots of inflexible people getting bogged down in lots of red tape. Weber's "universal" view of bureaucratic structure lies in contrast to the more modern approaches

Table 1.5   Characteristics of an Ideal Bureaucracy

According to Max Weber, bureaucracies are the ideal organizational form. To function effectively, however, they must possess the characteristics identified here.

Characteristics	*Description*
Formal rules and regulations	Written guidelines are used to control all employees' behaviors.
Impersonal treatment	Favoritism is to be avoided, and all work relationships are to be based on objective standards.
Division of labor	All duties are divided into specialized tasks and are performed by individuals with the appropriate skills.
Hierarchical structure	Positions are ranked by authority level in clear fashion from lower-level to upper-level ones.
Authority structure	The making of decisions is determined by one's position in the hierarchy; higher-ranking people have authority over those in lower-ranking positions.
Lifelong career commitment	Employment is viewed as a permanent, lifelong obligation on the part of the organization and its employees.
Rationality	The organization is committed to achieving its ends (e.g., profitability) in the most efficient manner possible.

to organizational design (see Chapter 13) in which it is recognized that different forms of organizational structure may be more or less appropriate under different situations. Although the bureaucracy may not have proven to be the perfect structure for organizing all work, many of Weber's ideas are still considered viable today.

Despite differences between Fayol's and Weber's principles for organizing work, both approaches assume that there is a single most effective way to structure organizations. Although, as noted earlier, such approaches seem simplistic by modern standards, we are indebted to Fayol, Weber, and other classical management theorists for calling our attention to the important effects of organizational design.

Organizational Behavior in the Modern Era

The pioneering contributions noted thus far set the stage for the emergence of the modern science of organizational behavior. Although the first doctoral degrees in OB were granted in the 1940s, the field's early growth was uneven. It was not until the late 1950s and early 1960s that OB became a going concern. By that time, active programs of research were going on, including investigations of such key processes as motivation and leadership and of the impact of organizational structure on productivity.

Stimulated by a report by the Ford Foundation in the 1960s, advocating that students trained in business receive firm grounding in the social sciences, the field of OB rapidly grew into one that borrowed heavily from other disciplines. In fact, the field of OB as we know it today may be characterized as a hybrid science that draws from many social science fields. For example, studies of motivation and work-related attitudes, dealing as they do with the processes of learning and perception, draw on psychology. Similarly, the study of group dynamics and leadership relies heavily on sociology. The topic of organizational communication, obviously, draws on research in the field of communication. And OB scientists look to the field of management science to understand the design of organizational hierarchies and other structural arrangements. Taken together, it is clear that modern OB has become a truly multifaceted and interdisciplinary field.

learning
objective

Organizational Behavior Today

Today, in the early part of the twenty-first century, the field of OB has added a few new characteristics worth noting. These reflect both changes that are occurring in the world as a whole and changes that have occurred as a result of advances in the science over the years. Although there are too many new developments to mention them all, a few current trends deserve to be pointed out.

- In keeping with the ever-growing globalization of business, the field of OB has been paying more attention than ever to the *cross-cultural aspects of behavior*, acknowledging that our understanding of organizational phenomena may not be universal. Today, research that considers the international generalizability of OB phenomena is considered key to understanding organizational competitiveness in a global society. Acknowledging this trend, you will find multicultural examples of OB throughout this book.

- The study of *unethical behavior in organizations* is considered more important than ever before. Indeed, OB scientists are fascinated by understanding the factors that lead people to make ethical or unethical decisions and by their willingness to engage in such antisocial behaviors as lying, cheating, stealing, and acting violently.[53] We will describe some of the factors that motivate people to behave unethically in Chapter 2.

■ There can be no doubt that today's workforce is more *diverse* than ever before. Minority groups already make up a quarter of the U.S. workforce, and their numbers are growing so rapidly that it soon may be inaccurate to refer to such groups as minorities.[54] Fortunately, diverse employees help bring a wide variety of perspectives to the workplace that tend to improve the quality of organizational decisions. On the other hand, this benefit is too often threatened by prejudice and discrimination against such individuals. These issues are a major concern to today's OB specialists (see Chapter 5).

■ The era of the employee who works from 9 to 5 and who stays with a single company all his or her life is rapidly fading. Today, many people are choosing to work part-time and to change jobs many times during their careers. These alternative work arrangements have important implications for the field of OB, as we will see in Chapter 4.

■ Traditionally, people either worked alone or in small groups in which they had clear-cut responsibilities. Today, however, because it is common for people to work as members of teams, it is not only individuals but also entire team products for which individuals are responsible. As a result, employees tend to have more responsibilities than ever before and are paid in ways that reflect their team's accomplishments. Naturally, such developments are important to the field of OB, and we will discuss them more fully in Chapter 9.

■ Organizations are facing *unrelenting change*—a fact that has not escaped the attention of OB scientists and practitioners. For example, as you will see in Chapter 14, the field pays a great deal of attention to how people cope with change, and it seeks ways of encouraging people to accept change. After all, unless people adapt to the changes, their organizations will find it difficult to thrive—or even to survive.

As you read this book, you will learn more about not only the traditional issues of concern in OB but also about these rapidly developing topics. One thing that makes the field of OB so interesting is that these trends, and many others, are all operating at once, making organizations highly concerned about a wide variety of OB principles and practices.

What Lies Ahead in This Book?

Now that you have a solid idea of what the field of OB is all about, you are in a good position to appreciate what to expect as you continue reading this book. In the chapters ahead, you will learn about a wide variety of organizational behavior phenomena. Our orientation will reflect the dual purposes of the field of OB— understanding and practical application. In other words, the focus will be on both basic processes as well as ways these can be applied to organizational practice. And, just to eliminate doubt about whether this material really matters in organizations, I will share lots of current examples to illustrate how OB principles have been followed within actual companies.

The book is organized around the three units of analysis described in this chapter— individuals, groups, and organizations. Specifically, Part II consists of Chapters 3–6, focusing on individual behavior. Part III, consisting of Chapters 7–11, examines group behavior. And finally, in Part IV, with Chapters 12–14, attention will be paid to organization-level processes. In a sense, these distinctions are artificial insofar as anything that happens in an organization is a blend of forces stemming from all three sources. With this in mind, you can expect to see several important connections between topics as you go through this book. These connections are indeed real and reflect the complexities of the field of OB as well as its multidisciplinary nature. Rather than finding them frustrating, I think you will come to appreciate the fascination that they hold. After all, the field of OB can be no more straightforward than people themselves—and, as you know, we are not all that simple to understand! So with all this in mind, I hope you enjoy your tour of the field of OB presented in the next 13 chapters.

You Be the **Consultant**

Designing the Office Environment

A large publishing company hires you to help design a new suite of offices in which proofreaders will be working. Your task is to determine the level of illumination that helps the proofreaders work most effectively. Answer the following questions relevant to this situation based on the material in this chapter.

1. What specific research method do you think would best provide an answer? Explain your answer.
2. How would managers adopting the Theory X philosophy differ from those adopting the Theory Y philosophy in approaching this issue?
3. What would be the major approach of Taylor's scientific management orientation to this matter?

Self-Assessment Exercise

Testing Your Assumptions About People at Work: Theory X or Theory Y?

What assumptions do you make about human nature? Are you inclined to think of people as primarily lazy and disinterested in working (a Theory X approach) or as willing to work hard under the right conditions (a Theory Y approach)? This exercise is designed to give you some insight into this question.

Directions

For each of the following eight pairs of statements, select the one that better reflects your feelings by marking the letter that corresponds to it.

1. (a) If you give people what they need to do their jobs, they will act very responsibly.
   (b) Giving people more information than they need will lead them to misuse it.

2. (c) People naturally want to get away with doing as little work as possible.

   (d) When people avoid working, it's probably because the work itself has been stripped of its meaning.

3. (e) It's not surprising to find that employees don't demonstrate much creativity on the job because people tend not to have much of it to begin with.

   (f) Although many people are, by nature, very creative, they don't show it on the job because they aren't given a chance.

4. (g) It doesn't pay to ask employees for their ideas because their perspective is generally too limited to be of value.

   (h) When you ask employees for ideas, you are likely to get some useful suggestions.

5. (i) The more information people have about their jobs, the more closely their supervisors have to keep them in line.

   (j) The more information people have about their jobs, the less closely they have to be supervised.

6. (k) Once people are paid enough, the less they tend to care about being recognized for a job well done.

   (l) The more interesting the work is that people do, the less likely they care about their pay.

7. (m) Supervisors lose prestige when they admit that their subordinates may have been right whereas they were wrong.

   (n) Supervisors gain prestige when they admit that their subordinates may have been right whereas they were wrong.

8. (o) When people are held accountable for their mistakes, they raise their standards.

   (p) Unless people are punished for their mistakes, they will lower their standards.

Scoring

1. Give yourself one point for selecting b, c, e, g, i, k, m, and p. The sum of these points is your Theory X score.

2. Give yourself one point for selecting a, d, f, h, j, l, n, and o. The sum of these points is your Theory Y score.

Discussion Questions

1. Which perspective did this questionnaire indicate that you more strongly endorse, Theory X or Theory Y? Is this consistent with your own intuitive conclusion?

2. Do you tend to manage others in ways consistent with Theory X or Theory Y ideas?

3. Can you recall any experiences that may have been crucial in defining or reinforcing your Theory X or Theory Y philosophy?

Group Exercise

Putting Your Common Sense About OB to the Test

Even if you already have a good intuitive sense about behavior in organizations, some of what you think may be inconsistent with established research findings (many of which are noted in this book). So that you don't have to rely on your own judgments (which may be idiosyncratic), working with others in this exercise will give you a good sense of what our collective common sense has to say about behavior in organizations. You just may be enlightened.

Directions

Divide the class into groups of approximately five students. Then within these groups discuss the following statements, reaching a consensus as to whether each is true or false. Spend approximately 30 minutes on the entire discussion.

1. People who are satisfied with one job tend to be satisfied with other jobs too.

2. Because "two heads are better than one," groups make better decisions than individuals.

3. The best leaders always act the same, regardless of the situations they face.

4. Specific goals make people nervous; people work better when asked to do their best.

5. People get bored easily, leading them to welcome organizational change.

6. Money is the best motivator.

7. Interpersonal conflict is likely in a highly diverse workforce.

8. People generally shy away from challenges on the job.

Scoring

Give your group one point for each item you scored as follows: 1 = True, 2 = False, 3 = False, 4 = False, 5 = False, 6 = False, 7 = False, and 8 = False. (Should you have questions about these answers, information bearing on them appears in this book as follows: 1 = Chapter 5, 2 = Chapter 9, 3 = Chapter 11, 4 = Chapter 6, 5 = Chapter 14, 6 = Chapter 6, 7 = Chapter 7, 8 = Chapters 2 and 6.)

Discussion Questions

1. How well did your group do? Were you stumped on a few?

2. Comparing your experiences to those of other groups, did you find that there were some questions that proved trickier than others (i.e., ones where the scientific findings were more counterintuitive)? If you did poorly, don't be frustrated. These statements are a bit simplistic and need to be qualified to

be fully understood. Have your instructor explain the statements that the class found most challenging.

3. Did this exercise give you a better understanding of the sometimes surprising (and complex) nature of behavior in organizations?

Notes

Case Notes

Icon Group, Ltd. (2003). *Kikkoman Corp.* London: Author. Yates, R. E. (1998). *The Kikkoman chronicles: A global company with a Japanese soul.* New York: McGraw-Hill. Kikkoman Web site (2003): www.kikkoman.com. Hoovers Online Web site (2003): www.hoovers.com.

Chapter Notes

[1] Miner, J. B. (2002). *Organizational behavior: Foundations, theories, analyses.* New York: Oxford University Press.

[2] Rogelberg, S. G. (2002). *Handbook of research methods in industrial and organizational psychology.* Malden, MA: Blackwell.

[3] Risher, H. (1999). *Aligning pay and results.* New York: AMACOM.

[4] Judge, T. A., & Church, A. H. (2000). Job satisfaction: Research and practice. In C. A. Cooper & E. A. Locke (Eds.), *Industrial and organizational psychology: Linking theory to practice* (pp. 166–198). Malden, MA: Blackwell.

[5] Hackman, J. R., Wageman, R., Ruddy, T. M., & Ray, C. L. (2000). Team effectiveness in theory and in practice. In C. A. Cooper & E. A. Locke (Eds.), *Industrial and organizational psychology: Linking theory to practice* (pp. 109–129). Malden, MA: Blackwell.

[6] Greenberg, J. (2001). Promote procedural justice to enhance acceptance of work outcomes. In E. A. Locke (Ed.), *A handbook of principles of organizational behavior.* Malden, MA: Blackwell.

[7] Benavides, F. G., Benach, J., Diez-Roux, A. V., & Roman, C. (2000). How do types of employment relate to health indicators? Findings from the Second European Survey on working conditions. *Journal of Epidemiology & Community Health, 54,* 494–501. Roberts, S. (2000, June 26). Integrating EAPs, work/life programs holds advantages. *Business Insurance, 34*(36), 3, 18–19. Vahtera, J., Kivimaeki, M., Pentti, J., & Theorell, T. (2000). Effect of change on the psychosocial work environment on sickness absence: A seven-year follow-up of initially healthy employees. *Journal of Epidemiology and Community Health, 54,* 484–493.

[8] The Corporate Research Foundation UK. (2000). *Britain's best employers: A guide to the 100 most attractive companies to work for.* New York: McGraw-Hill.

[9] Bollinger, D. (1996). *Aiming higher: 25 stories of how companies prosper by combining sound management and social vision.* New York: AMACOM.

[10] Katz, D., & Kahn, R. (1978). *The social psychology of organizations.* New York: Wiley.

[11] It all depends where you sit. (2000, August 14). *Business Week,* Frontier Section, p. F8.

[12] Bridges, W. (1994). *Job shift: How to prosper in a workplace without jobs.* Reading, MA: Addison-Wesley.

[13] See Note 12.

[14] Tomasko, R. M. (1990). *Downsizing: Reshaping the corporation for the future.* New York: AMACOM.

[15] Hendricks, C. F. (1992). *The rightsizing remedy*. Homewood, IL: Business One Irwin.

[16] Displaced workers summary. (2002, January). Bureau of Labor Statistics (at www.bls.gov/news.release/disp.nr0htm).

[17] McGinn, D., & Naughton, K. (2001, February 5). How safe is your job? *Newsweek*, pp. 36–43.

[18] Tomasko, R. M. (1993). *Rethinking the corporation*, New York: AMACOM.

[19] Bettis, R. A., Bradley, S. P., & Hamel, G. (1992). Outsourcing and industrial decline. *Academy of Management Review, 6*, 7–22.

[20] Haapaniemi, P. (1993, Winter). Taking care of business. *Solutions*, pp. 6–8, 10–13.

[21] See Note 20.

[22] Stewart, T. A. (1993, December 13). Welcome to the revolution. *Fortune*, pp. 66–68, 70, 72, 76, 78.

[23] Goranson, H. T. (1999). *The agile virtual enterprise*. Greenwich, CT: Quorum.

[24] Davidow, W. H., & Malone, M. S. (1992). *The virtual corporation*. New York: Harper Business.

[25] See Note 24 (quote, p. 99).

[26] See Note 24.

[27] International Telework Association and Council. (2001, October 23). News release: Number of teleworkers increases by 17 percent. www.telecommute.org/twa/twa2001/newsrelease.htm.

[28] Kugelmass, J. (1995). *Telecommuting: A manager's guide to flexible work arrangements*. New York: Lexington Books.

[29] DuBrin, A. J. (1994). *Contemporary applied management: Skills for managers* (4th ed.). Burr Ridge, IL: Irwin.

[30] Mariani, M. (2000, Fall). Telecommuters. *Occupational Outlook Quarterly*, pp. 10–17.

[31] Cascio, W. E. (1995). Whither industrial and organizational in a changing world of work? *American Psychologist, 50*, 928–939 (quote, p. 928).

[32] Lodge, G. C. (1995). *Managing globalization in the age of interdependence*. San Francisco: Pfeifer.

[33] Ogbonna, E. (1993). Managing organizational culture: Fantasy or reality? *Human Resource Management Journal, 3*(2), 42–54.

[34] DeCieri, H., & Dowling, P. J. (1995). Cross-cultural issues in organizational behavior. In C. L. Cooper & D. M. Rousseau (Eds.), *Trends in organizational behavior* (Vol. 2, pp. 127–145). New York: John Wiley & Sons.

[35] Hesketh, B., & Bochner, S. (1994). Technological change in a multicultural context: Implications for training and career planning. In H. C. Triandis, M. D. Dunnette, & L. Hough (Eds.), *Handbook of industrial and organizational psychology* (Vol. 4, pp. 190–240). Palo Alto, CA: Consulting Psychologists Press.

[36] Janssens, M. (1995). Intercultural interaction: A burden on international managers? *Journal of Organizational Behavior, 16,* 155–167.

[37] Lerman, R. I., & Schmidt, S. R. (2002). *An overview of economic, social, and demographic trends affecting the labor market*. Report to the Urban Institute for U.S. Department of Labor (at www.dol.gov).

[38] See Note 37.

[39] Mason, J. C. (1993, July). Working in the family way. *HRMagazine*, pp. 25–28.

[40] Shellenbarger, S. (1994, February 16). The aging of America is making "elder care" a big workplace issue. *Wall Street Journal*, p. A1.

[41] Fenn, D. (1993, July). Bottoms up. *Inc.*, pp. 57–60.

[42] Martinez, M. N. (1993). Family support makes business sense. *HRMagazine*, pp. 38–43.

[43] Meier, L., & Meagher, L. (1993, September). Teaming up to manage. *Working Woman*, pp. 31–32, 108.

[44] Mason, J. C. (1993, July). Working in the family way. *HRMagazine*, pp. 25–28.

[45] See Note 44.

[46] See Note 44.

[47] See Note 44.

[48] Carnevale, A. P., & Stone, S. C. (1995). *The American mosaic: An in-depth report on the future of diversity at work*. New York: McGraw Hill.

[49] See Note 48.

[50] Kanigel, R. (1997). *The one best way*. New York: Viking.

[51] Taylor, F. W. (1947). *Scientific management*. New York: Harper & Row.

[52] Drucker, P. F. (1974). *Management: Tasks, responsibilities, practices*. New York: Harper & Row.

[53] Verschoor, C. C. (1998). A study of the link between a corporation's financial performance and its commitment to ethics. *Journal of Business Ethics, 17*, 1509–1516.

[54] Bureau of Labor Statistics (2000).www.bls.gov.

Chapter Two

LEARNING OBJECTIVES

After reading this chapter, you will be able to:

1. **IDENTIFY** four different forms of organizational justice and the organizational impact of each.

2. **DESCRIBE** the nature of the interrelationships between distributive justice and procedural justice, and between interpersonal justice and informational justice.

3. **DESCRIBE** things that can be done to promote organizational justice.

4. **EXPLAIN** what is meant by ethical behavior and why organizations should be concerned about ethics.

5. **DESCRIBE** the individual and situational factors responsible for unethical behavior in organizations and methods for minimizing such behavior.

6. **EXPLAIN** what is meant by corporate social responsibility and the nature of the relationship between responsible behavior and financial profitability.

Organizational Justice, Ethics, and Corporate Social Responsibility

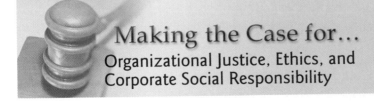

Making the Case for...
Organizational Justice, Ethics, and Corporate Social Responsibility

The NFL: The National "Fairness" League?

"Play fairly" is something we always admonish children, and doing so is expected of them even more emphatically if they grow up to be athletes. Indeed, the sanctity of athletic events is predicated on fairness. For an athlete to gain an unfair advantage by taking performance-enhancing drugs or by breaking a rule (e.g., using a "corked bat" in baseball) is not tolerated because it gives him or her an unfair advantage. With this in mind, the National Football League (NFL), the game's official governing body, has gone out of its way to ensure the existence of a "level playing field."

Within the NFL, a Competition Committee (composed of officials such as team owners and managers) is always tweaking the rules so as to make the game as fair as possible. Consider the simple coin toss used to determine which team will kick or receive the ball when a game begins. For 22 years, this was accomplished by having the captain of the visiting team call "heads or tails" as a coin was tossed into the air by a referee before the game. Then something happened. On Thanksgiving 1998, referee Phil Luckett misunderstood the call made by the Pittsburgh Steelers' Jerome Bettis, allowing the Detroit Lions to get possession of the ball at the beginning of a critical overtime period. To avoid such an "unfortunate incident" in the future, as NFL Commissioner Paul Tagliabue called it, the procedure was changed. Starting with the following weeks' games, the heads-or-tails calls are made before the coin is tossed, thereby allowing any uncertainties to be addressed before the outcome is determined.

To further ensure that the right decisions are made, the NFL uses an "instant replay rule." This allows coaches an opportunity to challenge (within certain limits) rulings made by officials on the field they believe are erroneous. Once a decision is challenged, a game official reviews a videotaped playback of the play in question and decides whether or not to reverse the earlier judgment. Following a seven-year hiatus, the procedure was reinstated by the NFL in 1999 in the wake of public outcries about blatantly erroneous calls by referees in several critical games during the previous season. Although the procedure is considered far from perfect, it is recognized as a useful way to enhance the fairness of the game.

The NFL's efforts to make the game of football as fair as possible go beyond the field itself to the financial books of the teams. Since 1994 the NFL has had a "salary cap" in effect, a rule that equalizes the total yearly amount that each team can pay its players (currently about $68 million). The underlying idea was that the game would be made fairer by preventing the wealthier teams from dominating the sport by "buying" the best athletes at prices the poorer teams could not afford. This practice has resulted in having a wider variety of teams win championships in recent years than ever before, eliminating the winning "dynasties" of past years. Many take this as evidence that today athletic talent plays a greater role than organizational wealth in creating winning football teams. Although this practice is not without controversy, NFL officials are convinced that it's in everyone's best interest to keep the game as fair as possible.

Football fans surely will argue whether the NFL's actions really promote the fairness of the game. Then again, controversy is natural in such situations. After all,

GOOD REASONS why you should care about...

Organizational Justice, Ethics, and Corporate Social Responsibility

You should care about organizational justice, ethics, and corporate social responsibility because:

1. Treating employees unfairly can adversely affect many different types of work attitudes and behaviors.

2. The public is growing increasingly intolerant of unethical corporate behavior, but managers can take steps to promote ethical behavior in organizations.

3. Consumers and investors tend to support socially responsible companies, enhancing their financial performance.

35

fans love to analyze and debate decisions about the sports they love. And few topics are as controversial as what should be done in the name of justice—particularly in the workplace, where well-intentioned parties often disagree about what's fair. Although this may be unclear, it is very clear that people care dearly about matters of justice on the job. Just ask any worker who feels that the small pay raise he received does not adequately reflect his important contributions, or someone who suspects that the boss is playing favorites by giving one of her coworkers more desirable work assignments. Workers in these cases are bound to cry foul, claiming that they have been treated unfairly. Indeed, people are very sensitive to matters of justice and injustice in the workplace and are inclined to express their feelings in significant ways. Not surprisingly, OB specialists have studied these dynamics in the growing field of *organizational justice*, one of the major topics covered in this chapter.[1]

The quest to maintain justice in the workplace is part of a broader concern that people have for *ethics*—doing the right thing—the second major topic we will discuss in this chapter. Given that great philosophers over the years have not reached consensus about what constitutes "the right thing" to do, we shouldn't be surprised that distinguishing between right and wrong in the workplace is rarely a straightforward matter.[2] Yet, it's clear from cases that have been in the news in recent years—Enron being the most visible, whose executives have been accused of various improprieties—that we often know what's wrong when we see it. And, as we will describe in this chapter, the field of OB provides a great deal of insight into why such unethical behavior occurs and can offer suggestions on how to curtail it.

As a natural outgrowth of the quest to behave ethically, many organizational leaders are going beyond merely doing what's right by proactively attempting to make things better in the communities in which they operate.[3] Indeed, many of today's organizations are demonstrating what is known as *corporate social responsibility*—not only attempting to meet prevailing legal and ethical standards but also exceeding them by embracing values that promote the greater welfare of society at large. Whether it involves donating money to charities, staffing community welfare projects, or taking steps to make our air and water clean, engaging in socially responsible behavior is of great concern to leaders of today's organizations. Here again, OB specialists have sought to explain this behavior, and their efforts will be outlined in this chapter.

Organizational Justice: Fairness Matters

Suppose you received a failing grade in a course. You don't like it, of course, but can you say that the grade is unfair? To answer this question, you would likely take several things into consideration. For example, does the grade accurately reflect how well you performed in the course? Were your scores added accurately and were they computed in an unbiased fashion? Has the professor treated you in a polite and professional fashion? Finally, has the professor communicated the grading process to you adequately? In judging how fairly you have been treated, questions such as these are likely to be raised, and your answers are likely to have a considerable impact on how you feel about your grade, the professor, and even the school as a whole. Moreover, they are likely to have a profound effect on how you respond, such as whether you quietly accept the grade, complain about it to someone, or even quit school entirely.

Although this example involves you as a student, the same kinds of considerations are likely to arise in the workplace. In that context, instead of talking about grades from professors, concerns about justice may take analogous forms. Does your salary reflect your work accomplishments? How was your performance evaluation determined? Were you treated with dignity and respect by your boss? And have you been given important job information in a thorough and timely manner? Matters such as these are relevant to **organizational justice**—the study of people's perceptions of fairness in organizations. The following discussion of organizational justice will focus on three important considerations—the major forms of organizational justice, the relationships between these forms, and tips for promoting justice in organizations.

Forms of Organizational Justice and Their Effects

learning objective

The idea that justice is a multifaceted concept follows from the variety of questions just raised previously to everything from *how much* you get paid to how well you are treated by your boss. Not surprisingly, OB scientists have recognized that organizational justice takes several different forms. These are known as *distributive justice, procedural justice, interpersonal justice*, and *informational justice* (see Figure 2.1).[4]

Figure 2.1   Forms of Organizational Justice and Their Effects

Organizational justice takes the four different forms identified here. Each of these forms of justice has been found to have different effects in organizations.

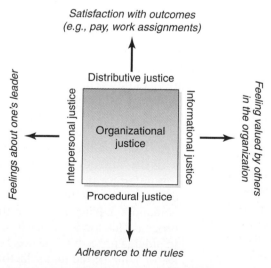

(Sources: Based on suggestions by Colquitt, 2001, and Greenberg, 1993; see Note 4.)

Distributive justice.   On the job, people are concerned with getting their "fair share" of resources. We all want to be paid fairly for the work we do and we want to be adequately recognized for our efforts and any special contributions we bring to the job. **Distributive justice** is the form of organizational justice that focuses on people's beliefs that they have received fair amounts of valued work-related outcomes (e.g., pay, recognition, etc.). For example, workers consider the formal appraisals of their performance to be fair to the extent that these ratings are based on their actual level of performance.[5]

As noted in Figure 2.1, distributive justice affects workers' feelings of satisfaction with their work outcomes, such as pay and job assignments. Naturally, people will be dissatisfied with such important outcomes when these fall below expected standards. (Related to this, as you will see in the discussion of *equity theory* appearing in Chapter 6, feelings of distributive justice can have a great impact on people's motivation to perform their jobs.) Let's look at a recent study.[6] In this investigation, researchers compared two groups of workers with respect to their feelings about distributive justice: a group of local workers from Singapore and a group of foreign workers, Chinese people who worked in Singapore. In this setting, foreign workers tend to not be paid commensurate with their skills. Not surprisingly, the foreign workers expressed higher levels of distributive injustice and were less productive on their jobs.

Procedural justice.   Recall our earlier example regarding receipt of a failing grade. In assessing the fairness of this situation you would want to know precisely how your grade was determined. After all, if the professor made an error in calculating your grade, it would be unfair for you to be penalized. In other words, fairness involves consideration of not only *how much* of various outcomes you receive (i.e., distributive justice) but also the process by which those outcomes are determined—that is, *procedural justice*. In other words, **procedural justice** refers to people's perceptions of the fairness of the procedures used to determine the outcomes they receive.

Again, let's consider as an example the formal appraisals of their performance that workers receive on the job. Research has shown that workers consider these ratings to be fair to the extent that certain procedures were followed, such as when raters were believed to be familiar with their work and when they believed that the standards used to judge them were applied to everyone.[7] As you might imagine, matters of procedural justice take a variety of different forms and are involved in many different situations. Case in point: On May 12, 1998, New York City cab drivers went on strike to protest Mayor Giuliani's imposition of new safety rules.[8] As it worked out, the drivers had little gripe with the rules themselves. However, they felt it was unfair for the mayor to impose the rules without consulting with them. In their eyes, fairness demanded having a voice in the decision-making process. This too is a consideration when it comes to judging procedural justice. For a more complete list of some of the major factors that people take into account when forming judgments about procedural justice, see Table 2.1.

On May 12, 1998, New York City cab drivers went on strike to protest Mayor Giuliani's imposition of new safety rules. The drivers had little gripe with the rules themselves. However, they felt it was unfair for the mayor to impose the rules without consulting with them. In their eyes, fairness demanded having a voice in the decision-making process.

Table 2.1	Procedural Justice Criteria

In forming judgments of procedural justice, people take different factors into consideration. Some of the major ones are identified here, along with descriptions and examples of each.

Criterion	*Description*	*Example*
Voice in the making of decisions	Perceptions of procedural justice are enhanced to the extent that people are given a say in the decisions affecting them.	Workers are given an opportunity to explain their feelings about their own work to a supervisor who is evaluating their performance.
Consistency in applying rules	To be fair, the rules used as the basis for making a decision about one person must be applied equally to making a decision about others.	A professor must use the same exact standards in evaluating the term papers of each student in the class.
Accuracy in use of information	Fair decisions must be based on information that is accurate.	A manager calculating the amount of overtime pay a worker is to receive must add the numbers accurately.
Opportunity to be heard	Fair procedures are ones in which people have a readily available opportunity to correct any mistakes that have been made.	Litigants have an opportunity to have a judge's decision reconsidered in the event that an error was made in legal proceedings. (See also the instant replay rule used by the NFL as described in the opening vignette).
Safeguards against bias	A person making a decision must not have any opportunity to bias the results.	Lottery drawings are held in such a manner that each number is selected in a completely random, unbiased fashion.

(Source: Based on Information in Greenberg, 1996; see Note 5.)

Maintaining procedural justice is a major concern of people in all types of institutions. In legal proceedings, for example, cases may be dismissed if unfair procedures are used to gather evidence. And, in organizations, people also reject decisions based on unfair procedures. In fact, following unfair procedures not only makes people dissatisfied with their outcomes (as in the case of distributive justice) but also leads them to reject the entire system as unfair.[9] Not surprisingly, as shown in Figure 2.1, procedural justice affects people's tendencies to follow organizational rules: Workers are inclined to not follow an organization's rules when they have reason to believe that organization's procedures are inherently unfair. And, of course, when this occurs, serious problems are likely to arise. Accordingly, everyone in an organization—especially top officials—would be well advised to adhere to the criteria for promoting procedural justice summarized in Table 2.1.

Interpersonal justice.   Imagine that you were just laid off from your job. You're not happy about it, of course, but suppose that your boss explains this situation to you in a manner that takes some of the sting out of it. Although your boss cannot do anything about this high-level corporate decision, he or she is very sensitive to the problems this causes you and expresses concern for you in a highly dignified manner. Research has shown that people experiencing situations such as this tend to accept their layoffs as being fair and hold positive feelings about their supervisors (see Figure 2.1). Importantly, such individuals are less inclined to sue their former employers on the grounds of wrongful termination than those who believe they were treated in an opposite manner—that is, in an insensitive and disrespectful fashion.[10] The type of justice demonstrated in this example is known as **interpersonal justice**. This refers to people's perceptions of the fairness of the manner in which they are treated by other people.

Informational justice.   Imagine that you are a heavy smoker of cigarettes and learn that your company has just imposed a smoking ban. Although you may recognize that it's the right thing to do, you are unhappy about it because the ruling forces you to change your behavior and break an addictive habit. Will you accept the smoking ban as fair and do your best to go along with it? Research suggests that you will do so only under certain circumstances—if you are given clear and thorough information about the need for the smoking ban (e.g., the savings to the company and improvements to the health of employees).[11] The form of justice illustrated in this example is known as **informational justice**. This refers to people's perceptions of the fairness of the information used as the basis for making a decision. Because detailed information was provided about the basis for implementing the smoking ban, informational justice was high, leading people to accept the fairness of the smoking ban.

A key explanation for this phenomenon is identified in Figure 2.1—namely, that informational justice prompts feelings of being valued by others in an organization. In other words, people believe that they are considered an important part of the organization when an organizational official takes the time to explain thoroughly to them the rationale behind a decision. And people experiencing such feelings may be expected to believe that they are being treated in a fair manner. (By now, you may be thinking about the four types of fairness in the organization in which you work. To help you assess these feelings in a systematic manner, complete the **Self-Assessment Exercise** on pages 65–67.)

learning
objective

Relationships Between Various Forms of Justice

Although I have been describing the various forms of organizational justice separately, it would be misleading to assume that they are completely independent of one another. In fact, researchers have found some well-established relationships between the various forms of justice.

The interactive relationship between distributive justice and procedural justice.
Imagine once again that you have received either an excellent grade or a poor grade

in a class. Given that most of us tend to perceive ourselves more positively than others see us (we will discuss such perceptual biases in Chapter 3), you are likely to believe that a high grade is more fairly deserved than a low grade. In other words, the positive outcome is likely to be perceived as being more distributively just than the low outcome. (The same would apply to other outcomes as well, such as pay or recognition on the job.) Now, imagine that your grade either was the result of a simple arithmetic error (i.e., procedural justice was low) or that it was computed in an accurate, unbiased fashion (i.e., procedural justice was high). Generally speaking, you will respond more positively to the fair procedure than the unfair procedure, thinking more favorably of the professor and the school as a whole. (Of course, the analogous effect also would apply in organizations.) So far, this is nothing new.

Consider, however, what happens when you combine these effects, looking at the overall relationship between the favorability of outcomes together with the fairness of procedures to arrive at those outcomes. This relationship, which takes the interactive form shown in Figure 2.2, has been very well established among scientists studying organizational justice.[12] Let's illustrate this relationship using the course grade example. The right side of the diagram describes what happens when the outcome is favorable—in other words, when you get a high grade. In this instance, you would be inclined to have a positive reaction because you are so very pleased with your high grade. Although you don't like the fact that it was not computed fairly, you are willing to overlook this given that you got what you wanted.

Now, however, look at the left side of the diagram, the part representing unfavorable outcomes. In this case, where you received a low grade, your feelings about the professor and even the school as a whole are likely to be influenced greatly by the fairness of the procedure. Specifically, it shows that you will be highly dissatisfied with the low grade when it results from an unfair procedure. After all, the grade doesn't reflect your true performance. However, your reactions are inclined to be far more positive when the low grade was based on a fair procedure. Again, although you don't particularly like the grade, believing that it was computed in an accurate and unbiased fashion (i.e., that it is procedurally fair) will get you to respond in a positive fashion. Put differently, although people's reactions to unfavorable outcomes are enhanced by fair procedures, their reactions to favorable outcomes are affected very little by the fairness of the procedure used.

This particular relationship is important to understand because it has very practical implications. In organizations, after all, it is not always possible to give people the favorable outcomes they desire. However, this does not necessarily mean that they will respond negatively. The possibility of negative reactions may be minimized by following fair procedures (and, of course, by ensuring that everyone involved is well aware of the fairness of the procedures followed). To borrow a phrase from Mick Jagger, "you can't always get what you want," but you are more likely to accept what you get when it was determined in a procedurally just manner.

The additive relationship between interpersonal justice and informational justice.
In contrast to the interactive relationship between distributive justice and procedural justice, the relationship between interpersonal justice and informational justice is far simpler. Research has shown that perceptions of justice are enhanced when people explain outcomes using a lot of detail (i.e., when informational justice

| **Figure 2.2** | The Relationship Between Outcome Favorability and Procedural Justice |

Many different studies have reported that the relationship between outcome favorability and procedural justice takes the form summarized here. Specifically, people's reactions to favorable outcomes are affected little by the fairness of the procedure whereas people's reactions to unfavorable outcomes are enhanced by the use of fair procedures.

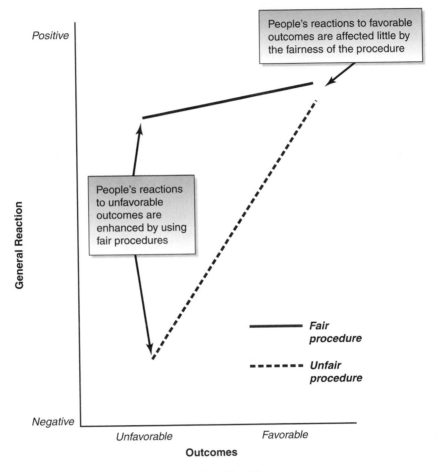

(Source: Based on suggestions by Brockner and Weisenfeld, 1996; see Note 12.)

is high) and also when people explain outcomes in a manner that demonstrates a considerable amount of dignity and respect (i.e., when interpersonal justice is high). What happens when these effects are combined—that is, when information is presented in a manner that is both socially sensitive and highly informative? Research findings provide a clear answer: The effects are additive. In other words, each of these factors contributes somewhat to people's perceptions of fairness, but together their effects are magnified.[13]

To illustrate this effect, which until now I have described only abstractly, consider an interesting experiment conducted a few years ago.[14] In this study, the researcher underpaid people who performed a clerical task by paying them far less than expected. Because distributive justice was violated, people reacted negatively. In fact, when it was possible to do so, they stole some of the money they had coming to them. However, the amount they stole depended on informational justice (how thoroughly the underpayment was described to them) and interpersonal justice (how much sensitivity was conveyed about the underpayment). The results were straightforward: People stole less when high amounts of informational justice were shown (i.e., when the underpayment was explained thoroughly) than when low amounts were shown (i.e., when the underpayment was explained in cursory fashion), and when high levels of interpersonal justice were shown (i.e., when the underpayment was explained in a highly sensitive and caring manner) than when low levels of interpersonal justice were shown (i.e., when the underpayment was explained in a more detached and insensitive fashion). Importantly, these two effects combined in additive fashion such that people stole least when together both informational justice and interpersonal justice were high (i.e., when thorough information was presented in a sensitive fashion) and stole most when together both informational justice and interpersonal justice were low (i.e., when cursory information was presented in an uncaring fashion).

This additive relationship between interpersonal justice and informational justice can be very valuable for supervisors to take into account when managing employees. The implications are straightforward: Sharing lots of information about outcomes makes workers accept those outcomes better as does presenting that information in a sensitive and caring fashion. However, being both highly informative *and* highly sensitive and caring in one's presentation style at the same time enhances feelings of justice and promotes positive behavior most effectively of all.

Suggestions for Promoting Organizational Justice

learning objective

The examples provided thus far make a compelling case for treating employees as fairly as possible. Indeed, workers who believe they are fairly treated are less inclined to respond negatively (such as by stealing from their employers or by suing them if laid off) and more inclined to respond positively (such as by adhering to organizational policies or by being more productive). And if these individual effects aren't sufficiently convincing, think about what it would be like if entire departments or work groups were composed of employees who felt unfairly treated. The cumulative impact would be dramatic, and that is precisely what was found by scientists conducting a recent study.[15] Analyzing 4,539 employees from 783 departments in 97 different hotels they found that departments composed of employees who felt unfairly treated suffered significantly higher rates of turnover and lower levels of customer satisfaction than those composed of employees who felt fairly treated. And, of course, these factors have enormous impact on a hotel's success. In view of these findings, there is good reason for managers to go out of their way to promote justice in the workplace. Fortunately, what we know about organizational justice points to some useful suggestions for doing so.

Pay workers what they deserve.   The practices of saving a little money by under-paying employees—or informally discouraging them from taking vacation days they are due, or asking them to work "off the clock"—are doomed to fail. Paying the "going wage" in your community for work of a certain type and not cheating workers out of what they have coming to them are far wiser investments. After all, workers who feel cheated are unmotivated to perform at high levels (see Chapter 6). Just as importantly, those who feel they have been dealt a distributive injustice will be inclined to "even the score" by stealing from their companies. And, of course, a company paying below-market wages is likely to lose because the best workers will be disinclined to remain working there or even to accept jobs there in the first place. Not giving workers what they have coming to them clearly is "penny wise and pound foolish," as the saying goes.

Offer workers a voice.   One of the best-established principles of procedural justice is that people will better accept outcomes when they have had some input into determining them than when they are not involved.[16] This is known as the **fair process effect**. Often promoting fairness in this manner is accomplished simply by conducting regular meetings with employees to hear what they have to say. The benefits of doing so result not only from making better-quality decisions (because it taps workers' expertise) but also from merely involving workers in the process. After all, workers whose input is solicited are inclined to feel better accepted as valued members of their organization than those who are ignored. As shown in Figure 2.3, this leads them to perceive both that the resulting outcome is fair and that the procedure used to determine it is fair. And, as noted earlier, perceptions of distributive justice and procedural justice are quite beneficial to organizations.

Figure 2.3   The Fair Process Effect: A Summary

According to the *fair process effect*, employees who are given voice in the making of decisions affecting them will feel valued by the decision-making authorities (e.g., top company leaders). In turn, this leads employees to believe that both the decision-making procedure and the outcomes resulting from it are fair. As a result, employees will accept and follow the decision and be more supportive of the organization itself.

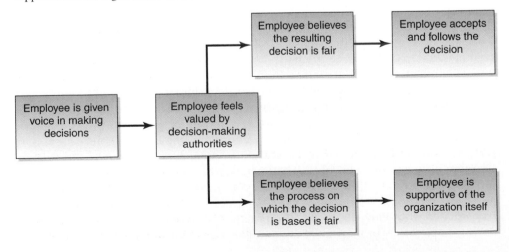

Openly follow fair procedures.   Table 2.1 identifies several standards to be followed in being procedurally fair. Applying rules in a consistent, unbiased, accurate, and correctable fashion is key to being procedurally fair, of course, but merely doing these things is insufficient. To reap the maximum benefits of your fair actions, it helps to ensure that others in the organization are keenly aware that you are doing so. Blatantly touting the fairness of one's actions not only may be inappropriately immodest, of course, but also may arouse suspicion about one's true motives ("why is she making such a big deal about how fair she is?"). At the same time, however, it is very useful to let people know that you are following fair procedures and to assure them of this by announcing all decisions publicly within the company and graciously explaining how they were made to anyone who wants to know. Making decisions in such an open fashion not only promotes perceptions of fairness but also demonstrates to workers precisely what they have to do to be recognized (see Chapter 10).

Explain decisions thoroughly in a manner demonstrating dignity and respect.   To be fair, both interpersonally and informationally, it is essential for managers to take great care in how they present decisions to their employees. Specifically, fairness demands giving employees lots of information about how decisions were made and explaining those decisions in a manner that demonstrates dignity and respect for them. This is especially important when the decisions made have a negative impact on workers. After all, it's bad enough to learn something negative (e.g., a pay cut or a layoff) without having a supervisor add insult to injury by not bothering to explain that decision thoroughly or by demonstrating a lack of concern for your feelings.

Illustrating this point, consider what it's like to have to live through a long pay freeze. Although it's bound to be painful, people may be more accepting of a pay freeze as fair if the procedure used to determine the need for the pay freeze is believed to be thorough and careful—that is, if "a fair explanation" for it can be provided. This was precisely what was found in an interesting study of manufacturing workers' reactions to a pay freeze.[17] Specifically, the researchers made comparisons between two groups of workers: those who received a thorough explanation of the procedures necessitating the pay freeze (e.g., information about the organization's economic problems), and those who received no such information. Although all workers were adversely affected by the freeze, those receiving the explanation better accepted it. In particular, the explanation reduced their interest in looking for a new job.

The practical lesson to be learned from this is important: Even if managers cannot do anything to eliminate distributive injustice (e.g., their "hands may be tied" by company policies), they may be able to reduce some of the sting by providing explanations as to *why* these unfortunate conditions are necessary and doing so in a sensitive and caring fashion. In fact, behaving in this manner can be one of the most effective cost-free things a manager can do.

Train workers to be fair.   Most people perceive themselves as fair individuals. However, as is clear from this section of the chapter, being fair involves several very specific things. And, when facing the everyday pressure to get the job done, managers may not be taking into account as many of the principles of organizational justice as they should. With this in mind, it has been found useful to train practicing managers on how to be fair (I will discuss the topic of training more thoroughly in

Chapter 3).[18] In general, these efforts have been quite successful. Managers who have been trained to treat their employees more fairly (i.e., by being trained in the various forms of justice and practice in bringing them about) reaped several key benefits compared to those who have not been trained to be fair. Not only are their employees less inclined to respond in a negative fashion (e.g., by stealing from the company), but the employees also are more inclined to pitch in and help others in the organization (a phenomenon known as *organizational citizenship behavior*, which I will describe in Chapter 7).

Ethical Behavior in Organizations

The history of American business is riddled with sordid tales of magnates who would go to any lengths in their quest for success, destroying in the process not only the country's natural resources and the public's trust but also the hopes and dreams of millions of people. For example, legends abound of how John D. Rockefeller, founder of Standard Oil, regularly bribed politicians and stepped all over people in his quest to monopolize the oil industry. I do not mean to imply that unsavory business practices are only a relic of the past. Far from it! As you know, they are all too common today—so much so that one newspaper reporter referred to ethical scandals as having reached "epidemic levels."[19] Just consider some of the major headlines from recent years:

- Hackers and data thieves plague businesses and government agencies.[20]
- Martha Stewart indicted for insider trading.[21]
- Enron officers cited for "cooking the books" to make millions for themselves (see Chapter 10).[22]
- Sears found to use fraudulent practices in its auto-repair business.[23]
- Nike accused of hiring children to manufacture clothing under dangerous working conditions.[24]
- Adelphia Communications officials charged with using corporate funds to make exorbitant personal purchases.[25]

Clearly, human greed has not faded from the business scene. However, something *has* changed—namely, the public's acceptance of unethical behavior on the part of organizations. Consider this statement by a leading expert on business ethics.

> Ethical standards, whether formal or informal, have changed tremendously in the last century. . . . Standards are considerably higher. Business-people themselves, as well as the public, expect more sensitive behavior in the conduct of economic enterprise. The issue is not just having the standards, however. It is living up to them.[26]

Not surprisingly—despite the spate of ethical crises that have gained the public's attention in recent years—growing intolerance of unethical business activity (and, cynically, fear of getting caught) has inspired business leaders to become more ethical than ever. According to a recent survey, between 2000 and 2003, workers report that top managers are more inclined to keep their promises, less inclined to engage in misconduct, less likely to feel pressure to be unethical, and perceive greater attention paid to practicing honesty and respect for others. At the same time, whatever ethical misdeeds they do witness are much more likely to be reported to organizational authorities.[27]

To the extent that people are increasingly intolerant of unethical business activity, it should not be surprising to learn that OB scientists are interested in understanding unethical practices and developing strategies for combating them. We will consider these issues in this section and the next section of this chapter. First, however, to prepare you for understanding ethical behavior in organizations, it helps to begin by addressing a fundamental question: What is ethics?

What Do We Mean by Ethics?

4
learning
objective

Although people often talk about ethics, it's not always clear what they mean. With this in mind, let's define some key terms. To understand what is meant by ethics, we first must understand the concept of *moral values*. When social scientists speak of **moral values** they are referring to people's fundamental beliefs regarding what is right or wrong, good or bad. One of the most important sources of moral values is the religious background, beliefs, and training we receive. Although people's moral values may differ, several are widely accepted. For example, most people believe that helping someone in need (e.g., being charitable) is the right thing to do whereas harming someone (e.g., killing) is wrong.

Based on these beliefs, people are guided in ways that influence the decisions they make and the actions in which they engage. These standards are what we mean by *ethics*. Thus, **ethics** refers to standards of conduct that guide people's decisions and behavior (e.g., not stealing from others is one such ethical standard).[28] With this in mind, organizational scientists acknowledge that it is not a company's place to teach employees values. After all, these come with people as they enter the workplace. However, it *is* a company's responsibility to set clear standards of behavior and to train employees in recognizing and following them.[29] (For a summary of the distinction between moral values and ethics, see Figure 2.4.) Just as organizations prescribe other kinds of behavior that are expected in the workplace (e.g., when to arrive and leave), so too should they prescribe appropriate ethical behavior (e.g., how to complete expense reports and what precisely is considered a bribe). Not surprisingly, most top business leaders recognize that clearly prescribing ethical behavior is a fundamental part of good management. After all, says Kent Druyversteyn, former vice president of ethics at General Dynamics, "Ethics is about conduct."[30]

In looking at Figure 2.4, please note the row of rounded boxes at the bottom. These identify some of the factors affecting moral values, ethics, decisions, and behavior. The ones corresponding to ethics and values are described in this section of the chapter. However, as indicated in the box in the lower right corner, the decisions people make and the behavior in which they engage are determined by a wide variety of considerations beyond ethics. Accordingly, these are discussed elsewhere throughout this book (note the references to other chapters in this book).

Why Should Companies Care About Ethical Behavior?

4
learning
objective

It's obvious, of course, that companies *should* do things to promote ethical behavior among employees simply because they are morally appropriate. To some top executives,

Figure 2.4   Moral Values Versus Ethics

As summarized here, *moral values* (which reside within an individual) provide the basis for *ethics* (which are standards of behavior that can be regulated by organizations). Ethical standards influence both decisions and behavior in the workplace, which also are affected by a host of other variables identified throughout this book.

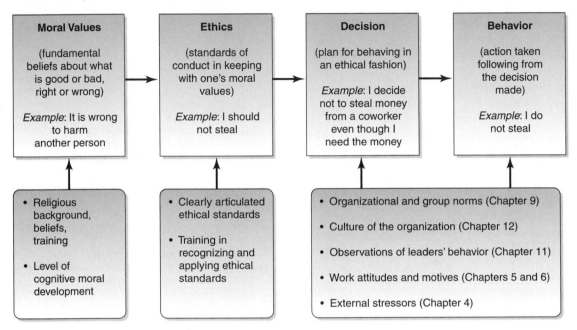

behaving ethically is an integral part of business. Take Levi Strauss & Co., for example, whose chairman, Robert D. Haas, has observed as follows:

> Levi has always treated people fairly and cared about their welfare. . . . In the past, however, that tradition was viewed as something separate from how we ran the business. We always talked about the "hard stuff" and the "soft stuff." The soft stuff was the company's commitment to our work force. And the hard stuff was what really mattered; getting pants out the door. What we've learned is that the soft stuff and the hard stuff are becoming increasingly intertwined. A company's values— what it stands for, what its people believe in—are crucial to its competitive success. Indeed, values drive the business. . . . Values are where the hard stuff and the soft stuff come together.[31]

Levi Strauss & Co. chairman, Robert D. Haas, has observed as follows: Levi has always treated people fairly and cared about their welfare. A company's values—what it stands for, what its people believe in—are crucial to its competitive success. Indeed, values drive the business.

All too often, as you know, forces deter even good people from doing the right thing. Pressure to meet "the bottom line" sometimes encourages people to do whatever it takes to make money, at least in the short run, even if it leads them to behave unethically. For example, some unscrupulous stockbrokers have been known to boost their own sales commissions by encouraging clients to make investments they know are questionable. Corporate leaders need to be concerned about this, if not for moral reasons, then out of recognition of two critical business realities—by being ethical, companies can (1) reap various financial benefits and (2) adhere to legal regulations.

Good ethics is good business.   People promoting ethical behavior among businesses agree that good ethics is good business. In other words, the idea is that although one may benefit in the short run by behaving unethically (e.g., the stockbroker in our example), being ethical pays off in the long run. These benefits take several forms, including the following:[32]

- *Improved financial performance:* Companies that make a clear commitment to ethics outperform those that make no such commitment on standard measures of financial success. In fact, one recent study reported that companies that make an explicit commitment to ethical behavior returned twice the value to shareholders than those that were more casual about ethical issues.[33]
- *Reduced operating costs:* Many efforts to reduce waste and to save energy designed to protect the natural environment also help save money.
- *Enhanced corporate reputation:* Many customers are loyal to companies that demonstrate their commitment to social causes. For example, The Body Shop has benefited by promoting the things it does to help the poor people from third world nations from whom they buy raw materials, courting customers who share their values.
- *Increased ability to attract and retain employees:* People generally like working at companies of which they can be proud and that treat them well. When talented employees are difficult to find, socially responsible companies have an easier job of getting people to work for them—and keeping them there.

If this evidence is not sufficiently convincing, then consider the other side of the coin. The evidence also is compelling that "bad ethics is bad business." Companies that survive ethical scandals do so under diminished capacity in large part because "the black eye" makes the public shy away from them—both as consumers and as stockholders—at least for a while.[34] Good examples from years past include Dow Corning (whose breast implants were found to be unsafe), Exxon (whose ship, the *Valdez*, spilled oil off the coast of Alaska), and the United Way (whose top official was accused of misusing agency funds). These misdeeds have cost their respective organizations dearly, and regaining the public's trust has proven to be a slow process. At the United Way, for example, although only one person, the president, was involved in the ethical scandal, completely independent and scrupulously ethical chapters of the esteemed philanthropic organization suffered severe reductions in donations (one-fifth of former donors stopped giving altogether and the remaining ones gave less) for at least five years.[35]

At the United Way, although only one person, the president, was involved in the ethical scandal, completely independent and scrupulously ethical chapters of the esteemed philanthropic organization suffered severe reductions in donations (one-fifth of former donors stopped giving altogether and the remaining ones gave less) for at least five years.

The lesson is clear: Even if company executives do not recognize the benefits of behaving ethically, they surely cannot afford to ignore the costs of behaving unethically.

Legal regulations.   Being ethical is not the same as following the law. In fact, a useful way to think of the law is as providing the minimum acceptable standard to which companies must adhere. Being ethical typically involves following a higher standard. Vin Sarni, former CEO of PPG, put this well when he said, "It is not enough simply to say that our conduct is lawful. The law is the floor. Compliance with it will be the absolute minimum with respect to the PPG associate, no matter where he or she works. Our ethics go beyond the legal code."[36] At the same time, it must be noted that the law plays a large role in governing ethical behavior within organizations. Some of the major laws enacted in the United States that influence ethical behavior in organizations are as follows:

- *False Claims Act (1986):* Provides procedures for reporting fraudulent behavior against U.S. government agencies and protects whistle-blowers (see Chapter 7) who do so.
- *Foreign Corrupt Practices Act (revised 1988):* Prohibits organizations from paying bribes to foreign officials for purposes of getting business.
- *Federal Sentencing Guidelines for Organizations (1991):* Provides guidelines for federal judges to follow when imposing fines on organizations whose employees engage in criminal acts.
- *Sarbanes-Oxley Act (2002):* Enacted to guard against future accounting scandals (such as occurred at Enron; see Chapter 10), this law initiates reforms in the standards by which public companies report accounting data.
- *Federal Prosecution of Business Organizations (2003):* To protect investors against unscrupulous acts by top executives (also in response to the Enron scandal), these revisions to the Federal Sentencing Guidelines for Organizations now focus on the role of boards of directors—the only parties in organizations with sufficient clout to prevent wrongdoing by high-ranking officials.[37]

Although all these laws are important when it comes to minimizing unethical behavior in organizations, the Federal Sentencing Guidelines for Organizations have been the most explicit when it comes to specifying precisely what organizations should do to discourage unethical behavior. The underlying rationale is that the more proactively organizations discourage criminal behavior by employees, the less they will be penalized should such behavior occur. (After all, an organization cannot directly control everything every employee does!) Specifically, the Federal Sentencing Guidelines for Organizations identify several specific actions which, if taken, will be recognized as efforts to discourage illegal behavior.[38] Not surprisingly, these behaviors, which are listed and described in Table 2.2, are widely followed by companies in their efforts to promote ethical behavior.

5
learning
objective

Why Do Some People Behave Unethically, at Least Sometimes—and What Can Be Done About It?

Management experts have long considered the matter of why some people behave unethically on at least some occasions. Put differently, is it a matter of good people who are led to behave unethically because of external forces acting on them (i.e.,

Table 2.2	Practices Encouraged by the Federal Sentencing Guidelines for Organizations

According to the Federal Sentencing Guidelines for Organizations, companies following the practices listed here will be punished less severely should one of its employees engage in criminal conduct.

- Standards for complying with the law should be specified clearly and widely disseminated (e.g., in publications and training programs).
- A high-level official should be responsible for overseeing these standards.
- A clear system for monitoring and auditing behavior should be in place so that criminal behavior can be detected when it occurs.
- Appropriate disciplinary action should be taken against employees who violate the standards.
- If an offense occurs, steps must be taken to prevent its recurrence.

(Source: Based on information reported by the Ethics and Policy Integration Centre, 2003; see Note 38.)

"good apples in bad barrels") or is it that bad people behave inappropriately in whatever setting they are in (i.e., "bad apples in good barrels")? Acknowledging the key role of leaders in determining the ethical climate of an organization, some scientists have considered the possibility that because of their profound influence, some unethical leaders (so-called "bad apples") have made their companies unethical as well (turning "good barrels into bad"), or poisoning the whole barrel, so to speak.[39] Although the relative importance of "apples" and "barrels" has yet to be firmly decided, it is clear that ethical and unethical behavior is determined by *both* of these classes of factors—that is, individual factors (the person) and situational factors (the external forces people confront in the workplace). In this section of the chapter, we will consider both sets of factors.

Individual Differences in Cognitive Moral Development

As you know from experience, people appear to differ with respect to their adherence to moral considerations. Some individuals, for example, refrain from padding their expense accounts, even if they believe they will not get caught, solely because they believe it is the wrong thing to do. They strongly consider ethical factors when making decisions. However, this is not true of everyone. Still others, as you know, would not think twice about padding their expense accounts, often rationalizing that the amounts of money in question are small and that "the company expects me to do it." A key factor responsible for this difference is what psychologists refer to as **cognitive moral development**—that is, differences among people in their capacity to engage in the kind of reasoning that enables them to make moral judgments. (Scientists measure people's cognitive moral development by systematically analyzing how people say they would resolve various ethical dilemmas. For practice analyzing an ethical dilemma, complete the Group Exercise on pages 67–68.)

The most well-known theory of cognitive moral development was introduced over three decades ago by the psychologist Lawrence Kohlberg.[40] According to **Kohlberg's theory of cognitive moral development**, people develop over the years in their capacity to understand what is right. Specifically, the theory distinguishes

Figure 2.5 Kohlberg's Theory of Cognitive Moral Development: A Summary

According to *Kohlberg's theory of cognitive moral development*, people develop the capacity to make moral decisions as they develop over the years by interacting with others. The three major levels of cognitive moral development are identified here.

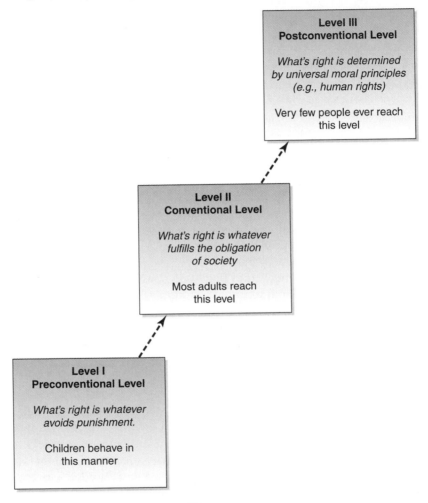

Level III
Postconventional Level

What's right is determined by universal moral principles (e.g., human rights)

Very few people ever reach this level

Level II
Conventional Level

What's right is whatever fulfills the obligation of society

Most adults reach this level

Level I
Preconventional Level

What's right is whatever avoids punishment.

Children behave in this manner

(Source: Based on information in Kohlberg, 1976; see Note 40.)

among three levels of moral development (for a summary, see Figure 2.5). The first level is referred to as the *preconventional level of moral reasoning*. People at this level (children and about one-third of all adults) haven't developed the capacity to assume the perspective of others. Accordingly, they interpret what is right solely with respect to themselves: It is wrong to do something if it leads one to be punished. Because their cognitive skills are not sufficiently advanced, such individuals generally cannot comprehend any argument you may make about something being wrong because it violates their social obligations to others.

As people interact with others over the years, most come to use higher level cognitive processes to judge morality. In a more sophisticated fashion, they judge right and wrong in terms of what is good for the others around them and society as a whole. This second level is referred to as the *conventional level of moral reasoning*. Approximately two-thirds of adults fall into this category. What they do is governed strongly by what's expected of them by others, and they carefully scour the social environment for cues as to "what's right." People who engage in conventional moral reasoning obey the law not only because they fear the repercussions of not doing so, but also because they recognize that doing so is the right thing to do insofar as it promotes the safety and welfare of society as a whole.

Finally, Kohlberg's theory also identifies a third level of cognitive moral development, the *postconventional level*. At this level, people judge what is right and wrong not solely in terms of their interpersonal and societal obligations but also in terms of complex philosophical principles of duty, justice, and rights. Very few people ever attain this level. Those who do, however, follow their own "moral compass," doing what they are convinced is truly right, even if others don't agree.

Research has found that people behave in very different ways as a function of their level of cognitive moral development. For example, as you might expect, people who are at higher levels of cognitive moral development (typically, conventional as opposed to preconventional) manifest their greater ethical behavior in several ways. Specifically, they are less inclined to harm others, less likely to misreport information even if it makes them look bad, and steal less from their employers.[41] Although efforts to raise people's level of moral reasoning through training have been successful, few such efforts have been used in organizations.[42] This is in large part because most workers already function at the conventional level, making them sensitive to efforts to promote ethical behavior predicated on changing the social norms that exist within organizations. We now will consider some of the key social dynamics that influence ethical behavior.

Situational Determinants of Unethical Behavior

As you might imagine, many different situational factors can lead people to behave unethically on the job. Although the list may be long, it is not too difficult to identify some of the major organizational influences on unethical behavior. Here, we will consider three of the most important ones—organizational norms encouraging unethical behavior, managerial values that discourage integrity, and the impact of unethical behavior by leaders. Although these factors surely are interrelated, it is worth identifying them separately so as to highlight their important effects on ethical behavior.

Some managerial values undermine integrity.   Most managers appear to believe that "good ethics is good business." However, some managers have developed ways of thinking that lead them to make unethical decisions. Given how very influential top leaders are when it comes to influencing others in their organizations, it should not be surprising that unethical managerial values promote unethical organizational decisions.[43] Several well-known forms of unethical thinking are as follows.[44]

■ **Bottom line mentality**—This line of thinking supports financial success as the only value to be considered. It promotes short-term decisions that are immediately financially sound, despite the fact that they may cause long-term problems for the organization.

■ **Exploitative mentality**—This view encourages "using" people in a way that promotes stereotypes and undermines empathy and compassion. This highly selfish perspective sacrifices concern for others in favor of benefits to one's own immediate interests.

■ **Madison Avenue mentality**—This perspective suggests that anything is right if the public can be made to see it as right. The idea is that executives may be more concerned that their decisions appear to be right than about their legitimate morality. This kind of thinking leads some companies to hide their unethical behavior (e.g., dumping toxic waste under cover of night) or to otherwise justify them as acceptable.

Recognizing the problems associated with these various orientations is not difficult. Their overemphasis on short-term monetary gain may lead to decisions that not only hurt individuals in the long run but also threaten the very existence of organizations.

Organizations sometimes encourage behavior that violates ethical standards.   It is easy to understand that people may behave unethically on the job to the extent that they are encouraged to do so. Consider, for example, how some business executives are expected to say nothing about ethically dubious behavior they've witnessed in the company. In fact, in many companies it is considered not only acceptable but also desirable to be secretive and deceitful. For example, the practice of **stonewalling**—willingly hiding relevant information—is quite common.

In 1968 B. F. Goodrich allegedly rewarded employees who falsified and withheld data on the quality of aircraft brakes to win certification. This illustrates how the *counternorms* of secrecy and deceitfulness were accepted and supported by the organization.

A major reason for this is that organizations may actually punish those who are too open and honest. As a case in point, consider the disclosure that in 1968 B.F. Goodrich allegedly rewarded employees who falsified and withheld data on the quality of aircraft brakes to win certification. This example illustrates how the *counternorms* of secrecy and deceitfulness were accepted and supported by the organization. By **counternorms** I am referring to accepted organizational practices that run contrary to society's prevailing ethical standards. For a summary of some of the most common counternorms found in organizations, see Figure 2.6.[45]

Workers emulate the unethical behavior of their superiors.   Probably very few organizational leaders condone and actively promote unethical behavior. However, many organizational officials promote unethical behavior unwittingly by way of the examples they set for their employees. For example, suppose a manager submits an expense report to her administrative assistant to prepare for submission to the accounting office. Included on it are several items the assistant knows are not legitimate (e.g., lavish meals with clients). Although the manager might not be thinking about it, by padding her expense account she is sending a message to her administrative assistant that stealing from the company is an acceptable practice. Despite what she might say publicly about not stealing, her behind-the-scenes actions tell a different story. As a result, the administrative assistant might not think twice about taking a few dollars from the company's petty cash box to purchase her lunch.

Figure 2.6   Ethical Norms Versus Organizational Counternorms

Although societal standards of ethics dictate the appropriateness of certain actions, counternorms that encourage and support opposite practices sometimes develop within organizations.

Ethical Norms		Organizational Counternorms
Be open and honest	vs.	Be secretive and deceitful
Follow the rules at all costs	vs.	Do whatever it takes to get the job done
Be cost-effective	vs.	Use it or lose it
Take responsibility	vs.	Pass the buck
Be a team player	vs.	Take credit for your own actions: grandstand

(Source: Based on suggestions by Jansen and Von Glinow, 1985; see Note 45.)

"After all," she may reason, "my boss takes a little extra money from the company, so it must be okay for me to do so too."

A recent survey of some 1,500 U.S. employees suggests that this is precisely what happens.[46] Specifically, employees who feel that the top managers in their organization act ethically themselves report seeing far less misconduct among their peers (15 percent) than those who feel that their top managers do not behave ethically themselves or who only talk about behaving ethically (56 percent). Obviously, when it comes to ethical conduct on the job, managers set an example by virtue of their own behavior, and their "actions speak louder than words." Putting it in the lingo of today's managers, to promote ethical behavior in their companies, it is essential for officials to "walk the talk."

Using Corporate Ethics Programs to Promote Ethical Behavior

Most companies today, particularly large ones, have in place some sort of formal, systematic mechanisms designed to promote ethics. These efforts, known as **corporate ethics programs**, are designed to create organizational cultures (see Chapter 12) that both make people sensitive to potentially unethical behavior and discourage them from engaging in them.

Components of corporate ethics programs.   Typically, corporate ethics programs consist of some combination of the following components.[47]

■ *A code of ethics.* A **code of ethics** is a document describing what an organization stands for and the general rules of conduct expected of employees (e.g., to avoid conflicts of interest, to be honest, and so on). In the mid-1990s, about 78 percent of all *Fortune* 1000 companies had codes of ethics in place, and that figure is higher today.[48] Some codes are highly specific, stating, for example, the maximum size of gifts that can be accepted, whereas others are far more general.

■ *Ethics training.* Codes of ethics are especially effective when they are used in conjunction with training programs that reinforce the company's ethical values.[49] In the absence of such training, too many codes come across as "window dressing," and are ignored, if they are even read at all. Ethics training efforts consist of everything ranging from lectures, videotapes, and case studies to more elaborate simulations. Citicorp, for example, has trained more than 40,000 employees in over 60 countries using an elaborate corporate ethics game, "The Work Ethic," that simulates ethical dilemmas that employees are likely to confront.[50]

> Citicorp has trained more than 40,000 employees in over 60 countries using an elaborate corporate ethics game, "The Work Ethic," that simulates ethical dilemmas that employees are likely to confront.

■ *Ethics audits.* Just as companies regularly audit their books to check on irregularities in their finances, they regularly should assess the morality of their employees' behavior so as to identify irregularities in this realm as well. Such assessments are known as **ethics audits**. These require actively investigating and documenting incidents of dubious ethical value, discussing them in an open and honest fashion, and developing a concrete plan to avoid such actions in the future. Conducting an ethics audit can be quite revealing. For some useful guidelines on how to do so, see Table 2.3.[51]

Table 2.3	**How to Conduct an Ethics Audit**

A thorough ethics audit can reveal a great deal about a company's commitment to ethics and the extent to which its efforts to foster ethical behavior are effective. However, to recognize these benefits, it is crucial to conduct an ethics audit in an appropriate manner. The following guidelines will help.

1. Ensure that top executives, such as the CEO, are committed to the ethics audit and appoint a committee to guide it.

2. Create a diverse team of employees to write questions regarding the company's ethical performance. These should focus on existing practices (e.g., codes of ethics) as well as prevailing norms about company practices (e.g., people regularly padding their expense accounts).

3. Carefully analyze official documents, such as ethical mission statements and codes of ethics, to see how clear and thorough they are.

4. Ask people questions about why they think various unethical behaviors have occurred.

5. Compare your company's ethical practices to those of other companies in the same industry.

6. Write a formal report summarizing these findings and present it to all concerned parties.

(Source: Based on suggestions by Ferrell et al., 2002; see Note 51.)

■ *An ethics committee.* An **ethics committee** is a group of senior-level managers from various areas of the organization who assist an organization's CEO in making ethical decisions. Members of the committee develop and evaluate company-wide ethics policies.

■ *An ethics officer.* An **ethics officer** is a high-ranking organizational official (e.g., the general counsel or vice president of ethics) who is expected to provide strategies for ensuring ethical conduct throughout an organization. Because the Federal Sentencing Guidelines for Organizations specify that a specific, high-level individual should be responsible for ethical behavior, many companies have such an individual in place.

■ *A mechanism for communicating ethical standards.* To be effective, ethics programs must clearly articulate—and reinforce—a company's ethical expectations to employees. With this in mind, growing numbers of companies are putting into place **ethics hot lines**, special phone lines that employees can call to ask questions about ethical behavior and to report any ethical misdeeds they may have observed. (For a particularly effective example of this, and other practices designed to encourage ethical behavior, see the accompanying **Winning Practices** section.)

The Effectiveness of Corporate Ethics Programs

By themselves, codes of ethics have only limited effectiveness in regulating ethical behavior in organizations.[54] However, an integrated ethics program that combines a code of ethics with additional components (e.g., an ethics officer, ethics training, etc.) can be quite effective. Specifically, it has been found that compared to companies that don't have ethics programs in place, within those that do, employees (a) are more likely to report ethical misconduct to company authorities, (b) are considered more accountable for ethics violations, and (c) face less pressure to compromise standards of business conduct.[55] Clearly, the ethics programs are being felt.

Additional evidence from a recent study shows that an ethics program also may effectively reduce employee theft, one particularly costly form of unethical behavior.[56] This investigation compared the rate of petty theft between two groups of employees who worked for the same financial services company—one whose office had a corporate ethics program in place for the past six months, and one in a distant city that had no ethics program in place. The ethics program consisted of a code of ethics, an ethics committee, and 10 hours of training. Prior to the study, employees were tested to identify their level of cognitive moral development. Some employees were found to be at the preconventional level whereas others were at the conventional level. The workers volunteered to complete a questionnaire sponsored by the company for one hour after work. They were told to expect "fair pay" for this task but were actually paid considerably less than their standard hourly wage ($2 as opposed to about $10). This motivated the workers to steal from the company in order to get even. In addition, workers were given an opportunity to steal by being allowed to take their own pay from a bowl of pennies in front of them while nobody watched. Because the researcher knew exactly how many pennies were in the bowl beforehand, it could be determined precisely how much money was taken. Amounts in excess of $2 were considered by the researcher to constitute theft.

Did those workers who had a code of ethics in place at their office steal less from the company than those who did not? As shown in Figure 2.7, the answer depended on the workers' level of cognitive moral development. Workers whose office did not

Winning **Practices**

Excelon Excels at Managing Ethics

In 2000, Exelon was formed by the merger of two electric utility companies, Unicom and PECO Energy. The creation of a new company provided an opportunity for an emphasis on ethics to be built into the company's structure from the ground floor. It was with this in mind that Eliecer Palacios, who was ethics and compliance director at Unicom at the time of the merger and who is now director of ethics and compliance at Exelon, got actively involved in the process of integrating the two companies.[52] Palacios believed that this was important insofar as large utilities face ethical challenges along several fronts, such as stock trading practices (e.g., avoiding insider trading), protection of the environment (e.g., avoiding air and water pollution), procurement (e.g., avoiding bribes and kickbacks), and following fair labor practices (e.g., avoiding harassment and discrimination). And, given that the energy industry is deregulated, customers have the opportunity to express their dissatisfaction with any ethical missteps by taking their business elsewhere. To avoid any ethical scandals, Palacios built in several safeguards to ensure that Exelon would remain "squeaky clean."

At the heart of the company's ethics initiatives is a 16-person Ethics and Compliance Committee. One of the key things this body does is review Exelon's code of ethics on a quarterly basis. Members, consisting of vice presidents and lower-level employees from throughout the company as well as several attorneys, carefully review the extent to which the company is meeting its legal and ethical obligations. Is it obeying the law? Is it meeting its obligations to shareholders, employees, and the environment? Among the specific things on which the committee focuses are the company's efforts at training its tens of thousands of employees on proper ethical behavior. Like other big companies, Exelon has a code of ethics, but unlike many, it is actively involved in ensuring that its employees both understand and follow it. With this in mind, Exelon employees are required to complete an intensive ethics training program using the company's intranet. On an annual basis, employees are required to be certified as having completed the training. Also unlike many companies, ethics training at Exelon involves more than only the lowest-level employees. Instead, everyone from entry level employees to the CEO is required to be trained and recertified annually.

In addition to its training efforts, Exelon maintains an active "helpline" that employees can call to lodge complaints about seemingly unethical behavior or to make inquiries about how to avoid unethical behavior. The helpline, staffed by Palacios and an assistant, receives about 300 calls per year. Most of these involve inquiries about behavior that is considered ethically appropriate (e.g., accepting gifts from a contractor valued at over $25 is considered inappropriate). Calls about allegations of waste, fraud, and abuse, although only about 10 to 15 percent of all received, also occur. All allegations are carefully investigated, and to ensure that these efforts are effective, the company strictly enforces a nonretaliation policy.

At its Web site, Exelon lists among its core values, "commitment in operating facilities safely, protecting the environment, and developing our businesses responsibly."[53] From the ethics initiatives reported here, it's clear that the company is going out of its way to translate these values into everyday practice.

Figure 2.7   The Effectiveness of an Ethics Program Depends on Cognitive Moral Development: Summary of Research Findings

A recent experiment compared the amount that employees stole from their company as a function of whether or not their office had an ethics program in place and their level of cognitive moral development. It was found that an ethics program had no appreciable effect on employee theft among workers at the preconventional level but that an ethics program successfully reduced employee theft among workers at the conventional level.

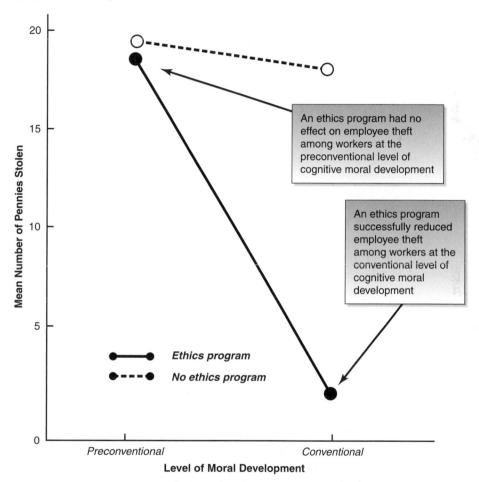

An ethics program had no effect on employee theft among workers at the preconventional level of cognitive moral development

An ethics program successfully reduced employee theft among workers at the conventional level of cognitive moral development

●——● Ethics program
●----● No ethics program

(Source: Based on data reported by Greenberg, 2002; see Note 56.)

have an ethics program in place stole an average of just under 20 cents regardless of their level of cognitive moral development. Likewise, people from offices that had an ethics program stole about the same amount when they were at the preconventional level of moral development. However, hardly any theft occurred at all among workers at the conventional level who worked at an office that had an ethics program in place. In other words, the ethics program was effective in combating employee theft, but only among employees who have attained a sufficiently high level of moral development for the program to have an effect on them. By contrast, among workers at the preconventional level of moral development, the ethics program apparently had little, if any, impact. Given that such individuals are unlikely to fully comprehend and accept their ethics training, this makes perfect sense.

Although the amount of theft examined in this study was small, the underlying conclusion to be drawn is straightforward. A corporate ethics program may have only limited effectiveness because it will influence only some workers—those who have reached a sufficiently high level of moral development. Fortunately, this constitutes about two-thirds of the population as a whole. Reaching the other one-third, those at the preconventional level, may well require other methods, such has emphasizing clear penalties for breaking the rules.

Beyond Ethics: Corporate Social Responsibility

Usually, when we think of business organizations, we focus on their financial responsibilities to stockholders and investors—that is, to make money. Of course, this is not their only responsibility. As we have been discussing all along, organizations also are responsible for obeying the law and to answering to yet a higher standard, behaving ethically. In addition to these considerations, many of today's organizations are going beyond their ethical responsibilities by taking proactive steps to help society at large by virtue of their philanthropic contributions. Together, these four types of responsibilities, shown in Figure 2.8 in the form of a pyramid—thus called the pyramid of **corporate social responsibility**—comprise what we have in mind when we speak of *corporate social responsibility*.[57]

What Is Corporate Social Responsibility?

The term **corporate social responsibility** is used to describe business decision making linked to ethical values, compliance with legal requirements, and respect for individuals, the community at large, and the environment. It involves operating a business in a manner that meets or exceeds the ethical, legal, and public expectations that society has of business. Some examples of highly socially responsible actions from companies around the world are as follows:[58]

- *Whole Foods Market*—This nationwide chain specializing in organic foods developed an initiative to use solar energy for 25 percent of its power.
- *Stonyfield Farms*—This dairy company donates 10 percent of net profits to charities that help protect and restore the earth, and it pays farmers extra to not use synthetic bovine growth hormones in the milk it buys to make yogurt.
- *Royal Dutch Shell*—This large oil company has agreed to not engage in mining or oil exploration activities in areas of the world that have special biological or cultural significance.
- *Boise Cascade*—Beginning in 2004, this paper and building materials company stopped harvesting timber from old-growth forests and endangered forests.
- *Natura Cosmeticos*—This Brazilian cosmetics firm promotes and supports local human rights initiatives (e.g., it does not use child labor), it promotes education, and it encourages its employees to volunteer for nonprofit organizations in their community.

Figure 2.8   The Pyramid of Corporate Social Responsibility

To be socially responsible, companies must meet the four different types of responsibilities identified here. The most basic responsibilities, financial, are shown at the bottom because organizations would go out of business if they failed to meet their financial responsibilities.

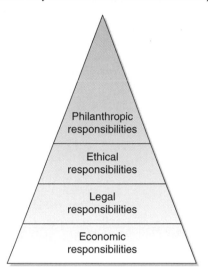

Philanthropic responsibilities

Ethical responsibilities

Legal responsibilities

Economic responsibilities

(Source: Based on suggestions by Carroll, 1991; see Note 57.)

- *Starbucks Coffee Co.* — Offering more than just a good cup of coffee, Starbucks has programs that benefit employees (e.g., retirement plans for even part-time workers), communities (e.g., promoting local charities), and the environment (e.g., developing reusable cups).
- *The Co-operative Bank* — One of the most innovative banks in the United Kingdom, the Co-operative Bank refrains from making socially irresponsible investments (e.g., it will not finance weapons deals, the fur trade, and companies involved in animal testing).

It is important to note that corporate social responsibility is not merely a collection of isolated practices or occasional gestures, nor does it involve initiatives motivated by marketing or public relations benefits. Instead, corporate social responsibility is a comprehensive set of policies, practices, and programs that are integrated throughout business operations and decision-making processes that are supported and rewarded by top management. Importantly, social responsibility involves more than simply making a few charitable donations; it must be a commitment to doing what's best for people and the community (as is the case with the companies spotlighted in these examples). In recent years, many of the largest companies in the United States have been going out of their way to behave in a variety of socially responsible ways. For a summary of some of the most socially responsible companies in a recent year, along with just a single noteworthy example of their commitment to social responsibility, see Table 2.4.[59]

Table 2.4	Top 10 Most Socially Responsible Companies in the United States in 2003

A research firm recently analyzed the level of corporate social responsibility among the largest companies in the United States in 2003. Basing their analysis on such key considerations as the companies' contributions to the community, attention to employees' needs, preservation of the environment, and advancement of minorities and women, the top 10 performers are listed here. As indicated, these companies excelled in different ways.

Rank	Company	Notable Socially Responsible Action
1	General Mills	Invested $2 million to create 150 jobs in the inner city of Minneapolis
2	Cummins Engine	Built a school serving 800 poor Brazilian children and their parents in a community near one of its manufacturing plants
3	Intel	On-the-job safety is emphasized so strongly that the accident rate among employees is 96 percent lower than the industry average
4	Procter & Gamble	Helped UNICEF fund tuberculosis vaccinations for 8 million children in developing countries
5	IBM	Donated $71 million in grants to help schools and $127 million in programs to help needy people around the world
6	Hewlett-Packard	Built a worldwide network of employee volunteers to develop ways to help the company to sustain the environment
7	Avon Products	Raised $250 million in support of breast cancer research, education, and screening for medically underserved women
8	Green Mountain Coffee	Pays poor Latin American coffee growers higher "fair trade price" for beans instead of the substantially lower "market price"
9	John Nuveen	Developed an educational program on financial literacy that is in use at over 1,300 schools
10	St. Paul	An active volunteer program gets employees involved in tutoring in schools, helping cleanup after natural disasters, and helping the homeless

(Sources: Based on information reported by Asmus, 2003, see Note 59; and the Web sites of the companies listed.)

Profitability and Social Responsibility: The Virtuous Circle

Do socially responsible companies perform better financially than those that are less socially responsible? The answer is not straightforward. Sometimes scientists find no clear connection, which is not surprising given the complexities of social responsibility and the fact that many different variables influence a company's financial performance. However, on many other occasions, they do find such a link. Consider, for example, that in the four decades from 1950 to 1990, highly socially responsible companies such as Johnson & Johnson, Coca-Cola, Gerber, IBM, Deere, Xerox, JCPenney, and Pitney Bowes grew at an annual rate of 11.3 percent compared to only 6.2 percent for other companies on the Dow Jones Industrials list over the same period.[60]

Although there are surely many different reasons for this, a key one, which I also mentioned in connection with ethics, is that people often support the socially responsible activities of organizations with their patronage and investments. With this in mind, there exist mutual funds that invest only in socially responsible companies and books that provide detailed information on the socially responsible (and irresponsible) behavior of companies that consumers and investors can use to guide their decisions.[61] Today, individuals who desire to support socially responsible companies by "voting with their dollars" can find it easy to get the information they need. That this may contribute to the financial well-being of a company is important, of course, since financial considerations are an organization's most basic responsibility (which is why they are at the base of the corporate social responsibility pyramid shown in Figure 2.8). That said, it is important to keep in mind that companies engage in socially responsible behavior for its own sake, not as a path to profitability.

> In the four decades from 1950 to 1990, highly socially responsible companies such as Johnson & Johnson, Coca-Cola, Gerber, IBM, Deere, Xerox, JCPenney, and Pitney Bowes grew at an annual rate of 11.3 percent compared to only 6.2 percent for other companies on the Dow Jones Industrials list over the same period.

Although profit may not be the primary objective for engaging in socially responsible behavior, it is clear that there is a strong link between the two. Moreover, this connection appears to be bidirectional in nature. The idea is straightforward: As noted earlier, companies that are highly socially responsible tend to perform well financially (i.e., they "do well by doing good"), and then because they have substantial resources, they can afford to allocate more resources (money, help from employees, etc.) to social causes (i.e., they "do good by doing well"). This relationship, which has been referred to as the **virtuous circle**, is summarized in Figure 2.9.[62]

With the virtuous circle in mind, it is not surprising to find that some of the world's most profitable organizations are also among the most philanthropic. For example, the highly profitable Microsoft Corporation regularly makes multimillion-dollar charitable contributions to worthwhile causes in the form of cash and software. In addition, a generous $24 million donation from its co-founder Bill Gates has made it possible for more good work to be accomplished around the world through the Bill and Melinda Gates Foundation. Although many big companies have been accused of exploiting people and harming society, examples like these make it clear that there is also another side to the story—and a very munificent and socially responsible one at that.[63]

Figure 2.9   The Virtuous Circle

It is been suggested that socially responsible companies perform well financially because they are supported by customers and investors. As a result, they become wealthier, making it easier for them to become even more philanthropic. This is known as the *virtuous circle*.

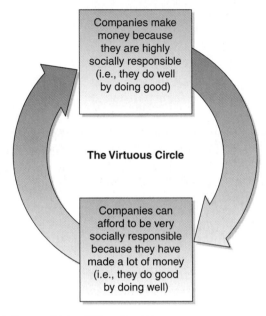

(*Source: Based on suggestions by Treviño and Nelson, 1999; see Note 30.*)

You Be the **Consultant**

Employee Theft in Convenience Stores

The district manager of a chain of 24-hour convenience stores is very concerned about her stores' rate of employee theft, which is currently about twice the industry average and rising rapidly. Because this problem has arisen suddenly, you and she suspect that it is in response to some recently introduced changes in the company's overtime policy. Managers who used to be paid time-and-a-half for each hour they worked over 40 are now paid a flat salary that typically results in lower total wages for the same amount of work. Answer the following questions based on the information in this chapter.

1. What form of justice appears to have been violated by the new pay policy? Explain your answer.

2. In this case, the new pay policy was implemented without first discussing it with store managers. Do you think that the theft rate might have been lower had this been done? What else could be done to reduce the growing theft rate?

3. The company's code of ethics expressly prohibits theft, but other than being handed a copy along with other company documents and forms upon being hired, hardly anyone pays attention to it. What do you think could be done, if anything, to enhance the effectiveness of the code of ethics as a weapon for combating the theft problem?

Self-Assessment Exercise

Assessing Organizational Justice Where You Work

To learn about how workers respond to various types of injustices they may experience in the workplace, scientists have found it useful to use rating scales like the one shown. By completing this scale, you will gain some useful insight into your own feelings about the fairness experienced in the organization in which you work.

Directions

1. Using the following scale, respond to each of the questionnaire items by selecting a number from 1 to 5 to indicate the extent to which it applies to you.

   1 = almost never

   2 = slightly

   3 = moderately

   4 = greatly

   5 = almost always

2. In responding to each item, think about a particular organization in which you work or, if you are a student, think about a particular class.

3. Where you see the word (*outcome*), substitute a specific outcome that is relevant to you (e.g., for a worker, pay; for a student, a grade).

4. Where you see the word (*superior*), substitute a specific authority figure that is relevant to you (e.g., for a worker, one's supervisor; for a student, one's teacher).

Scale

To what extent . . .

1. _____ Is it possible for you to express your views about your (outcome)?
2. _____ Are your (outcomes) generally based on accurate information?
3. _____ Do you have an opportunity to correct decisions made about your (outcome)?
4. _____ Are you rewarded appropriately for the effort you put into your work?
5. _____ Do the (outcomes) you receive reflect the quality of your work?
6. _____ Is your (outcome) in keeping with your performance?
7. _____ Are you treated politely by your (superior)?
8. _____ Does your (superior) treat you with dignity and respect?
9. _____ Does your (superior) refrain from making inappropriate comments?
10. _____ Does your (superior) communicate openly with you?
11. _____ Does your (superior) tell you things in a timely fashion?
12. _____ Does your (superior) explain decisions to you in a thorough fashion?

(Source: Adapted from Colquitt, 2001; see Note 4).

Scoring

1. Add your responses to questions 1, 2, and 3. This is your *distributive justice* score.

2. Add your responses to questions 4, 5, and 6. This is your *procedural justice* score.

3. Add your responses to questions 7, 8, and 9. This is your *interpersonal justice* score.

4. Add your responses to questions 10, 11, and 12. This is your *informational justice* score.

5. For each score, higher numbers (e.g., 12–15) reflect higher perceived amounts of the type of fairness in question, whereas lower scores (e.g., 3–6) reflect lower perceived amounts of that type of fairness.

Discussion Questions

1. With respect to what particular type of fairness did you score highest? What specific experiences contributed to this assessment?

2. With respect to what particular type of fairness did you score lowest? What specific experiences contributed to this assessment?

3. What kinds of problems resulted from any violations of any type of organizational justice you may have experienced? What could have been done to avoid these violations?

Group Exercise

Analyzing an Ethical Dilemma

More often than you might imagine, managers confront situations in which they have to decide the right thing to do. Such "ethical dilemmas," as they are known, are usually quite challenging. Discussing ethical dilemmas with others is often a useful way of shedding light on the ethical path by identifying ethical considerations that you may have overlooked on your own. This exercise will give you an opportunity to analyze an ethical dilemma.

Directions

1. Divide the class into multiple groups of three or four students.

2. Read the following ethical dilemma.

3. Working together with the others in your group, analyze the dilemma by answering the following questions:

   (a) As the vice president in this situation, what do you think you *would do*? What factors enter into your decision?

   (b) What do you think would be the *right thing* to do? Explain the basis for your answer.

Ethical Dilemma

You're the vice president of a medium-sized organization that uses chemicals in its production process. In good faith, you've hired a highly competent person to ensure that your company complies with all environmental laws and safety regulations. This individual informs you that a chemical the company now uses in some quantity is not yet on the approved EPA list, although it's undergoing review and is scheduled to be placed on the approval list in about three months because it's been found to be safe. You can't produce your product without the chemical, yet you're not supposed to use the chemical until it's approved. Waiting for approval would require shutting down the plant for three months, putting hundreds of people out of work, and threatening the company's very survival.

Source: Managing Business Ethics (2ⁿᵈ ed.) by Linda K. Treviño and Katherine A. Nelson, p. 10. © 1999 John Wiley & Sons.

Discussion Questions

1. Did the members of your group generally agree or disagree about what they would do in the situation described? What new viewpoints, if any, did you learn from others in your group?

2. Did the members of your group generally agree or disagree about what they thought was the right thing to do? What were the major points of agreement and disagreement?

3. In judging the right thing to do, what factors were taken into account (e.g., the law, the layoffs, etc.) and in what manner were they considered? Did you gain any new insight into the ethical dilemma by virtue of the viewpoints expressed by others? Explain.

Notes

Case Notes

Wilson, M. (2002, January 11). Understanding the NFL salary cap. *CasinoARTICLES.com.* From the World Wide Web at www.casinoarticles.com/pub/sports_nfl_football_salary_cap.html. National Football League. (1998, November 30). *NFL modifies coin toss procedure.* From the World Wide Web at www.nfl.com/news/981130coin.html. National Football League. (1999, August 21). *Commissioner's news conference.* From the World Wide Web at www.nfl.com/news/0123.tagliabue.html.

Chapter Notes

[1] Greenberg, J., & Colquitt, J. A. (2004). *Handbook of organizational justice.* Mahwah, NJ: Lawrence Erlbaum Associates.

[2] Werhane, P., Radin, T. J., & Bowie, N. E. (2003). *Employment and employee rights.* Malden, MA: Blackwell.

[3] Harvard Business School Press. (2003). *Harvard Business Review on corporate responsibility.* Boston: Author.

[4] Colquitt, J. A. (2001). On the dimensionality of organizational justice: A construct validation of a measure. *Journal of Applied Psychology, 86,* 386–400. Greenberg, J. (1993). The social side of fairness: Interpersonal and informational classes of organizational justice. In R. Cropanzano (Ed.), *Justice in the workplace: Approaching fairness in human resource management* (pp. 79–103). Hillsdale, NJ: Lawrence Erlbaum Associates.

[5] Greenberg, J. (1996). *The quest for justice on the job: Essays and experiments.* Thousand Oaks, CA: Sage.

[6] Ang, S., Van Dyne, L., & Begley, T. M. (2003). The employment relationships of foreign workers versus local employees: A field study of organizational justice, job satisfaction, performance, and OCB. *Journal of Organizational Behavior, 24,* 561–583.

[7] Greenberg, J. (2000). Promote procedural justice to enhance acceptance of work outcomes. In E. A. Locke (Ed.), *The Blackwell handbook of principles of organizational behavior* (pp. 181–195). Malden, MA: Blackwell.

[8] Allen, M. (1998, May 15). Giuliani threatens action if cabbies fail to cancel a protest. *New York Times*, p. C1.

[9] Greenberg, J., & Cropanzano, R. A. (2001). *Advances in organizational justice*. Stanford, CA: Stanford University Press.

[10] Lind, E. A., Greenberg, J., Scott, K. S., & Welchans, T. D. (2000). The winding road from employee to complainant: Situational and psychological determinants of wrongful termination claims. *Administrative Science Quarterly, 45*, 557–590.

[11] See Note 5.

[12] Brockner, J., & Weisenfeld, B. M. (1996). The interactive impact of procedural and outcome fairness on reactions to a decision: The effects of what you do depends on how you do it. *Psychological Bulletin, 120*, 189–208.

[13] See Note 5.

[14] Greenberg, J. (1993). Stealing in the name of justice: Informational and interpersonal moderators of theft reactions to underpayment inequity. *Organizational Behavior and Human Decision Processes, 54*, 81–103.

[15] Simons, T., & Roberson, Q. (2003). Why managers should care about fairness: The effects of aggregate justice perceptions on organizational outcomes. *Journal of Applied Psychology, 88*, 432–443.

[16] See Note 7.

[17] Schaubroeck, J., May, D. R., & Brown, F. W. (1994). Procedural justice explanations and employee reactions to economic hardship: A field experiment. *Journal of Applied Psychology, 79*, 455–460.

[18] Skarlicki, D. P., & Latham, G. P. (2004). Can leaders be trained to be fair? In J. Greenberg & J. A. Colquitt (Eds.), *Handbook of organizational justice*. Mahwah, NJ: Lawrence Erlbaum Associates.

[19] McConahey, M. (2003, June 8). Ethics scandals reach epidemic level. *Press Democrat* (Santa Rosa, California), p. A8. (Also on the World Wide Web at www.jim-carroll.com/acrobat/publicity/pressdemocrat-1.pdf)

[20] Hamm, S., Greene, J., Edwards, C., & Kerstetter, J. (2003, September 8). Epedemic: Crippling computer viruses and spam attacks threaten the information economy. *Business Week*, pp. 30–38, 40, 42.

[21] Weaver, J. (2003, June 4). Martha Stewart indicted on 9 counts. *MSNBC*. From the World Wide Web at stacks.msnbc.com/news/922014.asp.

[22] Zellner, W., & Forest, S. A. (2001, December 17). The fall of Enron. *Business Week*, pp. 30–34, 36.

[23] Ferrell, O. C., Fraedrich, J., & Ferrell, L. (2002). *Business ethics: Ethical decision making and cases* (5th ed.). Boston: Houghton Mifflin.

[24] Bies, R. J., & Greenberg, J. (2001). Dueling images of justice in the global economy: The swoosh, the sweatshops, and the sway of public opinion. In M. Gannon & K. Newman (Eds.), *Handbook of cross-cultural management* (pp. 320–334). Oxford, England: Blackwell.

[25] The Corporate Library. (2002, July). Spotlight topic: Adelphia scandal. From the World Wide Web at www.thecorporatelibrary.com/spotlight/scandals/adelq.html.

[26] Henderson, V. E. (1992). *What's ethical in business?* New York: McGraw-Hill.

[27] Ethics Resources Center. (2003). *2003 National business ethics survey*. Washington, DC: Author.

[28] Ethics Resource Center. (2003). *What is ethics?* From the World Wide Web at www.ethics.org/faq.html#eth_what.

[29] Salopek, J. J. (2001, July). Do the right thing. *American Society for Training and Development.* From the World Wide Web at www.astd.org/CMS/templates/index.html?template_id=1&articleid=26983.

[30] Treviño, L. K., & Nelson, K. A. (1999). *Managing business ethics* (2nd ed.). New York: John Wiley & Sons. (quote, p. 14)

[31] See Note 30. (quote, pp. 26–27)

[32] MAALA Business for Social Responsibility. (2002). Corporate social responsibility. Tel Aviv, Israel: Author (also at www.maala.com.). Verschoor, C. C. (1998). A study of the link between a corporation's financial performance and its commitment to ethics. *Journal of Business Ethics, 17,* 1509–1516. Embley, L. L. (1993). *Doing well while doing good.* Upper Saddle River, NJ: Prentice Hall.

[33] See Note 26.

[34] See Note 30.

[35] Johnson, D. C. (1997, November 9). United Way, faced with fewer donations, is giving away less. *New York Times,* p. A1.

[36] See Note 30. (quote, pp. 30–31)

[37] Kaplan, J. M. (2003, May/June). Justice Department revises corporate prosecution standards. *Ethikos, 16*(6), pp. 1–3, 13.

[38] Ethics and Policy Integration Centre (2003). Toward an effective ethics and compliance program: The Federal Sentencing Guidelines for Organizations. Washington, DC: Author. Available on the World Wide Web at www.ethicaledge.com/appendix1.html.

[39] Treviño, L. K., & Youngblood, S. A. (1990). Bad apples in bad barrels: A causal analysis of ethical decision-making behavior. *Journal of Applied Psychology, 75,* 378–385.

[40] Kohlberg, L. (1976). Moral stages and moralization: The cognitive-developmental approach. In T. Lickona (Ed.), *Moral development and behavior: Theory, research, and social issues* (pp. 2–52). New York: Holt, Rinehart, and Winston. Kohlberg, L. (1969). Stage and sequence: The cognitive-developmental approach to socialization. In D. A. Goslin (Ed.), *Handbook of socialization theory and research* (pp. 347–380). Chicago: Rand McNally.

[41] Greenberg, J. (2002). Who stole the money, and when? Individual and situational determinants of employee theft. *Organizational Behavior and Human Decision Processes, 89,* 895–1003. Blass, T. (1999). *Obedience to authority: Current perspectives on the Milgram paradigm.* Mahwah, NJ: Lawrence Erlbaum Associates. Grover, S. L. (1993). Why professionals lie: The impact of professional role conflict on reporting accuracy. *Organizational Behavior and Human Decision Processes, 55,* 251–272.

[42] Treviño, L. K. (1992). Moral reasoning and business ethics. *Journal of Business Ethics, 11,* 445–459.

[43] Brass, D. J., Butterfield, K. D., & Skaggs, B. C. (1998). Relationships and unethical behavior: A social-network perspective. *Academy of Management Review, 23,* 14–31.

[44] Wolfe, D. M. (1988). Is there integrity in the bottom line: Managing obstacles to executive integrity. In S. Srivastava (Ed.), *Executive integrity: The search for high human values in organizational life* (pp. 140–171). San Francisco: Jossey-Bass.

[45] Jansen, E., & Von Glinow, M. A. (1985). Ethical ambivalence and organizational reward systems. *Academy of Management Review, 10,* 814–822.

[46] See Note 27.

[47] Cassell, C., Johnson, P., & Smith, K. (1997). Opening the black box: Corporate codes of ethics in their organizational context. *Journal of Business Ethics, 16,* 1077–1093.

[48] Weaver, G. R., Treviño, L. K., & Cochran, P. L. (1996). Corporate ethics practices in the mid-1990s: An empirical study of the *Fortune* 1000. *Journal of Business Ethics, 18,* 283–294.

[49] Ethics Resource Center. (1994). *Ethics in American business: Policies, programs and perceptions.* Washington, DC: Author.

[50] See Note 29.

[51] Ferrell, O. C., Fraedrich, J., & Ferrell, L. (2002). *Business ethics* (5th ed.). Boston: Houghton Mifflin. Waddock, S., & Smith, N. (2000, Winter). Corporate responsibility audits: Doing well by doing good. *Sloan Management Review*, pp. 66–83.

[52] Singer, A. (2003, May/June). Excelon excels at reaching out. *Ethikos, 16*(6), pp. 7–9, 13.

[53] From the World Wide Web at www.exeloncorp.com/corporate/about/a_overview.shtml.

[54] Schwartz, M. (2001). The nature of the relationship between corporate codes of ethics and behaviour. *Journal of Business Ethics, 23*, 219–228.

[55] See Note 45.

[56] See Greenberg, 2002; Note 40.

[57] Carroll, A. B. (1991). The pyramid of corporate social responsibility: Toward the moral management of organizational stakeholders. *Business Horizons, 34*(4), 39–48.

[58] Brady, D. (2002, February 19). The right mix of (yogurt) cultures? *Business Week*, pp. 57–58. Key mining and oil companies pledge to keep hands off protected sites. (2003, September 7). *Business Respect Corporate Social Responsibility Dispatches No. 62.* From the World Wide Web at www.mallenbaker.net/csr/nl/62.html#anchor1058. U.S.: Boise Cascade announces zero old-growth wood policy. (2003, September 7). *Business Respect Corporate Social Responsibility Dispatches No. 62*. From the World Wide Web at www.mallenbaker.net/csr/nl/62.html#anchor1058. Waddock, S. A. (2001). *Leading corporate citizens*. Burr Ridge, IL: McGraw Hill/Irwin.

[59] Asmus, P. (2003, Spring). 2003 100 best corporate citizens. *Business Ethics*, pp. 6–10.

[60] Margolis, J. D., & Walsh, J. P. (2001). *People and profits? The search for a link between a company's social and financial performance*. Mahwah, NJ: Lawrence Erlbaum Associates. Labich, K. (1992, April 20). The new crisis in business ethics. *Fortune*, pp. 167–170, 172, 174, 176.

[61] McIntosh, M. (2003). *Raising a ladder to the moon: The complexities of corporate social and environmental responsibility*. New York: Palgrage Macmillan. Rayner, J. (2002). *Corporate social responsibility monitor*. London: Gee Publishing. Kinder, P. D., Lydenberg, S. D., & Domini, A. L. (1994). *Investing for good: Making money while being socially responsible*. New York: HarperCollins. Domini, A. L., Lydenberg, S. D., & Kinder, P. D. (1992). *The social investment almanac: A comprehensive guide to socially responsible investing*. New York: Henry Holt & Co.

[62] See Note 30.

[63] Clark, J., & Driscoll, W. (2003). *Globalization and the poor: Exploitation or equalizer*. New York: International Debate Education Association. Steele, J. R. (2003). *"Is this my reward?" An employee's struggles for fairness in the corporate exploitation of his inventions*. New York: Pencraft Press.

Chapter **Three**

LEARNING OBJECTIVES

After reading this chapter, you will be able to:

1. **DEFINE** personality and **DESCRIBE** various personality dimensions that are responsible for individual differences in organizational behavior.

2. **DISTINGUISH** between emotions and moods and **DESCRIBE** the effects of emotions and moods on behavior in organizations.

3. **DEFINE** social perception and **EXPLAIN** the processes by which people come to make judgments about what others are like.

4. **DESCRIBE** social identity theory and Kelley's theory of causal attribution and **DESCRIBE** the various biases that make the social perception process imperfect.

5. **DEFINE** learning and **DESCRIBE** the two basic kinds of learning that occur in organizations.

6. **EXPLAIN** various ways in which principles of learning are applied in organizations.

Individual Processes: Personality, Emotions, Perception, and Learning

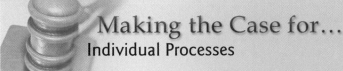

Making the Case for... Individual Processes

Building the Enterprise by Putting People First

In 1957 Jack Taylor, the sales manager of a Cadillac dealership in St. Louis, had an intriguing idea: Instead of selling cars outright, it might be more profitable to rent them repeatedly on a short-term basis. Enterprise Rent-A-Car was born. Rather than competing with industry giants Hertz and Avis, who targeted business travelers by offering rentals at airports, Taylor aimed Enterprise toward a different market—individuals seeking temporary replacements for their damaged or stolen cars. From this modest start, Enterprise Rent-A-Car has grown into a company with more than 50,000 employees in 5,150 offices, making it now the largest car rental company in North America. As the business was growing, Taylor's son, Andy, helped his father by working in rental branches, assisting customers, washing cars, doing whatever was needed. Learning all he could about the business, Andy Taylor worked his way up the ladder, eventually becoming CEO in

1991. Under his leadership, Enterprise quickly became a multibillion-dollar company that expanded into Europe and developed spin-off businesses.

The longer people work with Andy Taylor the more convinced they become that it is not just his business savvy that has made Enterprise so successful but also his special qualities—particularly, his infectious enthusiasm and his drive to succeed. He works tirelessly, acknowledging that "it doesn't matter how smart or talented you are if you are not willing to put in the work for future success." To ensure that they do, Taylor put a plan into place that rewards employees for their performance. From the assistant manager level upward, Enterprise employees are paid a salary plus a percentage of their branch's profits. As a result, they benefit directly from their hard work and those of their teammates with whom they work closely.

Taylor acknowledges that the business experience he got on the job was invaluable, saying, "Through my early experiences at Enterprise I was able to see firsthand the importance of customer service and employee development." So that today's employees can benefit from the same types of experiences, Enterprise promotes people from within the company. In fact almost all of the company's senior managers started out staffing rental offices and worked their way up the corporate ladder as management trainees. In fact, Taylor believes that advancing in Enterprise's training program is like picking up your M.B.A. on the job—"an M.B.A. without the IOU," as he puts it.

Taylor emphasizes that Enterprise's success comes not from an overarching focus on profit. Instead, he believes—and his company's history has shown—that profit follows naturally when you put people first. Indeed, making Enterprise a pleasant place for people to do business is the company's objective. One way Taylor does this is by visiting local offices to keep his finger on the pulse of the business—and to not pass up any opportunities to share his beliefs about the importance of keeping customers satisfied. He also puts people first by giving back to the community through generous donations (both personal and corporate) to local charity groups, such as the United Way. As Taylor put it, "It will be very satisfying if people say that, no matter now big our company got, we always stayed true to our goals of putting people first and always doing the right thing."

3 GOOD REASONS why you should care about...

Individual Processes

You should care about individual processes because:

1. Understanding people's personalities helps us know what to expect of them, and understanding our own personalities provides valuable insight into our own behavior.

2. The process by which we perceive others is fundamental to a wide variety of organizational activities.

3. Effectively training, managing, and disciplining employees requires knowing the basic principles of learning.

As straightforward as this case may be, it illustrates the importance of several basic psychological processes that are responsible for key aspects of people's behavior in organizations. Collectively, these are the **individual processes** to which we are referring in the title of this chapter—psychological processes that occur within individuals that cannot be seen but whose existence can be inferred on the basis of people's behavior. In particular, our account of Andy Taylor at Enterprise Rent-A-Car highlights the role of four such individual processes that we will discuss in this chapter, which account for a wide variety of forms of organizational behavior.

To begin, it is obvious that Andy Taylor is a very special individual. After all, it isn't everyone who works his way up from helping his father around the office to leading a multibillion-dollar business. But then again, like Andy Taylor, we all have our own special combination of characteristics that makes us distinct from others. It is this distinct pattern of traits that defines one's *personality*, the first topic we will examine in this chapter. Clearly, one of Taylor's most special qualities is his capacity to express his feelings about the things that matter most to him, such as putting people first—be they customers, employees, or members of the community. The nature of people's feelings—their *emotions* and *moods*—is the second topic covered in this chapter.

Among the things that have contributed to Andy Taylor's success as an executive appears to be his sensitivity to what others think about the company, cultivating the impression that Enterprise is a "people-first," community-spirited company. The process by which people come to make judgments of other individuals (and companies) is known as *social perception*—a topic that we also will cover in this chapter. Finally, this chapter will conclude with a discussion of another important individual process, *learning*. The importance of learning is illustrated in the Enterprise case by the careful attention given to the management training program and, of course, the hands-on experiences that Andy received as he worked his way up through the company.

As you will see from reading this chapter, the various individual processes that we touched on here are far broader in scope than this case suggests and account for a wide range of behavior in organizations. After reading this chapter, you will come away with a good understanding of some of the basic psychological processes that contributed to the success of Andy Taylor at Enterprise Rent-A-Car and, more importantly, that contribute to your own success in the world of organizations.

Personality: The Unique Differences Between Us

If our experience with other people tells us anything, it is that we are all in some way *unique*, and at least to a degree, we are all *consistent*. That is, we each possess a distinct pattern of traits and characteristics not fully duplicated in any other person, and these are generally stable over time. Thus, if you know someone who is courteous and outgoing today, he or she probably showed these traits in the past and is likely to continue showing them in the future. Moreover, this person will tend to show them in many different situations over time.

Together, these two facts form the basis for a useful working definition of **personality**—the unique and relatively stable pattern of behavior, thoughts, and emotions shown by individuals. In short, personality refers to the lasting ways in which any one person is different from all others. And, as you might imagine, personality characteristics can be very important on the job.[1] With this in mind, we will review several key personality dimensions that appear most relevant to OB.

The "Big Five" Dimensions of Personality

learning
objective

Although there are many different dimensions of personality that can be used to describe people, some are more important than others. One group of variables that scientists have found to be especially important is referred to as the **big five dimensions of personality**.[2] For a summary of these vital aspects of personality, see Table 3.1.

As you might imagine, the big five dimensions of personality play an important role in organizational behavior.[3] For example, research has shown that employees who are highly conscientious tend to perform better than those who are not so conscientious. Organizational scientists also have found that people who are highly extraverted tend to succeed on managerial and sales jobs—much as the stereotype suggests.[4] However, not all research findings are as easily explained. For example, neither agreeableness nor emotional stability have been linked to success in various kinds of job. This may well be because large numbers of disagreeable and unstable people leave their jobs early. As a result, those who are left behind, and whose performance is measured by the researchers, tend to be relatively agreeable and stable. Clearly, as you can see, personality plays an important—but often unpredictable—role when it comes to understanding behavior in organizations.

Table 3.1	The Big Five Dimensions of Personality

A cluster of personality traits known as the *big five dimensions of personality* has been found to account for important differences in the way people behave in organizations. These characteristics are described here.

Component of the Big Five	Description
Conscientiousness	The degree to which someone is hardworking, organized, dependable, and persevering (high in conscientiousness), as opposed to lazy, disorganized, and unreliable (low in conscientiousness)
Extraversion–introversion	The degree to which someone is gregarious, assertive, and sociable (extraverted), as opposed to reserved, timid, and quiet (introverted)
Agreeableness	The degree to which someone is cooperative and warm (highly agreeable), as opposed to belligerent and cold (highly disagreeable)
Emotional stability	The degree to which someone is insecure, anxious, and depressed (emotionally unstable), as opposed to secure, calm, and happy (emotionally stable)
Openness to experience	The extent to which someone is creative, curious, and cultured (open to experience), as opposed to practical and having narrow interests (closed to experience)

Type A and Type B Behavior Patterns

Think about the people you know. Can you identify someone who always seems to be in a hurry, is extremely competitive, and is often irritable? Now name someone who shows the opposite pattern—a person who is relaxed, not very competitive, and easygoing. The people you have in mind represent extremes on one key dimension of personality. The first individual would be labeled *Type A* and the second *Type B*. People categorized as **Type A** personalities show high levels of competitiveness, irritability, and time urgency (i.e., they are always in a hurry). In addition, they demonstrate certain stylistic patterns, such as loud and exaggerated speech, and a tendency to respond very quickly in many contexts. For example, during conversations they often begin speaking before others are finished. People classified as having a **Type B** personality show the opposite pattern; they are calmer and more relaxed.

Do people who are Type A's and Type B's differ with respect to job performance? Given their high level of competitiveness, it seems reasonable to expect that Type A's will work harder at various tasks than Type B's and, as a result, will perform at higher levels. In fact, however, the situation turns out to be more complex than this.[5] On the one hand, Type A's *do* tend to work faster on many tasks than Type B's, even when no pressure or deadline is involved. Similarly, they are able to get more done in the presence of distractions. In addition, Type A's often seek more challenges in their work than Type B's (e.g., given a choice, they tend to select more difficult tasks).

Despite these differences, Type A's do not always perform better than Type B's. For example, Type A's frequently do poorly on tasks requiring patience or careful, considered judgment. For the most part, they are simply in too much of a hurry to complete such work in an effective manner. A study comparing Type A and Type B nurses suggests why this may be so. Although Type A's were significantly more involved in their jobs and invested greater effort, they also were more overloaded (i.e., they took on too much to do) and experienced more conflict with respect to the various aspects of the job required of them. It is easy to understand how differences such as these may well interfere with any possible improvements in performance that may derive from effort alone.

These and other findings suggest that neither pattern has the overall edge when it comes to task performance. Although Type A's may excel on tasks involving time pressure or solitary work, Type B's have the advantage when it comes to tasks involving complex judgments and accuracy as opposed to speed.

Achievement Motivation: Striving for Success

You probably know some people who yearn for and focus on success, concentrating on doing what it takes to achieve it. Enterprise Rent-A-Car's Andy Taylor, described in the opening case, is a clear example. Others, as you know, are far less concerned about success. If it comes, fine, but if not, that's okay too. These individuals may be said to differ with respect to an important dimension of personality known as **achievement motivation** (sometimes termed the **need for achievement**). This may be defined as the strength of an individual's desire to excel—to succeed at difficult tasks and to do them better than anyone else.

People high in achievement motivation may be characterized as having a highly task-oriented outlook. That is, they are more concerned with getting things done than they are with having good relationships with others.[6] Also, because they are so interested in achieving success, people who have a high amount of achievement motivation tend to seek tasks that are moderately difficult and challenging. After all, a task that is too difficult is likely to lead to failure, and a task that is too easy doesn't offer sufficient challenge to suit them. The opposite pattern describes people who are low on achievement motivation. These individuals strongly prefer extremely difficult or extremely easy tasks because success is almost guaranteed if the task is easy enough, and failure can readily be justified by attributing it to external sources (i.e., the extreme difficulty of the task) if the task is too difficult (see Figure 3.1).[7]

As you might imagine, people who are high in achievement motivation strongly desire feedback on their performance. This allows them to adjust their aspirations (i.e., to shoot for easier or more difficult goals) and to determine when they have

Figure 3.1   Achievement Motivation and Attraction to Tasks

People who are high in achievement motivation are attracted to tasks of moderate difficulty, whereas people who are low in achievement motivation are attracted to tasks that are extremely easy or extremely difficult.

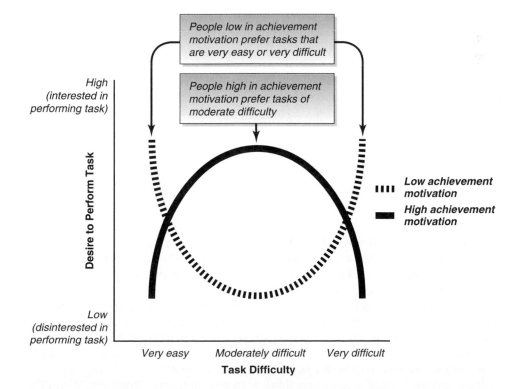

succeeded, allowing them to attain the good feelings about their accomplishments that they crave. As part of this tendency, people who differ with respect to achievement motivation are attracted to different kinds of jobs. People high in need achievement prefer jobs in which they receive feedback that tells them how well they are doing, whereas those low in need achievement have little such interest. Not surprisingly, it has been found that people high in achievement motivation prefer jobs in which pay is based on merit, whereas those low in achievement motivation prefer jobs in which pay is based on seniority.

Given their strong desire to excel, you may expect that people who are high in achievement motivation will have highly successful careers. To some extent, this is true. Such individuals tend to gain promotions more rapidly than those who are low in motivation, at least early in their careers. However, people who are high in achievement motivation are not necessarily superior managers. In part, this is because people who are high in achievement motivation tend to create situations in which they can receive credit for their performance while carefully monitoring others. As we will see later in this book (Chapter 13), such ways of structuring organizations are not always conducive to high performance.

Self-Monitoring: Controlling How We Present Ourselves to Others

Our opening case about Andy Taylor paints a clear picture of an individual who goes out of his way to present a certain image of himself (in this case, it's the image of a caring leader who is concerned about the people with whom he works and the customers and communities he serves). Because of his apparent sensitivity to what others think, Taylor may be said to have a high amount of the personality characteristic known as *self-monitoring*. Specifically, **self-monitoring** refers to the extent to which individuals attempt to exercise control over the way they present themselves to others.

Individuals who score high in measures of self-monitoring want to behave in socially acceptable ways and are especially sensitive to cues about the appropriateness of their behavior (e.g., they may be expected to pick up on such subtle signs of disapproval from others as a raised eyebrow). Their high concern about what others think of them may guide their behavior, such as by always doing what others think is right. People who are low in self-monitoring, by contrast, are more prone to be guided by their own attitudes and feelings than by the desires of others. These may be individuals who speak out sharply against company policies at meetings even if doing so offends others. The fact that this may make them look bad in the eyes of others is likely to be of little concern to them.

Because they are likely to tailor their behavior to the situation at hand, high self-monitors may perform especially well at tasks requiring sensitivity to others' feelings, such as sales positions.[8] At the same time, the bluntness of low self-monitors would likely make them poor choices for such positions. However, their willingness to speak their mind about things may make low self-monitors particularly well suited to tasks in which giving negative feedback is essential. Under such circumstances, high self-monitors may be so concerned about others' impressions of them that they may refrain from being as open as they should. Combining these observations, it is clear that the role of self-monitoring is particularly complex in the case of managerial jobs. On the one hand, the effective manager must not be so overly concerned about what others think as to refrain from telling them things they need to hear, even if they are unpleasant. On the other hand, individuals who are so unconcerned about what others think will be ineffective as managers because their insensitivity to others' feelings will insult people. Obviously, self-monitoring is a complex, and very important, personality variable in organizations.

Self-Efficacy: The "Can Do" Facet of Personality

Suppose that two individuals are assigned the same task by their supervisor, and that one is confident of her ability to carry it out successfully, whereas the other has some serious doubts on this score. Which person is more likely to succeed? Assuming that all other factors (e.g., differences in their ability and motivation) are held constant, it is reasonable to predict that the first will do better. Such an individual is higher in a personality variable known as **self-efficacy**—one's belief in his or her own capacity to perform a task. When considered in the context of a given task, self-efficacy is not, strictly speaking, an aspect of personality. However, based on direct experiences and vicarious experiences, people acquire general expectations about their ability to perform a wide range of tasks in many different contexts. Such generalized beliefs about self-efficacy are stable over time, and these can be viewed as a personality variable.

Self-efficacy is a good predictor of people's work behavior.[9] For example, in a study of university professors, it was found that self-efficacy was positively correlated with research productivity—that is, productivity increased as self-efficacy increased. In addition, it has been found that unemployed people who are trained in ways of enhancing their self-efficacy perceptions are more likely to look for jobs and, therefore, more likely to find jobs.[10] We also know that women who have taken physical self-defense training classes tend not only to be confident in their ability to defend themselves but also tend to be assertive on the job, as well.[11] Clearly, when it comes to a wide variety of behavior in organizations, self-efficacy is an important aspect of personality.

Self-Esteem: The Importance of Self-Evaluations

Beliefs about one's ability to perform specific tasks are an important part of the *self-concept*—individuals' conceptions of their own abilities, traits, and skills. Yet, they are only a small part. Another important aspect involves **self-esteem**—the extent to which people hold positive or negative views about themselves. People high in self-esteem evaluate themselves favorably, believing they possess many desirable traits and qualities. In contrast, people low in self-esteem evaluate themselves unfavorably, believing they are lacking in important respects and that they have characteristics that others consider unappealing. (To get a sense of your own self-esteem, complete the **Self-Assessment Exercise** on pages 106–107.)

Considerable evidence suggests that self-esteem is very important when it comes to a wide variety of organizational behavior.[12] For example, people who are low in self-esteem tend to be less successful in their job searches than those who are high in self-esteem. In addition, when people with low self-esteem are eventually employed, they are attracted to positions in larger organizations where they are unlikely to be noticed.

Once on the job, what can be expected of people who are low in self-esteem? The lower an employee's self-esteem, the less likely he or she is to take any active steps to solve problems confronted on the job (e.g., spending insufficient time to do a job). As a result, the employee's performance tends to suffer. By contrast, employees with high levels of self-esteem are inclined to actively attempt to acquire the resources needed to cope with work problems, and to use their skills and abilities to their fullest—and, as a result, perform at higher levels.[13] Interestingly, people with low self-esteem tend to be aware of their tendency to perform poorly. They are predisposed to evaluate themselves quite negatively (especially when ambiguity exists concerning their performance) and to believe that they are inherently responsible for their poor performance.

Although my comments thus far sound discouraging with respect to the fate of people with low self-esteem, I can conclude on a more positive note: Low self-esteem can be boosted. Although formal approaches are available, techniques that require the skills of a trained professional to implement (such as psychiatrists or clinical psychologists) can be very time consuming. Fortunately, there are things that you can do on an everyday basis in organizations to minimize people's feelings of low self-esteem. For an overview of some of these practices, see Table 3.2.

Emotions and Mood at Work

Just as stable aspects of ourselves—that is, our personalities—influence behavior in organizations, so too do more temporary feelings, such as our emotional states and our moods. If emotions and moods seem like they may be trivial, it's simply because their effects are so widespread that we take them for granted. However, their effects on the way we work can be considerable. Consider, for example, the following.

Table 3.2	Suggestions for Boosting Others' Low Self-Esteem

Although it is difficult to completely change key aspects of a personality, such as self-esteem, without intensive psychological help, there are several things that organizations can do to boost and maintain the self-esteem of their employees.

Suggestion	*Description*
■ Make people feel uniquely valuable.	Create opportunities for people to feel accepted by finding ways to make use of their unique skills and experiences.
■ Make people feel competent.	Recognize the good things that people do and praise them accordingly. That is, "catch someone in the act of doing something right."
■ Make people feel secure.	Employees' self-esteem will be enhanced when managers make their expectations clear and are forthright with them.
■ Make people feel empowered.	People given opportunities to decide how to do their jobs feel good about themselves and their work.

- It was a beautiful, sunny day—the kind that inspired Tonya to come up with lots of new ideas for her clients.
- Kimberly was so upset about not making any progress on her sales report that she left her desk and went to the gym to work out.
- It was a special day for Alex. He was so pleased that Shannon agreed to marry him that he made his way through his delivery route in half the usual time—and with a lively spring in his step.

Not only do scientists acknowledge that people's feelings at any given time are important, but they also recognize that two different kinds of feelings are involved—*emotions* and *mood*. Although you certainly have experienced different emotional states and different moods in your lives, and have seen them in others, you shouldn't assume that you know exactly how they influence behavior in organizations. As you will see, each of these states is far more complex than you might imagine.

Emotions: What Are They and How Do They Affect Us?

learning objective

By definition, **emotions** are overt reactions that express feelings about events. You get angry when a colleague takes advantage of you. You become sad when your best friend leaves to take a new job. And you become afraid of what the future holds when a larger firm merges with the company in which you've worked for 15 years. These are all examples of emotional reactions. The key thing to remember about emotions is that they have an object—that is, something or someone triggers them. Although it may seem that people have an infinite number of emotions, these all fit into the six basic categories shown in Table 3.3.[14]

We are interested in emotions in the field of OB because these are involved in three key aspects of how we work. I will review each of these here.

Emotional dissonance.   As you know, people sometimes are required to display emotions on the job that are inconsistent with how they actually feel. This phenomenon,

Table 3.3	Major Categories of Emotion and Associated Categories

Scientists have found it useful to categorize people's emotions into the six major categories (and several associated subcategories) identified here.

Category of Emotion	*Subcategories*
Anger	Disgust, envy, exasperation, irritation, rage, torment
Fear	Alarm, anxiety
Joy	Cheerfulness, contentment, enthrallment, optimism, pride, relief, zest
Love	Affection, longing, lust
Sadness	Disappointment, neglect, sadness, shame, suffering, sympathy
Surprise	(No subcategories)

(Source: Based on Weiss and Cropanzano, 1996; see Note 14.)

known as **emotional dissonance**, can be a significant source of work-related stress (a topic we will discuss in Chapter 4).[15]

You probably can think of several good examples of what may well be emotional dissonance. Imagine a flight crew of a major airline whose members are both tired and annoyed at the rude passengers whom they have encountered on a long flight. These individuals do not have the option of expressing how they really feel— or even, of expressing nothing at all. Instead, they are expected to act like everything is okay, thanking the passengers for choosing their airline and cheerfully saying goodbye (more like "b'bye") to them as they exit the plane. The conflict between the emotions they may be really feeling (anger) and those they are required to express (happiness) is considered a source of stress that eventually may take its toll on these individuals' well-being.[16]

Emotional intelligence.   Emotions also are important on the job insofar as people who are good at "reading" and understanding emotions in others, and who are able to regulate their own emotions, tend to have an edge when it comes to dealing with others. Recently, experts have come to recognize the importance of what is called **emotional intelligence**—that is, a cluster of skills related to the emotional aspects of life, such as the ability to monitor one's own and others' emotions, to discriminate among emotions, and to use such information to direct one's thoughts and actions.[17] Specifically, people who are considered to have high emotional intelligence (those said to have a high *EQ*) demonstrate four key characteristics.

- *Skill in regulating one's own emotions.* High EQs are good at self-regulation—that is, they are aware of their own feelings and display the most appropriate emotions. For example, if you know people who are especially good at calmly talking about their feelings instead of yelling at others at whom they are angry, chances are good that they have a high degree of emotional intelligence.

- *Ability to monitor others' emotions.* People with high EQs are very good at judging how they are affecting other people and behave accordingly. For example, such an individual would refrain from sharing bad news with a colleague who already is very upset about something in his or her life. Instead, he or she would be inclined to wait for a more appropriate time.

- *Interest in motivating oneself.* There are times when many of us feel frustrated and lack interest in whatever we are doing and want to quit. This is not the case for people with high EQs. Rather, such individuals are able to motivate themselves to sustain their performance, directing their emotions toward personal goals and resisting the temptation to quit.

- *Highly developed social skills.* People with high EQs also are very good at keeping a great number of relationships going over long periods of time. If you know people like this, you may realize that being this way is no accident. Such individuals are not only good at forming networks of relationships but also they are able to carefully coordinate their efforts with people and are good at working out ways of getting along with others, even during difficult periods.

As you might imagine, in the world of work, people who have highly developed emotional intelligence have an edge in many different ways. Consider entrepreneurs, for example. To be successful, such individuals usually have to be able to accurately judge what other people are like and to get along with others well enough to craft successful business deals. Not surprisingly, several aspects of emotional intelligence are related to the financial success of entrepreneurs.[18] Likewise, scientists who are well accepted by their colleagues and who, as a result, are well networked, tend to be up on the latest advances and as a result, tend to be more productive. Clearly, having high levels of emotional intelligence is a real plus when it comes to one's success on the job.[19]

Job performance.   Emotions play an important role on the job insofar as they interfere with job performance.[20] Will you work at your best when you are in a highly emotional state? Probably not. Someone who is excited because she is about to go on vacation or to attend an exciting sporting event the next day might not be focusing on the job as completely as she otherwise might in a less emotional state.

The negative impact of emotional states is even greater in the case of negative emotions. Consider, for example, an employee who is unhappy and upset because he received an unsatisfactory performance rating. This individual may be expected to be so distraught that he will lose the capacity to pay attention and become distracted from his work. Not only is this likely to impede task performance, but it also is likely to interfere with the potentially useful feedback that this individual might receive from the supervisor giving the evaluation. For this reason, successful managers recommend not even trying to get messages across to people while they are upset. In the case of the poorly performing employee, it may be best to wait until another time when the employee can be better focused to help him learn ways of improving.

Mood: Subtle Feelings with Big Impact

In contrast to emotions, which are highly specific and intense, we also have feelings that are more diffuse in scope, known as *moods*. Scientists define **mood** as an unfocused, relatively mild feeling that exists as background to our daily experiences. Whereas we are sure to recognize the emotions we are feeling, moods are more subtle and difficult to detect. For example, you may say that you are in a good mood or a bad mood, but this isn't as focused as saying that you are experiencing a certain emotion, such as anger or sadness.

Moods, as we all know, fluctuate rapidly, sometimes widely, during the course of a day. Whereas favorable feedback from our bosses may make us feel good, harsh criticism may put us in a bad mood. Such temporary shifts in feeling *states*—short-term differences in the way we feel—are only partly responsible for the mood that people demonstrate. Superimposed over these passing conditions are also more stable personality *traits*—consistent differences between people's predispositions toward experiencing positive or negative affect. Mood, in other words, is a combination of both who we are, personality-wise, and the conditions we face.[21]

Not surprisingly, then, the moods we experience can be based on our individual experiences (e.g., receiving a raise), as well as the general characteristics of our work groups or organizations (e.g., the extent to which they are upbeat, energetic, and enthusiastic). For example, the importance of having fun at work is emphasized at such companies as Southwest Airlines and Ben and Jerry's Homemade Ice Cream.[22] It's no wonder that people working for these companies are generally in a good mood.

Positive and negative affectivity.   As you might imagine, scientists are far more specific about classifying people's moods than saying that they are simply good or bad. A particularly popular way of doing so is by distinguishing between *positive and negative affectivity*. Some people, as you know, are generally energetic, exhilarated, and have a real zest for life. You know them to be "up" all the time. Such individuals may be said to be high in **positive affectivity**. By contrast, people who are low in positive affectivity are generally apathetic and listless.

Another dimension of mood is known as **negative affectivity**. It is characterized at the high end by people who are generally angry, nervous, and anxious, and at the low end, by those who feel calm and relaxed most of the time. As indicated in Figure 3.2, positive affectivity and negative affectivity are not the opposite of each other but are rather two separate dimensions.

It probably comes as no surprise that differences in people's characteristic mood levels play an important role in organizational behavior. For example, research comparing the performance of M.B.A. students making various simulated managerial decisions found that people showing high positive affectivity were superior to those showing high negative affectivity. They made decisions that were more accurate, more important to the group's effectiveness, and were rated by experts as having greater managerial potential. Emotional intelligence is so important that some organizations, such as the U.S. Air Force, are considering candidates' emotional intelligence when making key placement decisions.[23] Some organizations, such as Hong Kong Telecom, are even training employees in ways of increasing their

Figure 3.2   Positive and Negative Affectivity

Positive affectivity and negative affectivity are two independent dimensions. The mood states associated with high levels and low levels of each are shown here.

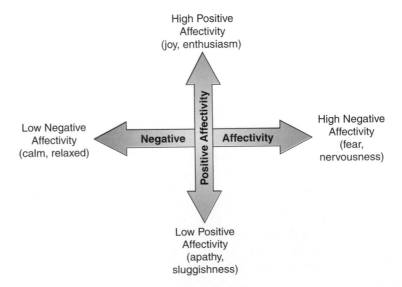

emotional intelligence. Although emotional intelligence is a new concept, it clearly holds a great
deal of promise when it comes to understanding
behavior in organizations.

Emotional intelligence is so important that some organizations, such as the U.S. Air Force, are considering candidates' emotional intelligence when making key placement decisions.

Mood and behavior.   Research has shown that
our moods influence the way we behave on the job
in several important respects. First, researchers
have shown that mood is related to memory. Specifically, we know that being in a positive mood helps people recall positive things and being in a negative mood helps people recall negative things.[24] This idea is known as **mood congruence**. For example, if
you go to work while you're in a good mood, chances are that this will help you
remember those things on the job that also put you in a good mood, such as the
friendly relationships you have with your coworkers. Likewise, if you are in a bad
mood, you are likely to recall negative things associated with work, such as a recent
fight with your boss.

Mood also biases the way we evaluate people and things. For example, people
report greater satisfaction with their jobs while they are in a good mood than while
they are in a bad mood.[25] Being in a good mood also leads people to judge others'
work more positively. The practical advice is clear: Make sure your boss is in a good
mood before he or she conducts your annual performance evaluation. It just may
make a difference!

Finally, it is important to note that mood strongly affects the extent to which
people help each other, cooperate with one another, and refrain from behaving
aggressively (forms of behavior we will discuss in more detail in Chapter 7). People
who are in a good mood also tend to be more generous and are inclined to help their
fellow workers who may need their assistance. So, if you need help with an important project on the job, it may be in your best interest to approach someone who is
in a good mood. People who are in a good mood also are inclined to work carefully
with others to resolve conflicts with them, whereas people in a bad mood are likely
to keep those conflicts brewing. As a result, if someone is in a bad mood, this might
not be the best time to sit down with her to discuss ways of settling an argument she
is having with you. Let it rest for now—or, better yet, help put that person in a good
mood before approaching this issue.

Social Perception: Understanding and Judging Others

What do the following organizational situations have in common? (1) You are interviewing a prospective employee for a new position in your company. (2) You apolo-
gize profusely after spilling a cup of coffee on your boss. (3) You complete a form
asking you to rate the strengths and weaknesses of your subordinates.

If you don't immediately see the connection, it's probably because these situations all involve a phenomenon that is so automatic that you probably never have
thought about it before. The answer is that they all involve understanding and evaluating others—in other words, figuring out what they are like. In our example, you

judge the applicant's qualifications, you make sure your boss's opinion of you is not negative, and you assess the extent to which your employees are doing their jobs properly. In each of these instances, you are engaging in **social perception**—the process of integrating and interpreting information about others so as to accurately understand them. As these examples illustrate, social perception is a very important process in a wide variety of organizational situations.[26] To better understand social perception, we will examine several different approaches to how the process works.

Social Identity Theory: Answering the Question, "Who Are You?"

3
learning
objective

How would you answer if someone asked, "Who are you?" There are many things you could say. For example, you could focus on individual characteristics, such as your appearance, your personality, and your special skills and interests—that is, your **personal identity**. You also could answer in terms of the various groups to which you belong, saying, for example, that you are a student in a particular organizational behavior class, an employee of a certain company, or a citizen of a certain country— that is, your **social identity**. The conceptualization known as **social identity theory** recognizes that the way we perceive others and ourselves is based on both our unique characteristics (i.e., personal identity) and our membership in various groups (i.e., social identity).[27] For an overview of this approach, see Figure 3.3.

Social identity theory claims that the way we identify ourselves is likely to be based on our uniqueness in a group. Say, for example, that you are the only business major in an English class. In this situation, you will be likely to identify yourself as "the business major," and so too will others come to recognize you as such. In other words, that will become your identity in this particular situation. Because we belong to many groups, we are likely to have several unique aspects of ourselves to use as the basis for establishing our identities (e.g., you may be the only left-handed person, the only one to have graduated college, or even the only one to have committed a crime). How do we know which particular bases for defining their personal identities people will choose?

Given the natural desire to perceive ourselves positively and to get others to see us positively as well, we are likely to identify ourselves with groups we believe to be perceived positively by others. We know, for example, that people in highly regarded professions, such as doctors, are more inclined to identify themselves with their profession than those who have lower-status jobs.[28] Likewise, people tend to identify themselves with winning sports teams by wearing the colors and logos of those teams. In fact, the tendency to wear clothing that identifies oneself as a fan of a certain team depends on how successful that team has been: The better a team has performed, the more likely its fans are to sport apparel that publicly identifies them with that team.[29]

In addition to explaining how we perceive ourselves, social identity theory also explains how we come to perceive others. Specifically, the theory explains that we focus on the differences between ourselves and other individuals as well as members of other groups (see the lower portion of Figure 3.3). In so doing, we tend to simplify things by assuming that people in different groups share certain qualities that make them different from ourselves—even if they really are not so different after all.

Not only do we perceive others as different from ourselves, but we also perceive them as different in negative ways. This is particularly so when we are com-

Figure 3.3   Social Identity Theory: An Overview

According to *social identity theory*, people identify themselves in terms of their individual charac-teristics and their group memberships. They then compare themselves to other individuals and groups to help define who they are, both to themselves and others.

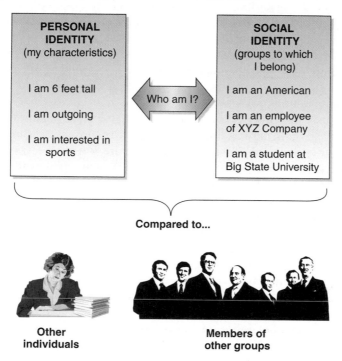

peting against them (see Chapter 7). Take athletic competitions, for example. If you ever have heard the negative things that students from one college or university say about those from other schools whom they are competing against in vari-ous sports, then you know quite well the phenomenon I am describing here. Although such perceptions tend to be exaggerations—and inaccurate, as a result—most of us stick with these perceptions, nevertheless. The reason is simple. Making such categorizations helps bring order to the world. After all, distinguish-ing between "the good guys" and "the bad guys" makes otherwise complex judg-ments quite simple. And, after all, bringing simplicity to a complex world is what social perception is all about.

Attribution: Judging What People Are Like and Why They Do What They Do

A question we often ask about others is "why?" Why did the manager use the wrong data in his report? Why did the chief executive develop the policy she did? When we ask such questions, we're attempting to get at two different types of information: (1) What is someone really like? (2) What made the person behave as he or she did? People attempt to answer these questions in different ways.

Making correspondent inferences: Using acts to judge dispositions.   Situations frequently arise in organizations in which we want to know what someone is like. Is your new boss likely to be tough or kind-hearted? Are your coworkers prone to be punctual or late? The more you know about what people are like, the better equipped you are to know what to expect and how to deal with them. How, then, do we go about identifying another's traits?

Generally speaking, the answer is that we infer others' traits based on what we are able to observe of their behavior. The judgments we make about what people are like based on what we have seen them do are known as **correspondent inferences**. Simply put, correspondent inferences are judgments about people's dispositions—their traits and characteristics—that correspond to what we have observed of their actions.

At first blush, this process seems deceptively simple. A person with a disorganized desk may be thought of as sloppy. Someone who slips on the shop floor may be considered clumsy. Such judgments might be accurate, but not necessarily! After all, the messy desk actually may be the result of a coworker rummaging through it to find some important documents. Similarly, the person who slipped could have encountered oily conditions under which anyone, even the least clumsy individual, would have fallen. In other words, it is important to recognize that the judgments we may make about someone may be inaccurate because there are many possible causes of behavior. For this reason, correspondent inferences may not always be accurate.

Another reason why correspondent inferences may be misleading is that people frequently conceal some of their traits—especially when these may be viewed as negative. So, for example, a sloppy individual may work hard in public to appear to be organized. Likewise, the unprincipled person may talk a good show about the importance of being ethical. In other words, people often do their best to disguise some of their basic traits. Not surprisingly, this makes the business of forming correspondent inferences risky, at best.

Causal attribution of responsibility: Answering the question "why?"   Imagine finding out that your boss just fired one of your fellow employees. Naturally, you'd ask yourself, "why did he do that?" Was it because your coworker violated the company's code of conduct? Or was it because the boss is a cruel and heartless person? These two answers to the question "why?" represent two major classes of explanations for the causes of someone's behavior: *internal* causes, explanations based on actions for which the individual is responsible, and *external* causes, explanations based on situations over which the individual has no control. In this case, the internal cause would be the person's violation of the rules, and the external cause would be the boss's cruel and arbitrary behavior.

Generally speaking, it is very important to be able to determine whether an internal or an external cause was responsible for someone's behavior. Knowing why something happened to someone else might better help you prepare for what might happen to you. For example, in this case, if you believe that your colleague was fired because of something for which she was responsible herself, such as violating a company rule, then you might not feel as vulnerable as you would if you thought she was fired because of the arbitrary, spiteful nature of your boss. In the later case, you might decide to take some precautionary actions, to do something to protect yourself from your boss, such as staying on his good side, or even giving up and finding a new job—before you are forced to. The key question of interest to social scientists is: How do people go about judging whether someone's actions were caused by internal or external causes?

An answer to this question is provided by **Kelley's theory of causal attribution**. According to this conceptualization, we base our judgments of internal and external causality on three types of information. These are as follows:

learning objective

- *Consensus*—the extent to which other people behave in the same manner as the person we're judging. If others do behave similarly, consensus is considered high; if they do not, consensus is considered low.

- *Consistency*—the extent to which the person we're judging acts the same way at other times. If the person does acts the same at other times, consistency is high; if he or she does not, then consistency is low.

- *Distinctiveness*—the extent to which this person behaves in the same manner in other contexts. If he or she behaves the same way in other situations, distinctiveness is low; if he or she behaves differently, distinctiveness is high.

According to the theory, after learning about these three factors, we combine this information to make our attributions of causality. Here's how. If we learn that other people act like this one (consensus is high), this person behaves in the same manner at other times (consistency is high), and that this person does not act in the same manner in other situations (distinctiveness is high), we are likely to conclude that this person's behavior stemmed from *external* causes. In contrast, imagine learning that other people do not act like this one (consensus is low), this person behaves in the same manner at other times (consistency is high), and that this person acts in the same manner in other situations (distinctiveness is low). In this case, we will probably conclude that this person's behavior stemmed from *internal* causes.

Because this explanation is highly abstract, let's consider an example to illustrate how the process works. Imagine that you're at a business lunch with several of your company's sales representatives when the sales manager makes some critical remarks about the restaurant's food and service. Further imagine that no one else in your party acts this way (consensus is low), you have heard her say the same things during other visits to the restaurant (consistency is high), and that you have seen her acting critically in other settings, such as the regional sales meeting (distinctiveness is low). What would you conclude in this situation? Probably that her behavior stems from internal causes. In other words, she is a "picky" person, someone who is difficult to please.

Now, imagine the same setting but with different observations. Suppose that several other members of your group also complain about the restaurant (consensus is high), that you have seen this person complain in the same restaurant at other times (consistency is high), but that you have never seen her complain about anything else before (distinctiveness is high). By contrast, in this case, you probably would conclude that the sales manager's behavior stems from external causes: The restaurant really *is* inferior. For a summary of these contrasting conclusions, see Figure 3.4.

Figure 3.4 Kelley's Theory of Causal Attribution

In determining whether another's behavior stems mainly from internal or external causes, we rely on the three types of information identified here.

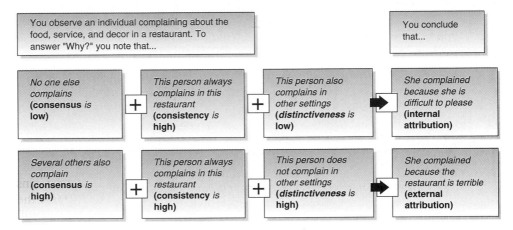

The Biased Nature of Social Perception

As you might imagine, people are far from perfect when it comes to making judgments of others. In fact, researchers have noted that there are several important types of biases that interfere with making completely accurate judgments of others.

The Fundamental Attribution Error

Despite what Kelley's theory says, people are *not* equally predisposed to reach judgments regarding internal and external causality. Rather, they are more likely to explain others' actions in terms of internal rather than external causes. In other words, we are prone to assume that others' behavior is due to the way they are, their traits and dispositions (e.g., "she's that kind of person"). So, for example, we are more likely to assume that someone who shows up for work late does so because she is lazy rather than because she got caught in traffic. This tendency is so strong that it is known as the **fundamental attribution error**.

This phenomenon stems from the fact that it is far easier to explain someone's actions in terms of his or her traits than to recognize the complex pattern of situational factors that may have affected their actions. As you might imagine, this tendency can be quite damaging in organizations. Specifically, it leads us to prematurely assume that people are responsible for the negative things that happen to them (e.g., "he wrecked the company car because he is careless"), without considering external alternatives, ones that may be less damning (e.g., "another driver hit the car"). And this can lead to inaccurate judgments about people.

The Halo Effect

Imagine that you are a supervisor of a worker whom you generally like and who performs her job well. There is only one problem, however: She usually arrives to work late, causing others in her work team to have to cover for her. You are well aware of the problem, but despite this, when it comes to evaluating this employee's performance, you tend to give her high ratings, overlooking this one problem. Why? The answer lies in what is called the **halo effect**. This refers to the tendency for a person's overall impression to bias his or her assessment of another on specific dimensions. This type of biased social perception is quite common. People want to have consistent perceptions of others and so they overlook the one characteristic that doesn't quite fit with the others. This occurs whether that characteristic is negative (as in this case) or positive. As you might imagine, whenever supervisors fail to provide their subordinates necessary feedback (be it positive or negative) on particularly important aspects of their work, they are missing the opportunity to change that behavior (if it is negative) or to maintain it (if it is positive).

The halo effect applies not only to individuals but to work teams as well (a topic we will discuss in Chapter 9). Consider, for example, the way we tend to bias our perceptions of the teams for which we root as sports fans. Because we desire to see our team in a favorable light, we attribute positive characteristics to it when it wins ("this is the greatest team ever"). However, if our team loses, we tend to blame the loss on the mistakes or poor performance of one particular player ("the team is still good, but that one player ruined it for us"). This is known as the **team halo effect**— the tendency for people to credit teams for their successes but not to hold them accountable for their failures.

The team halo effect has been demonstrated clearly in a recent study.[30] In this investigation researchers asked college students to recall either a successful team experience or an unsuccessful team experience in which they participated in their lives. They were then asked to complete a questionnaire indicating the extent to which they attributed that outcome to either the team as a whole or to the performance of a particular individual. The results, summarized in Figure 3.5, support the existence of the team halo effect. Specifically, whereas the team as a whole was believed to be much more responsible for good performance than for poor performance, specific team members were believed to be only slightly more responsible for good performance than for poor performance. In fact, participants attributed poor team performance more to certain individuals on the team than to the team as a whole.

Stereotypes: Fitting others into categories.   Inaccurate judgments about people can also stem from the preconceived ideas we hold about certain groups. Here, we are referring to **stereotypes**—beliefs that all members of specific groups share similar traits and behaviors. Expressions of stereotypes usually take the form: "People from group X possess characteristic Y." For example, what comes to mind when you think about people who wear glasses? Are they studious? Eggheads? Although there is no evidence of such a connection, it is interesting that for many people such an image lingers in their minds.

Deep down inside many of us know, and can articulate, that not all people from a specific group possess the characteristics—either negative or positive—with which we associate them. In other words, most of us accept that the stereotypes we use are at least partially inaccurate. After all, not *all* X's are Y; there are exceptions (maybe even quite a few!). If so, then why are stereotypes so prevalent? Why do we use them?

Figure 3.5 The Team Halo Effect: A Demonstration

According to the *team halo effect*, people tend to recognize teams more for their successes than for their failures. This effect was demonstrated in a recent experiment showing that people held teams much more responsible for good performance than for poor performance whereas individual team members were considered only slightly more responsible for good performance than for poor performance.

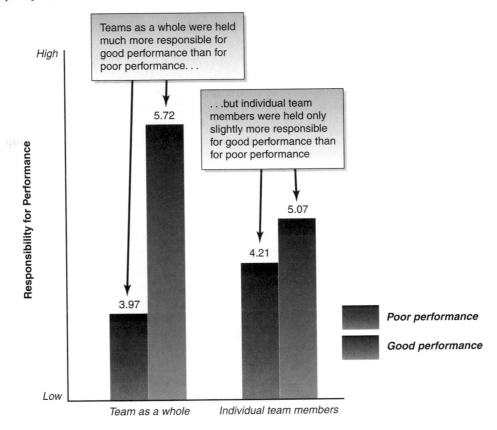

(Source: Based on data reported by Naquin and Tynan, 2003; see Note 30.)

To a great extent, the answer lies in the fact that people tend to do as little cognitive work as possible when it comes to thinking about others. That is, we tend to rely on mental shortcuts. If assigning people to groups allows us to assume that we know what they are like and how they may act, then we can save the tedious work of having to learn about them as individuals. After all, we come into contact with so many people that it's impractical—if not impossible—to learn everything about them we need to know. So, we rely on readily available information—such as someone's age, race, gender, or job type—as the basis for organizing our perceptions in a coherent way. If you believe that members of group *X* tend to have trait *Y*, then simply observing that someone falls into category *X* becomes the basis for your believing something about that individual (in this case, that he or she possesses *Y*). To the extent that the stereotype applies in this case, then the perception will be accurate. But in that case we are just lucky. More likely than not, such mental shorthand will lead us to judgments about people that are inaccurate—the price we pay for using stereotypes.

It is easy to imagine how the use of stereotypes can have powerful effects on the kinds of judgments people make in organizations. For example, if a personnel officer believes that members of certain groups are lazy, then he purposely may avoid hiring anyone belonging to those groups. The personnel officer may firmly believe that he is using good judgment—gathering all the necessary information and listening to the candidate carefully. Still, without being aware of it, the stereotypes he holds may influence the way he judges people. The result, of course, is that the fate of the individual in question is sealed in advance—not necessarily because of anything he or she may have done or said, but because of the mere fact that he or she belongs to a certain group. In other words, even people who are not being intentionally bigoted still may be influenced by the stereotypes they hold. The effects of stereotypes may be quite subtle and unintentional. (To give you a feel for some of the stereotypes people hold toward members of certain occupational groups, complete the **Group Exercise** on pages 107–108.)

Self-Fulfilling Prophecies: The Pygmalion Effect and the Golem Effect

In case it isn't already apparent just how important perceptions are in the workplace, consider the fact that the way we perceive others actually can dictate how effectively people will work. Put differently, perceptions can influence reality! This is the idea behind what is known as the **self-fulfilling prophecy**—the tendency for someone's expectations about another to cause that individual to behave in a manner consistent with those expectations.[31]

Self-fulfilling prophecies can take both positive and negative forms. In the positive case, holding high expectations of another tends to improve that individual's performance. This is known as the **Pygmalion effect**. This effect was demonstrated in a study of Israeli soldiers who were taking a combat command course.[32] The four instructors who taught the course were told that certain trainees had high potential for success, whereas the others had either normal potential or an unknown amount of potential. In reality, the trainees identified as belonging to each of these categories were assigned to that condition at random. Despite this, trainees who were believed to have high potential were found at the end of the training session to be more successful (e.g., they had higher test scores). This demonstrates the Pygmalion effect: Trainees whose instructors expected them to do well actually did so. Researchers also have found that the self-fulfilling prophecy works in the negative direction—that is, low expectations of success lead to poor performance. This is known as the **Golem effect**. Illustrating this phenomenon, researchers have found that paratroopers whose instructors expected them to perform poorly in their training class did, in fact, perform worse than those about whom instructors had no advance expectations.

The lesson to be learned from research on self-fulfilling prophecies is very clear: Managers should take concrete steps to promote the Pygmalion effect and to discourage the Golem effect. When leaders display enthusiasm toward people and express optimism about each person's potential, such positive expectations become contagious and spread throughout the organization. As a case in point, consider the great enthusiasm and support that Gordon Bethune showed toward employees of Continental Airlines in 1995 when he took over as that bankrupt company's CEO.[33] It would have been easy for him to be unsupportive and to show his disappointment with the workforce, but he did just the opposite. Only a few years after Bethune was at the helm, Continental turned around to become one of the most successful carriers in the sky today. Although the changes he made to the airline's systems and equipment helped, these things alone would not have been enough if the employees had felt like failures. Indeed, Gordon Bethune's acceptance and enthusiasm toward members of Continental's workforce contributed greatly to giving the encouragement needed to bring the airline "from worst to first."

> Gordon Bethune's acceptance and enthusiasm toward members of Continental's workforce contributed greatly to giving the encouragement needed to bring the airline "from worst to first."

Overcoming Bias in Social Perception: Some Guidelines

In most cases, people's biased perceptions of others are not the result of any malicious intent to inflict harm. Instead, biases in social perception tend to occur because we, as perceivers, are imperfect processors of information. We assume that people are internally responsible for their behavior because we cannot be aware of all the possible situational factors that may be involved—hence, we make the fundamental attribution error. Furthermore, it is highly impractical to be able to learn everything about someone that may guide our reactions—hence, we use stereotypes. This does not mean, however, that we cannot minimize the impact of these biases. Indeed, there are several steps that can be taken to help promote the accurate perception of others in the workplace. For an overview of several such suggestions, see Table 3.4.

We recognize that many of these tactics are far easier to say than to do. However, to the extent that you conscientiously attempt to apply these suggestions to your everyday interaction with others in the workplace, you will stand a good chance of perceiving people more accurately. And this, of course, is a fundamental ingredient in the recipe for managerial success.

Learning: Adapting to the World of Work

Question: What process is so broad and fundamental to human behavior that it may be said to occur in organizations—and throughout life, in general—continuously? The answer: **learning**. This process is so basic to our lives that you probably have a good sense of what learning is, but you may find it difficult to define. So, to make sure that we clarify exactly what it is, we formally define learning as a relatively permanent change in behavior occurring as a result of experience.

Several aspects of this definition bear pointing out. First, it's clear that learning requires that some kind of change occur. Second, this change must be more than temporary. Finally, it must be the result of experience—that is, continued contact with the world around us. Given this definition, we cannot say that short-lived performance changes on the job, such as those due to illness or fatigue, are the result of learning. Learning is a difficult concept for scientists to study because it cannot be directly observed. Instead, it must be inferred on the basis of relatively permanent

Table 3.4	Guidelines for Overcoming Perceptual Biases

Although perceptual biases are inevitable, the suggestions outlined here may be useful ways of reducing their impact.

Recommendation	*Explanation*
Do not overlook external causes of others' behavior.	Ask yourself if anyone else may have performed just as poorly under the same conditions. If the answer is yes, then you should not automatically assume that the poor performer is to blame. Good managers need to make such judgments accurately so that they can decide whether to focus their efforts on developing employees or changing work conditions.
Identify and confront your stereotypes.	Although it is natural to rely on stereotypes, erroneous perceptions are bound to result—and quite possibly at the expense of someone else. For this reason, it's good to identify the stereotypes you hold. Doing so will help you become more aware of them, taking a giant step toward minimizing their impact on your behavior.
Evaluate people based on objective factors.	The more objective the information you use to judge others, the less your judgments will be subjected to perceptual distortion.
Avoid making rash judgments.	It is human nature to jump to conclusions about what people are like, even when we know very little about them. Take the time to get to know people better before convincing yourself that you already know all you need to know about them. What you learn may make a big difference in the opinion you form.

changes in behavior. We will now consider two of the most prevalent forms of learning that occur in organizations—*operant conditioning* and *observational learning*.

Operant Conditioning: Learning Through Rewards and Punishments

Imagine you are a chef working at a catering company where you are planning a special menu for a fussy client. If your dinner menu is accepted and the meal is a hit, the company stands a good chance of adding a huge new account. You work hard at doing the best job possible and present your culinary creation to the skeptical client. Now, how does the story end? If the client loves your meal, your grateful boss gives you a huge raise and a promotion. However, if the client hates it, your boss asks you to turn in your chef's hat. Regardless of which of these outcomes occurs, one thing is certain: Whatever you did in this situation, you will be sure to do again *if* it succeeded, or you will avoid doing it again *if* it failed.

   This situation nicely illustrates an important principle of **operant conditioning** (also known as **instrumental conditioning**), namely, that our behavior produces

learning
objective

consequences and that how we behave in the future will depend on what those consequences are. If our actions have pleasant effects, then we will be more likely to repeat them in the future. If, however, our actions have unpleasant effects, we are less likely to repeat them in the future. This phenomenon, known as the **law of effect**, is fundamental to operant conditioning. Our knowledge of this phenomenon comes from the work of the famous social scientist B. F. Skinner.[34] Skinner's pioneering research has shown us that it is through the connections between our actions and their consequences that we learn to behave in certain ways. We summarize this process in Figure 3.6.

The various relationships between a person's behavior and the consequences resulting from it are known collectively as **contingencies of reinforcement**. We may identify four different kinds of contingencies, each of which describes the conditions under which rewards and punishments are either given or taken away. These are *positive reinforcement, negative reinforcement, punishment,* and *extinction*. As we discuss each of these next, you may find it useful to refer to the summary in Table 3.5.

Positive reinforcement.   A great deal of behavior is learned because of the pleasurable outcomes that we associate with it. In organizations, for example, people usually find it pleasant and desirable to receive monetary bonuses, paid vacations, and various forms of recognition. The process by which people learn to perform acts leading to such desirable outcomes is known as **positive reinforcement**. Whatever behavior led to the positive outcomes is likely to occur again, thereby strengthening that behavior. For a reward to serve as a positive reinforcer, it must be made contingent on the specific behavior sought. So, for example, if a sales representative is given a bonus after landing a huge account, the bonus will only reinforce the person's actions *if* he or she associates it with the landing of the account. When this

Figure 3.6   The Operant Conditioning Process

The basic premise of operant conditioning is that people learn by associating the consequences of their behavior with the behavior itself. In this example, the manager's praise increases the subordinate's tendency to perform the job properly in the future.

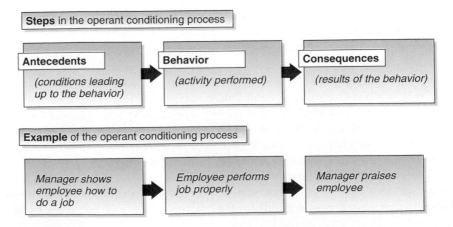

Table 3.5	Contingencies of Reinforcement

The four reinforcement contingencies may be defined in terms of the presentation or withdrawal of a pleasant or unpleasant stimulus. Positively or negatively reinforced behaviors are strengthened; punished or extinguished behaviors are weakened.

Stimulus Presented or Withdrawn	*Desirability of Stimulus*	*Name of Contingency*	*Strength of Response*	*Example*
Presented	Pleasant	Positive reinforcement	Increases	Praise from a supervisor encourages continuing the praised behavior.
	Unpleasant	Punishment	Decreases	Criticism from a supervisor discourages enacting the punished behavior.
Withdrawn	Pleasant	Extinction	Decreases	Failing to praise a helpful act reduces the odds of helping in the future.
	Unpleasant	Negative reinforcement	Increases	Future criticism is avoided by doing whatever the supervisor wants.

occurs, the individual will be more inclined in the future to do whatever it was that helped get the account.

Negative reinforcement.   Sometimes we also learn to perform acts because they permit us to avoid undesirable consequences. Unpleasant events, such as reprimands, rejection, probation, and termination, are some of the consequences faced for certain negative actions in the workplace. The process by which people learn to perform acts leading to the avoidance of such undesirable consequences is known as **negative reinforcement**, or **avoidance**. Whatever response led to the termination of these undesirable events is likely to occur again, thereby strengthening that response. For example, you may stay late at the office one evening to revise a sales presentation because you believe that the boss will "chew you out" if it's not ready in the morning. You learned how to avoid this type of aversive situation and behave accordingly.

Punishment.   Thus far, we have identified responses that are strengthened—either because they lead to the occurrence of positive consequences or the termination of negative consequences. However, the connection between a behavior and its consequences is not always strengthened; such links also may be weakened. This is what happens in the case of **punishment**. Punishment involves presenting an undesirable or aversive consequence in response to an unwanted behavior. A behavior accompanied by an undesirable outcome is less likely to recur if the person associates the negative consequences with the behavior. For example, if you are chastised by your boss for taking excessively long coffee breaks, you are considered punished for this action. As a result, you will be less likely to take long breaks again in the future.

Extinction.   The link between a behavior and its consequences also may be weakened by withholding reward—a process known as **extinction**. When a response that was once rewarded is no longer rewarded, it tends to weaken and eventually die out—or be *extinguished*. Let's consider an example. Suppose for many months you brought boxes of donuts to your weekly staff meetings. Your colleagues always thanked you as they gobbled them down. You were positively reinforced by their approval, so you continued bringing the donuts. Now, after several months of eating donuts, your colleagues have begun dieting. So, although tempting, your donuts go uneaten. After several several months of no longer being praised for your generosity, you will be unlikely to continue bringing donuts. Your once rewarded behavior will die out; it will be extinguished.

Observational Learning: Learning by Imitating Others

Although operant conditioning is based on the idea that we engage in behaviors for which we are directly reinforced, many of the things we learn on the job are *not* directly reinforced. Suppose, for example, on your new job you see many of your coworkers complimenting your boss on his attire. Each time someone says something flattering, the boss stops at his or her desk, smiles, and acts friendly. By complimenting the boss, they are reinforced by being granted his social approval. Chances are, after observing this several times, you too will eventually learn to say something nice to the boss. Although you may not have directly experienced the boss's approval, you would expect to receive it based on what you have observed from others. This is an example of a kind of learning known as **observational learning**, or **modeling**. It occurs when someone acquires new knowledge *vicariously*— that is, by observing what happens to others.

A great deal of what is learned about how to behave in organizations can be explained as the result of the process of observational learning. On the job, observational learning is a key part of many formal job instruction training programs. As we will explain in the next section, trainees given a chance to observe experts doing their jobs, followed by an opportunity to practice the desired skills, and then given feedback on their work tend to learn new job skills quite effectively. Observational learning also occurs in a very informal, uncalculated manner. For example, people who experience the norms and traditions of their organizations and who subsequently incorporate these into their own behavior may be recognized as having learned through observation.

Finally, it is important to note that people learn not only what to do by observing others but also what *not* to do. Specifically, research has shown that people observing their coworkers getting punished for behaving inappropriately on the job tend to refrain from engaging in those same actions themselves. As you might imagine, this is a very effective way for people to learn how to behave without ever experiencing any displeasure themselves.

Applications of Learning in Organizations

The principles of learning we have discussed thus far are used in organizations in many different ways. We will now discuss four systematic approaches to incorporating learning in organizations: *training, organizational behavior management, discipline,* and *knowledge management.*

Training: Learning and Developing Job Skills

Probably the most obvious use to which principles of learning may be applied in organizations is **training**—that is, the process through which people systematically acquire and improve the skills and abilities needed to improve their job performance. Just as students learn basic educational skills in the classroom, employees must learn their job skills. Training is used not only to prepare newly hired employees to meet the challenges of the jobs they will face but also to upgrade and refine the skills of existing employees. In fact, according to the American Society for Training and Development, American companies spend over $44 billion on training annually. For a summary of some of the most inventive training practices in use today, see Table 3.6.[35]

learning
objective

In view of this staggering investment, it is important to consider ways of enhancing the effectiveness of employee training.[36] Four major principles may be identified—participation, repetition, transfer of training, and feedback.

Participation.   People not only learn more quickly but also retain the skills longer when they have actively participated in the learning process. This applies to the learning of both motor tasks as well as cognitive skills. For example, when learning to swim, there's no substitute for actually getting in the water and moving your arms and legs. In the classroom, students who listen attentively to lectures, think about the material, and get involved in discussions tend to learn more effectively than those who just sit passively.

Repetition.   If you know the old adage "practice makes perfect," you are already aware of the benefits of repetition on learning. Perhaps you learned the multiplication table, or a poem, or a foreign language phrase by going over it repeatedly. Scientists have not only established the benefits of repetition on learning but also have shown that these effects are even greater when practice is spread out over time rather than when it is lumped together. After all, when practice periods are too long, learning can suffer from fatigue, whereas learning a little bit at a time allows the material to sink in.

Transfer of training.   As you might imagine, for training to be most effective, what is learned during training must be applied to the job. In general, the more closely a training program matches the demands of a job, the more effective the training will be. A good example is the elaborate simulation devices used to train pilots and astronauts. At a more down to earth level is the equipment used in many technical schools for people to learn skilled trades such as welding, computer repair, and radiation technology.

Feedback.   It is extremely difficult for learning to occur in the absence of feedback—that is, knowledge of the results of one's actions. Feedback provides information about the effectiveness of one's training.[37] Of course, unless you learn what you already are doing well and what behaviors you need to correct, you will probably be unable to improve your skills. For example, it is critical for people being trained as word processing operators to know exactly how many words they correctly entered per minute if they are to be able to gauge their improvement.

Table 3.6	Training: What Are Today's Companies Doing?

As summarized here, some of today's companies are investing considerable resources in training efforts and reaping huge dividends as a result.

Company	Training Effort	Result
Motorola	"Motorola University" trains over 100,000 employees each year in work-related skills.	Each dollar spent on training brings in $30 in increased productivity every three years.
Corning	For up to two years, apprentices are trained the equivalent of one day per week in becoming specialists in Celeor (a product used in catalytic converters).	Product defects dropped by 38 percent.
Harley-Davidson	A variety of courses are offered to dealers ("Dealer Operations Training") to help them become more effective.	Market share and profitability have risen steadily since training began.
Sears	Sears aims to train virtually all employees at "Sears University" to help make the company a better place at which to work and to shop.	Salespeople have become more knowledgeable, helping close more sales.
Siemens	In Munich, Germany, Siemens uses its own analysts and engineers to train other employees in the kinds of business challenges the company faces.	The program pays for itself and saved the company $11 million in 1999 alone.

(Sources: Based on information in Ewing, 1999, and Meister, 1998; see Note 35.)

One type of feedback that has become popular in recent years is known as **360-degree feedback**—the process of using multiple sources from around the organization to evaluate the work of a single individual. This goes beyond simply collecting feedback from superiors, as is customary, but extends to the gathering of feedback from other sources, such as one's peers, direct reports (i.e., immediate subordinates), customers, and even oneself.[38] Many companies, including General Electric, AT&T, Monsanto, Florida Power and Light, DuPont, Westinghouse, Motorola, Fidelity Bank, FedEx, Nabisco, and Warner-Lambert, have used 360-degree feedback to give more complete performance information to their employees, greatly improving not only their own work but overall corporate productivity as well.[39] To get a feel for how some companies are using this technique, see the accompanying **Winning Practices** Section.

Many companies, including General Electric, AT&T, Monsanto, Florida Power and Light, DuPont, Westinghouse, Motorola, Fidelity Bank, FedEx, Nabisco, and Warner-Lambert, have used 360-degree feedback to give more complete performance information to their employees, greatly improving not only their own work but overall corporate productivity as well.

Winning **Practices**

Using 360-Degree Feedback:
Three Profiles

If you think about it, the practice of giving questionnaires to various people in an organization to assess how large groups of them feel about each other can serve a lot of purposes. Not only might the survey findings be used to help assess job performance, but they also can be used for many other purposes as well. For example, 360-degree feedback can be used to systematically assess training needs, to determine new products and services desired by customers, to gauge team members' reactions to each other, and to learn about a variety of potential human resource problems.[40] To better understand these and other uses of this popular tool, we will now consider three specific examples of 360-degree feedback in action.[41]

- *Promoting change at the Landmark Stock Exchange.* The Landmark Stock Exchange is one of several smaller stock exchanges that operate in the United States. Eclipsed by the giant exchanges, such as the New York Stock Exchange and NASDAQ, Landmark has been striving to become the best marketplace in the world by providing faster and more accurate movement of stock than its well-known competitors. Meeting this objective requires a willingness to go along with rapid change and innovation. To see how it was doing in this regard, Landmark implemented a 360-degree feedback program that provided employees with feedback in such key areas as consulting others, inspiring others, team building, and networking. This feedback was then used as the basis for providing systematic training in ways to change any behaviors found lacking.
- *Developing leaders at Leher McGovern Bovis.* Leher McGovern Bovis (LMB) was responsible for the renovation and restoration of such New York City landmarks as the Statue of Liberty and Grand Central Terminal. LMB is unique in the construction industry in the attention it pays to developing its employees' leadership skills and preparing them for senior positions in the company. Company officials implemented a 360-degree feedback program that helped identify people's readiness for advancement to leadership positions within the company and the best candidates for management training. The 360-degree feedback program helped reduce turnover among project managers from 12 percent down to only 2 percent.

- *Identifying training and selection requirements at Northwestern Mutual Life Insurance Company.* To meet growing competition, Northwestern Mutual Life (NML) restructured its offices, which required them to identify many new managers. The company used a 360-degree feedback program to assess the potential of individual agents to be promoted to these new managerial positions. Also, by systematically noting shortcomings, they use this information to identify the most-needed forms of management training. NLM's 360-degree feedback program has made the task of selecting and training managers more effective than ever.

As these examples illustrate, 360-degree feedback can be a very successful tool to help meet a wide variety of organizational objectives. For this reason, it continues to be very popular and may be expected to remain in widespread use in the future.

Organizational Behavior Management: Positively Reinforcing Desirable Organizational Behaviors

Earlier, in describing operant conditioning, we noted that the consequences of our behavior determines whether we repeat it or abandon it. Behaviors that are rewarded tend to be strengthened and repeated in the future. With this in mind, it is possible to administer rewards selectively to help reinforce behaviors that we wish to be repeated in the future. This is the basic principle behind **organizational behavior management** (also known as **organizational behavior modification**, or more simply, **OB Mod**). Organizational behavior management may be defined as the systematic application of positive reinforcement principles in organizational settings for the purpose of raising the incidence of desirable organizational behaviors.

Organizational behavior management programs have been used successfully to stimulate a variety of behaviors in many different organizations.[42] For example, a particularly interesting and effective program has been used in recent years at Diamond International, the Palmer, Massachusetts, company of 325 employees that manufactures Styrofoam egg cartons. In response to sluggish productivity, a simple but elegant reinforcement was put into place. Any employee working for a full year without an industrial accident is given 20 points. Perfect attendance is given 25 points. Once a year, the points are totaled. When employees reach 100 points, they get a blue nylon jacket with the company's logo on it and a patch identifying their membership in the "100 Club." Those earning still more points receive extra awards. For example, at 500 points, employees can select any of a number of small household appliances. These inexpensive prizes go a long way toward symbolizing to employees the company's appreciation for their good work.

This program has helped improve productivity dramatically at Diamond International. After the OB Mod program began at Diamond International, output improved 16.5 percent, quality-related errors dropped 40 percent, grievances decreased 72 percent, and time lost due to accidents was lowered by 43.7 percent. The result of all of this has been over $1 million in gross financial benefits for the company—and a much happier workforce. Needless to say, this has been a very simple and effective organizational behavior management program. Although not all such programs are equally successful, evidence suggests that they are generally quite beneficial.

Discipline: Eliminating Undesirable Organizational Behaviors

Just as organizations systematically may use rewards to encourage desirable behavior, they also may use punishment to discourage undesirable behavior. Problems such as absenteeism, lateness, theft, and substance abuse cost companies vast sums of money, situations many companies attempt to manage by using **discipline**—the systematic administration of punishment.

After the OB Mod program began at Diamond International, output improved 16.5 percent, quality-related errors dropped 40 percent, grievances decreased 72 percent, and time lost due to accidents was lowered by 43.7 percent.

By administering an unpleasant outcome (e.g., suspension without pay) in response to an undesirable behavior (e.g., excessive tardiness), companies seek to minimize the undesirable behavior. In one form or another, using discipline is a relatively common practice. Survey research has shown, in fact, that 83 percent of companies use some form of discipline, or at least the threat of discipline, in response to undesirable behaviors. But, as you might imagine, disciplinary actions taken in organizations vary greatly. For a summary of commonly used disciplinary measures arranged in terms of severity, see Figure 3.7.[43]

The trick to disciplining effectively is to know how to administer punishment in a way that is considered fair and reasonable. Fortunately, research and theory have pointed to some effective principles that may be followed to maximize the effectiveness of discipline in organizations. We will now consider several of these.

Deliver punishment immediately after the undesirable response occurs.   The less time that passes between the occurrence of an undesirable behavior and the administration of a negative consequence, the more strongly people will make the connection between them. When people make this association, the consequence is likely to serve as a punishment, thereby reducing the probability of the unwanted behavior. Thus, it is best for managers to talk to their subordinates about their undesirable behaviors immediately after committing them. Expressing disapproval after several days or weeks have gone by will be less effective since the passage of time will weaken the association between behavior and its consequences.

Give moderate levels of punishment—neither too high nor too low.   If the consequences for performing an undesirable action are not very severe (e.g., rolling one's eyes as a show of disapproval), then they are unlikely to serve as a punishment. After all, it is quite easy to live with such a mild response. In contrast, consequences that are overly severe might be perceived as unfair and inhumane. When this occurs, not only might the individual resign, but also a strong signal will be sent to others about the unreasonableness of the company's actions.

Punish the undesirable behavior, not the person.   Effective punishment is impersonal in nature and focuses on the individual's actions rather than his or her personality. So, for example, when addressing an employee who is repeatedly caught taking excessively long breaks, it is unwise to say, "You're lazy and have a bad attitude." Instead, it would be better to say, "By not being at your desk when expected, you're making it more difficult for all of us to get our work done on time." Responding in this manner will be less humiliating for the individual. Additionally, focusing on exactly what people can do to avoid such disapproval (taking shorter breaks, in this case) increases the likelihood that they will attempt to alter their behavior in the desired fashion. By contrast, the person who feels personally attacked might not only "tune out" the message but also not know exactly how to improve.

Use punishment consistently—all the time, for all employees.   Sometimes managers attempting to be lenient turn a blind eye to infractions of company rules. Doing this may cause more harm than good insofar as it inadvertently reinforces the undesirable behavior (by demonstrating that one can get away with breaking the rules). As a result, it is considered most effective to administer punishment after each occurrence of an undesirable behavior. Similarly, it is important to show

Figure 3.7   A Continuum of Disciplinary Measures

Ranked from mildest to most severe, these are the most common disciplinary tactics used by supervisors.

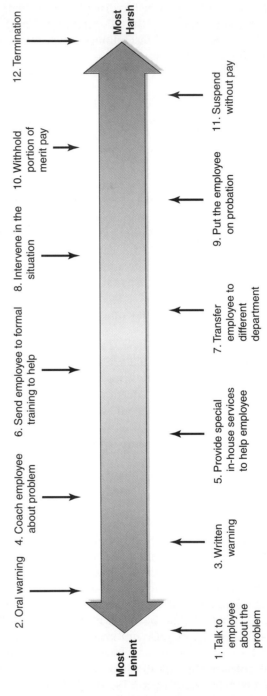

(*Source: Based on findings reported by Trahan and Steiner, 1994; see Note 43.*)

consistency in the treatment of all employees. In other words, everyone who commits the same infraction should be punished the same way, regardless of the person administering the punishment. When this occurs, supervisors are unlikely to be accused of showing favoritism.

Clearly communicate the reasons for the punishment given.   Making clear exactly what behaviors lead to what disciplinary actions greatly facilitates the effectiveness of punishment. Clearly communicated expectations helps strengthen the perceived connection between behavior and its consequences. Wise managers use their opportunities to communicate with subordinates to make clear that the punishment being given does not constitute revenge but rather an attempt to eliminate an unwanted behavior.

If, after reading all this, you are thinking that it is truly difficult to properly administer rewards and punishments in organizations, you have reached the same conclusion as experts in the field of organizational behavior. Indeed, one of the key skills that make some managers so effective is their ability to influence others by properly administering rewards and punishments (to practice this skill, see the **Group Exercise** on pages 107–109).

Knowledge Management: Sharing What Is Known

Thus far, our discussion of learning has focused on individuals. One by one, employees learn what they need to know and develop areas of expertise that are called on when needed to perform a certain job. However, there are occasions when there is somebody, somewhere in an organization needing to do something that requires special expertise but who doesn't know how to find it within the company. When this occurs, the company may waste time and money by "reinventing the wheel," developing expertise that already exists (if they only knew where to find it!). In other cases, if the necessary expertise is not tapped or new expertise is not developed, then either something will not get done properly, or it will not get done at all. Acknowledging this situation, in recent years many companies have instituted what is known as *knowledge management* programs. **Knowledge management** is defined as the process of gathering, organizing, and sharing a company's information and knowledge assets—that is, its **intellectual capital**. Typically, knowledge management programs involve using technology to establish repository databases and retrieval systems. Although only about a third of all companies have some type of knowledge management system in place, most others expect to implement such programs in the near future.[44]

A knowledge management plan is in place at British Petroleum (BP), where an employee-driven database available on the company's intranet contains information about the expertise of some 10,000 employees, making it a simple to task to determine "who knows what."[45] They also employ **knowledge managers**—individuals who are specifically charged with organizing the wealth of corporate knowledge represented by its people and ensuring that this information gets used effectively. Knowledge managers at BP actively seek out and summarize the lessons learned in various business units and distill the main points over the intranet. Harnessing knowledge in this way has led to considerable savings in the cost of construction and increased

A knowledge management plan is in place at British Petroleum (BP), where an employee-driven database available on the company's intranet contains information about the expertise of some 10,000 employees, making it a simple to task to determine "who knows what."

efficiency in the drilling of oilfields. Making it easy to find out whose brains to pick in an organization has proven very successful for many different companies. Indeed, some highly impressive results of implementing knowledge management programs have been reported. At IBM, for example, the sharing of information has made it possible for consultants to reduce the average time it takes to prepare a proposal from 200 hours down to 30 hours and for service representatives to slash in half the average amount of time required to repair one of its copy machines.

You Be the Consultant

Selecting, Training, and Appraising Employees

As human resources manager for a large information technology firm, you are responsible for three key functions—selecting prospective employees, training current employees, and appraising employees' job performance. Answer the following questions based on material in this chapter.

1. What personality characteristics would you recommend that the company seeks to find in its prospective employees? Which ones should it avoid? Explain your answers.

2. What types of biases and inaccuracies may be expected in the process of appraising employees' job performance? What can be done to minimize the impact of these factors?

3. Given that the company invests a great deal of money in its training program, you are interested in seeing that it works as effectively as possible. What specific steps can you take to ensure that learning of job skills occurs at a high level?

Self-Assessment Exercise

How Much Self-Esteem Do You Have?

To objectively measure self-esteem (and most other personality variables), scientists rely on paper-and-pencil questionnaires. This scale, adapted from ones actually used by scientists to measure self-esteem, should give you some insight into this important aspect of your personality. Because this measure is brief and not scientifically validated, you shouldn't draw any definitive conclusions about yourself from it. Still, completing it will give you *some* insight into your own self-esteem. Moreover, this exercise will give you a good feel for what these paper-and-pencil measures of personality are like in general.

Directions

For each of the following items, indicate whether you:

strongly disagree (SD)
disagree (D)
agree (A)
strongly agree (SA)

by marking the space provided.

_____   1. I believe I am a worthwhile person, who is as good as others.
_____   2. I have several positive qualities.
_____   3. For the most part, I consider myself a failure.
_____   4. Generally speaking, I can do things as well as others.
_____   5. I cannot be proud of too many things about myself.
_____   6. My feelings about myself are quite positive.
_____   7. In general, I am very pleased with myself.
_____   8. I really don't have a lot of self-respect.
_____   9. There are times when I feel useless.
_____   10. Sometimes I don't think I'm very good at all.

Scoring

1. For items 1, 2, 4, 6, and 7, assign points as follows: $SD = 1; D = 2; A = 3; SA = 4$.

2. For items 3, 5, 8, 9, and 10, assign points as follows: $SD = 4; D = 3; A = 2; SA = 1$.

3. Add the number of points in 1 and 2. This should range from 10 to 40. Higher scores reflect greater degrees of self-esteem.

Discussion Questions

1. Based on this questionnaire, how high or low is your self-esteem? Does your score make sense to you? In other words, does the questionnaire tell you something you already believed about yourself, or did it provide new insight?

2. Why do you think items 1, 2, 4, 6, and 7 are scored opposite from items 3, 5, 8, 9, and 10?

3. Do you think the techniques outlined in Table 3.1 on p. 75 may help raise your self-esteem?

Group Exercise
Disciplining a Generally Good Employee

Even the best employees sometimes behave inappropriately. When this occurs, managers confront a special challenge: How can they address the problem behavior without offending or turning off the employee in question? The following exercise will get you to think about handling this difficult, but not uncommon, type of dilemma.

Directions

1. Break into teams of two.

2. One member of each team should read the role of Michael M. The other individual should read the role of Michael's supervisor. Members of the class should read both roles.

3. After familiarizing themselves with their respective roles, the parties should discuss the situation as they would in a real organization.

Michael M.

You have been a laborer with a home construction company for almost four years, during which time you have developed an excellent record. You are an outstanding craftsman who always does meticulous work and completes his projects ahead of schedule. You have always gotten along well with your coworkers, and even customers have praised you for your kind and professional manner. You know that your boss likes you and is reluctant to fire you, so you have been taking advantage of him by showing up for work late—sometimes by as much as an hour. When your boss spoke to you about it, you admit to being late quite often but explain that this sometimes is necessary because you have to help send your children to school in the morning. Besides, you explain that because you work so quickly you make up for being late, so it shouldn't matter. However, you know that your company has a strict rule against being late ("three strikes and you're out"), and you are concerned about losing your job. You are worried about what your boss might say because you very much want to keep your job.

Michael M.'s Supervisor

Michael M. has been a laborer with your home construction company for almost four years, during which time he has developed an excellent record. He has been an outstanding craftsman who always does meticulous work and completes his projects ahead of schedule. Michael has always gotten along well with his coworkers, and even customers have praised him for his kind and professional manner. Employees like Michael are hard to find, making you very interested in keeping him happy so that he will continue to work for you. There has been one recurrent problem, however. Because he knows he is so good and that you are reluctant to fire him, Michael has been taking advantage of you by showing up for work late—sometimes by as much as an hour. When you have spoken to him about this, he admits to being late quite often but says that this sometimes is necessary because he has to help send his children to school in the morning. Besides, he claims that he works so quickly that he makes up for being late, so it shouldn't matter. However, your company has a strict rule against being late ("three strikes and you're out"), and you are concerned that by turning a blind eye to Michael, you are sending the message to the other employees that Michael is "above the law" and that you are "playing favorites" with him. You do not want to threaten your credibility by ignoring the problem, but you also don't want to risk making Michael quit.

Discussion Questions

1. Based on the guidelines for discipline described in this chapter, what specific steps should be taken to handle this situation?

2. As the roles were played out before you, what were the major strengths and weaknesses of the way Michael's supervisor handled the situation?

3. As Michael's supervisor, how would you be affected, if at all, by the fact that Michael's lateness resulted from the need to take care of his children? Did this matter? If so, how, and what would you do about it?

Notes

Case Notes

Schlereth, J. (2003, July–August). Putting people first. *BizEd*, pp. 16–20. *Hoover's Handbook of Private Companies* (2003). Enterprise Rent-A-Car (pp. 148–149). Austin, TX: Hoover's Online.

Chapter Notes

[1] Barrick, M., & Ryan, A. M. (2003). *Personality at work: Reconsidering the role of personality in organizations.* San Francisco: Jossey-Bass. Roberts, B. W., & Hogan, R. (2001). *Personality psychology in the workplace.* Washington, DC: American Psychological Association.

[2] Mount, M. K., & Barrick, M. R. (1998). Five reasons why the "Big Five" article has been frequently cited. *Personnel Psychology, 51*, 849–857.

[3] Hurtz, G. M., & Donovan, J. J. (2000). Personality and job performance: The big five revisited. *Journal of Applied Psychology, 85*, 869–879.

[4] Barrick, M. R., & Mount, M. K. (1993). Autonomy as a moderator of the relationships between the big five personality dimensions and job performance. *Journal of Applied Psychology, 78*, 111–118.

[5] Kirkcaldy, B. D., Shephard, R. J., & Furnham, A. F. (2002). The influence of Type A behavior and locus of control upon job satisfaction and occupational health. *Personality & Individual Differences, 33*, 1361–1371.

[6] Hirschfeld, R. R. (2002). Achievement orientation and psychological involvement in job tasks: The interactive effects of work alienation and intrinsic job satisfaction. *Journal of Applied Social Psychology, 32*, 1663–1681.

[7] McClelland, D. C. (1985). *Human motivation.* Glenview, IL: Scott, Foresman.

[8] Miller, J. S., & Cardy, R. L. (2003). Self-monitoring and performance appraisal: Rating outcomes in project teams. *Journal of Organizational Behavior, 21*, 609–626.

[9] Bandura, A., & Locke, E. A. (2003). Negative self-efficacy and goal effects revisited. *Journal of Applied Psychology, 88*, 87–99.

[10] Eden, D., & Aviram, A. (1993). Self-efficacy training to speed reemployment: Helping people to help themselves. *Journal of Applied Psychology, 78*, 352–360.

[11] Weielauf, J. C., Smith, R. E., & Cervone, D. (2000). Generalization effects of coping-skills training: Influence of self-defense training on women's efficacy beliefs, assertiveness, and aggression. *Journal of Applied Psychology, 85*, 625–633.

[12] Wiesenfeld, B. M., Brockner, J., & Thibault, V. (2000). Procedural fairness, managers' self-esteem, and managerial behaviors following a layoff. *Organizational Behavior and Human Decision Processes, 83*, 1–32.

[13] Richman, E. L., & Shaffer, D. R. (2000). "If you let me play sports:" How might sport participation influence the self-esteem of adolescent females? *Psychology of Women Quarterly, 24*, 189–199.

[14] Weiss, H. M., & Cropanzano, R. (1996). Affective events theory: A theoretical discussion of the structure, causes, and consequences of affective experiences at work. In B. M. Staw & L. L. Cummings (Eds.), *Research in organizational behavior* (Vol. 18, pp. 1–74). Greenwich, CT: JAI Press.

[15] Lord, R. G., Klimoski, R. J., & Kanfer, R. (2002). *Emotions in the workplace: Understanding the structure of emotions in organizational behavior*. San Francisco: Jossey-Bass. Morris, J. A., & Feldman, D. C. (1997). Managing emotions in the workplace. *Journal of Managerial Issues, 9*, 257–274.

[16] Zerbe, W. J. (2000). Emotional dissonance and employee well-being. In N. M. Ashkanazy, C. E. Haertel, & W. J. Zerbe (Eds.), *Emotions in the workplace: Research, theory, and practice* (pp. 189–214). Westport, CT: Quorum.

[17] Goleman, D. (1998). *Working with emotional intelligence*. New York: Bantam.

[18] Baron, R. A., & Markam, G. (in press). Social competence and entrepreneurs' financial success. *Journal of Applied Psychology*.

[19] Jordan, P. J., Ashkanazy, N. M., & Haertel, C. E. J. (2003). The case for emotional intelligence in organizational research. *Academy of Management Review, 28*, 195–197.

[20] See Note 14.

[21] George, J. M., & Brief, A. P. (1996). Motivational agendas in the workplace: The effects of feelings on focus of attention and work motivation. In B. M. Staw & L. L. Cummings (Eds.), *Research in organizational behavior* (Vol. 18, pp. 75–109). Greenwich, CT: JAI Press.

[22] Freiberg, K., Freiberg, J., & Peters, T. (1998). *Nuts!: Southwest Airlines crazy recipe for business and personal success*. New York: Bantam Doubleday. Cohen, B., Greenfield, J., & Mann, M. (1998). *Ben & Jerry's double dip: How to run a values-led business and make money, too*. New York: Fireside.

[23] Anonymous. (1998, January). Unconventional smarts. *Across the Board*, pp. 22–23.

[24] Clore, G. L., Schwartz, N., & Conway, M. (1994). Affective causes and consequences of social information processing. In R. S. Wyer, Jr. & T. K. Srull (Eds.), *Handbook of social cognition* (Vol. 1, pp. 323–417). Hillsdale, NJ: Lawrence Erlbaum Associates.

[25] Brief, A. P., Butcher, A. B., & Roberson, L. (1995). Cookies, disposition, and job attitudes: The effects of positive mood-inducing events and negative affectivity on job satisfaction in a field experiment. *Organizational Behavior and Human Decision Processes, 62*, 55–62.

[26] Forgas, J. P. (2000). *Handbook of affect and social cognition*. Mahwah, NJ: Lawrence Erlbaum Associates.

[27] Ashforth, B. E., & Mael, F. (1989). Social identity theory and the organization. *Academy of Management Review, 14*, 20–29.

[28] LaTendresse, D. (2000). Social identity and intergroup relations within the hospital. *Journal of Social Distress and the Homeless, 9,* 51–69.

[29] Cialdini, R. B., Borden, R. J., Thorne, A., Walker, M. R., Freeman, S., & Sloan, L. R. (1999). Basking in reflected glory: Three (football) field studies. In R. F. Baumeister (Ed.), *The self in social psychology* (pp. 436–445). Philadelphia: Psychology Press/Talor & Francis.

[30] Naquin, C. E., & Tynan, R. O. (2003). The team halo effect: Why teams are not blamed for their failures. *Journal of Applied Psychology, 88,* 332–340.

[31] Eden, D. (2003). Self-fulfilling prophecies in organizations. In J. Greenberg (Ed.), *Organizational behavior: State of the science* (2nd ed.) (pp. 91–122). Mahwah, NJ: Lawrence Erlbaum Associates.

[32] Eden, D., & Shani, A. B. (1982). Pygmalion goes to boot camp: Expectancy, leadership, and trainee performance. *Journal of Applied Psychology, 67,* 194–199.

[33] Bethune, G. (1999). *From worst to first: Behind the scenes of Continental's remarkable comeback.* New York: John Wiley & Sons.

[34] Nye, R. D. (1992). *The legacy of B. F. Skinner: Concepts and perspectives, controversies and misunderstandings.* Belmont, CA: Brooks/Cole.

[35] Ewing, J. (1999, November 15). Siemens: Building a "B-school" in its own backyard. *Business Week*, pp. 281–282. Meister, J. C. (1998). *Corporate universities.* New York: McGraw-Hill.

[36] Arthur, W., Jr., Bennett, W., Jr., Edens, P. S., & Bell, S. T. (2003). Effectiveness of training in organizations: A meta-analysis of design and evaluation features. *Journal of Applied Psychology, 88,* 234–245. Kraiger, K. (2001). *Creating, implementing, and managing effective training and development: State-of-the-art lessons for practice.* San Francisco: Jossey-Bass.

[37] Ilgen, D. R., & Moore, C. F. (1987). Types and choices of performance feedback. *Journal of Applied Psychology, 72,* 401–406.

[38] Hoffman, R. (1995, April). Ten reasons you should be using 360-degree feedback. *HRMagazine*, pp. 82–85.

[39] Bailey, C., & Fletcher, C. (2002). The impact of multiple source feedback on management development: Findings from a longitudinal study. *Journal of Organizational Behavior, 23,* 853–867. Edwards, M. R., & Ewen, A. J. (1996). *360° feedback: The powerful new model for employee assessment and performance improvement.* New York: AMACOM.

[40] Tornow, W. W., & London, M. (1998). *Maximizing the value of 360-degree feedback.* San Francisco: Jossey-Bass.

[41] Lepsinger, R., & Lucia, A. D. (1997). *The art and science of 360-degree feedback.* San Francisco: Jossey-Bass.

[42] Stajkovic, A. D., & Luthans, F. (2003). Behavioral management and task performance in organizations: Conceptual background, meta-analysis, and test of alternative models. *Personnel Psychology, 56,* 155–194.

[43] Trahan, W. A., & Steiner, D. D. (1994). Factors affecting supervisors' use of disciplinary actions following poor performance. *Journal of Organizational Behavior, 15,* 129–139.

[44] Wah, L. (1999, April). Behind the buzz. *Management Review*, pp. 17–26.

[45] McCune, J. C. (1999, April). Thirst for knowledge. *Management Review*, pp. 10–12.

Chapter **Four**

LEARNING OBJECTIVES

After reading this chapter, you will be able to:

1. **DESCRIBE** the basic nature of stress.

2. **IDENTIFY** the major causes and effects of organizational stress.

3. **IDENTIFY** steps that can be taken to control stress.

4. **DISTINGUISH** among the four major types of careers that exist.

5. **DESCRIBE** the major determinants of career choice.

6. **IDENTIFY** the major challenges people face as their careers develop.

Coping with Organizational Life: Stress and Careers

Parenthood and Dot-Coms: A Recipe for Stress

What do you get when you combine a job that requires an insane schedule with the demands of parenthood? The answer is *stress*—and lots of it. Just ask Melissa Lloyd, the only senior female executive at what used to be Hotlinks, now Newspaperlinks.Com, a small Internet start-up in Mountain View, California, that provides online bookmarking and search services. When she worked at Procter & Gamble, she could have taken advantage of the company's liberal benefits, such as maternity leave, flextime, and job sharing. But, as vice president of marketing for a 25-person company, these are not options. In the highly competitive and fast-moving world of the Internet, Hotlinks could afford neither giving up a key executive nor providing expensive day care facilities. The stubborn conflict between growing a company and growing a family forced Melissa to make some tough decisions.

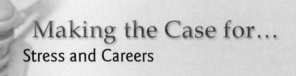

Making the Case for...
Stress and Careers

Acknowledging that her family came first, Melissa decided to take 12 weeks of unpaid leave (as covered by California law) and then return to work for 8- or 9-hour days instead of her usual 10- and 11-hour days. Others take a different route. According to Tuck Richards, an Internet consultant, many employees of high-tech start-up firms arrange for people such as friends, relatives, and professional nannies to take care of their families while they return to work as soon as physically possible. It's not that these individuals are unconcerned about their families. Rather, they are gambling that they will be able to make up for the present absence from their families by making it big and retiring in only a few years.

During the boom days of the Internet, during the late 1990s, hopes of making it rich led many to choose work ahead of their families. Back then, talk of family-friendly policies was limited because employees knew they were expected to stay at the office however long it took to get things done. Today, however, with Internet success stories the exception rather than the rule, it's more common for parents working at dot-coms to do what Melissa did by putting their families first.

Although the breakneck pace of Internet start-ups has slowed down, employees of such firms still are expected to put in long hours. And doing so still interferes with child-rearing, which remains a problem given that most of the employees of Internet companies are of child-rearing age. Generous benefits still aren't available, but today's start-up firms have developed several useful ways of adapting. In general, this means working smarter than ever before.

Some companies, such as Autobytel.com, the e-commerce car dealership, go out of their way to be incredibly nimble with employee scheduling, allowing employees to work whatever hours best suit their personal schedules. The Boston-based Internet consulting company Breakaway Solutions has found another way of dealing with the problem: It arranged for consultants to cut their travel time by 200 to 600 percent by opening smaller offices across the country. Although this isn't exactly cheap, Breakaway enjoys a 97 percent retention rate, which is almost unheard of in that industry. The company's efforts at making it possible to have both a work life and a family life is the key.

The various examples in this case all tell a common tale: Many of today's workers are suffering stress because they are forced to make difficult decisions between

Stress and Careers

You should care about stress and careers because:

1. Understanding how to manage stress can not only help you work effectively on your job but also can contribute to having a healthy life.

2. Knowing how to go about choosing a career can help you select the best possible career for yourself.

3. People often change their careers, and understanding how this occurs can ease the process of changing your own career.

their work lives and their personal lives. The case also reveals that something is being done about it. On her own, Melissa Lloyd sought to avoid stress in her life by taking a leave of absence. Many of today's more progressive companies are taking steps to make things less stressful for employees or attempting to avoid stress altogether. Employees of Autobytel.com have enough flexibility in scheduling their work to alleviate some sources of stress, and the use of small branch offices has cut the travel demands on consultants at Breakaway Solutions, which typically contributes to the stress of most consultants.

Stress clearly is a widespread aspect of organizational life today. The first part of this chapter is devoted to describing the problematic nature of stress in organizations and, of course, steps that can be taken to overcome it. As you know from experience, one of the most notable sources of stress is in the very nature of *careers*. Figuring out "what we want to be" is stressful, as is the subsequent process of dealing with the changing nature of our careers over the years. With this in mind, the second part of this chapter will be devoted to describing the dynamic nature of careers.

The Basic Nature of Stress

learning
objective

Stress is an unavoidable fact of organizational life today, taking its toll on both individuals and organizations. According to a recent survey, 90 percent of American workers report feeling stressed at least once a week and 40 percent describe their jobs as very stressful most of the time.[1] What stresses them? Lots of things, but having too much work to do and fear of being laid off are among people's most common concerns. As you might imagine, these sources of stress are both harmful to individual workers and costly to their organizations. In fact, about half of all American workers report that stress has adversely affected their health.[2] Not surprisingly, stress on the job has been linked to increases in accidents, lost productivity, and of course, phenomenal boosts in medical insurance. Overall, work-related stress has been estimated as costing American companies $200 billion to $300 billion annually.[3]

In view of these sobering statistics, it is clearly important to understand the nature of organizational stress. Formally, scientists define **stress** as the pattern of emotional and physiological reactions occurring in response to demands from within or outside organizations. In this chapter, we will review the major causes and effects of stress. Importantly, we also will describe various ways of effectively managing stress so as to reduce its negative impact. Before doing this, however, we will describe the basic nature of stress in more detail.

Stressors in Organizations

What do each of the following situations have in common?

- You are fired the day before you become eligible to receive your retirement pension.
- You find out that your company is about to eliminate your department.
- Your boss tells you that you will not be getting a raise this year.
- Your spouse is diagnosed with a serious illness.

The answer, besides that they are all awful situations, is that each situation involves external events (i.e., ones beyond your own control) that create extreme demands on you. Stimuli of this type are known as **stressors**, formally defined as any demands, either physical or psychological in nature, encountered during the course of living.

Scientists often find it useful to distinguish stressors in terms of how long-lasting they are. This results in the following three major categories (see Figure 4.1):

■ **Acute stressors** are those that bring some form of sudden change that threatens us either physically or psychologically, requiring people to make unwanted adjustments. For example, you may be assigned to a different shift at work, requiring you to get up earlier in the morning and to eat meals at different times. As your body's equilibrium is disrupted, you respond physiologically (e.g., by being tired) and emotionally (e.g., by being grouchy).

■ **Episodic stressors** are the result of experiencing lots of acute stressors in a short period of time, such as when you "have one of those days" in which everything goes wrong. In other words, you are experiencing particularly stressful episodes in life. This would be the case, for example, if within the course of a week you have a serious disagreement with one of your subordinates, you lose a major sales account, and then, to top it off, the pipes burst in your office, causing water to ruin your important papers and your computer. For a list of some of the most common episodic stressors, see Table 4.1.

■ **Chronic stressors** are the most extreme type of stressor because they are constant and unrelenting in nature, having a long-term effect on the body, mind, and spirit. For example, a person experiences chronic stressors if he or she is in a long-term abusive relationship with a boss or spouse or has a debilitating disease (e.g., arthritis or migraine headaches) that adversely affects his or her ability to work. In recent years, in which layoffs have been common, people have suffered stress due to considerable uncertainties about their future.

The Cognitive Appraisal Process

The Roman emperor and philosopher Marcus Aurelius Antonious (A.D. 121–180) is quoted as saying, "If you are distressed by anything external, the pain is not due to the thing itself, but to your estimate of it; and this you have the power to revoke at any moment." This observation is as true today as it was some 2,000 years ago, when first spoken. The basic idea is that the mere presence of potentially harmful events

Figure 4.1   Different Types of Stressors

Whereas acute stressors tend to be of brief duration, chronic stressors endure for a long period of time. Episodic stressors generally last for intermediate periods of time.

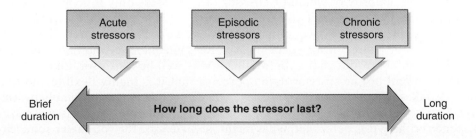

Table 4.1	Common Episodic Stressors in the Workplace

Many of the most commonly encountered stressors in organizations are episodic in nature. If you think about these, it's not difficult to recognize how they actually are composed of several different acute stressors. For example, fear of losing one's job includes concerns over money, threats to self-esteem, embarrassment, and other acute stressors.

- Lack of involvement in making organizational decisions
- Unrelenting and unreasonable expectations for performance
- Poor communication with coworkers
- Fear of losing one's job
- Spending long amounts of time away from home
- Office politics and conflict
- Not being paid fairly given one's level of responsibility and performance

or conditions in the environment is not enough for them to be stressors. For an event to become a stressor to someone, he or she must think of it as a stressor and acknowledge the danger and the difficulty of coping with it. As you think about the events or conditions you encounter, some may be considered especially threatening (warranting your concern) whereas others pose less of a problem to you (and can be ignored safely). Your assessment of the dangers associated with any potential stressor is based on **cognitive appraisal**—the process of judging the extent to which an environmental event is a potential source of stress. Let's consider this process more closely.

On some occasions, people appraise conditions instantly. Suppose, for example, you are camping in the woods when a bear looks like it's going to attack. You immediately assess that you are in danger and run away as fast as you can. This is a natural reaction, which biologists call a **flight response**. Indeed, making a rapid escape from a dangerous situation occurs automatically. So, without giving the matter much thought, you immediately flee from a burning office building because you judge the situation to be life-threatening. The situation is extreme, so you appraised it as dangerous automatically. In the blink of an eye, you recognized the danger and sought to escape. Although you may not have deliberated all the pros and cons of the situation, you did engage in a cognitive appraisal process: You recognized the situation as dangerous and took action instantly.

Most of the situations managers face are neither as extreme nor as clear-cut. In fact, the vast majority of would-be stressors are stressors only if people perceive them as such. For example, if you are an expert at writing sales reports and really enjoy doing them, the prospect of having to work extra hours on preparing one is not likely to be a stressor for you. However, for someone else who finds the same task to be an obnoxious chore, confronting it may well be a stressor. Likewise, the deadline might not be stressor if you perceive that it is highly flexible and that nobody takes it seriously or if you believe you can get an extension simply by asking. The point is simple: Whether or not an environmental event is a stressor depends on how it is perceived. What might be a stressor for you under some circumstances might not be a stressor at other times or even for someone else under the same conditions. Remember, it's all just a matter of how things are appraised cognitively.

As you might imagine, it is important to appraise potential threats as accurately as possible. For example, to think that everyone in your department is happy when, in fact, they are all planning to quit surely would be a serious mistake. Likewise, interpreting a small dip in sales as a sign of economic collapse would cause you needless worry and may spark panic in others. As such, it is important to recognize what you can do as a manager to ensure that you and those around you are assessing potential stressors accurately. For some recommendations in this regard, see Table 4.2.

Bodily Responses to Stressors

When we encounter stressors, our bodies (in particular, our sympathetic nervous systems and endocrine systems) are mobilized into action, such as through elevated heart rate, blood pressure, and respiration.[4] Arousal rises quickly to high levels, and

Table 4.2	Tips for Assessing Potential Stressors Accurately

It is important to recognize potential stressors and to take appropriate action. However, it can be very disruptive to mistakenly assume that something is a stressor when, in reality, nothing is wrong. With this in mind, here are some useful guidelines for appraising potential stressors accurately.

Suggestion	*Explanation*
Check with others.	Ask around. If others are not concerned about a situation, then maybe neither should you be concerned. Discussing the situation with people may alleviate any feelings of stress you may have had.
Look to the past.	Your best bet for deciding what to do may be to consider what has happened over the years. You may want to be concerned about something that has caused problems in the past, but worrying about conditions that haven't been problems before might only make things worse by distracting your attention from what really matters.
Gather all the facts.	It's too easy to jump to conclusions, seeing situations as problems that really aren't so bad. Instead of sensing a problem and assuming the worst, look for more objective information about the situation.
Avoid negative mental monologues.	Too often, people talk themselves into perceiving situations as being worse than they really are, thereby adding to stress levels. You should avoid such negative mental monologues, focusing instead on the positive aspects of the situations you confront.

many physiological changes take place. If the stressors persist, the body's resources eventually may become depleted, at which point people's ability to cope (at least physically) decreases sharply, and severe biological damage may result. It is these patterns of responses that we have in mind when we talk about stress.

To illustrate this, imagine that you are in an office building when you suddenly see a fire raging. How does your body react? As a natural, biological response, your body responds in several ways—both immediately after experiencing the stressor, a few minutes later, and after repeated exposure (see Figure 4.2). For example, certain chemicals are released that make it possible for us to respond. Adrenaline boosts our metabolism, causing us to breathe faster, taking in more oxygen to help us be stronger and run faster. Aiding in this process, blood flows more rapidly (up to four times faster than normal) to prime the muscles, and other fluids are diverted from less essential parts of the body. As a result, people experiencing stressful conditions

Figure 4.2   The Body's Reactions to Stress

As summarized here, the human body responds to stress in many different ways involving several different physiological mechanisms. These responses differ based on whether they occur immediately after perceiving a sensor, a few minutes later, or after repeated exposure to stressors.

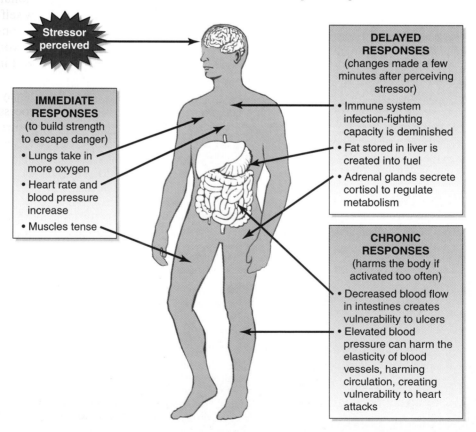

tend to experience dry mouths as well as cool, clammy, and sweaty skin. Other chemicals are activated that suppress the parts of the brain that control concentration, inhibition, and rational thought. (By the way, this is why people in emergency situations don't always think rationally or act politely.) In short, when exposed to stressors the body kicks into a self-protective mode, marshalling all its resources to preserve life. However, when this happens frequently, the chronic responses can be dangerous.

To the extent that people appraise various situations as stressors, they are likely to have stress reactions. And often these can have damaging behavioral, psychological, and/or medical effects. Indeed, physiological and psychological stress reactions can be so great that eventually they take their toll on the body and mind, resulting in such maladies as insomnia, cardiovascular disease, and depression. Such reactions are referred to as **strain**, defined as deviations from normal states of human function resulting from exposure to stressful events. (As you probably have seen in dealing with different people in your own lives, some individuals are far tougher than others. That is, they have the mental toughness to focus their minds and manage their emotions under stressful conditions.[5] To see how well you and your fellow team members fare in this regard, complete the **Group Exercise** on pages 149–150.)

Sometimes people find themselves worn down by chronic levels of stress. Such people are often described as suffering from **burnout**—a syndrome of emotional, physical, and mental exhaustion coupled with feelings of low self-esteem or low self-efficacy, resulting from prolonged exposure to intense stress and the strain reactions following from them.[6] Fortunately, some of the signs of burnout are clear, if you know what to look for. The distinct characteristics of burnout are summarized in Table 4.3.[7]

Let's summarize where we have been thus far. We have identified physical and psychological causes of stress known as stressors. Through the cognitive appraisal process, these lead to various physical and mental stress reactions. With prolonged exposure, physiological, behavioral, and psychological strain reactions result. Ultimately, in some cases, burnout occurs. For a summary of this process, see Figure 4.3.

Major Causes of Stress in the Workplace

learning
objective

Stress is caused by many different factors. For example, stress may caused by personal factors such as problems with family members, financial problems, and illness. Stress also may be caused by societal factors, such as concerns over crime, terrorism, and downturns in the economy. However, in this book, we are concerned mostly about job-related stress. What causes stress in work settings? Unfortunately, as you will see, the list is quite long; many different factors play a role in creating stress in the workplace.

Occupational Demands

Some jobs, such as emergency room physician, police officer, firefighter, and airline pilot, expose the people who hold them to high levels of stress. Others, such as college professor, janitor, and librarian, do not. This basic fact—that some jobs are much more stressful than others—has been confirmed by the results of a survey

Table 4.3	Symptoms of Burnout

Burnout is a serious condition resulting from exposure to chronic levels of stress. The symptoms of burnout, summarized here, are important to recognize so as to avoid making an already bad state of affairs even worse.

Symptom	*Description*
Physical exhaustion	Victims of burnout have low energy and feel tired much of the time. They also report many symptoms of physical strain, such as frequent headaches, nausea, poor sleep, and changes in eating habits (e.g., loss of appetite).
Emotional exhaustion	Depression, feelings of helplessness, and feelings of being trapped in one's job are all part of burnout.
Depersonalization	People suffering from burnout often demonstrate a pattern of attitudinal exhaustion known as *depersonalization*. They become cynical about others, derogating others and themselves, including their jobs, their organizations, and even life in general.
Feelings of low personal accomplishment	People suffering from burnout conclude that they haven't been able to accomplish much in the past, and assume that they probably won't succeed in the future.

(Source: Based on information in Bakker et al., 2000; see Note 6.)

Figure 4.3	Stressors, Stress, Strain, and Burnout

Stimuli known as *stressors* lead to *stress* reactions when they are cognitively appraised as threatening and beyond one's control. The deviations from normal states resulting from stress are known as *strain*. Prolonged stressful experiences can lead to *burnout*.

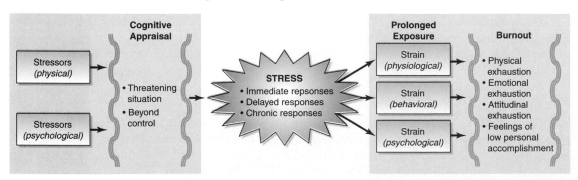

involving more than 130 different occupations.[8] For a listing of some of the most stressful jobs, see Table 4.4.

What, precisely, makes some jobs more stressful than others? Research has shown that several features of jobs determine the levels of stress they generate. Specifically, people experience greater stress the more their jobs require:

- making decisions
- constantly monitoring devices or materials
- repeatedly exchanging information with others
- working in unpleasant physical conditions
- performing unstructured rather than structured tasks

The greater the extent to which a job possesses these characteristics, the higher the level of stress that job produces among individuals holding it. Nurses and long-distance bus drivers perform jobs that match this profile—and, not surprisingly, people doing

Table 4.4   What Jobs Are Most—and Least—Stressful?

Using a variety of standards, scientists rated 250 different jobs regarding how stressful they are. Shown here are the rankings and stress scores for selected occupations. (Higher scores reflect greater levels of stress encountered.)

Rank Score	Stress Score	Rank Score	Stress Score
1. U.S. president	176.6	47. Auto salesperson	56.3
2. Firefighter	110.9	50. College professor	54.2
3. Senior executive	108.6	60. School principal	51.7
6. Surgeon	99.5	103. Market research analyst	42.1
10. Air traffic controller	83.1	104. Personnel recruiter	41.8
12. Public relations executive	78.5	113. Hospital administrator	39.6
16. Advertising account executive	74.6	119. Economist	38.7
17. Real estate agent	73.1	122. Mechanical engineer	38.3
20. Stockbroker	71.7	124. Chiropractor	37.9
22. Pilot	68.7	132. Technical writer	36.5
25. Architect	66.9	149. Retail salesperson	34.9
31. Lawyer	64.3	173. Accountant	31.1
33. General physician	64.0	193. Purchasing agent	28.9
35. Insurance agent	63.3	229. Broadcast technician	24.2
42. Advertising salesperson	59.9	245. Actuary	20.2

(Source: Reprinted by permission of the Wall Street Journal; © 1997 Dow Jones & Company, Inc. All rights reserved worldwide.)

these jobs tend to show many of the adverse signs of stress. This is not to imply that people do not experience stress in every job. In fact, as you can see from Table 4.5, many different causes of stress can be found in different types of jobs.[9]

Conflict Between Work and Nonwork

If you've ever known anyone who has had to face the demands of working while at the same time trying to raise a family—such as Melissa Lloyd, in this chapter's opening case—you are probably well aware of how difficult this situation can be. Not only must you confront the usual pressures to spend time at work while concentrating on what you're doing, but you also must pay attention to the demands placed on you by members of your family (e.g., to spend time with them). When people confront such incompatibilities in the various sets of obligations they have, they are said to experience **role conflict** (see Chapter 9). As you might expect, when we experience conflicts between our work and nonwork lives, something has to give. Not sur-

Table 4.5	Sources of Stress in Everyday Jobs

Although some jobs are inherently more stressful than others, even people holding everyday jobs in all fields confront significant sources of stress. Here are some examples.

Field	*Typical Jobs*	*Common Source of Stress*
Financial	Accountants, stock market traders, bank tellers, mortgage consultants	Clients are concerned about money, so they put lots of pressure on people working in this field.
Media	Newspaper, magazine, radio, or television journalists, reporters, editors	These people experience calm times followed by frantic activity as deadlines approach and as major events unfold.
Sales	Sales and marketing managers, advertising executives	These jobs create pressure to meet certain target objectives. Salespeople face pressure to always make good impressions.
Medical	Doctors, nurses, pharmacists, physical therapists	When human lives are at stake, the pressure to make the right decision is great. Also, dealing with human distress is very difficult on people.
Technology	Computer programmers and technicians, systems analysts	Workers in the information technology field face considerable pressure to stay abreast of very rapid changes.

(Source: Based on information in Heller and Hindle, 1998; see Note 9.)

prisingly, the more time people devote to their jobs, the more events in their non-work lives (e.g., personal errands) adversely affect their jobs (e.g., not being able to get the job done on time).

The stressful nature of role conflicts is particularly apparent in one group whose members are often expected to rapidly switch back and forth between the demands of work and family—a source of stress known as **role juggling**. This is an especially potent source of stress in one very large segment of the population—working parents.[10] Indeed, the more people, such as working mothers and fathers, are forced to juggle the various roles in their lives, the less fulfilling they find those roles to be, and the more stress they suffer in their lives. In a recent study, the same relationship was found among student athletes: The more successfully they were able to separate their distinct roles as students and as athletes, the less stress and the more well-being they experienced.[11]

Role Ambiguity: Stress from Uncertainty

Even if individuals are able to avoid the stress associated with role conflict, they still may encounter an even more common source of job-related stress: **role ambiguity**. This occurs when people are uncertain about several aspects of their jobs (e.g., the scope of their responsibilities, what's expected of them, how to divide their time among various duties). Most people dislike such uncertainty and find it quite stressful, but it is difficult to avoid. In fact, role ambiguity is quite common: 35 to 60 percent of employees surveyed report experiencing it to some degree.[12] Clearly, managers who are interested in promoting a stress-free workplace should go out of their way to help employees understand precisely what they are expected to do. As obvious as this may sound, such advice is all too frequently ignored in actual practice.

Overload: So Much Work, So Little Time

When the phrase "work-related stress" is mentioned, most people envision scenes in which employees are asked to do more work than they possibly can handle. Such an image is indeed quite legitimate, for such *overload* is an important cause of stress in many work settings. In fact, in today's business environment, where many companies are trimming staff size (the phenomenon known as *downsizing*, which we will discuss in Chapter 14), fewer employees are required to do more work than ever before. A distinction needs to be made, however, between **quantative overload**—the belief that one is required to do more work than possibly can be completed in a specific period—and **qualitative overload**—the belief that one lacks the required skills or abilities to perform a given job. Both are common sources of stress.

Today, as you know, overload is a problem when it comes to the management of information. Because we live in an information age, a period in which information is not only essential but also widely available, we are faced with more information than ever before. And with this comes pressure to store and process all that information in our heads as we strive to keep up with it all. This is known as **information anxiety**. As shown in Figure 4.4, information anxiety is a key source of overload.[13]

| **Figure 4.4** | Information Anxiety as a Source of Overload |

Advances in information technology have made it possible for people to come into contact with vast amounts of information. Pressure to process and store this information is a common source of *overload*—both quantitative and qualitative.

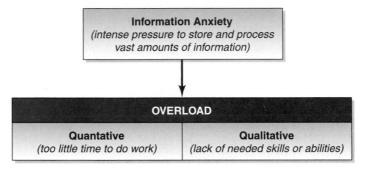

Responsibility for Others: A Heavy Burden

By virtue of differences in their jobs, some people, such as managers, tend to deal more with people than others. And people, as you probably suspect, can be a major source of stress. In general, individuals who are responsible for other people experience higher levels of stress than those who have no such responsibility. Such individuals are more likely to report feelings of tension and anxiety and are more likely to show overt symptoms of stress, such as ulcers or hypertension, than their counterparts in nonsupervisory positions.

This probably isn't too surprising if you think about it. After all, managers are often caught between the need to satisfy their staff members (e.g., giving them raises) while simultaneously meeting the demands of their own superiors (e.g., maintaining budgets). They also are often faced with meeting a wide variety of demands, creating responsibilities that often weigh heavily on them. Not surprisingly, many managers think of stress as a normal, everyday part of their jobs.

Importantly, managers who deal with people ineffectively—such as those who communicate poorly and who treat people unfairly—add stress to the lives of the people they supervise. As you surely know from your own experiences, a poor manager can be quite a significant source of stress. That said, it is clear that knowing and effectively practicing what you have learned about OB in this book can help alleviate stress among others in the workplace.

Lack of Social Support: The Costs of Isolation

According to an old saying, "misery loves company." With respect to stress, this statement implies that if we have to face stressful conditions, it's better to do so along with others (and with their support) rather than alone. Does this strategy actually work? In general, the answer is "yes." Research has shown that when individuals believe they have the friendship and support of others at work—that is, when they have **social support**—their ability to resist the adverse effects of stress increases. For example, a recent study found that police officers who felt they could talk to their colleagues about their reactions to a traumatic event (such as a shooting) experienced less stressful reactions than those who lacked such support.[14] Clearly, social support can be an important buffer against the effects of stress.[15]

Social support can come from many different sources. One of these is cultural norms (e.g., caring for the elderly is valued among the Japanese, thereby reducing the social isolation many elderly people otherwise experience). Another source of social support is social institutions (e.g., counseling from the church or school officials, help from the Red Cross). And, of course, probably the most important and valuable source of support comes from one's own friends and family members. These various sources help in several different ways.[16] These are as follows:

- *Boosting self-esteem*—Others can help make us feel better about ourselves.
- *Sharing information*—Talking to other people can help us learn about ways of coping with problems and give us a new perspective on things.
- *Providing diversion*—Spending time with others can be a friendly diversion from life's stressors, taking your mind off them.
- *Giving needed resources*—Time spent with others can result in them offering to help by giving money, advice, or other recourses needed to alleviate stress.

As we have shown here, not only does misery love company, but also company can help alleviate misery. This is something worth remembering the next time you feel stressed. Remember, don't go it alone. Friends can help, so seek them out.

Major Effects of Organizational Stress

By now, you probably are convinced that stress stems from many sources, and that it exerts important effects on the people who experience it. What may not yet be apparent, though, is just how powerful and far-reaching such effects can be. In fact, so widespread are the detrimental effects of stress (i.e., strain) that it has been estimated that their annual costs exceed 10 percent of the U.S. gross national product![17] For some other alarming statistics about stress, see Table 4.6.[18]

2
learning
objective

Lowered Task Performance—But Only Sometimes

The most current evidence available suggests that stress exerts mainly negative effects on task performance. For the most part, the greater the stress people encounter on the job, the more adversely affected their job performance tends to be.[19] In some cases, this is particularly serious. For example, in a recent study, people who were experiencing higher levels of stress were found to have higher chances of having an auto accident than those experiencing lower levels of stress.[20]

It is important to note that the adverse relationship between stress and job performance does not always hold. For example, some individuals seem to "rise to the occasion" and turn in exceptional performances at times of high stress. This may result from the fact that they are truly expert in the tasks being performed, making them so confident in what they are doing that they appraise a potentially stressful situation as a challenge rather than a threat. People also differ widely with respect to the impact of stress on task performance. Whereas some people seem to thrive on stress, finding it

Table 4.6	Some Alarming Statistics About Stress Today

Recent statistics tell a sobering story about the effects of stress today. In general, people are aware of the effects of stress in their lives but are still doing things that promote stress, creating dramatic costs in the workplace.

People feel the effects of stress:

- 36 percent feel used up at the end of the workday.
- 28 percent work so hard they do not have time or energy to spend with their families.
- 26 percent feel emotionally drained by their work.

People are contributing to their own stress levels:

- 83 percent of people would prefer to have a $10,000 per year raise than an extra hour per day at home.
- 71 percent of people are unwilling to make trade-offs between home and work.
- 49 percent of people indicate that they are not in control of how many hours they work.

Stress is costly:

- Unscheduled absences due to stress have tripled from 1995 to 1999, costing companies $602 per year for each employee.
- Among the industrialized nations, Americans work more but produce less than those in many other countries, making the cost of labor highly inefficient.
- On average, companies spend a quarter of their after-tax profits on medical bills.

(Sources: Based on data reported by Niemann, 1999, and Wah, 2000; see Note 18.)

exhilarating and improving their performance, others seek to avoid a high level of stress, finding it upsetting and a source of interference with job performance.

Desk Rage

A particularly unsettling manifestation of stress on the job that has become all too prevalent in recent years is known as **desk rage**—the lashing out at others in response to stressful encounters on the job. Just as angered drivers have been known to express their negative reactions to others in dangerous ways (commonly referred to as *road rage*), so too have office workers been known to behave violently toward others when stressed out by long hours and difficult working conditions. What makes desk rage so frightening is how extremely widespread it is and, as a recent survey indicates, the many different forms it takes (see Figure 4.5).[21]

Stress and Health: The Silent Killer

How strong is the link between stress and personal health? The answer, say medical experts, is "very strong, indeed." In other words, physiological strain reactions can be quite severe. In fact, some authorities estimate that stress plays a role in anywhere from 50 to 70 percent of all forms of physical illness.[22] Moreover, included in these

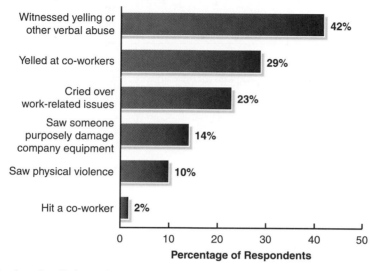

Figure 4.5   Common Forms of Desk Rage

Adults completing a survey described the negative signs of stress they either experienced directly or witnessed in the workplace. As summarized here, their responses indicated that *desk rage* took many different forms.

Witnessed yelling or other verbal abuse — 42%
Yelled at co-workers — 29%
Cried over work-related issues — 23%
Saw someone purposely damage company equipment — 14%
Saw physical violence — 10%
Hit a co-worker — 2%

Percentage of Respondents

(Source: Based on data collected by Inetegra Reality Resources as reported in Business Week, November 27, 2000; see Note 21).

figures are some of the most serious and life-threatening ailments known to medical science. A list of some of the more common ones is shown in Table 4.7. Even the most cursory look at this list must leave you with the conclusion that the health-related effects of stress are not only quite widespread but also extremely serious.

Reducing Stress: What Can Be Done?

3
learning objective

Stress stems from so many different factors and conditions that to eliminate it entirely from our lives is impossible. However, there still are many things that both companies and individuals can do to reduce stress and to minimize its harmful effects.[23] To ensure that these tactics are followed, many companies have introduced systematic programs designed to help employees reduce and/or prevent stress. The underlying assumption of these programs is that by minimizing employees' adverse reactions to stress, they will be healthier, less likely to be absent, and, consequently, more productive on the job—which, in turn, has beneficial effects on the bottom line.

Employee Assistance Programs

Employee assistance programs (EAPs) are systematic programs within organizations that provide employees with help for various personal problems (e.g., substance abuse, career planning, financial and legal problems). A recent survey of major companies found that nearly two-thirds have EAPs in place.[24] The Metropolitan Life Insurance Company (MetLife), for example, has one of the most extensive EAPs in use today. It offers toll-free telephone consultation for employees who

Table 4.7	Health-Related Consequences of Stress

Stress causes a variety of different health problems, including medical, behavioral, and psychological problems. Listed here are some of the major consequences within each category.

Medical Consequences	*Behavioral Consequences*	*Psychological Consequences*
Heart disease and stroke	Smoking	Family conflict
Backache and arthritis	Drug and alcohol abuse	Sleep disturbances
Ulcers	Accident proneness	Sexual dysfunction
Headaches	Violence	Depression
Cancer	Appetite disorders	
Diabetes		
Cirrhosis of the liver		
Lung disease		

(Sources: Based on material reported by Reivich and Shatté, 2002; see Note 25.)

The Metropolitan Life Insurance Company (MetLife), for example, has one of the most extensive EAPs in use today. It offers toll-free telephone consultation for employees who wish to talk about their problems, as well as on-site access to medical and psychological professionals.

wish to talk about their problems, as well as on-site access to medical and psychological professionals. As is always the case in such programs, anonymity is important. Employees seeking help are assured that nobody in their company will be able to learn that they have sought the services of the EAP.

Wellness Programs

Wellness programs are systematic efforts at training employees in a variety of things they can do to promote healthy lifestyles, such as workshops in which employees can learn many ways to reduce stress and maintain their health. Exercise, nutrition, and weight management counseling are among the most popular areas covered. About 56 percent of today's larger companies have wellness programs in place. Generally, such programs pay off handsomely. For example, at its industrial sites that offer wellness programs, DuPont has found that absenteeism is less than half of what it is at sites that do not offer such programs. Companies such as The Travelers Corporation and Union Pacific Railroad have enjoyed consistently high returns for each dollar they invest in employee wellness.

Stress Management Programs

Systematic efforts known as **stress management programs** involve training employees in a variety of techniques that they can use to become less adversely affected by stress. Some of the most commonly used techniques are described in Table 4.8.[25]

Table 4.8	Popular Stress Management Techniques

Growing numbers of companies are training their employees in techniques, such as those shown here, to help them manage their own stress. People seeking to manage their stress also can learn these techniques on their own by taking classes or by using self-help books and videotapes.

Technique	*Description*
Manage your time	Stress often is created by poor time management. It helps for people to learn such skills as prioritizing their activities, allocating their time realistically, and taking control of how they spend time.
Eat a healthy diet and be physically fit	Research makes it clear that reduced intake of salt and saturated fats and increased consumption of fiber- and vitamin-rich fruits and vegetables are steps that can greatly increase the body's ability to cope with the physiological effects of stress. Physical exercise also helps build resistance to the adverse effects of stress.
Relax and meditate	People can cope more effectively with work-related stressors when they have learned to relax. Meditation, the process of learning to clear one's mind of external thoughts, is especially useful in combating stress.
Get a good night's sleep	Lack of sleep makes us tired and unprepared to handle stressful situations. To get a good night's sleep, "clock out" mentally and never dwell on workplace problems as you try to fall asleep.
Avoid inappropriate self-talk	Avoid the temptation to think about how bad things will be if you fail. Dwelling on this only makes things worse.
Control your reactions	When facing stressful situations, don't allow your speech to become rapid and to intensify. Instead, make a conscious effort to speak calmly. Doing this can help reduce arousal and tension, making you calm. When facing rising tension, it also helps to take a short break—a time-out—to restore equilibrium.

(Sources: Based on suggestions by Reivich and Shatté, 2002, Abascal, Brucato, and Brucato, 2001, Cunningham, 2000; see Note 25.)

Stress management programs are used by about a quarter of all large companies today. Among them is the Equitable Life Insurance Company. Its "Emotional Health Program" offers training in a variety of ways that employees can learn to relax. (Although this is fairly typical, some other companies have used some more unusual stress management techniques. For a look at these, see the accompanying **Winning Practices** section.) The good news is that people can reap the benefits of stress management techniques even if their companies do not have stress management programs in place. Indeed, training classes (some of which may be found on

Winning Practices

Fighting—and Winning—the Battle Against Stress

Although many companies are doing things to help their employees reduce the effects of stress, some are being particularly creative in this regard.[26] Given how successful they've been, it is worthwhile to know about some of these novel practices.

You've heard of teachers taking sabbaticals—time off—so they can recharge and/or learn new skills. What you might not know is that growing numbers of companies are offering sabbaticals to their employees as well. Take Arrow Electronics, for example, the Melville, New York, company specializing in distributing electronic components to industrial and commercial customers. After working for seven years, employees are allowed to take a 10-week paid sabbatical during which they can do whatever they want. Company officials claim that the 1,400 employees who have taken advantage of this benefit return to their jobs refreshed and with greater appreciation for their work.

A quite different approach has been in use at Burmah Castrol, the multinational distributor of specialty lubricants and chemicals to business based in the United Kingdom. A few years ago, many of the company's top executives were asked to do more work in less time, resulting in them showing signs of stress-related illness. To alleviate these problems, the company physician trained employees in various biomedical techniques that helped them recognize signs of stress (e.g., adrenaline rushes and increased heartbeat) and showed them how to control these reactions by using various concentration techniques (i.e., "mind over matter"). Shortly thereafter, the signs of stress began to disappear.

Other companies take a far simpler approach. They help manage stress on a one-by-one basis by having employees look for signs that their colleagues may be suffering the adverse effects of stress. For example, in the restaurant business, where very long hours are the rule, employees of Hard Rock Café International are encouraged to do whatever it takes to help their fellow employees avoid stress. Case in point: When the wife of the general manager of the Hard Rock in San Diego went into labor on the restaurant's opening night, executives told him to join his wife instead of staying for the festivities. Although his presence was critical to the event, execs realized that people are the company's top asset and released him from his obligations so as to enhance his personal well-being at this important time in his life. This program appears to be working: Hard Rock has one of the lowest turnover rates in the restaurant industry today—about half the national average.

Despite their differences, these three examples illustrate an important point: Companies that invest in efforts to reduce the stress of their employees generally reap considerable benefits.

the Internet) and self-help books abound to help people practice such useful skills as time management, meditation, and other useful techniques.

The Nature of Careers

Thus far in this chapter we have focused on stress. Now, we turn our attention to one of the major causes of stress and one of the major contexts in which the effects of stress may be experienced—*careers*. Over the course of our lives we are likely to find ourselves holding a variety of different jobs in different organizations. In fact, the average American holds eight different jobs over his or her lifetime. In most cases, these positions are interconnected in some systematic way, weaving a path, however twisted and indirect, representing a career. We will describe the basic nature of careers in this section of the chapter and then in the remainder of the chapter elaborate on some of the key issues faced in conjunction with choosing a career and the challenges encountered as our careers develop over the years. First, let's begin with some basic definitions.

Basic Definitions

Formally, a **career** can be defined as the evolving sequence of work experiences over time. In everyday language, however, people often use the terms *job, occupation,* and *career* interchangeably, so it makes sense to distinguish among these terms before going any further. Simply put, a **job** is a predetermined set of activities one is expected to perform. An **occupation**, by contrast, is a coherent set of jobs.[27] So for example, a person working as a carpenter would be said to be have an occupation in the field of construction. Eventually, he or she may shift to occupations in the field of sales, such as home sales manager. Overall, this succession of jobs represents the individual's career. For a summary, see Figure 4.6.

Careers mean a great deal to individuals—both financially and psychologically. After all, the career path you take determines a great deal about how much money you will make throughout your life. Historically, some careers are more lucrative than others. For example, the average salary of people in finance, insurance, and real estate is over $55,000, whereas people who work in retail stores make only about $19,000.[28] Although money isn't everything, of course, these very large differences underscore the point that how much money you are likely to make depends greatly on your choice of career. Careers are important to us as individuals because they give us a sense of accomplishment and pride, and they also can give meaning to our lives (e.g., doctors who feel good about themselves because they save people's lives). Like it or not, your job defines your identity in the eyes of others. After all, when you meet someone at a party, the question often is asked, "What do you do?" Indeed, we define ourselves and others define us by the work we do.

Figure 4.6   Distinguishing Among Careers, Occupations, and Jobs

The typical *career* consists of several *occupations* (coherent sets of jobs), each of which is composed of a set of individual *jobs* (predetermined sets of activities). A hypothetical example is shown here.

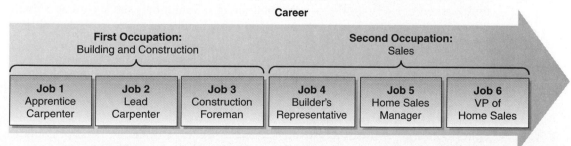

Types of Careers

Although everyone's career is unique, scientists who have studied careers have observed that there are some general patterns, or categories, into which the vast majority of careers fall.[29] Specifically, four different types of careers have been identified, and we now will describe each one (for a summary, see Figure 4.7).

4

learning objective

Steady-state careers.   Bob's family owns a small bakery, Main Street Bakery. When Bob was a young boy, he used to hang out at the bakery after school, and he became interested in that line of work. After getting a degree in hospitality management from the local community college, Bob took over the family business. For all his working life, some 40 years, he ran Main Street Bakery, where he baked fine breads, cakes, and pies. Over the years, Bob had several opportunities to sell the business and do something else, but he didn't. When it came time for him to retire, he simply handed over the family business to his own son.

Bob made a career choice that led him to a lifetime commitment to a single job, which is called a **steady-state career**. People who have steady-state careers are generally very satisfied with what they are doing. Also, because they work at their jobs for so long, they tend to become highly skilled experts at what they do. After all, for Bob to have stuck it out in the bakery as long as he did, he must like what he does and be pretty good at it, as well.

Linear careers.   Janice always loved tinkering with computers, even as a young girl. Nobody was surprised, therefore, when she did an internship at a software development firm before getting a bachelor's degree in computer science. After graduating, she took an entry-level position at a Silicone Valley start-up, where she did lots of different jobs and got great experience. After about four years, it became clear that the company wasn't going anywhere (except out of business, perhaps), so she moved on to a much larger company, where she took a position in which she helped develop and test new wireless products. Her assignments were small, at first, but after a few years, Janice found herself taking on larger and larger projects, until eventually, she became a vice president of technology for the company. It was a dream job for Janice, but she wanted more. At about the same time, the company decided to invest more of its resources in manufacturing and marketing and to outsource research and product development. So, Janice sold her stock in the company and started her own firm—not a competitor, but a lab that specialized in developing new wireless technology for her previous employer and lots of other companies as well.

Janice had what's known as a **linear career**. That is, she stuck with a certain field and worked her way up the occupational ladder. Sometimes she stayed at a single company, but at other times, she changed jobs. In all cases, however, she took on greater challenges. Linear careers are rather traditional paths. For many years, working one's way "up the corporate ladder" until "you made it" was considered the true sign of career success. Indeed, although achieving increasingly higher levels of success in a single line of work is a considerable accomplishment, it is no longer regarded as the only acceptable option for people today.

Spiral careers.   John always loved science, especially physics, so he kept going to school and getting higher degrees. Before he knew it, he had a Ph.D., and found that

Figure 4.7   Four Major Types of Careers

Scientists have found it useful to distinguish among the four different types of careers depicted here.

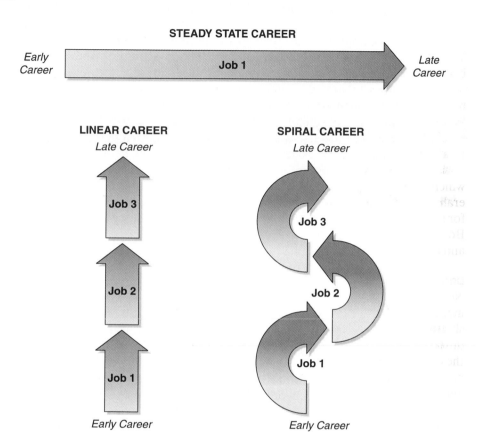

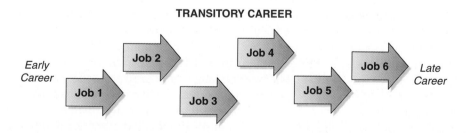

he enjoyed studying thermal dynamics. Fortunately, a local aeronautics lab was looking for someone in that area to conduct research, and they were impressed with John's accomplishments. Working there was satisfying for John for a few years, but research wasn't his passion. Then, one day, he was asked to give a talk about his work to a group of students at a small college nearby. John became hooked on teaching and soon took a job teaching physics courses at that same school. The pay wasn't great and the hours were long, but John enjoyed explaining physical principles in simple ways, and he proved to be pretty good at it. The students loved him—in part, because he made complex ideas more understandable than the textbook and far more fun, too. "If you don't like the textbook," he soon reasoned, "write one yourself." And so he did. Now, John has moved on to his third career—this time as an author of textbooks.

Over his working life, John moved between three jobs. First, he was a laboratory scientist; second, he was a professor; and third, he was an author. These jobs are very different from one another, and each requires different skills. However, John pieced them together such that each position built on the previous one. He did exciting, new, and different things with each career move, but they all drew on his interest in physics. In other words, he had what's called a **spiral career**—the kind of career in which people evolve through a series of occupations, each of which requires new skills and that builds on existing knowledge and skills. People who have spiral careers are not "job-hoppers," who move from one post to another. Rather, they are constantly growing and improving as they explore different facets of the same profession (physics, in John's case). Typically, people in spiral careers spend about 7 to 10 years in each position, enabling them to become pretty good at what they do.

Transitory careers.   After high school, Cheryl worked as a waitress while she tried to find a job as an actress. The tips were good, but after it became clear that Hollywood wasn't going to come calling, she took a job at an art gallery. She wasn't especially interested in art, but she had a friend who worked there, who helped her get the job. A few months later, she got bored and took a part-time job at a bookstore. To help make ends meet, she started a dog-walking and pet-sitting business for her neighbors, all while taking a few college classes at night. Although we could say more about the other jobs Cheryl had, you probably get the picture: She continuously moved from job to job, with little connection between them. In other words, Cheryl has what is known as a **transitory career**. People in transitory careers move between many different unrelated positions, spending about one to four years in each.

Although it may be tempting to dismiss Cheryl on the grounds that she is "trying to find herself," it would be unfair to assume that she is in any way inept. In fact, many people in transitory careers are those who have not been fortunate enough to discover the kind of work that allows them to derive satisfaction. In fact, many of the most successful people in the business world have been "late bloomers," who drifted between jobs until they found their calling. For example, before Ray Kroc founded McDonald's at age 52, he worked at such jobs as being an ambulance driver, a piano player, and a paper cup salesman.[30] Obviously, to say that he was anything other than a huge success, despite his transitory career, would be very misleading.

> Before Ray Kroc founded McDonald's at age 52, he worked at such jobs as being an ambulance driver, a piano player, and a paper cup salesman.

It also is important to acknowledge that some people simply do not find work the major source of fulfillment in their lives. Such individuals may elect to "make a career out of their hobbies," so to speak, preferring to devote their energy and talent to their avocations instead of their vocations. Perhaps you know someone who's a talented musician but who moves from one low-level "day job" to the next, so as to have time to play local gigs at night. Although such an individual may have a transitory career during the daytime, it's quite possible that his or her career is moving along in a very linear fashion after the sun goes down. Even if the hobby brings personal satisfaction instead of occupational recognition, it clearly would be unfair to think any less of such an individual.

Getting Started: Making Career Choices

5
learning
objective

"What do you want to be when you grow up?" This is a question you probably have heard many times in your youth (if not later in life, too!). As children, we learn about different careers, based mostly on the people with whom we come into contact in real life (e.g., teachers and doctors) and on television (e.g., athletes). This continues into our adult years as well, although as adults we come into contact with a broader range of professions and we have had experiences with some. With this in mind, we now will discuss three major factors that determine people's career choices.

Person–Job Fit: Holland's Theory of Occupational Choice

Why is it that you may decide to become a lawyer whereas your sister is interested in being an doctor, a police officer, a musician, or a chef—anything other than a lawyer? To a great extent, the answer lies in the notion of **person–job fit**, that is, the degree to which a particular job matches an individual's skills, abilities, and interests. This was the basic idea of John Holland, a scientist who specialized in studying occupational choice. Specifically, he believed that a person's occupational choice is based primarily on his or her personality (see Chapter 3).[31] His research has established two important findings:

- People from various occupations tend to have many similar personality characteristics.
- People whose characteristics match those of people in a given field are predisposed to succeed in that field.

So, for example, assume for argument's sake that successful lawyers tend to have certain characteristics in common: They are very inquisitive, detail oriented, and analytical—all characteristics that help them do their jobs well. According to *Holland's theory of vocational choice*, you would be attracted to the field of law to the extent that you share many of the same characteristics. In other words, because being a lawyer "suits you," and you "have what it takes" to succeed at that field, you are likely to select that occupation. In essence, **Holland's theory of vocational choice** says that people will perform best at occupations that match their traits and personalities.

Holland's theory is quite specific with respect to the various personality types and occupational types involved. Specifically, Holland identifies six different characteristics of work environments and the personality traits and interests of the people who are most successful in those environments. These are summarized in Figure 4.8. As you look at this diagram, you probably cannot help but consider what particular type best describes you. It is important to be very cognizant of this because the more closely your personality type matches the work you do, the more successful you will be and the less stress you are likely to encounter.[32]

Figure 4.8 Holland's Theory of Vocational Choice: An Overview

Holland's theory of vocational choice specifies that people are most satisfied with occupations that match their personalities. People are classified into any of six distinct personality types, each of which is associated with a particular work environment that best suits them. These pairings and the occupations that most closely match them are summarized here.

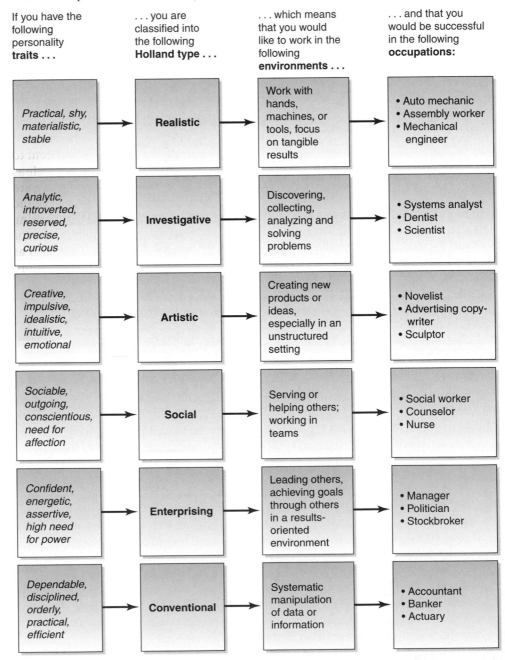

If you have the following personality traits . . .	. . . you are classified into the following Holland type . . .	. . . which means that you would like to work in the following environments . . .	. . . and that you would be successful in the following occupations:
Practical, shy, materialistic, stable	**Realistic**	Work with hands, machines, or tools, focus on tangible results	• Auto mechanic • Assembly worker • Mechanical engineer
Analytic, introverted, reserved, precise, curious	**Investigative**	Discovering, collecting, analyzing and solving problems	• Systems analyst • Dentist • Scientist
Creative, impulsive, idealistic, intuitive, emotional	**Artistic**	Creating new products or ideas, especially in an unstructured setting	• Novelist • Advertising copy-writer • Sculptor
Sociable, outgoing, conscientious, need for affection	**Social**	Serving or helping others; working in teams	• Social worker • Counselor • Nurse
Confident, energetic, assertive, high need for power	**Enterprising**	Leading others, achieving goals through others in a results-oriented environment	• Manager • Politician • Stockbroker
Dependable, disciplined, orderly, practical, efficient	**Conventional**	Systematic manipulation of data or information	• Accountant • Banker • Actuary

It's clear from Figure 4.8 that people in each type should work in certain environments, but what happens when these don't occur? Holland has noted that for people of each type there are second-best matches, third-best matches, and some jobs that constitute the worst possible match of all. These are summarized in Figure 4.9, known as **Holland's hexagon**. Interpreting this diagram is straightforward. The position of each Holland type around the hexagon indicates those occupations for which people are best suited and worst suited, based on their types. The closer a job environment comes to the associated personality type on this diagram, the more effective the person will be.

So for example, someone with an enterprising personality type is expected to be most successful when working in an occupation that permits enterprising qualities to come out (e.g., a sales job). However, neither people nor jobs fit perfectly into only a single category. As such, fairly good matches may occur in cases in which people in a certain category perform work in environments that favor adjacent types. So, for example, an enterprising person may perform reasonably well at jobs in social environments or in conventional environments, each of which is adjacent to the enterprising type in the hexagon. By the same token, poorer matches, such as with environments favoring artistic or realistic people, which are two steps away, are likely to be quite problematic for enterprising individuals. And, finally, we have the point along the hexagon that lies directly opposite—in the case of the enterprising type, it's the investigative environment. These represent the poorest matches. So, for example, we would expect people who do well in enterprising occupations (such as salesperson) to do poorly in occupations (such as scientist) that require the more analytical talents of the investigative type.

Figure 4.9   Holland's Hexagon

The diagram known as *Holland's hexagon* summarizes the relationship between each of the six personality and work environment types. According to Holland's theory of vocational choice, the closer these are, the more satisfied individuals will be with their occupational choices. Occupations with demands opposite each personality type (shown here with dashed lines) identify those for which people are most poorly suited.

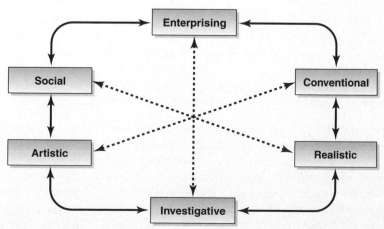

Holland's theory has been used widely by vocational counselors, professionals specializing in helping people find the kind of work that best suits them. The rationale is straightforward. People taking various vocational tests can determine how closely their traits and personality characteristics match those of people in various occupational groups. Then, using Holland's hexagon, people are encouraged to seek work in fields whose job incumbents tend to have those various qualities, and to avoid work in fields whose job incumbents have qualities that lie opposite their own along the hexagon. The happiest and most successful workers tend to be those for whom there is a close fit between their personality and their work environment. According to Holland, and supported by research, this is the key to successful career development.[33]

Career Anchors

Thus far, we've considered the extent to which a person's occupation matches his or her personality. However, another very important consideration when it comes to selecting careers has to do with the extent to which various jobs are in keeping with our images of ourselves. For example, suppose you think of yourself as a creative kind of person, someone who likes to build or produce new things on your own. Because of this, based on your experiences and knowledge, you may find yourself moving in directions that bring out your creative side. So, instead of managing a restaurant, for example, you might come to think of yourself as a chef, and be motivated to develop a new set of skills. In other words, these beliefs about yourself "anchor" your choice of careers—and, as such, they are known as *career anchors*.

Formally defined, a **career anchor** is a person's occupational self-concept, based on his or her self-perceived talents, abilities, values, needs, and motives.[34] As people spend time working, they gradually develop career anchors. Scientists studying careers have identified five major career anchors.[35] These are as follows:

- *technical or functional*—concentration on jobs focusing on specific content areas (e.g., auto mechanics, graphic arts)
- *managerial competence*—focus on jobs that allow for analyzing business problems and dealing with people
- *security and stability*—attraction to jobs that are likely to continue into the future (e.g., the military)
- *creativity or entrepreneurship*—primary interest in starting new companies from visions of unique products or services, but not necessarily running them
- *autonomy and independence*—attraction to jobs that allow for freedom from constraints and to work at one's own pace (e.g., novelists and creative artists)

Despite the fact that people have many interests and abilities, not all of these guide them toward careers. Instead, people regularly are attracted to careers that are in keeping with their particular career anchor. Scientists have used various questionnaires to assess people's career anchors. One of these, known as the Career Orientation Inventory, is regularly used by vocational counselors for purposes of helping people decide the kind of occupations to which they are best suited.

Job Opportunities

Let's face it: No matter how much you think you would like to be a shepherd, and how good a job you think you might do roaming through the pasture and tending the flock, job opportunities for shepherds are not exactly what they were in biblical days. Fortunately, most people tend to be highly rational when it comes to making career choices, favoring occupations in which opportunities are most likely to exist and avoiding positions in which opportunities are declining. For a summary of recent projections of the top 10 fastest-growing jobs by the U.S. Department of Labor, see Table 4.9.[36] As you look at these statistics, it's interesting to note that most of the growth is expected to come in computer-related occupations despite the collapse of many small technologically oriented companies in recent years. Apparently, although many firms are struggling for dominance in high-tech fields, that area is still expected to grow through 2010—and along with it, job opportunities.

Because openings in many high-tech jobs are expected to grow in the years ahead, these positions tend to capture people's attention when considering occupations they might want to enter. Not surprisingly, they also capture the attention of people administering vocational programs in high schools, technical schools, and colleges. To be popular with prospective students, these programs offer training in areas where the jobs are likely to be. The availability of such training opportunities also attracts people to the kind of jobs that require this training, creating the cycle shown in Figure 4.10.

Table 4.9   Fastest-Growing Occupations: 2000–2010

Computer-related jobs dominate the top 10 fastest-growing occupations for the first decade of the twenty-first century. The numbers represent thousands of jobs.

	Employment		Change	
Occupation	**2000**	**2010**	**Number**	**Percent**
Computer software engineers, applications	380	760	380	100
Computer support specialists	506	996	490	97
Computer software engineers, systems software	317	601	284	90
Network and computer systems administrators	229	416	187	82
Network systems and data communications analysts	119	211	92	77
Desktop publishers	38	63	25	67
Database administrators	106	176	70	66
Personal and home care aides	414	672	258	62
Computer systems analysts	431	689	258	60
Medical assistants	329	516	187	57

(Source: Bureau of Labor Statistics, U.S. Department of Labor, 2001; see Note 36.)

Figure 4.10   The Cyclical Nature of Job Growth, Training Opportunities, and Skilled Labor

As summarized here, the growth of high-tech companies leads to high-tech jobs, which leads to high-tech training, which leads to more people with high-tech skills, which further supports the growth of more high-tech jobs.

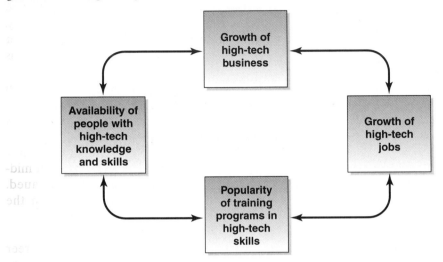

6
learning
objective

Challenges in Established Careers

Although getting started in one's career can be very difficult, so too do people face considerable challenges once they've been working for a while. We now will describe three such challenges.

Confronting the Career Plateau

While people in their 20s and 30s are figuring out what they want to be, the 40-something crowd faces different challenges. This is sometimes a difficult period in which people look down the road and realize that they never may fulfill their career aspirations. As you might imagine, this can be problematic for both employees and their organizations. Fortunately, however, as we will describe, something can be done to help.

The nature of the career plateau.   The point at which one's career has peaked and is unlikely to develop further is known as a **career plateau**. One way to identify a career plateau is by noting how long someone has been in his or her current position. Employees who have been in a particular post for five or more years would be considered immobile and to have reached a career plateau. Another popular approach for identifying a career plateau is subjective in nature. People may be considered to have plateaued whenever they no longer expect to move on to higher-status positions. Using either definition, about one employee in four is considered to have reached a career plateau.[37]

Although it is tempting to assume that employees whose careers have plateaued are no longer motivated or effective at their current jobs, this isn't always so. In fact, some people are quite satisfied to remain at their present jobs for a long time, finding it more relaxing and a source of contentment to be a "solid citizen" of the company instead of being one if its "fast trackers" or "high fliers." Of course, career plateauing can be a serious source of dissatisfaction for individuals who believe that the only path to contentment is via upward movement in the company. This is more likely to be the case among managers than for employees holding other jobs given that people in managerial positions tend to define their success in terms of upward advancement.

Today, as companies are reducing the sizes of their workforces and competition for good jobs is becoming intense, more people than ever are reaching career plateaus earlier than expected. Faced with poor chances for promotion and few alternatives for employment, they may feel unmotivated and simply stick out their jobs until they retire from them. If you think this picture is depressing, imagine how serious the problem becomes when companies are faced with large cohorts of mid-career employees who are unmotivated because their careers have plateaued. Surely, a workforce composed of people who are merely "going through the motions" will be neither very productive nor satisfied.

Career development interventions.   To avoid the problems associated with career plateaus, and other career-related issues, such as finding the right job or adjusting to new jobs, organizations have been relying on **career development interventions**. These are systematic efforts to help manage people's careers while simultaneously helping the organizations in which they work.

The career development interventions used in several companies are quite interesting. For example, at Chevron, employees are counseled to seek outside hobbies during periods in which their jobs offer little gratification. Some are encouraged to make lateral moves within the company in order to keep their work lives stimulating. Not only have Chevron employees done this, but so too have thousands of employees at General Motors, where the white-collar work-force has been reduced dramatically over the last few years. In fact, it has been reported that GM has spent some $10 million per year helping employees whose careers have reached plateaus find appropriate new positions within the company.

> At Chevron, employees are counseled to seek outside hobbies during periods in which their jobs offer little gratification.

Much of what goes on in career development interventions involves helping employees assess the skills and interests they have so that they may be placed into positions for which they are well suited. Some companies, such as Hewlett-Packard and Lawrence Livermore Laboratories, provide self-assessment exercises for this purpose. Others, such as Coca-Cola and Disneyland, rely on individualized counseling sessions in which employees meet with trained professionals. Still others, including AT&T, IBM, Ford, Shell Oil, and Kodak, take it a step further, offering organizational assessment programs through which employees are systematically tested to discover their profiles of skills and interests. (For an overview of what such tests look like, and a chance to examine your own career aspirations, see the **Self-Assessment Exercise** on pages 148–149.)

At the very least, companies such as CBS, Merck, Aetna, and General Electric all provide services, such as job posting systems and career resource centers, through which employees can learn about new career options within their companies. And, when companies find that they must reduce the size of their workforces, terminated employees at Exxon, Mutual of New York, General Electric, and other companies receive the services of **outplacement programs**. These generally include assistance in developing the skills needed to find new jobs (such as networking, interviewing skills, résumé writing, and the like). Despite these various differences, it is safe to characterize the vast majority of career development interventions as following the six steps listed in Figure 4.11.

Making Career Changes

Changing jobs, or even entire occupations, is quite common today. In fact, most new graduates with M.B.A. degrees expect to stay at their first jobs for no more than

Figure 4.11   Career Development Interventions: Step-by-Step

Although each specific career development intervention may be unique in various ways, most involve the six steps summarized here.

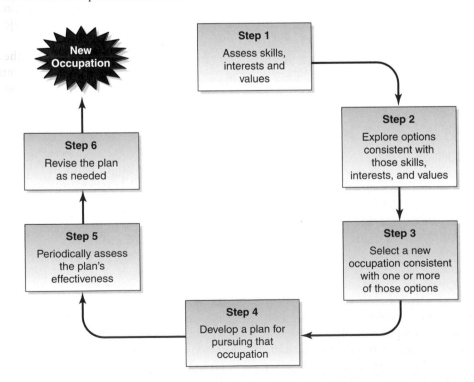

four years.[38] About two-thirds of all U.S. workers say that they would make major career changes if they could.[39] Each year, approximately 10 million workers do make major career changes. And, of those who made such career changes in recent years, 53 percent did so voluntarily, with the majority reporting that their incomes went up as a result.[40] People who make major career changes do so for a variety of reasons. The major ones are that they recognize that:

- They either don't like, or can't succeed at, their chosen profession.
- Prospects are poor for future employment in their present occupation.
- Their needs or interests have shifted, requiring a life change.

The traditional way of making a major career change is by starting completely anew. You may, for example, quit your present job, return to school for new training, and then begin starting over in your new career. People do this all the time. If you've done it, or if you know anyone who has, you probably know how very difficult it can be, both emotionally (because you're making a lot of changes at once) and financially (because you're likely to be without an income for a while, and then have a lower income).

For example, suppose that Michelle is a lawyer who specializes in computers. But she is unhappy and looking to make a brand-new start by becoming, say, a business teacher. The hard way of doing this would be for Michelle to give up her job and go back to college, where she studies both education and business. Then, after graduating and receiving her teaching credentials, she can look for a new job. Although this would take Michelle to that new place she desires, this way of making the change would be very disruptive. So how can Michelle go about making a major career change in such a way that minimizes the disruption in her life?

Career experts advise making the changes in two steps: first changing either your occupation or your field of expertise, and then changing the other.[41] In our example Michelle has a present occupation, lawyer, and desires a new one, teacher. She also has a present field, computers, and desires a new one, business. Using the two-step method, she first may change her field, such as by expanding her practice into business law. Then, after getting established in her new field, Michelle should consider changing occupations, such as by teaching a class or two during the evenings at a local community college. After a while, she might want to take on more teaching responsibilities and limit the size of her legal practice, until eventually she is teaching business on a full-time basis. It also would be possible for Michelle to first change her occupation (e.g., by teaching law) and then her field (shifting from law to business). Either way, there you have it—from computer lawyer to business teacher in two not-so-simple steps. Again, although this transition might not be easy for Michelle, it certainly is a lot more feasible than attempting to change both occupation and field at once (see summary in Figure 4.12).

Planning for Succession and Retirement

Preparation for retirement is an important issue faced during later life. Psychologically, there is a reorientation from being directed in one's life by work activities to an increased focus on leisure-time activities.

Figure 4.12   Making Career Changes: A Two-Step Process

Career experts advise that the most effective way to make a major career change is by changing your occupation and your field in two separate steps, as illustrated here.

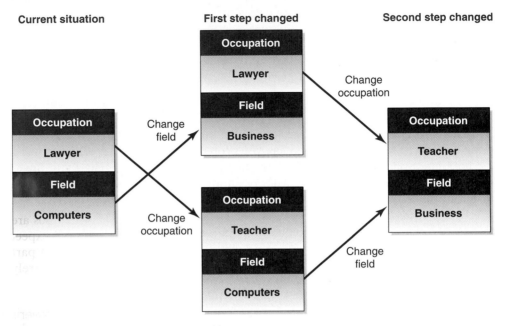

(Source: Based on suggestions by Bolles, 2002; see Note 1.)

Retirement.   The phase of people's lives in which they reach the end of their careers and stop working for their primary income is known as **retirement**. It's important to recognize that retirement does not necessarily imply inactivity, but rather, a different kind of activity.[42] Many retired people lead very active lives, such as by working part-time, engaging in volunteer work, spending time engaged in leisure pursuits, or some combination of these activities.

Generous pension plans coupled with more sophisticated investors and a generally good economy have made it possible for many people to retire earlier than ever. This, coupled with the fact that advances in health care enable people to live longer, makes it not unusual for people to spend 20 years or more in retirement.

People retire for either voluntary or involuntary reasons (see Figure 4.13). Sometimes people retire earlier than they originally planned—that is, involuntarily—because they fear that their jobs may be eliminated or because they are in ill health. In other words, like turnover and absenteeism, sometimes retirement is a form of withdrawal.[43] Fortunately, in most cases, retirement occurs voluntarily, with employees leaving their companies on good terms and happily moving on to the next stage of their lives. Research has shown that the underlying reason why people retire makes a difference in how their retirement goes.[44] Those who retire for work-related

Figure 4.13   Voluntary Versus Involuntary Retirement

Retirement can occur for voluntary or involuntary reasons, some of which are identified here.

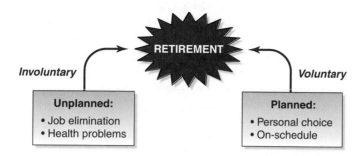

or health-related reasons tend to be less satisfied with their retirement than those who retire as planned, by personal choice.

Today, rather than retiring from work altogether, many people in their 60s are opting for brand new careers. In fact, only about 37 percent of recent retirees expect to never return to work. The rest plan on staying active by working at least part time.[45] Apparently, the image of retirees spending their golden years leisurely golfing and playing with their grandkids is fading fast. Speaking of golf, many professional golfers who find that aging makes it hard for them to compete against the likes of Tiger Woods no longer have to retire from the game. Instead, older golfers are discovering second careers by competing in the Senior PGA tour, where at age 50, they once again can rise to the top of their game.[46] Although precious few of us have the luxury of making a living by playing golf, many companies also are finding it beneficial to hire semiretired executives as consultants. Instead of putting these talented, experienced people out to pasture, so to speak, they are taking full advantage of the expertise they can bring to the job—especially as *mentors* to young employees.[47]

> Older golfers are discovering second careers by competing in the Senior PGA tour, where at age 50, they once again can rise to the top of their game.

Succession planning and mentoring.   Before people retire—whether to a world of leisure or to an entirely new career—high-level executives typically assist their companies to prepare for the void created by their departure. This process is known as **succession planning**—the systematic attempt to identify possible holders of particular positions ahead of time as preparation for top executives' departure.[48] After spending years building a successful business, it is unlikely that chief executives would feel comfortable retiring without taking steps to preserve what has been done and to ensure that the company is left in good hands. People generally also want to pass the baton to another whose goals and values match their own. And, of course, careful planning of this nature is in the best interest of the company as well.

Formal succession-planning efforts are more likely to occur in large organizations than small ones. Large firms generally have formal plans on record, specifying exactly who will move into certain positions once they are vacated. These typically include frequently updated information on the specific skills and qualifications of the individuals involved. Many succession plans identify **short-term successors**, individuals who are suitable candidates, at least temporarily, to fill a post vacated unexpectedly (e.g., through termination, resignation, or death).[49] This is not to say that leaders of small companies are unconcerned about succession. Indeed, their small size makes it crucial to consider how jobs will be filled in the event of an emergency. However, leaders of small companies are more likely to discuss these things among themselves than to have a formal plan specifying succession in any systematic fashion.

One way of identifying successors, particularly for top executives, is by having the retiring individual identify and develop a successor (over a course of years, if possible).[50] This may be accomplished through the process of **mentoring**, which involves having an experienced employee, known as a **mentor**, advise and counsel the professional development of a new employee, known as a **protégé**. If you've ever had an older, more experienced employee take you under his or her wing and guide you, then you probably already know how valuable mentoring can be. Indeed, mentoring is strongly associated with career success: The more mentoring people receive, the more promotions and pay raises they subsequently receive during their careers.[51]

Mentors do many important things for their protégés.[52] For example, they provide much needed emotional support and confidence. For those who are just starting out and are likely to be insecure about their abilities, this can be a big help. Mentors also help pave the way for their protégés' job success, such as by nominating them for promotions and by providing opportunities for them to demonstrate their competence. They also suggest useful strategies for achieving work objectives—especially ones that protégés might not generate for themselves. In doing all these things, they help bring the protégés to the attention of top management—a necessary first step for advancement. Finally, mentors often protect their protégés from the repercussions of errors and help them avoid situations that may be risky for their careers.[53]

As you might suspect, it is not only mentors and protégés who come out ahead from mentoring programs but also organizations themselves. At Scotiabank, for example, mentoring was used to reduce the time required for newly minted M.B.A.'s to become loan officers. This was necessary because these recent grads maintained traditional, not particularly service oriented, beliefs about banking that were holding them back. Through Scotiabank's Competency-Based Mentoring Program, however, branch managers reinforced what these new employees learned about service in their training programs. As a result, training time was reduced from a full year to nine months, allowing the bank to get these new employees fully functioning that much sooner. Clearly, mentoring can be very beneficial if it is handled properly. For a summary of some guidelines for effective mentoring, see Table 4.10.[54]

> At Scotiabank, for example, mentoring was used to reduce the time required for newly minted M.B.A.'s to become loan officers.

Table 4.10	10 Tips for Successful Mentoring

The long-term success of mentoring can be enhanced by adhering to the suggestions identified here. Both mentors and protégés should familiarize themselves with these guidelines before entering into a relationship.

Mentors should . . .

1. Be responsible *to* protégés, not *for* them.
2. Make the mentoring relationship fun and enjoyable.
3. Recognize that their involvement with their protégés extends beyond the workday.
4. Listen carefully to their protégés.
5. Openly acknowledge their failures as well as their successes.
6. Protect their protégés and expect their protégés to protect them.
7. Give their protégés not only directions but also options.
8. Recognize and encourage their protégés' small successes and accomplishments.
9. Encourage independent thinking among their protégés.
10. Focus not only on job skills but also on ethical values.

(Source: Based on suggestions by Clutterbuck and Ragins, 2002, Wickman and Sdodin, 1997; see Note 54.)

You Be the **Consultant**

Stressed-Out Employees Are Resigning

As the managing director of a large e-tail and catalog sales company, you are becoming alarmed about the growing levels of turnover your company has been experiencing lately among customer service representatives. It already has passed the industry average, and you are worried about the company's capacity to staff the call center and the warehouse during the busy holiday period. In conducting exit interviews, you learned that the employees who are leaving generally like their work and the pay they are receiving. However, they are displeased with the rude way their customers are treating them, and this is creating stress in their lives. They are quitting so they can take less stressful positions in other companies. Answer the following questions based on material in this chapter.

1. Assuming that levels of stress are high in the company, what problems would you expect to see in individuals, both physiologically and with respect to their job performance?

2. What steps can the company take to reduce the levels of stress encountered on the job?

3. You consider the possibility that the stress stems from having the wrong people in the jobs. What could you do to ensure that the people who work in your company are particularly well suited to the jobs they perform?

Self-Assessment Exercise

Finding the Right Occupation

An important part of selecting an appropriate occupation begins with understanding who you are and what special personality characteristics you bring with you to your job. This exercise is a highly simplified version of one kind of test that is sometimes used in career counseling and is similar in some respects to Holland's research described in this chapter.[55] Complete it to get a feel for what such tests are like and to learn something about your own occupational interests. Such a simple exercise cannot be completely accurate, of course, but considering your answers carefully may give you some interesting self-insights.

Directions

For each of the seven following sets of adjectives select the letter corresponding to the one adjective that best describes yourself.

1. (a) forceful   (b) enthusiastic   (c) systematic   (d) patient
2. (a) adventurous (b) outgoing   (c) diplomatic   (d) loyal
3. (a) demanding   (b) emotional   (c) conscientious (d) stable
4. (a) daring   (b) sociable   (c) conventional (d) team oriented

5. (a) decisive   (b) generous   (c) analytical   (d) calm
6. (a) self-assured   (b) convincing   (c) sensitive   (d) deliberate
7. (a) competitive   (b) trusting   (c) accurate   (d) passive

Scoring

1. Add the number of times you selected the adjectives corresponding to each letter.

2. If the majority of your choices were in the "a" category, you are likely to excel at jobs requiring the generation of new ideas, making decisions, solving problems, and taking charge. Positions in management might be right for you.

3. If the majority of your choices were in the "b" category, you are likely to excel at jobs requiring motivating others and generating enthusiasm in them, interacting with people and lending them assistance. Positions in teaching might be right for you.

4. If the majority of your choices were in the "c" category, you are likely to excel at jobs requiring careful following of orders and performing jobs with great care and precision. Positions in scientific laboratory work might be right for you.

5. If the majority of your choices were in the "d" category, you are likely to excel at jobs requiring patience and understanding of others, loyalty, and being a good listener. Positions in the clergy might be right for you.

Discussion Questions

1. What would you say are the underlying assumptions of this test, and are these reasonable?

2. Did you find it easy or difficult to describe yourself by using only these adjectives? Was it hard for you to select only one adjective? Why or why not?

3. Do you agree with the conclusions about the career best suited to your characteristics based on the scoring? Why or why not?

4. Did this exercise tell you something about yourself that you didn't know? Or did it merely confirm things you already believed? If so, does this limit the value of the test, or might it still be useful? Explain.

Group Exercise

Are You Tough Enough to Endure Stress?

A test known as the Attentional and Interpersonal Style (TAIS) inventory has been used in recent years to identify the extent to which a person can stay focused and keep his or her emotions under control—the core elements of performing well under high-pressure conditions (see Note 5). Completing this exercise (which is based on questions similar to those actually used by such groups as Olympic athletes and U.S. Navy Seals) will help you understand your own strengths and limitations in this regard. And, by discussing these scores with your teammates, you will come away with a good feel for the extent to which those with whom you work differ along this dimension as well.

Directions

1. Gather in groups of three or four people whom you know fairly well. If you are part of an intact group, such as a work team or a team of students working on a class project, meet with your fellow group members.

2. Individually, complete the following questionnaire by responding to each question as follows: "never," "rarely," "sometimes," "frequently," or "always."

_____ 1. When time is running out on an important project, I am the person who should be called on to take control of the schedule.

_____ 2. When listening to a piece of music, I can pick out a specific voice or instrument.

_____ 3. The people who know me think of me as being serious.

_____ 4. It is important to me to get a job completely right in every detail, even if it means being late.

_____ 5. When approaching a busy intersection, I easily get confused.

_____ 6. Just by looking at someone, I can figure out what he or she is like.

_____ 7. I am comfortable arguing with people.

_____ 8. At a cocktail party, I have no difficulty keeping track of several different conversations at once.

3. Discuss your answers with everyone else in your group. Item by item, consider what each person's response to each question indicates about his or her ability to focus.

Discussion Questions

1. What questions were easiest to interpret? Which were most difficult?

2. How did each individual's responses compare with the way you would assess his or her ability to focus under stress?

3. For what jobs is the ability to concentrate under stress particularly important? For what jobs is it not especially important? How important is this ability for the work you do?

Notes

Case Notes

Ehrenfeld, T. (2000, July 3). The parent trap. *The Industry Standard*, pp. 222–223, 225. www.autobytel.com/content/framed/index.cfm?id=4;4&action= InvestorRelations.

Chapter Notes

[1] Bolles, R. N. (2002). *What color is your parachute?* (2002 edition). Berkeley, CA: Ten Speed Press.

[2] Northwestern National Life Insurance Company. (1999). *Employee burnout: America's newest epidemic*. Minneapolis, MN: Author.

[3] Quick, J. C., Murphy, L. R., & Hurrell, J. J., Jr. (1992). *Stress and well-being at work*. Washington, DC: American Psychological Association.

[4] Selye, H. (1976). *Stress in health and disease*. Boston: Butterworths.

[5] Kane, K. (1997, October–November). Can you perform under pressure? *Fast Company*, pp. 54, 56. Enhanced Performance Web site: www.enhanced-performance.com.

[6] Bakker, A. B., Schaufeli, W. B., Sixma, H. J., Bosveld, W., & Van Dierendonck, D. (2000). Patient demands, lack of reciprocity, and burnout: A five-year longitudinal study among general practitioners. *Journal of Organizational Behavior, 21,* 425–441.

[7] See Note 6.

[8] Stress at work (1997, April 15). *Wall Street Journal,* p. A12.

[9] Heller, R., & Hindle, T. (1998). *Essential manager's manual*. New York: DK Publishing.

[10] Major, V. S., Klein, K. J., & Erhart, M. G. Work time, work interference with family, and psychological distress. *Journal of Applied Psychology, 87,* 427–436.

[11] Settles, I. H., Sellers, R. M., & Damas, A., Jr. (2002). One role or two? The function of psychological separation in role conflict. *Journal of Applied Psychology, 87,* 574–582.

[12] McGrath, J. E. (1976). Stress and behavior in organizations. In M. D. Dunnette (Ed.), *Handbook of industrial and organizational psychology* (pp. 1351–1398). Chicago: Rand McNally.

[13] Shedroff, N. (2000, November 28). Forms of information anxiety. *Business 2.0,* p. 220.

[14] Stephens, C., & Long, N. (2000). Communication with police supervisors and peers as a buffer of work-related traumatic stress. *Journal of Organizational Behavior, 21,* 407–424.

[15] Beehr, T. A., Jex, S. M., Stacy, B. A., & Murray, M. A. (2000). Work stressors and coworker support as predictors of individual strain and job performance. *Journal of Organizational Behavior, 21,* 391–405.

[16] Treharne, G. J., Lyons, A. C., & Tupling, R. E. (2001). The effects of optimism, pessimism, social support, and mood on the lagged relationship between stress and symptoms. *Current Research in Social Psychology, 7*(5), 60–81.

[17] Sullivan, S. E., & Bhagat, R. S. (1992). Organizational stress, job satisfaction, and job performance: Where do we go from here? *Journal of Management, 18,* 353–374.

[18] Nieman, C. (1999, July–August). How much is enough? *Fast Company*, pp. 108–116. Wah, L. (2000, January). The emotional tightrope. *Management Review,* pp. 38–43.

[19] Cropanzano, R., Rupp, D. E., & Byrne, Z. S. (2003). The interrelationship of emotional exhaustion to work attitudes, job performance, and organizational citizenship behaviors. *Journal of Applied Psychology, 88,* 160–169. Motowidlo, S. J., Packard, J. S., & Manning, M. R. (1986). Occupational stress: Its causes and consequences for job performance. *Journal of Applied Psychology, 71,* 618–629.

[20] Legree, P. J., Heffner, T. S., Psotka, J., Martin, D. E., & Medsker, G. J. (2003). Traffic crash involvement: Experiential driving knowledge and stressful contextual antecedents. *Journal of Applied Psychology, 88,* 5–26.

[21] The list: Desk rage. *Business Week* (2000, November 27), p. 12.

[22] Frese, M. (1985). Stress at work and psychosomatic complaints: A causal interpretation. *Journal of Applied Psychology, 70,* 314–328. Quick, J. C., & Quick, J. D. (1984). *Organizational stress and preventive management*. New York: McGraw-Hill.

[23] Latack, J. C., & Havlovic, S. J. (1992). Coping with job stress: A conceptual evaluation framework for coping measures. *Journal of Organizational Behavior, 13*, 479–508.

[24] Wah, L. (2000, January). The emotional tightrope. *Management Review*, pp. 38–43.

[25] Reivich, K., & Shatté, A. (2002). *The resilience factor*. New York: Broadway Books. Abascal, J. R., Brucato, D., & Brucato, L. (2001). *Stress mastery: The art of coping gracefully*. Upper Saddle River, NJ: Prentice Hall. Cunningham, J. B. (2000). *The stress management sourcebook* (2nd ed.). Los Angeles: Lowell House.

[26] See Note 39.

[27] Meager, N. (1995). Occupations. In N. Nicholson (Ed.), *The Blackwell encyclopedic dictionary of organizational behavior* (pp. 352–354). Cambridge, MA: Blackwell.

[28] Bureau of Labor Statistics (2002). News release, Table 4: State and industry average annual pay for 1999 and 2000. On the Internet at www.bls.gov/news.release/annpay.t04.htm.

[29] Driver, M. J. (1994). Careers: A review of personal and organizational research. In C. L. Cooper & I. T. Robertson (Eds.), *Key reviews in managerial psychology: Concepts and research for practice* (pp. 237–269). New York: John Wiley & Sons.

[30] Pepin, J. (2002, March). Burger meister: Ray Kroc. Time 100 Polls, on the Internet at www.time.com/time/time100/builder/profile/kroc.html. Love, J. F. (1995). *Grinding it out*. New York: Bantam.

[31] Holland, J. (1973). *Making vocational choices: A theory of careers*. Upper Saddle River, NJ: Prentice Hall. Gottfredson, G. D., & Holland, J. L. (1990). A longitudinal test of the influence of congruence: Job satisfaction, competency utilization, and counterproductive behavior. *Journal of Consulting Psychology, 37*, 389–398.

[32] Cluskey, G. R., & Vaux, A. (1997). Vocational misfit: Source of occupational stress among accountants. *Journal of Applied Business Research, 12*, 43–54.

[33] Savickas, M. L., & Spokane, A. R. (1999). *Vocational interests: Meaning, measurement, and counseling use*. Palo Alto, CA: Davies Black.

[34] Lawrence, B. (1995). Career anchor. In N. Nicholson (Ed.), *The Blackwell encyclopedic dictionary of organizational behavior* (pp. 44–45). Cambridge, MA: Blackwell.

[35] Schein, E. H. (1978). *Career dynamics: Matching individual and organizational needs*. Reading, MA: Addison-Wesley.

[36] United States Department of Labor, Bureau of Labor Statistics. (2001, December 3). *2000–2010 employment projections: Table 3b, Fastest growing occupations*. Available at www.bls.gov/news.release/ecopro.t06.htm.

[37] Nicholson, N. (1995). Career plateauing. In N. Nicholson (Ed.), *The Blackwell encyclopedic dictionary of organizational behavior* (pp. 49–50). Cambridge, MA: Blackwell.

[38] Branch, S. (1998, March 16). MBAs: What they really want. *Fortune*, p. 167.

[39] Penna Sanders & Sidney Career Consulting. (2001, November). *Taking the plunge*. Research report available at www.pennasanderssidney.com/research/report-taking theplunge.html.

[40] See Note 1.

[41] See Note 1.

[42] Hanisch, K. A. (1995). Retirement. In N. Nicholson (Ed.), *The Blackwell encyclopedic dictionary of organizational behavior* (pp. 490–491). Cambridge, MA: Blackwell.

[43] Hanisch, K. A., & Hulin, C. L. (1990). Job attitudes and organizational withdrawal: An examination of retirement and other voluntary withdrawal behaviors. *Journal of Vocational Behavior, 37*, 60–78.

[44] Hanisch, K. A. (1994). Reasons people retire and their relations to attitudinal and behavioral correlates in retirement. *Journal of Vocational Behavior, 45*, 1–16.

[45] Forum for Investor Advice (1999, July 26). Work 'til you drop. *Business Week*, p. 8.

46 Decker, J. P. (1999, November 22). Why pro golfers can't wait to hit the big five-oh. *Fortune*, p. 76.

47 Thornton, E. (1999, August 9). No room at the top. *Business Week*, p. 50.

48 Hirsch, W. (1995). Succession planning. In N. Nicholson (Ed.), *The Blackwell encyclopedic dictionary of organizational behavior* (pp. 544–545). Cambridge, MA: Blackwell.

49 Rothwell, W. J. (2000). *Effective succession planning: Ensuring leadership continuity and building talent from within.* New York: AMACOM.

50 Bianco, A., & Lavelle, L. (2000, December 11). The CEO trap. *Business Week*, pp. 86–92.

51 Darwin, A. (2000). Critical reflections on mentoring in work settings. *Adult Education Quarterly, 50*, 197–211.

52 Ragubsm, B. R., & Scandura, T. A. (1999). Burden or blessing? Expected costs and benefits of being a mentor. *Journal of Organizational Behavior, 20*, 493–509.

53 Ragins, B. R., Cotton, J. L., & Miller, J. S. (2000). Marginal mentoring: The effects of type of mentor, quality of relationship, and program design on work and career attitudes. *Academy of Management Journal, 43*, 1179–1194.

54 Clutterbuck, D., & Ragins, B. R. (2002). *Mentoring and diversity: An international perspective.* Burlington, MA: Butterworth-Heinemann. Wickman, F., & Sdodin, T. (1997). *Mentoring.* Chicago: Irwin.

55 Adapted from Morrison, E. K. (1994). *Leadership skills.* Tucson, AZ: Fisher Books.

Chapter Five

Work-Related Attitudes: Prejudice, Job Satisfaction, and Organizational Commitment

LEARNING OBJECTIVES

After reading this chapter, you will be able to:

1. **DISTINGUISH** among the concepts of prejudice, stereotypes, and discrimination.

2. **DISTINGUISH** between affirmative action plans and diversity management programs.

3. **DESCRIBE** four theories of job satisfaction.

4. **IDENTIFY** the consequences of having dissatisfied employees and **DESCRIBE** ways of boosting job satisfaction.

5. **DISTINGUISH** among three fundamental forms of organizational commitment.

6. **IDENTIFY** the benefits of having a committed workforce and **DESCRIBE** ways of developing organizational commitment.

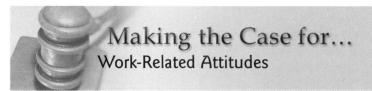

Making the Case for...
Work-Related Attitudes

"Islam 101": Basic Training at Ford After September 11 and the Iraq War

Under normal circumstances, it would not be necessary for employees of a large automotive manufacturing company to have any special knowledge of the Islamic world and the Muslim religion. But in the wake of the September 11, 2001, terrorist attacks and America's war with Iraq, circumstances were anything but normal. This was especially the case at Ford Motor Company, headquartered in Dearborn, Michigan, which happens to be home of one of the largest Arab American communities in the United States with many Muslim immigrants from Middle Eastern countries.

Following September 11, suspicions toward Ford's many Muslim employees grew, as did tensions that promised to threaten harmony in the workforce unless something was done. To neutralize these fears, a grassroots group of Middle Eastern workers was formed. Within days of the terrorist attack, they organized a fund-raising concert to aid the families of the victims. This helped people grieve together, making them feel better, but it did little to promote understanding of their world, which now was beginning to be the focus of ridicule by many of Ford's non-Islamic employees.

Recognizing that something had to be done, Mona Abdalall, who heads Ford's Interfaith Network (a group that represents seven different religious groups within the company), came up with a simple but elegant solution. She held an "Islam 101" meeting, designed to help people understand what Islam is all about. A high-ranking Muslim spiritual leader was brought in for the occasion, who reassured those gathered that the Koran (the Muslim bible) forbids killing in all forms. The terrorists, he explained, were radicals, who misinterpreted their religion, and were not at all like the millions of other peace-loving Muslims in the world.

When, to everyone's surprise, over 500 people showed up at this meeting, Abdalall, a 17-year employee at Ford, scheduled smaller, more intimate meetings of 60. The vast majority left the sessions with a better understanding of Islamic culture and the Muslim religion—an understanding that appears to be breeding tolerance and acceptance during a particularly difficult period.

When the 2003 U.S. war with Iraq began, anti-Muslim feelings reemerged, but once again stepping up those Islam 101 meetings helped promote interpersonal acceptance within the company. These efforts were especially useful after Saddam Hussein, the exiled Iraqi president, was captured by U.S. troops in December 2003. According to Samia Barnat, a manufacturing engineer who is Muslim, the results of these sessions are immediately noticeable. The year before the meetings, for example, coworkers used to offer her food during Ramadan, the month-long holiday, not realizing that Muslims fast during the days. Now, as more people have learned about her religious beliefs and customs, she feels better accepted.

Although regrettable that it took an unspeakable tragedy to bring about a new spirit of personal inquisitiveness and acceptance among its employees, Ford is surely fortunate that such feelings now exist. Instead of being ignorant about Islamic people—or, worse yet, harboring suspicions about them—Ford employees now have a greater understanding of this culture than ever before. This, in turn, has eased tensions and has made it easier for people of various races

3 GOOD REASONS why you should care about...

Work-Related Attitudes

You should care about work-related attitudes because:

1. We are all potential victims of prejudice and discrimination on the job; nobody is immune.

2. The more people are satisfied with their jobs and committed to their organizations, the less likely they are to be absent and to voluntarily resign.

3. Changing attitudes is not impossible. There are specific things that practicing managers and their organizations can do to enhance the work-related attitudes of employees.

and religions to work together in harmony. As a result, Ford can now draw on its valuable human capital to improve business. And this, in turn, keeps employees feeling good about working for the giant automaker, thereby keeping them on the job.

Obviously, such feelings about people and things—*attitudes*, as they are called—represent an important part of people's lives, particularly on the job. Indeed, people tend to have definite feelings about everything related to their jobs, whether it's the work itself, superiors, coworkers, subordinates, or even such mundane things as the food in the company cafeteria. Feelings such as these are referred to as **work-related attitudes**, the topic of this chapter. As you might imagine, our attitudes toward our jobs or organizations have profound effects not only on the way we perform but also on the quality of life we experience while at work. We will carefully examine these effects in this chapter. Specifically, our discussion of work-related attitudes will focus on three major targets—attitudes toward others (including a special kind of negative attitude known as *prejudice*), attitudes toward the job (known as *job satisfaction*), and attitudes toward the organization (known as *organizational commitment*).

Prejudice: Negative Attitudes Toward Others

How do you feel about your associate in the next cubicle? How about your boss or accountants in general? Our attitudes toward other people are obviously very important when it comes to understanding behavior in organizations. Such attitudes are highly problematic when they are negative, especially when these feelings are based on misguided beliefs that prompt harmful behavior. *Prejudice* is the term used to refer to attitudes of this type. Specifically, **prejudice** may be defined as negative feelings about people belonging to certain groups. Members of racial or ethnic groups, for example, are victims of prejudice when they are believed to be lazy, disinterested in working, or inferior in one way or another. Prejudicial attitudes often hold people back, creating an invisible barrier to success commonly known as the *glass ceiling* (as we discussed in Chapter 4, in the context of careers).

At the root of prejudicial feelings is the fact that people tend to be uncomfortable with those who are different from themselves. Today, differences between people in the workplace are not the exception but the rule. For example, not so long ago the American workforce was composed predominantly of white males. But that has been changing. White men now represent less than half of the current American workforce, and this figure is rapidly dropping. By 2008, 70 percent of new entrants to the workforce are expected to be women and people of color.[1] This is due to three key trends. First, there have been unequal shifts in the birth rate. Presently, three-quarters of the growth in the U.S. population is coming from African Americans, Hispanic Americans, and Asian Americans.[2] Second, growing numbers of foreign nationals are entering the American workforce, making it more ethnically diverse than ever before. Finally, we now see gender parity in the workforce.[3] About half of today's workforce is composed of women, and well over half of all adult American women work outside the home.

What do these demographic changes mean for organizations? Clearly, they bring with them several important challenges. White males, for example, must recognize that their era of dominance in the workplace is over. In fact, many white men, so used to being in the majority, are highly threatened by the prospect of losing this status.[4] For females and members of ethnic minority groups, barriers to success must be broken, and acceptance by others must be gained as old stereotypes and prejudicial attitudes fade away slowly. As you probably already know, this is not an easy thing to do.

Because prejudicial attitudes can have devastating effects on both people and organizations, we will examine them closely in this section of the chapter. To give you a feel for how serious prejudices can be, we describe specific targets of prejudice in the workplace and the special nature of the problems they confront. We will then follow up on this by describing various strategies that have been used to overcome prejudice in the workplace. Before doing this, however, we will take a closer look at the concept of prejudice and distinguish it from related concepts.

Anatomy of Prejudice: Some Basic Distinctions

When people are prejudiced, they rely on beliefs about people based on the groups to which they belong. So, to the extent that we believe that people from certain groups possess certain characteristics, knowing that individuals belong to that group will lead us to believe certain things about them. Beliefs such as these are referred to as **stereotypes**.

learning
objective

Stereotypes.   As you surely realize, stereotypes, whether positive or negative, are generally inaccurate. If we knew more about someone than whatever we assumed based on his or her membership in various groups, we would probably make more accurate judgments. However, to the extent that we often find it difficult or inconvenient to learn everything we need to know about someone, we frequently rely on stereotypes as a kind of mental shortcut. So, for example, if you believe that individuals belonging to group X are lazy, and you meet person A, who belongs to group X, you likely would believe that person A is lazy too. Although this may be logical, engaging in such stereotyping runs the risk of misjudging person A. He or she might not be lazy at all, despite the fact that you assumed so based on the stereotype.

Nonetheless, assume you believe person A to be lazy. How do you feel about lazy people? Chances are that you don't like them—that is, your evaluation of person A would be negative. Would you want to hire a lazy individual, such as A, for your company? Probably not. Thus, you would be predisposed against hiring A. Your prejudice toward person A is clear.

Discrimination.   Prejudicial attitudes are particularly harmful when they translate into actual behaviors. In such instances, people become the victims of others' prejudices— that is, **discrimination**. In other words, as summarized in Figure 5.1, prejudice is an attitude, whereas discrimination is a form of behavior consistent with that attitude.

Completing our example, you might refrain from hiring person A or giving him or her a positive recommendation. By acting this way, your behavior would be consistent with your attitude. Although this might be logical, it certainly is not in the best interest of the individual involved. After all, your behavior may be based on an attitude formed on the basis of inaccurate stereotypes. For this reason, it is important to identify ways of overcoming the natural tendency to base our attitudes on stereotypes and to unfairly discriminate between people on this basis. Later in this chapter we will outline some strategies shown to be effective in this regard. Before doing so, however, it would be useful to give you a feel for the seriousness of prejudicial attitudes in organizations today.

| Figure 5.1 | Prejudice Versus Discrimination: A Comparison |

Prejudice is an *attitude* consisting of negative beliefs (known as *stereotypes*), negative feelings about those beliefs, and negative predispositions toward people described by those stereotypes. These attitudes sometimes (but not always) lead to behavior consistent with that attitude—that is, *discrimination*.

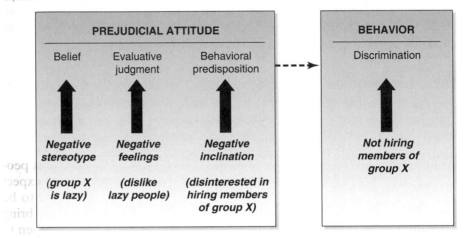

Everybody Is a Victim of Prejudice!

Unfortunate as it may be, we are all potential victims of prejudicial attitudes. Indeed, no matter what personal characteristics we may have, there may very well be people out there who are prejudiced against us. This is not surprising if you consider that people hold stereotypes about many different things. Whatever you look like, wherever you're from, whatever your interests, chances are good that at least some people will approach you with predisposed beliefs about what you're like. Sadly, for many groups of people, these beliefs have negative connotations, leading to discriminatory behavior. Here, we will describe some of the most prevalent targets of discrimination in American society today.

Prejudice based on age. As people are living longer and the birth rate is holding steady, the median age of Americans is rising all the time. Despite this trend—often referred to as the "graying of America"—prejudice against older people is all too common. Although U.S. laws (e.g., the Age Discrimination in Employment Act) have done much to counter employment discrimination against older workers, prejudices continue to exist.[5] Part of the problem resides in stereotypes that older workers are too set in their ways to train and that they will tend to be sick or accident-prone. As in the case of many attitudes, these prejudices are not founded on accurate information. In fact, survey findings paint just the opposite picture: A Yankelovich poll of 400 companies found that older workers are considered very good or excellent, especially in such critical areas as punctuality, commitment to quality, and practical knowledge.

It is not just older workers who find themselves victims of prejudice but younger ones as well. For them, part of the problem is that as the average age of the workforce advances (from an average of 29 in 1976 to 39 today), there develops a gap in expectations between the more experienced older workers who are in charge and the younger employees just entering the workforce.[6] Specifically, compared to older workers, who grew up in a different time, today's under-thirty employees view the world differently. They are more prone to question the way things are done, to not see the government as an ally, and to not expect loyalty. They are likely to consider self-development to be their main interest and are willing to learn whatever skills are necessary to make them marketable. These differing perspectives may lead older employees, who are likely to be their superiors, to feel uncomfortable with their younger colleagues.

Prejudice based on physical condition.   There are currently some 43 million Americans with disabilities, 14.6 million of whom are of working age, between 16 and 65. However, less than 30 percent of these individuals are working—and, among these, most work only part-time or irregularly. Clearly, there exist barriers that are keeping millions of potentially productive people from gainful employment. The most formidable barriers are not physical ones but attitudinal. Most people who are not physically challenged don't know how to treat and what to expect from those who are. Experts advise that people with disabilities don't want to be pitied; they want to be respected for the skills and commitment to work they bring to their jobs. That is, they wish to be recognized as whole people who just happen to have a disabling condition rather than a special class of "handicapped people."

Legal remedies have been enacted to help break down these barriers. For example, in the early 1990s, legislation known as the Americans with Disabilities Act (ADA) was enacted in the United States to protect the rights of people with physical and mental disabilities. Its rationale is straightforward: Simply because an employee is limited in some way does not mean that accommodations cannot be made to help the individual perform his or her job.[7] Companies that do not comply are subject to legal damages, and recent violators have paid dearly. However, probably the most important reason to refrain from discriminating against people with disabilities is not simply to avoid fines but more to tap into a pool of people who are capable of making valuable contributions if given an opportunity.

Prejudice against women.   There can be no mistaking the widespread—and ever growing—presence of women in today's workforce. Although 47 percent of all American workers are women, only about one large company in nine is headed by a woman.[8] Is this likely to change? Eighty-two percent of executives completing a recent *Business Week*/Harris poll indicated that it was not likely that their company would have a female CEO in the next 10 years. Thus, it appears that "women populate corporations, but they rarely run them."[9] For some recent data on the percentage of women holding top organizational positions, see Figure 5.2.[10] Equality for women in the workplace is improving, although it is a slow victory to be sure.

Why is this the case? Although sufficient time may not have passed to allow more women to work their way into the top echelons of organizations, there appear to be more formidable barriers. Most notably, it is clear that powerful *sex role stereotypes* persist, narrow-minded beliefs about the kinds of tasks for which women are most appropriately suited. For example, 8 percent of the respondents to the *Business*

Figure 5.2   Women Are Still Not Prevalent at the Top

Although women and men are almost equally represented in today's workforce, very few women have worked their way up to top positions in large organizations. Today, the percentage of executives holding the most powerful titles who are women is still quite small.

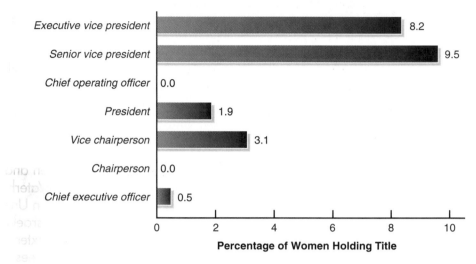

(Source: CATALYST, 2000; see Note 10.)

Week/Harris poll indicated that females are not aggressive or determined enough to make it to the top. Although this number is small, it provides good evidence of the persistence of a nagging — and highly limiting — stereotype. The existence of this problem has led growing numbers of women to venture out on their own. In fact, twice as many women as men are starting their own small businesses. As they do so, they may be expected to hire other women, potentially breaking the pattern of prejudicial behavior that has been prevalent for so long.

Prejudice based on sexual orientation.   Unlike people with physical disabilities, who are protected from discrimination by federal law, no such protection exists (yet, at least!) for another group whose members are frequently victims of prejudice — gay men and lesbian women. (However, several states and over 100 municipal laws have been enacted to protect the rights of gays and lesbians in the workplace.) Unfortunately, although more people than ever are tolerant of nontraditional sexual orientations, antihomosexual prejudice still exists in the workplace.[11] Indeed, about two-thirds of CEOs from major companies admit their reluctance to put a homosexual on a top management committee. Not surprisingly, without the law to protect them and with widespread prejudices against them, many gays and lesbians are reluctant to openly make their sexual orientations known.

Fears of being "discovered," exposed as a homosexual, represent a considerable source of stress among such individuals. For example, a gay vice president of a large office-equipment manufacturer admitted in a magazine interview that he'd like to become the company's CEO but fears that his chances would be ruined if his sexual orientation were to become known. If the pressure of going through working life with a disguised identity is disruptive, imagine the cumulative effect of such efforts on organizations in which several employees are homosexual. Such misdirection of energy can become quite a serious threat to productivity. In the words of consultant Mark Kaplan, "Gay and lesbian employees use a lot of time and stress trying to conceal a big part of their identity."[12] To work in an organization with a homophobic culture, to have to endure jokes slurring gays and lesbians, can easily distract even the most highly focused employees.

To help avoid these problems—and out of respect for diverse sexual orientations— many organizations have adopted internal fair employment policies that include sexual orientation. In addition, some companies are actively working to prohibit discrimination on the basis of sexual orientation. Extending this idea, still other companies are now offering fringe benefits, which traditionally have been offered exclusively to opposite-sex partners, to same-sex domestic partners as well. For example, companies such as Ben and Jerry's Homemade, Inc. (in Waterbury, Vermont), MCA, Inc. (in Universal City, California), and Beth Israel Medical Center (in New York) extend fringe benefits to their employees' partners regardless of whether they are of the same sex or the opposite sex. Clearly, although some companies are passively discouraging diversity with respect to sexual orientation, others encourage it, much to their own—and their employees'—advantages.

> Companies such as Ben and Jerry's Homemade, Inc. (in Waterbury, Vermont), MCA, Inc. (in Universal City, California), and Beth Israel Medical Center (in New York) extend fringe benefits to their employees' partners regardless of whether they are of the same sex or the opposite sex.

Prejudice based on race and national origin.
The history of the United States is marked by struggles over acceptance for people of various racial and ethnic groups. Although the American workplace is now more racially diverse than ever, it is clear that prejudice lingers on.

Not only do members of various minority groups believe they are the victims of prejudice and discrimination, but they are also taking action. For example, the number of complaints of discrimination based on national origin filed at the Equal Employment Opportunity Commission (EEOC) has been increasing steadily in recent years. Moreover, discrimination victims have been winning such cases. For example, in 1993 the Supreme Court of the state of Washington upheld a $389,000 judgment against a Seattle bank brought by a Cambodian American employee who was fired because of his accent.

Outside the courtroom, companies that discriminate pay in other ways as well— notably, in lost talent and productivity. According to EEOC Commissioner Joy Cherian, employees who feel victimized "may not take the initiative to introduce inventions and other innovations," adding, "every day, American employers are losing millions of dollars because these talents are frozen."[13] Some companies are taking concrete steps to help minimize these problems. For example, AT&T Bell Labs in Murray Hill, New Jersey, is working with managers to find ways of helping the company's many ethnic minority employees to be promoted more rapidly. Similarly, Hughes Aircraft Co. of Los Angeles has been assigning mentors to minority group employees to help teach them about the company's culture and the skills needed to succeed. Although both examples are only modest steps, they represent very encouraging trends intended to help reduce a long-standing problem.

Strategies for Overcoming Workplace Prejudice: Managing a Diverse Workforce

2
learning
objective

It's one thing to identify prejudicial attitudes and quite another to eliminate them. Two major approaches have been taken toward doing precisely this—*affirmative action plans* and *diversity management programs.*

Affirmative Action Plans

Traditionally, in the United States, **affirmative action plans** have been used to promote the ethical treatment of women and members of minority groups in organizations. Derived from civil rights initiatives of the 1960s, these generally involve efforts to give employment opportunities to qualified individuals belonging to groups that traditionally have been disadvantaged. The rationale is quite reasonable: By encouraging the hiring of qualified women and minority group members into positions in which they traditionally have been underrepresented, more people will be exposed to them, forcing them to see that their negative stereotypes were misguided. Then, as these stereotypes begin to crumble, prejudice will be reduced, along with the discrimination on which it is based.

After almost 40 years of experience with affirmative action programs, it is clear that there have been major gains in the opportunities that have become available to women and minority groups. Yet, they are not always well accepted.[14] Not surprisingly, several myths about affirmative action programs have developed over the years.[15] For a summary of these, and the facts that refute them, see Table 5.1.

Diversity Management Programs

In recent years, organizations have become increasingly proactive in their attempts to eliminate prejudice and have taken it upon themselves to go beyond affirmative action requirements. Their approach is not just to hire a broader group of people than usual but also to create an atmosphere in which diverse groups can flourish.[16] They are not merely trying to obey the law or attempting to be socially responsible (although they surely have these concerns) but they also recognize that diversity is a business issue. As one consultant put it, "A corporation's success will increasingly be determined by its managers' ability to naturally tap the full potential of a diverse workforce."[17] Indeed, research has established that there is, in fact, an advantage to having a diverse workforce. A recent study of the financial success of banks that actively pursued a growth strategy (i.e., those that were getting larger rather than smaller in size) found that the more highly diverse their workforce, the better they performed financially.[18] This, in turn, added value to these banks, giving them advantages over their competitors. Clearly, promoting diversity is a wise business strategy.

It is with this in mind that three-quarters of American organizations are adopting **diversity management programs**—efforts to celebrate diversity by creating supportive, not just neutral, work environments for women and minorities. Simply put, the underlying philosophy of diversity management programs is that women and minorities—anyone who may be different—be not just tolerated but also valued. This sentiment was expressed clearly by U.S. Coast Guard Admiral Thomas H. Collins, when he said, "Our ability to attract, develop, retain, and deploy a quality,

Table 5.1	Affirmative Action: Myth Versus Fact

Throughout the years, various myths about the ineffectiveness of affirmative action programs have become popular. However, as summarized here, these don't square with the facts.

Myth	*Fact*
Affirmative action has not led to increased representation of women and minorities in the workplace.	Gains have been substantial. Affirmative action programs have helped 5 million minority group members and 6 million white and minority women rise to higher positions.
Affirmative action programs reduce the self-esteem of women and racial minorities.	The opposite is true. By providing women and minority group members opportunities to succeed, their self-esteem actually increases.
Affirmative action plans bring unqualified people into the workplace.	Affirmative action programs specify that only qualified women and minority group members be hired.
The public no longer supports affirmative action programs.	This is overstated. Eighty percent of Americans currently believe that some sort of affirmative action is a good idea.
Although affirmative action programs may have been useful in the 1960s, they are less beneficial today.	The playing field is still far from level. For every dollar earned by men, women earn 74 cents, African American women earn 63 cents, and Hispanic women earn only 57 cents.

(Source: Based on information from Polus, 1996; see Note 15.)

diverse workforce is the key to the Coast Guard's success."[19] Indeed, the Coast Guard has been very actively involved in selecting highly diverse recruits and training them to value others despite their differences.

Diversity management programs consist of various efforts to not only create opportunities for diverse groups of people within organizations but also to train people to embrace differences between them. For example, Xerox's "Step-Up" program, in existence for some 40 years, has been one of the most thorough and sustained efforts to hire minority group members and train them to succeed. Similarly, Pacific Bell and US West also have made great strides at reaching out to minority group members (e.g., through internship programs), creating jobs for them in positions that have broad opportunities for advancement. Hewlett-Packard (HP) has extended such initiatives in its "Valuing Differences" program, an approach that focuses on not just giving people opportunities to succeed but valuing them *because* of their differences. HP officials rationalize that the broader the spectrum of differences in the workplace, the richer the depth of ideas on which

> Hewlett-Packard (HP) has extended such initiatives in its "Valuing Differences" program, an approach that focuses on not just giving people opportunities to succeed but valuing them *because* of their differences.

the organization can draw—hopefully, leading it to be more productive. Many different companies have been actively involved in a wide variety of diversity management activities.[20] For a small sampling of these, see Table 5.2, and for a close-up look at one particularly successful program, see the accompanying **Winning Practices** section.

Although most companies have been pleased with the ways their diversity management efforts have promoted harmony between employees, such programs are not automatically successful. For diversity management activities to be successful, experts caution that they must focus on accepting a range of differences among people. That is, they should not treat someone as special because he or she is a

Table 5.2	Diversity Management: Some Current Practices	

Many of today's companies are taking proactive steps to celebrate the diverse backgrounds of their employees. Summarized here are just a few illustrative practices.

Organization	*Name of Program*	*Description*
Pitney Bowes	Pitney Bowes Celebrates Diversity Around the World	Holds a weeklong outreach program consisting of over 100 events in which employees, customers, and community neighbors in 40 states and 11 countries recognize everyone else's ethnic backgrounds
DaimlerChrysler	Minority Dealer Program	Actively develops dealerships owned by members of the ethnic communities the company serves
Tellabs	You've Got ConneXions	Offers lavish rewards to employees for referring talented members of ethnic minorities
AT&T	Gay and Lesbian Awareness Week	Designates one week in which gay and lesbian issues are discussed and celebrated
Pace Food	Bilingual Operations	Presents all staff meetings and company publications in both English and Spanish
DuPont Corp.	Committee to Achieve Cultural Diversity	Holds focus groups that lead to career development programs for minority group members
City of Toronto	National Aboriginal Day	Showcases teaching circles, fashion shows, musicians, and traditional drummers and dancers to teach others about Aboriginal culture
NASA Glenn Research Center	Model Workplace Program	Offers multicultural training for all workers

(Source: Based on information from Gingold, 2000; see Note 20.)

Winning **Practices**

Diversity as a Competitive Weapon at Allstate

Although many companies have diversity management programs, the Allstate Insurance Co. uses its program as a strategic weapon. The idea is straightforward: By reflecting the racial and ethnic diversity of its customers, Allstate employees are more specific to needs that otherwise may go unrecognized and, therefore, unfulfilled, by a more homogeneous group of employees. According to Ed Liddy, Allstate's chairman, president, and CEO, "Our competitive advantage is our people and our people are diverse. Nothing less than an integrated diversity strategy will allow the company to excel."[21]

Allstate's diversity management program takes a broad perspective. Not limited to only gender and ethnicity, it also pays attention to diversity with respect to ages, sexual orientation, and religion. Specifically, it promotes diversity along three major fronts.

- Allstate recruiters visit historically black colleges and universities to attract members of the African American community. It also recruits from schools in Puerto Rico in an effort to expand its Hispanic customer base. From the many awards it has received for its efforts in these areas (e.g., the "Best Companies for Hispanics to Work"), such initiatives appear to be working. And, the more such recognition the company receives, the easier it is to attract more individuals from these groups.
- Attracting recruits is half the battle, but retaining them is far trickier. With this in mind, Allstate carefully trains all its employees that they are expected to show no bias toward others. It also goes out of its way to encourage minority candidates by showing them the route to promotion within the company. In

fact, minority candidates are considered seriously when it comes time to plan for succession up the ranks.

- Within their first six months on the job, all new Allstate employes receive diversity training (about three-quarters of a million person-hours have been spent thus far). This consists of classroom training that encourages people to recognize the way they see themselves and others as well as ways of sustaining a trusting environment among people who are different. Refresher courses also are given to managers from time to time.

Because it is an insurance company, it probably comes as no surprise to you that Allstate keeps careful statistical records of its diversity efforts and the company's financial success. Twice a year, the company's 53,000 employees complete a questionnaire known as the Diversity Index asking them to indicate, among other things, the extent to which they witness insensitive or inappropriate behavior at work, the amount of dignity and respect they are shown, and their beliefs about the company's commitment to delivering services to customers regardless of their ethnic background. Interestingly, the higher the overall score on the Diversity Index, the more managers are successful in promoting a diverse work environment, and the more satisfied they are. And the company's statistics show that when this happens Allstate does a better job of satisfying and retaining its customers. Indeed, Allstate is the top insurer of lives and automobiles among African Americans and also ranks as the top insurer of homes and lives among Hispanic Americans. Clearly, at Allstate, diversity is a highly successful business strategy.

member of a certain group, but because of the unique skills or abilities he or she brings to the job. To the extent that managers are trained to seek, recognize, and develop the talents of their employees without regard to the groups to which they belong, they will help break down the stereotypes on which prejudices are based. This, in turn, will bring down the barriers that made diversity training necessary in the first place. (One of the most difficult steps in eliminating prejudicial attitudes involves recognizing the sometimes subtle ways that these have infiltrated the culture of an organization. The **Group Exercise** on pages 182–183 presents a useful way to help identify these negative attitudes.)

learning
objective

Theories of Job Satisfaction: Attitudes Toward Jobs

Do people generally like their jobs? In general, only about half of all working Americans claim that they do, and this number has been dropping in recent years.[22] These feelings, reflecting attitudes toward their jobs, are known as **job satisfaction**. Because job satisfaction plays an important role in organizations, it makes sense to identify the factors that contribute to job satisfaction. As we will point out, a great deal of research, theory, and practice bears upon this question. Although there are many different approaches to understanding job satisfaction, four particular ones stand out as providing our best insight into this very important attitude—the *two-factor theory of job satisfaction, value theory*, the *social information processing model*, and the *dispositional model*.

Two-Factor Theory of Job Satisfaction

There is no more direct way to find out what causes people's satisfaction and dissatisfaction with their jobs than to ask them. Some 40 years ago, an organizational scientist assembled a group of accountants and engineers and asked them to recall incidents that made them feel especially satisfied and especially dissatisfied with their jobs.[23] His results were surprising: Different factors accounted for satisfaction and dissatisfaction. Rather than finding that the presence of certain variables made people feel satisfied and that their absence made them feel dissatisfied, as you might expect, he found that satisfaction and dissatisfaction stemmed from two different sources. For this reason, his approach is widely referred to as the **two-factor theory of job satisfaction.**

What are the two factors? In general, people were satisfied with aspects of their jobs that had to do with the work itself or with outcomes directly resulting from it. These included things such as chances for promotion, opportunities for personal growth, recognition, responsibility, and achievement. Because these variables are associated with high levels of satisfaction, they are referred to as *motivators*. However, dissatisfaction was associated with conditions surrounding the job, such as working conditions, pay, security, relations with others, and so on, rather than the work itself. Because these variables prevent dissatisfaction when present, they are referred to as *hygiene factors* (or *maintenance factors*).

Rather than a conceiving of job satisfaction as falling along a single continuum anchored at one end by satisfaction and at the other by dissatisfaction, this approach conceives of satisfaction and dissatisfaction as separate variables. Motivators, when present at high levels, contribute to job satisfaction but, when absent, do not lead to job dissatisfaction—just less satisfaction. Likewise, hygiene factors only contribute to dissatisfaction when absent but not to satisfaction when present. You may find the diagram in Figure 5.3 helpful in summarizing these ideas.

Two-factor theory has important implications for managing organizations. Specifically, managers would be well advised to focus their attention on factors known to promote job satisfaction, such as opportunities for personal growth. Indeed, several of today's companies have realized that satisfaction within their workforces is enhanced when they provide opportunities for their employees to develop their repertoire of professional skills on the job. With this in mind, front-line service workers at Marriott Hotels, known as "guest services associates," are hired not to perform a single task but to perform a wide variety of tasks, including checking guests in and out, carrying their bags, and so on. Because they perform a variety of different tasks, Marriott employees get to call on and develop many of their talents, thereby adding to their level of job satisfaction. (This approach, known as *job enrichment*, will be described more fully in Chapter 6 as a way to promote motivation.)

> Because they perform a variety of different tasks, Marriott employees get to call on and develop many of their talents, thereby adding to their level of job satisfaction.

Two-factor theory also implies that steps should be taken to create conditions that help avoid dissatisfaction—and it specifies the kinds of variables required to do so (i.e., hygiene factors). For example, creating pleasant working conditions may be quite

---

Figure 5.3   Two-Factor Theory of Job Satisfaction

According to the *two-factor theory*, job satisfaction and job dissatisfaction are not opposite ends of the same continuum but two separate dimensions. Some examples of *hygiene factors*, which lead to dissatisfaction, and *motivators*, which lead to satisfaction, are presented here.

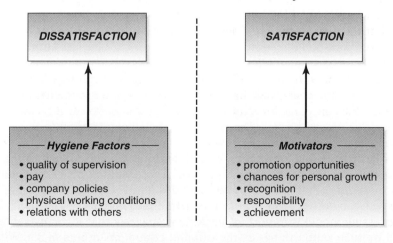

DISSATISFACTION

SATISFACTION

——— **Hygiene Factors** ———
- quality of supervision
- pay
- company policies
- physical working conditions
- relations with others

——— **Motivators** ———
- promotion opportunities
- chances for personal growth
- recognition
- responsibility
- achievement

helpful in getting people to avoid being dissatisfied with their jobs. Specifically, research has shown that dissatisfaction is great under conditions that are highly over-crowded, dark, noisy, have extreme temperatures, and poor air quality. These factors, associated with the conditions under which work is performed but not directly linked to the work itself, contribute much to the levels of job dissatisfaction encountered.

Value Theory

Another approach to job satisfaction, known as **value theory**, takes a broader look at the question of what makes people satisfied. This theory argues that almost any factor can be a source of job satisfaction so long as it is something that people value. The less people have of some aspect of the job (e.g., pay, learning opportunities) relative to the amount they want, the more dissatisfied they will be—especially for those facets of the job that are highly valued. Thus, value theory focuses on discrepancies between what people have and what they want: The greater those discrepancies, the more dissatisfied they will be.

This approach to job satisfaction implies that an effective way to satisfy workers is to find out what they want and, to the extent possible, give it to them. Believe it or not, this is sometimes easier said than done. In fact, organizations sometimes go through great pains to find out how to satisfy their employees. With this in mind, a growing number of companies, particularly big ones, have been systematically surveying their employees. For example, FedEx is so interested in tracking the attitudes of its employees that it has started using a fully automated online survey. The company relies on information gained from surveys of its 68,000 U.S.-based employees as the key to identifying sources of dissatisfaction and testing possible remedies.

> FedEx is so interested in tracking the attitudes of its employees that it has started using a fully automated online survey. The company relies on information gained from surveys of its 68,000 U.S.-based employees as the key to identifying sources of dissatisfaction

Social Information Processing Model

It's your first day on a new job. You arrive at the office excited about what you will be doing, but you soon discover that your coworkers are far less enthusiastic. "This job stinks," they all say, and you hear all the details when you hang out with them during lunch. Soon your own satisfaction with the job begins to fade. What once seemed exciting now seems boring, and your boss who once seemed so pleasant now looks more like an ogre. Your attitudes changed not because of any objective changes in the job or your boss but because you changed your outlook based on the messages you received from your coworkers.

The idea that people's attitudes toward their jobs are based on information they get from other people is inherent in the **social information processing model**. This approach specifies that people adopt attitudes and behaviors in keeping with the cues provided by others with whom they come into contact.[24] The social information processing model is important because it suggests that job satisfaction can be affected by such subtle things as the offhand comments others make. With this in

Figure 5.4   The Dispositional Model of Job Satisfaction

According to the dispositional model of job satisfaction, some people are consistently more satisfied with their jobs than others, even when they hold different jobs throughout their lives.

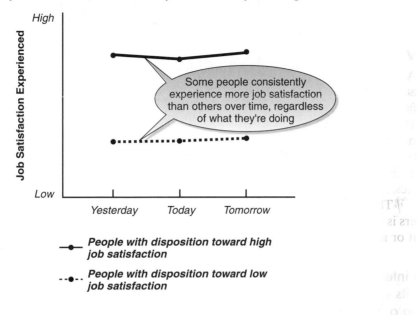

mind, it makes sense for managers to pay careful attention to what workers are thinking and feeling about their jobs. These things can be as important as actual characteristics of the jobs themselves when it comes to how people feel about them. This approach also suggests that managers should be very careful about what they say. A few well-chosen remarks may go a long way toward raising employees' job satisfaction. By the same token, a few offhand slips of the tongue may go a long way toward lowering morale.

Dispositional Model of Job Satisfaction

Do you know some people who always seem to like their jobs, no matter what they are doing, and others who are always grumbling about their jobs? If so, you are aware of the basic premise underlying what is known as the **dispositional model of job satisfaction**. This approach says that job satisfaction is a relative stable characteristic that stays with people over various situations.[25] According to this conceptualization, people who like the jobs they are doing at one time also tend to like the jobs they may be doing at another time, even if the jobs are different (see Figure 5.4).

Supporting this approach, researchers have found that people are consistent in liking or disliking their jobs over as long as a 10-year period, although they have had several different jobs during that time. Such evidence is in keeping with the idea that job satisfaction operates much like the stable dispositions toward positive and negative affect described in Chapter 3.

learning
objective

Consequences of Job Dissatisfaction—and Ways to Avoid Them

Thus far, we have been alluding to the negative effects of job dissatisfaction but without specifying exactly what these are. In other words, what consequences may be expected among workers who are dissatisfied with their jobs? Several effects have been well documented.

Employee Withdrawal: Voluntary Turnover and Absenteeism

As you might expect, people who are dissatisfied with their jobs want little to do with them—that is, they withdraw. An extreme form of employee withdrawal is quitting, formally referred to as **voluntary turnover**. Withdrawal also may take the form of *absenteeism*.

Organizations are highly concerned about these behaviors because they are very costly. The expenses involved in selecting and training employees to replace those who have resigned can be considerable. Even unscheduled absences can be expensive—averaging between $247 and $534 per employee, by one estimate. Although voluntary turnover is permanent, and absenteeism is a short-term reaction, both are effective ways of withdrawing from dissatisfying jobs.

As an example, consider the reactions of the highly dissatisfied bakery workers at the Safeway market in Clackamas, Oregon. So upset with their jobs (particularly the treatment they received from management) were the bakery's 130 employees that they frequently were absent, quit their jobs, and had on-the-job accidents. And these were no minor problems. In one year alone, accidents resulted in 1,740 lost workdays—a very expensive problem. Accidents only occurred, of course, when employees showed up. At unpopular times, such as Saturday nights, it was not unusual for as many as 8 percent of the workers to call in sick. Almost no one stayed for more than a year.

Consistent with this incident, research has shown that the more dissatisfied people are with their jobs, the more likely they are to be absent from work. This was demonstrated in a recent study of British health care workers whose questionnaire responses on a measure of job satisfaction were compared to records of their absenteeism over a two-year period.[26] Specifically, as summarized in Figure 5.5, workers whose levels of job satisfaction deteriorated over the study period also showed an increase in absenteeism, and those whose satisfaction increased over the study period also showed a decrease in absenteeism.

The same general relationship has been found in the case of turnover, although the relationship is more complex. Whether or not people will quit their jobs is likely to depend on several factors. Among them is likely to be the availability of other jobs. So, if conditions are such that alternative positions are available, people may be expected to resign in response to dissatisfaction. However, when such options are limited, voluntary turnover may be a less viable option. Hence, knowing that someone is dissatisfied with his or her job does not automatically suggest that he or she will be inclined to quit. Indeed, many people stay on jobs that they dislike.

The unfolding model of voluntary turnover.   As you might imagine, the decision to quit one's job is not taken lightly; people consider a variety of different factors

Figure 5.5   Job Satisfaction and Absence: Evidence of a Negative Relationship

A recent study tracing the levels of job satisfaction and absenteeism of health care workers over a two-year period found the relationship depicted here. Absenteeism went down among those whose satisfaction rose whereas absenteeism rose among those whose job satisfaction dropped.

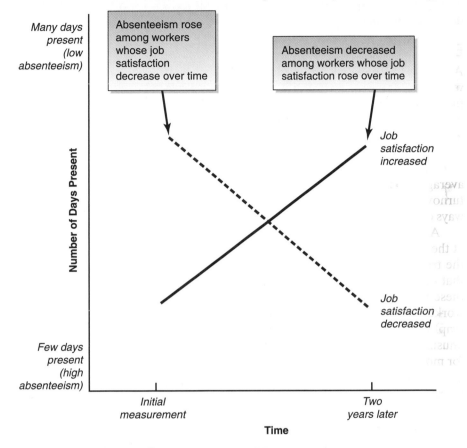

(*Source: Based on data reported by Hardy, Woods, and Wall, 2003; see Note 26.*)

before making such an important decision. These have been described in a recently proposed conceptualization known as the **unfolding model of voluntary turnover**, which is summarized in Figure 5.6.[27] According to this conceptualization, whether or not someone quits a job is said to depend on the way two key factors unfold. These are as follows:

- *Shock to the system*—An attention-getting event that gets employees to think about their jobs (e.g., merger with another company)
- *Decision frames*—A set of internalized rules and images regarding how to interpret something that has occurred (e.g., "Based on what I know from the past, is there an obvious response?")

Figure 5.6 The Unfolding Model of Voluntary Turnover

According to the *unfolding model of voluntary turnover*, people make decisions about staying or leaving their current jobs based on a complex set of cognitive processes. The major considerations are whether or not there is a shock to the system (i.e., if something occurs that makes you consider leaving) and your decision frame (i.e., the things you believe). The various decision paths are summarized here.

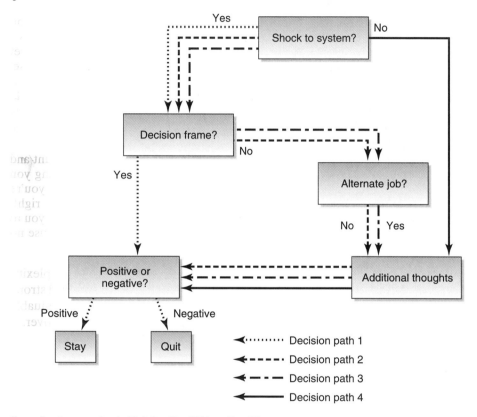

(Source: Based on suggestions by Mitchell and Lee, 2001; see Note 27.)

As shown in Figure 5.6, the unfolding model of voluntary turnover recognizes that four possible *decision paths* can result. Trace these paths through the diagram as you read about each.

1. In *Decision Path 1*, a shock to the system occurs that matches an existing decision frame. So, for example, suppose your company loses a large account. This unusual occurrence constitutes a shock to your system. Then you think about what occurred and assess what it means. If it has been your experience (directly or through others) that when accounts are lost, jobs are lost, you automatically will decide to quit. This doesn't take much consideration. Likewise, it's an easy decision for you if you reach the conclusion that lost accounts don't really mean anything, so you decide to stay.

2. In *Decision Path 2*, a shock to the system occurs, but in this case it fails to match a decision frame, and there is no specific job alternative. For example, suppose a lever-

aged buyout occurs (i.e., your company is taken over by another). This comes as a shock, but it's not exactly clear to you what it means. In such a case, you might assess how you feel about your organization. Upon further reflection, if you decide you like it, you probably will stay, especially since there is no alternative. If, however, this gets you to think about how bad the job is, you might decide to leave anyway, even without another job to fall back on. In either case, it's not immediately obvious to you what to do because you lack a decision frame, so you are forced to give the matter a lot of thought.

3. In *Decision Path 3*, a shock to the system occurs and it fails to match a decision frame, but here a specific job alternative is available. For example, suppose there's a leveraged buyout. Again, this comes as a shock, and you find it difficult to interpret because it does not match any existing decision frames. However, in this case, because there's an alternate job available, you compare your present job to this possible new one. If you think the future will be better by staying, you will be likely to do so. However, if you are so dissatisfied with your present job that you think the new one will be better, you will be inclined to leave. This, too, will be a difficult decision, although it's made easier by the presence of an alternative.

4. Finally, in *Decision Path 4*, there is no shock to the system (e.g., no lost account and no leveraged buyout). As a result, no decision frame is considered, leaving you unlikely to consider leaving in the first place. Under such circumstances, if you're feeling dissatisfied, you may be inclined to quit if other conditions are right. Otherwise, you probably would be unwilling to bother doing so, which leads you to stay. In either case, it may take a while for you to make the decision because no shock to the system has occurred.

Clearly, the unfolding model is quite complex. However, despite this complexity, and the fact that the conceptualization is new to the field of OB, it has received strong research support.[28] Accordingly, the unfolding model may be considered a valuable approach to understanding the relationship between job satisfaction and turnover.

Job Performance: Are Dissatisfied Employees Poor Workers?

How about those dissatisfied employees who remain on their jobs? Does their performance suffer? As in the case of withdrawal behaviors, the link between job performance and satisfaction is also quite modest. One key reason for this is that performance on some jobs is so carefully regulated (e.g., by the machinery required to do the work) that people may have little leeway to raise or lower their performance even if they wanted to. The weak negative association between job satisfaction and employee withdrawal and the weak positive association between job satisfaction and performance are good examples of the fact that attitudes are not perfect predictors of behavior. Indeed, the important work-related attitude, job satisfaction, has been found to be only modestly related, at best, to important aspects of job behavior.

The weak association between job satisfaction and performance appears to hold for most standard measures of performance, such as quantity or quality of work. However, when it comes to completely voluntary forms of work behavior, such as helping one's coworkers or tolerating temporary inconveniences without complaint, the connection to job satisfaction is much stronger. Such activities, which enhance social relationships and cooperation with the organization but go beyond the formal job requirements, are referred to as **organizational citizenship behaviors**. These forms of behavior, although not reflected in standard performance measures (e.g., sales figures), contribute greatly to the smooth functioning of organizations. The topic of organizational citizenship will be discussed more completely in Chapter 7. For now, we only will say that workers who feel satisfied with their jobs may be willing to help their organizations and others who have contributed to those positive feelings by engaging in acts of good organizational citizenship. In fact, research has shown that the more people are satisfied with their jobs, the greater the good citizenship contributions they tend to make.

Tips for Promoting Job Satisfaction

In view of the negative consequences of dissatisfaction, it makes sense to consider ways of raising satisfaction on the job. Although an employee's dissatisfaction might not account for all aspects of his or her performance, it is important to try to promote satisfaction if for no other reason than to make people happy. After all, satisfaction is a desirable end in itself. With this in mind, what can be done to promote job satisfaction? Based on the available research, we can offer several suggestions.

Pay people fairly.   People who believe that their organizations' pay systems are inherently unfair tend to be dissatisfied with their jobs. (We discussed the importance of fairness in Chapter 2 and will revisit this topic again in Chapter 6.) This not only applies to salary and hourly pay but also to fringe benefits. In fact, when people are given opportunities to select the fringe benefits they most desire, their job satisfaction tends to rise. This idea is consistent with value theory. After all, given the opportunity to receive the fringe benefits they most desire, employees may have little or no discrepancies between those they want and those they actually have.

Improve the quality of supervision.   It has been shown that satisfaction is highest among employees who believe that their supervisors are competent, treat them with respect, and have their best interests in mind. Similarly, job satisfaction is enhanced when employees believe that they have open lines of communication with their superiors.

For example, in response to the dissatisfaction problems that plagued the Safeway bakery employees described earlier, company officials responded by completely changing their management style. Traditionally, they were highly intimidating and controlling, leaving employees feeling powerless and discouraged. Realizing the problems caused by this iron-fisted style, they began loosening their highly autocratic ways, replacing them with a new openness and freedom. Employees were allowed to work together toward solving problems of sanitation and safety and were encouraged to make suggestions about ways to improve things. The results were dramatic: Workdays lost to accidents dropped from 1,740 a year down to 2, absenteeism fell from 8 percent to 0.2 percent, and voluntary turnover was reduced from almost 100 percent annually to less than 10 percent. Clearly, improving the quality of supervision went a long way toward reversing the negative effects of satisfaction at this Safeway bakery.

Decentralize organizational power.   Although we will consider the concept of *decentralization* more fully later in this book (e.g., in Chapters 8 and 13), it is worth introducing here. **Decentralization** is the degree to which the capacity to make decisions resides in several people, as opposed to one or just a handful. When power is decentralized, people are allowed to participate freely in the process of decision making. This arrangement contributes to their feelings of satisfaction because it leads them to believe that they can have some important effects on their organizations. By contrast, when the power to make decisions is concentrated in the hands of just a few, employees are likely to feel powerless and ineffective, thereby contributing to their feelings of dissatisfaction.

The changes in supervision made at the Safeway bakery provides a good illustration of moving from a highly centralized style to a highly decentralized style. The power to make certain important decisions was shifted into the hands of those who were most affected by them. Because decentralizing power gives people greater opportunities to control aspects of the workplace that affect them, it makes it possible for workers to receive the outcomes they most desire, thereby enhancing their satisfaction. This dynamic appears to be at work in many of today's organizations. For example, at the Blue Ridge, Georgia, plant of Levi Strauss, the sewing machine operators run the factory themselves. In a less extreme example, a committee of employees meets monthly with the CEO of Palms West Hospital (in Palm Beach County, Florida) to make important decisions concerning the hospital's operation. High satisfaction in these facilities can be traced in large part to the decentralized nature of decision-making power.

Match people to jobs that fit their interests.   People have many interests, and these are only sometimes satisfied on the job. However, the more people find that they are able to fulfill their interests while on the job, the more satisfied they will be with those jobs.

For example, a recent study found that college graduates were more satisfied with their jobs when the jobs were consistent with their college majors than when the jobs fell outside their fields of interest. It is, no doubt, with this in mind that career counselors frequently find it useful to identify people's nonvocational interests. For example, several companies, such as AT&T, IBM, Ford Motor Company, Shell Oil, and Kodak, systematically test and counsel their employees so they can effectively match their skills and interests to those positions to which they are best suited. Some companies, including Coca-Cola and Disneyland, go so far as to offer individualized counseling to employees so that their personal and professional interests can be identified and matched.

> Several companies, such as AT&T, IBM, Ford Motor Company, Shell Oil, and Kodak, systematically test and counsel their employees so they can effectively match their skills and interests to those positions to which they are best suited.

Organizational Commitment: Attitudes Toward Companies

Thus far, our discussion has centered around people's attitudes toward their jobs. However, to fully understand work-related attitudes we also must focus on people's attitudes toward the organizations in which they work—that is, their **organizational commitment**. The concept of organizational commitment is concerned with the degree to which people are involved with their organizations and are interested in remaining a part of them. A generation or two ago, most workers remained loyal to their companies throughout their working lives. However, today's workers are generally willing to move from job to job to advance their careers. For a look at some interesting statistics indicative of this trend, see Table 5.3.[29]

It is important to note that organizational commitment is generally independent of job satisfaction. Consider, for example, that a nurse may really like the kind of work she does but dislike the hospital in which she works, leading her to seek a similar job elsewhere. By the same token, a waiter may have positive feelings about the restaurant in which he works but may dislike waiting on tables. These complexities illustrate the importance of studying organizational commitment. Our presentation of this topic will begin by examining the different dimensions of organizational commitment. We will then review the impact of organizational commitment on organizational functioning and conclude by presenting ways of enhancing commitment.

5
learning
objective

Varieties of Organizational Commitment

Being committed to an organization is not only a matter of "yes or no" or even "how much." Distinctions also can be made with respect to "what kind" of commitment. Specifically, scientists have distinguished among three distinct forms of commitment, which we will review here (see summary in Figure 5.7).[30]

Continuance commitment.   Have you ever stayed on a job because you just don't want to bother to find a new one? If so, you are already familiar with the concept of **continuance commitment**. This refers to the strength of a person's desire to remain working for an organization due to his or her belief that it may be costly to leave. The longer people remain in their organizations, the more they stand to lose what they have invested in the organization over the years (e.g., retirement plans, close friendships). Many people are committed to staying on their jobs simply because they are unwilling to risk losing these things. Such individuals may be said to have a high degree of continuance commitment.

Table 5.3	Whatever Happened to Employee Loyalty?

Recent statistics tell a sobering tale about the low levels of employee commitment among members of today's workforce. Here are just a few.

- From August 1999 through January 2000, 66 percent of CEOs from the computer industry voluntarily resigned, as did 52 percent from the field of finance.
- A quarter of all employees indicate that they would leave their current job for a pay raise of only 10 percent. Fully half would leave for a 20 percent raise.
- Only 19 percent of new M.B.A.s expect to stay with their first employer for more than five years. Half expect to remain for three to five years.
- Among employees who are satisfied with their company's training programs, only 12 percent plan to leave within the next year, compared to 41 percent who are dissatisfied with the training they receive.

(Sources: See Note 29.)

Figure 5.7   Three Types of Organizational Commitment

Scientists have distinguished among the three different types of organizational commitment summarized here.

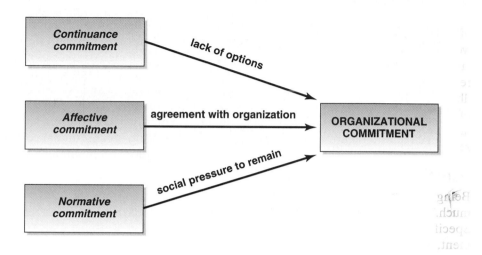

Signs suggest that today continuance commitment is not as high as it used to be. Traditionally, people sought jobs that would offer them lifetime employment. Many employees would stay on their jobs their whole working lives, starting at the bottom and working their way up to the top. But today that scenario is not readily found; the unspoken pact of job security in exchange for loyalty has all but faded from the organizational scene. In the words of a young project manager working at a New Jersey location of Prudential, "If the economy picked up, I'd consider a job elsewhere much sooner than before. I wouldn't bat an eye."[31] This expression of the willingness to leave one's job reflects a low degree of continuance commitment.

Affective commitment.   A second type of organizational commitment is **affective commitment**—the strength of people's desires to continue working for an organization because they agree with its underlying goals and values. People feeling high degrees of affective commitment desire to remain in their organizations because they endorse what the organization stands for and are willing to help it in its mission. Sometimes, particularly when an organization is undergoing change, employees may wonder whether their personal values continue to be in line with those of the organization in which they continue to work. When this happens, they may question whether they still belong and, if they believe not, they may resign.

A few years ago, Ryder Truck Company successfully avoided losing employees on this basis by publicly reaffirming its corporate values. Ryder was facing a situation in which the company was not only expanding beyond its core truck leasing business but also facing changes due to deregulation (e.g., routes, tariffs, taxes). To help guide employees through the tumultuous time, chief executive Tony Burns went out of his way to reinforce the company's core values—support, trust, respect, and striving. He spread the message far and wide throughout the company, using videotaped interviews, articles in the company magazine, plaques, posters, and even laminated wallet-size cards carrying the message of the company's core values. Along with other Ryder officials, Mr. Burns is convinced that reiterating the company's values was responsible for the high level of affective commitment that the company enjoyed during this turbulent period.

Normative commitment.   A third type of organizational commitment is **normative commitment**, which refers to employees' feelings of obligation to stay with the organization because of pressures from others. People who have high degrees of normative commitment are greatly concerned about what others would think of them for leaving. They would be reluctant to disappoint their employers and concerned that their fellow employees may think poorly of them for resigning. Normative commitment, like the other two forms of commitment, is typically assessed using a paper-and-pencil questionnaire. (To see what questions measuring organizational commitment look like and to assess your own degree of organizational commitment, see the **Self-Assessment Exercise** on pages 181–182.)

Why Strive for a Committed Workforce?

As you might imagine, people who feel deeply committed to their organizations behave differently than those who do not. Specifically, several key aspects of work behavior have been linked to organizational commitment.[32]

Committed employees are unlikely to withdraw.   The more highly committed employees are to their organizations, the less likely they are to resign and be absent (what we referred to as *withdrawal behavior* in the context of job satisfaction). Being committed leads people to stay on their jobs and to show up when they are expected to do so.[33]

This phenomenon has been demonstrated in a large-scale survey study in which dropout rates among U.S. Air Force cadets were traced over the four years required to get a degree. The more strongly committed to the service the cadets were upon entering the program, the less likely they were to drop out.[34] The finding that commitment levels could predict behavior so far into the future is a good indication of the importance of organizational commitment as a work-related attitude.

Committed employees are willing to make sacrifices for the organization.   Beyond remaining in their organizations, those who are highly committed to them demonstrate a great willingness to share and make sacrifices required for the organization to thrive. For example, when Chrysler Corp. was in serious financial trouble in the 1970s, Lee Iacocca as CEO demonstrated his commitment to help the company though its difficult period by reducing his annual pay to only $1. Although this move was clearly symbolic of the sacrifices the company wanted all employees to make, there is no doubt that Iacocca's actions cost him a great deal of real money. Had he been less committed to saving Chrysler, a company that is now highly successful, there would have been little incentive for him to be so generous. In fact, a less strongly committed CEO may have been expected to bail out altogether.

This example should not be taken as an indication that only highly magnanimous gestures result from commitment. In fact, small acts of good organizational

6
learning
objective

citizenship are also likely to occur among people who are highly committed to their organizations.[35] This makes sense if you consider that it would take people who are highly committed to their organizations to be willing to make the investment needed to give of themselves for the good of the company.

In view of these benefits of organizational commitment, it makes sense for organizations to take the steps necessary to enhance commitment among its employees. We will now describe various ways of doing this.

Ways to Develop Organizational Commitment

Some determinants of organizational commitment fall outside of managers' spheres of control, giving them few opportunities to enhance these feelings. For example, commitment tends to be lower when the economy is such that employment opportunities are plentiful. An abundance of job options surely will lower continuance commitment, and there's not too much a company can do about it. However, although managers cannot control the external economy, they can do several things to make employees want to stay working for the company—that is, to enhance affective commitment.

Enrich jobs.   People tend to be highly committed to their organizations to the extent that they have a good chance to take control over the way they do their jobs and are recognized for making important contributions. (We will discuss *job enrichment* as an approach to motivating employees in Chapter 6.) This technique worked well for Ford Motor Company. In the early 1980s, Ford confronted a crisis of organizational commitment in the face of budget cuts, layoffs, plant closings, lowered product quality, and other threats. In the words of Ernest J. Savoie, the director of Ford's Employee Development Office:

> The only solution for Ford, we determined was a total transformation of our company . . . to accomplish it, we had to earn the commitment of all Ford people. And to acquire that commitment, we had to change the way we managed people.[36]

With this in mind, Ford instituted its Employee Involvement program, a systematic way of involving employees in many aspects of corporate decision making. They not only got to perform a wide variety of tasks but also enjoyed considerable autonomy in doing them (e.g., freedom to schedule work, and to stop the assembly line if needed). A few years after the program was in place, Ford employees became more committed to their jobs—so much so, in fact, that the acrimony that usually resulted at contract renewal time had all but vanished. Although employee involvement may not be the cure for all commitment ills, it was clearly highly effective in this case.

Align the interests of the company with those of the employees.   Whenever making something good for the company also makes something good for its employees, those employees are likely to be highly committed to those companies. Many companies do this quite directly by introducing profit-sharing plans—that is, incentive plans in which employees receive bonuses in proportion to the company's profitability. Such plans are often quite effective in enhancing organizational commitment, especially when they are perceived to be administered fairly.

For example, the Holland, Michigan, auto parts manufacturer Prince Corporation gives its employees yearly bonuses based on several indices: the company's overall profitability, the employee's unit's profitability, and each individual's performance. Similarly, workers at Allied Plywood Corporation (a wholesaler of building materials in Alexandria, Virginia) receive cash bonuses based on company profits, but these are distributed monthly as well as yearly. The monthly bonuses are the same size for all, whereas the annual bonuses are given in proportion to each employee's individual contributions to total profit, days worked, and performance. These plans are good examples of some of the things companies are doing to enhance commitment. Although the plans differ, their underlying rationale is the same: By letting employees share in the company's profitability, they are more likely to see their own interests as consistent with those of their company. And, when these interests are aligned, commitment is high.

> The Holland, Michigan, auto parts manufacturer Prince Corporation gives its employees yearly bonuses based on several indices: the company's overall profitability, the employee's unit's profitability, and each individual's performance.

Recruit and select new employees whose values closely match those of the organization. Recruiting new employees is important not only because it provides opportunities to find people whose values match those of the organization but also because of the dynamics of the recruitment process itself. Specifically, the more an organization invests in someone by working hard to lure him or her to the company, the more that individual is likely to return the same investment of energy by expressing commitment toward the organization. In other words, companies that show their employees they care enough to work hard to attract them are likely to find those individuals strongly committed to the company.

In conclusion, it is useful to think of organizational commitment as an attitude that may be influenced by managerial actions. Not only might people be selected who are predisposed to be committed to the organization, but also various measures can be taken to enhance commitment in the face of indications that it is suffering.

You Be the Consultant

Addressing a Turnover Problem

The president of a small manufacturing firm comes to you with a problem: The company is spending a lot of money training new employees, but 75 percent of them quit after working less than a year. Worse, they take jobs at the company's biggest competitor. Answer the following questions relevant to this situation based on the material in this chapter.

1. Drawing on research and theory on job satisfaction, what would you suspect is the cause of the turnover? What advice can you offer about how to eliminate the problem?

2. Drawing on research and theory on organizational commitment, what would you suspect is the cause of the turnover? What advice can you offer about how to eliminate the problem?

3. Suppose you find out that the greatest levels of dissatisfaction exist among employees belonging to minority groups. What would you recommend doing to eliminate the prejudice that may be responsible for the turnover?

Self-Assessment Exercise

How Strongly Are You Committed to Your Job?

Questionnaires similar to the one presented here (which is based on established instruments) are used to assess three types of organizational commitment—continuance, affective, and normative.[37] Completing this scale will give you a good feel for your own level of job commitment and how this important construct is measured.

Directions

In the space to the left of each of the 12 statements that follow write the one number that reflects the extent to which you agree with it personally. Express your answers using the following scale: 1 = not at all, 2 = slightly, 3 = moderately, 4 = a great deal, 5 = extremely.

_____ 1. At this point, I stay on my job more because I have to than because I want to.

_____ 2. I feel I strongly belong to my organization.

_____ 3. I am reluctant to leave a company once I have been working there.

_____ 4. Leaving my job would entail a great deal of personal sacrifice.

_____ 5. I feel emotionally connected to the company for which I work.

_____ 6. My employer would be very disappointed if I left my job.

_____ 7. I don't have any other choice but to stay on my present job.

_____ 8. I feel like I am part of the family at the company in which I work.

_____ 9. I feel a strong obligation to stay on my job.

_____10. My life would be greatly disrupted if I left my present job.

_____11. I would be quite pleased to spend the rest of my life working for this organization.

_____12. I stay on my job because people would think poorly of me for leaving.

Scoring

1. Add the scores for items 1, 4, 7, and 10. This reflects your degree of *continuance commitment*.

2. Add the scores for items 2, 5, 8, and 11. This reflects your degree of *affective commitment*.

3. Add the scores for items 3, 6, 9, and 12. This reflects your degree of *normative commitment*.

Discussion Questions

1. Which form of commitment does the scale reveal you have most? Which do you have least? Are these differences great or are they highly similar?

2. Did the scale tell you something you didn't already know about yourself, or did it merely reinforce your intuitive beliefs about your own organizational commitment?

3. To what extent is your organizational commitment, as reflected by this scale, related to your interest in quitting your job and taking a new position?

Group Exercise

Auditing Organizational Biases

Is your organization biased against certain groups of people? Even if you answer "no," chances are good that you may have missed some subtle and unintentional forms of prejudice lurking about. This exercise is designed to help you uncover some of these.

Directions

1. Reproduce the checklist that follows, making one copy for each member of the class.

2. Guided by this checklist, gather the information indicated for the organization in which you work (or, if you don't work, for any organization to which you have access) and check off all items that apply.

3. In answering, either use your existing knowledge of the company or ask those who might know. (If you do ask others, be sure to tell them that it's for a class project!)

4. Report back to the class after one week.

Does Your Organization . . .

_____ have signs and manuals in English only although several employees speak other languages?

_____ ignore important holidays celebrated by people of certain cultures, such as Martin Luther King, Jr. Day, Yom Kippur, Cinco de Mayo, or Chinese New Year?

_____ limit social events to married people?

_____ restrict training opportunities available to women and people from minority groups?

_____ emphasize male-oriented sporting events, such as football?

_____ limit its recruitment efforts to colleges and universities that have predominately white students?

_____ hire predominately females for secretarial positions?

_____ discourage styles of dress that allow for the expression of varied cultural and ethnic backgrounds?

Discussion Questions

1. How many of the eight items did you check off? How about other members of the class? What was the class average?

2. What items represented the biggest sources of bias? What are the potential consequences of these actions?

3. What steps could be taken to change these practices? Do you think the company would be willing to cooperate?

Notes

Case Note

Garsten, E. (2002, January 13). Awareness of Islam aim of diversity effort at Ford. *Chicago Tribune*, p. S8.

Chapter Notes

[1] U.S. Bureau of Labor Statistics (2000). *Labor participation rates*. Washington, DC: Author.

[2] Gill, D. (1999, December 6). Diversity 101. *Business Week*, p. F12.

[3] Conlin, M., & Zellner, W. (1999, November 22). The CEO still wears wingtips. *Business Week*, pp. 85–86, 88, 90.

[4] Tsui, A. S., Egan, T. D., & O'Reilly, C. A., III. (1992). Being different: Relational demography and organizational attachment. *Administrative Science Quarterly, 37*, 549–579.

[5] Gregory, R. F. (2001). *Age discrimination in the American workplace: Old at a young age*. New Brunswick, NJ: Rutgers University Press.

[6] Raines, C. (1997). *Beyond generation X. A practical guide for managers*. Menlo Park, CA: Crisp.

[7] Magill, B. G. (1999). *Workplace accommodations under the ADA*. Washington, DC: Thompson Publishing Group.

[8] Morris, K. (1998, November 23). You've come a short way, baby. *Business Week*, pp. 82–83, 86, 88.

[9] Steinberg, R., & Shapiro, S. (1982), Sex differences in personality traits of female and male master of business administration students. *Journal of Applied Psychology, 67*, 306–310.

[10] CATALYST (2000). *The glass ceiling in 2000.* New York: Author (from the World Wide Web: www.catalystwomen.org/press/factslabor00.html. Bureau of Labor Statistics, 1999; Catalyst, 1999 Census of Women Corporate Officers and Top Earners; 1999 Census of Women Board Directors of the *Fortune* 1000).

[11] Hereck, G. M. (1998). *Stigma and sexual orientation: Understanding prejudice against lesbians, gay men, and bisexuals.* Newbury Park, CA: Sage.

[12] Martinez, M. N. (1993, June). Recognizing sexual orientation is fair and not costly. *HRMagazine*, pp. 66–68, 70–72 (quote, p. 68).

[13] Yang, C. (1993, June 21). In any language, it's unfair: More immigrants are bringing bias charges against employers. *Business Week*, pp. 110–112 (quote, p. 111).

[14] Kravitz, D. A., & Klineberg, S. L. (2000). Reactions to two versions of affirmative action among whites, blacks, and Hispanics. *Journal of Applied Psychology, 85*, 597–611.

[15] Pelus, S. (1996). Ten myths about affirmative action. *Journal of Social Issues, 52*, 25–31.

[16] Ragins, B. R., & Gonzales, J. A. (2003). Understanding diversity in organizations: Getting a grip on a slippery construct. In J. Greenberg (Ed.), *Organizational behavior: The state of the science* (2nd ed.) (pp. 125–163). Mahwah, NJ: Lawrence Erlbaum Associates.

[17] Thomas, R. R., Jr. (1992). Managing diversity: A conceptual framework. In S. E. Jackson (Ed.), *Diversity in the workplace* (pp. 306–317). New York: Guilford Press.

[18] Richard, O. C. (2000). Racial diversity, business strategy, and firm performance: A resource-based view. *Academy of Management Journal, 43*, 164–177.

[19] U.S. Coast Guard Diversity Policy Statement. (2003, March). Retrieved from the World Wide Web at www.uscg.mil/hq/g-w/g-wt/g-wtl/cgdiv.htm.

[20] Gingold, D. (2000, July 26). Diversity today. *Fortune*, special section.

[21] What's it like to work at Allstate? Diversity. (2003). From the World Wide Web at www.allstate.com/Careers/PageRender.asp?Page=diversity.htm.

[22] American Psychological Association Division 42 Online. *Letters for media interviews: Job satisfaction.* From the World Wide Web at www.division42.org/PublicArea/Media/PrReleases/job_satisfaction.html. Anderson, P. (2000, October 24). Job satisfaction: Oxymoron. CNN.com career trends. From the World Wide Web at www.cnn.com/2000/CAREER/trends/10/23/job.dissatisfaction/#chart.

[23] Herzberg, F. (1966). *Work and the nature of man.* Cleveland, OH: World.

[24] Salancik, G. R., & Pfeffer, J. R. (1978). A social information processing approach to job attitudes. *Administrative Science Quarterly, 23*, 224–252. Zalesny, M. D., & Ford, J. K. (1990). Extending the social information processing perspective: New links to attitudes, behaviors, and perceptions. *Organizational Behavior and Human Decision Processes, 47*, 205–246.

[25] Judge, T. A. (1992). Dispositional perspective in human resources research. In G. R. Ferris & K. M. Rowland (Eds.), *Research in personality and human resources management* (Vol. 10, pp. 31–72). Greenwich, CT: JAI Press.

[26] Hardy, G. E., Woods, D., & Wall, T. D. (2003). The impact of psychological distress on absence from work. *Journal of Applied Psychology, 88*, 306–314.

[27] Mitchell, T. R., & Lee, T. W. (2001). The unfolding model of voluntary turnover and job embeddedness: Foundations for a comprehensive theory of attachment. In B. M. Staw & R. I. Sutton (Eds.), *Research in organizational behavior* (Vol. 23, pp. 189–246). Oxford, UK: Elsevier.

[28] Lee, T. W., Mitchell, T. R., Holtom, B. C., McDaniel, L., & Hill, J. W. (1999). Theoretical development and extension of the unfolding model of voluntary turnover. *Academy of Management Journal, 42*, 450–462.

[29] Reingold, J. (1999, March 1). Why your workers might jump ship. *Business Week*, p. 8. Anonymous. (1999, July–August). To attract talent, you've gotta give 'em all. *Management Review*, p. 10. Anonymous. (1999, July–August). Employee loyalty surprisingly strong. *Management Review*, p. 9. The List: Hot Seat in the Corner Office (2000, February 14). *Business Week*, p. 8.

[30] Snape, E., & Redman, T. (2003). An evaluation of a three-component model of occupational commitment: Dimensionality and consequences among United Kingdom human resource management specialists. *Journal of Applied Psychology, 88*, 152–159. Meyer, J. P., Allen, N. J., & Smith, C. A. (1993). Commitment to organizations and occupations: Extension and test of a three-component conceptualization. *Journal of Applied Psychology, 78*, 538–551.

[31] O'Reilly, B. (1994, June 13). The new deal: What companies and employees owe each other. *Fortune*, pp. 45, 47, 50, 52 (quote, p. 45).

[32] Lee, K., Carswell, J. J., & Allen, N. J. (2000). A meta-analytic review of occupational commitment: Relations with person- and work-related variables. *Journal of Applied Psychology, 85*, 799–811.

[33] Clugston, M. (2000). The mediating effects of multidimensional commitment on job satisfaction and intent to leave. *Journal of Organizational Behavior, 21*, 477–486.

[34] Lee, T. W., Ashford, S. J., Walsh, J. P., & Mowday, R. T. (1992). Commitment propensity, organizational commitment, and voluntary turnover: A longitudinal study of organizational entry processes. *Journal of Management, 18*, 15–32.

[35] Hui, C., Lam, S. S. K., & Law, K. K. S. (2000). Instrumental values of organizational citizenship behavior for promotion: A field quasi-experiment. *Journal of Applied Psychology, 85*, 822–828.

[36] Rosen, R. H. (1991). *The healthy company*. Los Angeles: Jeremy P. Tarcher (quote, pp. 71–72).

[37] Meyer, J. P., & Allen, N. J. (1991). A three-component conceptualization of organizational commitment. *Human Resource Management Review, 1*, 61–89.

Chapter **Six**

What Motivates People to Work?

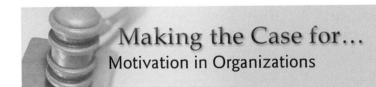
Making the Case for...
Motivation in Organizations

Keeping the Volunteers Working Hard at Amnesty International UK

Amnesty International (AI) refers to itself as "a worldwide movement of people who campaign for internationally recognized human rights." Its primary mission is to take action that prevents and ends mental and physical abuses of people around the world. Since its inception in 1961, the organization has been putting pressure on governments and other institutions to stop human rights abuses. In just 2003 alone, for example, AI has had a hand in ceasing hundreds of unlawful killings and acts of torture and releasing from prison hundreds more holding unpopular political beliefs. It brings pressure to bear on offending political regimes by writing letters, lobbying governmental organizations, and participating in events organized by international organizations such as the United Nations. Because most of AI's support comes from donations, it relies on a network of volunteers to keep it going—some 8,000 people in

100 nations (ranging from doctors and lawyers to everyday laborers).

Keeping the legions of volunteers working hard is one of the major challenges AI faces. In the U.K. office of AI, located in London, where there are 100 paid staff members, Veronique Du Pont coordinates the work of 70 volunteers. Their commitment to the cause of human rights is a big motivator, she explains, but the work they do is less than glamorous. Working in the mailroom, updating the computer database, filing, and writing routine correspondence seem a far cry from getting a political dissident out of a Colombian prison.

To keep the volunteers feeling the importance of the mundane work they do, Du Pont goes out of her way to point out how even this routine work is essential to making AI's campaigns successful. One way she does this is by holding regular meetings for volunteers and having them attend the various workshops the office puts on. As Du Pont points out, "Although volunteers are motivated by their involvement in the work, when they're doing quite mundane tasks, they need to feel integrated in Amnesty's projects. That means keeping volunteers informed and updated, and giving them access to information. Without a mutual respect between team members (volunteers or not) we wouldn't have happy volunteers."

If you talk to any of AI's London volunteers, it's clear that Du Pont's approach is working. Says Jamal, one of the volunteers, "I get a lot of satisfaction out of volunteering here. There are various events that help us to feel part of the organization." Among these, he cites the opportunity to attend various lectures about human rights and the work of the organization, as well as a field trip to AI's international headquarters.

Motivation in Organizations

You should care about motivation in organizations because:

1. Managers typically have a variety of opportunities to motivate employees by virtue of how they treat them.

2. In many different ways, motivated individuals tend to be better employees.

3. Jobs can be designed in such a manner as to make them inherently interesting to the individuals who perform them.

Motivating a large group of volunteers to perform mundane clerical tasks surely isn't easy, but it's clear that Veronique Du Pont has the right idea. She helps them feel involved in the important work that AI does by explaining how they contribute to the organization's efforts and by keeping them up-to-date on its activities. As you will see in this chapter, these are some of the key things it takes to motivate employees. We will discuss these and several other related ways of motivating employees in this chapter—identifying not only what you can do to motivate people but also precisely what makes various motivational techniques successful.

The question of exactly what it takes to motivate workers has received a great deal of attention by both practicing managers and organizational scientists.[1] In addressing this question, we examine five different approaches. Specifically, we will focus on motivating by (1) meeting basic human needs, (2) treating people fairly, (3) enhancing beliefs that desired rewards can be attained, (4) setting goals, and (5) designing jobs to make them more desirable. Before turning attention to these specific orientations, we first must consider a very basic matter—namely, what exactly is meant by the term *motivation*.

What Is Motivation? A Definition

learning objective

Scientists have defined **motivation** as the process of arousing, directing, and maintaining behavior toward a goal. As this definition suggests, motivation involves three components. The first component, *arousal*, has to do with the drive or energy behind our actions. For example, when we are hungry we are driven to seek food. The *direction* component involves the choice of behavior made. A hungry person may make many different choices—eat an apple, have a pizza delivered, go out for a burger, and so on. The third component, *maintenance*, is concerned with people's persistence, their willingness to continue to exert effort until a goal is met. The longer you would continue to search for food when hungry the more persistent you would be.

Putting it all together, it may help to think of motivation by using the analogy of driving a car. In this manner, arousal may be likened to the energy generated by the car's engine and fuel system. The direction it takes is dictated by the driver's manipulation of the steering wheel. Finally, maintenance may be thought of as the driver's determination to stay on course until the final destination is reached.

Despite this simple analogy, motivation is a highly complex concept. This is reflected by the fact that people often are motivated by many things at once, sometimes causing conflicts. For example, a factory worker may be motivated to make a positive impression on his supervisor by doing a good job, but at the same time, he may be motivated to maintain friendly relations with his coworkers by not making them look bad. This example has to do with job performance, and indeed, motivation is a key determinant of performance. However, it is important to note that *motivation is not synonymous with performance*. In fact, as we will explain later, even the most highly motivated employee may fall short of achieving success on the job—especially if he or she lacks the required skills or works under unfavorable conditions. Clearly, although motivation does not completely account for job performance, it surely is one important factor in bringing it about. Moreover, it is something about which managers can do something. With this in mind, you now are prepared to understand the different approaches to motivating people on the job.

Motivating by Meeting Basic Human Needs

learning objective

As our definition suggests, people are motivated to fulfill their needs—whether it's a need for food, as in our example, or other needs, such as the need for social approval. Companies that help their employees in this quest are certain to reap the benefits. In fact, companies that actively strive to meet the needs of their employees attract the best people and motivate them to do excellent work.[2]

Some insight into how this may come about is provided by Maslow's **need hierarchy theory**.[3] Maslow's basic idea is simple: People will not be healthy and well adjusted unless their needs are met. This idea applies whether we're talking about becoming a functioning member of society, Maslow's original focus, or a productive employee of an organization, a later application of his work. Specifically, Maslow identified five different types of needs that, he claimed, are activated in a specific order. These start at the lowest, most basic needs and work upward to higher-level needs (which is what makes it a hierarchy). Furthermore, these needs are not aroused all at once or in random fashion. Rather, each need is triggered only after the one beneath it in the hierarchy has been satisfied. The specific needs and the hierarchical order in which they are arranged are summarized in Figure 6.1. You may find it useful to refer to this overview as we describe each of Maslow's five categories of needs.

Physiological Needs

The lowest-order needs involve satisfying fundamental biological drives, such as the need for air, food, water, and shelter. These **physiological needs**, as they are called, are surely the most basic needs, because unless they are met people will become ill and suffer. For this reason, they are depicted at the base of the triangle in Figure 6.1.

There are many things that companies do to help meet their employees' basic physiological needs. Probably the simplest involves paying them a living wage, money that can be exchanged for food and shelter. But there's more to satisfying physiological needs than giving employees a paycheck. There are also coffee breaks and opportunities to rest. Even the cruelest, slave-driving bosses know the importance of giving workers time to relax and recharge their systems.

Figure 6.1   Need Hierarchy Theory

Maslow's *need hierarchy theory* specifies that the five needs shown here are activated in order, from lowest to highest. Each need is triggered after the one immediately below it in the hierarchy is satisfied.

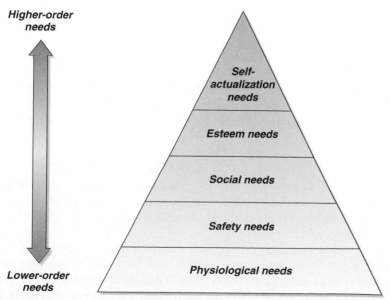

Staying physically healthy involves more than just resting; it also requires exercise, something that the sedentary nature of many of today's technologically advanced jobs does not permit. With this in mind, thousands of companies are providing exercise facilities for their employees. In fact, a recent survey found that the perk most desired by managers seeking new jobs is membership in a health club.[4] This makes perfectly good business sense. By keeping the workforce healthy and fit companies are paving the way for people to become productive. Some companies, such as Southern California Edison and Hershey Foods, have taken this thinking to the extreme. They offer insurance rebates to employees who live healthy lifestyles (e.g., physically fit nonsmokers) and raise the premiums of those at greater risk for illness. In this manner, not only are the insurance burdens distributed fairly, but also the incentives encourage wellness activities that promise to benefit both employers and employees.

> Southern California Edison and Hershey Foods offer insurance rebates to employees who live healthy lifestyles (e.g., physically fit nonsmokers) and raise the premiums of those at greater risk for illness.

Safety Needs

After physiological needs have been satisfied, the next level of needs is triggered— **safety needs**. These are concerned with the need to operate in an environment that is physically and psychologically safe and secure, one free from threats of harm.

Organizations help satisfy their employees' safety needs in several ways. For example, they protect shop workers from hazards in the environment by providing such basic services as security and fire-prevention, and by fitting them with goggles and hard hats. Even seemingly safe work settings, such as offices, can be riddled with safety hazards. This is why efforts are made to spare office workers from eye strain, wrist injuries (such as the increasingly prevalent carpal tunnel syndrome), and back pain by using ergonomically designed computer keyboards, desks, and chairs.

Psychological safety is important as well. By offering health and disability insurance, companies are promoting their employees' psychological well-being by assuring them that they will not be harmed financially in the event of illness. Although almost all companies offer health insurance benefits, a select few have taken psychological security to the extreme by having no-layoff policies. For over 70 years, Cleveland, Ohio's Lincoln Electric Company, for example, has not laid off a single worker.[5] When times are tough, they simply reassign their employees to other jobs. Knowing that your job will always be there regardless of economic conditions is surely a source of psychological reassurance.

Social Needs

Once people's physiological and safety needs have been satisfied, Maslow claims, **social needs** are activated. These refer to the need to be affiliative—that is, to be liked and accepted by others. As social animals we want to be with others and to have them approve of us.

Organizations do much to satisfy these needs when they sponsor social events, such as office parties and company picnics. For example, by holding its annual "Family Day" picnic near its Armonk, New York, headquarters, IBM employees enjoy good opportunities to socialize with their coworkers and their families.

Similarly, joining a company's bowling team or softball team also provides good opportunities to meet social needs within an organization. In discussing physiological needs we noted that many companies provide health club facilities for their employees. Besides keeping employees healthy, it's easy to see how such opportunities also help satisfy social needs. "Playing hard" with those with whom we also "work hard" provides good opportunities to fulfill social needs on the job.

Esteem Needs

Not only do we need to be liked by others socially, but we also need to gain their respect and approval. In other words, we have a **need for self-esteem**—that is, to achieve success and have others recognize our accomplishments. Consider, for example, reserved parking spots or plaques honoring the "employee of the month." Both are ways of demonstrating esteem for employees. So too are awards banquets in which worthy staff members' contributions are recognized.[6] The same thing is frequently done in print by recognizing one's organizational contributions on the pages of a corporate newsletter. For example, employees of the large pharmaceutical company Merck enjoyed the recognition they received for developing Proscar (a highly successful drug treatment for prostate enlargement) when they saw their pictures in the company newsletter. In fact, it meant more to Merck employees to have their colleagues learn of their success than it did to have their accomplishments touted widely, but to an anonymous audience, on the pages of the *New York Times*.

The practice of awarding bonuses to people making suggestions for improvement is another highly successful way to meet employees' esteem needs. Companies have used a variety of different rewards in this regard. For example, small prizes, such as VCRs and computers, are used routinely by companies such as Shell Oil, Campbell Soup, AT&T, and American Airlines to reward a wide range of special contributions. However, few companies have taken the practice of rewarding contributions to the same high art as Mary Kay Cosmetics. Not only are lavish banquets staged to recognize modest contributions to this company's bottom line, but top performers are awarded the most coveted prize of all—a pink Cadillac. As the company's late founder Mary Kay Ash put it, "There are two things people want more than sex and money . . . recognition and praise."[7] Companies that cannot afford such lavish gifts needn't be concerned about failing to satisfy their employees self-esteem needs. After all, sometimes the best recognition is nothing more than a heartfelt "thank you." Or, as Mark Twain put it, "I can live for two months on a good compliment."

> As Mary Kay Ash put it, "There are two things people want more than sex and money . . . recognition and praise."

Self-Actualization Needs

What happens after all an employee's lower-order needs are met? According to Maslow, people will strive for **self-actualization**—that is, they will work to become all they are capable of being. When people are self-actualized, they perform at their maximum level of creativity and become extremely valuable assets to their organizations.

For this reason, companies are interested in paving the way for their employees to self-actualize by meeting their lower-order needs.

As this discussion clearly suggests, Maslow's theory provides excellent guidance with respect to the needs that workers are motivated to achieve. Indeed, many organizations have taken actions that are directly suggested by the theory and have found them to be successful. For this reason, the theory remains popular with organizational practitioners. Scientists, however, have noted that specific elements of the theory—notably, the assertion that there are only five needs and that they are activated in a specific order—have not been supported. Despite this shortcoming, the insight that Maslow's theory provides into the importance of meeting human needs in the workplace makes it a valuable approach to motivation.

Motivating by Being Equitable

There can be little doubt about the importance of money as a motivator on the job. However, it would be overly simplistic and misleading to say that people only want to earn as much money as possible. Even the highest-paid executives, sports figures, and celebrities sometimes complain about their pay despite their multimillion-dollar salaries.[8] Are they being greedy? Not necessarily. Often the issue is not the actual amount of pay received, but rather, pay fairness. That is, how does the pay received compare to that of others who are doing similar work? As a case in point, consider the National Basketball Association's Houston Rockets. In recent years, low morale on this team was linked to the fact that it had three highly paid superstars who made multimillion-dollar salaries while the majority of the team's players made the league's minimum salary of $272,250.[9] Although you might not feel too sorry for someone who has to "rough it" on a quarter-million-dollar salary, many of these players felt underpaid because they thought that the stars who made eight or ten times more than they were not really eight or ten times better.

Organizational scientists have been actively interested in explaining exactly what constitutes fairness on the job and how people respond when they believe they have been unfairly treated. The major approach to this issue is known as *equity theory*.

Equity Theory: Balancing Outcomes and Inputs

Equity theory proposes that people are motivated to maintain fair, or equitable, relationships between themselves and others and to avoid those relationships that are unfair or inequitable.[10] To make judgments of equity people compare themselves to others by focusing on two variables: outcomes—what we get out of our jobs (e.g., pay, fringe benefits, prestige)—and inputs—the contributions made (e.g., time worked, effort exerted, units produced). It helps to think of these judgments in the form of ratios—that is, the outcomes received relative to the inputs contributed (e.g., $500 per week in exchange for working 40 hours). It is important to note that equity theory deals with outcomes and inputs as they are perceived by people, not necessarily objective standards. As you might imagine, well-intentioned people sometimes disagree about what constitutes equitable treatment.

According to equity theory, people make equity judgments by comparing their own outcome/input ratios to the outcome/input ratios of others. This so-called "other" may be someone else in one's work group, another employee in the organization, an individual working in the same field, or even oneself at an earlier point in time—in short, almost anyone against whom we compare ourselves. As shown in Figure 6.2, these comparisons can result in any of three different states: *overpayment inequity*, *underpayment inequity*, or *equitable payment*.

Let's consider an example. Imagine that Andy and Bill work together as copywriters in an advertising firm. Both men have equal amounts of experience, training and education, and work equally long and hard at their jobs. In other words, their inputs are equivalent. But suppose Andy is paid an annual salary of $30,000 while Bill is paid only $25,000. In this case, Andy's ratio of outcomes/inputs is higher than Bill's, creating a state of *overpayment inequity* for Andy (since the ratio of his outcomes/inputs is higher) but *underpayment inequity* for Bill (since the ratio of his outcomes/inputs is lower). According to equity theory, Andy, realizing that he is paid more than an equally qualified person doing the same work, will feel *guilty* in response to his *overpayment*. By contrast, Bill, realizing that he is paid less than an

---

Figure 6.2   Equity Theory: A Summary and Example

According to *equity theory*, people make judgments of equity or inequity by comparing the ratios of their own outcomes/inputs to the corresponding ratios of others. People are motivated to change inequitable relationships (such as the one shown on top) to equitable ones (such as the one shown on the bottom).

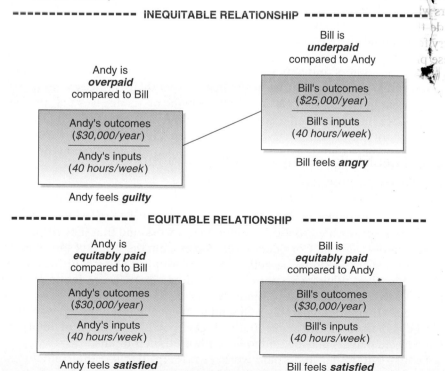

equally qualified person for doing the same work, will feel *angry* in response to his *underpayment*. Guilt and anger are negative emotional states that people are motivated to change. As a result, they will seek to create a state of *equitable payment* in which their outcome/input ratios are equal, leading them to feel *satisfied*.

Creating equity.   How can inequitable states be turned into equitable ones? The answer lies in adjusting the balance of outcomes and/or inputs. Among people who are underpaid, equity can be created by raising one's outcomes and/or lowering one's inputs. Likewise, those who are overpaid may either raise their inputs or lower their outcomes. In both cases, either action would effectively make the two outcome/input ratios equivalent. For example, the underpaid person, Bill, might lower his inputs, such as by slacking off, arriving at work late, leaving early, taking longer breaks, doing less work or lower-quality work—or, in an extreme case, quitting his job. He also may attempt to raise his outcomes, such as by asking for a raise, or even taking home company property, such as tools or office supplies. By contrast, the overpaid person, Andy, may do the opposite—raise his inputs or lower his outcomes. For example, he might put forth much more effort, work longer hours, and try to make a greater contribution to the company. He also might lower his outcomes, such as by working while on a paid vacation or not taking advantage of fringe benefits the company offers.

These are all specific *behavioral* reactions to inequitable conditions—that is, things people can *do* to turn inequitable states into equitable ones. However, people may be unwilling to do some of the things necessary to respond behaviorally to inequities. In particular, they may be reluctant to steal from their employers or unwilling to restrict their productivity for fear of getting caught "goofing off." In such cases, people may attempt to resolve inequity *cognitively* by changing the way they think about the situation. As noted earlier, because equity theory deals with perceptions, inequitable states may be redressed by altering one's thinking about their own and others' outcomes and inputs. For example, underpaid people may rationalize that others' inputs are really higher than their own (e.g., "I suppose she really *is* more qualified than me"), thereby convincing themselves that their higher outcomes are justified. Similarly, overpaid people may convince themselves that they really *are* better and deserve their relatively higher pay. So, by changing the way they see things, people can come to perceive inequitable situations as equitable, thereby effectively relieving their feelings of guilt and anger and transforming them into feelings of satisfaction.

Responding to inequities on the job.   There is a great deal of evidence to suggest that people are motivated to redress inequities at work and that they respond much as equity theory suggests. Consider two examples from the world of sports. Research has shown that professional basketball players who are underpaid (i.e., ones who are paid less than others who perform as well or better) score fewer points than those who are equitably paid.[11] Similarly, among baseball players, those paid less than others who play comparably well tend to change teams or even leave the sport when they are unsuccessful at negotiating higher pay. Cast in terms of equity theory, the underpaid players may be said to have lowered their inputs.

We also know that underpaid workers attempt to raise their outcomes. For example, in an organization studied by the author, workers at two manufacturing plants suffered an underpayment created by the introduction of a temporary pay cut of 15 percent.[12] During the 10-week period under which workers received lower pay, company officials noticed that theft of company property increased dramatically by approximately 250 percent. However, in another factory in which comparable work was done by workers paid at their normal rates, the theft rate remained low. This pattern suggests that employees may have stolen property from their company in order to compensate for their reduced pay. Consistent with this possibility, it was found that when the normal rate of pay was reinstated in the two factories, the theft rate returned to its normal, low level. These findings suggest that companies that seek to save money by lowering pay may merely be encouraging their employees to find other ways of making up for what they believe is rightfully theirs.

In closing this section, consider the examples we've given. First professional athletes performed worse, or even quit, when they received salaries that were not commensurate with their performance. Second, factory workers stole from their employers while they received lower pay than usual. Together, these examples clearly illustrate a key point explained by equity theory—namely, that people are highly motivated to seek equity and to redress the inequities they face on the job.

Managerial Implications of Equity Theory

Equity theory has important implications for ways of motivating people.[13] We will highlight two key ones here.

Avoid underpayment.   Companies that attempt to save money by reducing employees' salaries may find that employees respond in many different ways to even the score. For example, they may steal, or they may shave a few minutes off their workdays or otherwise withhold production.

In extreme cases, employees express their feelings of severe underpayment inequity by going on strike. This is exactly what happened in August 1997, when 185,000 members of the Teamsters Union went on strike against UPS, the world's largest package distribution company. Their claim was that the company was being unfair because it hired lots of part-time workers, who were paid less than full-time workers doing the same jobs. After a 16-day strike that cost UPS millions of dollars in lost revenue and that crippled package shipments throughout the world, a settlement was reached that the Teamsters believed would result in more equitable treatment for its members. This included limiting the use of part-timers and increasing hourly wages by $3.10 for full-timers and $4.10 for part-timers over five years.

> In August 1997 members of the Teamsters Union went on strike against UPS. Their claim was that the company was being unfair because it hired lots of part-time workers, who were paid less than full-time workers doing the same jobs.

Over the past few years, a particularly unsettling form of institutionalizing underpayment has materialized in the form of **two-tier wage structures**—payment systems in which newer employees are paid less than those hired to do the same work at an earlier point in time. Many of the major airlines adopted such a system in the 1980s, much to the chagrin of those involved, particularly by those in the lower tier.[14] When such a plan was instituted at the Giant Food supermarket chain, two-thirds of the lower-tier employees quit their jobs in the first three months. "It stinks," said a clerk at one Giant store in Los Angeles. "They're paying us lower wages for the same work."[15] Not surprisingly, proposals to introduce two-tier wage systems have met with considerable resistance among employees and, when applicable, the unions representing them.

This problem has been particularly severe among the growing legions of contingent, part-time, or permanent-temporary workers who have been staffing offices and factories in recent years (see Chapter 1). Because these individuals often receive lower pay and fewer fringe benefits than their full-time counterparts performing the same work, they tend to feel underpaid. It is with this in mind that some organizations have taken to putting contingent workers on different shifts or having them work in different locations than full-time, permanent employees so as to keep them from talking to each other and possibly making the inequities salient.[16] This practice—which amounts to attempting to hide an inequitable pay structure—cannot be condoned on ethical grounds. Moreover, making people feel underpaid is simply an unwise and ineffective managerial practice.

Avoid overpayment.   You may think that because overpaid employees work hard to deserve their pay, it would be a useful motivational technique to pay people more than they merit. There are several reasons why this would not work. First, the increases in performance shown in response to overpayment inequity tend to be only temporary. As time goes on, people begin to believe that they actually deserve the higher pay they're getting and bring their work level down to normal. A second reason why it is unwise to overpay employees is that when you overpay one employee, you are underpaying all the others. When the majority of the employees feel underpaid, they will lower their performance, resulting in a net *decrease* in productivity—and widespread dissatisfaction. Hence, the conclusion is clear: *Managers should strive to pay all employees equitably.*

I realize, of course, that this may be easier said than done. Part of the difficulty resides in the fact that feelings of equity and inequity are based on perceptions, and these aren't always easy to control. One approach that may help is to *be open and honest about outcomes and inputs.* People tend to overestimate how much their superiors are paid and, therefore, tend to feel that their own pay is not as high as it should be.[17] However, if information about pay is shared, inequitable feelings may not materialize.

Expectancy Theory: Believing You Can Get What You Want

Beyond seeking fair treatment on the job, people also are motivated by the belief that they can expect to achieve certain desired rewards by working hard to attain them. If you've ever put in long hours studying in the hopes of receiving an A in one of your classes, then you know what we mean. Believing that there may be a carrot dangling at the end of the stick, and that it may be attained by putting forth the appropriate effort, can be a very effective motivator. This is one of the basic ideas behind the popularity of pay systems known as *merit pay plans*, or *pay-for-performance plans*, which formally establish links between job performance and rewards. However, a recent survey found that only 25 percent of employees see a clear link between good job performance and their pay raises. Clearly, companies are not doing all that they can to take advantage of this form of motivation. To better understand this process, let's take a look at a popular theory of motivation that addresses this issue—**expectancy theory**.

Three Components of Motivation

Expectancy theory claims that people will be motivated to exert effort on the job when they believe that doing so will help them achieve the things they want.[18] It assumes that people are rational beings who think about what they have to do to be rewarded and how much the reward means to them before they perform their jobs. Specifically, expectancy theory views motivation as the result of three different types of beliefs that people have. These are (1) **expectancy**—the belief that one's effort will affect performance, (2) **instrumentality**—the belief that one's performance will be rewarded, and (3) **valence**—the perceived value of the expected rewards. For a summary of these components and their role in the overall theory, see Figure 6.3.

Expectancy. Sometimes people believe that putting forth a great deal of effort will help them get a lot accomplished. However, in other cases, people do not expect that their efforts will have much effect on how well they do. For example, an employee operating a faulty piece of equipment may have a very low *expectancy* that his or her efforts will lead to high levels of performance. Someone working under such conditions probably would not continue to exert much effort. After all, there is no

4
learning
objective

Figure 6.3 Overview of Expectancy Theory

Expectancy theory claims that motivation is the combined result of the three types of beliefs identified here—*expectancy*, *instrumentality*, and *valence of reward*. It also recognizes that motivation is only one of several determinants of job performance.

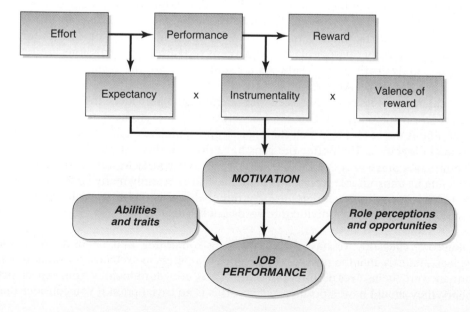

good reason to go on trying to fill a bucket riddled with holes. Accordingly, good managers will do things that help their subordinates believe that their hard work will lead them to do their jobs better. With this in mind, training employees to do their jobs better can be very effective in helping enhance expectancy beliefs (recall our discussion of training in Chapter 3). Indeed, a large part of working more effectively involves making sure that one's efforts will pay off.

Some companies have taken a more direct approach by soliciting and following their employees' suggestions about ways to improve their work efficiency. For example, United Electric Controls (a manufacturer of industrial temperature and pressure controls located in Watertown, Massachusetts) routinely asks its employees for ways to do their jobs more effectively. Since instituting this approach, not only have individual employees become more effective, but so too has the company. In fact, important indicators revealed that the company's performance improved dramatically after it began following its employees' suggestions (e.g., on-time deliveries rose from 65 percent to 95 percent).

> United Electric Controls routinely asks its employees for ways to do their jobs more effectively. Since instituting this approach, not only have individual employees become more effective, but so too has the company.

Instrumentality.   Even if an employee performs at a high level, his or her motivation may suffer if that performance is not appropriately rewarded—that is, if the performance is not perceived as *instrumental* in bringing about the rewards. So, for example, an extremely productive employee may be poorly motivated if he or she has already reached the top level of pay given by the company. Recognizing this possibility, several organizations have crafted pay systems that explicitly link desired performance to rewards.

Consider, for example, the pay plan instituted for IBM's 30,000 sales representatives. Previously, most of the pay these reps received was based on flat salary; their compensation was not linked to how well they did. Now, however, their pay is carefully tied to two factors that are essential to the company's success—profitability and customer satisfaction. So, instead of receiving commissions on the amount of the sale, as so many salespeople do, 60 percent of IBMers' commissions are tied to the company's profit on that sale. As a result, the more the company makes, the more the reps make. And, to make sure that the reps don't push only high-profit items that customers might not need, the remaining 40 percent of their commissions are based on customer satisfaction. Checking on this, customers are regularly surveyed about the extent to which their sales representatives helped them meet their business objectives. The better the reps have done in this regard, the greater their commissions. Since introducing this plan a few years ago, IBM has been effective in reversing its unprofitable trend. Although there are certainly many factors responsible for this turnaround, experts are confident that this practice of clearly linking desired performance to individual rewards is a key factor.

Valence.   Thus far, we have been assuming something that needs to be made explicit—namely, that the rewards the organization offers in exchange for desired performance are themselves desirable. In other words, using terminology from expectancy theory, they should have a positive *valence*. This is no trivial point if you consider that rewards are not equally desirable to everyone. For example, whereas a bonus of $200 may not be seen like much of a reward to a multimillionaire CEO, it may be quite valuable to a minimum-wage employee struggling to make ends meet. Valence is not just a matter of the amount of reward received but what that reward means to the person receiving it. (To help recognize those sources of reward that are currently most valuable to you personally, complete the **Self-Assessment Exercise** on pages 215–216.)

These days, with a highly diverse workforce, it would be erroneous to assume that employees are equally attracted to the same rewards. Some (e.g., single, young employees) might recognize the incentive value of a pay raise, whereas others (e.g., those taking care of families) might prefer additional vacation days, improved insurance benefits, and day care or elder care facilities. So, how can an organization find out what its employees want? Some companies have found a simple answer—asking them. For example, executives at PKF-Mark III (a construction company in Newton, Pennsylvania) have done just this. They put together a committee of employees representing a broad cross section of the company and allowed them to select exactly what fringe benefits they wanted most. This led to a package of fringe benefits that was highly desirable to the employees.

Many more companies have taken a completely individualized approach, introducing **cafeteria-style benefit plans**—incentive systems allowing employees to select their fringe benefits from a menu of available alternatives.[19] Given that fringe benefits represent almost 40 percent of payroll costs, more and more companies are recognizing the value of administering them flexibly. In fact, a recent survey found that such plans are in place in as many as half of all large companies (those employing over 5,000) and 22 percent of smaller companies (those with under 1,000 employees). For example, Primerica has had a flexible benefit plan in use since 1978—one that almost all of the employees believe is extremely beneficial to them. (Many of today's companies are doing highly creative things to ensure that their employees can achieve rewards that have value to them. For a summary of some of these practices, see the accompanying **Winning Practices** section.)

Emphasis on perception. It is important to emphasize that, like equity theory, expectancy theory focuses on people's perceptions of reality. It is *beliefs* about expectancy, instrumentality, and valence that matter as motivational forces. Of course, these beliefs are likely to be based at least in part on reality, but then again, people don't always perceive things accurately (a phenomenon we discussed in Chapter 3). For example, a worker might not have an accurate view of how his or her pay is really determined. In the absence of a clear system for communicating information about pay, as well as the absence of any motivation to misperceive that information, it's likely that some employees might have accurate perceptions of the extent to which their performance is linked to the pay they receive.

In keeping with the perceptual nature of expectancy theory, it makes sense that the things people believe about instrumentality, expectancy, and valence will be influenced by their moods (recall our discussion of mood in Chapter 2). A recent experiment demonstrated that this is, in fact, the case. In this study college students were asked to perform a task (solving anagrams) for as long as they wished after being put in a good mood (by being given a small gift) or a neutral mood (by not being given any gift).[21] Overall, the people who were put in a good mood showed

Winning Practices

Going "Beyond the Fringe" in Benefits: Especially Creative Reward Practices

Traditionally, someone who gets a new job receives not only a salary but also a standard set of fringe benefits, such as health insurance, life insurance, a paid vacation, and a retirement plan. These days, however, these basic benefits are not enough to bring job prospects through the door. The incentives that motivate today's employees are far more varied and, in many cases, truly lavish.[20]

Suppose, for example, you work at the Framingham, Massachusetts, corporate headquarters of the office supply chain, Staples, and that you have children who need to be cared for while you are at work. No problem. You simply drop them off at the company's brand-new, $1.4 million, 8,000-square-foot child care center near your office. Although there is a great need for on-site child care facilities, only 11 percent of today's companies, like Staples, offer them. This benefit makes it possible for Staples employees to concentrate on their work without having to worry about who's taking care of their children.

If you work at Staples, you also have available to you a wonderful concierge service, which runs all kinds of errands for busy employees (e.g., picking up dry cleaning, washing their cars), making their lives far easier. Staples isn't alone in offering concierge services. In fact, several com-panies have come into being in the past few years that offer concierge services to companies that seek them for their employees. For example, the San Francisco–based firm LesConcierges provides this service to employees of several well-known companies, including America Online and its sister company, CompuServe.

Some companies offer even more lavish benefits. For example, to attract employees to its out-of-the-way location in rural Wisconsin, Quad/Graphics, the printer, offers its employees rental apartments in its new $5 million complex. During its annual slow period, Rhino Foods (in Burlington, Vermont) helps its employees find jobs at other local businesses. Getting holidays off isn't so special; everyone gets them, right? Well, they might not be exactly the ones that you want to celebrate. This isn't a problem for employees of the Stamford, Connecticut, marketing firm Marquardt & Roche. This firm allows its employees to select any 11 out of 24 possible holidays.

Finally, some companies are even offering such benefits as pet insurance, auto financing, Internet access, home security systems, prepaid legal services, and even personal loans to their employees. Clearly, the days of finding so-called "standard" fringe benefits are over. What passes for standard today is anybody's guess.

greater motivation, as evidenced by their willingness to work for longer periods of time on the task (about 20 minutes, on average, for those put in a good mood, compared to about 16 minutes for those who were in a neutral mood). In a follow-up study, the researchers also measured participants' beliefs about the three components of expectancy theory: expectancy (the belief that a certain level of effort would result in a certain level of performance), instrumentality (the belief that they would be paid based on their performance), and valence (the attractiveness of the monetary prize they stood to win for performing at a certain level). As summarized in Figure 6.4, mood positively affected all three components of expectancy. Perceptions of expectancy, instrumentality, and valence all were higher among those who were in a good mood than those who were in a neutral mood. Clearly, these results highlight the motivational value of putting people in a good mood and suggest that this can be explained in terms of expectancy theory.

The Role of Motivation in Performance

Thus far, we have discussed the three components of motivation identified by expectancy theory. However, expectancy theory views motivation as just one of several determinants of job performance. As shown at the bottom of Figure 6.3, motivation combines with a person's skills and abilities, role perceptions, and opportunities to influence job performance.

It's no secret that the unique characteristics, special skills, and abilities of some people predispose them to perform their jobs better than others. For example, a tall, strong, well-coordinated person is likely to make a better professional basketball

Figure 6.4   The Effect of Mood on Expectancy, Instrumentality, and Valence

In a recently conducted experiment, the three components of expectancy theory—expectancy, instrumentality, and valence—were found to be higher among people who were in a positive mood than those who were in a neutral mood. This is in keeping with further evidence showing the higher motivation levels of those in positive moods.

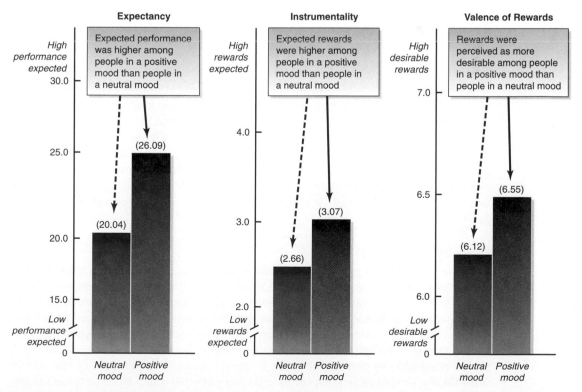

(Source: Based on data reported by Erez and Isen, 2002; see Note 21.)

player than a very short, weak, uncoordinated one—even if the shorter person is highly motivated to succeed. Recognizing this, it would be a mistake to assume automatically that someone performing below par is poorly motivated. Instead, some poor performers may be very highly motivated but lack the knowledge or skills needed to succeed. With this in mind, companies often make big investments in training employees to ensure that they have what it takes to succeed (see Chapter 3), regardless of their levels of motivation.

Expectancy theory also recognizes the role of *opportunities to perform* one's job. Even the best employees may perform at low levels if their opportunities are limited. This may occur, for example, if there is an economic downturn in a salesperson's territory or if the company's available inventory is insufficient to meet sales demand.

Finally, it is important to note that expectancy theory recognizes that job performance will be influenced by people's *role perceptions*—that is, what they believe is expected of them on the job. To the extent that there are uncertainties about what one's job duties may be, performance may suffer. For example, a shop foreman who believes his primary job duty is to teach new employees how to use the equipment may find that his performance is downgraded by a supervisor who believes he should be spending more time doing routine paperwork instead. In this case the foreman's performance wouldn't suffer due to any deficit in motivation but because of misunderstandings regarding what the job entails.

In conclusion, expectancy has done a good job of sensitizing managers to several key determinants of motivation, variables that frequently can be controlled. Beyond this, the theory clarifies the important—but not unique—role that motivation plays in determining job performance.

Goal Setting: Taking Aim at Performance Targets

Just as people are motivated to satisfy their needs on the job, to be paid fairly, and to act in ways consistent with their beliefs about reality, they also are motivated to strive for and to attain goals. The process of setting goals is one of the most important motivational forces operating on people in organizations.[22] The term **goal setting** refers to the process of setting goals in a manner that motivates workers to raise their performance. In this section, we will describe a prominent theory of *goal setting* and then identify some practical suggestions for setting goals effectively.

Goal-Setting Theory

Suppose that you are doing a task, such as word processing, when a performance goal is assigned. You are now expected, for example, to type 70 words per minute (wpm) instead of the 60 wpm you've been doing all along. Would you work hard to meet this goal, or would you simply give up? Some insight into the question of how people respond to assigned goals is provided by a conceptualization known as **goal setting theory**.[23] This theory claims that an assigned goal influences people's beliefs about being able to perform the task in question (i.e., the personality variable of **self-efficacy**, described in Chapter 3) and their personal goals. Both of these factors, in turn, influence performance.

Goal setting theory has been called "quite easily the single most dominant theory in the field [of organizational behavior]."[24] The basic idea behind goal setting theory is that a goal serves as a motivator because it causes people to compare their present capacity to perform with that required to succeed at the goal (for an overview of the theory, see Figure 6.5). To the extent that people believe they will fall short of a goal, they will feel dissatisfied and will work harder to attain it so long as they believe it is possible for them to do so. When they succeed at meeting a goal, they feel competent and successful.[25] Having a goal enhances performance in large part because the goal makes clear exactly what type and level of performance is expected.

The model also claims that assigned goals will lead to the acceptance of those goals as personal goals. In other words, they will be accepted as one's own. This is the idea of **goal commitment**—the extent to which people invest themselves in meeting a goal, their determination to reach a goal.[26] Indeed, it has been shown that people will become more committed to a goal to the extent that they desire to attain that goal and believe they have a reasonable chance of doing so.[27] Likewise, the more strongly people believe they are capable of meeting a goal, the more strongly they will accept it as their own. By contrast, workers who perceive themselves as being physically incapable of meeting performance goals, for example, are generally not committed to meeting them and do not strive to do so.[28]

Research also has shown that goal commitment combines with goal difficulty to influence task performance.[29] In other words, as shown in Figure 6.6, people perform at the highest levels when they are striving to meet difficult goals to which they are highly committed. By contrast, people will not work hard to achieve difficult

Figure 6.5 Goal Setting Theory: An Overview

According to *goal setting theory*, when people are challenged to meet higher goals, several things happen. First, they assess their desire to attain the goal as well as their chances of attaining the goal. Together, these judgments affect their *goal commitment*. Second, they assess the extent to which meeting the goal will enhance their beliefs in their own *self-efficacy*. When levels of goal commitment and self efficacy are high, people are motivated to perform at the goal level.

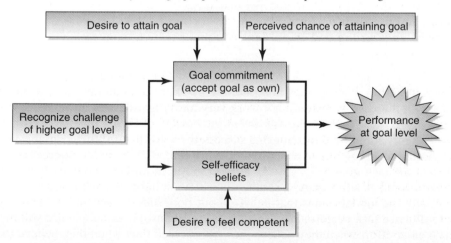

Figure 6.6　Effects of Goal Commitment and Goal Difficulty on Task Performance: A Summary

Research has shown that task performance is influenced by goal commitment and goal difficulty in the manner summarized here. That is, performance is highest when people are highly committed to attaining a difficult goal. However, people who are not committed to meeting a goal perform poorly on tasks at all levels of difficulty.

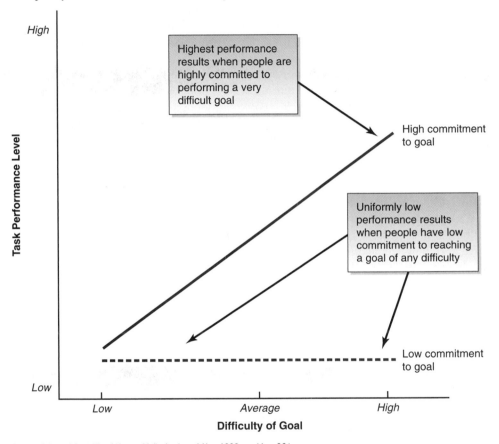

(Source: Adapted from Klein, Wesson, Hollenbeck, and Alge, 1999; see Note 29.)

goals when they are not highly committed to them. For example, suppose you don't care about getting good grades in school (i.e., you are not committed to achieving success). In this case, you would not work very hard regardless of how easy or difficult the course may be (see the flat line at the bottom of Figure 6.6). By contrast, if you are highly committed to achieving success, then a difficult (but acceptable) goal (e.g., getting a good grade in a very challenging course) will have more meaning to you than an easy goal (e.g., getting a good grade in an easy course) because it enhances your self-efficacy. As a result, you will work harder to achieve it.

Finally, the model claims that beliefs about both self-efficacy and goal commitment influence task performance. This makes sense insofar as people are willing to exert greater effort when they believe they will succeed than when they believe their efforts will be in vain.[30] Moreover, goals that are not personally accepted will have little capacity to guide behavior. In fact, research has shown that the more strongly people are committed to meeting goals, the better they will perform.[31] In general, Locke and Latham's model of goal setting has been supported by several studies, suggesting that is a valuable source of insight into how the goal setting process works.[32]

Guidelines for Setting Effective Performance Goals

Because researchers have been actively involved in studying the goal setting process for many years, it is possible to summarize their findings in the form of principles. These represent very practical suggestions that practicing managers can use to enhance motivation.

5
learning
objective

Assign specific goals.   In our word processing example, the supervisor set a goal that was very specific (70 wpm) and also somewhat difficult to attain (10 wpm faster than current performance). Would you perform better under these conditions than if the supervisor merely said something general, like "do your best to improve"? Decades of research on goal setting suggest that the answer is "yes."

Indeed, we know that people perform at higher levels when asked to meet specific high-performance goals than when they are directed simply to "do their best," or when no goal at all is assigned. People tend to find specific goals quite challenging and are motivated to try to meet them—not only to fulfill management's expectations, but also to convince themselves that they have performed well. Scientists have explained that attaining goals enhances employees' beliefs in their *self-efficacy*, which we noted in Chapter 3 refers to people's assessments of themselves as being competent and successful. And, when people believe that they can, in fact, succeed at a task, they will be motivated to work hard at it. For this reason people will be motivated to pursue specific goals, ones that readily enable them to define their accomplishments, enhancing their self-efficacy beliefs.

To demonstrate this principle, let's consider a classic study conducted at an Oklahoma lumber camp owned by Weyerhauser, a major producer of paper products.[33] The initial step in the paper-making process involves cutting down the trees and hauling them to the sawmill, where they are ground into pulp. For some time, the company was plagued by a problem: The loggers were only loading the trucks to about 60 percent of their maximum capacity. This resulted in wasted trips, adding considerably cost. To help solve this problem a goal setting program was introduced. A specific goal was set: The loggers were challenged to load the trucks to 94 percent of their capacity before returning to the mill.

How effective was this goal in raising performance? The results, summarized in Figure 6.7, show that the goal was extremely effective. In fact, not only was the specific goal effective in raising performance to the goal level in just a few weeks, but the effects were long-lasting as well. In fact, the loggers were found to sustain this level of performance as long as seven years later! The resulting savings logged in by the company have been considerable, a classic goal setting success story.

Importantly, these dramatic effects are not unusual, nor are they limited to this special setting. Rather, this study is just one of many that highlight the effectiveness of setting specific, challenging performance goals in a variety of organizational contexts. For example, specific goals have also been used to help improve many other kinds of

Figure 6.7   Goal Setting at a Logging Camp: An Impressive Demonstration

The performance of loggers loading timber onto trucks markedly improved after a specific, difficult goal was set. The percentage of the maximum possible weight loaded onto the trucks rose from approximately 60 percent before any goal was set to approximately 94 percent—the goal level—after the goal was set. Performance remained at this level as long as seven years.

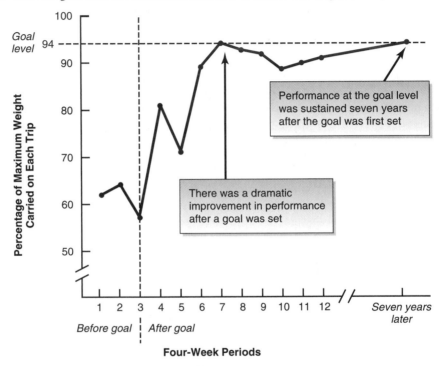

(*Source: Adapted from Latham and Baldes, 1975; see Note 33.*)

organizational behaviors, such as reducing absenteeism and lowering the occurrence of industrial accidents.

Assign difficult but acceptable performance goals.   The goal set at the logging camp was successful not only because it was specific, but also because it pushed crew members to a higher standard. Obviously, a goal that is too easy to attain will *not* bring about the desired increments in performance. For example, it you already type at 60 wpm, a goal of 50 wpm, although specific, would probably *lower* your performance. The key point is that a goal must be difficult as well as specific for it to raise performance.

At the same time, however, people will work hard to reach challenging goals so long as these are within the limits of their capability. When goals become too difficult, performance suffers because people reject those goals as unrealistic and unattainable. As an illustration, let's pick up our earlier example about working to achieve success in school. The point is that you may work much harder as a student in a class that challenges your ability than in one that is very easy. In all likelihood, however, you would probably give up trying if the goal was far too difficult (such as if the only way of passing was to get perfect scores on all exams—a standard you would reject as being unacceptable). In short, specific goals are most effective if they are set neither so low as to make success obvious nor so high that success is unattainable.

As you might imagine, this phenomenon occurs in organizations. For example, Bell Canada's telephone operators are required to handle calls within 23 seconds, and FedEx's customer service agents are expected to answer customers' questions within 140 seconds. Although both goals were initially considered difficult when they were imposed, the employees of both companies eventually met—or exceeded—these goals and enjoyed the satisfaction of knowing they succeeded at this task. At a General Electric manufacturing plant, specific goals were set for productivity and cost reduction. Those goals that were perceived as challenging but possible led to improved performance, whereas those thought to be unattainable led to decreased performance.

> At a General Electric manufacturing plant, specific goals were set for productivity and cost reduction. Those goals that were perceived as challenging but possible led to improved performance, whereas those thought to be unattainable led to decreased performance.

How should goals be set in a manner that strengthens employees' commitment to them? One obvious way of enhancing goal acceptance is to involve employees in the goal setting process. Research on workers' participation in goal setting has demonstrated that people better accept goals that they have been involved in setting than goals that have been assigned by their supervisors—and they work harder as a result.[34] Most of today's executives generally agree that it is a good idea to let employees figure out the best way to meet new goals. According to Bob Freese, CEO of Alphatronix Inc., in Research Triangle Park, North Carolina, "We let employees tell us when they can accomplish a project and what resources they need. Virtually always they set higher goals than we would ever set for them."[35]

Participation in the goal-setting process may have these beneficial effects for several reasons. First, people are more likely to better understand and appreciate goals they had a hand in setting themselves than those that are merely presented to them. Second, employees are likely to be committed to attaining goals they have set themselves because they must psychologically rationalize their decisions to set those goals.[36] (After all, one can hardly justify setting a specific goal and then not working to attain it.) Third, because workers often have more direct knowledge about what it takes to do a job than their supervisors, they are in a good position to come up with goals that are acceptably high but not unreasonable. For these various reasons, allowing people to participate in the setting of their own performance goals makes good sense.

Provide feedback concerning goal attainment.   The final condition for setting effective goals appears to be glaringly obvious, although it is not followed in practice as often as you might expect: Provide feedback about the extent to which goals have been met. Just as golfers can improve their games when they learn where their balls have landed, so too do workers benefit by feedback about how closely they are approaching their performance goals. Extending our golf analogy, when it comes to setting work goals effectively, "hooks" and "slices" need to be corrected.

A study of the performance of work crews in the U.S. Air Force illustrates the importance of using feedback in conjunction with goal setting.[37] A standardized index of job performance was used to measure five different groups repeatedly over a two-year period. During the first nine months, a baseline measure of effectiveness was taken that was used to compare the relative impact of feedback and goal setting. The groups then received feedback for five months (reports detailing how well they performed on various performance measures). Following this, the goal-setting phase of the study was begun. During this period, the crew members set goals for themselves with respect to their performance on various measures. Then, for the final five months, in addition to the feedback and goal setting, an incentive (time off from work) was made available to crew members who met their goals.

It was found that feedback and goal setting dramatically increased group effectiveness. Group feedback improved performance approximately 50 percent over the baseline level. The addition of group goal setting improved it 75 percent over baseline. These findings show that the combination of goal setting and feedback helps raise the effectiveness of group performance. Groups that know how well they're doing and have a target goal to shoot for tend to perform very well. Providing incentives, however, improved performance only negligibly. The real incentive seems to be meeting the challenge of performing up to the level of the goal.

In sum, goal setting is a very effective tool managers can use to motivate people. Setting a specific, acceptably difficult goal and providing feedback about progress toward that goal greatly enhance job performance. To demonstrate the effectiveness of goal setting in your own behavior, complete the **Group Exercise** on pages 216–217.

Designing Jobs That Motivate

6
learning
objective

As you may recall from Chapter 1, Frederick W. Taylor's approach to stimulating work performance was to design jobs so that people worked as efficiently as possible. No wasted movements and no wasted time added up to efficient performance, or so Taylor believed. However, Taylor failed to consider one important thing: The repetitive machine-like movements required of his workers were highly routine and monotonous. And, not surprisingly, people became bored with such jobs and frequently quit. Fortunately, today's organizational scientists have found several ways of designing jobs that may not only be performed very efficiently but are also highly pleasant and enjoyable. This is the basic principle behind **job design**, the process of creating jobs that people desire to perform because they are so inherently appealing.[38]

Job Enlargement: Doing More of the Same Kind of Work

If you've ever purchased a greeting card, chances are good that you've picked up at least one made by American Greetings, one of the largest greeting card companies in the United States. What you might not know is that that this Cleveland, Ohio–based organization recently redesigned some 400 jobs in its creative division. Now, rather than always working exclusively on, say, Christmas cards, employees will be able to move back and forth between different teams, such as those working on birthday ribbons, humorous mugs, and Valentine's Day gift bags. Similarly, employees at the Blue Ridge, Georgia, plant of Levi Strauss & Co. used to perform the same task all day on the assembly line, but now they have been trained to handle three different jobs. Employees at American

Greetings and Levi Strauss reportedly enjoy the variety, as do those at RJR Nabisco, Corning, and Eastman Kodak, other companies that have recently allowed employees to make such lateral moves.

Scientists have referred to what these companies are doing as **job enlargement**—the practice of giving employees more tasks to perform at the same level. There's no higher responsibility involved or any greater skills, just a wider variety of the same types of tasks. Enlarged jobs are said to be changed *horizontally* because people's level of responsibility stays the same. The idea behind job enlargement is simple: You can decrease boredom by giving people a greater variety of jobs to do.

> Employees at the Blue Ridge, Georgia, plant of Levi Strauss & Co. used to perform the same task all day on the assembly line, but now they have been trained to handle three different jobs.

Do job enlargement programs work? To answer this question, consider the results of a study comparing the job performance of people doing enlarged and unenlarged jobs.[39] In the unenlarged jobs different employees performed separate paperwork tasks such as preparing, sorting, coding, and keypunching various forms. The enlarged jobs combined these various functions into larger jobs performed by the same people. Although it was more difficult and expensive to train people to perform the enlarged jobs than the separate jobs, important benefits resulted. In particular, employees expressed greater job satisfaction and less boredom. And, because one person followed the whole job all the way through, greater opportunities to correct errors existed. Not surprisingly, customers were satisfied with the result.

In a follow-up investigation of the same company conducted two years later, however, it was found that not all the beneficial effects continued.[40] Notably, employee satisfaction leveled off, and the rate of errors went up, suggesting that as employees got used to their enlarged jobs they found them less interesting and stopped paying attention to all the details. Hence, although job enlargement may help improve job performance, its effects may be short-lived. It appears that the problem with enlarging jobs is that after a while people get bored with them, and they need to be enlarged still further. Because it is impractical to continue enlarging jobs all the time, the value of this approach is rather limited.

Job Enrichment: Increasing Required Skills and Responsibilities

As an alternative, consider another approach taken to redesign jobs. For many years, Procter & Gamble manufactured detergent by having large numbers of people perform a series of narrow tasks. Then, in the early 1960s, realizing that this rigid approach did little to utilize the full range of skills and abilities of employees, P&G executive David Swanson introduced a new way to make detergent in the company's Augusta, Georgia, plant. The technicians worked together in teams (see Chapter 9) to take control over large parts of the production process. They set production schedules, hired new coworkers, and took responsibility over evaluating each others' performance, including the process of deciding who was going to get raises. In short, they not only performed more tasks but also ones at higher levels of skill and responsibility. The general name given to this approach is **job enrichment**. Enriched jobs are said to be changed *vertically* because people's level of responsibility goes up. For a summary comparison between job enrichment and job enlargement, see Figure 6.8.

Figure 6.8 Job Enlargement and Job Enrichment: A Comparison

Redesigning jobs by increasing the number of tasks performed at the same level (*horizontal job loading*) is referred to as *job enlargement*. Redesigning jobs by increasing the employees' level of responsibility and control (*vertical job loading*) is referred to as *job enrichment*.

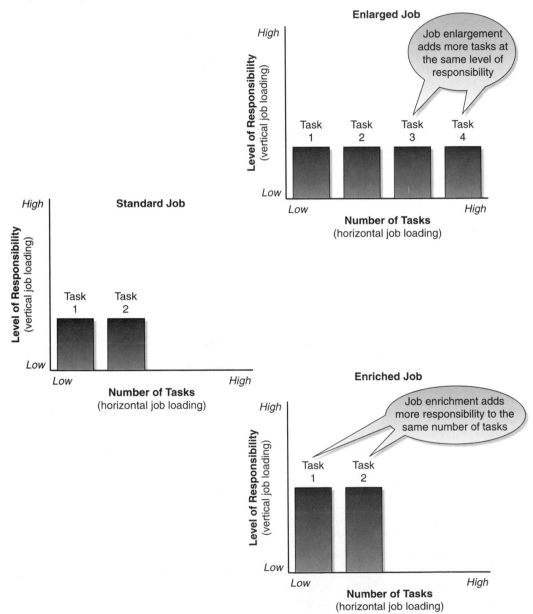

One of the best-known job enrichment programs was the one developed by Volvo, the Swedish auto manufacturer. In response to serious dissension among its workforce in the late 1960s, the company's president at the time, Pehr Gyllenhammar, introduced job enrichment in its Kalmar assembly plant. Cars were assembled by 25 groups of approximately 20 workers who are each responsible for one part of the car's assembly (e.g., engine, electrical system). In contrast to the usual assembly-line method of manufacturing cars used in Detroit, Volvo's work groups are set up so they can freely plan, organize, and inspect their own work. In time, workers became more satisfied with their jobs and the plant experienced a significant reduction in turnover and absenteeism.

Although job enrichment programs also have been successful at other organizations, several factors limit their popularity. First, there is the difficulty of implementation. Redesigning existing facilities so that jobs can be enriched is often prohibitively expensive. Besides, the technology needed to perform certain jobs makes it impractical for them to be redesigned. Another impediment is the lack of universal employee acceptance. Although many relish it, some people do *not* desire the additional responsibility associated with performing enriched jobs. In fact, when a group of American auto workers was sent to Sweden to work in a Saab engine assembly plant where jobs were highly enriched, five out of six indicated that they preferred their traditional assembly-line jobs. As one union leader put it, "If you want to enrich the job, enrich the paycheck."[41] Clearly, enriched jobs are not for everyone.

The Job Characteristics Model

Thus far, we have failed to specify precisely *how* to enrich a job. What elements of a job need to be enriched for it to be effective? An attempt to expand the idea of job enrichment, known as the **job characteristics model**, provides an answer to this important question.[42]

Basic elements of the job characteristics model.   This approach assumes that jobs can be designed to help people get enjoyment out of their jobs and care about the work they do. The model identifies how jobs can be designed to help people feel that they are doing meaningful and valuable work. In particular, it specifies that enriching certain elements of jobs alters people's psychological states in a manner that enhances their work effectiveness. Specifically, the model identifies five *core job dimensions* that help create three *critical psychological states*, leading, in turn, to several beneficial *personal and work outcomes* (see Figure 6.9).

The five critical job dimensions are *skill variety, task identity, task significance, autonomy*, and *feedback*. Let's take a closer look at these.

- *Skill variety* is the extent to which a job requires using several different skills and talents that an employee has. For example, a restaurant manager with high skill variety will perform many different tasks (e.g., maintaining sales records, handling customer complaints, scheduling staff, supervising repair work, and the like).
- *Task identity* is the degree to which a job requires doing a whole task from beginning to end. For example, tailors will have high task identity if they do everything associated with making an entire suit (e.g., measuring the client, selecting the fabric, cutting and sewing it, and altering it to fit).

Figure 6.9　The Job Characteristics Model: Basic Components

The *job characteristics model* stipulates that certain *core job dimensions* lead to certain *critical psychological states*, which in turn lead to several beneficial *personal and work outcomes*. The model also recognizes that these relationships are strongest among individuals with high levels of *growth need strength*.

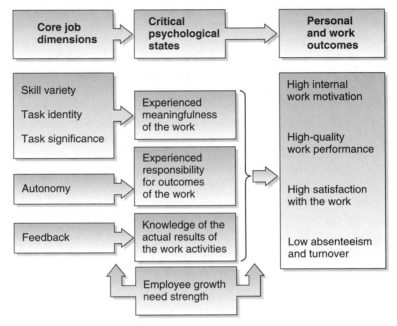

■ *Task significance* is the amount of impact a job is believed to have on others. For example, medical researchers working on a cure for a deadly disease surely recognize the importance of their work to the world at large. Even more modest contributions to the company can be recognized as being significant to the extent that employees understand the role of their jobs in the overall mission of the organization.

■ *Autonomy* is the extent to which employees have the freedom and discretion to plan, schedule, and carry out their jobs as desired. For example, in 1991 a team of Procter & Gamble employees was put in charge of making all the arrangements necessary for the building of a new $5 million facility for making concentrated Downy.

■ *Feedback* is the extent to which the job allows people to have information about the effectiveness of their performance. For example, telemarketing representatives regularly receive information about how many calls they make per day and the monetary values of the sales made.

The job characteristics model specifies that these job dimensions have important effects on various critical psychological states. Specifically, skill variety, task identity, and task significance jointly contribute to a task's *experienced meaningfulness*. A task is considered to be meaningful insofar as it is experienced as being highly important, valuable, and worthwhile. Jobs that provide a great deal of autonomy are said to make people feel *personally responsible and accountable for their work.* When they are free to decide what to do and how to do it, they feel more responsible for the results, whether good or bad. Finally, effective feedback is said to give employees *knowledge of the results of their work.* When a job is designed to provide people with information about the effects of their actions, they are better able to develop an understanding of how effectively they have performed and such knowledge improves their effectiveness.

The job characteristics model specifies that the three critical psychological states affect various personal and work outcomes—namely, people's feelings of motivation, the quality of work performed, satisfaction with work, absenteeism, and turnover. The higher the experienced meaningfulness of work, responsibility for the work performed, and knowledge of results, the more positive the personal and work benefits will be. When they perform jobs that incorporate high levels of the five core job dimensions, people should feel highly motivated, perform high-quality work, be highly satisfied with their jobs, be absent infrequently, and unlikely to resign from their jobs.

We should also note that the model is theorized to be especially effective in describing the behavior of individuals who are high in *growth need strength*—that is, people who have a high need for personal growth and development. People not particularly interested in improving themselves on the job are not expected to experience the theorized psychological reactions to the core job dimensions, nor consequently, to enjoy the beneficial personal and work outcomes predicted by the model. By introducing this variable, the job characteristics model recognizes the important limitation of job enrichment noted earlier—not everyone wants and benefits from enriched jobs.

Assessing the motivating potential of jobs. Based on the proposed relationship between the core job dimensions and their associated psychological reactions, the model claims that job motivation will be highest when the jobs performed rate high on the various dimensions. To assess this, a questionnaire known as the Job Diagnostic Survey (JDS) has been developed to measure the degree to which various job characteristics are present in a particular job. Based on responses to the JDS, we can make predictions about the degree to which a job motivates people who perform it.

The job characteristics model has been the focus of many empirical tests, most of which are supportive of many aspects of the model. One study conducted among a group of South African clerical workers found particularly strong support.[43] The jobs of employees in some of the offices in this company were enriched in accordance with techniques specified by the job characteristics model. Specifically, employees performing the enriched jobs were given opportunities to choose the kinds of tasks they perform (high skill variety), do the entire job (high task identity), receive instructions regarding how their job fit into the organization as a whole (high task significance), freely set their own schedules and inspect their own work (high autonomy), and keep records of their daily productivity (high feedback). Another group of employees, equivalent in all respects except that their jobs were not enriched, served as a control group.

After employees performed the newly designed jobs for six months, comparisons were made between them and their counterparts in the control group. With respect to most of the outcomes specified by the model, individuals performing redesigned jobs showed superior results. Specifically, they reported feeling more internally motivated and more satisfied with their jobs. There were also lower rates of absenteeism and turnover among employees performing the enriched jobs. The only outcome predicted by the model that was not found to differ was actual work performance; people performed equally well in enriched and unenriched jobs. Considering the many factors that are responsible for job performance (as discussed in connection with expectancy theory), this finding should not be too surprising.

Suggestions for enhancing the motivating potential of jobs.   The job characteristics model specifies several ways in which jobs can be designed to enhance their motivating potential. For example, instead of using several workers, each of whom performs a separate part of a whole job, it would be better to have each person perform the entire job. Doing so helps provide greater skill variety and task identity. For example, Corning Glass Works in Medford, Massachusetts, redesigned jobs so that people who assembled laboratory hot plates put together entire units instead of contributing a single part to the assembly process.

The job characteristics model also suggests that jobs should be set up so that the person performing a service (such as an auto mechanic) comes into contact with the recipient of the service (such as the car owner). Jobs designed in this manner will not only help the employee by providing feedback but also by enhancing skill variety (e.g., talking to customers in addition to fixing cars) and building autonomy (by giving people the freedom to manage their own relationships with clients). This suggestion has been implemented at Sea-Land Service, the large containerized ocean-shipping company. After this company's mechanics, clerks, and crane operators started meeting with customers, they became much more productive. Having faces to associate with the once abstract jobs they did clearly helped them take the jobs more seriously.

> At Sea-Land Service after mechanics, clerks, and crane operators started meeting with customers, they became much more productive. Having faces to associate with the once abstract jobs they did clearly helped them take the jobs more seriously.

Another implication of the job characteristics model is that jobs should be designed to give employees as much feedback as possible. The more people know how well they're doing (be it from customers, supervisors, or coworkers), the better equipped they are to take appropriate corrective action (recall our discussion in Chapter 3 about the importance of feedback). As a case in point, Childress Buick Co., a Phoenix, Arizona, auto dealership, once suffered serious customer dissatisfaction and employee retention problems before owner, Rusty Childress, began encouraging his employees to rely on feedback from customers and fellow employees to discover ways of doing their jobs better.

You Be the Consultant

Boosting Low Morale Among Employees

Suppose that you were just hired by executives of a large manufacturing company to help resolve problems of poor morale that have been plaguing the workforce. Turnover and absenteeism are high, and performance is at an all-time low. Answer the following questions relevant to this situation based on the material in this chapter.

1. Suppose, after interviewing the workers, you found that they believed that no one cared how well they were doing. What theories could help explain this problem? Applying these approaches, what would you recommend the company do to resolve this situation?

2. Company officials tell you that the employees are well paid, adding to their surprise about the low morale. However, your interviews reveal that the employees themselves feel otherwise. Theoretically, why is this a problem? What could be done to help?

3. "I'm bored with my job," an employee tells you, and you believe he speaks for many within the company. What could be done to make the jobs more interesting to those who perform them? What are the limitations of your plan? Would it work equally well for all employees?

Self-Assessment Exercise

What Rewards Do You Value?

According to expectancy theory, one thing companies can do to motivate employees is to give rewards that have positive valence to them. What work-related rewards have the greatest value to you? Completing this questionnaire will help you answer this question.

Directions

Following are 10 work-related rewards. For each, circle the number that best describes the value that particular reward has for you personally. Use the following scale to express your feelings: 1 = no value at all, 2 = slight value, 3 = moderate value, 4 = great value, 5 = extremely great value.

Reward	*Personal value*				
Good pay	1	2	3	4	5
Prestigious title	1	2	3	4	5
Vacation time	1	2	3	4	5
Job security	1	2	3	4	5
Recognition	1	2	3	4	5
Interesting work	1	2	3	4	5

Pleasant conditions	1	2	3	4	5
Chances to advance	1	2	3	4	5
Flexible schedule	1	2	3	4	5
Friendly coworkers	1	2	3	4	5

Discussion Questions

1. Based on your answers, which rewards do you value most? Which do you value least? Do you think these preferences will change as you get older and perform different jobs? If so, how?

2. To what extent do you believe that you will be able to attain each of these rewards on your job? Do you expect that the chances of receiving these rewards will improve in the future? Why or why not?

3. Do you believe that the rewards you value most are also the ones valued by other people? Are these reward preferences likely to be the same for all people everywhere or at least for all workers performing the same job in the same company?

Group Exercise
Demonstrating the Effectiveness of Goal Setting

The tendency for specific, difficult goals to enhance task performance is well established. The following exercise is designed to help you demonstrate this effect yourself. All you need is a class of students willing to participate and a few simple supplies.

Directions

1. Select a page of text from a book and make several photocopies. Then carefully count the words and number each word on one of the copies. This will be your score sheet.

2. Find another class of 30 or more students who don't know anything about goal setting. (We don't want their knowledge of the phenomenon to bias the results.) On a random basis, divide the students into three equal-size groups.

3. Ask the students in the first group ("baseline" group) to copy as much of the text as they can onto another piece of paper, giving them exactly one minute to do so. Direct them to work at a fast pace. Using the score sheet created in step 1, identify the highest number of words counted by any one of the students. Then multiply this number by 2. This will be the specific, difficult goal level.

4. Ask the students in another group ("specific goal" group) to copy the text on the same printed page for exactly one minute. Tell them to try to reach the specific goal number identified in step 3.

5. Repeat this process with the third group ("do your best" group) but instead of giving them a specific goal, direct them to "try to do your best at this task."

6. Compute the average number of words copied in the "difficult goal" group and the "do your best" group. Have your instructor compute the appropriate statistical test (a *t*-test, in this case) to determine the statistical significance of the difference between the performance levels of the groups.

Discussion Questions

1. Was there, in fact, a statistically significant difference between the performance levels of the two groups? If so, did students in the "specific goal" group outperform those in the "do your best" group, as expected? What does this reveal about the effectiveness of goal setting?

2. If the predicted findings were not supported, why do you suppose this happened? What was it about the procedure that may have led to this failure? Was the specific goal (twice the fastest speed in the "baseline" group) too high, making the goal unreachable? Or was it too low, making the specific goal too easy?

3. What do you think would happen if the goal was lowered, making it easier, or raised, making it more difficult?

Notes

Case Note

Amnesty International (2003). Facts and figures: The work of Amnesty International. From the World Wide Web at web.amnesty.org/pages/aboutai_facts. Voluntary Matters 3. (2003). *Amnesty International UK*. From the World Wide Web at www.voluntarymatters3.org/motivation/case_studies /case_study2.html.

Chapter Notes

[1] Porter, L. W., Bigley, G. A., & Steers, R. M. (2003). *Motivation and work behavior* (7th ed.). Burr Ridge, IL: McGraw-Hill/Irwin.

[2] Pfeffer, J. (1998). *The human equation*. Boston: Harvard Business School Press.

[3] Maslow, A. H. (1987). *Motivation and personality* (3rd ed.). Boston: Addison-Wesley.

[4] Where's my Stairmaster? (1999, October). *Across the Board*, p. 5.

[5] Against the grain. (1999, May). *Across the Board*, p. 1.

[6] Klubnik, J. P. (1995). *Rewarding and recognizing employees*. Chicago: Richard D. Irwin. Leverence, J. (1997). *And the winner is . . .* Santa Monica, CA: Merritt Publishing.

[7] Shepherd, M. D. (1993, February). Staff motivation. *U.S. Pharmacist*, pp. 82, 85, 89–93 (quote, p. 91).

[8] Langley, M. (2003, June 9). Big companies get low marks for lavish executive pay. *Wall Street Journal*, p. C1.

[9] Friedman, T. L. (1999). *The Lexus and the olive tree*. New York: Anchor Books.

[10] Colquitt, J. A., & Greenberg, J. (2003). Organizational justice: A fair assessment of the state of the literature. In J. Greenberg (Ed.), *Organizational behavior: The state of the*

science (2nd ed.) (pp. 165–210). Mahwah, NJ: Lawrence Erlbaum Associates. Adams, J. S. (1965). Inequity in social exchange. In L. Berkowitz (Ed.), *Advances in experimental social psychology* (Vol. 2, pp. 267–299). New York: Academic Press.

[11] Harder, J. W. (1992). Play for pay: Effects of inequity in a pay-for-performance context. *Administrative Science Quarterly, 37,* 321–335.

[12] Greenberg, J. (1993). Stealing in the name of justice: Informational and interpersonal moderators of theft reactions to underpayment inequity. *Organizational Behavior and Human Decision Processes, 54,* 81–103.

[13] Mowday, R. T., & Colwell, K. A. (2003). Employee reactions to unfair outcomes in the workplace: The contributions of Adams's equity theory to understanding work motivation. In L. W. Porter, G. A. Bigley, & R. M. Steers (Eds.), *Motivation and work behavior,* 7th ed. (pp. 65–82). Burr Ridge, IL: McGraw-Hill/Irwin.

[14] Martin, J. E., & Peterson, M. M. (1987). Two-tier wage structures: Implications for equity theory. *Academy of Management Journal, 30,* 297–316.

[15] Ross, I. (1985, April 29). Employers win big on the move to two-tier contracts. *Fortune,* pp. 82–92.

[16] Baron, J., & Kreps, D. M. (1999). *Strategic human resource management.* New York: John Wiley & Sons.

[17] Lawler, E. E., III. (1967). Secrecy about management compensation: Are there hidden costs? *Organizational Behavior and Human Performance, 2,* 182–189.

[18] Porter, L. W., & Lawler, E. E., III. (1968). *Managerial attitudes and performance.* Homewood, IL: Irwin.

[19] Schrage, M. (2000, April 3). Cafeteria benefits? Ha, you deserve a richer banquet. *Fortune,* p. 276.

[20] Boreman, A. M. (1999, October 19). Clean my house, and I'm yours forever. *Inc.,* p. 216. Emerging optional benefits. (1998, December), p. 8. Hickins, M. (1999, April). Creative "get-a-life" benefits. *Management Review,* p. 7. Nelson, B. (1994). *1001 ways to reward employees.* New York: Waterman. Palmer, A. T. (1999, April 26). Who's minding the baby? The company. *Business Week,* p. 32.

[21] Erez, A., & Isen, A. M. (2002). The influence of positive affect on the components of expectancy motivation. *Journal of Applied Psychology, 87,* 1055–1067.

[22] Wood, R. A., & Locke, E. A. (1990). Goal setting and strategy effects on complex tasks. In B. M. Staw & L. L. Cummings (Eds.), *Research in organizational behavior* (Vol. 12, pp. 73–110). Greenwich, CT: JAI Press.

[23] Locke, E. A., & Latham, G. P. (1990). *A theory of goal setting and task performance.* Upper Saddle River, NJ: Prentice Hall.

[24] Mitchell, T. R., & Daniels, D. (2003). Observations and commentary on resent research in work motivation. In L. W. Porter, G. A. Bigley, & R. M. Steers (Eds.), *Motivation and work behavior* (7th ed). (pp. 26–44). Burr Ridge, IL: McGraw-Hill/Irwin (quote, p. 29).

[25] Mento, A. J., Locke, E. A., & Klein, H. J. (1992). Relationship of goal level to valence and instrumentality. *Journal of Applied Psychology, 77,* 395–406.

[26] Wright, P. M., O'Leary-Kelly, A. M., Cortinak, J. M., Klein, H. J., & Hollenbeck, J. R. (1994). On the meaning and measurement of goal commitment. *Journal of Applied Psychology, 79,* 795–803.

[27] Klein, H. J. (1991). Further evidence on the relationship between goal setting and expectancy theories. *Organizational Behavior and Human Decision Processes, 49,* 230–257.

[28] Harrison, D. A., & Liska, L. Z. (1994). Promoting regular exercise in organizational fitness programs: Health-related differences in motivational building blocks. *Personnel Psychology, 47,* 47–71.

[29] Klein, J. J., Wesson, M. J., Hollenbeck, J., R., & Alge, B. J. (1999). Goal commitment and the goal-setting process: Conceptual clarification and empirical synthesis. *Journal of Applied Psychology, 84,* 885–896.

[30] Gellatly, I. R., & Meyer, J. P. (1992). The effects of goal difficulty on physiological arousal, cognition, and task performance. *Journal of Applied Psychology, 77,* 696–704.

[31] Wright, P. M. (1992). An examination of the relationships among monetary incentives, goal level, goal commitment, and performance. *Journal of Management, 18,* 677–693.

[32] Earley, P. C., & Litucy, T. R. (1991). Delineating goal and efficacy effects: A test of three models. *Journal of Applied Psychology, 76,* 81–98.

[33] Latham, G., & Baldes, J. (1975). The practical significance of Locke's theory of goal setting. *Journal of Applied Psychology, 60,* 122–126.

[34] Latham, G. P., Erez, M., & Locke, E. A. (1988). Resolving scientific disputes by the joint design of crucial experiments by the antagonists: Application to the Erez-Latham dispute regarding participation in goal setting. *Journal of Applied Psychology, 73,* 756–772.

[35] Finegan, J. (1993, July). People power. *Inc.*, pp. 62–63 (quote, p. 63).

[36] Donovan, J. J., & Williams, K. J. (2003). Missing the mark: Effects of time and causal attributions on goal revision in response to goal-performance discrepancies. *Journal of Applied Psychology, 88,* 379–390.

[37] Pritchard, R. D., Jones, S. D., Roth, P. L., Stuebing, K. K., & Ekberg, S. E. (1988). Effects of group feedback, goal setting, and incentives on organizational productivity. *Journal of Applied Psychology, 73,* 337–358.

[38] Morgenson, F. P., & Campion, M. A. (2003). Work design. In W. C. Borman, D. R. Ilgen, & R. J. Klimoski (Eds.), *Handbook of psychology, Vol. 12: Industrial and organizational psychology* (pp. 423–452). New York: John Wiley & Sons.

[39] Campion, M. A., & McClelland, C. L. (1991). Interdisciplinary examination of the costs and benefits of enlarged jobs: A job design quasi-experiment. *Journal of Applied Psychology, 76,* 186–198.

[40] Campion, M. A., & McClelland, C. L. (1993). Follow-up and extension of the interdisciplinary costs and benefits of enlarged jobs. *Journal of Applied Psychology, 78,* 339–351.

[41] Winpisinger, W. (1973, February). Job satisfaction: A union response. *AFL-CIO American Federationist*, pp. 8–10 (quote, p. 9).

[42] Hackman, J. R., & Oldham, G. R. (1980). *Work redesign.* Reading, MA: Addison-Wesley.

[43] Orpen, C. (1979). The effects of job enrichment on employee satisfaction, motivation, involvement, and performance: A field experiment. *Human Relations, 32,* 189–217.

Chapter **Seven**

LEARNING OBJECTIVES

After reading this chapter, you will be able to:

1. **DESCRIBE** two types of psychological contracts in work relationships and the types of trust associated with each.

2. **DESCRIBE** organizational citizenship behavior and ways in which it may be promoted.

3. **IDENTIFY** ways in which cooperation can be promoted in the workplace.

4. **DESCRIBE** competition and what makes it inevitable in organizations.

5. **DESCRIBE** the causes and effects of conflict in organizations.

6. **IDENTIFY** three forms of deviant organizational behavior and how to minimize their occurrence.

Interpersonal Behavior in the Workplace

Making the Case for...
Interpersonal Relationships at Work

Sendo's Smart Phone Battle with Microsoft

Although Birmingham, England, is better known for its steel mills than its advanced technology, this didn't deter Hugh Brogan from having high-tech dreams, and big ones at that. As CEO and cofounder of Sendo, England's only mobile phone manufacturer, Brogan envisioned making Web-enabled cellular "smart phones" that could be customized before sale to fit the needs of consumers, much like PCs. To bring his dream to realization, Brogan signed a deal with software giant Microsoft to codevelop the "Z100 Smartphone," relying on a streamlined version of the Windows operating system, code-named "Stinger."

In the months that followed, Brogan's dream rapidly turned into a nightmare. Although early prototypes of the Z100 were well received by industry analysts, a commercial version of the phone kept on getting postponed because the Stinger software wasn't ready. Because it's such a small company, these delays pushed

Sendo to the verge of bankruptcy, forcing Brogan to borrow $14 million from Microsoft just to stay afloat. A provision of the loan required Sendo to have a working version of the phone available by April 2002 to avoid default, but Sendo missed the deadline. The problem, Brogan claimed, was that Microsoft failed to meet its obligation to deliver the needed software. Microsoft agreed to not call in the loan but demanded an intense technical audit of Sendo's work on the Z100.

Only a few months later in October 2002, Orange, a Sendo competitor and Europe's second-largest mobile carrier, released its own version of a Microsoft-powered smart phone. Suspecting foul play, Sendo severed ties with Microsoft, canceled the Z100, and entered into a relationship with Nokia to use its software instead. On November 7, 2002, Brogan dropped this bomb on his 325 employees, noting that "we have to do this to save the company." His explanation was straightforward: "Microsoft double-crossed Sendo." Six weeks later, Sendo filed a lawsuit against the software giant alleging that it committed "fraud, theft of intellectual property, and conspiracy to destroy the start-up." Although it seems like it would not be in Microsoft's best interest to jeopardize its relationship with Sendo, Brogan has an explanation. Under the terms of their contract, Microsoft stood to get free access to Sendo's technology if Sendo went bankrupt, so that's precisely what Microsoft was attempting to make happen. Sendo's lawsuit alleges that Microsoft had a carefully constructed plan to gain its trust and "plunder" its technology while driving it to the brink of bankruptcy.

Microsoft officials have claimed that Sendo's allegations are baseless and that they are looking forward to establishing this in court. Although it has been observed that Brogan will have a hard time establishing that Microsoft was out to hurt his company, the matter is up to the courts to decide. As of now, at least, the case has not been settled.

3 GOOD REASONS why you should care about...

Interpersonal Behavior in the Workplace

You should care about interpersonal relationships at work because:

1. Cooperation between people can make life on the job not only more pleasant but more productive as well.

2. The effects of conflict can be beneficial in organizations, if managed properly, but harmful if mismanaged.

3. Managers can take several effective steps to reduce the likelihood of deviant organizational behavior, thereby avoiding its high costs.

On the surface, this case is just an ordinary corporate David versus Goliath tale. Reading between the lines, however, we find several important themes. Most obviously, there's the trust that turned to conflict as each party failed to meet the other's expectations. Add to this Sendo's allegations of misdeeds on the part of Microsoft and you have the makings of a bitter corporate feud. As you know, however, such dynamics are all too common among people in the workplace.

This tale reflects the kind of complex dynamics that occur all the time among people in organizations and are of major importance in the field of organizational behavior. Although you may not be involved in multimillion-dollar business deals, we all have been involved in situations in which people work at cross-purposes or even go out of their way to purposely harm one another. It is these processes of working with others and against them that is the focus of this chapter on **interpersonal behavior** at work. Specifically, we will summarize a wide array of interpersonal behaviors that occur in the workplace and describe how they influence the way people work and how they feel about their jobs and organizations.

Figure 7.1 identifies the major forms of interpersonal behavior in the workplace reviewed in this chapter. This diagram organizes interpersonal behaviors along a continuum ranging from those that involve working with others, shown on the left, to those that involve working against others, shown on the right. This forms a useful road map of how we will proceed in this chapter. Beginning on the left, we first will examine *prosocial behavior*—the tendency for people to help others on the job, sometimes even when there doesn't appear to be anything in it for them. Following this, we will discuss situations in which people help each other and receive help from them—that is, the tendency to *cooperate.* In the world of business, as you know, people and entire companies don't always work with each other; they also *compete* against each other—that is, as one tries to win, it forces the other to lose. Under such circumstances, it is not unusual for *conflict* to emerge, breeding ill-will. And, when taken to the extreme, this results in *deviant* behavior—extreme acts such as stealing from the company or even harming another person. Before examining these various

Figure 7.1 Varieties of Interpersonal Behavior

The five types of interpersonal behavior observed in organizations, and presented in this chapter, can be summarized as falling along a continuum ranging from those involving working with other people to those involving working against them.

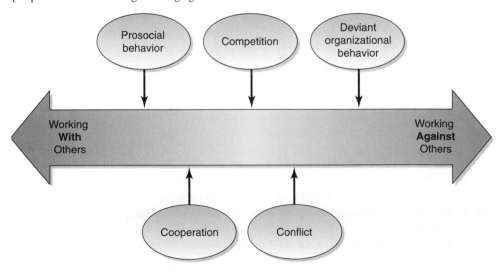

forms of behavior, we will begin by describing some of the basic dynamics that guide all forms of interpersonal behavior in the workplace.

The Dynamics of Interpersonal Relationships

To understand interpersonal behavior in organizations we must have an understanding of the basic building blocks of social relationships in general. What factors influence the kinds of relationships people develop between them? Although the answer to this question is more complicated than we can address here, we can identify two important factors—*psychological contracts* and *trust.*

Psychological Contracts: Our Expectations of Others

learning
objective

Whenever people have relationships with each other, they are bound to have certain expectations about what things will be like in that relationship. Leave a phone message for a friend, for example, and you expect him or her to return your call. Put in a fair day's work for your boss, and you expect to get paid in return. These examples illustrate what is known as the **psychological contract**—a person's beliefs about what is expected of another in a relationship.[1]

Although these are not legal contracts, they guide what we expect of others in much the same way. However, unlike legal contracts, in which the terms are made explicit, psychological contracts are perceptual in nature. Not surprisingly, there may well be differences of opinion regarding psychological contracts: What one person expects may not be exactly what the other expects. As you know from experience, such perceptual disagreements often make interpersonal relationships challenging.

As you might imagine, the nature of the psychological contracts we have with others depends on the kind of relationships we have with them. This is particularly clear in the workplace. Suppose, for example, that you are a temporary employee working in the order-fulfillment department of a large retail e-business during the busy holiday period. You know that your relationship with your employer will have a definite ending and that it is based on a clearly defined set of economic terms. You go to work each day as scheduled, you do your job as directed, you get your paycheck, and at the end of the season, it's over. In this case, you would be said to have a **transactional contract** with your employer.[2] This relationship is characterized by an exclusively economic focus, a brief time span, an unchanging nature, and is narrow and well defined in scope.

By contrast, other relationships between employers and employees are much closer and far more complex in nature. In fact, they operate more like marriages—long term in scope, ever changing, and not clearly defined. For example, if you have worked 20 years for the same boss in the same company, chances are good that your relationship is based not only on money but on friendship as well. You expect that relationship to last well into the future, and you recognize that it may well change over the years. In addition, your relationship with the boss has likely become quite complex and involves aspects of your lives that go beyond those of worker and supervisor. Such relationships are based on **relational contracts**. Compared to the transactional contracts that short-term employees are likely to have with their supervisors, long-term employees are likely to have relational contracts. For a summary of the defining characteristics of transactional and relational contracts, see Figure 7.2.

| Figure 7.2 | Two Kinds of Psychological Contracts: A Comparison |

Psychological contracts may be considered either transactional or relational. The characteristics of each type are summarized here.

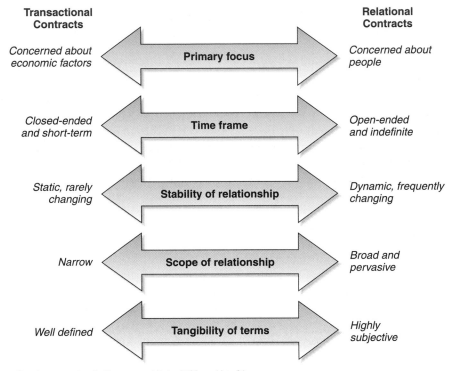

(*Source: Based on suggestions by Rousseau and Parks, 1993; see Note 2.*)

The Importance of Trust in Relationships

One thing that makes relationships based on transactional contracts so different from those based on relational contracts is the degree to which the parties trust each other. By **trust**, we are referring to a person's degree of confidence in the words and actions of another.[3] Suppose, for example, that your supervisor, the local sales manager, will be talking to his own boss, the district sales manager, about getting you transferred to a desirable new territory. You are counting on your boss to come through for you because he says he will. To the extent you believe that he will make a strong case on your behalf, you trust him. However, if you believe that his recommendation will not be too enthusiastic, or that he will not recommend you at all, you will trust him less.

Two major types of trust. These examples illustrate two different types of trust, each of which is linked to different kinds of relationships we have with others. The first is known as **calculus-based trust**, a kind of trust based on deterrence.[4] Calculus-based trust exists whenever people believe that another person will behave as promised out of fear of getting punished. We trust our employers to withhold the proper amount of taxes from our paychecks, for example, insofar as they risk fines and penalties from government agencies for failing to do so. People develop calculus-based trust slowly and incrementally: Each time they behave as promised, they build up the level of trust others have for them. This kind of trust is characteristic of professional relationships—the very kind in which people develop transactional contracts.

A second kind of trust, known as **identification-based trust**, is based on accepting and understanding the other person's wants and desires. Identification-based trust occurs when people know and understand each other so well that they are willing to allow that individual to act on his or her behalf. For example, you might allow your spouse or a very good friend to select furniture for your house based on the belief that his or her judgment will be much like yours and that this person would not make any decisions of which you would disapprove. In short, you trust this person. The example described earlier in which you allow your boss to discuss your transfer with a higher-ranking official also illustrates identification-based trust. As you might imagine, identification-based trust is likely to be found in very close relationships, be they personal or professional in nature—those based on relational contracts.

How does trust develop?   Even when people first meet, chances are good that they already have some level of trust or distrust in each other. What is responsible for this? In other words, what factors are responsible for the development of trust? Scientists have identified two important factors.

First, as you may already know from experience, some people tend to be more trusting than others. Indeed, the predisposition to be trusting of others is a personality variable (see Chapter 3). You probably know some people at the extremes in this regard: Whereas some individuals are cynical and hardly ever trust anyone, there are still others who are overly trusting of people, even when not warranted, to the point of being gullible.

Second, as you know, people develop reputations for being trustworthy or not trustworthy. That is, you may have learned by dealing with others directly that they will let you down and are not to be trusted. Importantly, based on their reputations, we also may judge people to be trustworthy or untrustworthy even if we have never met them. Because violating one's trust is such an affront, we are all very sensitive to this, making such information likely to be passed along to others—either by way of offering praise about never having been let down or by way of warning about the likelihood of getting let down (e.g., "Don't trust him!").

How to promote trust in working relationships.   Obviously, it is important to be thought of as being a trustworthy individual. The success of your relationships with others depends on it. That said, the question arises as to what we can do to get others to trust us. Clearly, the key is to not let others down. But this is easier said than done. Fortunately, there are specific things we all can do to build others' trust in us. These are as follows.

1. *Always meet deadlines.* If you promise to get something done on time, it is essential to meet that deadline. Although one or two incidents of lateness may be overlooked, people who are chronically late in meeting deadlines rapidly gain a reputation for being untrustworthy. And, when others believe that you will not meet important deadlines, they are likely to overlook you when it comes to getting any important career-building assignments.

2. *Follow through as promised.* It is not only important to do things on time but also to perform those tasks in the manner that others expect them to be done. Suppose, for example, that the manager of your department often gives you incomplete figures needed to prepare important sales reports for which you are responsible. His inconsistency (i.e., not behaving as promised) will lead you to be distrusting of him. And as this individual develops a reputation within the company for not being trustworthy, he or she may come across some serious barriers to promotion.

3. *Spend time sharing personal values and goals.* Remember, identification-based trust requires a keen understanding and appreciation of another person. And getting this understanding requires spending time together discussing common interests, common objectives, and the like. This has been the key to the success of Sir Adrian Cadbury, the former chairman of Cadbury Schweppes, the third largest soft drink company in the world.[5] By taking time to get to know his employees and by sharing ideas with them, Cadbury got to know what his employees are like as individuals. And this is key to developing trust.

> By taking time to get to know his employees and by sharing ideas with them, Cadbury got to know what his employees are like as individuals. And this is key to developing trust.

Prosocial Behavior: Helping Others

At Starbucks, founder and CEO Howard Schultz goes out of his way to help his employees.[6] Not only is he polite and attentive, as you might imagine, but he also does things to help them get ahead in life. Indeed, helping others is essential to making work not only a pleasant experience but a productive one for both individuals and their organizations as well. Scientists refer to such acts that benefit others in organizations as **prosocial behavior**. We will now discuss two important forms of prosocial behavior.

learning
objective

Organizational Citizenship Behavior: Above and Beyond Job Requirements

Imagine the following scene. It's coming up on 5:00 P.M. and you're wrapping up your work for the day. You're anxiously looking forward to getting home and relaxing. While this is going on, the scene is quite different at the next cubicle. One of your colleagues has been working feverishly to complete an important report but appears to have hit a snag. She now has little hope of getting the report on the boss's desk before he leaves for the day—that is, without your help. Pitching in to help your colleague is something you don't have to do. After all, there's nothing in your formal job description that makes it necessary for you to do so. What's more, you're quite weary after your own long day's work. However, when you see the bind your colleague is in, you put aside your own feelings and offer to stay and help her out.

In this case, although you're probably not going to win any medals for your generosity, you are being helpful, and you have gone "above and beyond the call of duty." Actions such as these, which exceed the formal requirements of one's job, are known as **organizational citizenship behavior** (or **OCB,** for short).[7] It is easy to imagine how such behaviors, although informal and sometimes minor in nature, play a very important role when it comes to the smooth functioning of organizations. The example we just gave of volunteering to help one of your coworkers is just one of five different forms that OCB can take. For a summary of all five, including examples of each, see Table 7.1.

Why does OCB occur?   As you know, people sometimes are selfish and do not engage in OCB. What, then, lies behind the tendency to be a good organizational citizen? Although there are several factors involved, evidence strongly suggests that people's beliefs that they are being treated fairly by their organization (especially their immediate supervisors) is a critical factor. The more people believe they are being treated fairly by the organization, the more they trust its management, and the more willing they are to go the extra mile to help out when needed.[8] By contrast, those who feel that their organizations are taking advantage of them are untrusting and not at all likely to engage in OCB.

Does OCB really matter?   As you might imagine, the affects of OCB are difficult to assess because OCB is generally not included as part of any standard performance measures that a company gathers about its employees. However, OCB does have important effects on organizational functioning. Specifically, people's willingness to engage in various types of OCB is related to such work-related measures as job satisfaction and organizational commitment, which, as described in Chapter 5, are related to organizational functioning in a number of complex ways.[9] In addition, being a good organizational citizen can have important effects on recruiting efforts. After all, the more positive statements current employees make about the companies where they are employed, the more effectively those companies will be able to

Table 7.1	Organizational Citizenship Behavior: Specific Forms and Examples

Organizational citizenship behavior (OCB) can take many different forms, most of which fall into the five major categories shown here.

Form of OCB	Examples
Altrusim	■ Helping a coworker with a project
	■ Switching vacation dates with another person
	■ Volunteering
Conscientiousness	■ Never missing a day of work
	■ Coming to work early if needed
	■ Not spending time on personal calls
Civic virtue	■ Attending voluntary meetings and functions
	■ Reading memos; keeping up with new information
Sportsmanship	■ Making do without complaint ("Grin and bear it!")
	■ Not finding fault with the organization
Courtesy	■ "Turning the other cheek" to avoid problems
	■ Not "blowing up" when provoked

recruit the best new employees.[10] In conclusion, although the effects of OCB may be indirect and difficult to measure, they can be very profound.

Tips for promoting OCB.   Given the importance of OCB, it makes sense to highlight some specific ways of bringing it about. Several potentially useful suggestions may be made.

1. *Go out of your way to help others.* The more you help your colleagues, the more likely they will be to help you. Soon, before you know it, with everyone helping everyone else, prosocial behavior will become the norm—that is, a widely accepted practice in the company.

2. *Be an example of conscientiousness.* Employees are inclined to model the citizenship behavior of their supervisors. If, as a manager, you set a good example by coming to work on time and not making personal phone calls, your subordinates may be expected to follow your lead. Although it might not be this easy, at least you have some credibility when you do insist that your subordinates refrain from these forms of poor citizenship.

3. *Fulfill psychological contracts.* Research has found that employees tend to be better, more conscientious organizational citizens to the extent that they believe their employers have fulfilled their psychological contracts with them.[11] After all, employees who feel let down by company officials would have little incentive to go the extra mile for them, doing as little as possible to get by, but no more.

4. *Make voluntary functions fun.* It only makes sense that employees will not be motivated to attend voluntary meetings or corporate functions of one kind or another (e.g., picnics, award banquets) unless these are enjoyable. People are more likely to show the good citizenship associated with attending corporate functions when the company makes it worthwhile for them to do so. After all, the more desirable it is for someone to be prosocial, the more likely that individual will be a good organizational citizen.

5. *Demonstrate courtesy and good sportsmanship.* When something goes wrong, don't "make a stink," rather, just "grin and bear it." Someone who "blows up" at the slightest provocation is not only a poor organizational citizen but also is one who may well discourage good citizenship among others.

Although these suggestions all seem like common sense, they certainly are not common practice. Even if you have only limited work experience you probably can tell a few tales about one or more individuals who behaved just the opposite of the manner outlined here. Keeping in mind just how unpleasant these people made life in your organization may be just the incentive you need to follow these guidelines. Doing so will keep you from becoming a bad organizational citizen yourself—and from encouraging others to follow suit.

Whistle-Blowing: Helping Through Dissent

Sometimes employees face situations in which they recognize that their organization is behaving in an improper fashion. To right the wrong they reveal the improper or illegal practice to someone who may be able to correct it—an action known as **whistle-blowing**.[12] Formally, whistle-blowing is the disclosure by employees of illegal, immoral, or illegitimate practices by employers to people or organizations able to take action.

Is whistle-blowing a prosocial action? From the point of view of society, it usually is. In many instances, the actions of whistle-blowers can protect the health, safety, or security of the general public. For example, an employee of a large bank who reports risky or illegal practices to an appropriate regulatory agency may be protecting thousands of depositors from considerable delay in recovering their savings. Similarly, an individual who blows the whistle on illegal dumping of toxic chemicals by his or her company may save many people from serious illness. For a summary of some actual cases of whistle-blowing, see Table 7.2.[13]

As you might imagine, blowing the whistle on one's employer is likely to be a very costly act for employees, as they often find themselves facing a long, uphill battle attempting to prove the wrongdoing. They also frequently face ostracism and losing their jobs in response to their disloyalty. For example, five agents from State Farm Insurance were fired recently after they accused the company of various consumer

Table 7.2	Whistle-Blowing: Some Examples

As the following examples illustrate, employees blow the whistle on many different types of organizations accused of committing a wide range of questionable activities.

Whistle-Blower	*Incident*
Coleen Rowley	This special agent wrote a letter to the FBI director (with copies to two key members of Congress) about the bureau's failure to take action that could have prevented the terrorist attacks of September 11, 2001.
Sherron Watkins	In 2001, she notified the press about her letter to her boss at Enron identifying the company's fictitious accounting practices.
Paul van Buitenen	Went public in 1999 with claims of fraud and corruption within the European Commission.
An unnamed U.S. Customs inspector	Alerted Congress of security problems at the Miami airport in 1995 after management took no action.
Tonya Atchinson	This former internal auditor at Columbia-HCA Healthcare Corp. charged the company with illegal Medicare billing.
Daniel Shannon	An in-house attorney for Intelligent Electronics protested the company's alleged misuse of marketing funds from computer manufacturers.
Robert Young	This agent for Prudential Insurance Co. in New Jersey accused company agents of encouraging customers to needlessly sell some policies and buy more expensive ones, boosting their commissions.
Bill Bush	This manager at the National Aeronautics and Space Administration (NASA) went public with the administration's policy of discouraging the promotion of employees older than 54 years of age.

(Sources: See Note 13.)

Six senior employees of the company that runs the 900-mile Trans-Alaskan pipeline chose to remain anonymous when voicing their complaints about safety violations to BP Amoco.

abuses.[14] Although various laws prevent employers from firing people directly because they blew the whistle, organizations frequently find alternative official grounds for dismissing "troublemakers."[15] It is not surprising, therefore, that six senior employees of the company that runs the 900-mile Trans-Alaskan pipeline chose to remain anonymous when voicing their complaints about safety violations to BP Amoco.[16] It is interesting to note that although whistle-blowing often involves considerable personal cost, the importance of the action motivates some people to go through with it.

Cooperation: Providing Mutual Assistance

Thus far, our discussion has focused on one person's giving help to another. However, it is probably even more common in organizations to find situations in which assistance is mutual, with two or more individuals, teams, or organizations working together toward some common goal. Such efforts are known as acts of **cooperation**. As you know from experience, people do not always cooperate with each other. As you might imagine, cooperation is essential to organizational success. Unless individuals, teams, and entire organizations cooperate with each other, all are likely to fall short of their objectives. With this in mind, it makes sense to consider the factors that bring about cooperation, both within organizations and between them as well.

3
learning
objective

Cooperation Within Organizations

Several factors affect the tendency for people to cooperate with each other within organizations. We will review some of the key ones here.

The reciprocity principle.   We all know that "the golden rule" admonishes us to do unto others as we would have them do unto us. However, this doesn't describe exactly the way people behave. Instead, of treating others as we would like to be treated, most people tend to treat others the way they have been treated in the past by them. In short, we are more inclined to follow a different principle: "an eye for an eye and a tooth for a tooth." Social scientists refer to this as the principle of **reciprocity**—the tendency to treat others as they have treated us.

To a great extent, the principle of reciprocity describes the way people behave when cooperating with others.[17] The key task in establishing cooperation in organizations is straightforward: getting it started. Once individuals or teams have begun to cooperate, the process may be largely self-sustaining. That is, one unit's cooperation encourages cooperation among the others. To encourage cooperation, therefore, managers should attempt to get the process under way.

Personal orientation.   As you know from experience, some people tend to be more cooperative by nature than others. In contrast, other people tend to be far more competitive—interested in doing better than others in one way or another. Not surprisingly, scientists have found that people can be reliably classified into four different categories in terms of their natural predispositions toward working with or against others.[18] These are as follows.

- **Competitors**—People whose primary motive is doing better than others, besting them in open competition.
- **Individualists**—People who care almost exclusively about maximizing their own gain and don't care whether others do better or worse than themselves.
- **Cooperators**—People who are concerned with maximizing joint outcomes, getting as much as possible for their team.
- **Equalizers**—People who are primarily interested in minimizing the differences between themselves and others.

Although there are individual differences, men as a whole tend to favor a competitive orientation, attempting to exploit others around them. By contrast, women tend to favor a cooperative orientation, preferring to work with other people rather than against them, and they also tend to develop friendly ties with others.[19] Still, it would be a mistake for managers to automatically assume that men and women automatically fall into certain categories. Instead, it is widely recommended that managers take the time to get to know their individual workers' personal orientations and then match these to the kinds of tasks to which they may be best suited. For example, competitors may be effective in negotiation situations whereas cooperators may be most effective in teamwork situations. (To get a sense of which category best describes you, complete the **Self-Assessment Exercise** on pages 248–249.)

Organizational reward systems.   It is not only differences between people that lead them to behave cooperatively but differences in the nature of organizational reward systems as well. Despite good intentions, companies all too often create reward systems that lead their employees to compete against each other. This would be the case, for example, in a company in which various divisions sell products that compete with each other. Sales representatives who receive commissions for selling their division's products have little incentive to help the company by attempting to sell another division's products. In other words, the company's reward system discourages cooperative behavior.

With an eye toward eliminating such problems and fostering cooperation, many of today's companies are adopting **team-based rewards**.[20] These are organizational reward systems in which at least a portion of an individual's compensation is based on the performance of his or her work group. The rationale behind these incentive systems is straightforward (and follows from the principle of reinforcement described in Chapter 3): People who are rewarded for contributing to their group's performance will focus their energies on group performance. In other words, they will cooperate with each other. Although there are many difficult challenges associated with setting up team-based reward programs that are manageable (e.g., based on measurable rewards that really matter) and that people find acceptable (e.g., ones that are administered fairly), companies that have met these challenges have reaped benefits in terms of increased job satisfaction and productivity.

learning
objective

Competition: The Opposite of Cooperation

Question: If cooperation is so beneficial, why does it not always occur? In other words, why do people or organizations with similar goals not always join forces? To a large extent, the answer is that some goals cannot be shared. There can be only one winner of the Super Bowl and one winner of the World Series; the teams cannot share these prizes. Similarly, when several large companies are courting the same small company as a takeover candidate, there can be only one winner as well. Such conditions breed **competition**—a pattern of behavior in which each person, group, or organization seeks to maximize its own gains, often at the expense of others. For a graphic summary of the differences between cooperation and competition, see Figure 7.3.

It is important to recognize that cooperation and competition might be occurring at the same time. That is, people may have **mixed motives**—the motive to cooperate and the motive to compete may be operating simultaneously. Take the game of baseball, for example. Players may cooperate with each other, such as when it comes to getting a double play (where the shortstop might flip a ground ball to the second baseman, who then throws it to the first baseman). At the same time, they also may be competing

Figure 7.3   Cooperation Versus Competition: A Comparison

When *cooperating* with each other, people work together to attain the same goal that they share. However, when *competing* against one another, each person works to attain the same goal to the exclusion of the other.

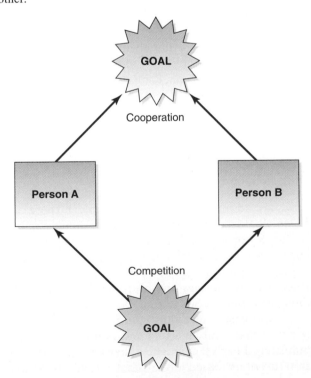

against each other for individual records. And, of course, they are working together to compete against the other team. Clearly, there are a lot of things going on in such situations: The motives to cooperate and to compete often coexist within the same situation.

In business, competition is the natural order of things. Employees in the same company compete for a promotion, companies compete for the same government contract, and of course, retail businesses compete for the same customers. In recent years, for example, several start-up companies, such as Victory and Excelsior-Henderson, have made high-quality motorcycles that compete very favorably with "cruisers" from the legendary Harley-Davidson.[21] They are trying to attract customers by offering more bike for the money, while Harley fans continue to be attracted to something less tangible—that company's reputation. Although only time will tell the outcome of this competition, it is clear that no matter what happens, there will always be companies competing against other companies.

Conflict: The Inevitable Result of Incompatible Interests

If we conceive of prosocial behavior and cooperation as being at one end of a continuum (as in Figure 7.1), then it makes sense to conceive of *conflict* as approaching the opposite end. In the context of organizations, **conflict** may defined as a process in which one party perceives that another party has taken or will take actions that are incompatible with one's own interests. As you might imagine, conflict occurs quite commonly in organizations. In fact, it has been estimated that about 20 percent of managers' time is spent dealing with conflict and its effects.[22] Considering this, it makes sense to examine the types of conflict that exist, the causes and consequences of conflict, and ways to effectively manage conflict that occurs in the workplace.

Types of Conflict

As you might imagine, all conflict is not alike. In fact, scientists have identified three major types of conflict that commonly occur.[23] These are as follows:

■ *Substantive conflict*—It is not unusual for people to have different viewpoints and opinions with respect to a decision they are making with others. This variety of conflict is known as **substantive conflict**. In most cases, substantive conflict can be very beneficial to helping groups make effective decisions because it forces the various sides to clearly articulate their ideas. (We will discuss group decision making more fully in Chapter 10.)

■ *Affective conflict*—When people experience clashes of personalities or interpersonal tension of some sort, the frustration and anger that result are signs of affective conflict. It is not unusual for affective conflict to result whenever people from different backgrounds are put together to perform tasks. Until they learn to accept one another, affective conflict is likely, resulting in disruption to group performance. After all, people who do not see the world in the same manner are likely to clash, and when they do, their joint performance tends to suffer.

■ *Process conflict*—In many work groups controversies arise about how they are going to operate—that is, how various duties and resources will be allocated and with whom various responsibilities will reside. This is known as process conflict. Generally, the more process conflict exists, the more group performance will suffer.[24]

As this discussion suggests, conflict takes several different forms and can have different effects—both positive and negative in nature. With this in mind, let's now turn to a discussion of the underlying causes of conflict.

Causes of Conflict

5
learning
objective

The conflicts we face in organizations may be viewed as stemming from a variety of causes, including both our interactions with other people and the organization itself. Here are just a few of the most important sources of organizational conflict.

Grudges.   All too often, conflict is caused when people who have lost face in dealing with someone attempt to "get even" with that person by planning some form of revenge. Employees involved in this kind of activity are not only going out of their way to harm one of their coworkers, but by holding a grudge, they also are wasting energy that could be devoted to more productive organizational endeavors.

Malevolent attributions.   Why did someone do something that hurt us? To the extent that we believe that the harm we suffer is due to an individual's malevolent motives (e.g., the desire to hurt us), conflict is inevitable. However, whenever we believe that we suffered harm because of factors outside someone's control (e.g., an accident), conflict is less likely to occur. (This is an example of the attribution process addressed in Chapter 3.) This causes problems in cases in which we falsely attribute the harm we suffer to another's negative intent when, in reality, the cause was externally based.

Destructive criticism.   Communicating negative feedback in organizations is inevitable. All too often, however, this process arouses unnecessary conflict. The problem is that some people make the mistake of using **destructive criticism**—that is, negative feedback that angers the recipient rather than helps this person do a better job. The most effective managers attempt to avoid conflict by using constructive criticism instead. For some important comparisons between these two forms of criticism, see Table 7.3.

Distrust.   The more strongly people suspect that some other individual or group is out to get them, the more likely they are to have a relationship with that person or group that is riddled with conflict. In general, companies that are considered great places in which to work are characterized by high levels of trust between people at all levels.

Competition over scarce resources.   Because organizations never have unlimited resources (such as space, money, equipment, or personnel), it is inevitable that conflicts will arise over the distribution of those resources. This occurs in large part because of a self-serving tendency in people's perceptions (see Chapter 3); that is, people tend to overestimate their own contributions to their organizations. Believing that we make greater contributions leads us to feel more deserving of resources than others. Inevitably, conflict results when others do not see it this way.

Table 7.3	Constructive Versus Destructive Criticism: A Comparison

The factors listed here distinguish constructive criticism (negative feedback that may be accepted by the recipient to improve his or her performance) from destructive criticism (negative feedback likely to be rejected by the recipient and unlikely to improve his or her performance).

Constructive Criticism	*Destructive Criticism*
Considerate—protects the recipient's self-esteem	Inconsiderate—harsh, sarcastic, biting
Does not contain threats	Contains threats
Timely—occurs as soon as possible after the substandard performance	Not timely—occurs after an inappropriate delay
Does not attribute poor performance to internal causes	Attributes poor performance to internal causes (e.g., lack of effort, motivation, ability)
Specific—focuses on aspects of performance that were inadequate	General—a sweeping condemnation of performance
Focuses on performance, not on the recipient	Focuses on the recipient—his or her personal characteristics
Motivated by desire to help the recipient improve	Motivated by anger, desire to assert dominance over the recipient, desire for revenge
Offers concrete suggestions for improvement	Offers no concrete suggestions for improvement

Consequences of Conflict: Both Good and Bad

The word *conflict* doubtlessly brings to mind negative images—thoughts of anger and confrontation. Indeed, there is no denying the many negative effects of conflict. But, as we already noted (and as we will describe further), conflict has a positive side as well. With this in mind, we will now identify the many consequences of conflict in organizations, both positive and negative.

Negative consequences of conflict.   The major problem with conflict, as you know from experience, is that it yields strong negative emotions. However, these emotional reactions mark only the beginning of a chain of reactions that can have harmful effects in organizations.

The negative reactions, besides being quite stressful, are problematic in that they may divert people's attention from the task at hand. For example, people who are focused on getting even with a coworker and making him look bad in front of others are unlikely to be attending to the most important aspect of their jobs. In particular, communication between individuals or teams may be so adversely affected that any coordination of effort between them is compromised. Not surprisingly, such lowered coordination tends to lead to decrements in organizational functioning. In short, organizational conflict has costly effects on organizational performance. For some helpful suggestions on how to avoid many of these problems, see Table 7.4.[25]

Table 7.4	How to Manage Conflict Effectively

Although conflict is inevitable, there are concrete steps that managers can take to avoid the negative consequences that result from conflict between people in the workplace.

■ Agree on a process for making decisions *before* a conflict arises. This way, when a conflict needs to be addressed, everyone knows how it is going to be handled.

■ Make sure everyone knows his or her specific areas of responsibility, authority, and accountability. Clarifying these matters avoids potential conflicts when people either ignore their responsibilities or overstep their authority.

■ Recognize conflicts stemming from faulty organizational systems, such as a pay system that rewards one department at the expense of another. In such cases, work to change the system rather than training employees.

■ Recognize the emotional reactions to conflict. Conflicts will not go away until people's hurt feelings are addressed.

■ Consider how to avoid problems rather than assign blame for them. Questions such as "Why did you do that?" only make things worse. It is more helpful to ask, "How can we make things better?"

■ Conflicts will not go away by making believe they don't exist; doing so will only make them worse. Avoid the temptation not to speak to the other party and discuss your misunderstandings thoroughly.

(Source: Based on suggestions by Bragg, 1999; see Note 25.)

Positive consequences of conflict. Have you ever worked on a team project and found that you disagreed with someone on a key matter? If so, how did you react? Chances are good that you fell short of sabotaging that person's work or acting aggressively. In fact, the conflict may have even brought the two of you to the table to have a productive discussion about the matter at hand. As a result of this discussion you may have even improved relations between the two of you and the quality of the decisions that resulted from your joint efforts. If you can relate to this scenario, then you already recognize an important fact about organizational conflict—that some of its effects are positive.

When asked recently about his management philosophy, Starbucks' CEO and founder Howard Schultz touted the importance of conflict and debate, saying, "If there's no tension, I don't think you get the best result."[26] As this successful business leader suggests, organizational conflict can be the source of several benefits. Among these are the following.

■ Conflict may improve the quality of organizational decisions (as in the preceding example).

■ Conflict may bring out into the open problems that have been previously ignored.

■ Conflict may motivate people to appreciate each others' positions more fully.

■ Conflict may encourage people to consider new ideas, thereby facilitating change.

In view of these positive effects of conflict, the key is to make sure that more of these benefits occur as opposed to costs. It is with this goal in mind that managers work so diligently to effectively manage organizational conflict. We will now examine some of the ways they go about doing this.

Reducing Conflict Through Negotiation

When conflicts arise between individuals, groups, or even entire organizations, the most common way to resolve them is to work together to find a solution that is acceptable to all the parties involved. This process is known as **bargaining** (or **negotiation**). Formally, we may define bargaining as the process in which two or more parties in dispute with each other exchange offers, counteroffers, and concessions in an attempt to find a mutually acceptable agreement.

Obviously, bargaining does not work when the parties rigidly adhere to their positions without budging—that is, when they "stick to their guns." For bargaining to be effective, the parties involved must be willing to adjust their stances on the issues at hand. And, for the people involved to be willing to make such adjustments, they must believe that they have found an acceptable outcome—one that allows them to claim victory in the negotiation process. For bargaining to be most effective in reducing conflict, this must be the case for all sides. That is, outcomes must be found for all sides that allow them to believe that they have "won" the negotiation process—results known as **win–win solutions.** In win–win solutions, everybody wins, precisely as the term implies.

Tips for negotiating win–win solutions.   Several effective ways of finding such win–win solutions may be identified. (For practice in putting these techniques to use, see the **Group Exercise** on pages 249–250.)

1. *Avoid making unreasonable offers.* Imagine that a friend of yours is selling a used car with an asking price of $10,000—the car's established "book value." If you were to attempt to "lowball" the seller by offering only $1,000, your bad-faith offer might end the negotiations right there. A serious buyer would offer a more reasonable price, say $9,000—one that would allow both the buyer and the seller to come out ahead in the deal. In short, extreme offers tend to anger opponents, sometimes ending the negotiation process on a sour note, allowing none of the parties to get what they want.

2. *Seek the common ground.* All too often people in conflict with others assume that their interests and those of the other party are completely incompatible. When this occurs, they tend to overlook the fact that they actually might have several areas of interest in common. When parties focus on the areas of agreement between them, it helps bring them together on the areas of disagreement. So, for example, in negotiating the deal for purchasing the used car, you might establish the fact that you agree to the selling price of $9,000. This verifies that the interests of the buyer and the seller are not completely incompatible, thereby encouraging them to find a solution to the area in which they disagree, such as a payment schedule. By contrast, if either party believed that they were completely far apart on all aspects of the deal, they would be less likely to negotiate a win–win solution.

3. *Broaden the scope of issues considered.* Sometimes parties bargaining with each other have several issues on the table. When this occurs, it is often useful to consider the various issues together as a total package. Labor unions often do this in negotiating contracts with company management whenever they give in on one issue in exchange for compensation on another issue. So, for example, in return for not

freezing wages, a company may agree to concede to the union's other interests, such as gaining representation on key corporate committees. In other words, compared to bargaining over single issues (e.g., the price of the used car), when the parties get to bargaining across a wide array of issues, it often is easier to find solutions that are acceptable to all sides.

4. *Uncover "the real" issues.* Frequently, people focus on the conflicts between them in only a single area although they may have multiple conflicts between them—some of which are hidden. Suppose, for example, that your friend is being extremely stubborn when it comes to negotiating the price of the used car. He's sticking firmly to his asking price, refusing to budge despite your reasonable offer, possibly adding to the conflict between you. However, it may be the case that there are other issues involved. For example, he may be trying to "get even" with you for harming him several years ago. In other words, what may appear to be a simple conflict between two people may actually have multiple sources. Finding long-lasting solutions requires identifying all the important issues—even the hidden ones—and bringing them to the table.

As you might imagine, it is almost always far easier to say these things than to do them. Indeed, when people cannot come to agreement about something, they sometimes become irrational, not seeking common ground and not taking the other's perspective needed to find a win–win solution, but only thinking of themselves. In such circumstances, third parties can be useful to break the deadlock. For a description of a popular approach for doing this, see the accompanying **Winning Practices** section.

Deviant Organizational Behavior

In recent years, TV news reports have aired an alarming number of accounts of disgruntled employees who have returned to their past places of employment to exact revenge on their former bosses by holding them at gunpoint—and, tragically, sometimes pulling the trigger. This scenario became so prominent among employees of the U.S. Postal Service in the late 1990s that the phrase "going postal" entered into our everyday language to describe this form of violence—clearly the most negative end of the continuum of positive to negative behaviors we have been describing in this chapter.

Although acts of physical violence have been the subject of news stories, they represent just one very extreme form of what OB scientists call **deviant organizational behavior**.[27] This refers to actions on the part of employees that intentionally violate the norms of organizations and/or the formal rules of society, resulting in negative consequences. *Workplace aggression,* which we have been describing, is only one extreme example of deviant organizational behavior. Another form that is less extreme and more common is known as **incivility**, which refers to a lack of regard for others, denying them the respect they are due. Yes, simply being rude to one of your coworkers is a type of deviant behavior. OB scientists are interested in reducing deviant organizational behavior because it can be a very disruptive and costly problem in terms of both the financial toll it takes on the company and the emotional toll it takes on employees.

Winning **Practices**

Settling Disputes Quickly and Inexpensively Out of Court: Alternative Dispute Resolution

When a customer canceled a $60,000 wedding reception, Anthy Capetola, a caterer from Long Island, New York, was able to fill that time slot with an event bringing in only half as much.[28] Although Capetola was harmed by the customer's actions, as you might imagine, that customer was unwilling to cough up the lost revenue. Many business owners in Capetola's shoes would seek restitution by taking the customer to court, resulting in a delay of many months, or even years, and a huge bill for litigation, not to mention lots of adverse publicity. Fortunately, in their contract, Capetola and the customer agreed to settle any future disagreements using what is known as **alternative dispute resolution** (**ADR**). This refers to a set of procedures in which disputing parties work together with a neutral party who helps them settle their disagreements out of court.

There are two popular forms of ADR—*mediation* and *arbitration*. **Mediation** involves having a neutral party (the *mediator*) work together with both sides to reach a settlement. Typically, mediators meet together and separately with each side and try to find a common ground that will satisfy everyone's concerns. Mediators do not consider who's wrong and who's right but set the stage for finding a resolution. And that they do! In fact, by one recent estimate mediators help disputing parties find solutions about 85 percent of the time. As you might imagine, however, for mediation to work the two sides must be willing to communicate with each other. When this doesn't happen, ADR may take the form of **arbitration**.

This involves having a neutral third party listen to the facts presented by each side who then makes a final, binding decision.

ADR is very popular these days because it helps disputants reach agreements rapidly (often in a matter of a day or two, compared to months or years for court trials) and inexpensively (usually for just a few thousand dollars split between the parties, compared to astronomical sums for attorney fees). Moreover, it keeps people who otherwise might end up in court out of the public eye, which could be damaging to their reputations—even the party in whose favor the judgment goes. Because it is low key and nonconfrontational, mediation is particularly valuable in cases in which the parties have an ongoing relationship (business or personal) that they do not want to go sour.[29] After all, the mediation process brings the parties together, helping them see each other's side—something that is usually lost for sure in the heat of a courtroom battle.

Not surprisingly, the popularity of ADR these days has led to the development of several companies specializing in rendering mediation and arbitration services. The largest of these, the American Arbitration Association, boasts offices in half the U.S. states, with a load pushing 80,000 cases per year. They maintain a file of some 18,000 arbitrators and mediators (typically lawyers, businesspeople, and former judges), enabling them to find a neutral party who is experienced in just about any kind of dispute that people are likely to have.

With examples ranging from murder to rudeness, it's an understatement to say that deviant organizational behavior is enormously broad in scope! Fortunately, scientists have devised a useful way of categorizing workplace deviance in a manner that helps us understand the various forms it takes.

Varieties of Deviant Behavior

The wide variety of behaviors that may be considered deviant can be categorized along two dimensions (see Figure 7.4).[30] First, deviant behavior may be distinguished in terms of the seriousness of its consequences. At the most serious extreme (shown on the right side of the diagram), we may find employees physically attacking and harming their past or present coworkers. Fortunately, physical violence doesn't occur all that often. Far more commonplace are acts that, although also considered deviant, are far less extreme (shown on the left side of the diagram), such as spreading malicious gossip about others, lying about your work, blaming others falsely, and the like. Scientists also categorize deviant organizational behavior with respect to the intended target. In this regard, we may distinguish between deviant acts designed to harm other individuals, such as one's bosses or coworkers (e.g., verbally abusing a coworker), and deviant acts designed to harm the organization itself

---

Figure 7.4   Dimensions and Categories of Deviant Organizational Behavior

Research has shown that deviant organizational behavior falls along the two dimensions shown here: seriousness (major or minor) and target of deviance (another person or the organization). Combining these two dimensions results in the four categories of behavior identified here, along with examples of each.

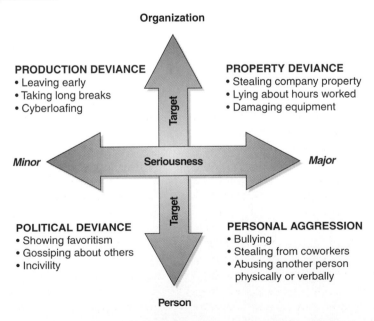

(*Sources: Based on findings reported by Bennett and Robinson, 2000; Robinson and Bennett, 1995; see Note 30.*)

(e.g., sabotaging company equipment). By combining these two dimensions, we get the four categories of deviant behavior shown in Figure 7.4.

Looking at Figure 7.4, you will find a broad variety of deviant behaviors ranging from some benign acts directed at the company, such as taking long breaks, to extreme acts aimed at other individuals, such as physical abuse. To give you a better feel for the nature of deviant organizational behavior, we now will take a closer look at three of the most prominent and widely studied forms of workplace deviance—*cyberloafing, workplace aggression,* and *employee theft.* To give you a feel for the wide variety of forms workplace deviance takes, our examples will draw from each of the four different categories we just described.

Cyberloafing: Deviant Behavior Goes High Tech

6
learning
objective

The advent of Internet technology has brought with it increased efficiency in accessing information and communicating with others—both of which are vital objectives. However, it also has created new ways for employees to loaf, or "goof off." Although workers have devised ways to slack off ever since people have been employed, access to the Internet and e-mail has provided tempting and more insidious opportunities than ever before. Employees who use their company's e-mail and/or Internet facilities for personal use are considered to be engaged in **cyberloafing**.[31]

In the United States, 40 million people have Internet and/or e-mail access at work and use it regularly, and they are referred to as online workers. However, further statistics reveal that much of what online workers are doing while online is not work related. For example:

- According to an MSNBC survey, one-fifth of all people who have visited pornographic Web sites have done so while on the job.
- One-third of workers surveyed by the Society of Financial Service Professionals reported playing computer games while at work.
- Eighty-three percent of employers surveyed by the Privacy Foundation indicated that their employees were using e-mail for personal purposes.

These and other forms of cyberloafing are costing U.S. organizations, both private and public, untold millions of dollars a year. In fact, just one $40,000/year employee can cost his or her employer as much as $5,000 annually by playing around on the Internet for one hour a day.

Executives are implicitly aware of this problem, and over three-quarters believe that some type of online monitoring and filtering efforts are needed. Recent polls found, however, that only about a third of online workers are monitored, and most of this monitoring is highly sporadic. In fact, only 38 percent acknowledge monitoring the online work of employees who already have been suspected of cyberloafing. Bottom line: Cyberloafing is a costly problem about which perilously little is being done.

Although various software products make it possible to monitor employees (Baltimore MIMEsweeper and Websense being the most widely used), and such products are growing in popularity, this technology is not a panacea. Although some problems are technical in nature, the most notable ones are social-psychological. Specifically, employees believe that being monitored constitutes an invasion of their privacy and reject the practice as being unfair.

Recent decisions in federal courts are in agreement. In September 2001, for example, the 27-judge Judicial Conference of the United States repealed a proposed monitoring policy for their own employees that they feared would violate their constitutional rights to privacy. Speaking for the group, federal appeals court judge Alex Kozinski objected to the policy's assertion that "court employees should have no expectation of privacy at any time while at work." The resulting policy permitted virtually no monitoring of employees' e-mail and only highly limited monitoring of their Internet use.

Where we stand now is quite interesting: Although cyberloafing is admittedly a widespread and costly problem, efforts aimed at addressing it that involve employee monitoring are not well accepted (or even legally permissible, in some cases). Clearly, the key is to find additional ways of discouraging people from cyberloafing. Admittedly, given the ancient problem of "goofing off" coupled with the vast opportunities to goof off provided by Internet access, cyberloafing looks like it's going to be a problem that stays around for years to come. Fortunately, organizational behavior specialists are now beginning to study this phenomenon, which hopefully will provide some helpful suggestions in the years to come.[32]

Workplace Aggression: Physical or Verbal Abuse and Bullying

Approximately 1.5 million Americans annually become victims of violence while on the job, costing some $4.2 billion.[33] Despite all the publicity given to workers going berserk and shooting up their offices, the good news is that such extreme acts of violence in the workplace occur very rarely. For example, only about 800 people are murdered at work each year in the United States (and even more in some other countries), and most of these crimes are committed by outsiders, such as customers.[34]

Despite their low occurrence, it is important to acknowledge such violent acts because they represent the visible "tip of the iceberg" of more prevalent forms of physical and verbal aggression that do occur. For example, even when guns are not involved, fistfights have been known to break out in offices and factories. Still, deviant acts of the physical variety occur far less frequently than verbal forms of aggression, such as threatening physical harm or by degrading or humiliating someone. If you've ever suffered verbal humiliation from another, you probably know only too well that such "sticks and stones," as the saying goes, can indeed be very harmful. Collectively, such acts of verbal and physical abuse are referred to as **workplace aggression**.[35]

Who engages in workplace aggression?   Recently, a study was conducted in which a group of employees were asked to report on the extent to which they behaved aggressively at work.[36] These individuals also completed various personality measures. Interestingly, the individuals who were most inclined to behave aggressively possessed characteristics that were associated with aggression. These were as follows:

- *High trait anger*—The tendency to respond to situations in a predominantly angry manner.
- *Positive attitude toward revenge*—The belief that it is justifiable to get back at others who have caused one harm.
- *Past experience with aggression*—A history that involves exposure to aggressive behavior.

These results are important because they suggest that some people are predisposed to behave more aggressively than others. In the future, as OB scientists come to understand this profile more fully, we will have a good chance of developing methods for screening those individuals who are most likely to behave aggressively on the job and keeping them out of the workplace altogether.

What job characteristics put people at risk for violence or aggression?   In addition to identifying individuals whose personal characteristics predispose them to behave aggressively, scientists also have considered the possibility that aggressive behavior is triggered by the nature of the work people perform. The possibility that people performing certain kinds of jobs are more likely to become victims of aggression than people performing other kinds of jobs surely is important to know in advance so that appropriate precautions can be taken. With this in mind, scientists recently conducted a study in which they assessed the relationship between two variables in a broad sample of workers—characteristics of the work they performed (i.e., the extent to which their jobs put them in a position to do certain things, such as caring for other people, handling valuable goods, etc.) and the extent to which they experienced various forms of violence or aggression at work.[37] Their findings were quite interesting: People whose jobs led them to exercise control over others or to handle various weapons (e.g., police officers) or to have contact with people on medication or to take physical care of others (e.g., nurses) were among the most likely to experience violence on the job. Figure 7.5 identifies the seven job characteristics that are most strongly associated with violence on the job.

Workplace bullying.   In recent years, OB specialists have become aware of a particularly widespread form of aggressive behavior known as **workplace bullying**.[38] This refers to the repeated mistreatment of an individual at work in a manner that endangers his or her physical or mental health.[39] Workplace bullying occurs by virtue of things people do intentionally to bring harm (e.g., chastising another) as well as things they don't do (e.g., withholding valuable information and training). Unlike harassment based on race or gender, bullying is not strictly illegal (unless, of course, it results in harm), and it is quite widespread. According to a recent survey, one in six workers in the United States has been the victim of bullying in the past year.[40] Typically, bullies tend to be bosses (81 percent) who are abusing their power. Interestingly, bullies are equally likely to be women as men, but the vast majority of the targets of bullying tend to be women (especially when the bullies are themselves women).[41] For a summary of the various forms of workplace bullying that exist, see Table 7.5.

The interesting thing about bullying is that it tends to repeat itself, thereby escalating its effects. For example, a bully's target is likely to complain to a higher-ranking organizational official. Typically, most higher-level managers will take some form of action (e.g., admonishing the bully) but will still leave the bully in place to strike again. This time, however, the bully is likely not only to strike again but also to retaliate with vengeance. Often this results in high levels of fear that paralyze the workplace, causing people to seek new jobs and exposing employers to litigation. Part of the difficulty in dealing with this problem is that bullies often are so highly effective that they bring other employees into their webs, getting them either to join in on the abuse or to agree to keep silent about it. Soon what appears to be the inappropriate behavior of a lone individual becomes a serious problem for the entire organization.

| Figure 7.5 | Job Characteristics That Put People at Risk for Violence |

According to a recent study, the seven job characteristics listed here were found to be most strongly related to experiencing violence on the job. Insofar as these are characteristic of the work performed by police officers and nurses, it is not surprising that individuals performing these jobs also were found to suffer the highest occurrences of violence.

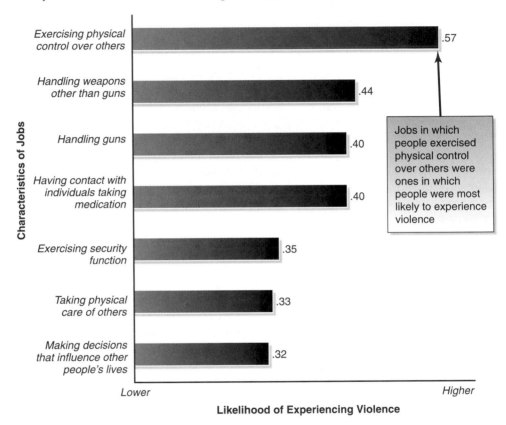

(Source: Based on data reported by LeBlanc and Kelloway, 2002; see Note 37.)

Today's workplace bully is not simply a grown-up version of the same person as the schoolyard bully who threatened to beat you up after school back in second grade. Rather, workplace bullies are best understood from the same perspective as those who perpetrate domestic violence—they are individuals whose needs to control others are so extreme that they are in need of psychological counseling. As you might imagine, the workplace bully, once rooted out, should be dealt with in a swift and effective manner. This might result in a leave of absence during which professional help is provided—or in many cases—termination. As you might imagine, of course, this is far easier said than done. After all, few among us would be willing to admit that we have a bully working in our midst, causing us to take only mild action, which, as we noted, can only make things worse. As in so many cases, the best

Table 7.5	Forms of Workplace Bullying

Workplace bullying takes a variety of forms. Some of the most prevalent are summarized here.

Category	*Description*
Constant Critic	■ Uses insulting and belittling comments, engages in name-calling ■ Constantly harangues the victim about his or her incompetence ■ Makes aggressive eye contact
Two-Headed Snake	■ Denies victims the resources needed to work ■ Demands that coworkers provide damning evidence against the victim ■ Assigns meaningless work as punishment
Gatekeeper	■ Isolates the victim; ignoring him or her with "the silent treatment" ■ Deliberately cuts the target out of the communication loop but expects the victim to have the missing information
Screaming Mimi	■ Yells, screams, and curses ■ Makes loud, angry outbursts and tantrums ■ Intimidates by slamming things and throwing objects

(Source: Based on information in Namie and Namie, 2000; see Note 41.)

offense here is likely to be "a good defense"—that is, to be on the lookout for bullies and to step in before they can get a foothold into the organization.

Although bullies are far too common in organizations, they still represent an extreme. Even the average worker who is not a bully or a "hothead" with a "short fuse" prone to "explode" may, if provoked, react strongly to adverse situations he or she has experienced. Frequent mergers and acquisitions make working conditions insecure for lots of people, causing almost anyone to behave aggressively from time to time.

Tips for avoiding workplace aggression. To keep such incidents from intensifying, it is important to recognize several things that managers can do to minimize the occurrence of aggression in the workplace. Here are three such tips.

1. *Establish clear disciplinary procedures.* It is not unusual for people to curb aggressive reactions in organizations that have clearly understood disciplinary procedures in place. Such programs not only send strong messages that inappropriate behavior will not be tolerated but also that it will be punished if it occurs. Such procedures go a long way toward deterring many forms of workplace aggression.[42]
2. *Treat people with dignity and respect.* Managers who belittle their subordinates and who fail to show them the dignity and respect they deserve unknowingly may be

promoting aggressive behavior. In some cases, this takes the form of people suing their former employers on the grounds of wrongful termination. Individuals who file such lawsuits are clearly striking back at their former employers, attempting to get even with them for harming them. Recent research has shown that the more unfairly people believe they have been treated on the job (i.e., the less dignity and respect they have been shown), the more likely they are to file lawsuits against their former employers.[43] Obviously, this provides a strong lesson to managers about the importance of treating people fairly, something that is easily under their control.

3. *Train managers in ways to recognize and avoid aggression.* Although we all recognize aggressive behavior when it occurs, too few of us know how to recognize potentially dangerous situations before they become serious. Managers should be trained in techniques for recognizing threats and be familiar with ways to defuse those threats. Probably the most significant tip in this regard is to take all threats seriously. Never assume that someone is merely making a joke. Talking calmly and rationally to someone who appears to be troubled can go a long way toward avoiding a potentially explosive situation.

Employee Theft

Retail stores are very concerned with problems of shoplifting, as you know. What you might not know, however, is that companies lose more money and goods from their own employees than from customers. Although estimates of costs of employee theft are quite varied, it is clear that the figures are staggering. For some recent figures on the costs and scope of employee theft in several types of organizations, see Table 7.6.[44]

To fully understand these statistics, we must consider an important fact: Almost everyone takes home some company property for personal purposes, but we are unlikely to consider doing this as theft. After all, you may say, "they expect it." Whether or not this is true, the taking of company property for nonbusiness uses constitutes **employee theft**. After all, who among us hasn't taken home a few pens or paper clips from the office at one time or another? Although these acts may seem innocent and innocuous enough, petty theft is so common that cumulatively it costs companies far more than the few acts of grand theft that grab newspaper headlines.[45]

Why do employees steal?   It's hardly surprising that many employees steal because they are troubled in some way (e.g., they are in serious debt or have a narcotics or gambling habit). Although this is undoubtedly true in some cases, it doesn't account for everyone.

Lots of people steal for a very simple reason—because *they see their coworkers doing it.* To the extent that everyone around you is taking home tools, office supplies, and even petty cash, it quickly seems not so inappropriate. After all, we rationalize, "everyone is doing it" and "the company expects us to do it." Although this doesn't make it right, of course, and it clearly costs the company money, people are quick to convince themselves that petty theft is "no big deal" and not worth worrying about.

Similarly, many employees engage in theft because in some companies *not* stealing goes against the *informal norms* of the work group.[46] Unspoken rules go a long way toward determining how people behave on the job (as we will discuss in Chapter 9), and in some companies an employee has to steal to feel accepted and to belong.

Finally, employees frequently also engage in theft because *they want to "even the score"* with employers who they believe have mistreated them. In fact, people who

Table 7.6	Employee Theft: Some Facts and Figures

The following statistics will give you a sense of the scope and serious nature of employee theft today.

- In the restaurant business, theft by employees costs between $15 billion and $25 billion per year.
- Although fewer consumers are stealing wireless phone service than ever before, there has been a significant rise in theft of service by employees of wireless companies.
- Most employees dislike the use of video surveillance cameras at work. At a Virginia restaurant, seven cashiers resigned the day before they believed closed-circuit surveillance cameras were going to be installed.
- Fraud cost American businesses about $400 billion a year.
- The average convenience store loses $20,000 per year due to employee theft.
- In Asian retail businesses, about 3 percent of the staff steal every day and 8 percent steal every week.
- Breaches of computer security are on the rise, but most of the people who break into corporate or government computers illegally are current employees rather than outsiders.

(Sources: See Note 44.)

believe they have been underpaid frequently steal from their employers because in so doing they are righting a wrong by taking what they should have had all along.

Tips for reducing employee theft.   Although you see security cameras just about everywhere, it's clear that they are not completely effective.[47] After all, many people keep on stealing. As a practicing manager, there are several things you can do to help chip away at the problem. Although you won't be able to stop theft completely, it's encouraging to know that you can make a difference by following these practical suggestions.

1. *Involve employees in the creation of a theft policy.* It is not always clear what constitutes theft. Does your company prohibit the use of personal phone calls or using the copy machine for personal purposes? If so, violating these policies constitutes theft of company resources, although chances are good that few will think of them as such. The trick is to develop very clear policies about employee theft and to involve employees in the process of doing so. The more involved they are, the more they will "buy into" the policies and follow them. Once such policies are developed, of course, it is critical to articulate them carefully in a formal document (such as a policy manual or code of ethics) and to carefully train all employees in them.

2. *Communicate the costs of stealing.* Chances are good that someone in the accounting department of any company has a good idea of how much the company is losing each year due to employee theft. To the extent that this information is shared with other employees, along with a clear indication of how it costs them (e.g., through smaller raises and bonuses), many employees will think twice before they take company property for personal use.

3. *Treat people fairly.* Many employees who steal from their employers are doing so because they are trying to strike back at employers whom they believe have treated them unfairly in the past. Indeed, underpaid employees may steal company property in an effort to take for themselves what they are not being given by their company.

4. *Be a good role model.* One of the most effective things managers can do to discourage theft is to not engage in theft themselves. After all, to the extent that employees see their managers making personal phone calls, padding their expense accounts, or taking home office supplies, they are left with the message that doing these kinds of things is perfectly acceptable. When it comes to discouraging employee theft, "walking the talk" is very important.

You Be the Consultant

Sabotage in the Workplace

Life in your company has become tumultuous. Not only are people always on each others' backs, but also sometimes they get downright hostile to each other, sabotaging others' work. Even those who have not been involved are suffering the consequences—getting sick over the stress that's always in the air—and good employees are resigning. Answer the following questions using the material in this chapter.

1. What possible causes of the problem would you consider and why?

2. Assuming that these causes are real, what advice would you offer about how to eliminate the problem?

3. What steps would you advise taking to help reduce the negative effects of stress that are likely to arise in this workplace?

Self-Assessment Exercise

Assessing Your Personal Orientation Toward Others

On page 231 you read descriptions of four different personal orientations toward others—*competitors, individualists, cooperators,* and *equalizers.* As you read these, you probably developed some ideas as to which orientation best describes you. This exercise is designed to help you find out.

Directions

Use the following scale to indicate how well each of the following statements describes you.

1 = Does not describe me at all/never
2 = Describes me somewhat/some of the time
3 = Describes me moderately/half of the time

4 = Describes me greatly/much of the time

5 = Describes me perfectly/all of the time

_____ 1. I don't care how much money one of my coworkers earns, so long as I make as much as I can.

_____ 2. When playing a game with a close friend, I always try to keep the score close.

_____ 3. So long as I do better than the next guy, I'm happy.

_____ 4. I will gladly give up something for myself if it can help my team get ahead.

_____ 5. It's important to me to be the best in the class, even if I'm not doing my personal best.

_____ 6. I feel badly if I do too much better than my friends on a class assignment.

_____ 7. I want to get an A in this class regardless of what grade others might get.

_____ 8. I enjoy it when the people in my work team all pitch in together to beat other teams.

Scoring

Insert the numbers corresponding to your answers to each of the questions in the spaces corresponding to those questions. Then add the numbers in each column (these can range from 2 to 10). The higher your score, the more accurately the personal orientation heading that column describes you.

Competitor	Individualist	Cooperator	Equalizer
3. _____	1. _____	4. _____	2. _____
5. _____	7. _____	8. _____	6. _____
Total = _____	Total = _____	Total = _____	Total = _____

Discussion Questions

1. What did this exercise reveal to you about yourself?

2. Were you surprised at what you learned, or was it something you already knew?

3. Do you tend to maintain the same orientation most of the time, or are there occasions in which you change from one orientation to another? What do you think this means?

Group Exercise

Negotiating the Price of a Used Car

This exercise is designed to help you put into practice some of the skills associated with being a good negotiator. In completing this exercise, follow the steps for negotiating a win–win solution found on pages 237–238.

Steps

1. Find a thorough description of a recent-model used car in the newspaper.

2. Divide the class into groups of six. Within each group, assign three students to the role of buyer and three to the role of seller.

3. Each group of buyers and sellers should meet in advance to plan their strategies. Buyers should plan on getting the lowest possible price; sellers should seek the highest possible price.

4. Buyers and sellers should meet to negotiate the price of the car within the period of time specified by the instructor. Feel free to meet within your groups at any time to evaluate your strategy.

5. Write down the final agreed-upon price and any conditions that may be attached to it.

Discussion Questions

1. Did you reach an agreement? If so, how easy or difficult was this process?

2. Which side do you think "won" the negotiation? What might have changed the outcome?

3. How might the negotiation process or the outcome have been different had this been a real situation?

Notes

Case Notes

Charny, B. (2003, January 14). Sendo sues Microsoft over "secret plan." *CNET News.com.* From the World Wide Web at zdnet.com.com/2100-1106-980463.html. Reinhardt, A., & Greene, J. (2003, February 10). Death of a dream. *BusinessWeek,* pp. 44–45.

Chapter Notes

[1] Rousseau, D. M. (2001). Schema, promise, and mutuality: The building blocks of the psychological contract. *Journal of Occupational and Organizational Psychology, 74,* 511–541. Robinson, S. L., & Morrison, E. W. (2000). The development of psychological contract breach violation: A longitudinal study. *Journal of Organizational Behavior, 21,* 525–546.

[2] Rousseau, D. M., & Parks, J. M. (1993). The contracts of individuals and organizations. In L. L. Cummings & B. M. Staw (Eds.), *Research in organizational behavior* (Vol. 15, pp. 1–43). Greenwich, CT: JAI Press. Turnley, W. H., & Feldman, D. C. (2000). Reexamining the effects of psychological contract violations: Unmet expectations and job dissatisfaction as mediators. *Journal of Organizational Behavior, 21,* 25–42.

[3] Lewicki, R. J., McAllister, D. J., & Bies, R. J. (1998). Trust and distrust: New relationships and realities. *Academy of Management Review, 23,* 438–458.

[4] Lewicki, R. J., & Wiethoff, C. (2000). Trust, trust development, and trust repair. In M. Deutsch & P. T. Coleman (Eds.), *The handbook of conflict resolution* (pp. 86–107). San Francisco: Jossey-Bass.

[5] Chapman, C. (2002, September/October). The human side of business. *BizEd,* pp. 20–25.

[6] Schultz, H., & Yang, D. J. (1999). *Pour your heart into it: How Starbucks built a company one cup at a time.* New York: Hyperion.

[7] Podsakoff, P. M., MacKenzie, S. B., Paine, J. B., & Bachrach, D. G. (2000). Organizational citizenship behaviors: A critical review of the theoretical and empirical literature and suggestions for future research. *Journal of Management, 26,* 513–563.

[8] Zellars, K. L., Tepper, B. J., & Duffy, M. K. (2002). Abusive supervision and subordinates' organizational citizenship behavior. *Journal of Applied Psychology, 87,* 1068–1076.

[9] See Note 1.

[10] Fomburn, C. J. (1996). *Reputation.* Boston: Harvard Business School Press.

[11] Turley, W. H., Bolino, M. C., Lester, S. W., & Bloodgood, J. M. (2003). The impact of psychological contract fulfillment on the performance of in-role and organizational citizenship behaviors. *Journal of Management, 29,* 187–206. Coyle-Shapiro, J. A-M. (2002). A psychological contract perspective on organizational citizenship behavior. *Journal of Organizational Behavior, 23,* 927–946.

[12] Gundlach, M. J., Scott, D. S., & Martinko, M. J. (2003). The decision to blow the whistle: A social information processing framework. *Academy of Management Review, 28,* 107–123. Miceli, M., & Near, J. (1992). *Blowing the whistle.* Lexington, MA: New Lexington Press.

[13] Fricker, D. G. (2002, March 27). Enron whistle-blower honored in Dearborn. From the World Wide Web at www.freep.com/money/business/htm. Anonymous. (2000, April). Paul van Buitenen: Paying the price of accountability. *Accountancy, 125*(1), 280. Taylor, M. (1999, September 13). Another Columbia suit unsealed. *Modern Healthcare, 29*(37), 10. Ettore, B. (1994, May). Whistleblowers: Who's the real bad guy? *Management Review,* pp. 18–23.

[14] Gjersten, L. A. (1999). Five State Farm agents fired after accusing company of consumer abuse. *National Underwriter, 103*(51), 1, 23.

[15] Martucci, W. C., & Smith, E. W. (2000). Recent state legislative development concerning employment discrimination and whistle-blower protections. *Employment Relations Today, 27*(2), 89–99.

[16] Jones, M., & Rowell, A. (1999). Safety whistleblowers intimidated. *Safety and Health Practitioner, 17*(8), 3.

[17] Falk, A., Gachter, S., & Kovacs, J. (1999). Intrinsic motivation and extrinsic incentives in a repeated game with incomplete contracts. *Journal of Economic Psychology, 20,* 251–284.

[18] Knight, G. P., Dubro, A. F., & Chao, C. (1985). Information processing and the development of cooperative, competitive, and individualistic social values. *Developmental Psychology, 21,* 37–45.

[19] Knight, G. P., & Dubro, A. F. (1984). Cooperative, competitive, and individualistic social values: An individualized regression and clustering approach. *Journal of Personality and Social Psychology, 46,* 98–105.

[20] Kirkman, B. L., & Shapiro, D. L. (2000). Understanding why team members won't share: An examination of factors related to employee receptivity to team-based rewards. *Small Group Research, 31,* 175–209. DeMatteo, J. S., Eby, L. T., & Sundstrom, E. (1998). Team-based rewards: Current empirical evidence and directions for future research. In B. M. Staw & L. L. Cummings (Eds.), *Research in organizational behavior* (Vol. 20, pp. 141–183). Greenwich, CT: JAI. Heneman, R.L. (2000). *Business-driven compensation policies.* New York: Amacom.

[21] Teerlink, R., & Ozley, L. (2000). *More than a motorcycle: The leadership journey at Harley-Davidson.* Boston: Harvard Business School Press.

[22] Thomas, K. W., & Schmidt, W. H. (1976). A survey of managerial interests with respect to conflict. *Academy of Management Journal, 10,* 315–318.

[23] Dirks, K. T., & McLean Parks, J. (2003). Conflicting stories: The state of the science of conflict. In J. Greenberg (Ed.), *Organizational behavior: The state of the science,* 2nd ed. (pp. 283–324). Mahwah, NJ: Lawrence Erlbaum Associates.

[24] Jehn, K., & Mannix, E. (2001). The dynamic nature of conflict: A longitudinal study of intragroup conflict and performance. *Academy of Management Journal, 44,* 238–251.

[25] Bragg, T. (1999, October). Ten ways to deal with conflict. *IIE Solutions,* pp. 36–37.

[26] Resume: Howard Schultz (2002, September 9). *BusinessWeek Online.* From the World Wide Web at www.businessweek.com/magazine/content/02_36/b3798005.htm.

[27] Lee, M. (1998, October 12). "See you in court—er, mediation." *Business Week Enterprise,* pp. ENT22, ENT24.

[28] Bordwin, M. (1999). Do-it-yourself justice. *Management Review,* pp. 56–58.

[29] Greenberg, J. (2004). Deviance. In N. Nicholson, P. Audia, & M. Pillutla (Eds.), *Blackwell encyclopedia of organizational behavior,* 2nd ed. Malden, MA: Blackwell. Bennett, R. J., & Robinson, S. L. (2003). The past, present, and future of workplace deviance research. In J. Greenberg (Ed.), *Organizational behavior: The state of the science* (pp. 247–282). Mahwah, NJ: Lawrence Erlbaum Associates. Vardi, Y., & Weitz, E. (2003). *Misbehavior in organizations: Theory, research, management.* Mahwah, NJ: Lawrence Erlbaum Associates.

[30] Bennett, R. J., & Robinson, S. L. (2000). The development of a measure of workplace deviance. *Journal of Applied Psychology, 85,* 349–360. Robinson, S. L., & Bennett, R. J. (1995). A typology of deviant workplace behaviors: A multidimensional scaling study. *Academy of Management Journal, 38,* 555–572.

[31] Bidoli, M., & Eedes, J. (2001, February 16). Big Brother is watching you. *Future Company.* From the World Wide Web at www.futurecompany.co.za/2001/02/16/covstory.htm.

[32] Mastrangelo, P., Everton, W., & Jolton, J. (2001). *Computer misuse in the workplace.* Unpublished manuscript. University of Baltimore. Lim, V. K. G., Loo, G. L., & Teo, T. S. H. (2001, August). *Perceived injustice, neutralization and cyberloafing at the workplace.* Paper presented at the Academy of Management, Washington, DC.

[33] See Note 29.

[34] National Institute for Occupational Safety and Health, Centers for Disease Control and Prevention. (1993). *Homicide in the workplace.* [Document \# 705003]. Atlanta, GA: Author.

[35] Jockin, V., Arvey, R. D., & McGue, M. (2001). Perceived victimization moderates self-reports of workplace aggression and conflict. *Journal of Applied Psychology, 86,* 1262–1269.

[36] Douglas, S. C., & Martinko, M. J. (2001). Exploring the role of individual differences in the prediction of workplace aggression. *Journal of Applied Psychology, 86,* 547–559.

[37] LeBlanc, M. M., & Kelloway, E. K. (2002). Predictors and outcomes of workplace violence and aggression. *Journal of Applied Psychology, 87,* 444–453.

[38] Varita, M., & Jari, R. (2002). Gender differences in workplace bullying among prison officers. *European Journal of Work and Occupational Psychology, 11,* 113–126.

[39] Cowie, H., Naylor, P., Rivers, I., Smith, P. K., & Pereira, B. (2002). Measuring workplace bullying. *Aggression and Violent Behavior, 7,* 33–51.

[40] Namie, G. (2000). *U.S. hostile workplace survey, 2000.* Benicia, CA: Campaign Against Workplace Bullying.

[41] Namie, G., & Namie, R. (2001). *The bully at work.* Naperville, IL: Sourcebooks.

[42] Trevino, L. K., & Weaver, G. R. (1998). Punishment in organizations: Descriptive and normative perspectives. In M. Schminke (Ed.), *Managerial ethics: Moral management of people and processes* (pp. 99–114). Mahwah, NJ: Erlbaum.

[43] Lind, E. A., Greenberg, J., Scott, K. S., & Welchans, T. D. (2000). The winding road from employee to complainant: Situational and psychological determinants of wrongful-termination claims. *Administrative Science Quarterly, 45,* 557–590 .

[44] Kooker, N. R. (2000, May 22). Taking aim at crime—stealing the profits: Tighter controls, higher morale may safeguard bottom line. *Nation's Restaurant News, 34*(21), 114–118. Young, D. (2000, May 1). Inside jobs. *Wireless Review, 17*(9), 14–20. Rosner, B. (1999, October). How do you feel about video surveillance at work? *Workforce, 78*(10), 26–27. Anonymous. (1999, May). As new CCTV system goes live, cashiers quit. *Security, 36*(5), 40. Wells, J. T. (1999, August). A fistful of dollars. *Security Management, 43*(8), 70–75. Vara, B. (1999, June). The "steal trap." *National Petroleum News, 91*(6), 28–31. Wimmer, N. (1999, June). Fingers in the till. *Asian Business, 35*(6), 59–60. Golden, P. (1999, May). Dangers without, dangers within. *Electronic Business, 25*(5), 65–70.

[45] Jabbkerm, A. (2000, March 29). Agrium seeks $30 million in damages in embezzlement case. *Chemical Week, 162*(13), 22.

[46] Greenberg, J. (1998). The cognitive geometry of employee theft: Negotiating "the line" between taking and stealing. In R. W. Griffin, A. O'Leary-Kelly, & J. M. Collins (Eds.), *Dysfunctional behavior in organizations: Non-violent dysfunctional behavior* (pp. 147–194). Stamford, CT: JAI Press.

[47] Greenberg, J., & Tomlinson, E. (in press). Methodological issues in the study of employee theft. In R. Griffin & A. O'Leary-Kelley (Eds.), *The dark side of organizational behavior.* San Francisco, CA: Pfeiffer.

Chapter **Eight**

LEARNING OBJECTIVES

After reading this chapter, you will be able to:

1. **DEFINE** communication and **DESCRIBE** the various steps in the communication process.

2. **RECOGNIZE** the differences between formal and informal communication in organizations.

3. **DISTINGUISH** between verbal communication—both traditional and computer mediated—and nonverbal communication, and the factors that make each effective.

4. **IDENTIFY** various inspirational techniques that can be used to enhance one's effectiveness as a communicator.

5. **DESCRIBE** what it takes to be a supportive communicator.

6. **EXPLAIN** how to meet the challenges associated with communicating with people from different cultures.

Organizational Communication

Without Mr. Sam, Wal-Mart Still Listens—Only Not as Much

The late Sam Walton, founder of Wal-Mart, never fit the image of the hard-driving business tycoon who readily sacrifices the well-being of his employees in exchange for boosting his company's bottom line. Then again, Walton never had to choose between people and profits because, as he saw it, they were inextricably connected. Despite Wal-Mart's meticulous attention to cost-cutting methods that helped the company prosper, Walton always insisted that the key to the company's success was its homespun, rural American values embracing open and honest communication with people. "If you're good to people, and fair with them, and demanding of them, they will eventually decide that you're on their side," Walton says in his autobiography.

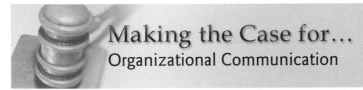

Making the Case for...
Organizational Communication

Showing that he meant this, it was not unusual for Walton to make unscheduled in-person visits to stores. Coming through the front door, "Mr. Sam," as he was called, would announce his presence on the PA system, grab some crackers off the shelf, and set up shop with associates in the back of the store, where he would spend hours chatting with them, carefully listening to their ideas and concerns. More than just demonstrating his folksiness by dropping in for an occasional chat, Walton also initiated an open-door policy that encouraged workers to bring their concerns to top managers at any time (a practice that was new when Walton started it but that since has been copied widely in the retail world). Communicating with employees was so central to Walton's business philosophy that he emphasized it as one of *Sam's Rules for Building a Business*: "Communicate everything you possibly can to your partners. The more they know, the more they'll understand. The more they understand, the more they'll care. Once they care, there's no stopping them."

When Sam Walton died in 1992, many believe that at least some of this philosophy passed on with him. The blue aprons donned by store employees that used to boast, "Our people make the difference" now read, "How may I help you?" Although it may be a small thing, some think that the change is telling of a company that shifted its concern from its employees to its customers. Company spokesman Jay Allen disagrees, noting, "If we didn't . . . operate in an open-door environment, we would not be living up to the expectations that our associates have of us."

Although Sam Walton is no longer around to visit his employees, he would be pleased to know that the business he built is now five times larger than it was at the time of his death. In fact, with 3,500 stores generating $220 billion in annual revenue and three times the number of employees as General Motors, Wal-Mart is easily the largest company in the United States. However, many claim that this rapid expansion, along with the practice of keeping stores open 24 hours a day, has led to a deterioration of communication between workers and managers—a fate that Mr. Sam would have found unacceptable. As one analyst put it, "Managers (most of whom work the day shift and get in at 7 A.M.) barely interact with the employees who work the peak afternoon and evening selling times. Expecting the personal touch in stores this huge . . . seems like wishful thinking at best." To some company veterans who longingly recall sharing ideas with Mr. Sam—even if nothing happened as a result—today's Wal-Mart may have "everyday low prices" but not the same everyday connection to its employees.

GOOD REASONS why you should care about...

Organizational Communication

You should care about organizational communication because:

1. Although managers spend a great deal of time communicating with others, they tend not to do so as effectively as possible.

2. Properly managing organizational communication is key to individual and organizational effectiveness.

3. Being a good communicator can help you advance to a higher organizational position.

Sam Walton was a special individual, to be sure, but the key to his success demonstrated in this case—good communication with employees—is not at all mysterious. *Communication* is a basic function of all managers' jobs—the processes through which people send information to others and receive information from them. Although few have honed their communication skills to the same high level as Mr. Sam, fundamental communication skills are a basic ingredient for organizational success. Everyone involved in organizations, from the lowest-level employee to the head of a large corporation, needs to be able to communicate effectively. Fortunately, improving communication skills, at least somewhat, is a manageable task. With this in mind, this chapter will focus on two key aspects of communication: how the communication process works and how to improve communication in organizations.

learning
objective

The Communication Process

For organizations to function, individuals and teams must coordinate their efforts and activities carefully. Waiters must take their customers' orders and pass them along to the chef. Store managers must describe special promotions to their sales staffs. And the football coach must tell his team what plays to run. Clearly, communication is the key to these attempts at coordination. Without it, people would not know what to do, and groups and organizations would not be able to operate effectively—if at all!

With this in mind, it should not be surprising that communication has been referred to as "the social glue . . . that continues to keep organizations tied together,"[1] and "the essence of organizations."[2] Given the importance of communication in organizations, you may not be surprised to learn that managers spend as much as 80 percent of their time in one form of communication or another (e.g., writing reports, sending e-mails, talking to others in person, etc.). I will begin discussing organizational communication by formally describing the communication process and then describing some of the forms it takes. Then, building on this foundation, I will describe several ways of improving organizational communication.

Steps in the Communication Process

Formally, **communication** is defined as the process by which a person, group, or organization (the *sender*) transmits some type of information (the *message*) to another person, group, or organization (the *receiver*). Figure 8.1 clarifies this definition and further elaborates on the process.

Encoding.   The communication process begins when one party has a message it wishes to send another (either party may be an individual, a group, or an entire organization). It is the sender's mission to transform the idea into a form that can be sent to and understood by the receiver. This is what happens in the process of **encoding**—translating an idea into a form, such as written or spoken language, that can be recognized by a receiver. We encode information when we select the words we use to send an e-mail message or when we speak to someone in person.

Transmission via communication channels.   After a message is encoded, it is ready to be transmitted over one or more **channels of communication** to reach the desired

Figure 8.1   The Communication Process

Communication generally follows the steps outlined here. Senders *encode* messages and *transmit* them via one or more communication channels to receivers, who then *decode* these messages received. The process continues as the original receiver then sends *feedback* to the original sender. Factors distorting or limiting the flow of information—known collectively as *noise*—may enter into the process at any point.

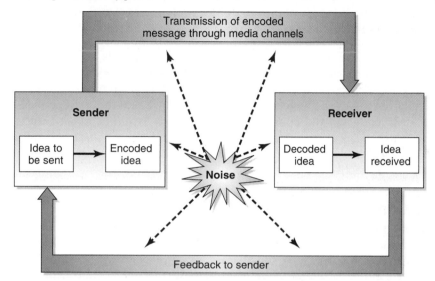

receiver. There are many different pathways over which information travels, including telephone lines, radio and television signals, fiber-optic cables, mail routes, and even the airwaves that carry the vibrations of our voices. Thanks to modern technology, people sending messages have a wide variety of communication channels available to them for sending both visual and oral information. Whatever channel is used, the communicator's goal is the same: to send the encoded message accurately to the desired receiver.

Decoding.   Once a message is received, the recipient must begin the process of **decoding**—that is, converting that message back into the sender's original ideas. This can involve many different processes, such as comprehending spoken and written words, interpreting facial expressions, and the like. To the extent that a sender's message is accurately decoded by the receiver, the ideas understood will be the ones intended.

As you might imagine, our ability to comprehend and interpret information received from others is far from perfect. This would be the case, for example, if we were conducting business in a foreign country and lacked the language skills needed to understand the speaker. However, even when it comes to understanding one's own native language, it's only too easy to imagine how we sometimes misunderstand what others intend to say.

Feedback.   Once a message has been decoded, the process of communication can continue but in reverse. In other words, the person receiving the message now becomes the sender of a new message. This new message is then encoded and transmitted along a communication channel to the intended recipient, who then decodes it. This part of the communication process is known as **feedback**—providing information about the impact of messages on receivers. Receiving feedback allows senders to determine whether their messages have been understood properly. Of course, once received, feedback can trigger another idea from the sender, initiating yet another cycle of communication and triggering another round of feedback. It was with this cyclical nature of the communication process in mind that we characterize the communication process in Figure 8.1 as being continuous.

Noise.   Despite its apparent simplicity, it probably comes as no surprise that the communication process rarely operates as flawlessly as I have described it here. As you will see, there are many potential barriers to effective communication. **Noise** is the name given to factors that distort the clarity of messages that are encoded, transmitted, or decoded in the communication process. Whether noise results from unclear writing (i.e., poorly encoded messages), a listener's inattentiveness (i.e., poorly decoded messages), or static along a telephone line (i.e., faulty communication media), ineffective communication is inevitably the result.

learning
objective

Formal Communication in Organizations

Imagine a CEO of a large conglomerate announcing plans for new products to a group of stockholders. Now, imagine a supervisor telling her subordinates what to do that day on the job. Both examples describe situations in which someone is sharing official information with others who need to know this information. This is referred to as **formal communication**. The formally prescribed pattern of interrelationships existing between the various units of an organization is commonly described by using a diagram known as an **organization chart**. Such diagrams provide a graphic representation of an organization's structure, an outline of the planned, formal connections between its various units—that is, who is supposed to communicate with whom.

An organization chart revealing the structure of a small part of a fictitious organization, and an overview of the types of communication expected to occur within it, is shown in Figure 8.2. Each box represents a particular job, as indicated by the job titles noted. The lines connecting the boxes show the formal lines of communication between the individuals performing those jobs—that is, who is supposed to communicate with whom. This particular organization chart is typical of most in that it shows that people communicate formally with those immediately above them and below them, as well as those at their own levels.

Downward communication.   Formal communication differs according to people's positions in an organization chart. Suppose, for example, that you are a supervisor. How would you characterize the formal communication that occurs between you and your subordinates—that is, communication down the organization chart? Typically, *downward communication* consists of instructions, directions, and orders—that is, messages telling subordinates what they should be doing. We also would expect to find feedback on past performance flowing in a downward direction. A sales manager, for example, may tell the members of her sales force what products they should be promoting.

Figure 8.2   The Organization Chart: A Summary of Formal Communication Paths

Diagrams known as *organization charts* indicate the formal pattern of communication within an organization. They reveal which particular people, based on the jobs they hold, are required to communicate with each other. The types of messages generally communicated across different levels are identified here.

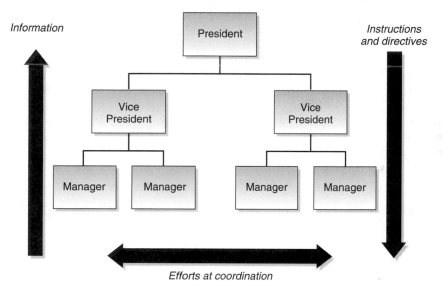

As formal information slowly trickles down from one level of an organization to the next lowest level (as occurs when information is said to "go through channels"), it becomes less accurate. This is especially true when that information is spoken. In such cases, it is not unusual for at least part of the message to be distorted and/or omitted as it works its way down from one person to the next lowest-ranking person. (Anyone who has ever played the game of "telephone" has experienced this firsthand.) To avoid these problems, many companies have introduced programs in which they communicate formal information to large numbers of people at different levels all at one time.

Upward communication.   When information flows from lower levels to higher levels within an organization, such as messages from subordinates to their supervisors, it is known as *upward communication*. Typically, such messages involve information that managers need to do their jobs, such as data required to complete projects. This may include suggestions for improvement, status reports, reactions to work-related issues, and new ideas.

Although logically upward communication is the opposite of downward communication, there are some important differences between them resulting from difference in status between the communicating parties. For example, it has been established that upward communication occurs far less frequently than downward communication. In fact, one classic study found that 70 percent of assembly-line workers initiated communication with their supervisors less than once a month.

And, when people do communicate upward, their conversations tend to be far shorter than the ones they have with others at their own level.

Even more importantly, when upward communication does occur, the information transmitted is frequently inaccurate. Given that employees are interested in "putting their best foot forward" when communicating with their bosses, they have a tendency to highlight their accomplishments and to downplay their mistakes. As a result, negative information tends to be ignored or disguised. This tendency for people to purposely avoid communicating bad news to their supervisors is known as the **MUM effect**. We are concerned about this phenomenon because supervisors can only make good decisions when they have good information available to them. And, when subordinates are either withholding or distorting information so as to avoid looking bad, the accuracy of the information communicated is bound to suffer. As one executive put it, "All of us have our share of bonehead ideas. Having someone tell you it's a bonehead idea before you do something about is really a great blessing."[3] Unfortunately, this does not occur as much as many executives would like. In fact, a recent survey has found that although 95 percent of CEOs say that they have an open-door policy and will not harm those who communicate bad news, still half of all employees believe that they will be jeopardizing their positions by sharing bad news, and frequently refrain from doing so.[4]

> Although 95 percent of CEOs say that they have an open-door policy and will not harm those who communicate bad news, still half of all employees believe that they will be jeopardizing their positions by sharing bad news.

Horizontal communication.   Within organizations messages don't only flow up and down the organization chart, but sideways as well. **Horizontal communication** is the term used to identify messages that flow laterally, at the same organizational level. Messages of this type are characterized by efforts at coordination, attempts to work together. Consider, for example, how a vice president of marketing would have to coordinate her efforts with people in other departments when launching an advertising campaign for a new product. This would require the coordination of information with experts from manufacturing and production (to see when the products will be available) as well as those from research and development (to see what features people really want).

Unlike vertical communication, in which the parties are at different organizational levels, horizontal communication involves people at the same level. Therefore, it tends to be easier and friendlier. It also is more casual in tone and occurs more readily given that there are fewer social barriers between the parties. This is not to say that horizontal communication is without its potential pitfalls. Indeed, people in different departments sometimes feel that they are competing against each other for valued organizational resources, leading them to show resentment toward one another. And when an antagonistic, competitive orientation replaces a friendly, cooperative one, work is bound to suffer.

Informal Communication: Beyond the Organization Chart

Imagine a group of workers standing around the coffee machine chatting about how tough the big boss is or who was dancing with whom at the company party. These are also examples of organizational communication, but because they involve the sharing of unofficial information, they would be considered examples of **informal communication**.

It's probably obvious to you that a great deal of information communicated in organizations goes far beyond sending formal messages up, down, or across organization charts. Such information is shared without any formally imposed obligations or restrictions.

Hearing it "through the grapevine."   When people communicate informally, they are not bound by their organizational positions. Anyone can tell anything to anyone else. Although it clearly would be inappropriate for a mail room clerk to share his thoughts with a vice president about matters of corporate policy, both parties may be perfectly at ease exchanging funny stories. The difference lies in the fact that the funny stories are unofficial in nature and are communicated informally—that is, without following the formal constraints imposed by the organization chart.

When anyone can tell something informally to anyone else, it results in a very rapid flow of information along what is commonly called **the grapevine**. This term refers to the pathways along which unofficial information travels. In contrast to formal organizational messages, which might take several days to reach their destinations, information traveling along the organizational grapevine tends to flow very rapidly. In fact, it is not unusual for some messages to reach everyone in a large organization in a matter of a few hours. This happens not only because informal communication crosses organizational boundaries and is open to everyone, but also because it generally is transmitted orally, and oral messages not only reach more people but also do so more quickly than written messages.

As we noted earlier, however, oral messages run the risk of becoming inaccurate as they flow between people. Because of the possible confusion grapevines can cause, some people have sought to eliminate them. However, they are not necessarily bad. In fact, informally socializing with our coworkers can help make work groups more cohesive, and they also may provide excellent opportunities for the pleasant social contacts that make life at work enjoyable. Moreover, the grapevine remains one of the most efficient channels of communication. Indeed, about 70 percent of what people learn about their companies they pick up by chatting with coworkers in the cafeteria, at the coffee machine, or in the corridors.[5]

Rumors: The downside of informal communication.   Although the information communicated along the grapevine may be accurate in some respects, it may be inaccurate in others. In extreme cases information may be transmitted that is almost totally without any basis in fact and is unverifiable. Such messages are known as **rumors**. Typically, rumors are based on speculation, someone's overactive imagination, and wishful thinking, rather than on facts.

Rumors race like wildfire through organizations because the information they contain is usually so interesting and vague. This ambiguity leaves messages open to embellishment as they pass orally from one person to the next. Before you know it, almost everyone in the organization has heard the rumor, and its inaccurate message comes to be taken as fact ("Everyone knows it, so it must be true"). Hence, even if there may have been, at one point, some truth to a rumor, the message quickly grows untrue.

If you personally have ever been the victim of a rumor, you know just how troublesome it can be. Now, imagine how many times more serious the consequences may be when an organization falls victim to a rumor. Two extreme cases come to mind. In the late 1970s, a rumor circulated in Chicago that McDonald's hamburgers contained worms.

In the late 1970s, a rumor circulated in Chicago that McDonald's hamburgers contained worms. Also, in June 1993 stories appeared in the press stating that people had found syringes in cans of Pepsi-Cola. Although both rumors were proven to be completely untrue, they cost both McDonald's and Pepsi considerable sums of money.

Also, in June 1993 stories appeared in the press stating that people had found syringes in cans of Pepsi-Cola. Although both rumors were proven to be completely untrue, they cost both McDonald's and Pepsi considerable sums of money due to lost sales, not to mention the costs of investigation and advertising.

With this in mind, the question arises: What can be done to counter the effects of rumors? You may be tempted to consider directly refuting a rumor. This approach works best whenever a rumor is highly implausible and is challenged immediately by an independent source. This was precisely what occurred when the Food and Drug Administration (FDA) carefully investigated Pepsi-Cola and announced that there were not, nor could there have been, syringes in cans of Pepsi. In the case of McDonald's, direct refutations (in the form of signs from the FDA stating that McDonald's used only wholesome ground beef in its burgers) had little effect because the rumor had spread so rapidly. In fact, directly challenging the rumor only led some customers to raise questions about why such official government statements were necessary in the first place, thereby fueling the rumor. What worked best at countering the rumor, research showed, was reminding people about other things they already believed about McDonald's (e.g., that it is a clean, family-oriented place).[6] Not surprisingly, advertising campaigns (including public relations efforts by politicians rumored to be involved in various scandals) frequently devote more time to redirecting the public's attention away from negative thoughts and toward positive ones that they already have.

3

learning objective

Communicating With and Without Words: Verbal and Nonverbal Communication

By virtue of the fact that you are reading this book, I know that you are familiar with **verbal communication**—transmitting and receiving ideas using words. Verbal communication can be either oral—that is, using spoken language, such as face-to-face talks or telephone conversations—or written, such as faxes, letters, or e-mail messages. It also can occur either with the assistance of computers (in which case it is known as computer-mediated communication) or without the assistance of computers (in which case it is known as traditional communication). Despite their differences, these forms of communication share a key feature: They all involve the use of words. As you know, however, people also communicate a great deal without words, nonverbally—that is, by way of their facial gestures, body language, the clothes they wear, and even where at a table they choose to sit. This is referred to as **nonverbal communication**. In this section I will describe verbal communication media, both traditional and computer mediated, as well as nonverbal communication.

Traditional Verbal Media: Their Forms and Effectiveness

As you already know, organizations rely on a wide variety of verbal media. Some forms are considered rich because they are highly interactive and rely on a great deal of information. A face-to-face discussion is a good example. A telephone conversation may be considered a little less rich because it doesn't allow the parties to see each other. At the other end of the continuum are communications media that are considered lean because they are static (one-way) and involve much less information. Flyers and bulletins are good examples insofar as they are broadly aimed and focus on a specific issue. Letters also are a relatively lean form of communication. However, because letters are aimed at a specific individual, they may be considered not as lean as bulletins. For a summary of this continuum, please refer to Figure 8.3.[7]

Forms of written communication.   Although organizations rely on a wide variety of written media, two particular forms—*newsletters* and *employee handbooks*—deserve special mention because of the important roles they play. **Newsletters** are regularly published internal documents describing information of interest to employees regarding an array of business and nonbusiness issues. Traditionally, these are printed on paper, but today a great many company newsletters are published online, using the company's **intranet**—a Web site that only can be accessed by a company's employees. Many companies have found newsletters to be useful devices for explaining official policies and reminding everyone of important decisions made at group meetings. At the Widemeyer-Baker Group, a 75-person media relations firm, for example, employees use the company's intranet site to access an online newsletter that provides key information about what's going on in the company.[8] Particularly popular is a column called "The Buzz," which serves as a sort of electronic water cooler around which people gather to share information about others in the company.

> At the Widemeyer-Baker Group, a 75-person media relations firm, employees use the company's intranet site to access an online newsletter that provides key information about what's going on in the company.

Figure 8.3   A Continuum of Traditional Verbal Communication Media

Traditional verbal communication media may be characterized along a continuum ranging from highly rich, interactive media (e.g., face-to-face discussions) to lean, static media (e.g., flyers and bulletins).

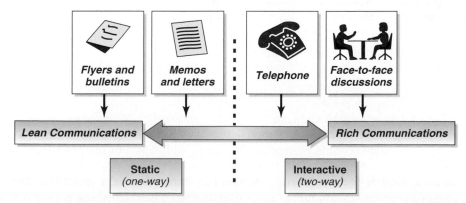

(Source: Based on information in Lengel and Daft, 1988; see Note 7.)

Employee handbooks also are important vehicles of internal organizational communication. These are formal documents describing basic information about the organization—its formal policies, mission, and underlying philosophy. Handbooks are widely used today. Not only do they do an effective job socializing new employees into the company (see Chapter 4), but the explicit statements they provide also may help avoid serious misunderstandings and conflict between employees and their company's top management (see Chapter 7).

The effectiveness of verbal media: Matching the medium and the message.   Given that people in organizations spend so much of their time using both oral and written communication, it makes sense to ask: Which is more effective? As you might imagine, the answer is rather complex. For example, we know that communication is most effective in organizations when it uses multiple channels—that is, *both* oral and written messages.[9] Oral messages help get people's immediate attention. Then written follow-ups are helpful because they provide permanent documents to which people later can refer. Oral messages also have the benefit of allowing for immediate two-way communication between parties, whereas written messages frequently are either one-way or take too long for a response. Not surprisingly, in organizations two-way communications (such as face-to-face discussions and telephone calls) occur more frequently than one-way communications (e.g., memos).

The matter of how effectively a particular communications medium works depends on the kind of message being sent. In general, managers prefer using oral media when communicating ambiguous messages (e.g., directions on how to solve a complex technical problem) but written media for communicating clear messages (e.g., sharing a price list). This makes sense if you think about it. After all, when a message is ambiguous, managers will find it easier to express themselves orally, especially given that spoken messages often provide immediate feedback, making it possible to tell how well the other person is getting the point. However, when it comes to clear messages, putting them in writing is more effective insofar as it makes it easier for others to refer to them later on when needed. Not surprisingly, managers who follow this particular pattern of matching media with messages tend to be more effective on the job than those who do not do so. This suggests that demonstrating sensitivity to communicating in the most appropriate fashion is an important determinant of managerial success.

Computer-Mediated Communication

Today, a great deal of the verbal communication in which we engage in organizations occurs with the assistance of computers, a process known as **computer-mediated communication**. Although people continue to talk to others in person, of course, various forms of online communication, such as e-mail messaging, Web conferencing, and instant messaging, have become common in the workplace.[10] Not surprisingly, OB scientists have been involved in examining the nature and impact of this phenomenon.

Comparing face-to-face and online communication.   In recent years, our understanding of communication media has expanded from distinguishing between oral and written media to communication that occurs orally in one of two ways—either face-to-face or online. Comparing these two forms of communication is particularly important given the growing popularity of online conferencing, the practice of communicating with others virtually, using online technology that makes it possible to communicate with others live via Internet connections. Because the price of computer-based telecommunications equipment has been dropping, businesses have found online conferencing to be a highly cost-effective alternative to getting people together to discuss things in person. This leads to an important question: How do online communications between people differ from in-person discussions?

A recent study examined this question by comparing groups of people who were brought together to have in-person discussions on a defined topic with an approximately equal number of people who were brought together to discuss the same topic via an online conference.[11] This particular conference did not provide visual contact with others using Web cameras (i.e., it was not a videoconference). Rather, participants merely shared their remarks with others by typing them on a computer keyboard. Although both groups discussed the topic for approximately the same amount of time, one hour, the groups differed significantly in several different ways. As summarized in Figure 8.4, compared to members of online groups, members of face groups made fewer comments, but the comments they made were longer and more detailed. In other words, online participants were generally less likely to elaborate on the statements they made, failing to share equally deep insight into their ideas. Also, because members of online groups could not be seen, they were more inclined to rely on simple statements of agreement (e.g., "that's a good idea") in situations in which members of face-to-face groups would just nod. These findings suggest that face-to-face and online discussions may be used for different purposes. For example, market researchers may rely on online discussions to gather people's general and immediate reactions to new products. However, if they want to tap more detailed opinions, face-to-face discussions would appear to be a better choice.

Using "emoticons" to express emotions in e-mail.   Today, e-mail is one of the most common forms of communication, and some predict that it will even surpass face-to-face communication in popularity in the near future. As useful and as indispensable as e-mail has become, people sometimes find it frustrating to use e-mail to express their emotions. After all, traditional e-mail is limited to alphanumeric characters and lacks the nonverbal information that makes face-to-face communication so rich. Although you can change the tone of your voice or make a face to express how you feel about something, it's harder to do this using only the tools of the keyboard.

In recent years, however, people have, rather ingeniously, developed simple graphic representations of facial expressions to express emotions. Known as **emoticons**, short for "emotional icons," these are created by typing characters such as commas, hyphens, and parentheses, which are viewed by tilting one's head to the left (treating left as top). The most common emoticons are as follows:

:-)   smile

:-(frown

;-)   wink

People generally use emoticons to qualify their emotions in important ways, such as to communicate sarcasm. For example, the presence of the smiley face in the

Figure 8.4   Face-to-Face Versus Online Communication: An Experimental Comparison

A recent study compared the way people communicate with one another in person versus when having live online discussions. It was found that although members of online groups made more comments, the comments made by members of face-to-face groups were longer and more detailed. Also, because online groups could not use nonverbal gestures to communicate their points, they relied more heavily on brief verbal statements to indicate their agreement with others.

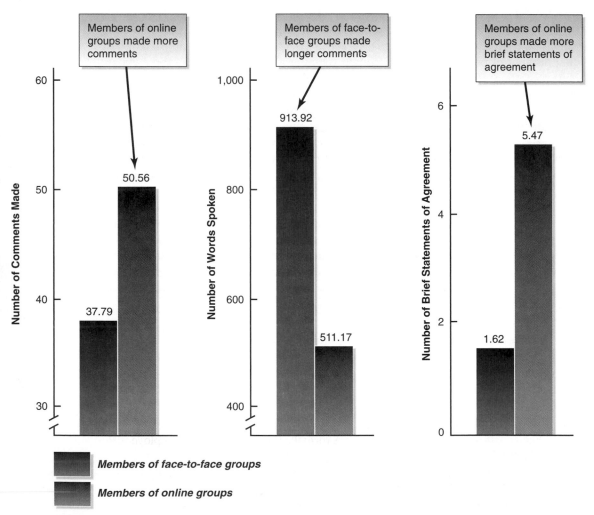

(Source: Based on data reported by Schneider et al., 2002; see Note 11.)

message, "he's really smart :-)" may be used to connote that the person in question is really not so smart at all.

However, recent research has revealed that emoticons do *not* always qualify the meanings of written messages.[12] For example, a negative message accompanied by a wink or a frown was not seen as being any more sarcastic or negative in tone than the words by themselves. For example, sending the message "That class was awful ;-)" was perceived to be as sarcastic as "That class was awful." Likewise, saying "That class was awful :-(" was perceived as negatively as "That class was awful." In the case of positive statements, the effects were interesting. Saying "That class was great :-)" suggested that the speaker was happier than saying "that class was great," but it did not send the message that the class was any better. In other words, emoticons don't always have the effects that the communicator intended. One possible reason for this is that emoticons tend to be overused, and as a result, their impact has diminished over time.

Additional research has shown some interesting sex differences in the use of emoticons.[13] In general, women use emoticons more frequently than men. However, when men are communicating with women, they use emoticons more frequently than they do when they are communicating with other men. This is in keeping with research showing that in general men feel more comfortable expressing their emotions to women than to other men. Interestingly, men and women use emoticons differently. Whereas women use emoticons to be humorous, men use them to be teasing and sarcastic. Yeah, right ;-).

In conclusion, you should be careful using emoticons because they don't always do a good job of getting your message across. In fact, using emoticons is more likely to send a message about the gender of the communicator than it is to qualify the emotional meaning of the message itself.

Nonverbal Communication

It has been estimated that people communicate at least as much *nonverbally* (i.e., without words) as they do verbally.[14] Indeed, there can be no doubt that many of the messages we send others are transmitted without words. Here are just a few examples of how we communicate nonverbally in organizations.

- *Mode of dress*—Much of what we say about ourselves to others comes from the way we dress. For example, despite the general trend toward casual clothing in the workplace, higher-status people tend to dress more formally than lower-ranking employees.[15]
- *Waiting time*—Higher-status people, such as managers and executives at all ranks, tend to communicate their organizational positions nonverbally by keeping lower-ranking people waiting to see them—a gesture that sends the message that one's time is more important.[16]
- *Seating position*—Higher-ranking people also assert their higher status by sitting at the heads of rectangular tables, a position that not only has become associated with importance over the years but that also enables important people to maintain eye contact with those for whom they are responsible.[17]

As you read this, you may be asking yourself, "What can I do to present myself more favorably to those around me on the job?" Specifically, what can you do nonverbally to cultivate the impression that you have the qualities of a good leader and that you are worthy of promotion? Just as you can say certain things to enhance

Table 8.1	How to Communicate Your Leadership Potential Nonverbally

People who are self-confident not only speak and write with assurance, but they also project their capacity to lead others in the various nonverbal ways summarized here.

- Stand and sit using an erect posture. Avoid slouching.
- When confronted, stand up straight. Do not cower.
- Nod your head to show that you are listening to someone talk.
- Maintain eye contact and smile at those with whom you are talking.
- Use hand gestures in a relaxed, nonmechanical way.
- Always be neat, well groomed, and wear clean, well-pressed clothes.

(Source: Based on suggestions by DuBrin, 2001; see Note 18.)

your image as a strong, effective employee, there also are several things you can do nonverbally that will enhance your image. For a summary of these, see Table 8.1.

learning objective

Improving Your Communication Skills

There can be no doubt that successful employees at all levels, from the lowest-ranking person to the CEO, stand to benefit by improving their verbal communication skills. Although there are far too many ways of improving your verbal communication than I possibly can review here, two general approaches are worthy of mention. These include using inspirational tactics and being a supportive communicator.

Use Inspirational Communication Tactics

Effective leaders know how to inspire others when they communicate with them. To become an effective leader, or even a more effective employee, it helps to consider several key ways of inspiring others when communicating with them.[18] These are as follows.

- *Project confidence and power with emotion-provoking words.* The most persuasive communicators attempt to inspire others by sprinkling their speech with words that provoke emotion. For example, it helps to use phrases such as "bonding with customers" instead of the more benign "being friendly." Effective communicators also use words in ways that highlight their power in an organization. For some linguistic tips in this regard, see Table 8.2.[19]
- *Be credible.* Communicators are most effective when they are perceived to be credible. Such perceptions are enhanced when one is considered trustworthy, intelligent, and knowledgeable. Bill Joy of Sun Microsystems (considered "the Thomas Edison of the Internet"), for example, has considerable credibility in the computer business because he is regarded to be so highly intelligent. At the very least, credibility is enhanced by backing up your claims with clear data. People might not believe you unless you support your ideas with objective information.
- *Pitch your message to the listener.* The most effective communicators go out of their way to send messages that are of interest to listeners. Assume that people will pay greatest

Table 8.2	How to Project Confidence with Your Words

The most powerful and confident people tend to follow certain linguistic conventions. By emulating the way they speak, you, too, can enhance the confidence you project.

Rule	*Explanation or Example*
Always know exactly what you want.	The more committed you are to achieving a certain end, the more clearly and powerfully you will be able to sell your idea.
Use the pronoun *I* unless you are a part of a team.	This allows you to take individual credit for your ideas.
Downplay uncertainty.	If you are unsure of your opinion, make a broad but positive statement, such as "I am confident this new accounting procedure will make things more efficient."
Ask very few questions.	You may come across as being weak or unknowledgeable if you have to ask what something means or what's going on.
Don't display disappointment when your ideas are challenged.	It is better to act as though opposition is expected and to explain your viewpoint.
Make bold statements.	Be bold about ideas, but avoid attacking anyone personally.

(Source: Based on suggestions by DuBrin, 2001; see Note 18.)

attention when they are interested in answering the question "how is what you are saying important to me?" People will attend most carefully to messages that have value to them. Jürgen E. Schrempp, the CEO of DaimlerChrysler, appeared to have this rule in mind when he explained how his plan for organizing the company into three divisions would result in higher salaries and bonuses for them, as well as greater autonomy.

■ *Avoid "junk words" that dilute your message.* Nobody likes to listen to people who constantly use phrases such as "like," "know what I mean?" and "you know." Such phrases send the message that the speaker is ill-prepared to express himself or herself clearly and precisely. Because many of us use such phrases in our everyday language, it helps to practice by tape-recording what you are going to say so you can keep track of the number of times you say these things. Make a conscious effort to stop saying these words, and use your tape-recordings to monitor your progress.

■ *Use front-loaded messages.* The most effective communicators come right out and say what they mean. They don't beat around the bush, and they don't embed their most important message in a long speech or letter. Instead, they begin by making the point they are attempting to communicate and then use the remainder of the message to illustrate it and flesh out the details.

■ *Cut through the clutter.* People are so busy these days that they easily become distracted by the many messages that come across their desks (see Figure 8.5).[20] The most effective communicators attempt to cut through the clutter, such as by making their messages interesting, important, and special. Dull and uninspiring messages are likely to get lost in the shuffle.

Figure 8.5 We Are Bombarded by Messages

The average U.S. office worker receives 189 messages per day—that's over 23 per hour. As summarized here, they come in many different forms.

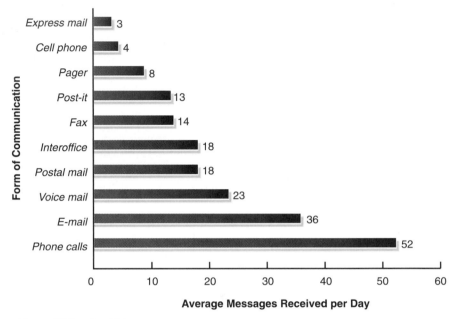

(Source: Wurman, 2000; see Note 20.)

5

learning objective

Be a Supportive Communicator

Thus far, I have been describing a way of being an effective communicator by being forceful and inspiring people. Good communicators, as you know, are also highly people oriented, requiring a low-key approach. To communicate effectively with others, we need to show that we are interested in what the other person has to say and respond in ways that strengthen the relationship between ourselves and the target of our messages. In short, we need to demonstrate what is called **supportive communication**. Doing this requires adhering to the following rules.[21]

- *Focus on the problem instead of the person.* Although people are generally receptive to ways of making things better, we all naturally resist suggestions that we somehow need to change ourselves. Saying, for example, "you need to be more creative," would lead most of us to become defensive and turn off the speaker. However, saying something more supportive, like "see if you can find a way of finding more solutions to this problem," is bound to meet with a far better reaction.

- *Match your words and your body language.* You can be a far more effective communicator when the things you say with your body match the words you use. For example, sending the message that you are excited about someone's idea is amplified by verbally explaining your satisfaction and nonverbally showing your excitement, such as by sitting up, looking alert, and opening your eyes widely. By contrast, crossing your arms, closing your eyes, and slumping while saying the same words would only detract from your message—if it even comes across at all.

- *Acknowledge the other person's ideas.* Even if you disagree with what someone is saying, you don't want to make that individual feel badly about expressing his or her ideas. Not only is this rude, but also it is a good way of getting people to keep their ideas to themselves, which interferes with effective management. So, for example, if you have to reject someone's suggestion, don't make that person feel badly by suggesting that the idea was silly and devoid of merit. Instead, it would be far more supportive to highlight the good aspects of that person's ideas but explain precisely why it would be inappropriate to implement it right now.

- *Keep the conversation going.* One sure way to block the exchange of ideas is to say or do things that stop conversations in their tracks. Long pauses may do this, as will saying things that change the topic. Effective communication requires keeping the conversation going, and this can be accomplished by listening carefully to what someone says and building on it when responding.

Encourage Open Feedback

In theory, it's simple: If accurate information is the key to effective communication, then organizations should encourage feedback since, after all, feedback is a prime source of information. However, we say "in theory" because it is natural for workers to be afraid of the repercussions they may face when being extremely open with their superiors. Likewise, high-ranking officials may be somewhat apprehensive about hearing what's really on their workers' minds. In other words, people in organizations may be reluctant to give and to receive feedback—a situation that can wreak havoc on organizational communication.

These problems would be unlikely to occur in an organizational climate in which top officials openly and honestly seek feedback and in which lower-level workers believe they can speak their minds with impunity. But how can this be accomplished? Although this is not easy, several successful techniques for opening feedback channels have been used by organizations. Some of the more popular approaches are listed next. However, for a close-up look at one company's novel approach to addressing this problem, see the accompanying **Winning Practices** section.

- **360-degree feedback**—Formal systems in which people at all levels give feedback to others at different levels and receive feedback from them, as well as outsiders—including customers and suppliers. This technique is used in such companies as Alcoa, BellSouth, General Mills, Hewlett-Packard, Merck, Motorola, and 3M.

- **Suggestion systems**—Programs that invite employees to submit ideas about how something may be improved. Employees are generally rewarded when their ideas are implemented. For example, the idea of mounting film boxes onto cards that hang from display stands, which is so common today, originally came from a Kodak employee.

- **Corporate hot lines**—Telephone lines staffed by corporate officials ready to answer questions and listen to comments. These are particularly useful during times when employees are likely to be full of questions because their organizations are undergoing change. For example, AT&T used hot lines in the early 1980s during the period of its antitrust divestiture.

Winning **Practices**

Mistake of the Month

If your company has an important message to communicate to customers, the press, employees, financial analysts, or any such group, Delahaye Medialink can do research to help you find the most effective way of communicating with them. Given that this Portsmouth, New Hampshire–based company is in the communication research business, it probably comes as no surprise that it uses a particularly effective, yet counterintuitive, way of communicating within its ranks.[22]

It all started in 1989 when founder and CEO Katie Paine made a serious mistake: She overslept, causing her to miss a flight to an important meeting with a client. Despite her obvious embarrassment, Paine learned a vital lesson about the importance of getting up on time from her big mistake. But why, she thought, should this lesson be kept solely with her? After all, sharing it with others stood to benefit them as well. With this in mind, the next day Paine went to a staff meeting, where she put a $50 bill on the table and challenged her colleagues to tell a worse story about their own mistakes. That they did. One salesperson described how he went on a sales call without his business cards, and another admitted to having scheduled a presentation at Coca-Cola but left the presentation materials behind.

So many people learned so many things about ways to mess things up—and how to

avoid them—that the "Mistake of the Month" soon became a feature of staff meetings at Delahaye. It works like this. At each monthly staff meeting, a half-hour is devoted to identifying and discussing everyone's mistakes. Each is written on a board, and everyone gets to vote on two categories of mistakes—the one from which they learned the most and the one from which they learned the least. The person whose mistake is identified as helping the most is awarded a highly coveted downtown parking space for the next month. The person from whose mistake people learned the least are required to speak at the next meeting about what they are doing to ensure that it will never happen again. The time spent on this exercise is considered a wise investment insofar as it allows all employees to learn from everyone else's mistakes.

During the program's first 10 years, more than 2,000 mistakes have been identified—but few ever have been repeated, creating a positive effect on the company's work. Paine also notes that the program helps her identify steps she needs to take to improve things at Delahaye. She also notes that sharing mistakes has been "a bonding ritual," adding "once you go through it, you're a member of the club."

Use simple language. No matter what field you're in, chances are good that it has its own special language—its **jargon**. Although jargon may greatly help communication within specialized groups, it can severely interfere with communication among the uninitiated.

The trick to using jargon wisely is to know your audience. If the individuals with whom you are communicating understand the jargon, using it can help facilitate communication. However, when addressing audiences whose members are unfamiliar with specialized language, simple, straightforward language is bound to be most effective. In either case, the rationale is the same: Communicators should speak the language of their audiences. Although you may be tempted to try to impress your audience by using big words, you may have little impact on them if they don't understand you. Our advice is clear: Follow the **K.I.S.S. principle**—that is, **k**eep **it** **s**hort and **s**weet.

Avoid overload.   Imagine this scene: You're up late one night at the end of the term as you're writing a paper and studying for finals (or at least trying to) all at the same time. Your desk is piled high with books when your roommate comes in to explain what you should do to prepare for the end-of-semester party. If this sounds at all familiar to you, then you probably know only too well that it's unlikely that you'd be able to give everything you're doing your most careful attention. After all, when people are confronted with more information than they can process at any given time, their performance tends to suffer. This condition is known as **overload**.

As we noted earlier (recall Figure 8.5), these days we tend to be bombarded by messages so regularly that we take overload for granted. Staying competitive in today's hectic world often requires doing many things at once—but without threatening the performance that often results when communication channels are overloaded. Fortunately, several things can be done to avoid, or at least minimize, the problem of overload. These suggestions apply both to in-person communications and electronic communications. These are as follows.

- *Rely on gatekeepers.* People whose jobs require them to control the flow of information to potentially overloaded individuals, groups, or organizations are known as **gatekeepers**. In making appointments for top executives, administrative assistants are providing a gatekeeping service.
- *Practice queuing.* A "queue" is a line. So, **queuing** involves lining up incoming information so that it can be attended to in an orderly fashion. Air traffic controllers do this when they "stack" incoming planes in a holding pattern so as to prevent them from tragically "overloading" the runway. And, as you know, physicians rely on queuing by requiring their nonemergency patients to make appointments and then seeing them only in the appointed order.
- *Screen phone calls.* The practice of screening phone calls is a good way to avoid overload because it allows you to take control over your time by taking the calls you want now and allowing the others to roll over into voice mail (which you can then answer at your convenience).
- *Filter your e-mail.* An easy way to become overloaded with information is by paying attention to unwanted e-mail messages—commonly called **spam**, but officially referred to as unsolicited commercial e-mail messages (UCE) by network administrators. In recent years, workers have been plagued by so much spam that it has been estimated that the average companies loses about 10 days of productivity per year due to time lost by dealing with spam—even if employees spend as little as 5 seconds on each unwanted message.[23] Fortunately, free or very low-cost spam filters can be downloaded to help combat the problem.

Walk the Talk

When it comes to effective communication, action definitely speaks louder than words. Too often, communication is hampered by the practice of saying one thing but meaning another. And, whenever implicit messages (e.g., "we may be cutting jobs") contradict official messages (e.g., "don't worry, the company is stable"), confusion is bound to result.

This is especially problematic when the inconsistency comes from the top. In fact, one of the most effective ways of fostering effective organizational communication is for CEOs to "walk the talk," that is, to match their deeds to their words. After all, a boss would lose credibility if she told her employees "my door is always open to you" but then was never available for consultation. Good communication demands consistency. And, for the words to be heard as loud as the actions, they must match up.

Be a Good Listener

Effective communication involves more than just presenting messages clearly. It also involves doing a good job of comprehending others. Although most of us take listening for granted, effective listening is an important skill. In fact, given that managers spend about 40 percent of their time listening to others but are only 25 percent effective, listening is a skill that could stand to be developed in most of us. When we speak of *effective listening* we are not referring to the passive act of just taking in information that so often occurs. Rather, effective listening involves three important elements.

- Being nonjudgmental while taking in information from others.
- Acknowledging speakers in ways that encourage them to continue speaking.
- Attempting to advance the speaker's ideas to the next step.

It is worthwhile to consider what we can do to improve our own effectiveness as listeners. Fortunately, experts have offered several good suggestions, some of which are summarized in Table 8.3.[24] Although it may require some effort, incorporating these suggestions into your own listening habits cannot help but make you a more effective listener.

Given its importance, it should not be surprising that many organizations are working hard to improve their employees' listening skills. For example, Unisys has long used seminars and self-training audiocassettes to train thousands of its employees in effective listening skills. Such systematic efforts at improving listening skills represent a wise investment insofar as good listening definitely pays off. Indeed, research has shown that the more effective one is as a listener, the more likely he or she is to get promoted to a management position—and to perform effectively in that role. (To practice your own listening skills, and to help others do the same, see the **Group Exercise** section on pages 282–283.)

6
learning
objective

Meeting the Challenges of Cross-Cultural Communication

By this point in the chapter, you are likely to have reached the conclusion that effective communication in organizations cannot be taken for granted. Making things even more challenging are two fundamental facts of contemporary organizational life: (1) the global nature of business relationships and (2) the multilingual nature of

Table 8.3	Tips for Improving Your Listening Skills

Being a good listener is an important skill that can enhance the effectiveness of communication in organizations. Although it may be difficult to follow the suggestions outlined here, the resulting benefits make it worthwhile to try to do so.

Suggestion	*Description*
Do not talk while being spoken to.	It is difficult, if not impossible, to listen to another while you are speaking to that person.
Make the speaker feel at ease.	Help the speaker feel that he or she is free to talk as desired.
Eliminate distractions.	Don't focus on other things: Pay attention only to the speaker.
Show empathy with the speaker.	Try to put yourself in the speaker's position, and make an effort to see his or her point of view.
Be as patient as possible.	Take the time needed to hear everything the speaker has to say.
Hold your arguments.	If you're busy forming your own arguments, you cannot focus on the speaker's points.
Ask questions.	By asking questions, you demonstrate that you are listening and make it possible to clarify areas of uncertainty.

(Source: Based on suggestions by Morrison, 1994; see Note 24.)

the workforce. As you might imagine, these characteristics pose critical challenges that must be met for organizations to be as effective as they must to thrive—or even to survive.

Communicating in a Global Economy

It's no secret that businesses operate in a global economy. Approximately two-thirds of large companies in Europe, Australia, and New Zealand have employees in six or more countries (compared to 56 percent of Asian companies, 43 percent of North American companies, and 33 percent of Latin American companies).[25] Keeping this economy going requires a keen understanding of the complexities of communicating with people from different countries. This is far easier said than done—and mistakes readily can offend your hosts, even unintentionally.

Imagine, for example, that you are at home in a large U.S. city, where you are entertaining a group of potential business partners from abroad. As you enter a restaurant, you find it odd that your guests are reluctant to check their coats, taking them to the table instead, although the inside temperature is quite comfortable. Upon prompting, your guests admit that they heard all about the crime problem in the United States and were advised against ever letting something of value out of their sight. If you are not immediately offended, you would feel at the very least uncomfortable about the message your visitors are sending about their trust of Americans—a likely problem given that you are considering partnering with them. Clearly, when visiting abroad, it pays to not only learn the language spoken there (even if only somewhat, as a gesture of politeness) but also to familiarize yourself carefully with the local customs.[26] As a quick summary of some of the most easily recognized pitfalls of international communication, see Figure 8.6. (To see how familiar you are with the unique ways people from different cultures communicate, see the **Self-Assessment Exercise** on pages 281–282.)

Challenges of cross-cultural communication.   Three key factors make communicating with people from different cultures a difficult task. First, different words may mean different things to different people. For example, as hard as it might be for people from countries with long-standing capitalist economies to realize, Russians have difficulty understanding words such as *efficiency* and *free market*, which have no direct translation in their own language. People who have never known a free-market econ-

---

Figure 8.6   "When in Rome": Understanding National Customs

Understanding differences in local customs is essential when conducting business in today's global economy. A few important customs that might come as a surprise to American businesspeople are summarized here.

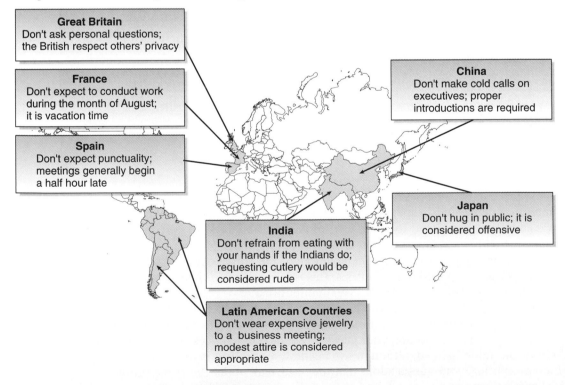

Great Britain
Don't ask personal questions; the British respect others' privacy

France
Don't expect to conduct work during the month of August; it is vacation time

Spain
Don't expect punctuality; meetings generally begin a half hour late

China
Don't make cold calls on executives; proper introductions are required

Japan
Don't hug in public; it is considered offensive

India
Don't refrain from eating with your hands if the Indians do; requesting cutlery would be considered rude

Latin American Countries
Don't wear expensive jewelry to a business meeting; modest attire is considered appropriate

(Sources: Based on information in Marx, 2001, and Lewis, 2000; see Note 26.)

omy while they were growing up certainly may find it difficult to grasp the concept. It is, therefore, not surprising to find that communication barriers have been found to exist among American executives who are attempting to conduct business in Russia.[27]

Second, different cultures sometimes have very different cultural norms about using certain words. Take the simple word *no*, for example. Although the term exists in the Japanese language, the Japanese people are reluctant to say no directly to someone because doing so is considered insulting. For this reason, they often rely on other ways of saying no that can be quite difficult for foreigners to understand (see Table 8.4).[28] As such, it frequently is considered wise for foreign visitors to other countries to learn not only the language of that country but the customs about using language as well.

Third, cross-cultural communication is made difficult by the fact that in different languages even the same word can mean different things. Just imagine, for example, how confused an American executive might become when she speaks to her counterpart in Israel, where the same Hebrew word, *shalom*, means both "hello" and "good-bye" (as well as "peace"). Confusion is bound to arise. The same may be said for cultural differences in the tone of speech used in different settings. Whereas Americans might feel free to say the word *you* in both formal and informal situations, the Spanish have different words in each (*tu* for informal speech and *usted* for formal speech). To confuse these may be tantamount to misinterpreting the nature of the social setting, a potentially costly blunder—and all because of a failure to recognize the subtleties of cross-cultural communication.

Guidelines for avoiding pitfalls in cross-cultural communications.   Communication between people of different cultures can be promoted by taking into account several basic rules. To avoid misunderstandings that can ruin business relationships, it is

Table 8.4	How to Say No in Japan

Although most Americans are not reluctant to come out directly and say "no" when necessary, doing so is frowned on by Japanese culture. As such, the Japanese rely on the following more indirect ways of communicating "no."

- Saying "no" in a highly vague and roundabout manner
- Saying "yes or no" in an ambiguous fashion
- Being silent and not saying anything at all
- Asking questions that change the topic
- Responding in a highly tangential manner
- Leaving the room
- Making a polite excuse
- Saying, "yes, but . . ."
- Delaying the answer, such as by promising a future letter

(Source: Based on information in Hodgson, Sango, and Graham, 2000; see Note 28.)

especially important for people to follow these guidelines when conducting business with people from other countries.[29] These are as follows.

- *Learn local cultural rules.* By acknowledging that there are likely to be cultural differences between yourself and people from another country, learn what you can do to avoid embarrassing these people. Many Americans make this mistake, for example, when they publicly praise Asian visitors. Although this would be considered a very kind thing to do in American culture, Asians are likely to find it a source of discomfort inasmuch as their cultures value group performance more highly than individual performance. Pay special attention to rules of etiquette regarding how to address people (by first name, last name, or title). To avoid embarrassment, it's a good idea to check with local experts to ensure that you are doing this correctly.

- *Don't take anything for granted.* It is important when communicating with people from other nations to challenge your cultural assumptions. Don't assume, for example, that everyone values the same things that you do. Although it may come as a shock to many Americans, concepts such as equal achievement, autonomy, and individual accomplishment are not recognized as appropriate throughout the world.

- *Show respect for everyone.* We often find it funny when someone says or does something that runs counter to what we expect. However, giggling or telling someone that they have a funny accent is not only disrespectful, but also it imposes a tall barrier to effective communication. In this connection, it helps to focus on *what* people are saying rather than how they are saying it or how they look.

- *Speak slowly, clearly, and in straightforward language.* Even after you have studied a foreign language for a few years in high school or college, you may be surprised to find just how little you understand when you visit a country where that is the native language. "If they only spoke more slowly and clearly," you think to yourself, "I'd probably understand them." Indeed, you might. With this in mind, it's important for you to speak slowly and clearly (but not loudly!) when talking to people in languages that are not their native tongue. Moreover, it's important to avoid colloquial words or phrases that you take for granted but that they might not know.

- *Try to speak the local language—at least a little.* People always appreciate the effort you make to speak their language, so give it a try. It's a good way to show goodwill and to break the barrier between you. Whatever you do, however, check with a native speaker to make sure that your pronunciation is accurate and that you are not offending anyone by using the wrong words or gestures.

- *Beware of nonverbal differences.* The same gestures that mean one thing in one country may mean quite another in another country. For example, an American may not think twice about hugging a colleague who has done well or touching another's arm to acknowledge him or her. However, these same acts would be considered not only inappropriate but also offensive to people from Korea. Bottom line: You have not completely learned a foreign language until you have learned its nonverbal language as well.[30] For some examples of cross-cultural differences in nonverbal behavior, see Figure 8.7.

The Multilingual Workforce: "You Say Tomato, I Say Domates, or Pomidor, or Tomate."

In the Book of Genesis, the Bible tells us of the Tower of Babel that the descendants of Noah built to reach up to heaven and make them like God. However, the story tells us that God prevented them from completing the tower by confusing

Figure 8.7   Beware of Nonverbal Miscommunication in Different Countries

Although people preparing to conduct business abroad may study their host country's language, they frequently fail to learn differences in the nonverbal language. As summarized here, this can lead to some serious miscommunication.

When a person from the United States does this	it means . . .	BUT	When the same thing is done by a person from	it means . . .
 stands close to another while talking	the speaker is considered pushy		 Italy	the speaker is behaving normally
 looks away from another	the speaker is shy		 Japan	the speaker is showing deference to authority
 extends the palm of his or her hand	the person is extending a greeting, such as a handshake		 Greece	the person is being insulted
 joins the index finger and thumb to form an "O"	"okay"		 Tunisia	"I'll kill you"

(Sources: Based on information in Hossell, 2003, and Knapp and Hall, 2001; see Note 30.)

their language so that they could no longer understand one another. From that time forward, according to the Bible, the peoples of the earth would speak different languages. Just as language differences kept the tower from completion in Biblical times, so too do language differences between people threaten to interfere with people's work today.

Just because you go to work at an American company in the United States, there's no assurance that everyone around you will be a native speaker of English. Especially in states like California and New York, where as many as one person in four is foreign born, there's good reason to expect that many of your coworkers will speak English with a foreign accent—if they speak it at all. The communication challenges this situation creates are not difficult to imagine. After all, business operations are sure to falter when people cannot understand each other because they are speaking different languages.

To combat this problem, several companies have implemented *English-only rules*, requiring all employees to speak only English while on the job. The underlying idea is that workplaces in which people speak only one language will be ones in which communications are clear and efficient and in which safety is enhanced. In recent years, however, the courts have not looked favorably on such policies, claiming they interfere with an employee's rights to use whatever language he or she wishes. For example, a Washington court awarded a Cambodian-born immigrant $389,000 by the bank that employed him, ruling that he was unfairly denied a promotion because of his lack of fluency in English.[31] Legally, for companies to insist that their employees speak fluent English, they must establish clearly that an employee who cannot do so will perform poorly on the job.

> Fluency in English is important for sales associates at Longo Toyota in El Monte, California, where three-quarters of the sales staff speak at least one additional language.

Instead of insisting that everyone speak only English, companies with diverse customer bases generally are delighted to have employees who speak several different languages. For example, fluency in English is important for sales associates at Longo Toyota in El Monte, California, where three-quarters of the sales staff speak at least one additional language (in fact, 20 different languages are spoken at Longo!). This has helped the dealership sell cars to people from the community who were not as well served by the competition, helping it become one of the top-grossing car dealerships in the United States.

Although it often is useful to be able to speak a second language, most U.S. companies find it necessary to ensure that its employees speak English so that they can understand instructions, notices, and memos. With this in mind, many businesses have arranged for their employees to take classes in English as a second language. This is done at Kayem Foods, a meat processing and packaging company in Chelsea, Massachusetts, where English is a second language for 60 to 70 percent of the employees, most of whom have Spanish or Polish as their native tongues. This is so important that it's not relegated to something the company hopes workers will do on their own time off the job. Rather, teachers are brought into the facility to train workers during their shifts.

Learning to communicate in English is particularly important in the hospitality industry, where doing so is required to cater to American tourists. For example, before the Four Seasons Hotel and Resort opened on the southern tip of the island of Bali in Indonesia, none of the 10,000 applicants could speak English. In fact, nobody could pass a simple test of English required to perform any of the 580 jobs the resort was attempting to fill. The solution was intensive training in English language terms used in the hospitality industry—nine hours per day for almost a month. Although staff members might not be able to understand the entire language, they know enough English to serve its customers' needs.

In some locations, a company's customer base is so ethnically diverse that it must go out of its way to hire employees who speak foreign languages. What happens, however, if the one or two employees who speak an unusual language are not available? Detroit Edison, the electric utility company serving ethnically diverse southeast Michigan, has faced this challenge by using AT&T's Language Line service. This service provides around-the-clock translation services in any of 140 different languages by accessing a toll-free phone number. Customers who speak a language that is unknown to any of Detroit Edison's service representatives are put on a conference call with someone from the company and the Language Line service. In conclusion, it's easy to see how very important it is for people to respond to the challenge of using language—be it one or many—to communicate effectively with coworkers and customers.

You Be the Consultant

A Crisis in Communicating Coordination

"Everyone is moving in different directions; no one seems to have any sense of what the company is and where it is going. Making things worse, people around here aren't paying any attention to each other, and everyone is doing his or her own thing." These are the words of an operations director of a large credit card processing center, who asks you to look into these problems in your capacity as manager of human resources. Answer the following questions relevant to this situation based on the material in this chapter.

1. Casting the problem as one of poor communication between company officials and lower-level employees, what steps could be taken to fill everyone in on the company's plans, goals, and activities?

2. What specific tactics would you advise the company's management use to improve communication within?

3. In what ways might differences in nationality be responsible for this state of affairs, and what can be done to help improve communication despite these differences?

Self-Assessment Exercise

How Familiar Are You with Foreign Communication Practices?

Expert communicators in today's global business world must have considerable familiarity with cultural differences in communication style around the world. This questionnaire is designed to assess your familiarity with many such communication practices. It is important to note that although people in any given country are not all alike, their cultural backgrounds lead them to share certain communication styles and practices.

Directions

Match the countries in the left-hand column to the communication characteristic that best describes its people, listed in the column on the right.

1. _____ Russia
2. _____ Brazil
3. _____ Germany
4. _____ Australia
5. _____ Japan
6. _____ Philippines
7. _____ Poland
8. _____ France
9. _____ Great Britain
10. _____ India

a. Chivalry and old-fashioned gallantry are important; first names are reserved for use only with close friends.

b. Show respect for speakers by being silent; tend to be shy and to refrain from open disagreement.

c. Women are deferent to men; good bargainers, who expect you to negotiate with them.

d. Raise their voice and use gestures when excited; formal dress and style are typical at meetings.

e. Punctuality is important; perfectionists, who demand lots of information from others.

f. Use humor a great deal, such as to break up tension; take time to make decisions.

g. Talk tough when they believe they have an advantage; tend to drink between meetings.

h. Being an hour or two late is not unusual; leadership is based on family name, age, and connections.

i. Very talkative and long-winded; tend to interrupt conversations with their own ideas.

j. Tend to be cynical and distrust people who praise them too enthusiastically.

(Source: Based on information in Rosen et al., 2000, see Note 25; and Lewis, 2000, see Note 26.)

Scoring

Using the following key, count how many correct matches you made.

1 = g, 2 = i, 3 = e, 4 = j, 5 = b, 6 = h, 7 = a, 8 = d, 9 = f, 10 = c

Discussion Questions

1. How many correct matches did you make? How does this figure compare to how you expected to score before you began this exercise?

2. Based on your own experiences, to what extent do you believe these descriptions are generally accurate as opposed to merely stereotypic?

3. How would you characterize your own culture relative to those described in this exercise?

Group Exercise

Sharpening Your Listening Skills

Are you a good listener, a *really* good listener? Do you understand exactly what others are saying and get them to open up even more? Most of us tend to think that we are much better than we really are when it comes to this important skill. After all, we've been listening to people our whole lives—and, with that much practice, we must be at least reasonably acceptable. However, being a truly effective listener is an active skill, and it takes some practice to master. The following exercise will help you gain some insight into your own listening skills.

Directions

1. Divide the class into pairs of people who do not already know each other. Arrange the chairs so that the people within each pair are facing one another but are separated from the other pairs.

2. Within each pair, select one person as the speaker and the other as the listener. The speaker should tell the listener about a specific incident on the job in which he or she was somehow harmed (e.g., disappointed by not getting a raise, being embarrassed by another, getting fired, and so on), and how he or she felt about it. This discussion should last about 10 to 15 minutes.

3. Listeners should carefully attempt to follow the suggestions for good listening summarized in Table 8.3 (on page 275). To help, the instructor should discuss these with the class.

4. After the conversations are over, review the suggestions with your partner. Discuss which ones the listener followed and which ones were ignored. Try to be as open and honest as possible about assessing your own and the other's strengths and weaknesses. Speakers should consider the extent to which they felt the listeners were really paying careful attention to them.

5. Now repeat steps 2 through 4 but change roles. Speakers now become listeners, and listeners now become speakers.

6. As a class, share your experiences as speakers and listeners.

Discussion Questions

1. What did this exercise teach you about your own skills as a listener? Are you as good as you thought? Do you think you can improve?

2. Was there general agreement or disagreement in the class about each listener's strengths and weaknesses? Explain.

3. Which particular listening skills were easiest and which were most difficult for you to put into practice? Do you think there may be certain conditions under which good listening skills may be especially difficult to implement?

Notes

Case Notes

Slater, R. (2003). *The Wal-Mart decade: How a newgeneration of leaders turned Sam Walton's legacy into the world's #1 company.* New York: Portfolio. Gimein, M. (2002, March 18). Sam Walton made us a promise. *Fortune*, pp. 120–124, 128, 130. Walton, S. (1993). *Made in America: My story.* New York: Bantam.

Chapter Notes

[1] Roberts, K. H. (1984). *Communicating in organizations*. Chicago: Science Research Associates (quote, p. 4).

[2] Weick, K. E. (1987). Theorizing about organizational communication. In F. M. Jablin, L. L. Putnam, K. H. Roberts, & L. W. Porter (Eds.), *Handbook of organizational communication* (pp. 97–122). Newbury Park, CA: Sage.

[3] Daft, R. L., Lengel, R. H., & Trevino, L. K. (1987). Message equivocality, media selection, and manager performance: Implications for information systems. *MIS Quarterly, 11*, 355–366.

[4] Stromberg, R. M. (1998, September). No, it couldn't happen here. *American Management Association International*, p. 70.

[5] Poe, R., & Courter, C. L. (1998, September). The great coffee grapevine. *Across the Board*, p. 7.

[6] Walton, E. (1961). How efficient is the grapevine? *Personnel, 28*, 45–49.

[7] Lengel, R. H., & Daft, R. L. (1988). The selection of communication media as an executive skill. *Academy of Management Executive, 2*, 225–232.

[8] Esterson, E. (1998). Inner beauties. *Inc. Tech*, pp. 78–80, 84, 86, 88, 90.

[9] Jablin, F. M., & Putnam, L. L. (2000). *The new handbook of organizational communication: Advances in theory, research, and methods*. Thousand Oaks, CA: Sage.

[10] Thurlow, C., Lengel, L., & Tomic, A. (2004). *Computer-mediated communication*. Thousand Oaks, CA: Sage.

[11] Schneider, S. J., Kerwin, J., Frechtling, J., & Vivari, B. A. (2002). Characteristics of the discussion in online and face-to-face focus groups. *Social Science Computer Review, 20*, 31–42.

[12] Walther, J. B., & Addario, K. P. (2001). The impacts of empticons on message interpretation in computer-mediated communication. *Social Science Computer Review, 19*, 324–347.

[13] Wolf, A. (2000). Emotional expression online: Gender differences in emoticon use. *CyberPsychology & Behavior, 3*, 827–833.

[14] Hickson, M. L., Stacks, D. W., & Moore, N-J. (2003). *Nonverbal communication: Studies and applications* (4th ed.). Los Angeles, CA: Roxbury Publishing.

[15] Rafaeli, A., Dutton, J. Harquail, C., & Mackie-Lewis, S. (1997). Navigating by attire: The use of dress by female administrative employees. *Academy of Management Journal, 40*, 9–45.

[16] Greenberg, J. (1989). The organizational waiting game: Time as a status-asserting or status-neutralizing tactic. *Basic and Applied Social Psychology, 10*, 13–26.

[17] Zweigenhaft, R. L. (1976). Personal space in the faculty office: Desk placement and student–faculty interaction. *Journal of Applied Psychology, 61*, 628–632.

[18] Dubrin, A. J. (2001). *Leadership* (3rd ed.). Boston: Houghton Mifflin.

[19] Tannen, D. (1998, February 2). How you speak shows where you rank. *Fortune*, p. 156.

[20] Wurman, R. S. (2000). *Understanding*. Newport, RI: TED Conferences.

[21] Whetten, D. E., & Cameron, K. S. (2002). *Developing management skills* (5th ed.). Upper Saddle River, NJ: Prentice Hall.

[22] Labarre, P. (1998, November). Screw up, and get smart. *Fast Company*, p. 58.

[23] Computer Mail Services. (2003). *Spam calculator*. On the World Wide Web at www.cmsconnect.com.

[24] Morrison, K. E. (1994). *Leadership skills*. Tucson, AZ: Fisher Books.

[25] Rosen, R., Digh, P., Singer, M., & Phillips, C. (2000). *Global literacies*. New York: Simon & Schuster.

[26] Marx, E. (2001). *Breaking through culture shock*. London: Nicholas Brealey Publishing. Lewis, R. D. (2000). *When cultures collide*, rev. ed. London: Nicholas Brealey Publishing.

[27] Mellow, C. (1995, August 17). Russia: Making cash from chaos. *Fortune*, pp. 145–146, 148, 150–151.

[28] Hodgson, J. D., Sango, Y., & Graham, J. L. (2000). *Doing business with the new Japan*. Oxford, England: Rowman & Littlefield. Ueda, K. (1974). Sixteen ways to avoid saying no in Japan. In J. C. Condon & M. Saito (Eds.), *International encounters with Japan*, pp. 185–192. Tokyo: Simul Press.

[29] See Notes 25 and 26.

[30] Hossell, K. P. (2003). *Body language*. Oxford, England: Heinemann Library. Knapp, M. L., & Hall, J. A. (2001). *Nonverbal communication in human interaction*. Belmont, CA: Wadsworth. Axtell, R. E. (1997). *Gestures: The do's and taboos of body language around the world*. New York: Wiley.

[31] Dutton, G. (1998, December). One workforce, many languages. *Management Review*, pp. 42–47.

Chapter **Nine**

LEARNING OBJECTIVES

After reading this chapter, you will be able to:

1. **DEFINE** what is meant by a *group* and **IDENTIFY** different types of groups operating within organizations.

2. **DESCRIBE** the importance of *norms, roles, status,* and *cohesiveness* within organizations.

3. **EXPLAIN** how individual performance in groups is affected by the presence of others (*social facilitation*) and the number of others with whom one is working (*social loafing*).

4. **DEFINE** what *teams* are and **DESCRIBE** the various types of teams that exist in organizations.

5. **DESCRIBE** the evidence regarding the effectiveness of teams in organizations.

6. **EXPLAIN** the factors responsible for the failure of some teams to operate as effectively as possible and steps that can be taken to build successful teams.

Group Processes and Work Teams

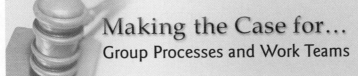

Making the Case for...
Group Processes and Work Teams

Taking Teamwork to the Net

What do you get when you put together 40,000 people working for 80 different suppliers at 187 locations around the world? The answer, hope officials from Lockheed Martin Aeronautics Co., is the Joint Strike Fighter—a supersonic stealth fighter plane it is producing for the U.S. Defense Department. Agreeing to deliver the totally new, state-of-the-art aircraft—what it calls the F-35—in only four years, Lockheed won the biggest manufacturing contract ever, some $200 billion. How does the company plan to carry out such a monumental task? In a word, "teamwork," says President Dain M. Hancock. "Almost everything we now do is a team activity," he observed recently, on the occasion of being honored as the National Management Association's "Executive of the Year."

From Lockheed's Fort Worth, Texas, headquarters, a 75-member tech group links together the various engineers and suppliers designing the aircraft, along with officials from the U.S. Air Force,

286

Navy, and Marines as well as Great Britain's Defense Ministry and eight other allies—each of whom not only can track the plane's progress but also can make changes along the way if necessary. What makes all this teamwork possible and keeps it running smoothly is a new generation of Web technologies that allows for a "true virtual connection" among all the parties. According to one defense industry analyst, this advanced technology moves several steps beyond sending information between PCs, allowing "people separated by oceans [to] interact with one another as if there were not even a wall between them."

More than simply allowing people to collaborate in real time, the new Web technology makes it possible to "use the Web as a giant electronic Yellow Pages—to find experts to do many of these jobs and then to collaborate with them over the Net on a minute-by-minute basis." The upshot of this, envisions tech market expert George Colony, CEO of Forrester Research, is a level of collaboration between companies that is so tight that workers eventually may come to identify themselves less with the company for which they work than the particular projects on which they are working—a result, he predicts, that "could reshape the traditional corporation."

As you might imagine, however, officials at Lockheed Martin are concerned far more with the day-to-day realities of using the Web technology to move ideas and subassemblies between various technical experts and government officials than with any future prognostications. For now, signs are that if there are any weak spots in the teamwork technology, it's more a matter of people than machines. Two potential sticking points seem to be emerging. First, there's training people in the collaboration software itself, which given the high-tech orientation of Lockheed Martin's employees, has not been a problem (although the software has met with mixed results within one large law firm that attempted using it, for precisely this reason). Second, there's the loss of face time that usually occurs when people are collaborating with one another. Can today's "digital workspaces" completely replace more traditional actions between people—particularly in the creative process, and with regard to the building of personal relationships that is necessary for teamwork to succeed? As in the case of all things, of course, time will tell. Meanwhile, Lockheed is heading its F-35 "into the digital wilderness with no thought of turning tail."

3 GOOD REASONS why you should care about...

Group Processes and Work Teams

You should care about group processes and work teams because:

1. The dynamics among people in groups is largely responsible for both the success and failure of many work groups, as well as the satisfaction of the individuals working in them.

2. Groups and teams can be very effective if you know how to manage them properly.

3. Teams are a fact of organizational life—the most popular way of coordinating the activities of people on the job. Knowing how they operate and how to manage them effectively will give you an edge.

As you might imagine, the extremely sophisticated technology-dependent approach to teamwork used at Lockheed Martin Aeronautics represents just the tip of a very deep iceberg. Although this company's high-tech approach to *work teams* may be extreme, to be sure, at its core lies an ingredient common to all work teams—the underlying need to coordinate large numbers of people and getting them to make important contributions to a project. Today, work teams are extremely popular in all kinds of organizations. People in offices and factories everywhere are called on to coordinate their efforts toward achieving important organizational goals, and teams are often used as the vehicle for making this possible. Acknowledging that they don't always operate as successfully as they do at Lockheed Martin Aeronautics (or anywhere near as ambitiously), we will describe the general effectiveness of teams and outline steps that can be taken to make teams as productive as possible.

To help you understand the underlying factors that contribute to team success and failure, we first must turn attention to the basic nature of *groups* in general. As you know, a great deal of the work performed in organizations is done by people working together in groups. In view of this, it makes sense to understand the types of groups that exist and the variables governing the interrelationships between them and individuals—commonly referred to as *group dynamics*. **Group dynamics** focuses on the nature of groups—the variables governing their formation and development, their structure, and their interrelationships with individuals, other groups, and the organizations within which they exist.[1] Because groups exist in all types of social settings, the study of group dynamics has a long history in the social sciences—including OB.[2]

In the first half of this chapter we will draw on this work. Specifically, we will describe the nature of groups by defining what groups are, identifying various types of groups and why they form, explaining the various stages through which groups develop, and describing the dynamics of the way groups are structured. Following this, we will shift our attention to how effectively groups operate. Specifically, we will describe how people are affected by the presence of others, how the cultural makeup of a group affects performance, and the tendency for people to withhold their individual performance under certain conditions.

Groups at Work: Their Basic Nature

To understand the dynamics of groups and their influence on individual and organizational functioning, we must begin by raising some basic questions—namely, what is a group and what types of groups exist?

What Is a Group?

learning
objective

Imagine three people waiting in line at the cashier's stand at a supermarket. Now compare them to the board of directors of a large corporation. Which collection would you consider to be a "group"? Although in our everyday language we may refer to the people waiting in line as a group, they clearly are not a group in the same sense as the members of the board. Obviously, a group is more than simply a collection of people. But what exactly is it that makes a group a group?

Social scientists have formally defined a **group** as a collection of two or more interacting individuals with a stable pattern of relationships between them who share common goals and who perceive themselves as being a group.[3] To help us examine this definition more closely, let's take a closer look at the various elements of this definition.

- *Social interaction.* One of the most obvious characteristics of groups is that they are composed of *two or more people in social interaction.* In other words, the members of a group must have some influence on each other. The interaction between the parties may be either verbal (such as sharing strategies for a corporate takeover) or non-verbal (such as exchanging smiles in the hallway), but the parties must have some impact on each other to be considered a group.

- *Stability.* Groups also must possess a *stable structure.* Although groups can change, and often do, there must be some stable relationships that keep group members together and functioning as a unit. A collection of individuals that constantly changes (e.g., the people inside an office waiting room at any given time) cannot be thought of as a group. To be a group, a greater level of stability would be required.

- *Common interests or goals.* A third characteristic of groups is that their *members share common interests or goals.* For example, members of a stamp collecting club constitute a group that is sustained by the mutual interest of members. Some groups form because members with common interests help each other achieve a mutual goal. For example, the owners and employees of a sewing shop constitute a group formed around a common interest in sewing and the common goal of making money.

- *Recognition as being a group.* Finally, to be a group, the individuals involved must *perceive themselves as a group.* Groups are composed of people who recognize each other as a member of their group and can distinguish these individuals from non-members. The members of a corporate finance committee or a chess club, for example, know who is in their group and who is not. In contrast, shoppers in a checkout line probably don't think of each other as being members of a group. Although they stand physically close to each other and may have passing conversations, they have little in common (except, perhaps, a shared interest in reaching the end of the line) and fail to identify themselves with the others in the line.

By defining groups in terms of these four characteristics, we have identified a group as a very special collection of individuals. As we shall see, these characteristics are responsible for the important effects groups have on organizational behavior. To better understand these effects, we will now review the wide variety of groups that operate within organizations.

Types of Groups

What do the following have in common: a military combat unit, three couples getting together for dinner, the board of directors of a large corporation, and the three-person cockpit crew of a commercial airliner? As you probably guessed, the answer is that they are all groups. But, of course, they are very different kinds of groups, ones people join for different reasons.

Formal groups.   The most basic way of identifying types of groups is to distinguish between *formal groups* and *informal groups* (see Figure 9.1). **Formal groups** are created by the organization and are intentionally designed to direct members toward some important organizational goal. One type of formal group is referred to as a **command group**—a group determined by the connections between individuals who

Figure 9.1   Varieties of Groups in Organizations

Within organizations one may find formal groups (such as *command groups* and *task groups*) and informal groups (such as *interest groups* and *friendship groups*).

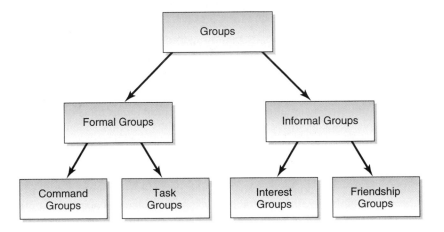

are a formal part of the organization (i.e., those who legitimately can give orders to others). For example, a command group may be formed by the vice president of marketing who gathers together her regional marketing directors from around the country to hear their ideas about a new national advertising campaign. The point is that command groups are determined by the organization's rules regarding who reports to whom and usually consist of a supervisor and his or her subordinates.

A formal organizational group also may be formed around some specific task. Such a group is referred to as a **task group**. Unlike command groups, a task group may be composed of individuals with some special interest or expertise in a specific area regardless of their positions in the organizational hierarchy. For example, a company may have a budget committee whose members make recommendations about how company funds should be spent. It may be composed of accounting and finance specialists, corporate vice presidents, and workers from the shop floor. Whether they are permanent committees, known as **standing committees**, or temporary ones formed for special purposes (such as a committee formed to recommend solutions to a parking problem), known as **ad hoc committees** or **task forces**, task groups are common in organizations.

Informal groups.   As you know, not all groups found in organizations are as formal as those we've identified. Many groups are informal in nature. **Informal groups** develop naturally among an organization's personnel without any direction from the management of the organization within which they operate. One key factor in the formation of informal groups is a common interest shared by its members. For example, a group of employees who band together to seek union representation, or who march together to protest their company's pollution of the environment, may be called an **interest group**. The common goal sought by members of an interest group may unite workers at many different organizational levels. The key factor is that membership in an interest group is voluntary—it is not created by the organization but is encouraged by an expression of common interests.

Of course, sometimes the interests that bind individuals together are far more diffuse. Groups may develop out of a common interest in participating in sports, or going to the movies, or just getting together to talk. These kinds of informal groups are known as **friendship groups**. A group of coworkers who hang out together during lunch may also bowl or play cards together after work. Friendship groups extend beyond the workplace because they provide opportunities for satisfying the social needs of workers that are so important to their well-being.

Informal work groups are an important part of life in organizations. Although they develop without direct encouragement from management, friendships often originate out of formal organizational contact. For example, three employees working along side each other on an assembly line may get to talking and discover their mutual interest in basketball and decide to get together to shoot baskets after work. As we will see, such friendships can bind people together, helping them cooperate with each other, having beneficial effects on organizational functioning.

The Basic Building Blocks of Group Dynamics

Now that you understand exactly what a group is, you are prepared to appreciate the basic elements that account for the dynamics of people in groups. Specifically, I will describe four basic building blocks of groups: the various parts played by group members (*roles*), the rules and expectations that develop within groups (*norms*), the prestige of group membership (*status*), and the members' sense of belonging (*cohesiveness*).

2
learning
objective

Roles: The Hats We Wear

One of the primary structural elements of groups is members' tendencies to play specific roles in group interaction, often more than one. Social scientists use the term *role* in much the same way as a director of a play would refer to the character who plays a part. Indeed, the part one plays in the overall group structure is what we mean by a role. More formally, a **role** is defined as the typical behaviors that characterize a person in a social context.[4]

In organizations, many roles are assigned by virtue of an individual's position within an organization. For example, a boss may be expected to give orders, and a teacher may be expected to lecture and to give exams. These are behaviors expected of the individual in that role. The person holding the role is known as a **role incumbent**, and the behaviors expected of that person are known as **role expectations**. The person holding the office of the president of the United States (the role incumbent) has certain role expectations simply because he or she currently has that post. When a new president takes office, that person assumes the same role and has the same formal powers as the previous president. This is the case although the new president may have very different ideas about key issues facing the nation.

Think of committees to which you have belonged. Was there someone who joked and made people feel better, and another member who worked hard to get the group to focus on the issue at hand? This is not at all unusual. In fact, as groups develop, various members come to play different roles in the social structure—a process referred to as **role differentiation**. The emergence of different roles in groups is a naturally occurring process. In general, three roles commonly emerge in groups. These are as follows:

■ The **task-oriented role**. This refers to the person who, more than anyone else, helps the group reach its goal.

■ The **socioemotional role**. This refers to the group member who is quite supportive and nurturant, someone who makes everyone else feel good. Such a person is said to play a **socioemotional role**.

■ The **self-oriented role**. This refers to group members who tend to do things for themselves, often at the expense of the group.

Norms: A Group's Unspoken Rules

One feature of groups that enhances their orderly functioning is the existence of group norms. **Norms** may be defined as generally agreed upon informal rules that guide group members' behavior.[5] They represent shared ways of viewing the world. Norms differ from organizational rules in that they are not formal and written. In fact, group members may not even be aware of the subtle group norms that exist and regulate their behavior. Yet, they have profound effects on behavior. Norms regulate the behavior of groups in important ways, such as by fostering workers' honesty and loyalty to the company, establishing appropriate ways to dress, and dictating when it is acceptable to be late for or absent from work.

If you recall the pressures placed on you by your peers as you grew up to dress or wear your hair in certain styles, you are well aware of the profound normative pressures exerted by groups. Some norms, known as **prescriptive norms**, dictate the behaviors that should be performed. Other norms, known as **proscriptive norms**, dictate specific behaviors that should be avoided. For example, groups may develop prescriptive norms to follow their leader or to help a group member who needs assistance. They may also develop proscriptive norms to avoid absences or to refrain from telling each other's secrets to the boss.

Sometimes the pressure to conform to norms is subtle, as in the dirty looks given a manager by his peers for going to lunch with one of the assembly-line workers. At other times normative pressures may be quite severe, such as when one production worker sabotages another's work because he is performing at too high a level and making his coworkers look bad. Although our examples emphasize the underlying social dynamics responsible for how groups develop norms, this is only one reason. There are, in fact, several factors responsible for the formation of norms.[6] For a summary of these, see Table 9.1.

Status: The Prestige of Group Membership

Have you ever been attracted to a group because of the prestige accorded its members? You may have wanted to join a certain fraternity or sorority because it is highly regarded by the students. No doubt, members of championship-winning football teams proudly sport their Super Bowl rings to identify themselves as members of that highly regarded team. Clearly, one potential reward of group membership is the status associated with being in that group. Even within social groups, different

Table 9.1	Group Norms: How Do They Develop?

Group norms develop in the four ways summarized here.

Basis of Norm Development	*Example*
1. Precedents set over time	Seating location of each group member around a table
2. Carryovers from other situations	Professional standards of conduct
3. Explicit statements from others	Working a certain way because you are told "that's how we do it around here"
4. Critical events in group history	After the organization suffers a loss due to one person's divulging company secrets, a norm develops to maintain secrecy

(Source: Based on Feldman, 1984; see Note 6.)

members are accorded different levels of prestige. Fraternity and sorority officers, and committee chairpersons, for example, may be recognized as more important members of their respective groups. This is the idea behind **status**—the relative social position or rank given to groups or group members by others.[7] Status may be recognized as both formal and informal in nature.

Formal and informal status.   **Formal status** refers to attempts to differentiate between the degrees of formal authority given employees by an organization. This is typically accomplished through the use of **status symbols**—objects reflecting the position of an individual within an organization's hierarchy. Some examples of status symbols include job titles (e.g., director); perquisites, or perks, (e.g., a reserved parking space); the opportunity to do desirable and highly regarded work (e.g., serving on important committees); and luxurious working conditions (e.g., a large, private office that is lavishly decorated).[8]

Symbols of **informal status** within organizations are also widespread. These refer to the prestige accorded individuals with certain characteristics that are not formally recognized by the organization. For example, employees who are older and more experienced may be perceived as higher in status by their coworkers. Those who have certain special skills (such as the home-run hitters on a baseball team) also may be regarded as having higher status than others. In some organizations, the lower value placed on the work of women and members of minority groups by some individuals also can be considered an example of informal status in operation.[9]

Status and influence: A key relationship.   One of the best-established findings in the study of group dynamics is that higher-status people tend to be more influential than lower-status people. (As will be described in Chapter 11, *influence* refers to the capacity to affect others in some fashion.) This phenomenon may be seen in a classic study of decision making in three-man bomber crews.[10] After the crews had difficulty solving a problem, the experimenter planted clues to the solution with either a low status group member (the tail gunner) or a high-status group member (the pilot). It was found that the solutions offered by the pilots were far more likely to be adopted than the same solutions presented by the tail gunners. Apparently, the greater status accorded the pilots (because they tended to be more experienced and hold higher military ranks) was responsible for the greater influence they wielded.

Cohesiveness: Getting the Team Spirit

One obvious determinant of any group's structure is its **cohesiveness**—the strength of group members' desires to remain part of their groups. Highly cohesive work groups are ones in which the members are attracted to each other, accept the group's goals, and help work toward meeting them. In very uncohesive groups, the members dislike each other and may even work at cross-purposes.[11] In essence, cohesiveness refers to a *we-feeling*, an *esprit de corps*, a sense of belonging to a group.

Determinants of cohesiveness.   Several important factors have been shown to influence the extent to which group members tend to "stick together." These are as follows:

- *Severity of initiation.* The greater the difficulty people overcome to become a member of a group, the more cohesive the group will be.[12] The rigorous requirements for gaining entry into elite groups, such as the most prestigious medical schools and military training schools, are partly responsible for the high degree of camaraderie found in such groups. Having "passed the test" tends to keep individuals together and separates them from those who are unwilling or unable to "pay the price" of admission.

- *External threat.* Group cohesion also tends to be strengthened under conditions of high external threat or competition. When workers face a "common enemy," they tend to draw together. Such cohesion not only makes workers feel safer and better protected, but also aids them by encouraging them to work closely together and coordinate their efforts toward the common enemy. Good examples of cohesion in response to shared external threat may be seen in the way employees of normally competing restaurants in New York City banded together to feed the hungry in the aftermath of the September 11, 2001, terrorist attacks and the August 14, 2003, power blackouts.

> Good examples of cohesion in response to shared external threat may be seen in the way employees of normally competing restaurants in New York City banded together to feed the hungry in the aftermath of the September 11, 2001, terrorist attacks and the August 14, 2003, power blackouts.

- *Group size.* As you might imagine, cohesiveness tends to be greater in smaller groups. Generally speaking, groups that are too large make it difficult for members to interact and, therefore, for cohesiveness to reach a high level.

- *History of success.* "Nothing succeeds like success," as they say, and groups with a history of success tend to be highly cohesive. It is often said that "everyone loves a winner," and the success of a group tends to help unite its members as they rally around their success. For this reason, employees tend to be loyal to successful companies—and sports fans tend to be loyal to winning teams.

Beware—cohesiveness can be a double-edged sword.   Thus far, our discussion has implied that cohesiveness is a positive thing. Indeed, it can be. For example, people are known to enjoy belonging to highly cohesive groups. Members of closely knit work groups participate more fully in their group's activities, more readily accept their group's goals, and are absent from their jobs less often than members of less cohesive groups.[13] Not surprisingly, cohesive groups tend to work together quite well and are sometimes exceptionally productive with low levels of voluntary turnover.[14]

However, highly cohesive groups also can be problematic. For example, if a highly cohesive group's goals are contrary to the organization's goals, that group is in a position to inflict a great deal of harm to an organization by working against its interests.[15] Highly cohesive group members who conspire to sabotage their employers are a good example. With this in mind, it's important to recognize that when it comes to performance group cohesiveness is a double-edge sword: Its effects can be both helpful and harmful.

Individual Performance in Groups

3
learning
objective

Now that we have reviewed the basic nature of groups, we will turn to an aspect of group dynamics most relevant to the field of organizational behavior—the effects of groups on individual performance. Specifically, we will take a look at two different issues in this connection: how people's work performance is affected by the presence of others and how performance is affected by group size.

Social Facilitation: Working in the Presence of Others

Imagine that you have been taking piano lessons for 10 years and you now are about to go on stage for your first major solo concert performance. You have been practicing diligently for several months, getting ready for the big night. Now, you are no longer alone in your living room but on stage in front of hundreds of people. Your name is announced and silence breaks the applause as you take your place in front of the concert grand. How will you perform now that you are in front of an audience? Will you freeze, forgetting the piece you practiced, or will the audience spur you on to your best performance yet? In other words, what impact will the presence of the audience have on your behavior?

The social facilitation effect.   After studying this question for over a century, using a wide variety of tasks and situations, social scientists found that the answer to this question is not straightforward.[16] Sometimes people were found to perform better in the presence of others than when alone, and sometimes they were found to perform better alone than in the presence of others. This tendency for the presence of others to enhance an individual's performance at times and to impair it at other times is known as **social facilitation**. (Although the word *facilitation* implies improvements in task performance, scientists use the term *social facilitation* to refer to both performance improvements and decrements stemming from the presence of others.)

The obvious question is this: Under what conditions will performance be helped by the presence of others and under what conditions will it be hindered? Research has shown that the answer depends on how well people know the task they are performing (for a summary, see Figure 9.2). When people are performing tasks they know quite well (e.g., a musical piece they have played for years), they generally perform better in front of an audience than alone. However, when people are performing tasks with which they are unfamiliar (e.g., a piece of music that is new to their repertoires), they generally perform better alone than in the presence of others.

Figure 9.2 The Social Facilitation Effect: A Summary

According to the phenomenon of *social facilitation*, a person's performance on a task will be influenced by the presence of others. Compared to performance when doing the task alone, performance in front of an audience will be enhanced if that task is well learned but impaired if it is not well learned.

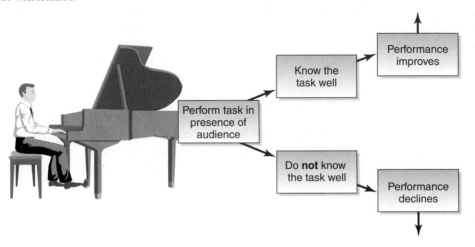

Social facilitation and performance monitoring. It's easy to imagine how the social facilitation effect may have a profound influence on organizational behavior. For example, consider the effects it may have on people whose work is monitored, either by others who are physically present or by connections made via computer networks. The rationale behind performance monitoring—the practice of supervisors observing subordinates while working—is that it will encourage people to perform at their best. But does it really work this way?

The concept of social facilitation suggests that monitoring should improve task performance only if the people monitored know their tasks extremely well. However, if they are relatively new to the job, their performance would suffer when monitored. In fact, research suggests that this is precisely what happens.[17] For employees who are not well practiced at their jobs, performance monitoring does not have the intended effects. Accordingly, supervisors seeking to raise employees' performance levels by introducing performance monitoring should carefully consider the effects of social facilitation before doing so.

Social Loafing: "Free Riding" When Working with Others

Have you ever worked with several others helping a friend move into a new apartment, each carrying and transporting part of the load from the old place to the new one? Or how about sitting around a table with others stuffing political campaign letters into envelopes and addressing them to potential donors? Although these tasks may seem quite different, they actually share an important common characteristic: performing each requires only a single individual, but several people's work can be pooled to yield greater outcomes. Insofar as each person's contributions can be added together with another's, such tasks have been referred to as **additive tasks**.[18]

The social loafing effect.   If you've ever performed additive tasks, such as the ones described here, there's a good chance that you found yourself working not quite as hard as you would have if you did them alone. Does this sound familiar to you? Indeed, a considerable amount of research has found that when several people combine their efforts on additive tasks, each individual contributes less than he or she would when performing the same task alone.[19] As suggested by the old saying "Many hands make light the work," a group of people would be expected to be more productive than any one individual. However, when several people combine their efforts on additive tasks, each individual's contribution tends to be less. Five people working together raking leaves will *not* be five times more productive than a single individual working alone; there are always some who go along for a "free ride." In fact, the more individuals who are contributing to an additive task, the less each individual's contribution tends to be—a phenomenon known as **social loafing**.[20]

This effect was first noted almost 70 years ago by a scientist who compared the amount of force exerted by different size groups of people pulling on a rope.[21] Specifically, he found that one person pulling on a rope alone exerted an average of 63 kilograms of force. However, in groups of three, the per-person force dropped to 53 kilograms, and in groups of eight it was reduced to only 31 kilograms per person— less than half the effort exerted by people working alone! Social loafing effects of this type have been observed in many different studies conducted in recent years.[22] The general form of the social loafing effect is portrayed in Figure 9.3. (To demonstrate the social loafing effect firsthand, complete the **Group Exercise** at the end of this chapter.)

Is social loafing a universal phenomenon?   A simple way of understanding social loafing is that it occurs because people are more interested in themselves (getting the most for themselves while doing the least) than their fellow group members (who are forced to do their work for them). If you've ever attempted to go along for a "free ride" on a class project by not contributing your fair share, then you know what I mean. In considering this phenomenon, an interesting question arises: Is social loafing equally likely to occur all around the world?

To begin considering this question, it probably isn't surprising that social loafing occurs in the United States because Americans tend to be to be highly individualistic. In **individualistic cultures** people highly value individual accomplishments and personal success. However, in other countries, such as Israel and the People's Republic of China, people place a high value on shared responsibility and the collective good of all. Such nations are referred to as having **collectivistic cultures**. In such cultures, people working in groups would not be expected to engage in social loafing because doing so would have them fail in their social responsibility to the group (a responsibility that does not prevail in individualistic cultures). In fact, to the extent that people in collectivistic cultures are strongly motivated to help their fellow group members, they would be expected to be more productive in groups than alone. That is, not only wouldn't they loaf, but also they would work especially hard!

These ideas were tested in an interesting experiment.[23] Managers from the United States, Israel, and the People's Republic of China were each asked to complete

Figure 9.3 The Social Loafing Effect

When individuals work together on additive tasks, the greater the size of the group, the less effort each individual tends to exert. This phenomenon is known as *social loafing*.

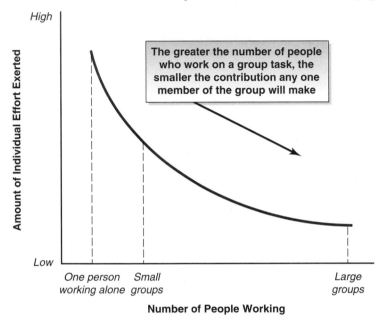

an exercise simulating the daily activities of managers, such as writing memos, filling out forms, and rating job applicants. They were all asked to perform this task as effectively as they could for a period of one hour but under one of two different conditions: either *alone* or as part of a *group* of ten. Individual and group performance was then compared. Did social loafing occur, and in which countries? The results, summarized in Figure 9.4, show that social loafing occurred in the United States. That is, individual performance was significantly lower among people working in groups than those working alone. However, the opposite was found in each of the two highly collectivistic cultures, the People's Republic of China and Israel. In these nations, people not only failed to loaf in groups, but also they worked *harder* than they did alone. Because they strongly identified with their groups and were concerned about the welfare of its members, members of collectivistic cultures placed their group's interests ahead of their own.

It is important to note that culture plays an important part in determining people's tendencies to engage in social loafing. Although it may be tempting to think of social loafing as an inevitable aspect of human nature, it appears that the phenomenon is not as universal as you might think. Instead, loafing appears to be a manifestation of cultural values: Among cultural groups in which individualism is stressed, individual interests guide performance, but among groups in which collectivism is stressed, group interests guide performance.

Figure 9.4   Social Loafing: Not a Universal Phenomenon

Researchers compared the performance of people from the United States, Israel, and the People's Republic of China who worked alone and in groups on a managerial task. Although individual performance alone was lower than performance as part of a group in the United States (i.e., *social loafing* occurred), the opposite was found in China and Israel. Compared to the more *individualistic* nature of American culture, the highly *collectivistic* nature of Chinese and Israeli cultures discouraged people in these nations from letting down their fellow group members.

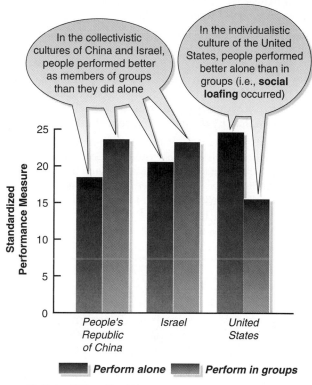

(Source: Based on data reported by Earley, 1993; see Note 23.)

Suggestions for overcoming social loafing.   Obviously, the tendency for people to reduce their effort when working with others could be a serious problem in organizations. Fortunately, there are several ways in which social loafing can be overcome.

- *Make each performer identifiable.* Social loafing may occur when people feel they can get away with "taking it easy"—namely, under conditions in which each individual's contributions cannot be determined. A variety of studies on the practice of *public posting* support this idea.[24] This research has found that when each individual's contribution to a task is displayed where it can be seen by others (e.g., weekly sales figures posted on a chart), people are less likely to slack off than when only overall group (or company-wide) performance is made available. In other words, the more one's individual contribution to a group effort is highlighted, the more pressure each person feels to make a group contribution. Thus, social loafing can be overcome if one's contributions to an additive task are identified: Potential loafers are not likely to loaf if they fear getting caught.

■ *Make work tasks more important and interesting.* Research has revealed that people are unlikely to go along for a free ride when the task they are performing is believed to be vital to the organization.[25] For example, research has found that the less meaningful salespeople believe their jobs are, the more they engage in social loafing—especially when they think their supervisors know little about how well they are working.[26] To help in this regard, corporate officials should deliberately attempt to make jobs more intrinsically interesting to employees. To the extent that jobs are interesting, people may be less likely to loaf.

■ *Reward individuals for contributing to their group's performance.* Social loafing may be overcome by encouraging people's interest in their group's performance.[27] Doing this (e.g., giving all salespeople in a territory a bonus if they jointly exceed their sales goal) may help employees focus more on collective concerns and less on individualistic concerns, increasing their obligations to their fellow group members. This is important, of course, in that the success of an organization is more likely to be influenced by the collective efforts of groups than by the individual contributions of any one member.

■ *Use punishment threats.* To the extent that performance decrements may be controlled by threatening to punish the individuals slacking off, loafing may be reduced. This effect was demonstrated in a experiment involving members of high school swim teams who swam either alone or in relay races during practice sessions.[28] Confirming the social loafing effect, students swam faster alone than as part of relay teams when no punishment was threatened. However, when the coach threatened them with having to swim "penalty laps," the social loafing effect did not occur.

Teams: Empowered Work Groups

In recent years, as organizations have been striving to hone their competitive advantages, many have been organizing work around specific kinds of groups known as *teams*. Because the team movement frequently takes different forms, some confusion has arisen regarding exactly what teams are. In this section we will clarify the basic nature of teams by describing their key characteristics and then identifying the various types of teams that exist.

learning
objective

What Is a Team?

At the Miller Brewing Company in Trenton, Ohio, groups ranging from six to nineteen employees work together to perform all operations, including brewing, packaging, and distributing Miller Genuine Draft beer. They schedule their own work assignments and vacations, conduct assessments of their peers' performance, maintain the equipment, and perform other key functions. Each group is responsible for meeting prespecified targets for production, quality, and safety—and to help, data regarding costs and performance are made available to them.

Clearly, these groups are different in key respects from the ones we have been describing this far, such as a company's budget committee. The Miller employees are all members of special kinds of groups known as *teams*. Formally, we define a **team** as a group whose members have complementary skills and are committed to a common purpose or set of performance goals for which they hold themselves mutually accountable. Applying this definition to our description of the way work is done at Miller's Trenton plant, it's clear that teams are in use at this facility.

Given the complicated nature of teams, I will highlight some of their key characteristics and distinguish teams from the traditional ways in which work is structured.[29] As you read these descriptions, you might find it useful to refer to Table 9.2 as a summary.

Teams are organized around work processes rather than functions. Instead of having traditional departments focusing on a specialized function (such as engineering, planning, quality control, and so on), it is likely that team members have many different skills and come together to perform key processes, such as designing and launching new products, manufacturing, and distribution. As an example, Sterling Winthrop (an Austalian manufacturer of liquid analgesics) used to have 21 different departments working on various aspects of the manufacturing process. Today, all facets of production (e.g., ordering supplies, blending the formulation, scheduling work, etc.) are carried out by members of teams who work together on the production process.

Teams "own" the product, service, or processes on which they work. By this, I mean that people feel part of something meaningful and understand how their work fits into the big picture (recall our discussion of the motivating properties of these kinds of beliefs described in Chapter 6). For example, employees at Florida's Cape Coral Hospital work in teams within four "minihospitals" (surgical, general, specialty medical, and outpatient)—not only to boost efficiency but also to help them feel more

> Employees at Florida's Cape Coral Hospital work in teams within four "minihospitals" (surgical, general, specialty medical, and outpatient)— not only to boost efficiency but also to help them feel more responsible for their patients.

Table 9.2	Teams Versus Traditional Work Structures: Some Key Distinctions

Teams differ from traditional work structures with respect to the six key distinctions identified here.

Traditional Structure	*Teams*
Design around functions	Design around work processes
No sense of ownership over the work products	Ownership of products, services, or processes
Workers have single skills	Team members have many skills
Outside leaders govern workers	Team members govern themselves
Support staff and skills are found outside the group	Support staff and skills are built into teams
Organizational decisions are made by managers	Teams are involved in making organizational decisions for themselves

(Source: Adapted from Wellins, Byham, and Dixon, 1994; see Note 29.)

responsible for their patients. By working in small units, team members have greater contact with patients and are more aware of the effects of their work on patient care. This is in contrast to the traditionally more distant ways of organizing hospital work, in which employees tend to feel less connected to the results of their actions.

Members of teams are trained in several different areas and have a variety of different skills. For example, at Milwaukee Insurance, policies are now processed by team members who rate applications, underwrite policies, and enter them into the computer system. Before the switch to teams, these three tasks were performed by specialists in three separate departments. In fact, this type of separation of tasks is typical within traditional work groups. Before the advent of work teams, it was usual for people to learn only single jobs and perform them over and over again unless there was some specific need for retraining (or interest in doing so on the part of the employee). In work teams, however, this practice of learning to perform a variety of different tasks, known as **cross-training**, occurs regularly. Cross-training involves efforts to learn the jobs performed by one's team members.

A recently conducted experiment explains precisely why cross-training is effective.[30] The participants in this study were college students who performed a military combat simulation game in a laboratory setting. Each person was carefully trained to perform a specific task (e.g., pilots learned how to fly, radar specialists learned how to interpret radar screens, and so on). In addition, some of the participants also were trained in how to perform the task of other group members. The performance of teams composed of members who were cross-trained was compared with the performance of teams whose members were not cross-trained. (In this simulation game, good performance required "killing" enemy targets while keeping one's plane from being shot.) Overall, the performance of the cross-trained group was higher than the performance of the group whose members were not cross-trained.

By including additional questionnaire measures to assess *how* the teams operated, the researchers were able to determine precisely why this occurred. The process, summarized in Figure 9.5, appears to work as follows. When people are cross-trained, they develop what are called **shared mental models**—that is, a common understanding regarding how their team operates, including how people are expected to work together and who does what at particular points in time. These shared mental models, in turn, help people to understand how to coordinate their efforts with others and, of course, how to assist others who may need help (i.e., how to back them up). And, as you might expect, these particular skills contribute to team success. By contrast, people who were not cross-trained failed to develop any shared mental models with their teammates, thereby lowering the degree of coordination and backup capacity that contributed to team success.

Teams govern themselves—at least to some extent. Because team members tend to be so highly trained and involved in a variety of organizational activities, it often is unnecessary for them to be governed closely in the traditional manner in which bosses supervise their subordinates. Instead, many team leaders serve as *coaches* who help team members achieve their goals rather than as traditional, more authoritarian leaders (see Chapter 11). In other words, teams are **empowered** to make decisions on their own behalf.

Figure 9.5	How Does Cross-Training Impact Team Effectiveness?

Recent research has established that cross-training promotes team effectiveness in the manner identified here. The process of cross-training helps create *shared mental models* (common views about how a team should operate), which in turn facilitate high levels of coordination within teams and the capacity for members to provide needed backup. These factors ultimately promote the success of cross-trained teams.

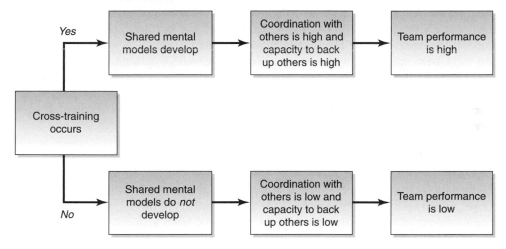

(Source: Based on suggestions by Marks et al., 2002; see Note 30.)

Here's a case in point. At Texas Instruments' defense electronics plant, teams appoint their own leaders, called "coordinators," who do exactly what the name implies—they work to ensure the smooth interaction between the efforts of team members. At other companies, such as Mine Safety Appliances, team members take turns as "captains," handling all the paperwork for a few weeks until the job is rotated to someone else. It is important to note, however, that not all teams enjoy such total self-regulatory freedom. As you might imagine, because many company officials are reluctant to give up power, complete self-governance by teams does not always occur. Still, at least some degree of self-governance tends to occur in today's work teams.

In teams, support staff and responsibilities are built in.   Traditionally, such functions as maintenance, engineering, and human resources operate as separate departments that provide support to other groups requiring their services. Insofar as this often causes delays, teams often include members who have expertise in these crucial support areas. For example, at K Shoes, a British footwear manufacturing firm, there are no longer any quality inspectors. Instead, all team members are trained in matters of inspection and quality control techniques. Sometimes organizations hire people with highly advanced or specialized skills who are assigned to work as members of several teams at once. For example, this is done at Texas Instruments to

> At K Shoes, a British footwear manufacturing firm, there are no longer any quality inspectors. Instead, all team members are trained in matters of inspection and quality control techniques.

give teams access to specialized engineering services. Regardless of how it's done, the point is that teams do not rely on outside support services to get their jobs done; they are relatively self-contained and self-sufficient.

Teams are involved in making company-wide decisions.   Traditionally, high level managers are used to make important organizational decisions. In work teams, however, this responsibility tends to fall on the shoulders of teams. For example, team members at Tennessee Eastman, a manufacturer of chemicals, fibers, and plastics, participate actively on company-level committees that develop policies and procedures affecting everyone. The underlying idea is that the people who are closest to the work performed should be the ones most involved in making the decisions. As noted earlier, the reluctance of some corporate leaders to completely empower teams may temper this process somewhat. In other words, although some companies may be reluctant to give teams total decision-making power, the granting of at least some decision-making authority is a hallmark of modern teams.

Types of Teams

According to one expert, major U.S. companies are now either using some form of teams or are seriously considering them for the future. Although there has been a great amount of recent interest in teams, they have been around the workplace in one form or another for some time. In fact, many large corporations (e.g., Cummins Engine, General Motors, and Ford Motor Company) have been using them for quite a few years—with some, such as Procter & Gamble, for four decades.

In view of their widespread popularity, it should not be surprising that there are many different kinds of teams. I will summarize some of the major kinds of teams here in terms of some of the key ways they may be distinguished from one another.

Work teams and improvement teams.   One way of distinguishing between teams has to do with their major *purpose* or *mission*. In this regard, some teams—known as **work teams**—are primarily concerned with the work done by the organization, such as developing and manufacturing new products, providing services for customers, and so on. Their principle focus is on using the organization's resources to effectively create its products (either goods or services). The examples I've given thus far fall into this category. Other teams—known as **improvement teams**—are primarily oriented toward the mission of increasing the effectiveness of the processes that are used by the organization. For example, Texas Instruments has relied on teams to help improve the quality of operations at its plant in Malaysia.

Temporary and permanent teams.   A second way of distinguishing between types of teams has to do with *time*. Specifically, some teams are only **temporary** and are established for a specific project with a finite life span. For example, a team set up to develop a new product would be considered temporary because as soon as its job is done, it disbands. However, other kinds of teams are **permanent** and remain intact as long as the organization is operating. For example, teams focusing on providing effective customer service tend to be permanent parts of many organizations.

Work groups and self-managed work teams.   Teams also differ with respect to the degree of autonomy they have. Typically, this is reflected in terms of two key factors: the degree of responsibility people have and the degree to which they are held accountable for their own work outcomes. Along the resulting continuum we may identify three kinds of groups and teams (see Figure 9.6). These are as follows.

■ At the low-autonomy extreme are **work groups**, in which leaders make decisions on behalf of group members, whose job it is to follow the leader's orders. This traditional form is becoming less popular, as more organizations are allowing employees to make their own key decisions.

■ At the high-autonomy extreme are **self-managed work teams** (or **self-directed teams**). In such teams, small numbers (typically about 10) take on duties once performed by their supervisors, such as making work assignments, deciding on the pace of work, and so on.[31] About 20 percent of U.S. companies use self-managed work teams, and this figure is growing rapidly.

Figure 9.6   A Continuum of Autonomy

Work groups and teams differ with respect to the degree of autonomy they have. In *work groups*, bosses have responsibility over decisions and are accountable for work outcomes. The workers themselves have very little autonomy. By contrast, in *self-managed work groups*, the workers themselves have responsibility over decisions and are accountable for work outcomes. They are highly autonomous. *Semiautonomous work groups* fall between these two extremes.

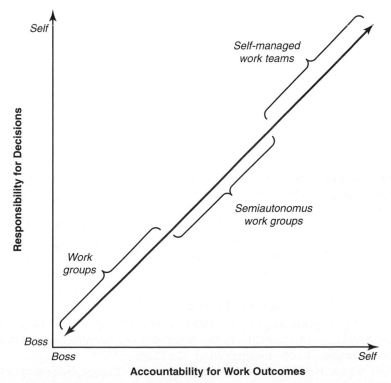

■ Between these two extremes are **semiautonomous work groups**. These are groups whose members who have some, but not complete, freedom to make decisions on their own behalf. Many companies making the move to self-managed work teams try using semiautonomous work groups along the way just to ensure that everyone involved is ready for the resulting freedom and responsibility that go with self-management.

Intact and cross-functional teams.   Another way to distinguish teams is with respect to the team's connection to the organization's overall authority structure—that is, the connection between various formal job responsibilities. In some organizations, **intact teams** work together all the time and do not apply their special knowledge to a wide range of products. Teams in such organizations, such as Ralston-Purina, do not have to stray from their areas of expertise.

With growing frequency, however, teams are crossing over various functional units (e.g., marketing, finance, human resources, and so on). Such teams, referred to as **cross-functional teams**, are composed of employees at identical organizational levels but from different specialty areas. Cross-functional teams are an effective way of bringing people together from throughout the organization to cooperate on large projects. To function effectively, the boundaries between cross-functional teams must be permeable—that is, employees must be members of more than one team. For example, members of an organization's manufacturing team must carefully coordinate their activities with members of its marketing team. To the extent that people are involved in several different kinds of teams, they may gain broader perspectives and make more contributions that are important to their various teams. Chrysler used cross-functional teams to develop its popular Neon automobile, and Boeing used them to develop its latest 777 aircraft.

> Chrysler used cross-functional teams to develop its popular Neon automobile, and Boeing used them to develop its latest 777 aircraft.

Physical and virtual teams.   The teams I have been describing thus far may be considered **physical teams** insofar as they involve people who physically meet to work together. Although teams have operated this way for many years, and will continue to do so, technology has made it possible for teams to exist without ever having their members get together physically. Teams of this sort—that operate across space, time, and organizational boundaries, communicating with each other only through electronic technology—are known as **virtual teams**.[32] Easily one of the most clear-cut examples of a virtual team is the one at Lockheed Martin Aerospace described in detail in this chapter's opening case (see pages 286–287).

Effective Team Performance

In recent years, the popular press has been filled with impressive claims about the success of teams in improving quality, customer service, productivity, and the bottom line.[33] For a sampling of the findings cited, see Table 9.3.[34]

Clearly, we are led to believe that teams in general can produce very impressive results. However, it is important to consider whether or not such claims are valid. In

Table 9.3	The Effectiveness of Teams: Some Impressive Results

Teams have helped many organizations enjoy dramatic gains in productivity. Here is a sampling of these impressive results.

Company	*Result*
Wilson Sporting Goods	Average annual cost savings of $5 million
Kodak Customer Assistance Center	Accuracy of responses increased 100 percent
Corning	Defects dropped from 1,800 ppm to 3 ppm
Sealed Air	Waste reduced by 50 percent
Exxon	$10 million saved in six months
Carrier	Unit turnaround reduced from two weeks to two days
Xerox	Productivity increased by 30 percent
Westinghouse	Product costs down 60 percent
Texas Instruments	Costs reduced by more than 50 percent

(Sources: Based on information in Redding, 2000; and Bianchard and Bowles, 2001; see Note 34.)

this section we will examine evidence bearing on this question. Following this, we will focus on some of the obstacles to team success. Then building on this, in the final section of the chapter we will consider some of the things that can be done to help promote highly successful teams.

How Successful Are Teams? A Look at the Evidence

Now that you understand the basic nature of teams, you are prepared to consider a key question: How successful are teams in organizations? The most direct way to learn about companies' experiences with work teams is to survey the officials of organizations that use them. One large-scale study did precisely this.[35] The sample consisted of several hundred of the 1,000 largest companies in the United States. About 47 percent used some work teams, although these were typically in place in only a few selected sites as opposed to the entire organization. Where they were used, however, they were generally highly regarded. Moreover, teams were viewed as becoming increasingly popular over time.

Case studies.   These optimistic results are further supported by in-depth case studies of numerous teams in many different organizations.[36] Research of this type, although difficult to quantify and to compare across companies, provides some interesting insight into what makes teams successful and why.

Consider, for example, the work teams used in General Motors' battery plant in Fitzgerald, Georgia. The 320 employees at this facility operate in various teams, including managers working together in *support teams*, middle-level employees (such as foremen and technicians) working in *coordination teams*, and *employee teams*, natural work units of three to nineteen members performing specific tasks.

5
learning
objective

Although the teams work closely together, coordinating their activities, they function almost as separate businesses. Because employees must perform many different tasks in their team, they are not paid based on their positions but for their knowledge and competence. In fact, the highest-paid employees are individuals who have demonstrated their competence (usually by highly demanding tests) on all the jobs performed in at least two different teams. This is GM's way of rewarding people for broadening their perspectives, appreciating "the other guy's problems." By many measures, the Fitzgerald plant has been very effective. Its production costs are lower than comparable units in traditionally run plants. Employee satisfaction surveys also reveal that job satisfaction at this plant is among the highest found at any General Motors facility. Although this is only one example, many companies in a wide variety of businesses have reported successes using work teams.[37]

Empirical studies.   Although case studies report successful experiences with teams, they are not entirely objective. After all, companies may be unwilling to broadcast their failures to the world. This is not to say that case studies cannot be trusted. Indeed, when the information is gathered by outside researchers (such as those on which we have reported here), the stories they tell about how teams are used, and the results of using them, can be quite revealing.[38] Still, there is a need for completely objective, empirical studies of team effectiveness.

Research objectively assessing the effectiveness of work teams has been performed in recent years. In one such investigation comparisons were made between various aspects of work performance and attitudes of two groups of employees at a railroad car repair facility in Australia: those who were assembled into teams that could freely decide how to do their jobs and those whose work was structured in the more traditional, nonautonomous fashion.[39] After the work teams had been in place for several months, it was found that they had significantly fewer accidents as well as lower rates of absenteeism and turnover. Not all empirical studies, however, paint such an optimistic picture of the benefits of work teams. For example, in one study examining work teams in an English manufacturing plant it was found that employees were more satisfied with their jobs in teams than those who worked in conventional arrangements (in which individuals took orders from a supervisor), but they were individually no more productive.[40] However, because the use of teams made it possible for the organization to eliminate several supervisory positions, the company became more profitable.

Overall, what can we conclude? Are teams effective? Taken together, research suggests that teams are well received. Most people enjoy working in teams, at least after they have adjusted to them (which can take some work). Certainly, teams help enhance commitment among employees, and as we described in Chapter 5, there are benefits to be derived from this (e.g., reduced absenteeism and turnover). From an organizational perspective, teams appear to be an effective way of eliminating layers of management, thereby allowing more work done to be done by fewer people, which also can be a valuable money-saving contribution. All of these benefits are tangible. However, it is important to keep in mind that teams are not always responsible for making individuals and organizations any more productive. Cases of companies becoming wildly successful after adopting teams, although compelling, cannot always be generalized to all teams in all situations.

Potential Obstacles to Success: Why Do Some Teams Fail?

6
learning
objective

Although we have reported many success stories about teams, we also have hinted at several possible problems and difficulties in implementing them. After all, working in a team demands a great deal, and not everyone may be ready for them. (To see if you are predisposed to work as a member of a team, complete the **Self-Assessment Exercise** on pages 316–317.) Fortunately, we can learn a great deal from the experiences of failed teams. Specifically, analyses of failed attempts at introducing teams into the workplace suggest several obstacles to team success, pitfalls that can be avoided if you know about them.[41] Here are some of the most common ones.

- *Lack of cooperation.* Some teams fail because their members are unwilling to cooperate with one another. This is what happened a few years ago at Dow Chemical Company's plastics group in Midland, Michigan, where a team was put into place to create a new plastic resin.[42] Some members (those in the research field) wanted to spend several months developing and testing new options, whereas others (those on the manufacturing end) wanted to slightly alter existing products and start up production right away. Neither side budged, and the project eventually stalled. By contrast, when team members share a common vision and are committed to attaining it, they are generally very cooperative with each other, leading to success.

- *Lack of support.* It is not unusual for teams to fail because they do not receive the proper support needed by upper management. Consider, for example, the experience at the Lenexa, Kansas, plant of the Puritan-Bennett Corporation, a manufacturer of respiratory equipment.[43] After seven years of working to develop improved software for its respirators, product development teams have not gotten the job done, despite the fact that the industry average for such tasks is only three years. According to Roger J. Dolida, the company's director of research and development, the problem is that management never made the project a priority and refused to free up another key person needed to do the job. As he put it, "If top management doesn't buy into the idea . . . teams can go nowhere."[44]

- *Reluctance to relinquish control.* Traditional supervisors work their way up the corporate ladder by giving orders and having them followed. However, team leaders have to build consensus and must allow team members to make decisions together. As you might expect, letting go of control isn't always easy for some to do. This problem emerged at Bausch & Lomb's sunglasses plant in Rochester, New York.[45] In 1989 some 1,400 employees were put into 38 teams. By 1992 about half the supervisors had not adjusted to the change, despite receiving thorough training in how to work as part of a team. They argued bitterly with team members whenever their ideas were not accepted by the team, and eventually they were reassigned.

- *Failure to cooperate with other teams.* Teams don't operate in a vacuum. To be successful, they must carefully coordinate their efforts with other teams. Not doing so is a recipe for failure. This problem occurred in General Electric's medical systems division when it assigned two teams of engineers, one in Waukesha, Wisconsin, and another in Hino, Japan, the task of creating software for two new ultrasound devices.[46] Not cooperating with one another, each team pushed features that made its products popular only in their own countries and duplicated each other's efforts. When teams met, language and cultural barriers separated them, further distancing the teams from each other. Without close cooperation between teams (as well as within them!), organizations are not likely to reap the benefits they hoped for when creating teams in the first place.[47]

How to Develop Successful Teams

Now that you understand the track record of teams and some of the factors that make them fallible, you are in a good position to understand the various steps that can be taken to develop successful work teams. As you might imagine, making teams work effectively is no easy task. Success is not automatic. Rather, teams need to be carefully nurtured and maintained for them to accomplish their missions.[48] As one expert expressed it, "Teams are the Ferraris of work design. They're high performance but high maintenance and expensive."[49] What, then, could be done to help make teams as effective as possible? Based on analyses of successful teams, several keys to success may be identified.[50]

Provide Training in Team Skills

To be effective, team members must have the right blend of skills needed for the team to contribute to the group's mission. Rather than simply putting teams together and hoping they will work, many companies are taking proactive steps to ensure that team members will get along and perform as they should. Formal efforts directed toward making teams effective are referred to as **team building**. Team building is usually used when established teams are showing signs of trouble, such as when members lose sight of their objectives and when turnover is high. Workers having high degrees of freedom and anonymity require a depth of skills and knowledge that surpasses that of people performing narrower, traditional jobs. For this reason, successful teams are those in which investments are made in developing the skills of team members and leaders. In the words of one expert, "Good team members are trained, not born."[51]

Illustrating this maxim is Development Dimensions International, a printing and distribution facility for a human resource company, located in Pittsburgh, Pennsylvania. This small company has each of its 70 employees spend some 200 hours in training (in such areas as interaction skills, customer service skills, and various technical areas) during their first year—even more for new leaders. Then, after this initial period, all employees receive a variety of training on an ongoing basis.

Key areas of team training.   Two areas of emphasis are essential to the success of any team training effort—training in being a team member and training in self-management.

■ *Being a team member.* Linda Godwin, a mission specialist at NASA's Johnson Space Center in Houston, likens team success to the kind of interpersonal harmony that must exist within space shuttle crews. "We have to be willing to compromise and to make decisions that benefit everyone as a whole," says Godwin, a veteran of two successful shuttle missions.[52] In this regard, there are several key interpersonal skills in which training is most useful, and these are summarized in Table 9.4.

■ *Self-management.* For teams to operate effectively, members must be able to manage themselves. However, most employees are used to being told what to do and don't

Table 9.4	Interpersonal Skills Required by Team Members

Experts have advocated that team members be trained in the various interpersonal skills summarized here (many of which are described elsewhere in this book).

Skill	*Description*
Advocating	Ways of persuading others to accept one's point of view (see Chapter 11)
Inquiring	Listening effectively to others and drawing information out of them (see Chapter 8)
Tension management	Managing the tension that stems from conflict with others (see Chapter 7)
Sharing responsibility	Learning to align personal and team objectives (see Chapter 9)
Leadership	Understanding one's role in guiding the team to success (see Chapter 9)
Valuing diversity	Acceptance—and taking advantage of—differences between members (see Chapter 5)
Self-awareness	Willingness to criticize others constructively and to accept constructive criticism from others (see Chapters 7 and 8)

(Source: Based on information in Caudron, 1994; see Note 51.)

know how to manage their own behavior. Specifically, this involves the various skills summarized in Figure 9.7.[53]

Team training exercises.   Typically, team building involves having team members participate in several different exercises designed to help employees learn how to function effectively as team members. Among the most widely used are the following.[54]

- *Role definition exercises.* Are team members doing what others expect them to be doing? Teams whose members answer "no" are destined for trouble. To avoid such problems, some team-building exercises ask members to describe their own roles and the roles of others on their team. Members then systematically discuss these perceptions and highlight areas of disagreement so these can be worked on.

- *Goal-setting exercises.* As described in Chapter 6, successful performance is enhanced by the setting of goals. As a team-building strategy, team members meet to clarify the various goals toward which they are working and to identify ways they can help achieve them.

- *Problem-solving exercises.* Building successful teams requires ensuring that members are able to work together at solving important problems. To help in this regard, some team-building sessions require members to get together to systematically identify and discuss ways of solving problems more effectively.

- *Interpersonal process exercises.* Some of the most popular team-building exercises involve activities that attempt to build trust and to open communication among members. The underlying idea is that those members who harbor hostility toward each other or who have hidden agendas are unlikely to work together well. There is usually

Figure 9.7   Self-Management Skills: A Key to Team Success

For teams to function successfully, it is essential for members to know how to manage themselves. Training in self-management focuses on the five skills summarized here.

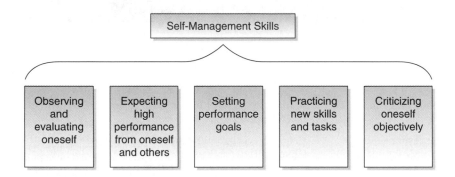

a fun aspect to interpersonal process training as well. Black & Decker, for example, had members of its design team participate in a Spider Web activity requiring members to crawl through a large web of woven rope suspended between two trees without touching the rope. The underlying idea is that by helping each other through these exercises, team members can develop more positive relationships with each other and come to learn how they can influence each other's potential back on the job. In doing this, companies have used such diverse activities as trekking in the wilderness, going through obstacle courses, and having paintball wars. For a close-up example of one extreme form of building teams through interpersonal processes, see the accompanying **Winning Practices** section.

Is team building effective?   Although these various meetings and physical exercises may be fun, we must ask if they have any value? In other words, are they worth the time and money invested in them? The answer is: *only sometimes*. For team-building exercises to be effective they must be applied correctly. Too often, exercises are used without first thoroughly analyzing precisely what the team needs. When it comes to team building, one size does not fit all! Another problem is that team-building exercises often are used as a one-time panacea. For them to be most effective, however, team-building exercises should be repeated regularly to keep the team in tip-top shape or, at least, at the very first sign of problems. And then, when on the job, everyone should be reminded of the lessons learned off-site.

Compensate Team Performance

Because the United States and Canada are highly individualistic cultures, most North American workers are used to highly individualistic compensation systems—ones that recognize individual performance. However, when it comes to teams, it is also very important to recognize group performance. Teams are no places for hot shots who want to make their individual marks—rather, teams require "team players." And the more organizations reward employees for their teams' successes, the more strongly team spirit will be reinforced. Several companies in which teams are

Winning **Practices**

Altrec.com: Extreme Team Building in Action (and Lots of It!)

In the fast-paced, eat-or-be-eaten world of e-business, start-up companies have few options but to grow big overnight. Mike Morford, CEO of Altrec.com, which sells outdoor and travel gear online, was well aware of this as he planned a way to develop a senior team that could pull off the nearly impossible task of finding large investors while keeping at bay two equally hungry competitors.[55] Although his team of 10 star soloists looked good on paper, he realized that six were new to the company, and for things to gel, they had to learn to work together as a team.

Instead of bringing everyone together in the company's comfortable conference room in Bellevue, Washington, Morford opted for a more rugged venue—a 75-mile stretch of Idaho's lower Salmon River, one of the country's wildest waterways. There, in temperatures that reached 100 degrees, rode the fate of the company on an 18-foot rubber raft. They had four days to come up with a six-month plan for the company. If they didn't become a cohesive team by the end of the run, they faced a threat more ominous than business failure—"the Slide," at high water, the largest rapids in North America. The rationale was simple enough: The lessons learned about teamwork in the course of navigating the minefield of unknown hazards on the trip could be taken back to the office, where the more conventional hazards of e-business confronted them.

Although the technical specialists looked forward to the adventure (some more than others), they all were somewhat skeptical about whether the "touchy-feely" trip would be anything more than a fun adventure. The first three days were just plain scary, but on the fourth, the team faced a "sink-or-swim" challenge. Amidst what the guide called particularly "flippy" rapids, the raft rose straight up into the air and plummeted from a height of a story and a half, dumping everyone into the water. Fortunately, everyone came out okay—or even better than okay, as they learned how to help each other confront a force bigger than themselves.

The real challenge began immediately after the adventure, as Altrec.com's senior management team put its words into practice. Two particular strategies emerged. First, team members realized there was tension due to the fact that nobody knew exactly what a particular employee was supposed to be doing. Because this individual happened to be close friends with Morford, everyone just sidestepped the issue and resentment grew. During the trip, everyone agreed on a way to tackle the problem, and a plan was put in place to address it. Second, the team developed a strategy for development in four key areas: communication, feedback, decision making, and respect. After seeing his team in action, Morford, who welcomed a return to the dry and safe harbor of his office back in Bellevue, learned an important lesson himself: He had assembled a group of aggressive decision makers, and his job was to leverage, but not cripple, that strength.

Although everyone claimed to have enjoyed the adventure, back at the office, team members were no more than cautiously optimistic about what the future held for the company and the extent to which their river trip helped at all. If, after six months, the individuals begin working together as a team, none of the skeptical engineers is likely to bad-mouth the "touchy-feely" experience they had on—and in—the Salmon River.

The Hannaford Brothers retail food distribution company in New York and Westinghouse's defense and commercial electronics plant in Texas rely on gainsharing plans to reward teams. These plans reward team members for reaching company-wide performance goals, allowing them to share in their companies' profits.

widely used—including the Hannaford Brothers retail food distribution company in New York and Westinghouse's defense and commercial electronics plant in Texas—rely on gain-sharing plans to reward teams. These plans reward team members for reaching company-wide performance goals, allowing them to share in their companies' profits.

In view of the importance of team members having a variety of different skills, many companies, including Milwaukee Insurance, Colgate-Palmolive, and Sterling Winthrop, have taken to paying employees for their demonstrated skills as opposed to their job performance. Such as system is known as skill-based pay. A highly innovative skill-based pay system has been in use at Tenessee Eastman. This company's "pay-for-applied-skills-and-knowledge" plan—or *PASK,* as it is known—requires employees to demonstrate their skills in several key areas, including technical skills and interpersonal skills. The pay scale is carefully linked to the number of skills acquired and the level of proficiency attained. By encouraging the development of vital skills in this manner, the company is ensuring that it has the resources for its teams to function effectively.

Communicate the Urgency of the Team's Mission

Team members are prone to rally around challenges that compel them to meet high performance standards. As a result, the urgency of meeting those standards should be expressed. For example, a few years ago, employees at Ampex Corporation (a manufacturer of videotape equipment for the broadcasting industry) worked hard to make their teams successful when they recognized the changes necessitated by the shift to digital technology. Unless the company met these challenges, the plug surely would be pulled. Realizing that the company's very existence was at stake, work teams fast-forwarded Ampex into a position of prominence in its industry by ramping up development of digital recording technology.

Promote Cooperation Within and Between Teams

Team success requires not only cooperation within teams but between teams as well. As one expert put it, "Time and time again, teams fall short of their promise because companies don't know how to make them work together with other teams. If you don't get your teams into right constellations, the whole organization can stall."[56] Boeing successfully avoided such problems in the course of developing its 777 passenger jet—a project involving some 200 teams.

As you might imagine, on such a large project coordination of effort between teams is essential. To help, regular meetings were held between various team leaders who disseminated information to members. And team members could go wherever needed within the organization to get the information required to succeed. As one Boeing employee, a team leader, put it, "I can go the chief engineer. Before, it was unusual just to see the chief engineer."[57] Just as importantly, if after getting the information they need, team members find problems, they are empowered to take action without getting management's approval. According to Boeing engineer, Henry Shomber, "We have the no-messenger rule. Team members must make decisions on the spot. They can't run back to their functions [department heads] for permission."[58]

Select Team Members Based on their Skills or Potential Skills

Insofar as the success of teams demands that they work together closely on a wide variety of tasks, it is essential for them to have a complementary set of skills. This includes not only job skills but also interpersonal skills (especially since getting along with one's teammates is very important). With this in mind, at Ampex (noted earlier) three-person subsets of teams are used to select their own new members because they have the best idea about what skills are needed and who would best fit into the teams. It is also frequently important for teams to project future skills that may be needed and to train team members in these skills. With this in mind, work teams at Colgate-Palmolive Company's liquid detergents plant in Cambridge, Ohio, initially received 120 hours of training in such skills as quality management, problem solving, and team interaction, and subsequently received advanced training in all these areas.

In an effort to keep team members' skills fresh, it is important to regularly confront members with new facts. Fresh approaches are likely to be prompted by fresh information, and introducing new facts may present the kind of challenges that teams need to say innovative. For example, when information about pending cutbacks in defense spending was introduced to teams at Florida's Harris Corporation (an electronics manufacturer), new technologies were developed that positioned the company to land large contracts in nonmilitary government organizations—including a $1.7 billion contract to upgrade the FAA's air traffic control system.

A Cautionary Note: Developing Successful Teams Requires Patience

It is important to caution that, although these suggestions are important, they alone do not ensure the success of work teams. Many other factors, such as the economy, the existence of competitors, and the company's financial picture, also are important determinants of organizational success. Still, the fact that these practices are followed in many highly successful teams certainly makes them worthy of consideration.

However, developing effective teams is difficult, and the path to success is riddled with obstacles. It is also time-consuming. According to management expert Peter Drucker, "You can't rush teams. It takes five years just to learn to build a team and decide what kind you want."[59] And it may take most organizations over a decade to make a complete transition to teams. Clearly, teams are not an overnight route to success. But

> According to management expert Peter Drucker, "You can't rush teams. It takes five years just to learn to build a team and decide what kind you want."

with patience and careful attention to the suggestions outlined here, teams have ushered many companies into extraordinary gains in productivity. For this reason, they must be considered a viable option for organizing work groups.[60]

You Be the **Consultant**

Using Teams to Enhance Performance

A large manufacturing company has been doing quite well over the years but is now facing dramatic competition from overseas competitors that are undercutting its prices and improving on the quality of its goods. The company president has read a lot about teams in popular business magazines and has called on you as a consultant to help implement a transition to teams for the organization. Answer the following questions relevant to this situation based on the material in this chapter.

1. What would you tell the company president about the overall record of teams in being able to improve organizational performance?

2. The company president notes that the current employees tend to have relatively poor skills and are generally disinterested in acquiring new ones. Will this be a problem when it comes to using teams? Why or why not?

3. The company president tells you that several people in the company—including some top executives— are a bit concerned about relinquishing some of their power to teams. Is this likely to be a problem, and if so, what can be done to help alleviate it?

Self-Assessment Exercise

Are You a Team Player?

Let's face it, some people find it easier to work in teams than others. Are you already a "team player," or have you not yet developed the skills needed to work effectively with others in teams? Knowing where you stand along this dimension may come in handy when it comes to considering a new job or planning your next work assignment. The following questionnaire will give you insight into this question.

Directions

1. Read each of the following statements and carefully consider whether or not it accurately describes you on the job most of the time.

2. Then, on the line next to each statement, write "yes" if the statement describes you most of the time, or "no" if it does not describe you most of the time. If you are uncertain, write a question mark ("?").

3. Do your best to respond to all items as honestly as possible.

Most of the time, on the job, I . . .

_____ 1. demonstrate high ethical standards.
_____ 2. deliver on promises I make.
_____ 3. take initiative, doing what's needed without being told.
_____ 4. follow the norms and standards of the groups in which I work.

_____ 5. put team goals ahead of my own.

_____ 6. accurately describe my team to others in the organization.

_____ 7. pitch in to help others learn new skills.

_____ 8. do at least my share of the work.

_____ 9. coordinate the work I do with others.

_____ 10. try to attend all meetings and arrive on time for them.

_____ 11. come to meetings prepared to participate.

_____ 12. stay focused on the agenda during team meetings.

_____ 13. share with others new knowledge I may have about the job.

_____ 14. encourage others to raise questions about the way things are.

_____ 15. affirm positive things about others' ideas before noting concerns.

_____ 16. listen to others without interrupting them.

_____ 17. ask others questions to make certain I understand them.

_____ 18. make sure I attend to a speaker's nonverbal messages.

_____ 19. praise others who have performed well.

_____ 20. give constructive, nonjudgmental feedback to others.

_____ 21. receive constructive feedback without acting defensively.

_____ 22. communicate ideas without threats or ridicule.

_____ 23. explain the reasoning behind my opinions.

_____ 24. demonstrate my willingness to change my opinions.

_____ 25. speak up when I disagree with others.

_____ 26. show disagreement in a tactful, polite manner.

_____ 27. discuss possible areas of agreement with others with whom I am in conflict.

(Source: Based on material appearing in McDermott et al., 1998; see Note 60.)

Scoring

1. Count the number of times you responded by saying "yes."

2. Then count the number of times you responded by saying "no."

3. Add these two numbers together.

4. To compute your *team player score*, divide the number of times you said yes (step 1) by the total (step 3). Then multiply by 100. Your score will be between 0 and 100. Higher scores reflect greater readiness for working in teams.

Discussion Questions

1. What was your score, and how did it compare to those of others in your class?

2. What does this questionnaire reveal about the ways in which you are best equipped to work in teams?

3. What does this questionnaire reveal about the ways in which you are most deficient when it comes to working in teams? What do you think you could do to improve your readiness for working in teams?

Group Exercise

Demonstrating the Social Loafing Effect

The social loafing effect is quite strong and is likely to occur in many situations in which people make individual contributions to an additive group task. This exercise is designed to demonstrate the effect firsthand in your own class.

Directions

1. Divide the class into groups of different sizes. Between five and ten people should work alone. In addition, there should be a group of two, a group of three, a group of four, and so on, until all members of the class have been assigned to a group. (If the class is small, assign students to groups of vastly different sizes, such as two, seven, and fifteen.) Form the groups by putting together at tables people from the same group.

2. Each person should be given a page or two from a telephone directory and a stack of index cards. Then have the individuals and the members of each group perform the same additive task—copying entries from the telephone directory onto index cards. Allow exactly 10 minutes for the task to be performed, and encourage everyone to work as hard as they can.

3. After the time is up, count the number of entries copied.

4. For each group, and for all the individuals, compute the average per-person performance by dividing the total number of entries copied by the number of people in the group.

5. At the board, the instructor should graph the results. Along the vertical axis show the average number of entries copied per person. Along the horizontal axis show the size of the work groups—one, two, three, four, and so on. The graph should look like the one in Figure 9.2.

Discussion Questions

1. Was the social loafing effect demonstrated? What is the basis for your conclusion?

2. Did members of smaller groups feel more responsible for their group's performance than members of larger groups?

3. What could have been done to counteract any "free riding" that may have occurred in this demonstration?

Notes

Case Notes

Keenan, F., & Ante, S. E. (2002, February 18). The new teamwork. *BusinessWeek Online*. From the Web at www.businessweek.com:/print/magazine/content/02_07/b3770601.htm?bw. Hancock, D. M. (2001). Upon being honored as the National Management Association's executive of the year for 2001. From the Web at www.lmaeronautics.com/news/speeches/hancock/dmh_nma2001.html.

Chapter Notes

[1] Turner, M. E. (2000). *Groups at work: Theory and research*. Mahwah, NJ: Lawrence Erlbaum Associates. Cartwright, D., & Zander, A. (1968). Origins of group dynamics. In D. Cartwright & A. Zander (Eds.), *Group dynamics: Research and theory* (pp. 3–21). New York: Harper & Row.

[2] Toothman, J. (2000). *Conducting the experiential group: An introduction to group dynamics*. New York: John Wiley. Bettenhausen, K. L. (1991). Five years of groups research: What we have learned and what needs to be addressed. *Journal of Management, 17*, 345–381.

[3] Nowak, A., Vallacher, R. R., & Miller, M. E. (2003). Social influence and group dynamics. In T. Millon & M. J. Lerner (Eds.), *Handbook of psychology: Vol. 5, Personality and social psychology* (pp. 383–418). New York: John Wiley & Sons. Forsyth, D. L. (1999). *Group dynamics* (3rd ed.). Belmont, CA: Wadsworth.

[4] Podsakoff, P. M., & MacKenzie, S. B. (1997). Kerr and Jermier's substitutes for leadership model: Background, empirical assessment, and suggestions for future research. *Leadership Quarterly, 8*, 117–125. Biddle, B. J. (1979). *Role theory: Expectations, identities, and behavior*. New York: Academic Press.

[5] Hackman, J. R. (1992). Group influences on individuals in organizations. In M. D. Dunnette & L. M. Hough (Eds.), *Handbook of industrial and organizational psychology* (2nd ed.) (Vol. 3, pp. 199–268). Palo Alto, CA: Consulting Psychologists Press.

[6] Janicik, G. A., & Bartel, C. A. (2003). Talking about time: Effects of temporal planning and time awareness norms on group coordination and performance. *Group Dynamics, 7*, 122–134. Feldman, D. C. (1984). The development and enforcement of group norms. *Academy of Management Review, 9*, 48–53.

[7] Wilson, S. (1978). *Informal groups: An introduction*. Upper Saddle River, NJ: Prentice Hall.

[8] Greenberg, J. (1988). Equity and workplace status: A field experiment. *Journal of Applied Psychology, 73*, 606–613.

[9] Jackson, L. A., & Grabski, S. V. (1988). Perceptions of fair pay and the gender wage gap. *Journal of Applied Social Psychology, 18*, 606–625.

[10] Torrance, E. P. (1954). Some consequences of power differences on decision making in permanent and temporary three-man groups. *Research Studies: Washington State College, 22*, 130–140.

[11] Hare, A. P. (1976). *Handbook of small group research* (2nd ed). New York: Free Press.

[12] Aronson, E., & Mills, J. (1959). The effects of severity of initiation on liking for a group. *Journal of Abnormal and Social Psychology, 59*, 178–181.

[13] Cartwright, D. (1968). The nature of group cohesiveness. In D. Cartwright & A. Zander (Eds.), *Group dynamics: Research and theory* (3rd ed.), (pp. 91–109). New York: Harper & Row.

[14] George, J. M., & Bettenhausen, K. (1990). Understanding prosocial behavior, sales performance, and turnover: A group-level analysis in a service context. *Journal of Applied Psychology, 75*, 698–709.

[15] Douglas, T. (1983). *Groups: Understanding people gathered together*. New York: Tavistock.

[16] Aiello, J. R., & Douthirt, E. A. (2001). Social facilitation from Triplett to electronic performance monitoring. *Group Dynamics, 5*, 163–180.

[17] Aiello, J. R., & Svec, C. M. (1993). Computer monitoring of work performance: Extending to social facilitation framework to electronic presence. *Journal of Applied Social Psychology, 23*, 537–548.

[18] Steiner, I. D. (1972). *Group processes and productivity*. New York: Academic Press.

[19] Shepperd, J. A. (1993). Productivity loss in performance groups: A motivation analysis. *Psychological Bulletin, 113*, 68–81.

[20] Latané, B., Williams, K., & Harkins, S. (1979). Many hands make light the work: The causes and consequences of social loafing. *Journal of Personality and Social Psychology, 37*, 822–832.

[21] Kravitz, D. A., & Martin, B. (1986). Ringelmann rediscovered: The original article. *Journal of Personality and Social Psychology, 50*, 936–941.

[22] Karau, S. J., & Williams, K. D. (1993). Social loafing: A meta-analytic review and theoretical integration. *Journal of Personality and Social Psychology, 65*, 681–706.

[23] Earley, P. C. (1993). East meets West meets Mideast: Further explorations of collectivistic and individualistic work groups. *Academy of Management Journal, 36*, 319–348.

[24] Nordstrom, R., Lorenzi, P., & Hall, R. V. (1990). A review of public posting of performance feedback in work settings. *Journal of Organizational Behavior Management, 11*, 101–123.

[25] Bricker, M. A., Harkins, S. G., & Ostrom, T. M. (1986). Effects of personal involvement: Thought-provoking implications for social loafing. *Journal of Personality and Social Psychology, 51*, 763–769.

[26] George, J. M. (1992). Extrinsic and intrinsic origins of perceived social loafing in organizations. *Academy of Management Journal, 35*, 191–202.

[27] Albanese, R., & Van Fleet, D. D. (1985). Rational behavior in groups: The free-riding tendency. *Academy of Management Review, 10*, 244–255.

[28] Miles, J. A., & Greenberg, J. (1993). Using punishment threats to attenuate social loafing effects among swimmers. *Organizational Behavior and Human Decision Processes, 56*, 246–265.

[29] Wellins, R. S., Byham, W. C., & Dixon, G. R. (1994). *Inside teams*. San Francisco: Jossey-Bass.

[30] Marks, M. A., Sabella, M. J., Burke, C. S., & Zaccaro, S. J. (2002). The impact of cross-training on team effectiveness. *Journal of Applied Psychology, 87*, 3–13.

[31] Robbins, H., & Finley, M. (2000). *The new why teams don't work*. San Francisco: Barrett-Koehler.

[32] Willmore, J. (2003). *Managing virtual teams*. London: Spiro Press. Hoefling, T. (2003). *Working virtually: Managing people for successful virtual teams and organizations*. London: Stylus Publications.

[33] Sheridan, J. H. (1990, October 15). America's best plants. *Industry Week*, pp. 28–64.

[34] Blanchard, K. H., & Bowles, S. M. (2001). *High five: The magic of working together*. New York: William Morrow. Redding, J. C. (2000). *The radical team handbook*. New York: John Wiley & Sons. Fisher, K. (1993). *Leading self-directed work teams*. New York: McGraw-Hill.

[35] Lawler, E. E., III., Mohrman, S. A., & Ledford, G. E., Jr. (1992). *Employee involvement and total quality management*. San Francisco: Jossey-Bass.

[36] Hackman, J. R. (Ed.) (1990). *Groups that work (and those that don't)*. San Francisco: Jossey-Bass.

[37] Wellins, R. S., Byham, W. C., & Wilson, J. M. (1991). *Empowered teams*. San Francisco: Jossey-Bass.

[38] Blanchard, K. H., & Bowles, S. M. (2001). *High five: The magic of working together*. New York: William Morrow.

[39] Pearson, C. A. L. (1992). Autonomous workgroups: An evaluation at an industrial site. *Human Relations, 45*, 905–936.

[40] Wall, T. D., Kemp, N. J., Jackson, P. R., & Clegg, C. W. (1986). Outcomes of autonomous workgroups: A long-term field experiment. *Academy of Management Journal, 29*, 280–304.

[41] Robbins, H., & Finley, M. (1995). *Why teams don't work*. Princeton, NJ: Peterson's/Pacesetters Books.

[42] Stern, A. (1993, July 18). Managing by team is not always as easy as it looks. *New York Times*, p. B14.

[43] See Note 42.

[44] See Note 42.

[45] See Note 42.

[46] See Note 42.

[47] West, M. A. (2004). *Effective teamwork*. Oxford, England: Blackwell. Maginn, M. D. (1994). *Effective teamwork*. Burr Ridge, IL: Business One Irwin.

[48] Salas, E., Edens, E., & Nowers, C. A. (2000). *Improving teamwork in organizations*. Mahwah, NJ: Lawrence Erlbaum Associates.

[49] Dumaine, B. (1994, September 5). The trouble with teams. *Fortune*, pp. 86–88, 90, 92 (quote, p. 86).

[50] Barner, R. W. (2001). *Team troubleshooter*. Palo Alto, CA: Davies Black. Maruca, R. F. (2000, November). Unit of one. *Fast Company*, pp. 109–140.

[51] LeStorti, A. (2003). *When you're asked to do the impossible: Principles of business teamwork and leadership from the U.S. Army's elite rangers*. Guilford, CT: Lyons Press. Caudron, S. (1994, February). Teamwork takes work. *Personnel Journal*, pp. 41–46, 49 (quote, p. 43).

[52] Caudron, 1994; see Note 51 (quote, p. 42).

[53] Stewart, G. L., & Manz, C. C. (1997). Leadership for self-managing work teams: A typology and integrative model. In. R. P. Vecchio (Ed.), *Leadership: Understanding the dynamics of power and influence in organizations* (pp. 396–410). Notre Dame, IN: University of Notre Dame Press.

[54] Sundstrom, E., DeMeuse, K. P., & Futrell, D. (1990). Work teams: Applications and effectiveness. *American Psychologist, 45*, 128–137.

[55] Balf, T. (1999, November). Extreme off-site. *Fast Company*, pp. 384–388, 390, 396, 398.

[56] See Note 49 (quote, p. 88).

[57] See Note 49 (quote, p. 90).

[58] See Note 49 (quote, p. 88).

[59] Anonymous. (1994, December). The facts of life for teambuilding. *Human Resources Forum*, p. 3.

[60] McDermott, L. C., Brawley, N., & Waite, W. W. (1998). *World class teams*. New York: John Wiley & Sons.

Chapter Ten

LEARNING OBJECTIVES

After reading this chapter, you will be able to:

1. **IDENTIFY** the steps in the decision-making process and DESCRIBE the effects of culture on decision making.

2. **DESCRIBE** the different varieties of decisions people make in organizations.

3. **EXPLAIN** the three major approaches to individual decision making (the *rational-economic model*, the *administrative model*, and *image theory*).

4. **IDENTIFY** various factors that contribute to imperfect decision making in organizations.

5. **DESCRIBE** the conditions under which individuals make better decisions than groups and groups make better decisions than individuals.

6. **EXPLAIN** how various structural techniques (the *stepladder technique*, the *Delphi technique*, and the *nominal group technique*) as well as various computer-based techniques (*electronic meeting systems*, *computer-mediated communication*, and *group decision support systems*) may be used to improve the quality of decisions made by groups.

Making Decisions in Organizations

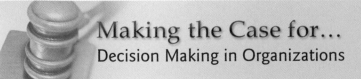

Making the Case for...
Decision Making in Organizations

The Enron–Arthur Andersen Scandal: Decision Making Gone Awry

In July 1985, the Houston Natural Gas company merged with InterNorth to form Enron. In the years that followed, shrewd financial dealings led the fledgling company to become one of the world's richest and most powerful companies, eventually reaching number five on the *Fortune* 500. Or so it seemed. That was until December 2, 2001, when the company filed for Chapter 11 bankruptcy protection—just days after announcing a $1.2 billion loss.

As the story unfolded, it became clear that the demise of Enron was no ordinary business failure. Rather, Enron's collapse was the inevitable result of a complex web of lies, deceit, and unethical decisions by company officials that led to the ongoing illusion that Enron was in excellent financial condition when the truth was quite the opposite. By way of some questionable accounting practices, actual losses were reported as profits (a jump of 37.6 percent in

2001 alone), in deals that put some $30 million in the pocket of Enron CEO Ken Lay. Despite Lay's obvious windfall, the company's collapse led to the loss of jobs and vaporized the pension savings for 4,000 company employees. It also sent reverberations through the stock market amid fears that there may be "other Enrons out there."

In January 2002, the U.S. Justice Department launched an investigation of Enron that painted a picture of ongoing blatant financial mismanagement and greed that spread beyond Enron to its accounting firm, the then-highly regarded Arthur Andersen. As soon as it became apparent that it was going to be investigated by the Securities and Exchange Commission, Andersen officials are alleged to have ordered employees to destroy thousands of documents that could connect it to the questionable business practices of its client. Indicted by a federal grand jury, Andersen was cited with undermining the justice system by destroying "tons" of paperwork and by attempting to purge electronic data, even working around-the-clock to do it.

Andersen officials have claimed that these actions were neither directed by high-ranking officials, nor did they conform to company policy. Rather, they say that these acts stemmed from poor decisions by a few rogue employees in the Houston office, who subsequently were fired, including a partner in the firm, David Duncan, who is alleged to have spearheaded the destruction operations. Although the truth may never be known, it's clear that Andersen suffered greatly from its association with Enron. Not wanting to be linked to an accounting firm whose ethics may be questioned, major clients such as Delta Airlines and FedEx fired Andersen, leading the company to falter. As many as 7,000 Andersen employees have lost their jobs and the company's German operations have been purchased by competitor Ernst & Young.

Few cases in the annals of business have been as serious and as far-reaching as the tales of corruption at Enron and its beleaguered accounting firm, Arthur Andersen, that unfolded on the pages of the business press in recent years. The resulting changes in accounting practices and government regulation of business are sure to be monumental. Yet, at the heart of all this lies a process that is very fundamental to human beings and of considerable concern to the field of OB—the making of *decisions*. Whether guided by greed or power, some Enron officials decided to engage in business practices that were intentionally misleading.

3 GOOD REASONS why you should care about...

Decision Making in Organizations

You should care about decision making in organizations because:

1. Human decision making is inherently imperfect, although these imperfections can be overcome if you know what they are and how they operate.

2. Functioning effectively in today's business environment requires awareness of cultural differences in the way people make decisions.

3. Groups are widely used to make organizational decisions despite the fact they often are ineffective at dealing with the kinds of tasks they are likely to face.

Then, guided by the desire to protect its client, Andersen officials made decisions to cover up Enron's misdeeds. When viewed from this perspective, it's clear that understanding how people come to make decisions can be quite important.

Although the decisions you make as an individual may be less monumental than those associated with the Enron scandal, they are very important to you. For example, personal decisions about what college to go to, what classes to take, and what company to work for can have a major impact on the direction your life takes. If you think about the difficulties involved in making decisions in your own life, you surely can appreciate how complicated—and important—the process of decision making can be in organizations, where the stakes are often considerable and the impact is widespread. In both cases, however, the essential nature of **decision making** is identical. It may be defined as the process of making choices from among several alternatives.

Management experts agree that decision making represents one of the most common and most crucial work roles of executives.[1] Every day people in organizations make decisions about a wide variety of topics ranging from the mundane to the monumental.[2] Understanding how these decisions are made, and how they can be improved, is an important goal of the field of organizational behavior. As such, you will find a great deal of insight devoted to these matters in this chapter. Before considering this, we begin the chapter by examining the general nature of the decision-making process and the wide variety of decisions made in organizations.

The Fundamental Nature of Decision Making

I begin this chapter by describing the fundamental nature of decision making. Specifically, I will focus on two things. First, I will describe a general model of the decision-making process. Second, I will address a fundamental question about decision making: Are we all alike in the way we make decisions?

learning
objective

A General Model of Decision Making

Traditionally, scientists have found it useful to conceptualize the process of decision making as a series of steps that groups or individuals take to solve problems.[3] A general model of the decision-making process can help us understand the complex nature of organizational decision making (see Figure 10.1). This model highlights two important aspects of the decision-making process: *formulation*, the process of understanding a problem and making a decision about it, and *implementation*, the process of carrying out the decision made. As I outline this model, keep in mind that all decisions might not fully conform to the neat, eight-step pattern described (e.g., steps may be skipped and/or combined). However, for purposes of pointing out the general way the decision-making process operates, the model is quite useful.

1. *Identify the problem.* To decide how to solve a problem, one must first recognize and identify it. For example, an executive may identify as a problem the fact that the company cannot meet its payroll obligations. This step isn't always as easy as it sounds. People frequently distort, omit, ignore, and/or discount information around them that provides important cues regarding the existence of problems. This, of course, is problematic. After all, a problem cannot be solved if it is never recognized.

Figure 10.1   The Decision-Making Process

The process of decision making tends to follow the eight steps outlined here. The running example illustrates how a particular problem—insufficient funds to meet payroll obligations—can be applied to each step.

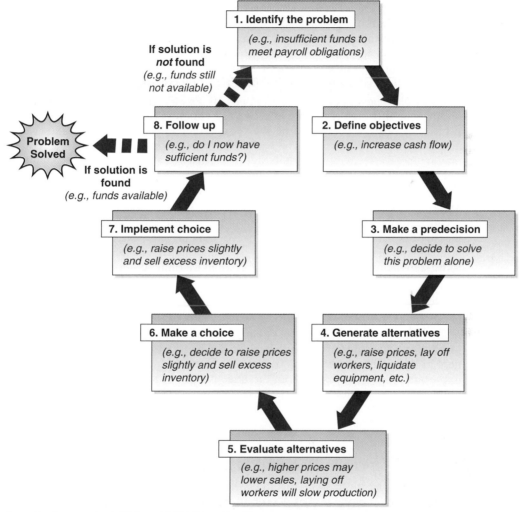

1. Identify the problem
(e.g., insufficient funds to meet payroll obligations)

If solution is *not* found
(e.g., funds still not available)

8. Follow up
(e.g., do I now have sufficient funds?)

Problem Solved

If solution is found
(e.g., funds available)

2. Define objectives
(e.g., increase cash flow)

7. Implement choice
(e.g., raise prices slightly and sell excess inventory)

3. Make a predecision
(e.g., decide to solve this problem alone)

6. Make a choice
(e.g., decide to raise prices slightly and sell excess inventory)

4. Generate alternatives
(e.g., raise prices, lay off workers, liquidate equipment, etc.)

5. Evaluate alternatives
(e.g., higher prices may lower sales, laying off workers will slow production)

(Source: Based on suggestions by Wedley and Field, 1983; see Note 3.)

2. *Define objectives.* After a problem is identified, the next step is to define the objectives to be met in solving it. It is important to conceive of problems in such a way that possible solutions can be identified. The problem identified in our example may be defined as "inadequate cash flow." By looking at the problem in this way, the objective is clear: Increase available cash reserves. Any possible solution to the problem should be evaluated relative to this objective.

3. *Make a predecision.* A **predecision** is a decision about how to make a decision. By assessing the type of problem in question and other aspects of the situation, managers

may opt to make a decision themselves, delegate the decision to another, or have a group make the decision. Predecisions should be based on research that tells us about the effectiveness of decisions made under different circumstances, many of which we will review later in this chapter. Much of this information is summarized in computer programs known as **decision support systems (DSS)**. These techniques are generally quite effective in helping people make decisions about complex problems.

4. *Generate alternatives.* Possible solutions to the problem are identified in this stage. Whenever possible in attempting to come up with solutions, people tend to rely on previously used approaches that may provide ready-made answers. In our example, some possible ways of solving the revenue shortage problem include reducing the workforce, liquidating unnecessary equipment, or increasing sales.

5. *Evaluate alternative solutions.* Because not all possible alternatives may be equally feasible, the fifth step calls for evaluating the various alternatives identified. Which solution is best? What would be the most effective way of raising the revenue needed to meet the payroll? The various alternatives need to be identified. Some may be more effective than others, and some may be more difficult to implement than others. For example, although increasing sales would certainly help, that is much easier said than done. It is a solution, but not an immediately practical one.

6. *Make a choice.* After several alternatives are evaluated, one that is considered acceptable is chosen. As we will describe shortly, different approaches to decision making offer different views of how thoroughly people consider alternatives and how optimal their chosen alternatives are. Choosing which course of action to take is the step that most often comes to mind when we think about the decision-making process.

7. *Implement the chosen alternative.* In following this step, whatever alternative was chosen is now carried out.

8. *Follow-up.* Monitoring the effectiveness of the decisions they put into action is important to the success of organizations. Does the problem still exist? Have any new problems been caused by implementing the solution? In other words, it is important to seek feedback about the effectiveness of any attempted solution. For this reason, the decision-making process is presented as circular in Figure 10.1. If the solution works, the problem may be considered solved. If not, a new solution will have to be attempted.

Cultural Differences in Decision Making

Having outlined the basic steps through which people go in making decisions, you may assume that everyone makes decisions the same way. This would be misleading. Although the basic steps involved in making decisions may be identical, there are widespread differences in the way people from various nations go about making decisions.[4] Because we take for granted our own ways of making decisions, differences between people from different cultures may seem strange to us. However, it is important to become aware of such differences when doing business with people from around the world. Accordingly, it makes sense to ask how people from different countries differ in the way they make decisions.

Recognizing problems.   As I noted earlier, decision making begins by observing a problem. As obvious as this may seem, people from different countries do not always agree on what constitutes a problem. Suppose, for example, you are managing a large construction project and discover that your most important supplier will deliver some important materials several months late. If you are from the United States, Canada, or Western Europe, you may decide to get another supplier. However, if you are from Thailand, Indonesia, or Malaysia, you would be likely to accept the situation as fate and allow the project to be delayed.

Preference for decision-making unit.   In the United States, where people tend to have a highly **individualistic orientation** (i.e., their primary focus is on themselves as individuals), people tend to make decisions by themselves. However, in Asian countries, people have a more **collectivistic orientation** (i.e., their primary focus is on the groups to which they belong). As such, it would be inconceivable for a Japanese businessperson to make a decision without first checking with his or her colleagues. Individuals from such cultures are inclined to make group decisions rather than individual ones.

Who makes the decisions?   In Sweden, employees at all levels expect to be involved in making whatever decisions involve them. In fact, employees of the Scandinavian auto manufacturers Saab and Volvo routinely make decisions about how to do their jobs. In India, by contrast, the hierarchy of an organization matters a great deal. People there expect decisions to be made by others of higher rank. Empowered decision making (which I will describe more fully later in this chapter) is not well accepted.

> Employees of the Scandinavian auto manufacturers Saab and Volvo routinely make decisions about how to do their jobs.

Time taken to make decisions.   In the United States, we generally respect people who make decisions quickly, referring to them as "decisive," a quality that is valued. In other cultures, however, time urgency is downplayed. For example, in the Middle East, quickly reaching a decision is seen as a sign of being overly hasty. In Egypt, the more important the matter, the more time one is expected to take when making a decision about it.

As these examples illustrate, there are some interesting and important differences in how people from various countries formulate and implement decisions. Understanding such differences is an important first step toward developing appropriate strategies for conducting business at a global level.[5]

Varieties of Organizational Decisions

learning
objective

Consider for a moment the variety of decisions likely to be made in organizations. Some decisions have consequences that don't matter much (e.g., what brand of paper clips to order for the company supply closet), whereas others are far-reaching (e.g., whether and how to count disputed ballots in a presidential election). People sometimes make decisions in situations in which the likely outcomes are relatively well known (e.g., the decision to underwrite life insurance on the basis of actuarial data), whereas at other times the outcomes are much more uncertain (e.g., the decision to invade a hostile nation for purposes of freeing hostages). Finally, some decisions are issued from the top (e.g., an order from the department head that work will begin sharply at 8:00 A.M.) whereas other decisions are made by the very individuals who will be affected by them (e.g., a team whose members decide whom to hire).

These examples illustrate the three major characteristics of organizational decisions I will now describe: (1) how structured or unstructured the situation is, (2) how much certainty or risk is involved in the decision, and (3) how much employees are involved in making the decisions affecting them.

Programmed Versus Nonprogrammed Decisions

Think of a decision that is made repeatedly, according to a preestablished set of guidelines. For example, a word processing operator may decide to make a backup diskette of the day's work, or a manager of a fast-food restaurant may decide to order hamburger buns as the supply starts to get low. Decisions such as these are known as **programmed decisions**—routine decisions, made by lower-level personnel, that rely on predetermined courses of action.

By contrast, people also make **nonprogrammed decisions**—ones for which there are no ready-made solutions. The decision maker confronts a unique situation in which the solutions are novel. The research scientist attempting to find a cure for a rare disease faces a problem that is poorly structured. Unlike the order clerk whose course of action is clear when the supply of paper clips runs low, the scientist in this example must rely on creativity rather than preexisting answers to solve the problem at hand.

Certain types of nonprogrammed decisions are known as **strategic decisions**. Typically, because these decisions have important long-term implications for the organization, they are made by coalitions of high-level executives.[6] Strategic decisions reflect a way of directing an organization in some specified fashion—that is, according to an underlying organizational philosophy or mission. For example, an organization may make a strategic decision to grow at a specified yearly rate or to be guided by a certain code of corporate ethics (see Chapter 2). Both of these decisions are likely to be considered "strategic" because they guide the future direction of the organization. Some excellent examples of highly successful strategic decisions may be found in Table 10.1.[7]

Certain Versus Uncertain Decisions

Think of how easy it would be to make decisions if we knew exactly what the future held in store. Making the best investments in the stock market would simply be a matter of looking up the changes in tomorrow's newspaper. Of course, we never know for sure what the future holds, but we can be more certain at some times than others. Certainty about the factors on which decisions are made is highly desired in organizational decision making.

Degrees of certainty and uncertainty are expressed as statements of risk. All organizational decisions involve some degree of risk—ranging from complete certainty (no risk) to complete uncertainty, "a stab in the dark" (high risk). To make the best possible decisions in organizations, people seek to "manage" the risks they take—that is, to minimize the riskiness of a decision by gaining access to information relevant to the decision.

| Table 10.1 | Strategic Decisions: Some Highly Successful Examples |

Decisions that guide the future directions of organizations are known as *strategic decisions*. Some of the best-known and most successful strategic decisions are shown here.

Company	Decision Made
Toyota	In the aftermath of World War II, the company decided to emphasize high-quality manufacturing techniques.
Coca-Cola	During World War II, the company developed brand loyalty by selling bottles of Coke to members of the armed services.
IBM	In 1924, founder Thomas Watson, Sr., changed the company's name from the Computing-Tabulating-Recording Company to International Business Machines although it had no international operations at the time, boldly declaring its ambitions.
Microsoft	In 1981, Bill Gates decided to license MS-DOS to IBM, which relinquished control of the operating system for all non-IBM personal computers.
Apple	Steve Jobs decided to build his company around sales of a simple computer that could be used by individuals.
Sears	In 1905, the company decided on a way to bring its products to a wider audience by introducing a mail-order catalog.
Johnson & Johnson	In 1982, the company pulled all bottles of Tylenol capsules off store shelves after a few capsules were found to be poisoned.
Sony	In 1980, the company introduced the Walkman after officials noticed that young people like to have music with them wherever they go.
Hewlett-Packard	In 1979 the company decided to exploit an engineer's observation that metal heated in a certain way tended to splatter, resulting in the development of the ink-jet printer.

(Source: Based on material in Crainer, 1998; see Note 7.)

What makes an outcome risky or not is the probability of obtaining the desired outcome. Decision makers attempt to obtain information about the probabilities, or odds, of certain events occurring given that other events have occurred. For example, a financial analyst may report that a certain stock has risen 80 percent of the time that the prime rate has dropped, or a meteorologist may report that the precipitation probability is 50 percent (i.e., in the past it rained or showed half the time certain atmospheric conditions existed). These data may be considered reports of *objective probabilities* because they are based on concrete, verifiable data. Many decisions are also based on subjective probabilities—personal beliefs or hunches about what will happen. For example, a gambler who bets on a horse because it has a name similar to one of his children's, or a person who suspects it's going to rain because he just washed his car, is basing these judgments on *subjective probabilities*.

Obviously, uncertainty is an undesirable characteristic in decision-making situations. We may view much of what decision makers do in organizations as attempting to reduce uncertainty so they can make better decisions. In general, what reduces uncertainty in decision-making situations? The answer is *information*. Knowledge about the past and the present can be used to help make projections about the future. A modern executive's access to data needed to make important decisions may be as close as the nearest computer terminal. A variety of online information services are designed to provide organizational decision makers with the latest information relevant to the decisions they are making.

Of course, not all information needed to make decisions comes from computers. Many managerial decisions are also based on the decision maker's experiences and intuition. This is not to say that top managers rely on subjective information in making decisions (although they might), but that their history of past decisions—both successes and failures—is often given great weight in the decision-making process. In other words, when it comes to making decisions, people often rely on what has worked for them in the past. (To help reduce the riskiness of their decisions, many of today's top company officials are relying on high-tech devices. For a look at how this is done in a popular retail store, see the **Winning Practices** section.)

Top-Down Versus Empowered Decisions

Traditionally, the job of making all but the most menial decisions has belonged to managers.[9] Subordinates collect information and give it to their superiors, who then use it to make decisions. Known as **top-down decision making**, this approach puts the power to make decisions in the hands of managers, leaving lower-level workers with little or no opportunity to make decisions.

Today, however, a new approach has come into vogue. The idea of **empowered decision making** allows employees to make the decisions required to do their jobs without seeking supervisory approval. As the name implies, this approach gives employees the power to do their jobs effectively. The rationale is straightforward: Allow the people who actually do certain jobs to make decisions about them. This practice is generally very useful insofar as it is likely to lead to effective decisions. In addition, it helps build commitment to decisions. After all, people are more committed to the results of decisions they made themselves than those their bosses have made for them.

> The Ritz-Carlton hotel chain, renown for its service, has empowered chambermaids to authorize expenditures up to $2,000 per day for maintenance of hotel facilities they find to be in need of repair.

The Ritz-Carlton hotel chain offers a good example of empowered decision making. This upscale hotel chain, renown for its service, has empowered chambermaids to authorize expenditures up to $2,000 per day for maintenance of hotel facilities they find to be in need of repair. So, instead of filling out a form to repair, say, a broken lamp, which normally would get passed from one person to another for approval, chambermaids now can go straight to the appropriate person who can get the job done. What's more, they are empowered to follow up by making sure that the repair has been made and overseeing its reinstallation in the hotel.

Winning **Practices**

Adaptive Agents as Decision Aids

To make good decisions, it helps to know in advance how things will work out. With this in mind, scientists are developing sophisticated computer models that capture the rules of complex human behavior. The so-called **adaptive agents** created by engineers and consultants at PricewaterhouseCoopers are software-based "people" programmed to behave in the same ways as human beings.[8] Their goal is ambitious: to be able to mimic what people will do in certain situations, thereby allowing managers to see the impact of their decisions without ever making them in the real world.

This would be the ultimate way of reducing the uncertainty of decisions. Although even the most sophisticated computer programs cannot perfectly predict the future, they will be able to provide extremely useful information to decision makers about likely outcomes. I use the future tense here because this technology is in its infancy. Still, optimistic about how it will facilitate complex decision making, several companies have invested in its development, hoping to bring this technology to fruition. For example, Macy's is relying on using the technology to help it determine the number of salespeople to schedule in each store department and where to locate service desks and cash registers within stores. Macy's also wants to know how a sales associate's age, gender, and length of service will influence sales by consumers. US West also has expressed interest in the technology, hoping to be able to predict how both competitors and customers will respond to different pricing and promotion plans.

As useful as this technology is, scientists freely admit that they have a long way to go before it's perfected. Still, it already has seen some successes. For example, the group at PricewaterhouseCoopers has developed 40,000 adaptive agents for a major entertainment company. Cloned from a survey of actual moviegoers, programming these agents has made it possible to forecast first-week box-office receipts 30 percent more accurately than traditional methods.

The real benefit from creating adaptive agents comes from the fact that you can simulate in just a few months what it otherwise would take entire days or weeks to find out. And, of course, mistakes have no cost because you're playing "what if" games with a simulated public. Those of you who have crashed airplanes while playing with flight simulation programs surely can appreciate the safety of using simulated decisions. At the same time, just as what you learn about real flying using a flight simulator can be invaluable, so too can what you learn about the behavior of real people when using simulated ones.

As promising as this technology may be, experts caution that it's only as good as the assumptions built into it (which, of course, require considerable research in organizational behavior). And, although it could be useful as a decision aid, it certainly won't be replacing actual human decision makers anytime soon.

How Are Individual Decisions Made?

Now that we have identified the types of decisions people make in organizations, we are prepared to consider the matter of how people go about making them. Perhaps you are thinking, "What do you mean, you just think things over and do what you think is best?" Although this may be true, you will see that there's a lot more to decision making than meets the eye. In fact, scientists have considered several different approaches to how individuals make decisions. Here we will review three of the most important ones.

The Rational-Economic Model: In Search of the Ideal Decision

We all like to think that we are "rational" people who make the best possible decisions. But what exactly does it mean to make a *rational* decision? Organizational scientists view **rational decisions** as ones that maximize the attainment of goals, whether they are the goals of a person, a group, or an entire organization.[10] What would be the most rational way for an individual to go about making a decision? Economists interested in predicting market conditions and prices have relied on a **rational-economic model** of decision making, which assumes that decisions are optimal in every way. An economically rational decision maker will attempt to maximize his or her profits by systematically searching for the *optimum* solution to a problem. For this to occur, the decision maker must have complete and perfect information and be able to process all this information in an accurate and unbiased fashion.[11]

In many respects, rational-economic decisions follow the same steps outlined in our analytical model of decision making (see Figure 10.1). However, what makes the rational-economic approach special is that it calls for the decision maker to recognize *all* alternative courses of action (step 4) and to accurately and completely evaluate each one (step 5). It views decision makers as attempting to make *optimal* decisions.

Of course, the rational-economic approach to decision making does not fully appreciate the fallibility of the human decision maker. Based on the assumption that people have access to complete and perfect information and use it to make perfect decisions, the model can be considered a *normative* (also called *prescriptive*) approach—one that describes how decision makers ideally ought to behave so as to make the best possible decisions. It does not describe how decision makers actually behave in most circumstances. This task is undertaken by the next major approach to individual decision making, the *administrative model*.

The Administrative Model: The Limits of Human Rationality

As you know from your own experience, people generally do not act in a completely rational-economic manner. To illustrate this point, consider how a personnel department might select a new receptionist. After several applicants are interviewed, the personnel manager might choose the best candidate seen so far and stop interviewing. Had the manager been following a rational-economic model, he or she would have had to interview all possible candidates before deciding on the best one. However, by ending the search after finding a candidate who was just good enough, the manager is using a much simpler approach.

The process used in this example characterizes an approach to decision making known as the **administrative model**.[12] This conceptualization recognizes that decision makers may have a limited view of the problems confronting them. The number of solutions that can be recognized or implemented is limited by the capabilities of the decision maker and the available resources of the organization. Also, decision makers do not have perfect information about the consequences of their decisions, so they cannot tell which one is best.

How are decisions made according to the administrative model? Instead of considering all possible solutions, decision makers consider solutions as they become available. Then they decide on the first alternative that meets their criteria for acceptability. Thus, the decision maker selects a solution that may be just good enough, although not optimal. Such decisions are referred to as **satisficing decisions**. Of course, a satisficing decision is much easier to make than an optimal decision. In most decision-making situations, satisficing decisions are acceptable and are more likely to be made than optimal ones.[13] The following analogy is used to compare the two types of decisions: *Making an optimal decision is like searching a haystack for the sharpest needle, but making a satisficing decision is like searching a haystack for a needle just sharp enough with which to sew.*

As we have noted, it is often impractical for people to make completely optimal, rational decisions. The administrative model recognizes the **bounded rationality** under which most organizational decision makers must operate. The idea is that people lack the cognitive skills required to formulate and solve highly complex business problems in a completely objective, rational way.[14] In addition, decision makers limit their actions to those that fall within the bounds of current moral and ethical standards—that is, they use **bounded discretion**.[15] So, although engaging in illegal activities such as stealing may optimize an organization's profits (at least in the short run), ethical considerations strongly discourage such actions.

It should not be surprising that the administrative model does a better job than the rational-economic model of describing how decision makers actually behave. The approach is said to be *descriptive* (also called *proscriptive*) in nature. This interest in examining the actual, imperfect behavior of decision makers, rather than specifying the ideal, economically rational behaviors that decision makers ought to engage in, lies at the heart of the distinction between the administrative and rational-economic models. Our point is not that decision makers do not want to behave rationally, but that restrictions posed by the innate capabilities of the decision makers preclude "perfect" decisions.

Image Theory: An Intuitive Approach to Decision Making

If you think about it, you'll probably realize that some, but certainly not all, decisions are made following the logical steps of our general model of decision making. Consider Elizabeth Barrett Browning's poetic question "How do I love thee? Let me count the ways."[16] It's unlikely that anyone would ultimately answer the question by carefully counting what one loves about another (although many such characteristics can be enumerated). Instead, a more intuitive-based decision making is likely, not only for matters of the heart but for a variety of important organizational decisions as well.[17]

The point is that selecting the best alternative by weighing all the options is not always a major concern when making a decision. People also consider how various decision alternatives fit with their personal standards as well as their personal goals and plans. The best decision for someone might not be the best for someone else. In other words, people may make decisions in a more automatic, *intuitive* fashion than is traditionally recognized. Representative of this approach is **image theory**.[18] This approach to decision making is summarized in Figure 10.2.

Image theory deals primarily with decisions about adopting a certain course of action (e.g., should the company develop a new product line?) or changing a current course of action (e.g., should the company drop a present product line?). According to the theory, people make adoption decisions on the basis of a simple two-step process. The first step is the *compatibility test*, a comparison of the degree to which a particular course of action is consistent with various images—particularly individual principles, current goals, and plans for the future. If any lack of compatibility exists with respect to these considerations, a rejection decision is made. If the compatibility test is passed, then the *profitability test* is carried out. That is, people consider the extent to which using various alternatives best fits their values, goals, and plans. The decision is then made to accept the best candidate. These tests are used within a certain *decision frame*—that is, with consideration of meaningful information about the

---

Figure 10.2   Image Theory: An Overview and Example

According to image theory, decisions are made in a relatively automatic, intuitive fashion following the two steps outlined here.

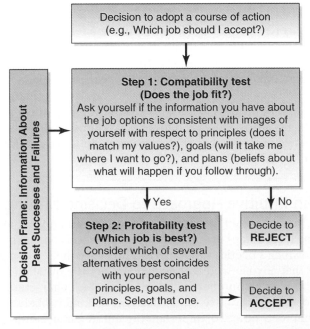

(Source: Adapted from Beach and Mitchell, 1990; see Note 18.)

decision context (such as past experiences). The basic idea is that we learn from the past and are guided by it when making decisions. The example shown in Figure 10.2 highlights this contemporary approach to decision making.

According to image theory, the decision-making process is very rapid and simple. The theory suggests that people do not ponder and reflect over decisions but make them using a smooth, intuitive process with minimal cognitive processing. If you've ever found yourself saying that something "seemed like the right thing to do," or "something doesn't feel right," you're probably well aware of the kind of intuitive thinking that goes on in a great deal of decision making. Recent research suggests that when it comes to making relatively simple decisions, people tend to behave as suggested by image theory.[19] For example, it has been found that people decide against various options when past evidence suggests that these decisions may be incompatible with their images of the future.[20]

To summarize, we have described three major approaches to individual decision making. The rational-economic approach represents the ideal way optimal decisions may be made. However, the administrative model and image theory represent ways that people actually go about making decisions. Both approaches have received support, and neither should be seen as a replacement for the other. Instead, several different processes may be involved in decision making. Not all decision making is carried out the same way: Sometimes decision making might be analytical, and sometimes it might be more intuitive. Modern organizational behavior scholars recognize the value of both approaches. Something both approaches have in common is that they recognize the fallibility of the human decision maker. With this in mind, we will now turn our attention to the imperfect nature of human decisions.

The Imperfect Nature of Human Decisions

learning objective

We all like to think of ourselves as "rational" people who make **rational decisions**— that is, decisions that maximize the attainment of individual, team, or organizational goals. However, as you know from experience, people do not always act in completely rational ways. It's not that decision makers do not want to behave rationally or that they are somehow irrational. Rather, innate limits in people's ability to make decisions as well as impediments in the work environment make it virtually impossible to make completely rational, perfect decisions.

To illustrate this point, consider how a personnel department might select a new receptionist. After several applicants are interviewed, the personnel manager might choose the best candidate seen so far and stop interviewing. Had the person been completely rational, he or she would have had to interview *all* possible candidates before deciding on the best one. But, he did not. Instead, the manager in this example used a far simpler approach, one that typifies the way people go about making decisions.

Characteristics of Decisions in Organizations

Because people are not machines, we don't always make perfect decisions—in fact, we rarely, if ever, do so. And whatever limitations we have as human decision makers are aggravated by the realities of life in organizations. These limitations can be characterized in several key ways.

Decision makers have a limited view of the problems confronting them.   The number of solutions that can be recognized or implemented is limited by the capabilities of the decision maker and the available resources of the organization. Also, because decision makers do not have perfect information about the consequences of their decisions, they cannot tell which one is best. The idea is that people lack the cognitive skills required to formulate and solve highly complex business problems in a completely objective, rational way—what is known as **bounded rationality**.[21]

Decision makers consider solutions as they become available.   Although it might be best to consider all possible solutions, making an **optimal decision**, people don't do so. Instead, they decide on the first alternative that meets their criteria for acceptability. Thus, the decision maker selects a solution that may be just good enough, although not optimal. Such decisions are referred to as **satisficing decisions**. In most situations satisficing decisions are acceptable and are more likely to be made than optimal ones. The following analogy has been used to compare the two types of decisions: making an optimal decision is like searching a haystack for the sharpest needle, but making a satisficing decision is like searching a haystack for a needle just sharp enough with which to sew.

Decision makers face time constraints.   An unavoidable fact of life in contemporary organizations is that people often have only limited amounts of time to make important decisions. The rapid pace with which businesses operate these days results in severe pressures to make decisions almost immediately. Among firefighters, emergency room doctors, and fighter pilots, it's clear that time is of the essence. But even those of us who toil in less dramatic settings also face the need to make good decisions quickly. The practice of thoroughly collecting information, carefully analyzing it, and then leisurely reviewing the alternatives is a luxury few modern decision makers can afford. In a recent survey, 77 percent of a broad cross section of managers polled felt that the number of decisions they were required to make each day has increased, and 43 percent reported that the time they can devote to making decisions has decreased.[22] Often the result is that as people are rushed into action, bad—and inevitably, costly—decisions are made.

Decision makers are sensitive to political "face-saving" pressure.   In other words, people may make decisions that help them look good to others, although the resulting decisions might not be in the best interest of their organizations. Decisions frequently are made with an eye toward cultivating a good impression, although they may not always be the best ones for their organizations.

Systematic Biases in Individual Decisions

Beyond the fundamental limitations of people's capacity to process information, it also is important to be aware of the fact that people approach the decisions they make in ways that are systematically biased.[23] I will describe several of these types of biases here.

Framing effects: "Half full or half empty?"   One well-established decision-making bias has to do with the tendency for people to make different decisions based on how the problem is presented to them—that is, the **framing** of a problem. Scientists have found that problems framed in a manner that emphasizes the positive gains to be received tend to encourage conservative decisions (i.e., decision makers are said to be *risk averse*), whereas problems framed in a manner that emphasizes the potential losses to be suffered lead to *risk-seeking* decisions. Consider the following example:

> The government is preparing to combat a rare disease expected to take 600 lives. Two alternative programs to combat the disease have been proposed, each of which, scientists believe, will have certain consequences. Program A will save 200 people, if adopted. Program B has a one-third chance of saving all 600 people, but a two-thirds chance of saving no one. Which program do you prefer?

When such a problem was presented to a group of people, 72 percent expressed a preference for Program A, and 28 percent for Program B. In other words, they preferred the "sure thing" of saving 200 people over the one-third possibility of saving them all. However, a curious thing happened when the description of the programs was framed in negative terms. Specifically:

> Program C was described as allowing 400 people to die, if adopted. Program D was described as allowing a one-third probability that no one would die, and a two-thirds probability that all 600 would die. Now which program would you prefer?

Compare these four programs. Program C is just another way of stating the outcomes of Program A, and Program D is just another way of stating the outcomes of Program B. However, Programs C and D are framed in negative terms, which led to opposite preferences: 22 percent favored Program C and 78 percent favored Program D. In other words, people tended to avoid risk when the problem was framed in terms of "lives saved" (i.e., in positive terms) but to seek risk when the problem was framed in terms of "lives lost" (i.e., in negative terms).

Scientists believe that such effects are due to the tendency for people to perceive equivalent situations framed differently as not really equivalent. In other words, focusing on the glass as "half full" leads people to think about it differently than when it is presented as being "half empty," although they might recognize intellectually that the two are really the same. Such findings illustrate that people are not completely rational decision makers but are systematically biased by the cognitive distortions created by simple differences in the way situations are framed.

Heuristics.   Framing effects are not the only cognitive biases to which decision makers are subjected. It also has been established that people often attempt to simplify the complex decisions they face by using **heuristics**—simple rules of thumb that guide them through a complex array of decision alternatives. Although heuristics are potentially useful to decision makers, they represent potential impediments to decision making. Two very common types of heuristics may be identified.

- **The availability heuristic**—This is the tendency for people to base their judgments on information that is readily available to them—although it may be inaccurate. Suppose, for example, that an executive needs to know the percentage of entering college freshmen who go on to graduate. There is not enough time to gather the appropriate statistics, so she bases her judgments on her own recollections of when she was a college student. If the percentage she recalls graduating, based on her own experiences, is higher or lower than the usual number, her estimate will be off accordingly.

- **The representativeness heuristic**—This is the tendency to perceive others in stereotypical ways if they appear to be typical representatives of the category to which they belong. For example, suppose you believe that accountants are bright, mild-mannered individuals, whereas salespeople are less intelligent but much more extroverted. Furthermore, imagine that there are twice as many salespeople as accountants at a party. You meet someone at the party who is bright and mild-mannered. Although mathematically the odds are two-to-one that this person is a salesperson rather than an accountant, chances are you will guess that the individual is an accountant because she possesses the traits you associate with accountants.

It is important to note that heuristics do not always deteriorate the quality of decisions made. In fact, they can be quite helpful. People often use rules of thumb to help simplify the complex decisions they face. For example, management scientists employ many useful heuristics to aid decisions regarding such matters as where to locate warehouses or how to compose an investment portfolio. We also use heuristics in our everyday lives, such as when we play chess ("control the center of the board") or blackjack ("hit on 16, stick on 17"). However, the representativeness heuristic and the availability heuristic may be recognized as impediments to superior decisions insofar as they discourage people from collecting and processing as much information as they should. Making judgments based on only readily available information or on stereotypical beliefs, although making things simple for the decision maker, does so at a potentially high cost—poor decisions.

Escalation of commitment: Throwing good money after bad.   It is inevitable that some organizational decisions will be unsuccessful. What would you say is the rational thing to do when a poor decision has been made? Intuitively, it makes sense for the ineffective action to be stopped or reversed, to "cut your losses and run." However, people don't always respond this way. In fact, it is not unusual to find that ineffective decisions are sometimes followed up with still further ineffective decisions.

Imagine, for example, that you have invested money in a company, but as time goes on, it appears to be failing. Rather than lose your initial investment, you may invest still more money in the hope of salvaging your first investment. The more you invest, the more you may be tempted to save those earlier investments by making later investments. That is to say, people sometimes may be found "throwing good money after bad" because they have "too much invested to quit." This phenomenon is known as **escalation of commitment**—the tendency for people to continue to support previously unsuccessful courses of action because they have sunk costs invested in them. For a summary of the escalation of commitment phenomenon, see Figure 10.3.

Although this might not seem like a rational thing to do, this strategy is frequently followed. Consider, for example, how large banks and governments may invest money in foreign governments in the hope of turning them around even though such a result becomes increasingly unlikely. Similarly, the organizers of Expo '86 in British Columbia

Figure 10.3   Escalation of Commitment

According to the *escalation of commitment* phenomenon, people who have repeatedly made poor decisions will continue to support those failing courses of action in the future so that they may justify their original decisions.

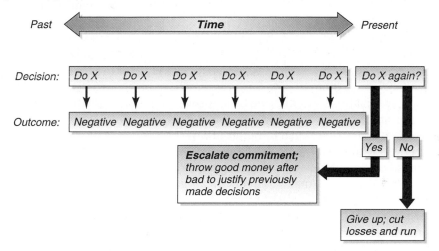

continued pouring money into the fair long after it became apparent that it would be a big money-losing proposition.[24]

Why do people do this? If you think about it, you may realize that the failure to back your own previous courses of action in an organization would be taken as an admission of failure—a politically difficult act to face in an organization. In other words, people may be very concerned about "saving face"—looking good in the eyes of others. Scientists believe that this tendency for self-justification is primarily responsible for people's inclination to protect their beliefs about themselves as rational, competent decision makers by convincing themselves and others that they made the right decision all along and are willing to back it up.

Group Decisions: Do Too Many Cooks Spoil the Broth?

learning
objective

Decision-making groups are a well-established fact of modern organizational life. Groups such as committees, study teams, task forces, or review panels are often charged with the responsibility for making important business decisions. They are so common, in fact, that it has been said that some administrators spend as much as 80 percent of their time in committee meetings. Given this, it is important to consider the strengths and weaknesses of using groups to make organizational decisions.

Group Decisions: A Double-Edged Sword

There is little doubt that much can be gained by using decision-making groups. Several potential advantages of this approach may be identified. First, bringing people together may increase the amount of knowledge and information available for making good decisions. In other words, there may be a *pooling of resources*. A related benefit is that in decision-making groups there can be a *specialization of labor*. With enough people around to share the workload, individuals can perform only those tasks at which they are best, thereby potentially improving the quality of the group's efforts. Another benefit is that group decisions are likely to enjoy *greater acceptance* than individual decisions. People involved in making decisions may be expected to understand those decisions better and be more committed to carrying them out than decisions made by someone else.

Of course, there are also some problems associated with using decision-making groups. One obvious drawback is that groups are likely to *waste time*. The time spent socializing before getting down to business may be a drain on the group and be very costly to organizations. Another possible problem is that potential disagreement over important matters may breed ill will and *group conflict*. Although constructive disagreement can actually lead to better group outcomes, highly disruptive conflict may interfere with group decisions. Finally, we may expect groups to be ineffective sometimes because of members' *intimidation by group leaders*. A group composed of several "yes" men or women trying to please a dominant leader tends to discourage open and honest discussion of solutions.

Given the several pros and cons of using groups to make decisions, we must conclude that *neither groups nor individuals are always superior*. Obviously, there are important trade-offs involved in using either one to make decisions.

Comparing Group and Individual Decisions: When Are Two (or More) Heads Better Than One?

Since there are advantages associated with both group and individual decision makers, a question arises as to when each should be used.[25] That is, under what conditions might individuals or groups be expected to make superior decisions?

When are groups superior to individuals?   Imagine a situation in which an important decision has to be made about a complex problem—such as whether one company should merge with another. This is not the kind of problem about which any one individual working alone would be expected to make a good decision. Its highly complex nature may overwhelm even an expert, thereby setting the stage for a group to do a better job.

Whether a group actually will do better than an individual depends on several important considerations. First, who is in the group? Successful groups are composed of heterogeneous group members with complementary skills.[26] So, for example, a group composed of lawyers, accountants, real estate agents, and other experts may make much better decisions on the merger problem than would a group composed of specialists in only one field. Indeed, the diversity of opinions offered by group members is one of the major advantages of using groups to make decisions.

Second, for a group to be successful, its members also must be able to freely communicate their ideas to each other in an open, nonhostile manner. Conditions under which one individual (or group) intimidates another from contributing his or her expertise can easily negate any potential gain associated with composing groups of heterogeneous experts. After all, having expertise and being able to make a contribution by using that expertise are two different things. Only when the contributions of the most qualified group members are given the greatest weight does the group derive any benefit from those members' presence. Thus, for groups to be superior to individuals, they must be composed of a heterogeneous collection of experts with complementary skills who can freely and openly contribute to their group's product.

In contrast to complex decision tasks, imagine a situation in which a judgment is required on a simple problem with a readily verifiable answer. For example, imagine that you are asked to translate a phrase from a relatively obscure language into English. Groups might do better than individuals on such a task only because the odds are increased that someone in the group knows the language and can perform the translation on behalf of the group. However, there is no reason to expect that even a large group will be able to perform such a task better than a single individual who has the required expertise. In fact, an expert working alone may do even better than a group because that expert may be distracted by others and may suffer from having to convince them of the correctness of his or her solution. For this reason, exceptional individuals tend to outperform entire committees on simple tasks. In such cases, for groups to benefit from a pooling of resources, there must be some resources to pool. The pooling of ignorance does not help. In other words, the question "Are two heads better than one?" can be answered this way: On simple tasks, two heads may be better than one *if* at least one of those heads has enough of what it takes to succeed.

In summary, whether groups perform better than individuals depends on the nature of the task performed and the expertise of the people involved. For an overview of these key considerations, refer to Figure 10.4.

Figure 10.4 Comparing Group and Individual Decisions

As summarized here, groups make better decisions than individuals under some conditions, but individuals make better decisions than groups under others.

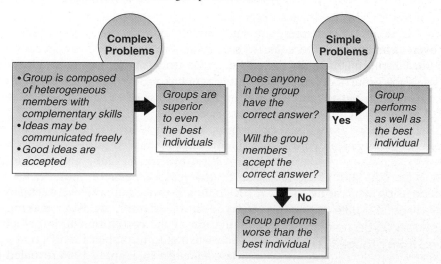

When are individuals superior to groups? Most of the problems faced by organizations require a great deal of creative thinking. For example, a company deciding how to use a newly developed adhesive in its consumer products is facing decisions on a poorly structured task. Although you would expect that the complexity of such creative problems would give groups a natural advantage, this is not the case. In fact, research has shown that on poorly structured, creative tasks, individuals perform better than groups.[27]

An approach to solving creative problems commonly used by groups is **brainstorming**. This technique was developed by an advertising executive as a tool for coming up with creative, new ideas.[28] The members of brainstorming groups are encouraged to present their ideas in an uncritical way and to discuss freely and openly all ideas on the floor. Specifically, members of brainstorming groups are required to follow four main rules: (1) avoid criticizing others' ideas, (2) share even far-out suggestions, (3) offer as many comments as possible, and (4) build on others' ideas to create your own.

Does brainstorming improve the quality of creative decisions? To answer this question, researchers conducted a study comparing the effectiveness of individuals and brainstorming groups working on creative problems.[29] Specifically, participants were given 35 minutes to consider the consequences of situations such as "What if everybody went blind?" or "What if everybody grew an extra thumb on each hand?" Clearly, the novel nature of such problems requires a great deal of creativity. Comparisons were made of the number of solutions generated by groups of four or seven people and a like number of individuals working on the same problems alone. The results were clear: Individuals were significantly more productive than groups.

In summary, groups perform worse than individuals when working on creative tasks. A great part of the problem is that some individuals feel inhibited by the presence of others even though one rule of brainstorming is that even far-out ideas may be shared. To the extent that people wish to avoid feeling foolish as a result of saying silly things, their creativity may be inhibited when in groups. Similarly, groups may inhibit creativity by slowing down the process of bringing ideas to fruition.

Groupthink: Too Much Cohesiveness Can Be a Dangerous Thing

One reason groups may fare so poorly on complex tasks lies in the dynamics of group interaction (see Chapter 9). When members of a group develop a very strong group spirit—high levels of *cohesiveness*—they sometimes become so concerned about not disrupting the like-mindedness of the group that they may be reluctant to challenge the group's decisions. When this happens, group members tend to isolate themselves from outside information, and the process of critical thinking deteriorates. This phenomenon is referred to as **groupthink**.

The concept of groupthink was proposed initially as an attempt to explain ineffective decisions made by U.S. government officials that led to fiascoes such as the Bay of Pigs invasion in Cuba and the Vietnam War.[30] Analyses of each of these cases have revealed that the president's advisers actually discouraged more effective decision making. An examination of the conditions under which the decision was made to launch the ill-fated space shuttle *Challenger* in January 1986 revealed that

An examination of the conditions under which the decision was made to launch the ill-fated space shuttle Challenger in January 1986 revealed that it too resulted from groupthink.

it too resulted from groupthink.[31] Post-hoc analyses of conversations between key personnel suggested that the team that made the decision to launch the shuttle under freezing conditions did so while insulating itself from the engineers who knew how the equipment should function. Given that NASA had such a successful history, the decision makers operated with a sense of invulnerability. They also worked so closely together and were under such intense pressure to launch the shuttle without further delay that they all collectively went along with the launch decision, creating the illusion of unanimous agreement.

Groupthink occurs not only in governmental decision making, of course, but also in the private sector (although the failures may be less well publicized). For example, analyses of the business policies of large corporations such as Lockheed and Chrysler have suggested that it was the failure of top-management teams to respond to changing market conditions that at one time led them to the brink of disaster. The problem is that members of very cohesive groups may have considerable confidence in their group's decisions, making them unlikely to raise doubts about these actions (i.e., "the group seems to know what it's doing"). As a result, they may suspend their own critical thinking in favor of conforming to the group.[32] When group members become fiercely loyal to each other, they may ignore potentially useful information from other sources that challenges the group's decisions. The result of this process is that the group's decisions may be completely uninformed, irrational, or even immoral.

Fortunately, there are several strategies can effectively combat groupthink. A few proven techniques are summarized in Table 10.2. Given the extremely adverse effects groupthink can have on organizations, practicing managers would be wise to press these simple suggestions into action.

Structural Approaches for Improving Group Decisions

6
learning
objective

As explained in this chapter, certain advantages can be gained from sometimes using individuals and sometimes using groups to make decisions. A decision-making technique that combines the best features of groups and individuals, while minimizing the disadvantages, would be ideal.[33] Here, I will describe three special techniques that do so—the *stepladder technique*, the *Delphi technique*, and the *nominal group technique*. All represent ways in which a group's activities may be structured so as to improve decision making.

The Stepladder Technique

Another way of structuring group interaction is known as the **stepladder technique**.[34] This approach minimizes the tendency for group members to be unwilling to present their ideas by adding new members to a group one at a time and requiring each to present his or her ideas independently to a group that already has discussed the problem at hand. To begin, each of two people works on a problem independently, and then they come together to present their ideas and discuss solutions jointly. While the two-person group is working, a third person working alone also considers the problem. Then this

| Table 10.2 | Guidelines for Avoiding Groupthink |

The suggestions outlined here have been shown to be effective when it comes to avoiding the critical problem of groupthink.

Suggestion	*Explanation*
Use subgroups	Because the decision made by any one group may be the result of groupthink, basing decisions on the recommendations of two or more subgroups is a useful check. If the different groups disagree, a discussion of their differences is likely to raise important issues. However, if the two groups agree, you can be relatively confident that their conclusions are not the result of groupthink.
Admit shortcomings	When groupthink occurs, group members feel very confident that they are doing the right thing. Such feelings discourage people from considering opposing information. However, if group members acknowledge some of the flaws and limitations of their decisions, they may be more open to corrective influences. This may help avoid the illusion of perfection that contributes to groupthink.
Hold second-chance meetings	As people get tired of working on problems, they may hastily reach agreement on a solution. Before implementing a decision, hold sessions in which group members are asked to express any doubts and to propose any new ideas they may have (known as *second-chance meetings*). Second-chance meetings can be useful devices for seeing if a solution still seems good even after "sleeping on it."
Promote open inquiry	Remember, groupthink arises in response to group member's reluctance to "rock the boat." Group leaders should encourage members to be skeptical of all solutions and to avoid reaching premature agreements. It sometimes helps to play the role of *devil's advocate*, that is, to intentionally find fault with a proposed solution. Many executives have found that raising a nonthreatening question to force both sides of an issue can be a very helpful way to improve the quality of decisions.

individual presents his or her ideas to the group and joins in a three-person discussion of a possible solution. During this period a fourth person works on the problem alone and then presents his or her ideas to the group and joins into a four-person group discussion. After each new person has been added to the group, the entire group works together at finding a solution. (For a summary of the steps in this technique, see Figure 10.5.)

In following this procedure, it is important for each individual to be given enough time to work on the problem before he or she joins the group. Then each person must be given enough time to present thoroughly his or her ideas to the

Figure 10.5   The Stepladder Technique

By systematically adding new individuals into decision-making groups, the stepladder technique helps to increase the quality of the decisions made.

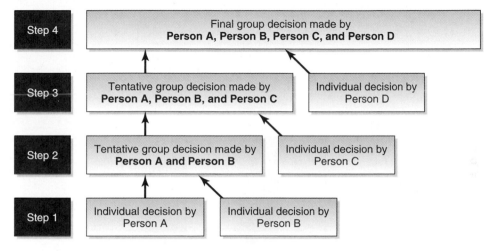

(Source: Adapted from Rogelberg and O'Connor, 1998; see Note 34.)

group. Groups then must have sufficient time to discuss the problem at hand and reach a preliminary decision before the next person is added. The final decision is made only after all individuals have been added to the group.

The rationale underlying this procedure is that by forcing each person to present independent ideas without knowing how the group has decided, the new person will not be influenced by the group, and the group is required to consider a constant infusion of new ideas. If this is so, then groups solving problems using the stepladder technique would be expected to make better decisions than conventional groups meeting all at once to discuss the same problem. Research has found that this is precisely what happens. In a recent study, scientists compared the quality of decisions made by four-person groups that met in conventional fashion with that of groups that used the stepladder technique.[35] Both groups read a story about a plane that crashed in a remote northern location and were asked to make decisions about the particular gear the crew members needed most to survive. After scoring the decisions with respect to quality (based on comparisons with the decisions made by expert wilderness survivors), it was found that the stepladder groups did better. In other words, stepladder groups made higher-quality decisions than conventional groups (see Figure 10.6).

The Delphi Technique

According to Greek mythology, people interested in seeing what fate the future held for them could seek the counsel of the Delphic oracle. Today's organizational decision makers sometimes consult experts to help them make the best decisions as

Figure 10.6   The Effectiveness of the Stepladder Technique

In a recent experiment, scientists compared the relative decision quality of groups meeting in conventional fashion with those using the stepladder technique. As noted here, groups using the stepladder technique generated higher-quality decisions.

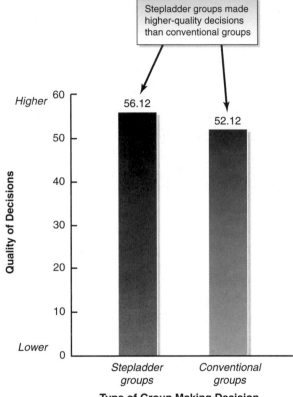

(Source: Based on data reported by Rogelberg et al., 2002; see Note 35.)

well. A technique developed by the Rand Corporation, known as the **Delphi technique**, represents a systematic way of collecting and organizing the opinions of several experts into a single decision.[36] The steps in the process are summarized in Figure 10.7.

The Delphi process starts by enlisting the cooperation of experts and presenting the problem to them, usually in a letter. Each expert then proposes what he or she believes is the most appropriate solution. The group leader compiles all of these individual responses and reproduces them so they can be shared with all the other experts in a second mailing. At this point, each expert comments on the others' ideas and proposes another solution. These individual solutions are returned to the leader, who compiles them and looks for a consensus of opinions. If a consensus is reached, the decision is made. If not, the process of sharing reactions with others is repeated until a consensus is eventually obtained.

Figure 10.7   Steps in the Delphi Technique

The *Delphi technique*, outlined here, allows decisions to be made by several experts without encountering many of the disadvantages of face-to-face groups.

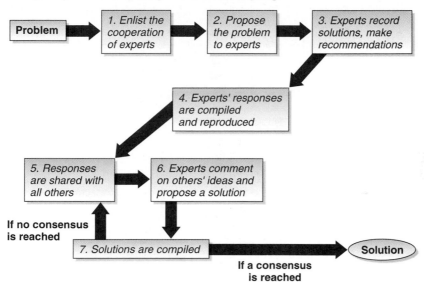

The obvious advantage of using the Delphi technique to make decisions is that it allows the collection of expert judgments without the great costs and logistical difficulties of bringing many experts together for a face-to-face meeting. However, the Delphi process can be very time-consuming. Sending out letters, waiting for everyone to respond, transcribing and disseminating the responses, and repeating the process until a consensus is reached can take quite a long time—often several months. Given this limitation, the Delphi approach would not be appropriate for making decisions in crisis situations or whenever else time is of the essence. However, the approach has been successfully employed to make decisions such as what items to put on a conference agenda and what the potential impact of implementing various new policies would be.

The Nominal Group Technique

When there are only a few hours available to make a decision, group discussion sessions can be held in which members interact with each other in an orderly, focused fashion aimed at solving problems. The **nominal group technique (NGT)** brings together a small number of individuals (usually about seven to ten) who systematically offer their individual solutions to a problem and share their personal reactions to others' solutions. The technique is referred to as nominal because the individuals involved form a group in name only. Participants do not attempt to agree as a group on any solution but rather vote on all the solutions proposed. For an outline of the steps in the process, see Figure 10.8.

Figure 10.8   Steps in the Nominal Group Technique

The *nominal group technique*, whose steps are summarized here, structures face-to-face meetings in a way that allows for the open expression and evaluation of ideas.

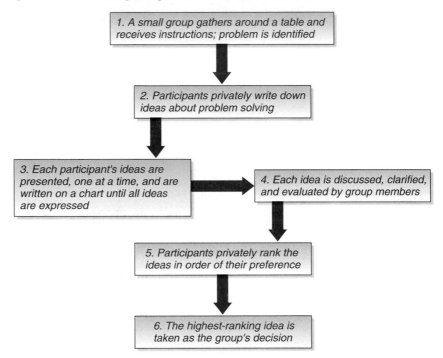

1. A small group gathers around a table and receives instructions; problem is identified

2. Participants privately write down ideas about problem solving

3. Each participant's ideas are presented, one at a time, and are written on a chart until all ideas are expressed

4. Each idea is discussed, clarified, and evaluated by group members

5. Participants privately rank the ideas in order of their preference

6. The highest-ranking idea is taken as the group's decision

As shown in Figure 10.8, the nominal group process begins by gathering group members together around a table and identifying the problem at hand. Members then write down their solutions. Next, one at a time, each member presents his or her solutions to the group as the leader records these on a chart. This process continues until all ideas have been expressed. Following this, each solution is discussed, clarified, and evaluated by the group members. Each member is given a chance to voice his or her reactions to each idea. After all the ideas have been evaluated, the group members privately rank-order their preferred solutions. The idea given the highest rank is taken as the group's decision.

Although nominal groups traditionally meet in face-to-face settings, advances in modern technology enable nominal groups to meet even when their members are far away from each other. Specifically, a technique known as **automated decision conferencing** has been used, in which individuals in different locations participate in nominal group conferences by means of telephone lines or direct satellite transmissions. The messages may be sent either via characters on a computer monitor or images viewed during a teleconference. Despite their high-tech look, automated decision conferences are really just nominal groups meeting in a manner that approximates face-to-face contact.

The NGT has several advantages and disadvantages. We have already noted that it can be used to arrive at group decisions in only a few hours. Another benefit is that it discourages any pressure to conform to the wishes of a high-status group member because all ideas are evaluated and the preferences are expressed in private balloting. The technique must be considered limited, however, in that it requires the use of a trained group leader. In addition, using NGT successfully requires that only one narrowly defined problem be considered at a time. So, for very complex problems, many NGT sessions would have to be run—and only if the problem under consideration can be broken down into smaller parts.

Computer-Based Approaches to Promoting Effective Decisions

6
learning
objective

Now that we have reviewed traditional, structural techniques for improving decision-making effectiveness, we will move on to examining several new technology-based approaches that have been used in recent years. Given the widespread use of computers in the workplace, it probably comes as no surprise that attempts have been made to put computers to use in improving the quality of group decisions. For the most part, these techniques are not especially sophisticated and make good use of widely available and inexpensive computer technology. As a result, they stand to be widely used to the extent that they are effective. With this in mind, we will examine three such techniques: *electronic meeting systems, computer-assisted communication,* and *group decision support systems.*

Electronic Meeting Systems

Although nominal groups traditionally meet in face-to-face settings, advances in modern technology enable them to be formed even when members are in distant locations. Specifically, **electronic meeting systems**, as they are known, involve holding teleconferences in which individuals in different locations participate in group conferences by means of telephone lines or direct satellite transmissions.[37] The messages may be sent either via characters on a computer monitor or images viewed during a teleconference. Despite their high-tech look, automated decision conferences are really just nominal groups meeting in a manner that approximates face-to-face contact. And, for the most part, they have proven to be equally effective.

Because electronic meetings allow for groups to assemble more conveniently than face-to-face meetings, they are growing in popularity. Presently, such companies as GE Appliances, US West, Marriott Corp., and Sun Microsystems regularly rely on electronic meetings—and with the rapidly decreasing costs of communication technology, more organizations are hopping on the bandwagon all the time.

Such companies as GE Appliances, US West, Marriott Corp., and Sun Microsystems regularly rely on electronic meetings—and with the rapidly decreasing costs of communication technology, more organizations are hopping on the bandwagon all the time.

Computer-Assisted Communication

Another way of leveraging technology to facilitate group decision making involves using **computer-assisted communication**, which refers to the sharing of information, such as text messages and data relevant to the decision, over computer networks. (The term *computer-mediated communication*, identified in Chapter 8, means essentially the same thing.) The underlying idea of computer-assisted communication is that on-screen messages provide an effective means of sending some forms of information that can help groups make better decisions. In Chapter 8 we described some ways in which computer-assisted communication differs from face-to-face communication, but now we turn to a more specific question: Does computer-assisted communication facilitate decision making? In other words, does being able to communicate with other team members via computer help teams make more effective decisions than they would make without computer assistance?

Research suggests that the answer is "only sometimes."[38] Recently, a study was conducted that compared the effectiveness of three-person groups whose members were allowed only to speak to each other (the talk-only condition) with other three-person groups whose members also were allowed to send text messages to one another over a computer network (the computer-assisted communication condition).[39] Participants were asked to perform a task that simulated the kind of deci-

Figure 10.9   Computer-Assisted Communication Improves Decision Making Among People Who Are Open to Experience

Computer-assisted communication involves the sharing of information (e.g., text messages and data relevant to them) over computer networks. Research simulating a military decision-making situation has shown that the effectiveness of this technique depends on people's openness to experience. As summarized here, computer-assisted communication improved the decision-making performance of three-person teams only when they were composed of individuals who scored highly on a personality test measuring openness to experience. However, individuals who were not open to experience were not helped by computer-assisted communication.

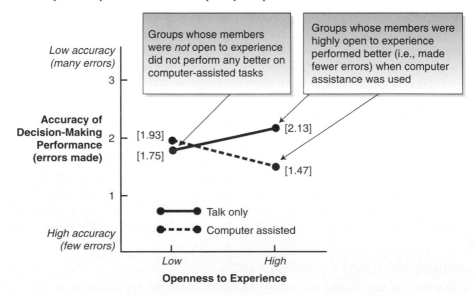

(Source: Based on data reported by Colquitt et al., 2002; see Note 39.)

sions made in a military "command and control" situation. This involved assessing the threat risk of aircraft spotted on a computer screen (based on such information as speed and size) after they were trained to perform this task. The teams' decisions were scored on the basis of accuracy and then were compared to one another. The results, summarized in Figure 10.9, revealed that the effectiveness of the teams' decisions depended on another variable.

Specifically, teams using the computer-assisted communication made better decisions than teams using verbal communication only when they were composed of individuals whose scores on a personality test indicated that they were highly open to experience. People scoring high on **openness to experience** tend to have intellectual curiosity, value learning, have an active imagination, and are intrigued by artistic endeavors. By contrast, people scoring low on this measure tend to be exactly the opposite. Apparently, because computer-assisted communication was new to many of the participants, its effectiveness was limited to those who were most accepting of the new technology and who possessed the creativity to use the technology in an efficient manner. These individuals reaped the benefits associated with the computer assistance. However, those who were less open to experience failed to perform better when using computer-assisted communication—actually, they performed slightly worse. Apparently, the computer-assisted communication was not much "assistance" to them, after all.

Because it provides a useful means of exchanging crucial information, one might be inclined to assume that computer-assisted communication is an effective way to improve group decision quality. And, because it can be adopted readily and inexpensively, some may be tempted to put it into practice. However, given that it appears not to be effective for everyone, implementing computer-assisted communications on a widespread basis would be unwise—at least, it may be premature. Perhaps, after such systems are in use for a while and people become familiar with them, even those who are not open to experiences will find them acceptable. Furthermore, training on how to integrate computer-assisted communication with more traditional forms also could compensate for any lack of openness. For the moment, however, those implementing computer-assisted communication systems would be wise to proceed with caution.

Group Decision Support Systems

Another approach to using technology to improve the effectiveness of decisions that has received attention in recent years is known as **group decision support systems (GDSS)**. These are interactive computer-based systems that combine communication, computer, and decision technologies to improve the effectiveness of group problem-solving meetings. They often involve having people type their ideas into a computer program and discuss these ideas anonymously with others in chat rooms. A record of these discussions is then left for all to examine as needed. Their underlying rationale is straightforward: The quality of group decisions stands to be improved insofar as this process removes some of the impediments to decision making. In this sense, just as decision support systems, described earlier (see page 326), can be used to identify effective ways of making decisions, so too can group decision support systems.

One of the reasons why face-to-face groups sometimes make poor decisions is that group members do not always share information they have available to them that might help the group. As we discussed earlier, in connection with the phenomenon of groupthink, this may occur because people sometimes censor unpopular ideas voluntarily, even if these are good ideas that can improve the quality of group decisions. This is where GDSS can be useful. Groups using GDSS may avoid this problem insofar as the anonymous recording of ideas makes people less reluctant to share them and makes it easier than ever to have access to them. In this manner, some of the most potent impediments to group decision quality can be eliminated. Recent research has found that this is, in fact, exactly what happens in groups using GDSS. An experiment was conducted comparing the effectiveness of groups of managers asked to solve simulated management problems in face-to-face groups and using GDSS.[40] As expected, the results showed that compared to face-to-face groups, groups using GDSS not only shared considerably more information, but they also made far better decisions as a result.

For now, it seems that group decision support systems appear to be quite effective. However, because they are very new, we don't yet know all the conditions under which they will continue to be successful. As OB researchers conduct further research on this topic, we surely will learn more about this promising technique in the future.

You Be the **Consultant**

Making Decisions Effectively

A business associate refers you to the president of a growing environmental management firm. The fact that the company is new and operates in a changing business environment makes all of its decisions especially crucial. As such, you are hired to assist in guiding the president in helping the company make decisions in the most effective possible way. Answer the following questions relevant to this situation based on the material in this chapter.

1. The president has been making decisions about how to deal with governmental regulations all by himself. Should he consider delegating this task to a group instead? Why or why not?

2. What individual biases would be expected to interfere with the quality of the decisions made by individuals in this company?

3. In what ways might the group interaction limit the quality of decisions made? What steps can be taken to overcome these problems?

Self-Assessment Exercise

Are You Risk Seeking or Risk Averse?

It's one thing to read about the effects of framing on riskiness but quite another to experience it firsthand. This exercise will help you demonstrate the effects of framing for yourself.

Directions

Read each of the following descriptions of hypothetical situations. Then, for each, answer the following question: *Which project will you select: Alpha or Beta?*

Situation 1:   You are an executive whose policies have resulted in a $1 million loss for your company. Now you are considering two new projects. One of them, Alpha, will provide a definite return of $500,000. The other, Beta, will provide a 50-50 chance of obtaining either a $1 million return or a $0 return.

Situation 2:   You are considering one of two new projects to conduct in your company. One of them, Alpha, will provide a definite return of $500,000. The other, Beta, will provide a 50-50 chance of obtaining either a $1 million return or a $0 return.

Discussion Questions

1. What choice did you make in Situation 1? Most people would select Beta in such a situation because it gives them a 50-50 chance of undoing the loss completely. Such a risk-seeking decision is likely in a situation in which people are focusing on undoing loss.

2. What choice did you make in Situation 2? Most people would select Alpha in such a situation because it gives them a sure thing, a "bird in the hand." Such a risk-averse decision is likely in a situation in which people are focusing on gains received.

3. Given that both situations are mathematically identical, why should people prefer one or the other?

Group Exercise

Running a Nominal Group: Try It Yourself

A great deal can be learned about nominal groups by running one—or, at least, by participating in one—yourself. Doing so will not only help illustrate the procedure but also demonstrate how effectively it works.

Directions

1. Select a topic suitable for discussion in a nominal group composed of students in your class. It should be a topic that is narrowly defined and on which people have many different opinions (these work best in nominal groups). Some possible examples include:

   ■ What should your school's student leaders be doing for you?

   ■ What can be done to improve the quality of instruction in your institution?

   ■ What can be done to improve the quality of jobs your school's students receive when graduating?

2. Divide the class into groups of approximately ten. Arrange each group in a circle, or around a table, if possible. In each group, select one person to serve as the group facilitator.

3. Following the steps outlined in Figure 10.8, facilitators should guide their groups in discussions regarding the focal question identified in step 1. Allow approximately 45 minutes to one hour to complete this process.

4. If time allows, select a different focal question and a different group leader, and repeat the procedure.

Discussion Questions

1. Collectively, how did the group answer the question? Do you believe that this answer accurately reflected the feelings of the group? How do you think your group experiences would have differed had you used a totally unstructured, traditional face-to-face group instead of a nominal group?

2. How did the various groups' answers compare? Were they similar or different? Why?

3. What were the major problems, if any, associated with the nominal group experience? For example, were there any group members who were reluctant to wait their turns before speaking up?

Notes

Case Notes

Bryce, R. (2004). *Pipe dreams: Greed, ego, and the death of Enron.* New York: PublicAffairs. Fox, L. (2003). *Enron: The rise and fall.* New York: John Wiley & Sons. Teather, D. (2002, January 21). Arthur Andersen pins blame on Enron. From the Web at www.guardian.co.uk/enron/story/0,11337,636598,00.html. Left, S. (2002, March 27). Ex-Andersen boss was "sacrificial lamb." From the Web at www.guardian.co.uk/enron/story/0,11337,674980,00.html. Enron auditor faces criminal charges. (2002, March 15). From the Web at news.bbc.co.uk/hi/english/business/newsid_1873000/1873758.stm. Saporito, B. (2002, February 20). How Fastow helped Enron fall. From the Web at www.time.com/time/business/article/0,8599,201871,00.html.

Chapter Notes

[1] Mintzberg, H. J. (1988). *Mintzberg on management: Inside our strange world of organizations.* New York: Free Press.

[2] Allison, S. T., Jordan, A. M. R., & Yeatts, C. E. (1992). A cluster-analytic approach toward identifying the structure and content of human decision making. *Human Relations, 45*, 411–422.

[3] Wedley, W. C., & Field, R. H. (1984). A predecision support system. *Academy of Management Review, 9*, 696–703.

[4] Brett, J. (2001). *Negotiating globally. How to negotiate deals, resolve disputes, and make decisions across cultural boundaries.* San Francisco: Jossey-Bass. Adler, N. J. (1991). *International dimensions of organizational behavior.* Boston: PWS Kent.

[5] Roth, K. (1992). Implementing international strategy at the business unit level: The role of managerial decision-making characteristics. *Journal of Management, 18*, 769–789.

[6] Greenhalgh, L. (2001). *Managing strategic relationships: The key to business success.* New York: Free Press.

[7] Crainer, S. (1998, November). The 75 greatest management decisions ever made. *Management Review*, pp. 16–23.

[8] Byrne, J. A. (1998, September 21). Virtual management. *Business Week*, pp. 80–82.

[9] Simon, H. (1977). *The new science of management decisions* (2nd ed.). Upper Saddle River, NJ: Prentice Hall.

[10] Linstone, H. A. (1984). *Multiple perspectives for decision making.* New York: North-Holland.

[11] Simon, H. A. (1979). Rational decision making in organizations. *American Economic Review, 69*, 493–513.

[12] March, J. G., & Simon, H. A. (1958). *Organizations.* New York: Wiley.

[13] See Note 12.

[14] Simon, H. A. (1957). *Models of man.* New York: Wiley.

[15] Shull, F. A., Delbecq, A. L., & Cummings, L. L. (1970). *Organizational decision making.* New York: McGraw-Hill.

[16] Browning, E. B. (1850/1950). *Sonnets from the Portuguese.* New York: Ratchford and Fulton.

[17] Mitchell, T. R., & Beach, L. R. (1990). ". . . Do I love thee? Let me count . . ." Toward an understanding of intuitive and automatic decision making. *Organizational Behavior and Human Decision Processes, 47*, 1–20.

[18] Beach, L. R., & Mitchell, T. R. (1990). Image theory: A behavioral theory of image making in organizations. In B. Staw and L. L. Cummings (Eds.), *Research in organizational behavior* (Vol. 12, pp. 1–41). Greenwich, CT: JAI Press.

[19] Dunegan, K. J. (1995). Image theory: Testing the role of image compatibility in progress decisions. *Organizational Behavior and Human Decision Processes, 62,* 71–86.

[20] Dunegan, K. J. (1993). Framing, cognitive modes, and image theory: Toward an understanding of a glass half full. *Journal of Applied Psychology, 78,* 491–503.

[21] Gigerenzer, G., & Selten, R. (2001). *Bounded rationality: The adaptive toolbox.* Cambridge, MA: MIT Press.

[22] Hurry up and decide (2001, May 14). *Business Week,* p. 16.

[23] Brownstein, A. L. (2003). Biased predecision processing. *Psychological Bulletin, 129,* 545–568.

[24] Ross, J., & Staw, B. M. (1986). Expo '86: An escalation prototype. *Administrative Science Quarterly, 31,* 274–297.

[25] Forman, E., H., & Selly, M. A. (2001). *Decision by objectives: How to convince others that you are right.* London: World Scientific.

[26] Salas, E., & Klein, G. (2001). *Linking expertise and naturalistic decision making.* Mahwah, NJ: Erlbaum.

[27] Hill, G. W. (1982). Group versus individual performance: Are $N + 1$ heads better than one? *Psychological Bulletin, 91,* 517–539.

[28] Osborn, A. F. (1957). *Applied imagination.* New York: Scribner's.

[29] Bouchard, T. J., Jr., Barsaloux, J., & Drauden, G. (1974). Brainstorming procedure, group size, and sex as determinants of the problem-solving effectiveness of groups and individuals. *Journal of Applied Psychology, 59,* 135–138.

[30] Janis, I. L. (1982). *Groupthink: Psychological studies of policy decisions and fiascoes* (2nd ed.). Boston: Houghton Mifflin.

[31] Morehead, G., Ference, R., & Neck, C. P. (1991). Group decision fiascoes continue: Space shuttle *Challenger* and a revised groupthink framework. *Human Relations, 44,* 539–550.

[32] Kray, L. J., & Galinsky, A. D. (2003). The debiasing effect of counterfactual mind-sets: Increasing the search for disconfirmatory information in group decisions. *Organizational Behavior and Human Decision Processes, 91,* 69–81.

[33] Nutt, P. C. (2002). *Why decisions fail.* San Francisco: Berrett-Koehler.

[34] Rogelberg, S. G., & O'Connor, M. S. (1998). Extending the stepladder technique: An examination of self-paced stepladder groups. *Group Dynamics, 2*(2), 82–91. Rogelberg, S. G., Barnes-Farrell, J. L., & Lowe, C. A. (1992). The stepladder technique: An alternative group structure facilitating effective group decision making. *Journal of Applied Psychology, 77,* 730–737.

[35] Robelberg, S. G., O'Connor, M. S., & Sederburg, M. (2002). Using the stepladder technique to facilitate the performance of audio conferencing groups. *Journal of Applied Psychology, 87,* 994–1000.

[36] Dalkey, N. (1969). *The Delphi method: An experimental study of group decisions.* Santa Monica, CA: Rand Corporation.

[37] Harmon, J., Schneer, J. A., & Hoffman, L. R. (1995). Electronic meetings and established decision groups: Audioconferencing effects on performance and structural stability. *Organizational Behavior and Human Decision Processes, 61,* 138–147.

[38] Alge, B. J., Wiethoff, C., & Klein, H. J. (2003). When does the medium matter? Knowledge-building experiences and opportunities in decision-making teams. *Organizational Behavior and Human Decision Processes, 91,* 26–37.

[39] Colquitt, J. A., Hollenbeck, J. R., Ilgen, D. R., LePine, J. A., & Sheppard, L. (2002). Computer-assisted communication and team decision-making performance: The

moderating effect of openness to experience. *Journal of Applied Psychology, 87*, 402–410.

[40] Huang, W. W., Wei, K-K., Watson, R. T., & Tan, B. C. Y. (2003). Supporting virtual team-building with a GSS: An empirical investigation. *Decision Support Systems, 34*, 359–367. Lam, S. S. K., & Shaubroeck, J. (2000). Improving group decisions by better pooling information: A comparative advantage of group decision support systems. *Journal of Applied Psychology, 85*, 564–573.

Chapter **Eleven**

After reading this chapter, you will be able to:

1. **DEFINE** leadership and **EXPLAIN** the major sources of power leaders have at their disposal.

2. **DESCRIBE** the trait approach to leadership and **IDENTIFY** the major characteristics of effective leaders.

3. **IDENTIFY** the types of behavior that have been most strongly associated with effective leadership.

4. **DESCRIBE** the basic tenets of three major contingency theories of leadership (*LPC contingency theory*, the *path-goal theory*, and *situational leadership theory*) and how they may be applied.

5. **IDENTIFY** the emerging trends and challenges in leadership practice.

6. **DESCRIBE** various approaches that can be taken to develop leaders in organizations.

The Quest for Leadership

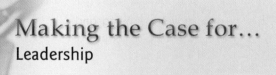

Making the Case for...
Leadership

Rudolph Giuliani: From "The Boss" to "Consoler in Chief" in One Tragic Day

If it's true that out of tragedy emerges something good, as they say, then from the September 11, 2001, terrorist attacks must emerge something truly exceptional. In the eyes of many, it's New York City's mayor at the time, Rudolph Giuliani, who inspired an army of disaster workers while healing the psychological wounds of a city—ultimately a whole country—in shock and mourning.

By the time the plane hit the south tower of the World Trade Center, it already was clear that Giuliani had taken charge of the city in chaos. He immediately set up a makeshift command center in a tent at ground zero but had to move it to a nearby firehouse when the second tower imploded, almost killing him. From there, he ran the city government, making rapid-fire decisions about rescue and security operations. But the mayor rarely stood still. He constantly made the rounds between hospitals, where he visited the injured, and the scene of the attack, where he consoled the families of the missing who waited desperately for word about their loved ones.

Some of his most inspired moments came when the mayor took to the airwaves to calm and comfort the people of New York—and the nation. "Tomorrow, New York is going to be here. And we're going to rebuild, and we're going to be stronger than we were before," he reassured everyone. With the president out of sight for most of September 11, "Giuliani became the voice of America," said *TIME* magazine, calling him "Person of the Year" for 2001 and adding, "Every time he spoke, millions of people felt a little better." In his autobiography, aptly titled *Leadership*, Mayor Giuliani now admits that he expressed far more optimism about the future than the facts warranted. But, as he learned by studying his idol, Winston Churchill (the British prime minister who kept London together with his inspiring words at the beginning of World War II), the beleaguered citizens of his city needed strong reassurance and were destined to pull together if they got it.

For over seven years before the terrorist attacks, Mayor Giuliani, dubbed "the boss" by his aides, was known for ruling New York City with an iron fist. "He's arrogant," said New York's Police Commissioner Bernard Kerik. "But you know what? He gets it done!" He always was more respected for his successes in improving the city than loved for the way he went about it. September 11 changed all that. In the days that followed, he not only performed critical roles as crisis manager, doing so masterfully, but he also showed a loving and compassionate side of himself that previously was hidden to all but his closest aides. Rising to the occasion by offering spiritual comfort for an embattled city, Mayor Giuliani's eloquence under fire led him to be dubbed "consoler in chief." Author F. Scott Fitzgerald (1896–1940) once said, "Show me a hero and I will write you a tragedy." With the tragedy already written by terrorists, Mayor Giuliani surely emerged as the hero—and an unlikely one at that.

Whatever your political beliefs may be, you certainly cannot raise questions about Mayor Giuliani's grace under fire. He immediately seized control of the apocalyptic crisis, getting vast armies of government officials and volunteers to work together, and doing so in a manner that inspired confidence and demonstrated compassion—both of which were precisely what was needed. To label him

GOOD REASONS why you should care about...

Leadership

You should care about leadership because:

1. An organization's success is greatly determined by the quality of its leadership.

2. There are steps that anyone can take to enhance his or her effectiveness as a leader.

3. Changing business practices, such as globalization and the use of the Internet, have important implications for the practice of leadership.

a hero is an understatement, but to call him a *leader* is truly instructive, for Giuliani's actions on those fateful late summer days embody precisely what the best leaders do—they inspire others to get the job done in a manner that demonstrates concern for people. Although the mayor is truly a rare example of leadership in action, he is in many ways representative of the legions of unsung heroes who lead organizations day in and day out—albeit, quite fortunately, under far less cataclysmic conditions.

If you gathered a group of top executives and asked them to identify the single most important determinant of organizational success, most likely would reply "effective leadership." Indeed, it is widely believed in the world of business that *leadership* is the key ingredient in the recipe for corporate achievement. And this view is by no means restricted to organizations. As you know, leadership also is important when it comes to politics, sports, and many other activities.

Is this view justified? Do leaders really play crucial roles in shaping the fortunes of organizations? Over a century of research on this topic suggests that they do. Effective leadership, it appears, is indeed a key determinant of organizational success. In view of this, I will devote this chapter to describing various approaches to the study of leadership as well as their implications for managerial practice. Before launching into this discussion, however, I will begin by defining what we mean by leadership and distinguish it from some other terms with which it is frequently associated.

What Is Leadership? Some Fundamental Issues

Although we all have a good intuitive idea about what leadership is and what leaders are like, it is important to begin this chapter with a formal definition of leadership and an overview of the ways in which leaders influence their followers.

learning objective

A Definition

When you think of a leader, what image comes to mind? For many, a leader is an individual—often with a title reflecting a high rank in an organization (e.g., president, director, etc.)—who is influential in getting others to behave as required by the organization. Indeed, social scientists think of leaders as people who have a great deal of influence over others. Formally, **leadership** is defined as the process by which an individual influences others in ways that help attain group or organizational goals.[1]

From this definition, it may seem that *leaders* and *managers* are quite similar. Indeed, the two terms are often used interchangeably. However, this is misleading insofar as they are conceptually distinct.[2] The primary function of a *leader* is to create the essential purpose or mission of the organization and the strategy for attaining it. By contrast, the job of the *manager* is to implement that vision. He or she is responsible for achieving that end, taking the steps necessary to make the leader's vision a reality. The reason for the confusion is that the distinction between establishing a mission and implementing it is often blurred in practice. After all, many leaders, such as top corporate executives, are frequently called on not only to create a vision but also to help implement it. Similarly, managers are often required to lead those who are subordinate to them while also carrying out their leader's mission. With this in mind, it has been observed that too many so-called leaders get bogged down in the managerial aspects of their job, creating organizations that are "over-managed and underled."[3]

How Do Leaders Influence Others? Sources of Leadership Power

As our definition suggests, leaders influence others. To fully understand how leaders operate, it is necessary to identify how exactly they come by the power to exert influence. The basis for a leader's power resides in his or her formal position as well as the way followers respond to his or her personal qualities.[4]

Position power.   A great deal of the power that people have in organizations comes from the posts they hold in those organizations. In other words, they are able to influence others because of the formal power associated with their jobs. This is known as **position power**. For example, there are certain powers that the president of the United States has simply due to the authority given to the officeholder (e.g., signing bills into law, making treaties, and so on). These formal powers remain vested in the position and are available to anyone who holds that position. When the president's term is up, these powers transfer to the new officeholder. There are four bases of position power. These are as follows.

- **Legitimate power**—The power that someone has because others recognize and accept his or her authority. For example, students recognize that their instructors have the legitimate power (i.e., authority) to make class policies and to determine grades.

- **Reward power**—The power to control the rewards others receive. For example, a supervisor has the power to reward one of her subordinates by recommending a large pay raise.

- **Coercive power**—The capacity to control punishment. For example, a boss may tell you to do something "my way or else." Typically, dictators are inclined to use coercive power, whereas leaders avoid it whenever possible.

- **Information power**—The power a person has by virtue of his or her access to valuable data or knowledge. Traditionally, people in top positions have available to them unique sources of information that are not available to others (e.g., knowledge of company performance, market trends, and so on). As they say, "knowledge is power," and such information greatly contributes to the power of people in many jobs.

As you read these descriptions of the different sources of position power, you may find yourself wondering what you could do to enhance your own position power where you are working. If so, don't feel self-conscious about being "power hungry." To the contrary, you may find it comforting to know that building a strong power base is an important first step toward being an effective leader. With this in mind, you may find it interesting to review the various suggestions for enhancing position power summarized in Table 11.1.

Personal power.   In addition to the power leaders derive from their formal positions in organizations, they also derive power from their own unique qualities or characteristics. This is known as **personal power**. There are four sources of personal power, as follows.

- **Rational persuasion**—The power leaders have by virtue of the logical arguments and factual evidence they provide to support their arguments. Rational persuasion is widely used by top executives, such as when they present detailed reports in making a case as to why certain organizational policies should be changed.

- **Expert power**—The power leaders have to the extent that others recognize their expert knowledge on a topic. For example, athletes do what their coaches tell them in large part because they recognize and respect their coaches' expertise.

Table 11.1	Position Power: How to Get It

The following suggestions identify various ways of enhancing one's position power in organizations.

Suggestion	*Rationale*
Expand your network of communication contacts.	The more contacts you have, the more information you will have, and the more others will count on you.
Make some of your job responsibilities unique.	People have power to the extent that they are the only ones who can perform certain tasks.
Perform more novel tasks and fewer routine ones.	People who perform routine tasks readily can be replaced by others, whereas those who perform novel tasks are more powerful because they are indispensable.
Increase the visibility of your job performance by joining task forces and making contact with senior people.	The more involved you are in organizational decisions, and the more important others consider your input to be, the more power you will have.
Become involved with activities that are central to the organization's top priorities.	People performing peripheral activities have far less power than those whose activities are in line with the organization's primary mission and its top priorities.

- **Referent power**—The power that individuals have because they are liked and admired by others. For example, senior managers who possess desirable qualities and good reputations may have referent power over younger managers who identify with them and wish to emulate them.

- **Charisma**—The power someone has over others because of his or her engaging and magnetic personality. As I will describe later in this chapter, people with this characteristic are highly influential and inspire others to do things.

As I have outlined here, leaders derive power from a variety of sources, some of which are based on the nature of the positions they hold and some of which are based on their individual characteristics. In the remainder of this chapter I will describe various approaches to understanding how leaders rely on these sources of power to attain group and organizational goals.

The Trait Approach: Are Some People "Born Leaders"?

Common sense tells us that some people have more of "the right stuff" than others and are just naturally better leaders. And, if you look at some of the great leaders throughout history, such as Martin Luther King, Jr., Alexander the Great, and Abraham Lincoln, to name just a few, it is clear that such individuals certainly appear to be different from ordinary folks. The question is, "How are they different?" That is, what is it that makes great leaders so great?

2
learning
objective

Great Person Theory

For many years, scientists have devoted a great deal of attention to the matter of identifying the specific traits and characteristics that are associated with leadership success. In so doing, they have advanced what is known as the **great person theory**—the approach that recognizes that great leaders possess key traits that set them apart from most others. Furthermore, the theory contends that these traits remain stable over time and across different groups. Most organizational scientists today accept the idea that traits *do* matter—namely, that certain traits, together with other factors, contribute to leaders' success in business settings.[5] Specifically, as one team of scientists put it, "Leaders do not have to be great men or women by being intellectual geniuses or omniscient prophets to succeed, but they do need to have the 'right stuff' and this stuff is not equally present in all people."[6] (With this in mind, you may find it interesting to consider who the great leaders throughout the ages have been—a task that you will complete in the **Group Exercise** on pages 388–389.)

What are these traits? Table 11.2 lists and describes some of the key ones. Although you will readily recognize and understand most of these characteristics (e.g., drive, honesty and integrity, self-confidence), some require further clarification. For example, **leadership motivation** refers to a leader's desire to influence others—essentially, his or her interest in assuming a leadership role. It also is important to understand the role of **flexibility**—the ability to recognize what actions are required in a given situation and then to act accordingly. The most effective leaders are not prone to behave in the same ways all the time but, rather, to be adaptive, matching their styles to the demands of the situations they face. Today's most effective business leaders do an exceptional job of adapting to changing conditions. This

Table 11.2	Characteristics of Successful Leaders

Research indicates that successful leaders demonstrate the traits listed here.

Trait or Characteristic	*Description*
Drive	Desire for achievement; ambition; high energy; tenacity; initiative
Honesty and integrity	Trustworthy; reliable; open
Leadership motivation	Desire to exercise influence over others to reach shared goals
Self-confidence	Trust in own abilities
Cognitive ability	Intelligence; ability to integrate and interpret large amounts of information
Knowledge of the business	Knowledge of industry and relevant technical matters
Creativity	Originality
Flexibility	Ability to adapt to needs of followers and requirements of situation

quality is not only desirable but also essential for leaders of companies competing in the rapidly growing online marketplace.[7]

Transformational Leaders: Special People Who Make Things Happen

If you think about the great leaders throughout history, the names of Rev. Dr. Martin Luther King, Jr., and President John F. Kennedy are certain to come to mind. These individuals surely were effective at envisioning ways of changing society and then bringing these visions to reality. People who do things to revitalize and transform society or organizations are known as **transformational leaders**.[8] Rev. King's famous "I have a dream" speech inspired people to adopt the civil rights movement, and President Kennedy's shared vision of "landing a man on the moon and returning him safely to earth" before 1970 inspired the "space race" of the 1960s. For these reasons, they are considered transformational leaders. Although these examples are useful, we must ask: Exactly what makes a leader transformational? The key characteristics of transformational leaders are as follows.

- *Charisma*—Transformational leaders have a mission and inspire others to follow them, often in a highly emotional manner.
- *Self-confidence*—Transformational leaders are highly confident in their ability and judgment, and others readily become aware of this.
- *Vision*—Transformational leaders have ideas about how to improve the status quo and do what it takes to change things for the better, even if it means making personal sacrifices.
- *Environmental sensitivity*—Transformational leaders are highly realistic about the constraints imposed on them and the resources needed to change things. They know what they can and cannot do.
- *Intellectual stimulation*—Transformational leaders help followers recognize problems and show them ways of solving them.
- *Interpersonal consideration*—Transformational leaders give followers the support, encouragement, and attention they need to perform their jobs well.
- *Inspiration*—Transformational leaders clearly communicate the importance of the company's mission and rely on symbols (e.g., pins and slogans) to help focus their efforts.
- *Morality*—Transformational leaders tend to make decisions in a manner showing advanced levels of moral reasoning (recall this concept from Chapter 2). For a summary of some recent evidence in this regard, see Figure 11.1.[9]

> In the world of business, a good example of a transformational leader is Jack Welch, the recently retired, illustrious CEO of General Electric.

In the world of business, a good example of a transformational leader is Jack Welch, the recently retired, illustrious CEO of General Electric (GE).[10] Under Welch's leadership, GE underwent a series of changes with respect to the way it does business.[11] At the individual level, GE abandoned its highly bureaucratic ways and now does a good job of listening to its employees. Not surprisingly, GE has consistently ranked among

Figure 11.1   Transformational Leadership and Morality: Evidence of a Connection

In a sample of workers from Canada and the United Kingdom scientists assessed the degree to which leaders were judged by their subordinates as having the characteristics of transformational leaders. These leaders also were assessed in terms of the degree of moral reasoning they displayed on a paper-and-pencil test. The findings, summarized here, were clear: More transformational leaders demonstrated higher levels of moral reasoning.

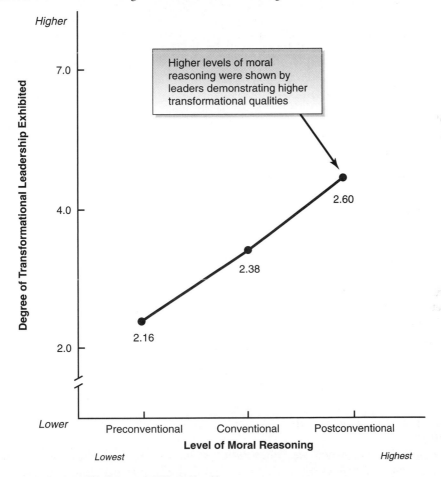

Higher levels of moral reasoning were shown by leaders demonstrating higher transformational qualities

(Source: Based on data reported by Turner et al., 2002; see Note 9.)

the most admired companies in its industry in *Fortune* magazine's annual survey of corporate reputations (including a number-one ranking in several recent years!).[12] In the 1980s, Welch bought and sold many businesses for GE, using as his guideline the fact that GE would only keep a company if it placed either number one or number two in market share. If this meant closing plants, selling assets, and laying off personnel, he did it and got others to follow suit, earning him the nickname "Neutron Jack." Did Welch transform and revitalize GE? Having added well over $100 billion of value to the company, making it the most valuable company in the United States, there can be no doubt about it.[13]

What we know about the effectiveness of transformational leadership goes beyond anecdotal examples and is based on sound scientific research.[14] Overall, transformational leadership is positively related to key aspects of job performance. For example, a study of secondary school teachers found that the more highly transactional their schools' principals were (as measured using a special questionnaire), the more they engaged in organizational citizenship behavior (see Chapter 7), and the higher were the levels of job satisfaction and organizational commitment among the teachers (Chapter 5).[15] Further research has shown managers at FedEx who are rated by their subordinates as being highly transformational tend to be higher performers and are recognized by their superiors as being highly promotable.[16] These studies and others suggests that the benefits of being a transformational leader are considerable.[17]

Although this is a useful conclusion as it stands, it raises an important question of interest to OB scientists: Why? Specifically, what is it about being a transformational leader that leads to improved performance among followers? Recently, a study was done that sheds light on this question. The researchers assessed the transformational leadership behavior of platoon leaders in the U.S. Army by administering a questionnaire to the soldiers who worked under them on military exercise missions.[18] They also used judgments by military experts to assess the performance of these leaders' platoons as a whole. The findings were clear: The more strongly the leaders demonstrated transformational characteristics, the more successfully their platoons performed. So far, this is consistent with other studies. However, in this research, the scientists went a step further by also assessing another key variable — the soldiers' perceptions of the degree of cohesiveness in their platoons (as you may recall from Chapter 9, cohesiveness has to do with the extent to which people pull together to get the job done). This proved to be an important piece of the puzzle. As summarized in Figure 11.2, the more platoon leaders were recognized as being transformational, the more cohesive were their platoons, and this, in turn, was one key determinant of how well those platoons performed. Thus, cohesiveness is a partial explanation for the successful impact of transformational leaders.

In view of this rather convincing evidence regarding the effectiveness of transformational leadership, you may be asking yourself how to become more of a transformational leader yourself. Although it isn't easy to take charge of transforming

---

Figure 11.2   Transformational Leadership and Group Performance: The Important Role of Group Cohesiveness

A recent study found that transformational leadership among military platoon leaders led to improved performance among platoons. Group cohesiveness was found to play an important role in this process. Transformational leaders tended to raise the cohesiveness levels of their platoons, which in turn improved their effectiveness in military maneuvers.

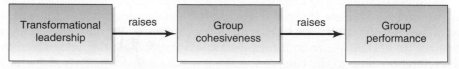

(Source: Based on suggestions by Bass et al., 2003; see Note 18.)

Table 11.3	Guidelines for Becoming a Transformational Leader

Being a transformational leader is not easy, but following the suggestions outlined here may help leaders transform and revitalize their organizations.

Suggestion	*Explanation*
Develop a vision that is both clear and highly appealing to followers.	A clear vision will guide followers toward achieving organizational goals and make them feel good about doing so.
Articulate a strategy for bringing that vision to life.	Don't present an elaborate plan; rather, state the best path towards achieving the mission.
State your vision clearly and promote it to others.	Visions must not only be clear but also made compelling, such as by using anecdotes.
Show confidence and optimism about your vision.	If a leader lacks confidence about success, followers will not try very hard to achieve that vision.
Express confidence in followers' capacity to carry out the strategy.	Followers must believe that they are capable of implementing a leader's vision. Leaders should build followers' self-confidence.
Build confidence by recognizing small accomplishments toward the goal.	If a group experiences early success, it will be motivated to continue working hard.
Celebrate successes and accomplishments.	Formal or informal ceremonies are useful for celebrating success, thereby building optimism and commitment.
Take dramatic action to symbolize key organizational values.	Visions are reinforced by things leaders do to symbolize them. For example, one leader demonstrated concern for quality by destroying work that was not up to standards.
Set an example; actions speak louder than words.	Leaders serve as role models. If they want followers to make sacrifices, for example, they should do so themselves.

(Source: Based on suggestions by Yukl, 2002; see Note 1; and Bass, 1998; see Note 8.)

one's organization, you may find it worthwhile to consider the ways of developing your transformational qualities summarized in Table 11.3.

The Behavior Approach: What Do Leaders Do?

The great person theory paints a somewhat fatalistic picture, suggesting that some people are, by nature, more prone to being effective leaders than others. After all, some of us have more of "the right stuff" than others. However, other approaches to leadership—particularly, those focusing on what leaders do rather than who leaders are—paint a more encouraging picture for those of us who aspire to leadership positions. This orientation is known as the **behavior approach**. By emulating the behavior of successful leaders the possibility exists that anyone may become an effective leader.

Two Critical Leadership Behaviors

Precisely what behaviors hold the key to leadership success? Although the answer to this question is quite complex, we can safely point to two very important leadership behaviors. The first is showing a *concern for people*, also known as **consideration**. In describing your boss, would you say that he or she cares about you as a person, is friendly, and listens to you when you want to talk? If so, he or she may be said to demonstrate a high amount of consideration.

The second main type of leadership behavior is showing a *concern for getting the job done*, also known as **initiating structure**. In describing your boss, would you say that he or she gives you advice, answers your questions, and lets you know exactly what is expected of you? If so, he or she may be said to demonstrate a high amount of initiating structure.

A large body of research suggests that leaders do differ greatly along these two dimensions. In these classic investigations subordinates completed questionnaires in which they described their leaders' behavior. Those leaders scoring high on initiating structure were mainly concerned with production and focused primarily on getting the job done. They engaged in actions such as organizing work, inducing subordinates to follow rules, setting goals, and making expectations explicit. In contrast, leaders scoring lower on this dimension showed less tendency to engage in these actions.

Leaders at the high end of the consideration dimension were primarily concerned with establishing good relations with their subordinates and being liked by them. They engaged in actions such as doing favors for subordinates, explaining things to them, and assuring their welfare. People who scored low on this dimension didn't care much about how they got along with subordinates.

> Leaders are likely to be most successful when they demonstrate high concern for both people (showing consideration) *and* production (initiating structure). Indeed, this is precisely what New York City's Mayor Rudolph Giuliani did in the aftermath of September 11.

It has been well established that leaders are likely to be most successful when they demonstrate high concern for both people (showing consideration) *and* production (initiating structure). Indeed, this is precisely what New York City's Mayor Rudolph Giuliani did in the aftermath of September 11. Showing consideration is beneficial insofar as it leads to high levels of group morale and low levels of turnover and absenteeism. At the same time, high levels of initiating structure are useful in promoting high levels of efficiency and performance. Not surprisingly, highly skilled leaders combine both orientations into their overall styles to produce favorable results.

Recently, two top executive recruiters analyzed the specific behaviors that characterize the way America's 50 most successful business leaders behave.[19] They found that these individuals shared a commitment to behaving in certain ways. Specifically, they all did the following.

- Demonstrated the utmost integrity in whatever they did.
- Developed strategies for building on what the company does best.
- Built a skilled management team whose members shared their own values.

- Communicated so well that they inspired others to achieve greatness.
- Made it possible for their organizations to make changes rapidly.
- Developed compensation systems that reinforced the company's mission.

Interestingly, this list is completely consistent with the well-established findings about the importance of paying attention to both people and the work itself. However, it provides a highly specific and very insightful list of some specific forms these behaviors take.

Developing Successful Leader Behaviors: Grid Training

How can one go about developing these two forms of leadership behavior—demonstrating concern for production and concern for people? A technique known as **grid training** proposes a multistep process designed to cultivate these two important skills.[20]

The initial step consists of a *grid seminar*—a session in which an organization's managers (who have been previously trained in the appropriate theory and skills) help organization members analyze their own management styles. This is done using a specially designed questionnaire that allows managers to determine how they stand with respect to their *concern for production* and their *concern for people*. Each participant's approach on each dimension is scored using a number ranging from 1 (low) to 9 (high).

Managers who score low on both concern for production and concern for people are scored 1,1, showing evidence of *impoverished management*. A manager who is highly concerned about production but shows little interest in people scores 9,1, demonstrating the *task management* style. In contrast, those who show the opposite pattern—high concern with people but little concern with production—are described as having a *country club* style of management; they are scored 1,9. Managers scoring moderately on both dimensions, the 5,5 pattern, are said to follow a *middle-of-the-road* management style. Finally, there are individuals who are highly concerned with both production and people, those scoring 9,9. This is the most desirable pattern, representing what is known as *team management*. These various patterns are represented in a diagram like that shown in Figure 11.3, known as the *managerial grid®*.

After a manager's position along the grid is determined, training begins to improve concern over production (planning skills) and concern over people (communication skills) to reach the ideal *9,9* state. This consists of organization-wide training aimed at helping people interact more effectively with each other. Then training is expanded to reducing conflict between groups that work with each other. Additional training includes efforts to identify the extent to which the organization is meeting its strategic goals and then comparing this performance to an ideal. Next, plans are made to meet these goals, and these plans are implemented in the organization. Finally, progress toward the goals is continuously assessed, and problem areas are identified.

Grid training is widely considered an effective way of improving the leadership behaviors of people in organizations. Indeed, the grid approach has been used to train hundreds of thousands of people in developing the two key types of leadership behavior.

Figure 11.3 The Managerial Grid®

A manager's standing along two basic dimensions—concern for production and concern for people—can be illustrated by means of a diagram such as this, known as the managerial grid®. To promote effective leadership, managers are trained to demonstrate high amounts of both dimensions.

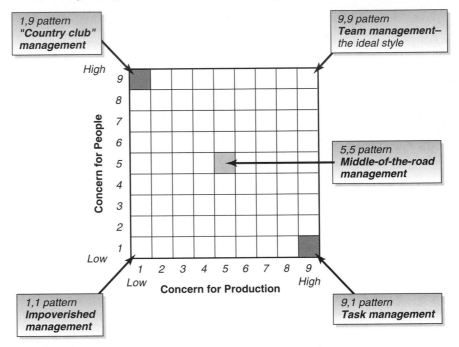

(*Source: Based on suggestions by Blake and Mouton, 1969, 1982; see Note 20.*)

4

learning objective

Contingency Theories of Leader Effectiveness

It should be clear by now that leadership is a complex process. It involves intricate social relationships and is affected by a wide range of variables. In general, it may be said that leadership is influenced by two main factors—the characteristics of the individuals involved and the nature of the situations they face. This basic point lies at the heart of several approaches to leadership known as **contingency theories** of leader effectiveness. According to this approach, there is no one best style of leadership. Instead, they suggest that certain leadership styles may prove most effective under certain conditions. Contingency theories seek to identify the conditions and factors that determine whether, and to what degree, leaders will enhance the performance and satisfaction of their subordinates. We will describe three such approaches.

LPC Contingency Theory: Matching Leaders and Tasks

Earlier, I explained that the behaviors associated with effective leadership fall into two major categories—concern for people and concern for production. Both types of behavior contribute to a leader's success. However, a more refined look at this issue leads us to ask exactly when each type of behavior works better. That is, under what conditions are leaders more successful when they demonstrate a concern for people compared to a concern for production?

The basics of the theory.   This question is addressed by a widely studied approach to leadership known as **LPC contingency theory**. The contingency aspect of the theory is reflected by the assumption that a leader's contribution to successful performance by his or her group is determined by the leader's own traits in conjunction with various features of the situation. Different levels of leader effectiveness occur under different combinations of conditions. To fully understand leader effectiveness, both types of factors must be considered.

The theory identifies *esteem (liking) for least preferred coworker* (**LPC** for short) as the most important personal characteristic. This refers to a leader's tendency to evaluate in a favorable or unfavorable manner the person with whom she or he has found it most difficult to work. Leaders who perceive this person in negative terms (low LPC leaders) are primarily concerned with attaining successful task performance. In contrast, those who perceive their least preferred coworker in a positive light (high LPC leaders) are mainly concerned with establishing good relations with subordinates. LPC is considered a leadership style that is relatively fixed and cannot be changed.

Which type of leader—one low in LPC or one high in LPC—is more effective? As suggested by the word *contingency* in the name, the answer is: "It depends." And what it depends on is the degree to which the situation is favorable to the leader—that is, how much it allows the leader to have control over subordinates. This, in turn, is determined largely by three factors: (1) the nature of the *leader's relations with group members* (the extent to which he or she enjoys their support and loyalty), (2) the *degree of structure* in the task being performed (the extent to which task goals and subordinates' roles are clearly defined), and (3) the leader's *position power* (as described earlier in this chapter). Combining these three factors, the leader's situational control can range from very high (positive relations with group members, a highly structured task, and high position power) to very low (negative relations, an unstructured task, and low position power).

What types of leaders are most effective under these various conditions? According to the theory, low LPC leaders (ones who are task oriented) are superior to high LPC leaders (ones who are relations or people oriented) when situational control is either very low or very high. In contrast, high LPC leaders have an edge when situational control falls within the moderate range (refer to Figure 11.4).

The rationale for these predictions is quite reasonable. Under conditions of low situational control, groups need considerable guidance to accomplish their tasks. Without such direction, nothing would get done. For example, imagine a military combat group led by an unpopular platoon leader. Any chance of effectiveness this person has would result from paying careful attention to the task at hand rather than hoping to establish better relations with the group. (In fact, in the military, it is often said that a leader in an emergency is better off giving wrong orders than no orders whatsoever.) Since low LPC leaders are more likely to provide structure than high LPC leaders, they usually will be superior in such cases.

Similarly, low LPC leaders are also superior under conditions that offer the leader a high degree of situational control. Indeed, when leaders are liked, their

Figure 11.4   LPC Contingency Theory

According to *LPC contingency theory*, low LPC leaders (i.e., ones who are primarily task oriented) will be more effective than high LPC leaders (ones who are primarily people oriented) when situational control is either very low or very high. However, when situational control is moderate, high LPC leaders will be more effective than low LPC leaders.

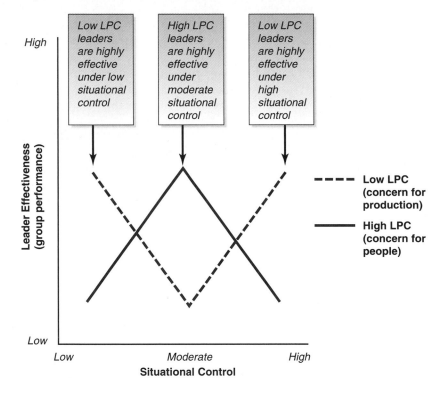

power is not challenged, and when the demands of the task make it clear what a leader should be doing, it is perfectly acceptable for them to focus on the task at hand. Subordinates expect their leaders to exercise control under such conditions and accept it when they do so. And this leads to task success. For example, an airline pilot leading a cockpit crew is expected to take charge and to not seek the consensus of others as she guides the plane onto the runway for a landing. Surely, she would be less effective if she didn't take charge but instead asked the copilot what he thought she should do.

Things are different, however, when situations offer leaders moderate situational control. Consider, for example, a situation in which a leader's relations with subordinates are good, but the task is unstructured, and the leader's power is somewhat restricted. This may be the case within a research and development team attempting to find creative new uses for a company's products. Here, it would be clearly inappropriate for a low LPC leader to impose directives. Rather, a highly nurturing leader who is considerate of the feelings of others would likely be more effective—that is, a high LPC leader.

Applying LPC contingency theory. Practitioners have found LPC contingency theory to be quite useful when it comes to suggesting ways of enhancing leader effectiveness. Because the theory assumes that certain kinds of leaders are most effective under certain kinds of situations and that leadership style is fixed, the best way to enhance effectiveness is to fit the right kind of leaders to the situations they face.

This involves completing questionnaires that can be used to assess both the LPC score of the leader and the amount of situational control he or she faces in the situation. Then, using these indexes, a match can be made such that leaders are put into the situations that best suit their leadership styles—a technique known as **leader match**. This approach also focuses on ways of changing the situational control variables—leader–member relations, task structure, and leader position power—when it is impractical to change leaders. For example, a low LPC leader either should be moved to a job in which situational control is either extremely high or extremely low. Alternatively, the situation should be changed (such as by altering relations between leaders and group members or by raising or lowering his or her position power) to increase or decrease the amount of situational control encountered. Several companies, including Sears, have used the leader match approach with great success. In fact, research has found that this approach is a very effective way of improving group effectiveness.

> Several companies, including Sears, have used the leader match approach with great success.

Path-Goal Theory: Leaders as Guides to Valued Goals

In defining leadership, I indicated that leaders help their groups or organizations reach their goals. This basic idea plays a central role in the **path-goal theory** of leadership.[21] In general terms, the theory contends that subordinates will react favorably to leaders who are perceived as helping them make progress toward various goals by clarifying the paths to such rewards. Specifically, the theory contends that the things a leader does to help clarify the nature of tasks and reduce or eliminate obstacles will increase subordinates' perceptions that working hard will lead to good performance and that good performance, in turn, will be recognized and rewarded. And, under such conditions (as you may recall from our discussion of expectancy theory in Chapter 6), motivation will be enhanced (which may help enhance performance).

How, precisely, can leaders best accomplish these tasks? Again, as in the case of LPC contingency theory, the answer is: "It depends." (In fact, this answer is your best clue to identifying any contingency theory.) And what it depends on is a complex interaction between key aspects of *leader behavior* and certain *contingency* factors. Specifically, with respect to leader behavior, path-goal theory suggests that leaders can adopt four basic styles:

- **Instrumental** (directive): an approach focused on providing specific guidance, establishing work schedules and rules
- **Supportive:** a style focused on establishing good relations with subordinates and satisfying their needs

- **Participative:** a pattern in which the leader consults with subordinates, permitting them to participate in decisions
- **Achievement oriented:** an approach in which the leader sets challenging goals and seeks improvements in performance

According to the theory, these styles are not mutually exclusive; in fact, the same leader can adopt them at different times and in different situations. Indeed, as described earlier in this chapter, showing such flexibility is key to being an effective leader. (Recognizing that it is important to adopt these styles, many of today's leaders have adopted an approach to leadership known as coaching. For a look at this orientation to leadership, see the accompanying **OB to the Rescue** section.)

OB to the Rescue

Leadership Lessons from Sports Coaches

If you have ever played on a sports team, you have experienced firsthand the important leadership function of a coach. What did your coach do? Chances are that he or she was actively involved in helping you in the following ways:

- Analyzing ways of improving your performance and extending your capabilities.
- Creating a supportive climate, one in which barriers to development are eliminated.
- Encouraging you to improve your performance, no matter how good you already may be.

Coaching has been around for a long time, but only recently has coaching emerged as a philosophy of leadership in organizations.[22]

In recent years, some of the most successful athletic coaches (such as the former Notre Dame football coach, Lou Holtz) and team executives (such as the Green Bay Packers' executive vice president and general manager, Ron Wolf) have written books describing what makes coaching a unique form of leadership.[23] The key, they explain, is the special trust that develops in relationships between coaches and players. Team members acknowledge the coach's expertise and trust the coach to have his or her own best interests, as well as the entire team's best interests, in mind. At the same time, coaches believe in their team members' capacities to profit from their advice. In other words, coaching is a partnership in which both the coach and the team member play an important part in achieving success.

Additional dimensions of the coach's leadership power have been described by basketball hall of famer and former U.S. Senator Bill Bradley.[24] A key to coaching, Bradley emphasizes, is to get players to commit to something bigger than themselves. In sports this may mean winning a championship, and in other businesses it may mean landing a huge contract or surpassing a long-standing sales record. Focusing on the goal itself, and identifying how each individual may contribute to it, is key.

Bradley also advises that the best coaches don't do all the talking when someone gets out of line. Rather, they harness the power of team members to put pressure on the problem person. As a case in point, consider what happened when the New York Knicks' Scottie Pippin angrily took himself out of a 1994 semifinal championship game after Coach Phil Jackson called for teammate Toni Kukoc to make the final, game-

(continued)

deciding shot. Naturally, Coach Jackson came down hard on Pippin in his postgame interview, but that was mostly for show. The real work in getting Pippin to see the error of his ways came not from the coach but from his teammates. After the game, the coach left the locker room, announcing that the team had something to say to Pippin. Then, one by one, members of the Knicks expressed their disappointment in Pippin for letting down the team. Seeing the error of his ways, Pippin apologized on the spot and immediately went back to being the team player he had been all along. Had the coach not orchestrated this session, the effects would not have been as successful.

One way coaches can be supportive of their team members and earn their trust is to refrain from bad-mouthing team members to others. Athletic coaches who use the media to send critical messages to their players live to regret it, Bradley tells us. However, behind the closed doors of the locker room, it's quite a different story. In that setting, there's no such thing as being too frank. The same applies in the office or shop as well. A manager who complains to other managers what a poor job one of her employees has been doing is not only making herself look bad but also, more importantly, betraying that employee's trust. And, as we said earlier, trust is at the heart of the coaching game.

Which of these styles is best for maximizing subordinates' satisfaction and motivation? The answer depends on several characteristics of subordinates. For example, if followers are high in ability, an instrumental style of leadership may be unnecessary; instead, a less structured, supportive approach may be preferable. On the other hand, if subordinates are low in ability, they may need considerable guidance to help them attain their goals. Similarly, people high in need for affiliation (that is, those desiring close, friendly ties with others) may strongly prefer a supportive or participative style of leadership. Those high in the need for achievement may strongly prefer an achievement-oriented leader, one who can guide them to unprecedented levels of success.

The theory suggests that the most effective leadership style also depends on several aspects of the work environment. Specifically, path-goal theory predicts that when tasks are unstructured and nonroutine, an instrumental approach by the leader may be best; much clarification and guidance are needed. However, when tasks are structured and routine, such leadership may get in the way of good performance and may be resented by subordinates who think the leader is engaging in unnecessary meddling. (See Figure 11.5 for an overview of all these aspects of path-goal theory.)

Situational Leadership Theory: Adjusting Leadership Style to the Situation

Another theory of leadership, **situational leadership theory**, is considered a contingency theory because it focuses on the best leadership style for a given situation. Specifically, the scientists who developed the theory argue that leaders are effective when they select the right leadership style for the situation they face.[25] Specifically, this depends on the maturity of followers—that is, their readiness to take responsibility for their own behavior. This, in turn, is based on two variables with which we

Figure 11.5 Path-Goal Theory

According to *path-goal theory*, perceptions among employees that leaders are helping them attain valued goals enhance their motivation and job satisfaction. Such perceptions are encouraged when a leader's style is consistent with the needs and characteristics of subordinates and various aspects of the work environment.

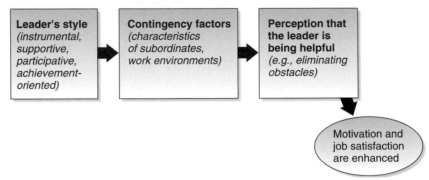

(Source: Based on suggestions by House, 1996; see Note 21.)

are already familiar: (1) task behavior (the degree to which followers have the appropriate job knowledge and skills—that is, their need for guidance and direction) and (2) relationship behavior (the degree to which followers are willing to work without taking direction from others—that is, their need for emotional support).

As shown in Figure 11.6, by combining high and low levels of these independent dimensions, four different types of situations are identified (denoted by *S* in the diagram), each of which is associated with a leadership style that is most effective.

- *Lower-right corner of Figure 11.6 (S1):* Situations in which followers need a great deal of direction from their leaders but don't need much emotional support from them. The practice of *telling* followers what to do is most useful in such situations. That is, giving followers specific instructions and closely supervising their work may be the best approach.

- *Upper-right corner of Figure 11.6 (S2):* Situations in which followers still lack the skill to be able to succeed, although in this case, they require more emotional support. Under these conditions, *selling* works best. Being very directive may make up for the follower's lack of ability, while being very supportive will help get them to go along with what the leader is asking of them.

- *Upper-left corner of Figure 11.6 (S3):* Conditions in which followers need very little guidance with respect to how to do their jobs but considerable emotional hand-holding and support to motivate them. That is, low levels of task behavior but high levels of relationship (supportive) behavior are required. A *participating* style of leadership works well in such situations because it allows followers to share their expertise while enhancing their desire to perform.

- *Lower-left corner of Figure 11.6 (S4):* Followers are both willing and able to do what is asked of them. In other words, low levels of task behavior and low levels of relationship behavior are required. Under such conditions, *delegating* is the best way to treat followers—that is, turning over to them the responsibility for making and implementing their own decisions.

Figure 11.6   Situational Leadership Theory

Situational leadership theory specifies that the most appropriate leadership style depends on the amount of emotional support followers require in conjunction with the amount of guidance they require to do their jobs.

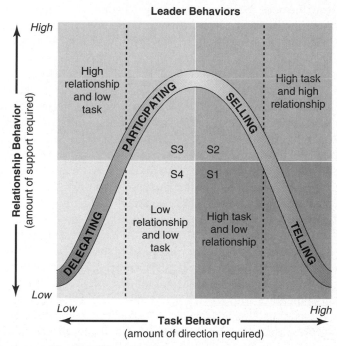

(Source: Adapted from Hersey and Blanchard, 1988; see Note 25.)

According to this situational leadership theory, leaders must be able to (1) diagnose the situations they face, (2) identify the appropriate behavioral style, and then (3) implement that response. Because the situations leaders face may change all the time, leaders must constantly reassess them, paying special attention to their followers' needs for guidance and emotional support. To the extent that they do so, they are likely to be effective.

Specialized training in these skills has been found to be quite useful. In fact, the approach has been widely used to train leaders at such corporate giants as Xerox, ExxonMobil, and Caterpillar, as well as the U.S. military services. (Which style of leadership are you most prone to follow in your treatment of others? To give you some insight into this question, complete the **Self-Assessment Exercise** on pages 387–388.)

Emerging Trends and Challenges in Leadership Practice

Now that your understanding of the nature of leadership has a solid foundation, you are prepared to appreciate several emerging trends and challenges that leaders face in today's rapidly changing business environment. I will describe four such issues: the practice of co-leadership, as well as the implications for leadership associated with the use of teams and the digital economy.

5
learning
objective

Co-CEOs: The Buck Splits Here

Traditionally, companies have only one chief executive officer (CEO), a top leader in charge of the company. These days, however, many companies are finding that there's good reason to have two talented leaders in charge—**co-CEOs**, who share power.[26] This trend has grown in popularity as the business world has become more global and complex, dictating the need for more than one top leader. Also, the wave of megamergers has led to the growth of co-CEOs as the newly created companies scramble to find places for the CEOs of the formerly individual firms. Moreover, the sheer size and geographic challenges of running these megacorporations make having two CEOs somewhat of a necessity. For example, since Chrysler and Daimler-Benz merged in 1998, the new DaimlerChrysler has had as co-CEOs the former CEOs of the individual companies. Actually, the DaimlerChrysler case is far from unique. In one recent year alone, three of the top 10 largest mergers have led to the sharing of power by co-CEOs.[27]

Co-CEO arrangements frequently are well received following mergers and acquisitions because they are friendly in tone (in contrast to the hostile takeovers that occurred in the 1980s). When the leaders of the two formerly separate companies work well together, they send a strong message to the rank-and-file employees that they are expected to do the same. However, co-CEOs don't exist only in newly merged firms. Unilever, for example, the world's second-largest consumer products company, has had co-CEOs since 1930. Instead of having two CEOs at once, Royal Dutch Shell has two executives who alternate turns as CEOs (one from Royal Dutch Petroleum and the other from Shell Transport and Trading).

Unfortunately, not all such "professional marriages" are successful. In fact, some experts say that companies with co-CEOs are unstable.[28] In the case of the proposed merger of pharmaceutical giants Galaxo-Welcome and Smithkline Beecham, arguments about who would lead were so intense that the deal was canceled before it ever occurred. Attempts at installing co-CEOs failed the mergers between Time-Life and Warner Brothers (forming Time-Warner) and that between INA Corp. and Connecticut General (forming Cigna Corp). In both cases, after the two CEOs tore their companies apart with their acrimony, the power-sharing arrangements were disbanded. Both companies now have single CEOs.

> In the case of the proposed merger of pharmaceutical giants Galaxo-Welcome and Smithkline Beecham, arguments about who would lead were so intense that the deal was canceled before it ever occurred.

At this time, the future of co-leadership is not clear. Although it works sometimes, it's just as likely to fail. The keys to its success seem to be (a) the willingness of each party to yield power to the other and (b) the recognition by each party that the other makes a vital contribution to the company. When these criteria are met, co-CEOs have a chance at sharing leadership successfully. Otherwise, it's unlikely to succeed.

The Challenge of Leading Teams

Traditionally, leaders make strategic decisions on behalf of followers, who are responsible for carrying them out. In many of today's organizations, however, where teams predominate (see Chapter 9), leaders are called on to provide special resources to team members, who are empowered to implement their own missions in their own ways. Instead of "calling the shots," team leaders help subordinates take responsibility for their own work. As such, they are very different from the traditional, "command and control" leaders we have been discussing.[29] As Table 11.4 suggests, leading teams is very different from leading individuals in the traditional manner.

Clearly, the special nature of teams makes the leader's job very different. Although appreciating these differences is easy, making the appropriate adjustments may be extremely challenging—especially for individuals who are well practiced in the traditional, "command and control" ways of leadership. However, given the prevalence of teams in today's work environment, the importance of making the adjustments cannot be overstated. With this in mind, here are a few guidelines that should be followed to achieve success as a team leader.

1. Instead of directing people, *team leaders work at building trust and inspiring teamwork*. One way this can be done is by encouraging interaction among all members of the team as well as among the team and its customers and suppliers. Another key ingredient is take initiatives to make things better. Instead of taking a reactive, "if it ain't broke, don't fix it" approach, teams may be led to success by individuals who set a good example for improving the quality of their team's efforts.

2. Rather than focusing simply on training individuals, effective *team leaders concentrate on expanding team capabilities*. In this connection, team leaders function primarily as coaches, helping team members by providing all members with the skills needed to perform the task, removing barriers that might interfere with task success, and finding

Table 11.4	Leading Groups Versus Leading Teams

The popularity of teams in today's organizations has important implications for how leaders go about fulfilling their roles. Some of the key differences between leading traditional work groups and leading teams are summarized here.

In Traditional Work Groups, Leaders . . .	*But, in Teams, Leaders . . .*
Tell people what to do.	Ask people what they think and share responsibility for organizing and doing the work.
Take all the credit.	Share the limelight with all their teammates.
Focus on training employees.	Concentrate on expanding their team's capabilities by functioning primarily as coaches who build confidence in team members, cultivating their untapped potential.
Relate to others individually.	Create a team identity by helping the team set goals, helping members meet them, and celebrating when they have been met.
Work at reducing conflict between individuals.	Make the most of team differences by building respect for diverse points of view and ensuring that all team members' views are expressed.
React to change.	Recognize that change is inevitable and foresee it, better preparing the organization to make appropriate adaptations.

the resources required to get the job done. Likewise, team leaders work at building the confidence of team members, cultivating their untapped potential.

3. Instead of managing one-on-one, *team leaders attempt to create a team identity.* In other words, leaders must help teams understand their missions and recognize what they're doing to help fulfill it. In this connection, team leaders may help the group set goals—pointing out ways they may adjust their performance when they do not meet them and planning celebrations when team goals are attained.

4. Although traditional leaders have worked at preventing conflict between individuals, *team leaders are encouraged to make the most of team differences.* Without doubt, it is a considerable challenge to meld a diverse group of individuals into a highly committed and productive team, but doing so is important. This can be done by building respect for diverse points of view, making sure that all team members are encouraged to present their views and respecting these ideas once they are expressed.

5. Unlike traditional leaders who simply react to change, *team leaders should foresee and influence change.* To the extent that leaders recognize that change is inevitable (a point we will emphasize in Chapter 14), they may be better prepared to make the various adaptations required. Effective team leaders continuously scan the business environment for clues as to changes that appear to be forthcoming and help teams decide how to be responsive to them.

In conclusion, leading teams is a far cry from leading individuals in the traditional directive (or even a participative) manner. The special nature of teams makes the leader's job very different. Although appreciating these differences is easy, making the appropriate adjustments may be extremely challenging—especially for individuals who are well practiced in the ways of traditional leadership. However, given the prevalence of teams in today's work environment, the importance of making the adjustments cannot be overstated. Leading new teams using old methods is a surefire formula for failure.

Leading in the Digital Age

Most of what we know about leading people is derived from the era in which (a) there were clear hierarchies in organizations and everyone knew who was in charge, (b) changes were made slowly, and (c) people expected to follow their leaders' orders. Many of these characteristics do not apply to today's organizations, and none describe the high-tech world of Internet businesses. In today's digital economy, organizations are highly **decentralized**—that is, power to make decisions is spread out among many different people. What's more, the pace of change is so blindingly fast that leaders rarely have the luxury of making decisions with careful deliberation. Finally, unlike traditional workers, many of today's employees demand independence and autonomy. In short, they are reluctant to be led in the traditional sense of having someone tell them precisely what to do.

As you might imagine, these considerations have important implications for the way today's dot-com leaders are required to operate. Some of the most important implications of the Internet economy for leadership are as follows.[30]

■ *Growth occurs so quickly that strategies have to be changed constantly.* For example, Meg Whitman, president and CEO of eBay, says that the company grows so rapidly (often 40 to 50 percent each quarter!) that it becomes an entirely different company

every few months.[31] Leaders cannot take anything for granted, except the fact that whatever
they decided to do yesterday may need to be
changed tomorrow.

■ *Leaders of Internet companies are not expected to
have all the answers.* The highly technical nature of
the business and the rapid pace of change make it
impossible for just one or two people to make all
the right decisions. According to Jonathan Buckeley, CEO of Barnesandnoble.com,
today's leaders "must be evangelists for changing the system, not preserving it."[32]

> Meg Whitman, president and CEO of eBay, says that the company grows so rapidly (often 40 to 50 percent each quarter!) that it becomes an entirely different company every few months.

■ *Showing restraint is critical.* There are so many opportunities available to Internet
companies today that executives can too easily enter into a bad deal. For example,
Andrew Jarecki, cofounder and CEO of Moviefone, Inc., ignored the many suggestions he received to go into business with a big portal before agreeing to what proved
to be the right deal—acquisition by AOL for $386 million in stock.

■ *Hiring and retaining the right people is more important than ever.* In the world of the
Internet, the average tenure of a senior executive is only 18 months. Constant change
means that the people who are hired for today's jobs must meet the demands of tomorrow's jobs as well. As Jay Walker, founder and vice chairman of Priceline.com, puts it,
"You've got to hire ahead of the curve," adding, "If you wait until you're actually doing
[as much business as you expect] to hire the necessary talent, then you'll be too late."[33]

■ *Today's leaders must not take anything for granted.* When Mark Cuban and his partner
founded Broadcast.com (before selling it to Yahoo! four years later for $5.7 billion),
they made lots of incorrect decisions. Instead of sticking by them, they quickly
adjusted their game plan to fit the realities they faced.

■ *Internet leaders must focus on real-time decision making.* Traditional leaders were
trained to gather lots of data before making carefully researched decisions. According
to Ruthann Quindlen, partner in Institutional Venture Partners, leaders can no longer
afford to do so: "If your instinct is to wait, ponder, and perfect, then you're dead. . . .
Leaders have to hit the undo key without flinching."[34]

As I have outlined here, many of the traditional ways of leading need to be
adjusted to accommodate today's Internet economy. Before you think of ignoring
everything you learned about leadership in this chapter, please note that the
Internet world does *not* require us to rewrite all the rules about good leadership. For
example, showing concern for people and concern for production have not gone out
of style! In fact, to successfully accommodate the fast-paced, modern era, they may
be considered more important than ever.

Leadership Development: Bringing Out the Leader Within You

learning
objective

In case it's not clear by now, being an effective leader isn't easy. If you happen to be
fortunate enough to be born with "the right stuff," it helps. It also helps to find yourself in the kind of situation in which an opportunity exists to demonstrate your
capacity as a leader (as was the case with New York's Mayor Giuliani, described in
this chapter's opening case). However, anyone can improve his or her leadership
skills, honing his or her capacity to inspire others in an organization. Although we all

cannot become a Jack Welch (the highly successful former CEO of General Electric described earlier), it is possible for anyone to develop the skills needed to become more successful than he or she already is as a leader.

The systematic process of training people to expand their capacity to function effectively in leadership roles is known as **leadership development**. In recent years, many organizations have invested heavily in leadership development efforts, recognizing that effective leadership is a source of competitive advantage for an organization. Such efforts have focused on the following three major areas of emphasis.

- Developing networks of social interaction between people, close ties within and between organizations.
- Developing trusting relationships between individuals (see Chapter 7).
- Developing common values and shared visions with others.

In essence, these skills focus on the development of emotional intelligence—one of the key characteristics of effective leaders we described earlier.

All leadership development programs are based on two key assumptions: (1) Leadership makes a difference in an organization's performance, and (2) it is possible for leaders to be developed.[35] However, the various leadership development tools go about the mission of promoting leadership skills in different ways. We now identify some of the most widely used techniques.[36]

360-Degree Feedback

In Chapter 3 we described *360-degree feedback*, which is the process of using multiple sources from around the organization to evaluate the work of a single individual. Here we note that this practice has proven to be an effective way for leaders to learn what key others, such as peers, direct reports, and supervisors, think about them.[37] This is a useful means of identifying aspects of an individual's leadership style that are in need of change. Its basic assumption is that a person's performance is likely to vary across different contexts, suggesting that different people will have different perspectives on someone's leadership.

The practice of collecting 360-degree feedback is extremely popular these days. In fact, nearly all of the *Fortune* 500 companies rely on this technique in one way or another.[38] However, collecting feedback and taking appropriate action based on it are two entirely different things. After all, many people are threatened by negative feedback and defend against it psychologically by dismissing it as invalid. Even those who agree with it might not be willing to change their behavior (a topic we will revisit in Chapter 14). Furthermore, even the most well-intentioned leaders may fail to take action on the feedback they receive if that information is too complex or inconsistent, which may well occur. To help in this regard, many companies have found that leaders who have face-to-face meetings with others in which they get to discuss the feedback they receive are particularly likely to follow up in an effective manner.[39]

Networking

Far too often, leaders find themselves isolated from things that are going on in other departments. As a result, when they need help, they don't know where to look within their organizations. As a leadership development tool, **networking** is designed to break down these barriers. Specifically, it is aimed at helping leaders learn to whom they should turn for information and finding out the problem-solving resources that are available to them. Networking is so important to Accenture, the worldwide consulting firm, for example, that it holds an annual five-day seminar designed to give its global partners a chance to meet one another and to exchange views. The goal is to allow partners to strengthen their personal networks, making it possible to address problems and take on projects that otherwise would have been overlooked.

Networking is so important to Accenture, the worldwide consulting firm, for example, that it holds an annual five-day seminar designed to give its global partners a chance to meet one another and to exchange views.

Networking is beneficial to leadership development because it promotes peer relationships in work settings. These relationships are valuable insofar as they involve mutual obligations, thereby promoting cooperation. What's more, they tend to be long-lasting. In fact, it is not unusual for some peer relationships to span an entire 30-year career. Importantly, personal networks tend to be effective because they transcend organizational boundaries, thereby bringing together people from different parts of an organization who otherwise would not normally come into contact with one another.

Executive Coaching

A highly effective method of developing leaders involves custom-tailored, one-on-one learning aimed at improving an individual leader's performance. This approach, known as **executive coaching**, is an extension of the practice of *career coaching* described in Chapter 4. Coaching can be either a one-time process aimed at addressing some specific issues, or it can be an ongoing, continuous process. In either case, executive coaching typically includes an integrative assessment of a leader's strengths and weaknesses along with a comprehensive plan for improvement. Specifically, executive coaching programs tend to follow the specific steps outlined in Figure 11.7.

In some organizations, being assigned a coach is seen as a remedial measure and a sign of weakness. In such cases, any benefits of coaching may be minimized because leaders fail to get involved in the process out of embarrassment. For this reason, organizations that use coaches are advised to provide these services to an entire executive group, thereby removing any stigma associated with coaching and putting all leaders on an equal footing. Research has found that executive coaching is particularly effective when it is used following a formal training program. In fact, the customized, one-on-one coaching provided after a standardized training program was found to increase leaders' productivity by 88 percent.[40]

Mentoring

In Chapter 4, we described the formal process of mentoring, in which employees receive support, either formally or informally, from more experienced colleagues in the organization as a means of helping them develop their careers. Again, in Chapter 5 we discussed how minority group members stand to benefit by having

Figure 11.7   Steps in the Executive Coaching Process

The process of executive coaching generally follows the four steps outlined here.

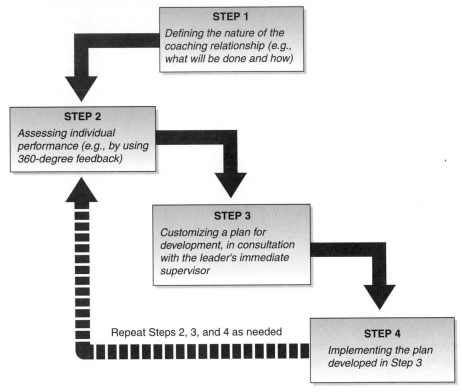

STEP 1

Defining the nature of the coaching relationship (e.g., what will be done and how)

STEP 2

Assessing individual performance (e.g., by using 360-degree feedback)

STEP 3

Customizing a plan for development, in consultation with the leader's immediate supervisor

Repeat Steps 2, 3, and 4 as needed

STEP 4

Implementing the plan developed in Step 3

(Source: Based on information in Chapman et al., 2003; see Note 40.)

relationships with *mentors*, more senior associates who help show them the ropes. Although mentoring is unlikely to include a formal assessment of a leader's strengths and limitations, it is inclined to be focused on personal and professional support. Recent research shows that officials from a wide array of organizations consider mentoring one of the most effective forms of leadership development they have in place.[41]

A potential problem with mentoring is that protégés may become so highly connected to their mentors that they fail to think independently. Soon what a protégé does is just what the mentor would have done. Although this can be beneficial, it is also potentially quite limiting, leading to a narrowness of thought. This problem is especially likely to occur in the case of executive coaching because protégés making important decisions may fear straying from the tried-and-true solutions of their mentors. And whenever this occurs, the organization is denied any fresh, new perspective that the less seasoned executive might be able to provide.

Job Assignments

When it comes to leadership, the phrase "experience is the best teacher" seems to hold true. Indeed, one of the most effective ways of training leaders is by assigning them to positions that promise to give them needed experience. With this in mind, several companies intentionally assign personnel to other countries so they can broaden their experiences. For example, Coca-Cola recently transferred over 300 professional and managerial employees from the United States to facilities in other countries for one year in an effort to develop their skills before returning them home to assume new positions of leadership. Gillette International does the same thing on a regular basis, assigning prospective leaders to positions at foreign affiliates for periods of one to three years. In many ways, this may be thought of as developing baseball players by sending them to the minor leagues. Likewise, teams from the National Football League are able to develop their players by sending them to compete in NFL Europe teams.

> Coca-Cola recently transferred over 300 professional and managerial employees from the United States to facilities in other countries for one year in an effort to develop their skills before returning them home to assume new positions of leadership.

For job assignments to serve their developmental function, it is necessary for the newly assigned positions to provide the kind of opportunities that make learning possible. Ideally, the new positions are ones that give developing leaders opportunities to try out different approaches to leadership so they can see what works for them. In other words, they should have the latitude to try different approaches, even if they fail. It is important to keep in mind that the purpose of the job assignment is to facilitate learning, in which case failure is inevitable. However, should an emphasis be placed on job performance instead, it's unlikely that the new assignment will have the intended benefits and is destined to be looked upon unfavorably.

Action Learning

Traditionally, much of the learning that takes place when people learn to lead occurs in the classroom. The problem with this approach, however, is that shortly after the formal training sessions are over, people revert to their old ways, resulting in little if any developmental progress. To combat this problem, many organizations have been turning to **action learning**, which is a continuous process of learning and reflection that is supported by colleagues and that emphasizes getting things done.[42] The underlying assumption of action learning is that leaders develop most effectively when they are working on real organizational problems.[43]

Citibank used action learning to help develop its leaders, who were having difficulty thinking about problems from a broad perspective.[44] Specifically, they took the following steps.

1. The issues to be worked on were selected by heads of business units. These had to be ones that affected total Citibank performance.
2. Participants were selected from throughout the world based on a thorough review of their talents.

3. A three-day orientation session was held off-site in which team-building skills were practiced (these are discussed in Chapter 9).

4. For two to three weeks, data were collected about effective banking practices from both inside and outside Citibank.

5. These findings were systematically analyzed and recommendations were developed.

6. Findings were presented to area heads and the CEO in 90-minute meetings.

7. A one-day debriefing session was held with a coach. These sessions focused on recommendations, team processes, and individual development opportunities.

8. One to two weeks later, senior managers followed up and made decisions regarding the various recommendations.

Although the business imperatives that drive action learning are often different, this basic process is generally quite similar across companies. Action learning has been used not only at Citibank but also at such organizations as General Electric (to develop new markets), ARAMARK (to promote cross-cultural opportunities), Shell Oil (to alter perceptions of the company's financial strength), and even the U.S. Army (to share lessons from battlefield experiences).[45] Because action learning is a general idea that takes different forms in different organizations, its effectiveness has been difficult to assess. However, available research generally confirms the effectiveness of training leaders by using the kind of active approaches described here instead of more passive, classroom training methods (see also the discussion of the factors that make training effective in Chapter 3).

You Be the **Consultant**

A Controlling Leadership Style

The president and founder of a large office furniture manufacturer tells you, "Nobody around here has any respect for me. The only reason they listen to me is because this is my company." Company employees report that he is a highly controlling individual who does not let anyone do anything for themselves.

1. What behaviors should the president attempt to emulate to improve his leadership style? How may he go about doing so?

2. Under what conditions would you expect the president's leadership style to be most effective? Do you think that these conditions might exist in his company?

3. Would your advice be any different if he were in charge of a small Internet start-up firm instead of a large manufacturing company?

Self-Assessment Exercise

Determining Your Leadership Style

As noted on pages 375–377, *situational leadership theory* identifies four basic leadership styles. To be able to identify and enact the most appropriate style of leadership in any given situation, it is first useful to understand the style to which you are most predisposed. This exercise will help you gain such insight into your own leadership style.

Directions

Following are eight hypothetical situations in which you have to make a decision affecting you and members of your work group. For each, indicate which of the following actions you are most likely to take by writing the letter corresponding to that action in the space provided.

- *Action A.* Let the members of the group decide themselves what to do.

- *Action B.* Ask the members of the group what to do but make the final decision yourself.

- *Action C.* Make the decision yourself but explain your reasons.

- *Action D.* Make the decision yourself, telling the group exactly what to do.

_____1. In the face of financial pressures, you are forced to make budget cuts for your unit. Where do you cut?

_____2. To meet an impending deadline, someone in your secretarial pool will have to work late one evening to finish typing an important report. Who will it be?

_____3. As coach of a company softball team, you are required to trim your squad to 25 players from 30 currently on the roster. Who goes?

_____4. Employees in your department have to schedule their summer vacations so as to keep the office appropriately staffed. Who decides first?

_____5. As chair of the social committee, you are responsible for determining the theme for the company ball. How do you do so?

_____6. You have an opportunity to buy or rent an important piece of equipment for your company. After gathering all the facts, how do you make the choice?

_____7. The office is being redecorated. How do you decide on the color scheme?

_____8. Along with your associates you are taking a visiting dignitary to dinner. How do you decide what restaurant to go to?

Scoring

1. Count the number of situations to which you responded by marking *A*. This is your *delegating* score.

2. Count the number of situations to which you responded by marking *B*. This is your *participating* score.

3. Count the number of situations to which you responded by marking *C*. This is your *selling* score.

4. Count the number of situations to which you responded by marking *D*. This is your *telling* score.

Discussion Questions

1. Based on this questionnaire, what was your most predominant leadership style? Is this consistent with what you would have predicted in advance?

2. According to situational leadership theory, in what kinds of situations would this style be most appropriate? Have you ever found yourself in such a situation, and if so, how well did you do?

3. Do you think that it would be possible for you to change this style if needed?

Group Exercise
Identifying Great Leaders in All Walks of Life

A useful way to understand the great person theory is to identify those individuals who may be considered great leaders and then to consider what it is that makes them so great. This exercise is designed to guide a class in this activity.

Directions

1. Divide the class into four equal-size groups, arranging each in a semicircle.

2. In the open part of the semicircle, one group member—the recorder—should stand at a flip chart, ready to write down the group's responses.

3. The members of each group should identify the 10 most effective leaders they can think of—living or dead, real or fictional—in one of the following fields: business, sports, politics/government, or humanitarian endeavors. One group should cover each of these domains. If more than 10 names come up, the group should vote on the 10 best answers. The recorder should write down the names as they are identified.

4. Examining the list, group members should identify the traits and characteristics that the people on the list have in common that distinguish them from others who are not on the list. In other words, what is it that makes these people so special? The recorder should write down the answers.

5. One person from each group should be selected to present his or her group's responses to members of the class. This should include both the names of the leaders identified and their special characteristics.

Discussion Questions

1. How did the traits identified in this exercise compare to the ones described in Table 11.2 as important determinants of leadership? Were they similar or different? Why?

2. To what extent were the traits identified in the various groups different or similar? In other words, were different characteristics associated with leadership success in different walks of life? Or were the ingredients for leadership success universal?

3. Were some of some traits identified surprising to you, or were they all what you would have expected?

Notes

Case Notes

Giuliani, R. W. (2002). *Leadership*. New York: Hyperion. Pooley, E. (2002, January 7). Person of the year 2001: Mayor of the world. *Time*, pp. 40–46.

Chapter Notes

[1] Yukl, G. (2002). *Leadership in organizations* (5th ed.). Upper Saddle River, NJ: Prentice Hall.
[2] Weathersby, G. B. (1999, March). Leadership vs. management. *Management Review*, p. 5.
[3] See Note 1.
[4] Yukl, G. (2000). Use power effectively. In E. A. Locke (Ed.), *The Blackwell handbook of principles of organizational behavior* (pp. 241–256). Oxford, England: Blackwell.
[5] Kirkpatrick, S. A., & Locke, E. A. (1991). Leadership: Do traits matter? *Academy of Management Executive, 5*, 41–60.
[6] See Note 5 (quote, p. 58).
[7] Editorial. (2000, January 10). The best managers: What it takes. *Business Week*, p. 158.
[8] Bass, B. M. (1998). *Transformational leadership: Industry, military, and educational impact*. Mahwah, NJ: Erlbaum.

[9] Turner, N., Barling, J., Epitropaki, O., Butcher, V., & Milner, C. (2002). Transformational leadership and moral reasoning. *Journal of Applied Psychology, 87*, 304–311.

[10] Colvin, G. (1999, November 22). The ultimate manager. *Fortune*, pp. 185–187. Slater, R. (1999). *Jack Welch and the GE way*. New York: McGraw-Hill.

[11] Tichy, N. M. (1993). *Control your destiny or someone else will*. New York: Doubleday Currency.

[12] Stewart, T. A. (1998, March 2). America's most admired companies. *Fortune*, pp. 70–82.

[13] Colvin, C. (2000, December 18). America's best and worst wealth creators. *Fortune*, pp. 207–208, 210, 212, 214, 216.

[14] Judge, T. A., & Bono, J. E. (2000). Five-factor model of personality and transformational leadership. *Journal of Applied Psychology, 85*, 751–765.

[15] Koh, W. L., Steers, R. M. & Terborg, J. R. (1995). The effects of transformational leadership on teacher attitudes and student performance in Singapore. *Journal of Organizational Behavior, 16*, 319–333.

[16] Hater, J. J., & Bass, B. M. (1988). Superiors' evaluations and subordinates' perceptions of transformational and transactional leadership. *Journal of Applied Psychology, 73*, 695–702.

[17] Hauser, M., & House, R. J. (2000). Lead through vision and values. In E. A. Locke (Ed.), *The Blackwell handbook of principles of organizational behavior* (pp. 257–273). Oxford, England: Blackwell.

[18] Bass, B. M., Avolio, B. J., Jung, D. I., & Berson, Y. (2003). Predicting unit performance by assessing transformational and transactional leadership. *Journal of Applied Psychology, 88*, 207–218.

[19] Neff, T. J., & Citrin, J. W. (1999). *Lessons from the top*. New York: Doubleday.

[20] Blake, R. R., & Mouton, J. S. (1982). Management by grid principles or situationalism: Which? *Group and Organization Studies, 7*, 207–210. Blake, R. R., & Mouton, J. S. (1969). *Building a dynamic corporation through grid organizational development*. Reading, MA: Addison-Wesley.

[21] House, R. J. (1996). Path-goal theory of leadership: Lessons, legacy, and a reformulated theory. *Leadership Quarterly, 7*, 323–352.

[22] Whitworth, L., House, H., Sandahl, P., & Kimsey-House, H. (1998). *Co-active coaching: New skills for coaching people toward success in work and life*. Palo Alto, CA: Davies-Black.

[23] Holtz, L. (1998). *Winning every day*. New York: Harper Business. Wolfe, R. (1998). *The Packer way*. New York: St. Martins.

[24] Bradley, Bill. (1998). *Values of the game*. New York: Artisan.

[25] Hersey, P., & Blanchard, K. H. (1988). *Management of organizational behavior*. Upper Saddle River, NJ: Prentice Hall.

[26] Bennis, W., & Heenan, D. A. (1999). *Co-leaders: The power of great partnerships*. New York: Wiley.

[27] Troiano, P. (1999, February). Sharing the throne. *Management Review*, pp. 39–43.

[28] Sirower, M. (2000). *The synergy trap: How companies lose the acquisition game*. New York: The Free Press.

[29] Sheard, A. G., & Kakabadse, A. P. (2001). Key roles of the leadership landscape. *Journal of Managerial Psychology, 17*, 129–144. Zenger, J. H., Musselwhite, E., Hurson, K., & Perrin, C. (1994). *Leading teams: Mastering the new role*. Homewood, IL: Business One Irwin.

[30] Labarre, P. (1999, June). Unit of one: Leaders.com. *Fast Company*, pp. 95–98, 100, 102, 104, 108, 110, 112.

[31] Lashinsky, A. (2003, September 1). Meg and the machine. *Fortune*, pp. 68–72, 76, 78.

[32] See Note 30 (quote, p. 96).

[33] See Note 30 (quote, p. 100).

[34] See Note 30 (quote, p. 104).

[35] Pernick, R. (2001). Creating a leadership development program: Nine essential tasks. *Public Personnel Management, 30,* 429–444.

[36] Day, D. V. (2001). Leadership development: A review in context. *Leadership Quarterly, 11,* 581–613.

[37] Atwater, L. E., Ostroff, C., Yammarino, F. J., & Fleenor, J. W. (1998). Self–other agreement: Does it really matter? *Personnel Psychology, 51,* 577–598.

[38] London, M., & Smither, J. W. (1995). Can multi-source feedback change perceptions of goal accomplishments, self-evaluations, and performance related outcomes? Theory-based applications and directions for research. *Personnel Psychology, 48,* 803–839.

[39] Walker, A. G., & Smither, J. W. (1999). A five-year study of upward feedback: What managers do with their results matters. *Personnel Psychology, 52,* 393–423.

[40] Chapman, T., Best, B., & Van Casteren, P. (2003). *Executive coaching: Exploding the myths.* New York: Palgrave Macmillan. Olivero, G., Bane, D. K., & Kopellman, R. E. (1997). Executive coaching as a transfer of training tool: Effects of productivity in a public agency. *Public Personnel Management, 26,* 461–469.

[41] McCauley, C. D., & Van Velsor, E. (2003). *The Center for Creative Leadership handbook of leadership development.* San Francisco: Jossey-Bass. Giber, D., Carter, L., & Goldsmith, M. (1999). *Linkage: Inc.'s best practices in leadership development handbook.* Lexington, MA: Linkage Press.

[42] Brobank, A., & McGill, I. (2003). *The action learning handbook.* London: Kogan Page. Marquardt, M. J., & Revans, R. (1999). *Action learning in action.* Palo Alto, CA: Davies-Black.

[43] Edmonstone, J. (2003). *The action learner's toolkit.* Hampshire, England: Gower Publishing. Pedler, M. (1997). Interpreting action learning. In J. Burgoyne & M. Reynolds (Eds.), *Management learning: Integrating perspectives in theory and practice* (pp. 248–264). London: Sage.

[44] Dotlich, D. L., & Noel, J. L. (1998). *Action learning: How the world's top companies are recreating their leaders and themselves.* San Francisco: Jossey-Bass.

[45] See Note 44.

Chapter **Twelve**

LEARNING
OBJECTIVES

After reading this chapter,
you will be able to:

1. **DEFINE** organizational culture
   and **IDENTIFY** the various
   functions it serves in organizations.

2. **DESCRIBE** the major types of
   organizational culture identified in
   the *competing values framework.*

3. **IDENTIFY** the factors
   responsible for creating
   organizational culture, for
   transmitting it, and for getting it to
   change.

4. **DEFINE** creativity and
   DESCRIBE the basic components
   of individual and team creativity.

5. **DESCRIBE** various approaches
   to promoting creativity in
   organizations.

6. **IDENTIFY** the basic components
   of innovation and the various stages
   of the innovation process.

Culture, Creativity, and Innovation

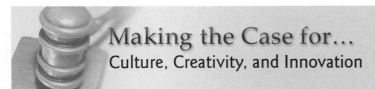

Making the Case for...
Culture, Creativity, and Innovation

IDEO: Where Silliness Is Taken Seriously

Although you probably never heard of IDEO, you most certainly are familiar with the products it has designed, including the optical computer mouse (for Apple Computer), the stand-up toothpaste tube (for Procter & Gamble's Crest), and 3Com's sleek Palm V personal digital assistant. IDEO's team of product design specialists even created the 25-foot robotic whale used in the movie *Free Willy.* Although we take such products for granted, coming up with them, as you might imagine, requires incredibly creative people. CEO and founder David Kelley knows that maintaining IDEO's status as the largest product design firm in the United States requires keeping ideas flowing from his 350-person staff, which is something he doesn't take for granted.

The key to nurturing creativity at IDEO is having fun—not just telling a few jokes but also playing games and acting goofy. Having fun for the sake of nurturing creativity permeates the atmosphere at IDEO. For example, when employees are not playing miniature golf or tossing Nerf balls in the corridors, they may be found racing desk chairs on the streets outside the company's Palo Alto, California, headquarters. According to Jim Hackett, CEO of Steelcase (which bought an equity stake in IDEO after being impressed with its operations), this way of operating "appeals to the childlike aspirations of all of us to be continually creative," adding that at IDEO, "work doesn't look like work."

Although Kelley's approach is unconventional, there is a method to his madness. By creating an atmosphere in which people are encouraged to play and have fun, he believes that the barriers that keep people from sharing ideas with each other will be broken down. In other words, if you're willing to throw a Nerf ball at your boss, you also might be willing to toss a few crazy ideas across the table. In Kelley's own words, "You can be playful when everybody feels they're just as important as the next person." Given the company's phenomenal success at coming up with innovative new product designs, his approach seems to be working.

As its clients noticed IDEO's innovative—and highly effective—way of nurturing creativity, they soon became interested not only in *what* the firm designs but also in *how* it goes about doing so. After several such inquiries, Kelley decided to diversify IDEO's services by teaching its customers its own special recipe for creativity. In fact, with clients such as NEC, Kodak, Canon, McDonald's, and Samsung, creativity training now accounts for a quarter of IDEO's revenues. Acknowledging the adage that genius is 99 percent perspiration and 1 percent inspiration, Dennis Boyle, one of IDEO's trainers, says, "Most companies have that 99 percent. It's that 1 percent that's really hard, and that's why our clients are asking us to work with their people and not just their products."

Culture, Creativity, and Innovation

You should care about organizational culture, creativity, and innovation because:

1. Organizational culture exerts profound influences on employees, both positive and negative.

2. Managers play an important role in creating, transmitting, and changing organizational culture.

3. Individual and team creativity is an important determinant of an organization's capacity to be innovative. This, in turn, is largely responsible for organizational success.

The question of how this elusive 1 percent is developed is one of the key issues I will describe in this chapter. In so doing, I will identify some of the approaches that IDEO takes, as well as several other successful approaches for enhancing *creativity*. As you probably know, people in some organizations, such as IDEO, regularly take novel, ingenious, and cutting-edge approaches to the problems they face. So too do employees in companies such as 3M, General Electric, and Rubbermaid routinely do the nonroutine.

What accounts for such differences? Why are some organizations more *innovative* than others? It's tempting to speculate that because people have different personalities, the organizations in which they work are likely to be different from each other as well. However, when you consider that entire organizations are often so consistently different from each other, it's apparent that there's more involved than simply differences in the personalities of the employees. In fact, even in companies where employees are constantly changing, the organizations themselves do not reinvent themselves. In fact, it is often the new employees who themselves change rather than their organizations. In a sense, then, organizations have a stable existence of their own, apart from the unique combination of people of which they are composed at any given time. This is the idea behind *organizational culture*—the shared beliefs, expectations, and core values of people in an organization.[1]

Because organizational culture is a key determinant of individual creativity and an organization's tendency toward innovation, I will begin this chapter by examining the concept of organizational culture. Specifically, I will begin by describing the basic nature of organizational culture, including the role it plays in organizations. Then I will describe the processes through which organizational culture is formed and maintained. Finally, I will review the effects of organizational culture on individual and organizational functioning and examine when and how culture is subject to change. Then, after having described the nature of organizational culture, I will turn attention to questions of creativity and innovation, including not only basic descriptions but also specific tips and suggestions regarding how to bring out your own creativity and how to make your own company more innovative.

Organizational Culture: Its Basic Nature

So that you can fully appreciate organizational culture, I will begin by offering a formal definition and then explain key features of its basic nature.

Organizational Culture: A Definition

learning
objective

Scientists define **organizational culture** as a cognitive framework consisting of assumptions and values shared by organization members.[2] For example, organizations tend to have different absence cultures—that is, the employees share different understandings about the appropriateness of taking off from work. At one organization, for example, healthy employees may feel that it's appropriate to call in sick if they have unused sick days available. However, at other companies, people wouldn't think of taking off unless they really are ill. In both of these companies, employees take for granted these various *assumptions* about sick leave. They are said to be ingrained into the organizational culture and are taken for granted.

As the definition indicates, organizational culture also reflects different *values* that are shared by members of the organization. By **values**, I am referring to stable, long-term beliefs about what is important. For example, some companies consider their employees as valuable only insofar as they contribute to production, much as they view machinery. Such organizations, where people do not feel valued, are considered having **toxic organizational cultures**. A recent survey found that 48 percent of people believe they work in toxic cultures.[3] Organizations with toxic cultures tend to lose good employees. By contrast, organizations that treat people well—said to have **healthy organizational cultures**—tend to have very low turnover. Examples of companies with healthy cultures include Hewlett-Packard, the Men's Wearhouse, and Starbucks. Indeed, having a healthy organizational culture can pay off handsomely on the bottom line.[4]

> Examples of companies with healthy cultures include Hewlett-Packard, the Men's Wearhouse, and Starbucks.

Despite widespread differences in organizational culture, in all companies organizational culture serves three vital functions. Specifically, organizational culture does the following.

1. *Provides a sense of identity for members.* The more clearly an organization's shared perceptions and values are defined, the more strongly people can associate themselves with their organization's mission and feel a vital part of it.

2. *Generates commitment to the organization's mission.* Sometimes it's difficult for people to go beyond thinking of their own interests: How will this affect me? However, a strong, overarching culture reminds people of what their organization is all about.

3. *Clarifies and reinforce standards of behavior.* Culture guides employees' words and deeds, making it clear what they should do or say in a given situation, thereby providing stability to behavior.

Cultures Within Organizations: One or Many?

The discussion thus far has implied that each organization has only a single, uniform culture—one set of shared values and expectations. In fact, this is rarely the case. Instead, organizations, particularly large ones, typically have *several* cultures operating within them.

In general, people tend to have more attitudes and values in common with others in their own fields of work or their own company units than they do with those in other fields or other parts of the organization. These various groups may be said to have several different **subcultures**—cultures existing within parts of organizations rather than entirely through them. These typically are distinguished with respect to either functional differences (i.e., the type of work done) or geographic distances (i.e., the physical separation between people). Indeed, research suggests that several subcultures based on occupational, professional, or functional divisions usually exist within any large organization.

This is not to say, however, that there also may not be a **dominant culture**, a distinctive, overarching "personality" of an organization—the kind of culture to which we have been referring. An organization's dominant culture reflects its core values, dominant perceptions that are generally shared throughout the organization. Typically, although members of subcultures may share additional sets of values, they generally also accept the core values of their organizations as a whole. Thus, subcultures should not be thought of as a bunch of separate cultures but rather as "mini" cultures operating within a large, dominant culture.

Major Types of Organizational Culture: The Competing Values Framework

As you might imagine, just are there are many different organizations, there also are many different types of organizational culture. Although each organization may be unique in several ways, key similarities in underlying organizational cultures may be noted. Fortunately, organizational scientists have developed useful ways of organizing and identifying these cultures. One of the most popular approaches is known as the **competing values framework**.[5] According to this approach, the cultures of organizations differ with respect to two sets of opposite values, that is, the extent to which the organization values (1) flexibility and discretion as opposed to stability, order, and control, and (2) attention to internal affairs as opposed to what's going on in the external environment. By combining both dimensions, as shown in Figure 12.1, scientists have been able to identify the following four unique types of organizational culture.

■ **Hierarchy culture.** Organizations described as having a *hierarchy culture* (shown in the lower left corner of Figure 12.1) have an internal focus and emphasize stability and control. Here the most effective leaders are good coordinators of projects and emphasize a smooth-running organization, often relying on formal rules and policies to do so. Governmental agencies and large corporations tend to fall into this category. At

Figure 12.1   The Competing Values Framework

According to the *competing values framework*, the cultures of organizations can be distinguished in terms of the two opposite dimensions identified here. Combining these two sets of competing values results in the four types of organizational cultures shown.

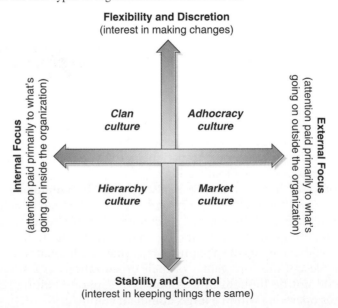

(Source: Adapted from Cameron and Quinn, 1999; see Note 5.)

McDonald's, for example, key values center on maintaining efficient and reliable production, and to ensure this, both the equipment used and the procedures followed—described in a 350-page manual—are designed with this in mind.

At McDonald's key values center on maintaining efficient and reliable production, and to ensure this, both the equipment used and the procedures followed—described in a 350-page manual—are designed with this in mind.

■ **Market culture.** The term *market culture* describes organizations that are concerned with stability and control but are external in their *orientation culture* (see the lower-right corner of Figure 12.1). In such organizations, the core values emphasize competitiveness and productivity, emphasizing bottom-line results. They do this by carefully identifying the markets in which they are going to compete and then by taking a very hard-driving, results-oriented approach to getting things done. A prototypical example is General Electric under the guidance of former CEO Jack Welch, who made it clear that the company would sell any businesses in which it was not number one or number two.

■ **Clan culture.** An organization is said to have a *clan culture* when it has a strong internal focus along with a high degree of flexibility and discretion (see the upper-left corner of Figure 12.1). With goals that are highly shared by members of the organization and high levels of cohesiveness (see Chapter 9), such organizations feel more like extended families than economic entities. This depicts the culture at People Express Airlines, a new airline in the 1980s, where management was highly informal and the employees (who also owned stock in the company) governed themselves. Soon after People Express merged with the more traditionally run Frontier Airlines (where workers were unionized and had more adversarial relationships with management) in 1985, serious culture clashes led to its demise.

■ **Adhocracy culture.** Organizations that have an *adhocracy culture* emphasize flexibility while also paying a great deal of attention to the external environment (see upper-right corner of Figure 12.1). Typical of contemporary organizations, which often have to make rapid changes in the way they operate (see Chapter 14), the adhocracy culture is characterized by recognizing that to succeed organizations need to be highly innovative (a concept we will describe later in this chapter) and by constantly assessing what the future requires for it to survive, let alone grow. Typical of companies with adhocracy cultures are those in the aerospace, software development, and filmmaking businesses, where it is widely recognized that highly innovative products and services are essential to success.

The Formation and Maintenance of Organizational Culture

3
learning
objective

Now that we have described what organizational culture is and how it operates, we are prepared to consider two more issues that are important: how culture is initially created and how it is sustained—that is, what keeps it going once it is created.

How Is Organizational Culture Created?

Now that you know what organizational culture is, it is natural to ask how it is created in the first place. Three major factors contribute to the emergence of organizational culture.

Company founders. First, organizational culture may be traced, at least in part, to the founders of the company.[6] These individuals often possess dynamic personalities, strong values, and a clear vision of how the organization should operate. Because they are on the scene first and play a key role in hiring initial staff, their attitudes and values are readily transmitted to new employees. The result is that these views become the accepted ones in the organization and persist as long as the founders are on the scene.

> The culture at Microsoft calls for working exceptionally long hours, in large part because that's what cofounder Bill Gates has always done.

For example, the culture at Microsoft calls for working exceptionally long hours, in large part because that's what cofounder Bill Gates has always done. Sometimes the founder's values can continue to drive an organization's culture even after that individual is no longer with the organization. For example, the late Ray Kroc founded the McDonald's restaurant chain on the values of good food at a good value served in clean, family-oriented surroundings—key cultural values that persist today.

Experience with the environment. Second, organizational culture often develops out of an organization's experience with the external environment. Every organization must find a niche for itself in its industry and in the marketplace. As it struggles to do so in its early days, it may find that some values and practices work better than others. For example, one company may determine that delivering defect-free products is its unique market niche; by doing so, it can build a core of customers who prefer it to competing businesses. As a result, the organization may gradually acquire a deep, shared commitment to high quality. In contrast, another company may find that selling products of moderate quality but at attractive prices works best. As a result, a dominant value centering on *price leadership* takes shape. In these and countless other ways, an organization's culture is shaped by its interaction with the external environment.

Contact with others. Third, organizational culture develops out of contact between groups of individuals within an organization. As this occurs, people's interpretations of events and actions are likely to be shared, promoting the development of organizational culture. In other words, organizational culture reflects the fact that people assign similar meaning to various events and actions so that they come to perceive the key aspects of the world, those relevant to the organization's work, in a similar manner (see Chapter 3).

Tools for Transmitting Culture

How are an organization's cultural values transmitted between employees? In other words, how do people come to learn about their organization's culture? Several key mechanisms are involved: *symbols, stories, jargon, ceremonies*, and *statements of principle*.

Symbols: Objects that say more than meets the eye. First, organizations often rely on **symbols**—material objects that connote meanings that extend beyond their intrinsic content. For example, some companies use impressive buildings to convey the organization's strength and significance, showing that it is a large, stable place. Other companies rely on slogans to symbolize their values, including such classic examples as General Electric's "Progress is our most important product," or Ford's "Quality is job one." Corporate cars (or even jets!) also are used to convey information about certain aspects of an organization's culture, such as who wields power. Material symbols are potent tools for sending messages about organizational culture. (To demonstrate this phenomenon for yourself, try the **Group Exercise** on pages 419–420.)

Stories: "In the old days, we used to . . .".   Organizations also transmit information about culture by virtue of the **stories** that are told in them, both formally and informally. Stories illustrate key aspects of an organization's culture, and telling them can effectively introduce or reaffirm those values to employees.[7] For example, employees of Nike are told tales about how the company was founded in an effort to underscore the company's abiding commitment to athletes (for some examples, see Table 12.1).[8] It is important to note that stories need not involve some great event, such as someone who saved the company with a single wise decision, but may be small tales that become legends because they so effectively communicate a message.

Jargon: The special language that defines a culture.   Even without telling stories, the everyday language used in companies helps sustain culture. For example, the slang or *jargon* that is used in a company helps its employees define their identities as members of an organization. For example, someone who works in a human resources

Table 12.1	The Nike Story: Just Telling It—And Keeping It Alive

New employees at Nike are told stories that transmit the company's underlying cultural values. The themes of some of the most important Nike stories are summarized here along with several of the ways the company helps keep its heritage alive.

New employees are told the following stories . . .

- Founder Phil Knight was a middle-distance runner who started the business by selling shoes out of his car.
- Knight's running coach and company cofounder, Bill Bowerman, developed the famous "waffle sole" by pouring rubber into the family waffle iron.
- The late Steve Prefontaine, coached by Bowerman, battled to make running a professional sport and was comitted to helping athletes.

To ensure that these tales of Nike's heritage are kept alive, the company . . .

- Takes new hires to the track where Bowerman coached and the site of Prefontaine's fatal car crash.
- Has created a "heritage wall" in its Eugene, Oregon, store.
- Requires salespeople to tell the Nike story to employees of the retail stores that sell its products.

(Source: Based on information in Ransdell, 2000; see Note 8.)

department may be found talking about the FMCS (Federal Medication and Conciliation Service), ERISA (the Employee Retirement Income Security Act), BFOQs (bona fide occupational qualifications), RMs (elections to vote out a union), and other acronyms that sound odd to the uninitiated. Over time, as organizations— or departments within them—develop unique language to describe their work, their terms, although strange to newcomers, serve as a common factor that brings together individuals belonging to a corporate culture or subculture.

Ceremonies: Special events that commemorate corporate values.   Organizations also do a great deal to sustain their cultures by conducting various types of *ceremonies*. Indeed, ceremonies may be seen as celebrations of an organization's basic values and assumptions. Just as a wedding ceremony symbolizes a couple's mutual commitment and a presidential inauguration ceremony marks the beginning of a new presidential term, various organizational ceremonies also celebrate some important accomplishment. For example, one accounting firm celebrated its move to much better facilities by throwing a party, a celebration signifying that it "has arrived" or "made it to the big time." Such ceremonies convey meaning to people inside and outside the organization. As one expert put it, "Ceremonies are to the culture what the movie is to the script . . . values that are difficult to express in any other way."[9]

Statements of principle: Defining culture in writing.   A fifth way in which culture is transmitted is via the direct *statements of principle*. Some organizations have explicitly written their principles for all to see. For example, Forrest Mars, the founder of the candy company M&M Mars, developed his "Five Principles of Mars" that still guide his company today.[10] These are quality (everyone is responsible for maintaining quality), responsibility (all employees are responsible for their own actions and decisions), mutuality (creating a situation in which everyone can win), efficiency (most of the company's 41 factories operate continuously), and freedom (giving employees opportunities to shape their futures).

Organizational Culture: Its Effects and Capacity to Change

By now, you probably are convinced that organizational culture plays an important role in the functioning of organizations. To make this point explicit, I now will examine the various ways in which organizational culture has been found to affect organizations and the behavior of individuals in them. Because some of these effects might be undesirable, organizations are sometimes interested in changing their cultures. Accordingly, we also will consider why and how organizational culture might be changed.

The Effects of Organizational Culture

Organizational culture exerts many effects on individuals and organizational processes—some dramatic and others more subtle. Culture generates strong pressures on people to go along, to think and act in ways consistent with the existing culture. Thus, if an organization's culture stresses the importance of product quality and excellent service, its customers generally will find their complaints handled politely and efficiently. If, instead, the organization's culture stresses high output at any cost, customers seeking service may find themselves on a much rockier road. An organization's culture can strongly affect everything from the way employees dress (e.g., the white shirts traditionally worn by male employees of IBM) and the amount of time allowed to elapse before meetings begin to the speed with which people are promoted.

Organizational performance.   Turning to the impact of culture on organizational processes, research has focused on the possibility of a link between culture and performance.[11] We know, for example, that to influence performance, organizational culture must be strong. In other words, approval or disapproval must be expressed to those who act in ways that are consistent or inconsistent with the culture, respectively, and there must be widespread agreement on values among organizational members. Only if these conditions prevail will a link between organizational culture and performance be observed.

Positive work-related attitudes.   This idea has important implications both for individuals and for organizations. First, it suggests that people seeking employment should examine carefully the prevailing culture of an organization before deciding to join it. If they don't, they run the risk of finding themselves in a situation where their own values and those of their company clash. Second, it also suggests that organizations should focus on attracting individuals whose values match their own (what is referred to as **person–culture fit**). This involves identifying key aspects of organizational culture, communicating these aspects to prospective employees, and selecting those for whom the person–organization fit is best.

Although it may be difficult and time-consuming to communicate key aspects of an organization's culture to prospective employees, the effort appears to be well worthwhile insofar as people whose individual values more closely fit the values of their organizations tend to be more satisfied with their jobs and committed to their organizations (recall these work-related attitudes from Chapter 5).[12] Moreover, employees whose personal values fail to match the values of their organizations tend to leave their jobs after a while because they don't fit in. Accordingly, it makes sense for prospective employers and prospective employees to screen one another very carefully before entering into a work relationship. Although values can change somewhat over time, a serious clash between individual and organizational values is a sure sign of problems to come.

Why and How Does Organizational Culture Change?

learning
objective

My earlier comments about the relative stability of organizational culture may have left you wondering if and when organizational culture ever changes. Why isn't it simply passed from one generation of organizational members to the next in a totally static manner? The basic answer, of course, is that the world in which all organizations operate constantly changes (see Chapter 14). External events such as shifts in market conditions, new technology, altered government policies, and many other factors change over time, necessitating changes in an organization's mode of doing business—and, hence, its culture.

Composition of the workforce.   Over time, the people entering an organization may differ in important ways from those already in it, and these differences may impinge on the existing culture of the organization. For example, people from different ethnic or cultural backgrounds may have contrasting views about various aspects of behavior at work. For instance, they may hold dissimilar views about style of dress, the importance of being on time (or even what constitutes "on time" behavior), the level of deference one should show to higher-status people, and even what foods should be served in the company cafeteria. In other words, as large numbers of people with different backgrounds and values enter the workplace, changes in organizational culture may be expected to follow.

Mergers and acquisitions.   Another and even more dramatic source of cultural change is *mergers* and *acquisitions*, events in which one organization purchases or otherwise absorbs another.[13] When this occurs, there is likely to be a careful analysis of the financial and material assets of the acquired organization. However, it is rare that any consideration is given to the acquired organization's culture. This is unfortunate because there have been several cases in which the merger of two organizations with incompatible cultures has led to serious problems referred to as **culture clashes**. As you might imagine, life in companies with incompatible cultures tends to be conflict-ridden and highly disruptive, often resulting in arguments and considerable uncertainty about what to do. In some cases, organizations have even been known to disband because of extreme culture clashes. For several good examples of culture clashes resulting from mergers and acquisitions, see Table 12.2.[14]

Planned organizational change.   Even if an organization doesn't change by acquiring another, cultural change still may result from other planned changes, such as conscious decisions to alter the internal structure or the basic operations of an organization (a topic we will describe in detail in Chapter 14). Once such decisions are reached, many practices in the company that both reflect and contribute to its culture may change. A good example of this can be seen in IBM.[15] In response to staggering losses IBM realized that one of its problems was that it was heavily bureaucratic, making it difficult for lower-level people to make on-the-spot decisions. As a result, IBM changed the nature of its corporate structure from one in which there was a steep hierarchy with many layers of management to a "delayered" one with far fewer managers. As you might imagine, the newly "rightsized" IBM developed a new corporate culture. Once known for a highly rigid, autocratic culture in which decision making was centralized in the hands of just a few, the reorganized IBM is now much more open and democratic in its approach than ever before. (For another example of a deliberate effort to alter organizational culture, see this chapter's accompanying **Winning Practices** section.)

> Once known for a highly rigid, autocratic culture in which decision making was centralized in the hands of just a few, the reorganized IBM is now much more open and democratic in its approach than ever before.

Responding to the Internet.   There can be no doubt that the Internet is a major influence on organizational culture these days. Compared to traditional businesses, where things move slowly and people look at change skeptically, the culture of

Table 12.2 Organizational Culture Clashes: Four Examples

Four major examples of culture clashes in the past few decades are summarized here, along with the cast of characters. As you read about these, think about what it must have been like to work in these companies at the time the clashes were occurring.

Original Company and CEO at Time of Merger	Original Company and CEO at Time of Merger	New Company (Merger Date) and Original Officers	Nature of Culture Conflict
AOL Steve Case, CEO	**Time Warner** Gerald M. Levin, CEO	**AOL Time Warner** (2001), renamed **Time Warner** (2003), Steve Case, CEO	The first "bricks-and-clicks" media empire to be formed suffered as AOL officials spent money in reckless fashion (far more lavishly than accurate accounting methods suggest would have been prudent), whereas the more conservative Time Warner officials were not accustomed to such high-flying ways. Although AOL Time Warner was officially a business entity, from the perspective of organizational culture, no merger ever really occurred. It was with this in mind that the company dropped the AOL from its name in 2003, returning to Time Warner.
Chrysler Robert J. Eaton, CEO	**Daimler-Benz** Jüergen E. Schrempp, CEO	**DaimlerChrysler** (1998) Robert J. Eaton and Jüergen E. Schrempp, co-CEOs	The so-called "merger of equals" was decidedly unequal. Executives' lifestyles were in sharp contrast. Those who came from Chrysler traveled together to meetings in minivans and flew economy class. However, Daimler-Benz officials arrived in chauffeur-driven Mercedes-Benz sedans and flew first class. While spending six months working this out, executives ignored important corporate problems.
RJ Reynolds Tylee Wilson, CEO	**Nabisco** Ross Johnson, CEO	**RJR Nabisco** (1988) Ross Johnson, CEO	Nabisco executives had a fast-paced lifestyle with perks such as corporate jets, penthouse apartments, and lavish parties. RJ Reynolds was characterized by a strong work ethic, much less autonomy for employees, and a deep commitment to its local community. A bitter feud erupted and Johnson fired RJ Reynolds executives.
HFS (franchising company) Henry Silverman, CEO	**CUC International (membership-club company)** Walter Forbes, CEO	**Cendant (1997)** Henry Silverman, CEO; and Walter Forbes, chairman of the board	Silverman was a control freak who insisted on seeing and knowing everything. However, Forbes saw himself as a visionary and left the details to others. Power clashes grew, eventually leading someone to blow the whistle on CUC officials for creating phony profits. The resulting scandal harmed the company greatly.

(Source: Based on information from references cited in Note 14.)

Winning **Practices**

Alberto-Culver Undergoes an Organizational Culture Makeover

In 1955 Leonard and Bernice Lavin purchased a beauty supply company that made hundreds of different products. Immediately they discontinued the entire line except for one product—a conditioning hairdressing. Taking the name "Culver" from the man from whom they bought the company and a chemist named "Alberto" who developed the original hairdressing formula for Hollywood movie studies, they came up with their new company name, Alberto-Culver. That name and the original product, Alberto VO5, remain to this day. As the years went on, the company located in suburban Chicago, developed new products, and acquired other companies, eventually reaching $2 billion in sales today. Besides Alberto VO5, brands such as Mrs. Dash seasonings, the Sally Beauty Company chain of stores, and the St. Ives line of botanically based cosmetic products all are from Alberto-Culver.[16]

In the early 1990s turnover was high and sales were flat, prompting Carol Lavin Bernick, president of Alberto-Culver North America, to intervene. Confident that the company's products were not to blame, she turned attention to the company's culture. It was a cold and indifferent place in which to work. Employees were in the dark about company operations, and even the most productive people were highly dissatisfied, eventually leaving. Realizing that something had to be done, she took several concrete steps to humanize the culture at Alberto-Culver.[17] Specifically, her key moves were as follows.

- 1993: A program was launched in which certain individuals called "growth development leaders" (GDLs) were honored by being selected to mentor a dozen or so other employees in such matters as the company's family-friendly benefit policies and career development.
- 1995: Bernick attempted "to open" the culture by giving detailed annual speeches on "the state of the company."
- 1997: The first "Business Builders Awards" were given to individuals and teams who went beyond their job requirements in ways that had a great impact on the company's growth and profitability.
- 1998: Brief statements describing how each employee contributes to the company's profitability, called "individual economic values" (IEVs), were developed to help employees recognize precisely how their work helps the business.
- 1998: A list of 10 core cultural values was formalized (honesty, ownership, trust, customer orientation, commitment, fun, innovation, risk taking, speed and urgency, and teamwork), which employees are expected to be able to recite by heart.

In only a few years, these efforts to transform the culture at Alberto-Culver North America had beneficial effects on the bottom line. From 1994 through 2001, sales increased 83 percent and pretax profit jumped 336 percent. As importantly, Bernick attributes changes in the corporate culture as responsible for dramatic reductions in turnover and newfound ease in acquiring other companies. In fact, the founder of one recently purchased company agreed to the acquisition not because Alberto-Culver was the highest bidder but because, as he says, he "had a good feeling about its culture."

Internet businesses is agile, fast-paced, and receptive to new solutions.[18] Information sharing is key, as such organizations not only accept but also embrace the expansion of communication networks and business relationships across organizational boundaries. When traditional brick-and-mortar businesses expand into e-commerce, changes in their organizational culture follow suit. We see this, for example, at the venerable investment firm, Merrill Lynch, which launched a Web site for trading stock in an effort to compete with brokerage firms such as E*Trade, which do business only online. The organizational culture at this venerable, traditional firm has become far more fast-paced ever since it adapted to the Internet economy.

To conclude, it is clear that although organizational culture is generally stable, it is not immutable. In fact, culture often evolves in response to outside forces (e.g., changes in workforce composition) as well as deliberate attempts to change the design of organizations (e.g., through mergers and corporate restructuring). An important aspect of culture that organizations frequently strive to change is the degree to which it approaches problems in creative and innovative ways. With this in mind, we will now turn attention to the topics of *creativity* and *innovation* in organizations.

Creativity in Individuals and Teams

4
learning
objective

Although you probably have no difficulty recognizing creativity when you see it, defining creativity can be a bit more challenging. Scientists define **creativity** as the process by which individuals or teams produce novel and useful ideas.[19] With this definition to guide us, I will explain how the process of creativity operates. Specifically, I will begin by describing the components of individual and team creativity and then outline several steps you can take to enhance your own creativity.

Components of Individual and Team Creativity

Creativity in individuals and teams has three basic components—domain-relevant skills, creativity-relevant skills, and intrinsic task motivation.

Domain-relevant skills.   Whether it's the manual dexterity required to play the piano or to use a computer keyboard, or the sense of rhythm and knowledge of music needed to conduct an orchestra, specific skills and abilities are necessary to perform these tasks. In fact, any task you might undertake requires certain talents, knowledge, or skills. These skills and abilities that we already have constitute the raw materials needed for creativity to occur. After all, without the capacity to perform a certain task at even a basic level, one has no hope of demonstrating creativity on that task. For example, before he can even begin to create stunning automotive stunts, a stunt driver must have the basic skills of dexterity and eye–hand coordination required to drive a car.

Creativity-relevant skills.   Beyond the basic skills, being creative also requires additional skills—special abilities that help people approach the things they do in novel ways. Specifically, when fostering creativity, it helps to do the following.

- *Break mental sets and take new perspectives.* Creativity is enhanced when people do not limit themselves to old ways of doing things. Restricting oneself to the past can inhibit creativity. Take a fresh look at even the most familiar things. This involves what is known as **divergent thinking**—the process of reframing familiar problems in unique ways. Divergent thinking often is promoted by asking people to identify as many unusual uses for common objects as possible.

■ *Understand complexities.* Instead of making things overly simplistic, don't be afraid to consider complex ways in which ideas may be interrelated.

■ *Keep options open and avoid premature judgments.* Creative people are willing to consider all options. To do so, they consider all the angles and avoid reaching conclusions prematurely. People are particularly good at this when they are new to an organization and, therefore, don't know enough to accept everything the way it is. With this in mind, some companies actually prefer hiring executives from outside their industry.

■ *Follow creativity heuristics.* People sometimes follow certain strategies, known as **creativity heuristics**, to help them come up with creative new ideas. These are rules that people follow to help them approach tasks in novel ways. They may involve such techniques as considering the counterintuitive and using analogies.

■ *Use productive forgetting.* Sometimes our creativity is inhibited when we become fixated on certain ideas that we just can't seem to get out of our heads. With this in mind, it helps to practice **productive forgetting**—the ability to abandon unproductive ideas and temporarily put aside stubborn problems until new approaches can be considered.

To help individuals and groups become more creative, many organizations invite employees to participate in training exercises designed to promote some of these skills. (These may include exercises similar to the one described in the **Self-Assessment Exercise** on pages 417–418. Try the exercise described here to experience firsthand how it may help your own creative juices flow.)

Intrinsic task motivation. The first two components of creativity, domain-relevant skills and creativity-relevant skills, focus on what people are *capable* of doing. However, the third component, intrinsic task motivation, refers to what people are *willing* to do. The idea is simple: For someone to be creative, he or she must be interested in performing the task in question. In other words, there must be a high degree of **intrinsic task motivation**—the motivation to do work because it is interesting, engaging, or positively challenging. Someone who has the capacity to be creative but who isn't motivated to do what it takes to produce creative outcomes certainly wouldn't be considered creative. People are most likely to be highly creative when they are passionate about their work.[20]

Intrinsic task motivation tends to be high under several conditions. For example, when an individual has a *personal interest* in the task at hand, he or she will be motivated to perform it—and may go on to do so creatively. However, anyone who doesn't find a task interesting surely isn't going to perform it long enough to demonstrate any signs of creativity. Likewise, task motivation will be high whenever an individual perceives that he or she has internal reasons to be performing that task. People who come to believe that they are performing a task for some external reason—such as high pay or pressure from a boss—are unlikely to find the work inherently interesting and are unlikely to show much creativity when performing it.

Putting it all together. As you might imagine, the components of creativity are important because they can be used to paint a picture of when people will be creative. In this connection, scientists claim that people will be at their most creative when they have high amounts of all three of these components (see Figure 12.2).

Figure 12.2 Components of Creativity

Scientists claim that people will be at their most creative when they exhibit high levels of the three factors shown here.

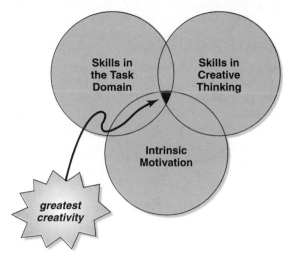

(Source: Adapted from Amabile, 1988; see Note 19.)

Specifically, it has been claimed that there is a multiplicative relationship among these three components of creativity. Thus, if any one component is low, the overall level of creativity will be low. In fact, people will not be creative at all if any one of these components is at zero (i.e., it is completely missing). This makes sense if you think about it. After all, you would be unlikely to be creative at a job if you didn't have the skills needed to do it, regardless of how motivated you were to be creative and how well practiced you were at coming up with new ideas. Likewise, creativity would be expected to be nonexistent if either creativity-relevant skills or motivation were zero. The practical implications are clear: To be as creative as possible, people must strive toward attaining high levels of all three components of creativity.

A Model of the Creative Process

Although it isn't always obvious to us how people come up with creative ideas, scientists have developed a model that outlines the various stages of the creative process.[21] This model specifies that the process of creativity occurs in the following four stages.

1. *Prepare to be creative.* Although we often believe that our most creative ideas come "out of thin air," people are at their most creative when they have made suitable preparations. This involves gathering the appropriate information and concentrating on the problem.

2. *Allow ideas to incubate.* Because ideas take time to develop, creativity can be enhanced by putting the problem out of our conscious minds and allowing it to incubate. If you've ever been successful at coming up with a fresh approach to a problem

by putting it aside and working on something else, you know what I am describing. The phrase "sleep on it" captures this stage of the process.

3. *Document insight.* At some point during the first two stages, you are likely to come up with a unique idea. However, that idea may be lost if it is not documented. With this in mind, many people carry small voice recorders that allow them to capture their ideas before they become lost in the maze of other ideas. Likewise writers keep diaries, artists keep sketch pads, and song writers keep tape recorders handy to capture ideas whenever inspiration strikes.

4. *Verify ideas.* Coming up with an idea is one thing but verifying that it's any good is quite another. Assessing the usefulness of an idea requires consciously thinking about it and verifying it, such as by seeing what others have to say about it. In other words, you want to see if the ideas that came to you in a moment of inspiration in the middle of the night are any good in the morning light.

Knowing about the creative process is particularly useful insofar as it can be applied to promoting individual and team productivity. I will now turn to the process of doing so.

5
learning
objective

Promoting Creativity in Organizations

Highly creative people are an asset to any organization. But what exactly do organizations do to promote creativity within their ranks? In general terms, the answer lies in things that we can do as individuals and that organizations can do as a whole. Several major approaches may be identified.

Training People to Be Creative

It is true that some people, by nature, are more creative than others. Such individuals are inclined to approach various situations in new ways and tend not to be bogged down by previous ways of doing things.[22] However, there still are skills that anyone can develop to become more creative. Generally, training people to become more creative involves three steps.[23]

Encourage openness to new ideas.   Many good ideas go undeveloped because they are not in keeping with the current way of doing things. Becoming more creative requires allowing oneself to be open to new ideas or, as it is often described, *thinking outside the box*. Some companies do this by sending their employees on *thinking expeditions*—trips specifically designed to put people in challenging situations in an effort to help them think differently and become more creative. According to the CEO of a company that specializes in running such expeditions for clients, these trips "push people out of their 'stupid zone'—a place of mental and physical normalcy—so that they can start to think differently," adding that "it's an accelerated unlearning experience."[24]

Doing precisely this, General Mills recently did something novel to promote thinking outside the (cereal) box. To develop creative new ideas about how to improve efficiency in their Betty Crocker factories, General Mills officials went to an unlikely place—the pit of a NASCAR auto race track, where they carefully studied how pit crews changed tires on race cars in the midst of a race.[25] What they learned led them to creative new ways of making the changes necessary to swap factory configurations from one product to another, ultimately reducing the process from 4.5 hours to only 12 minutes. Clearly, General Mills' openness to new ideas led to some creative new ways of solving a problem.

Take the time to understand the problem.   Meaningful ideas rarely come to those who don't fully understand the problem at hand. Only when time is taken to understand the many different facets of the issue can people be equipped to develop creative solutions. Consider, for example, BrightHouse, the 17-employee Atlanta-based company that specializes in developing new ideas for its clients (among them have been Coca-Cola, Home Depot, and Georgia-Pacific).[26] For a fee of $500,000, the entire staff of BrightHouse devotes a full 10 weeks to the issues their clients have in mind (e.g., how to improve on billboard advertising at Turner Field, the home of baseball's Atlanta Braves).

> To develop creative new ideas about how to improve efficiency in their Betty Crocker factories, General Mills officials went to the pit of a NASCAR auto race track, where they carefully studied how pit crews changed tires on race cars in the midst of a race. What they learned led them to creative new ways of making the changes necessary to swap factory configurations from one product to another, ultimately reducing the process from 4.5 hours to only 12 minutes.

Develop divergent thinking.   As I noted earlier, divergent thinking involves taking new approaches to old problems. Teaching people various tactics for divergent thinking allows problems to incubate, setting the stage for creative new ideas to develop. One popular way of developing divergent thinking is known as **morphology**. A morphological analysis of a problem involves identifying its basic elements and combining them in systematically different ways. (For an example of this approach, and for a chance to practice it yourself, see the **Self-Assessment Exercise** on pages 417–418.)

Developing Creative Work Environments

Thus far, I have identified ways of making people more creative as individuals. In conjunction with these approaches, it also is useful for organizations to take concrete steps to change work environments in ways that bring out people's creativity. Several such approaches may be identified.[27]

Ensure autonomy.   It has been established that people are especially creative when they are given the freedom to control their own behavior—that is, they have *autonomy* (see Chapter 6) and are *empowered* to make decisions (see Chapter 10). At the Japanese video game manufacturer, Nintendo, creativity is so important that no one considers it odd when designers leave work to go see a movie or a play.

> At the Japanese video game manufacturer Nintendo, creativity is so important that no one considers it odd when designers leave work to go see a movie or a play.

Provide exposure to other creative people.   It is widely assumed that workers are likely to be creative when they are surrounded by other creative individuals. After all, being around creative people inspires one to be creative oneself. Moreover, one can learn creativity-relevant skills from creative individuals. Although this is true under some circumstances, research suggests that the picture is not so simple. Specifically, the effect of having creative coworkers on a person's own creativity depends on the extent to which that individual is closely monitored by his or her supervisor.

A researcher conducting a recent study administered questionnaires to a group of employees to assess the extent to which they believed they were surrounded by creative coworkers as well as their beliefs about how closely they were monitored by their supervisors.[28] In addition, supervisors who were familiar with the work of each of these employees were asked to rate the degree of creativity they demonstrated in their work. The results, summarized in Figure 12.3, show that the presence of creative coworkers promoted creativity when supervisory monitoring was low but that it actually discouraged creativity when supervisory monitoring was high.

Figure 12.3 When Do Creative Coworkers Boost Creativity? Research Findings

The effects of having creative coworkers present on a worker's level of creativity has been found to depend on the degree to which the worker is closely monitored by his or her supervisor. According to a recent study, having creative coworkers boosted creativity when close supervisory monitoring was low (because they provided encouragement and demonstrated creativity-relevant skills). However, having creative coworkers actually lowered creativity when close supervisory monitoring was high (because workers were so concerned about not doing anything out of the ordinary that they merely "played it safe" by imitating the behavior of others).

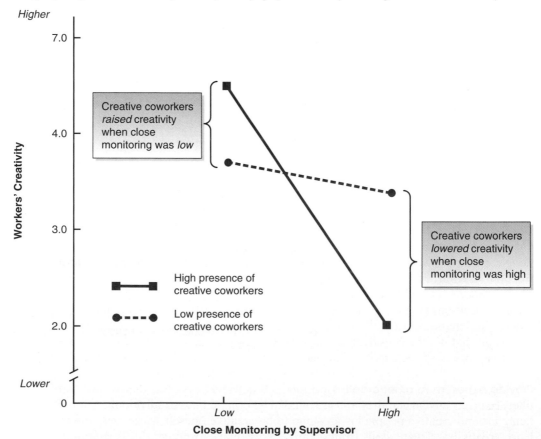

(Source: Based on data reported by Zhou, 2003; see Note 28.)

These findings may be explained as follows. Workers who feel that they are constantly being watched, evaluated, and controlled by their bosses were reluctant to take the chances required to behave in a creative fashion for fear of doing something that is considered inappropriate. As a result, they tended to "play it safe" by simply imitating what others are doing, thereby demonstrating less creativity than they were capable of showing. By contrast, employees who are not closely monitored by their supervisors are likely to be more willing to experiment with new ideas, thereby allowing them to reap the creative benefits of having creative coworkers around them.

Allow ideas to cross-pollinate.   People who work on just one project run the risk of getting stale, whereas those who work on several are likely to come into contact with different people and have a chance of applying an idea they picked up on one project to another project. This is done all the time at IDEO, the company described in this chapter's opening case. For example, in coming up with an idea about how to develop a more comfortable handle for a scooter, designers might use ideas they picked up while working on a project involving the design of a more comfortable computer mouse.

Make jobs intrinsically interesting.   Research has shown that people are inclined to be creative when they are intrinsically interested in the work they do. After all, nobody will want to invest the effort it takes to be creative at a task that is uninteresting. With this in mind, creativity can be promoted by enhancing the degree to which tasks are intrinsically interesting to people. The essence of the idea is to turn work into play by making it interesting. For some specific suggestions on how to do this, see Table 12.3.

Table 12.3	Boosting Creativity by Making Jobs More Intrinsically Interesting

As summarized here, several specific features of the work environment can boost a job's intrinsic interest and, hence, the degree to which people are likely to cemonstrate creativity.

Characteristic	*Description*
Challenge	People are likely to be creative at tasks they find interesting because they are required to work hard at them.
Autonomy	People are likely to be interested their work and creative in performing it when they are free to determine how to do it.
Work group support	Intrinsic interest in a task is enhanced, as is creativity, when others share ideas about it and have the skills needed to perform it.
Supervisory and organizational encouragement	Workers are likely to be interested in performing a job, and to do it creatively, when they believe their immediate supervisor, or the organization as a whole, encourages their efforts.
Absence of organizational impediments	People will be interested in working and likely to be creative when key organizational impediments are eliminated, such as political problems, negative criticism of new ideas, and pressure to maintain the status quo.

(Source: Based on suggestions from Amabile, 2000; see Note 19.)

This approach is used routinely at Play, a marketing agency in Richmond, Virginia. Instead of coming up with ideas by sitting in boring meetings, staff members are encouraged to play (much like IDEO, described in this chapter's opening case). For example, to aid the process of coming up with an new marketing campaign for the Weather Channel, employees spent time in a corner office developing costumes for superheroes. According to cofounder Andy Stefanovich, the idea is simple: "When you turn work into a place that encourages people to be themselves, have fun, and take risks, you fuel and unleash their creativity. The best ideas come from playful minds. And the way to tap into that playfulness is to play—together."[29]

Set your own creative goals.   Being free to do as you wish does not necessarily imply goofing off. In fact, the freedom to make your own decisions pays off most handsomely when people set their own creative goals. For example, the famous inventor Thomas A. Edison set the goal of having a minor invention every 10 days and a major invention every six months. This kept Edison focused on being creative—and, with over 1,000 patents in his name, he clearly did an outstanding job of meeting his goals. It is important to underscore that I'm not talking about strict external pressure to be creative, which rarely results in anything positive. However, creativity is aided when people are encouraged to set their own goals about being creative.

Support creativity at high organizational levels.   Nobody in an organization is going to go out of his or her way to be creative if it is not welcomed by the bosses. Supervisors, team leaders, and top executives must encourage employees to take risks if they are to have any chance of being creative. At the same time, this involves accepting any failures that result. This idea is embraced by Livio D. DeSimone, the CEO of 3M, one of the most innovative companies in the world. "Failure is not fatal," he says, adding, "Innovations are simply chance breakthroughs. And when you take a chance, theirs is always the possibility of a failure."[30] Showing that he means it, DeSimone introduced a "30/4" rule—that is, 30 percent of sales were to come from products that had been around for no more than four years. This goal really sparked the creative fires, and this goal was met only two years after it was introduced.

3M has established an honorary society that recognizes extraordinary contributions to its science and technology. Members include individuals who have invented such ubiquitous products as Post-it Notes, Scotch Magic Transparent Tape, and Scotchgard fabric protector.

Although most companies recognize their employees' accomplishments with some form of monetary reward, 3M takes things a step further by giving a variety of special, highly coveted awards to employees who have been among the most creative. For example, 3M has established an honorary society that recognizes extraordinary contributions to its science and technology. Members include individuals who have invented such ubiquitous products as Post-it Notes, Scotch Magic Transparent Tape, and Scotchgard fabric protector. Obviously, 3M goes out of its way to ensure that its employees are highly creative—and, to a large degree, this focus has been responsible for the company's century-long record of success.

The Process of Innovation

learning
objective

Now that you know about the process of creativity, you are prepared to understand situations in which people implement their creative skills for the sake of improving their organizations. This is the process of **innovation**—the successful implementation of creative ideas within an organization. To understand this process I will review the various stages through which innovation progresses. Before doing this, however, I will begin by identifying the various components of innovation.

Components of Innovation: Basic Building Blocks

Earlier, I depicted individual creativity as having three components—motivation, resources, and skills. As it works out, these same components are involved in organizational innovation as well, albeit in somewhat different ways.

Motivation to innovate.   Just as individual creativity requires that people are motivated to do what it takes to be creative, organizational innovation requires that organizations have the kinds of cultures that encourage innovation. When top executives fail to promote a vision of innovation and accept the status quo, change is unlikely. However, at companies such as Microsoft, where leaders (including president and cofounder Bill Gates) envision innovation as being part of the natural order of things, it is not surprising that innovative efforts are constantly underway.

Resources to innovate.   Again, a parallel to individual creativity is in order. Just as people must have certain basic skills to be creative, so too must organizations possess certain basic resources that make innovation possible. For example, to be innovative, at the very least, organizations must have what it takes in terms of human and financial resources. After all, unless the necessary skilled people and deep pockets are available to do what it takes to innovate, stagnation is likely to result.

At Hewlett-Packard (HP), for example, a whopping 5 to 6 percent of revenues (some $1 billion) are spent on research and development—over twice as much as its competitors—to ensure that the company stays competitive in the home and office printer business by constantly generating new and improved products.[31] By doing precisely this (e.g., introducing 100 new printers in the fall of 2003, alone), HP's printer business has grown in profitability even while its other units (e.g., Compaq computers) have been flat, successfully taking on upstarts, such as Dell, whose printers sell at about 10 percent less.

> At Hewlett-Packard (HP), 5 to 6 percent of revenues (some $1 billion) is spent on research and development—over twice as much as its competitors—to ensure that the company stays competitive in the home and office printer business by constantly generating new and improved products.

Innovation management.   Finally, just as individuals must hone special skills needed to be creative, so too must organizations develop special ways of managing people to encourage innovation—that is, *skills in innovation management*. Most notable in this regard is the matter of *balance*. Specifically, managers help promote

Figure 12.4 Skills in Innovation Management: A Careful Balancing Act

Managing innovation requires carefully balancing the three matters identified here.

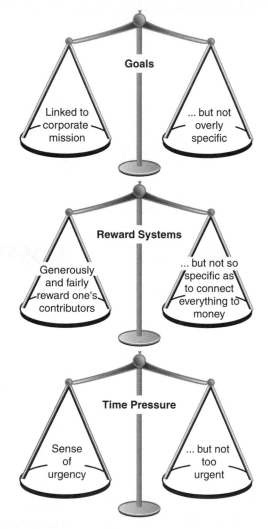

(Source: Based on information reported by Amabile, 1988; see Note 19.)

innovation when they show balance with respect to three key matters: goals, reward systems, and time pressure (see Figure 12.4).

- Organizational innovation is promoted when *goals* are carefully linked to the corporate mission. However, they should not be so specific as to tie the hands of those who put them into practice. Innovation is unlikely when such restrictions are imposed.

- *Reward systems* should generously and fairly recognize individuals' contributions, but they should not be so specific as to connect literally every move to a bonus or some type of monetary reward. To do so discourages people from taking the kinds of risks that make innovation possible.

■ Innovation management requires carefully balancing the *time pressures* under which employees are placed. If pressures are too great, people may be unimaginative and offer routine solutions. By the same token, if pressure is too weak, employees may have no sense of time urgency and believe that the project is too unimportant to warrant any creative attention on their part.

Stages of the Organizational Innovation Process

Any CEO who snaps her fingers one day and expects her troops to be innovative on command will surely be in for disappointment. Innovation does not happen all at once. Rather, innovation occurs gradually, through a series of stages. Scientists have identified five specific stages through which the process of organizational innovation progresses.[32] I now will describe each of these five stages (see the summary in Figure 12.5).

Stage 1: Setting the agenda.   The first stage of the process of innovation begins by setting the agenda for innovation. This involves creating a *mission statement*—a document describing an organization's overall direction and general goals for accomplishing that movement. The component of innovation that is most involved

Figure 12.5   The Process of Innovation

The innovation process consists of the various components and follows the steps shown here.

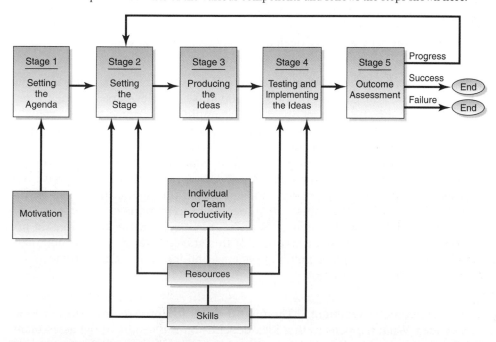

(Source: Adapted from Amabile, 1988; see Note 19.)

here is motivation. After all, the highest-ranking officials of the organization must be highly committed to innovation before they will initiate a push toward it.

As a case in point, consider HP, mentioned earlier. Head of the printer division, Vyomesh Joshi, acknowledges that to keep his company's printers from becoming commodities, his company must innovate. "Innovation is still important in this business," he says, putting up the $1 billion annual investment in research and development required to bring it to fruition.[33]

Stage 2: Setting the stage.   Once an organization's mission has been established, it is prepared to set the stage for innovation. This may involve narrowing down certain broad goals into narrower, more specific tasks and gathering the resources to meet them. It also may involve assessing the environment, both outside and inside the organization, searching for anything that may either support or inhibit later efforts to "break the rules" by being creative. Effectively setting the stage for innovation requires using the skills necessary for innovation management as well as full use of the organization's human and financial resources.

Stage 3: Producing the ideas.   This stage of the process involves coming up with new ideas and testing them. It is in this third stage that individual and small group creativity enters the picture. As a result, all of the components of individual creativity mentioned earlier are involved. What's more, these may combine in important ways with various organizational factors. For example, an individual who has the skills and motivation to be highly creative might find his motivation waning as he attempts to introduce novel ideas in an organization that is not committed to innovation and that fails to make the necessary resources available. By contrast, the highly innovative nature of an organization may bring out the more creative side of an individual who may not have been especially creative.

Stage 4: Testing and implementing the ideas.   This is the stage where implementation occurs. Now, after an initial group of individuals has developed an idea, other parts of the organization get involved. For example, a prototype product may be developed and tested, and market research may be conducted. In short, input from the many functional areas of the organization is provided.

I note in Figure 12.4 that skills in innovation management are very important in this stage of the process. In large part this is because for good ideas to survive it is necessary for them to be "nourished" and supported throughout the organization. Even the best ideas may be "killed off" if people in some parts of the organization are not supportive. For this same reasoning, resources in the task domain are another important component involved in this stage. After all, unless adequate amounts of money, personnel, material systems, and information are provided, the idea will be unlikely to survive.

Stage 5: Outcome assessment.   The final stage of the process involves assessing the new idea. What happens to that idea depends on the results of the assessment. Three outcomes are possible. If the resulting idea (e.g., a certain product or service) has been a total success, it will be accepted and carried out in the future. This ends the process. Likewise, the process is over if the idea has been a complete failure. In this case, there is no good reason to continue. However, if the new idea shows promise and makes some progress toward the organization's objectives but still has problems, the process starts all over again at stage 2.

Although this five-stage process does not account for all innovations you may find in organizations, this general model does a good job of identifying the major steps through which most innovations go as they travel along their path from a specific organizational need to a product or service that meets that need.

You Be the Consultant
Promoting a Creative Organizational Culture

The president of your organization, a small manufacturing company, has been complaining that sales are stagnant. A key problem, you discover, is that the market for the products your firm makes is fully developed—and, frankly, the products themselves are not very exciting. No one seems to care about doing anything innovative. Instead, the employees seem more interested in doing things the way they have always done them. Answer the following questions based on the material in this chapter.

1. What factors do you suspect are responsible for the way the culture in this organization has developed over the years?

2. What do you recommend should be done to enhance the creativity of this company's employees?

3. What could be done to help make the company's products more innovative?

Self-Assessment Exercise
Morphology in Action: Using the Idea Box

One day the marketing director of a company that makes laundry hampers was tinkering with ways of boosting sales in a stagnant, mature market.[34] To trigger his imagination, he thought explicitly about something that most of us take for granted—the basic parameters of laundry hampers. Specifically, he noted that they differed in four basic ways: the materials of which they were made, their shape, their finish, and how they are positioned. For each of these dimensions, he identified five different answers, resulting in the chart at the top of p. 418, known as an *idea box*.

Then, by randomly combining one item from each column—net material, cylindrical shape, painted finish, and positioning on a door—the marketing director came up with a completely new idea. It was a laundry hamper made to look like a basketball net: about a yard of netting attached to a cylindrical hoop, hung from a backboard attached to the back of a door.

IMPROVE DESIGN FOR LAUNDRY HAMPER

	Material	Shape	Finish	Position
1	Wicker	Square	Painted	Sits on Floor
2	Plastic	Cylindrical	Painted	On Ceiling
3	Paper	Rectangle	Clear	On Wall
4	Metal	Hexagonal	Luminous	Chute to Basement
5	Net Material	Cube	Neon	On Door

(Source: Reprinted with permission from Thinkertoys *by Michael Michalko. Berkeley, California: Ten Speed Press.)*

With some quick math, you can see that this particular idea box generates 500 different combinations. Given that this is a far greater number of ideas than you could probably generate without the aid of the idea box, it makes sense to practice generating idea boxes for situations you face in which creative new solutions are required. Nurture your own creativity by following the four simple steps identified by creativity expert Michael Michalko.[35]

Steps for Generating an Idea Box

1. *Specify the challenge you are facing.* Although you may not be interested in developing exciting new laundry baskets, you must start at the same point indicated in our example—that is, by identifying exactly what you are attempting to do.

2. *Select the parameters of your challenge.* Material, shape, finish, and position were the parameters of the laundry basket problem. What are yours? To help determine if the parameter you are considering is important enough to add, ask yourself if the challenge would still exist without that parameter.

3. *List variations.* Our example shows five variations of each parameter, but feel free to list as many key ones as you can. After all, as your idea box grows larger, it gets increasingly difficult to spot new ideas. (For example, if your idea box had 10 parameters, each of which contained 10 variations, you'd face 10 billion potential combinations to consider—hardly a practical task!)

4. *Try different combinations.* After your idea box is completed, work your way through the box to find some of the most promising combinations. Begin by examining the entire box and then eventually limit yourself to the most promising combinations.

Discussion Questions

1. Have you ever used the idea box, or something similar to it, before now? If so, how effectively has it worked?

2. For what kinds of challenges is the idea box most useful and least useful?

3. It has been said that generating an idea box is similar to writing a poem. How is this so?

Group Exercise

What Does Your Workspace Say About Your Organizational Culture?

Newcomers' impressions of an organization's culture depend greatly on the visual images of that organization they first see. Even without knowing anything about an organization, just seeing the workplace sends a message, intentional or unintentional, regarding what that organization is like. The following exercise is designed to demonstrate this phenomenon.

Directions

1. Each member of the class should take several photographs of his or her workplace and select the three that best capture, in his or her own mind, the essence of what that organization is like.

2. One member of the class should identify the company depicted in his or her photos, describe the type of work it does, and present the photos to the rest of the class.

3. Members of the class should then rate the organization shown in the photos using the following dimensions. Circle the number that comes closest to your feelings about the company shown.

unfamiliar	: 1 : 2 : 3 : 4 : 5 : 6 : 7 :	familiar
unsuccessful	: 1 : 2 : 3 : 4 : 5 : 6 : 7 :	successful
unfriendly	: 1 : 2 : 3 : 4 : 5 : 6 : 7 :	friendly
unproductive	: 1 : 2 : 3 : 4 : 5 : 6 : 7 :	productive
not innovative	: 1 : 2 : 3 : 4 : 5 : 6 : 7 :	innovative
uncaring	: 1 : 2 : 3 : 4 : 5 : 6 : 7 :	caring
conservative	: 1 : 2 : 3 : 4 : 5 : 6 : 7 :	risky
closed	: 1 : 2 : 3 : 4 : 5 : 6 : 7 :	open

4. Take turns sharing your individual reactions to each set of photos. Compare the responses of the student whose company pictures were examined with those of the students who were seeing the photos for the first time.

5. Repeat this process using the photos of other students' organizations.

Discussion Questions

1. For each set of photos examined, how much agreement or disagreement was there within the class about the companies rated?

2. For each set of photos examined, how close did the descriptions of members of the class come to the photographers' assessments of their own companies?

In other words, how well did the photos capture the culture of the organization as perceived by an "insider"?

3. As a whole, were people more accurate in assessing the culture of companies with which they were already familiar than those they didn't already know? If so, why do you think this occurred?

Notes

Case Notes

Kelley, T., & Littman, J. (2001). *The art of innovation: Lessons in creativity from IDEO, America's leading design firm.* New York: Doubleday. Myerson, J. (2001). *IDEO: Masters of innovation.* New York: te Neues Publishing. Garner, R. (2000, April). Innovation for fun and profit. *Upside*, pp. 88–90, 92, 94, 96. Anonymous. (1999, September 13). Seriously silly. *Business Week*, p. F14. Brown, E. (1999, April 12). A day at Innovation U. *Fortune*, pp. 163–165.

Chapter Notes

[1] Schneider, B. (1990). *Organizational climate and culture.* San Francisco: Jossey-Bass.

[2] Schein, E. H. (1999). *The corporate culture survival guide.* San Francisco: Jossey-Bass. Schein, E. H. (1985). *Organizational culture and leadership.* San Francisco: Jossey-Bass.

[3] Anonymous. (1999, April). Toxic shock? *Fast Company*, p. 38.

[4] Webber, A. M. (1998, November). Danger: Toxic company. *Fast Company*, pp. 152–159.

[5] Cameron, K. S., & Quinn, R. E. (1999). *Diagnosing and changing organizational culture: Based on the competing values framework.* Reading, MA: Addison-Wesley. Berrio, A. A. (2003). Organizational culture assessment using the competing values framework: A profile of Ohio State University extension. *Journal of Extension, 41*(2). Published exclusively on the World Wide Web at www.joe.org/joe/2003april/a3.shtml.

[6] Martin, J., Sitkin, S. B., & Boehm, M. (1985). Founders and the elusiveness of a cultural legacy. In P. J. Frost, L. F. Moore, M. R. Louis, C. C. Lundberg, & J. Martin (Eds.), *Organizational culture* (pp. 99–124). Beverly Hills, CA: Sage.

[7] Martin, J. (2001). *Organizational culture: Mapping the terrain.* Newbury Park, CA: Sage. Martin, J. (1982). Stories and scripts in organizational settings. In A. Hastorf & A. Isen (Eds.), *Cognitive social psychology* (pp. 255–306). New York: Elsevier.

[8] Ransdell, E. (2000, January–February). The Nike story? Just tell it. *Fast Company*, pp. 44, 46.

[9] Neuhauser, P. C. (1993). *Corporate legends and lore: The power of storytelling as a management tool.* New York: McGraw-Hill (quote, p. 63).

[10] Brenner, J. G. (1999). *The emperors of chocolate: Inside the secret world of Hershey and Mars.* New York: Random House.

[11] Weiner, Y. (1988). Forms of value systems: A focus on organizational effectiveness and cultural change and maintenance. *Academy of Management Review, 13*, 534–545.

[12] O'Reilly, C. A., & Chatman, J. (1996). Culture as social control: Corporations, cults, and commitment. In B. M. Staw & L. L. Cummings (Eds.), *Research in organizational behavior* (Vol. 18, pp. 157–200). Greenwich, CT: JAI Press. O'Reilly, C. A., Chatman, J., & Caldwell, D. F. (1991). People and organizational culture: A profile comparison approach to assessing person–organization fit. *Academy of Management Journal, 34*, 487–516.

[13] Walter, G. A. (1985). Culture collisions in mergers and acquisitions. In P. J. Frost, L. F. Moore, M. R. Louis, C. C. Lundberg, & J. Martin (Eds.), *Organizational culture* (pp. 301–314). Beverly Hills, CA: Sage.

[14] Klein, A. (2003). *Stealing time*. New York: Simon & Schuster. Vlasic, B., & Stertz, B. A. (2001). *Taken for a ride: How Daimler-Benz drove off with Chrysler*. New York: Harper Business. Naughton, K. (2000, December 11). A mess of a merger. *Newsweek*, pp. 54–57. Elkind, P. (1998, November 9). A merger made in hell. *Fortune*, pp. 134–138, 140, 142, 144, 146, 149, 150. Burrough, B., & Helyar, J. (1990). *Barbarians at the gate*. New York: Harper Collins. Muller, J. (1999, November 29). Lessons from a casualty of the culture wars. *Business Week*, p. 198. Muller, J. (1999, November 15). The one-year itch at DaimlerChrysler. *Business Week*, p. 42.

[15] Carroll, P. (1993). *Big blues: The unmaking of IBM*. New York: Crown.

[16] Alberto-Culver: Our story. From the World Wide Web at www.alberto.com/ACCorpWeb/Pages/OurStory/OurStory.html#.

[17] Bernick, C. L. (2001). When your culture needs a makeover. *Harvard Business Review, 79*(6), 53–56, 58, 60–61.

[18] Fischer, I., & Frontczak, D. (1999, September). Culture club. *Business 2.0*, pp. 196–198.

[19] Amabile, T. M. (1988). A model of creativity and innovation in organizations. In B. M. Staw & L. L. Cummings (Eds.), *Research in organizational behavior* (Vol. 10, pp. 123–167). Greenwich, CT: JAI Press.

[20] Amabile, T. M. (2000). Stimulate creativity by fueling passion. In E. A. Locke (Ed). *The Blackwell handbook of principles of organizational behavior* (pp. 331–341). Oxford, England: Blackwell.

[21] Kabanoff, B., & Rossiter, J. R. (1994). Recent developments in applied creativity. In C. Cooper & I. T. Robertson (Eds.), *International review of industrial and organizational psychology* (Vol. 9, pp. 283–324). London: Wiley.

[22] Michalko, M. (1998, May). Thinking like a genius: Eight strategies used by the supercreative, from Aristotle and Einstein and Edison. *The Futurist*, pp. 21–25.

[23] Kabanoff, B., & Bottiger, P. (1991). Effectiveness of creativity training and its reaction to selected personality factors. *Journal of Organizational Behavior, 12*, 235–248.

[24] Muoio, A. (2000, January–February). Idea summit. *Fast Company*, pp. 151–156, 160, 162, 164 (quote, p. 152).

[25] Gogoi, P. (2003). Thinking outside the cereal box. *Business Week*, pp. 74–75.

[26] Sittenfeld, C. (1999, July–August). This old house is a home for new ideas. *Fast Company*, pp. 58, 60.

[27] Oldham, G. R., & Cummings, A. (1996). Employee creativity: Personal and contextual factors at work. *Academy of Management Journal, 39*, 607–634.

[28] Zhou, J. (2003). When the presence of creative coworkers is related to creativity: The role of supervisor close monitoring, developmental feedback, and creative personality. *Journal of Applied Psychology, 88*, 413–422.

[29] Dahle, C. (2000, January–February). Mind games. *Fast Company*, pp. 169–173, 176, 178–179.

[30] Sutton, R. I., & Hargadon, A. (1996). Brainstorming groups in context: Effectiveness in a product design firm. *Administrative Science Quarterly, 41*, 685–718. (quote, p. 702).

[31] Elgin, B. (2003, July 14). Can HP's printer biz keep printing money? *Business Week*, pp. 68–70.

[32] See Note 19.

[33] See Note 31.

[34] Michalko, M. (1991). *Thinkertoys*. Berkeley, CA: Ten Speed Press.

[35] See Note 34.

Chapter **Thirteen**

LEARNING OBJECTIVES

After reading this chapter, you will be able to:

1. **DEFINE** organizational structure and **DISTINGUISH** among five aspects of organizational structure that are typically represented in an organization chart.

2. **DISTINGUISH** among the three types of departmentalization: functional organizations, product organizations, and matrix organizations.

3. **DEFINE** organizational design and **DISTINGUISH** between classical and neoclassical approaches to organizational design.

4. **DESCRIBE** the contingency approach to organizational design.

5. **IDENTIFY** five emerging approaches to organizational design.

6. **DISTINGUISH** between *conglomerates* and *strategic alliances* as two types of interorganizational designs.

Designing Effective Organizations

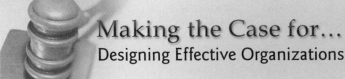

Making the Case for...
Designing Effective Organizations

Commercial Metals Company "Steels" the Show

When builders repaired the Pentagon after the September 11 terrorist attack, they turned to the Commercial Metals Company (CMC) for ultrastrong structural steel girders. To industry insiders, the choice seemed obvious. Since 1915, companies building bridges, skyscrapers, vehicles, and industrial equipment have relied on CMC to provide steel and metal products of every conceivable type. The company's high-quality products coupled with its reputation for outstanding service have paid off on the bottom line. Even in the economically rocky years of the early 2000s, CMC managed to reap big profits, enjoying an increase in net earnings of 70 percent in the period from 2001 to 2002 alone.

Says company president and CEO Stanley A. Rabin, the key to the company's success can be described in a single word—*efficiency*. Indeed, CMC operates a network of companies that carefully feed one another in a manner that minimizes waste. The company is organized into three segments: manufacturing, recycling, and marketing and distribution. The manufacturing segment consists of two companies, CMC Steel Group, which operates four "minimills" and over 70 manufacturing plants located throughout the Southeast and Southwest, and the Howell Metals Company, which manufactures copper tubes in Virginia. A constant supply of raw materials is ensured by CMC's Secondary Metals Processing division, its recycling segment. Operating 34 metals processing plants across the sunbelt, it is one of the largest processors of scrap metals in the United States, providing metal products of all types to steel mills (including the company's own facilities) and manufacturing plants.

Supporting these two divisions is CMC's third major segment of the organization, the marketing and distribution segment. This portion of the business, which itself is composed of four different divisions, focuses on marketing the company's finished products as well as buying and selling raw materials for use in manufacturing. One of these is the international division, which knits together CMC's operations in 130 countries around the world and coordinates business ventures with companies in other nations (e.g., Australia and Ireland). To help promote the manufacturing business, the marketing and distribution segment also performs vital service functions for its customers, such as providing technical information, financing, transportation and shipping, and even insurance. In short, if it's something that a metals customer may need, this segment of CMC is there to provide it. And the more seamlessly customers have their needs met, the more metal products they buy from the other segments of the organization.

To say that nothing goes to waste at CMC is an understatement. Take scrap, for instance. For a quarter century the company has been holding an annual "Scrap Can Be Beautiful" contest for art students at a Dallas area high school (where the company is headquartered). The company donates scrap metal to students in a metal sculpture class and awards cash prizes for the best entries. Some of the projects are displayed in the corporate office for a year, others are displayed in local galleries and museums, and still others are auctioned off to benefit Dallas area arts organizations.

GOOD REASONS
why you should care about...

Designing Effective Organizations

You should care about organizational design because:

1. To understand how organizations function you must know about their structural elements, their basic building blocks.

2. The design of organizations has profound effects on organizational functioning.

3. The way organizations are designed has been changing in recent years and will continue to change in the years ahead.

It's safe to assume that a great part of CMC's success can be attributed to the tight interconnections among the various segments of the business. Each serves and feeds the others. CMC's success raises an important question: Is this approach, which works so well at CMC, a model for all companies to follow? Putting the question more generally, how should companies organize themselves into separate units to be most effective? This question is a venerable one in the field of business—and, as I shall explain in this chapter, a very important one.

OB researchers and theorists have provided considerable insight into the matter by studying what is called *organizational structure*—the way individuals and groups are arranged with respect to the tasks they perform—and *organizational design*—the process of coordinating these structural elements in the most effective manner.[1] As you may suspect, finding the best way to structure and design organizations is no simple matter. However, because understanding the structure and design of organizations is key to fully appreciating their functioning, organizational scientists have devoted considerable energy to this topic. I will describe these efforts in this chapter. To begin, I will identify the basic structural dimensions of organizations. Following this, I will examine how these structural elements can be most effectively combined into productive organizational designs. In so doing, I will cover some of the traditional ways of designing organizations as well as some of the rapidly developing organizational forms emerging today.

Structural Dimensions of Organizations

learning
objective

Think about how a simple house is constructed. It is composed of a wooden frame positioned atop a concrete slab covered by a roof and siding materials. Within this basic structure are separate systems operating to provide electricity, water, and telephone services. It is possible to extend this analogy to the structure of organizations. Let's use as an example an organization with which you are familiar—your college or university. It is probably composed of various departments working together to serve special functions. Individuals and groups are dedicated to tasks such as teaching, providing financial services, maintaining the physical facilities, and so on. Of course, within each group, even more distinctions can be made between the jobs people perform. For example, it's unlikely that the instructor for your OB course is also teaching seventeenth-century French literature.

This illustrates our main point: An organization is not a haphazard collection of people but a meaningful combination of groups and individuals working together purposefully to meet organizational goals. The term **organizational structure** refers to the formal configuration between individuals and groups with respect to the allocation of tasks, responsibilities, and authority within organizations.

Unlike the structure of a house, we cannot see the structure of an organization; it is an abstract concept. However, the connections between various clusters of functions of which an organization is composed can be represented in the form of a diagram known as an **organization chart**. Specifically, an organization chart may be considered a representation of an organization's internal structure. Organization charts are useful tools for specifying how various tasks or functions are interrelated within organizations. For example, look at the chart depicting part of a hypothetical manufacturing organization shown in Figure 13.1. Each box represents a specific

Figure 13.1	Organization Chart of a Hypothetical Manufacturing Firm

An *organization chart*, such as this one, identifies pictorially the various functions performed within an organization and the lines of authority between people performing those functions.

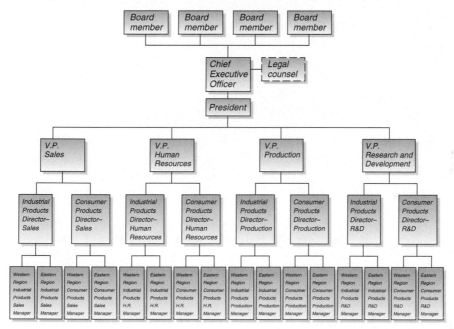

job, and the lines connecting them reflect the formally prescribed lines of communication between the individuals performing those jobs (see Chapter 8). To specialists in organizational structure, however, such diagrams reveal a great deal more.

Division of Labor

The standard organization chart reflects the fact that the many tasks to be performed within an organization are divided into specialized jobs, a process known as the **division of labor**. The more that tasks are divided into separate jobs, the more those jobs are *specialized* and the narrower the range of activities that job incumbents are required to perform. For example, the jobs performed by members of a pit crew for a race car are divided into highly specialized functions, such as refueling, changing tires, and so on. In theory, the fewer tasks a person performs, the better he or she may be expected to perform them, freeing others to perform the tasks that they perform best. (I say "in theory" because if specialization is too great, people may lose their motivation to work at a high level and performance may suffer; see Chapter 6.) Taken together, an entire organization is composed of people performing a collection of specialized jobs. This is probably the most obvious feature of an organization that can be observed from the organization chart.

As you might imagine, the degree to which employees perform specialized jobs is likely to depend on the size of the organization. The larger the organization, the more the opportunities for specialization are likely to exist. For example, someone in the advertising department of a large agency is likely to specialize in a certain, narrowly defined task, such as writing radio jingles, whereas someone working at a smaller agency is likely to have to perform a much wider variety of tasks, including preparing copy for print ads, meeting with clients, and maybe even sending out the bills.

Hierarchy of Authority

Organization charts provide information about who reports to whom—what is known as **hierarchy of authority**. The diagram reveals which particular lower-level employees are required to report to which particular individuals immediately above them. In our hypothetical example in Figure 13.1, the various regional salespeople (at the bottom of the diagram) report to their respective regional sales directors, who report to the vice president of sales, who reports to the president, who reports to the chief executive officer, who reports to the members of the board of directors. As we trace these reporting relationships, we work our way up the organization's hierarchy. In this case, the organization has six levels. Organizations may have many levels, in which case their structure is considered *tall*, or only a few, in which case their structure is considered *flat* (see Figure 13.2).

In recent years, a great deal has appeared in the news about organizations restructuring their workforces by flattening them out. Although it has not been uncommon for large companies to lay off people in low-level jobs, in recent years, middle managers and executives, who long believed they were secure in their positions, found themselves unemployed as their companies "downsized," "rightsized," "delayered," or "retrenched" by eliminating entire layers of organizational structure. Even the U.S. Army has downsized by 30 percent in recent years.[2] The underlying assumption behind these changes is that fewer layers reduce waste and enable people to make better decisions (by moving them closer to the problems at hand), thereby leading to greater profitability. Although some layers of hierarchy are necessary, too many can be needlessly expensive. Moreover, as technology advances, fewer people are needed to carry out management roles.

Span of Control

Over how many individuals should a manager have responsibility? The earliest management theorists and practitioners alike (dating back to the Roman legions) addressed this question. When you look at an organization chart, the number of people formally required to report to each individual manager is immediately clear. This number constitutes what is known as a manager's **span of control**. Those responsible for many individuals are said to have a *wide* span of control, whereas those responsible for fewer individuals are said to have a *narrow* span of control. In our organization chart (Figure 13.2), the CEO is responsible for only the actions of the president, giving this individual a narrower span of control than the president himself or herself, who has a span of control of five individuals.

When a manager's span of control is wide, the organization itself has a flat hierarchy. In contrast, when a manager's span of control is narrow, the organization itself has a tall hierarchy. This is demonstrated in Figure 13.2. The diagram at the top shows a *tall* organization—one in which there are many layers in the hierarchy and the span of control is relatively narrow (i.e., the number of people supervised is low). By con-

Figure 13.2   Span of Control in Tall Versus Flat Organizations

Each of the two organizations depicted here has 31 employees, but they are structured differently. In the *tall organization*, shown on top, the hierarchy has many layers and managers have a *narrow span of control*. However, in the *flat organization*, shown on the bottom, the hierarchy has fewer layers and managers have a *wide span of control*.

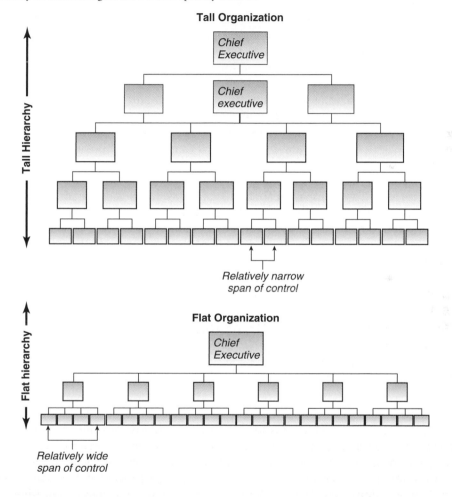

trast, the diagram at the bottom of Figure 13.2 shows a *flat* organization—one in which there are only a few levels in the hierarchy, and the span of control is relatively wide. Although both organizations depicted here have 31 positions, these are arranged differently.

It is not possible to specify the "ideal" span of control that should be sought. Instead, it makes better sense to consider what form of organization is best suited to various purposes. For example, because supervisors in a military unit must have tight control over subordinates and get them to respond quickly and precisely, a narrow span of control is likely to be effective. As a result, military organizations tend to be extremely tall. In contrast, people working in a research and development lab must have an open exchange of ideas and typically require little managerial guidance to be successful. Units of this type tend to have very flat structures. (As you might imagine, there may be widespread differences with respect to spans of control in different types of organizations. To learn about this possibility, complete the **Group Exercise** on pages 453–454.)

Line Versus Staff Positions

The organization chart shown in Figure 13.1 reveals an additional distinction that deserves to be highlighted—that between *line positions* and *staff positions*. People occupying **line positions** (e.g., the various vice presidents and managers) have decision-making power. However, the individual shown in the dotted box—the legal counsel—cannot make decisions but provides advice and recommendations to be used by the line managers. For example, such an individual may help corporate officials decide whether a certain product name can be used without infringing on copyright restrictions. This individual may be said to hold a **staff position**. In many of today's organizations, human resources managers may be seen as occupying staff positions because they may provide specialized services regarding testing and interviewing procedures as well as information about the latest laws on personnel administration.

Differences between line and staff personnel are not unusual. Specifically, staff managers tend to be younger, better educated, and more committed to their fields than to their organizations. Line managers might feel more committed to their organizations not only because of the greater opportunities they have to exercise decisions but also because they are more likely to perceive themselves as part of a company rather than as an independent specialist whose identity lies primarily within his or her specialty area.

Centralization Versus Decentralization

During the first half of the twentieth century, as companies grew larger and larger, they shifted power and authority into the hands of a few upper-echelon administrators—executives whose decisions influenced the many people below them in the organizational hierarchy. In fact, during the 1920s Alfred P. Sloan, Jr., then president of General Motors, introduced the notion of a "central office," the place where a few individuals made policy decisions for the entire company. Another part of Sloan's plan involved pushing lower and lower down the organizational hierarchy decisions regarding the day-to-day operation of the company, thereby allowing those individuals who were most affected to make the decisions. This process of delegating power from higher to lower levels within organizations is known as **decentralization**. It is the opposite of **centralization**, the tendency for just a few powerful individuals or groups to hold most of the decision-making power.

Recent years have seen a marked trend toward increasingly greater decentralization.[3] As a result, organization charts tend to show fewer staff positions, as decision-making authority is pushed farther down the hierarchy. Many organizations have moved toward decentralization to promote managerial efficiency and to improve employee satisfaction (the result of giving people greater opportunities to take responsibility for their own actions). For example, in recent years thousands of staff jobs have been eliminated at companies such as 3M, Eastman Kodak, AT&T, and GE as these companies have decentralized. In particular, people working in research and development positions are likely to enjoy the autonomy to make decisions that decentralization allows. With this in mind, many companies heavily involved in research and development—including parts of Hewlett-Packard, Intel Corporation, Philips Electronics, and AT&T's Bell Laboratories—have shifted to more decentralized designs. By contrast, people working on production jobs are likely to be

> In recent years thousands of staff jobs have been eliminated at companies such as 3M, Eastman Kodak, AT&T, and GE as these companies have decentralized.

less interested in taking responsibility for decisions and may enjoy not having to take such responsibility. For a summary of the relative advantages and disadvantages of centralization, see Table 13.1.

Research has indicated that the way people respond to different levels of centralization is based on their perceptions of fairness: That is, centralization is perceived as being more fair under some circumstances and less fair under others.[4] This is demonstrated clearly in one recent study.[5] A team of researchers examined the degree to which employees from a variety of different organizations perceived that their work unit was centralized, as measured in terms of their frequency of participation in organizational decisions (the more people believe to have participated, the less centralized their unit was labeled as being). They also measured these workers' perceptions of interactional justice—that is (as you may recall from Chapter 2), their beliefs that they are treated in a sensitive and respectful manner by the organization.

As shown in Figure 13.3, the researchers found that the relationship between these variables depended on the employees' organizational level. Specifically, high-level employees perceived that they were treated fairly regardless of the degree to which organizational decisions were centralized. This reflects the general tendency for high-level workers, who tend to enjoy relatively high levels of participation as a whole, to feel positively about their work. By contrast, level of centralization made a very big difference for low-level employees. Specifically, the more low-level workers were allowed to participate in the making of decisions (i.e., the less decision making was considered centralized), the more fairly they believe they were treated. This reflects the tendency for lower level employees to place a high value on participation because as a whole they tend to get it so little. As a result, the more low-level employees are given an opportunity to participate, the more positively this reflects on the fairness of the organization in their eyes.

Table 13.1　　Decentralization: Benefits When Low and When High

Various benefits are associated with low decentralization (high centralization) and high decentralization (low centralization) within organizations.

Low Decentralization *(High Centralization)*	*High Decentralization* *(Low Centralization)*
Eliminates the additional responsibility not desired by people performing routine jobs	Can eliminate levels of management, making a leaner organization
Permits crucial decisions to be made by individuals who have the "big picture"	Promotes greater opportunities for decisions to be made by people closest to problems

Figure 13.3   The Perceived Fairness of Centralization: Research Findings

A recent study found that low-level employees perceived that they were treated more fairly when their organizations were low in centralization—that is, when they believed they had good opportunities to participate in the making of decisions. However, the effects of centralization were minimal in the case of high-level employees (for whom participation tends to be high to begin with).

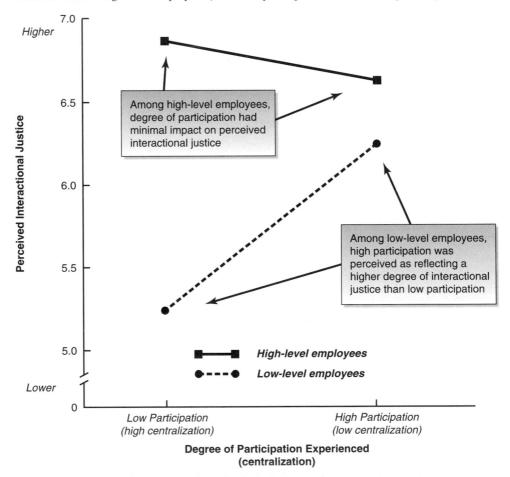

(Source: Based on data reported by Schminke, Cropanzano, and Rupp, 2002; see Note 5.)

2
learning
objective

Departmentalization: Ways of Structuring Organizations

Thus far, I have been talking about "the" organization chart of an organization. Typically, such charts, like the one shown in Figure 13.1, divide the organization according to the various functions performed. However, this is only one option. Organizations can be divided up not only by function but also by product or market, and by a combination of both. I will now take a closer look at these various ways of breaking up organizations into coherent units—that is, the process of **departmentalization**.

Functional Organizations: Departmentalization by Task

Because it is the form organizations usually take when they are first created, and because it is how we usually think of organizations, the **functional organization** can be considered the most basic approach to departmentalization. Essentially, functional organizations departmentalize individuals according to the functions they perform, with people who perform similar functions assigned to the same department. For example, a manufacturing company might consist of separate departments devoted to basic functions such as production, sales/marketing, research and development, and human resources (recall Figure 13.1).

Naturally, as organizations grow and become more complex, additional departments are added or deleted as the need arises. Consider, for example, something that is beginning to happen at Johnson & Johnson (J&J). Although this company has long been highly decentralized, certain functions are now beginning to become centralized (e.g., the legal and human resources operations). This makes it possible for resources to be saved by avoiding duplication of effort, resulting in a higher level of efficiency. Not only does this form of organizational structure take advantage of economies of scale (by allowing employees performing the same jobs to share facilities and not duplicating functions), but it also allows people to specialize, thereby performing only those tasks at which they are most expert. The result is a highly skilled workforce—a direct benefit to the organization.

Partly offsetting these advantages, however, are several potential limitations. The most important of these stems from the fact that functional organizational structures encourage separate units to develop their own narrow perspectives and to lose sight of overall organizational goals. For example, in a manufacturing company, an engineer might see the company's problems in terms of the reliability of its products and lose sight of other key considerations, such as market trends, overseas competition, and so on. Such narrow-mindedness is the inevitable result of functional specialization—the downside of people seeing the company's operations through a narrow lens.

Product Organizations: Departmentalization by Type of Output

Organizations—at least successful ones—do not stand still; they constantly change in size and scope. As they develop new products and seek new customers, they might find that a functional structure doesn't work as well as it once did. Manufacturing a wide range of products using a variety of different methods, for example, might put a strain on a manufacturing division of a functional organization. Similarly, keeping track of the varied tax requirements for different types of business (e.g., restaurants, farms, real estate, manufacturing) might pose quite a challenge for a single financial division of a company. In response to such strains, a **product organization** might be created. This type of departmentalization creates self-contained divisions, each of which is responsible for everything to do with a certain product or group of products. For a look at the structure of a hypothetical product organization, see Figure 13.4.

When organizations are departmentalized by products, separate divisions are established, each of which is devoted to a certain product or group of products. Each unit contains all the resources needed to develop, manufacture, and sell its products. The organization is composed of separate divisions, operating independently, the heads of which report to top management. Although some functions might be centralized

Figure 13.4   Structure of a Typical Product Organization

In a *product organization*, separate units are established to handle different product lines. Each of these divisions contains all the departments necessary for it to operate as an independent unit.

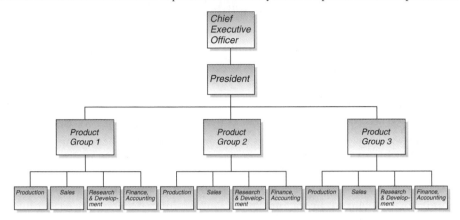

within the parent company (e.g., human resource management or legal staff), on a day-to-day basis each division operates autonomously as a separate company or, as accountants call them, "cost centers" of their own.

Consider, for example, how separate divisions of General Motors are devoted to manufacturing cars, trucks, locomotives, refrigerators, auto parts, and the like. The managers of each division can devote their energies to one particular business. Organizations may be beneficial from a marketing perspective as well. Consider, for example, the example of Honda's 1987 introduction of its line of luxury cars, Acura. By creating a separate division, manufactured in separate plants and sold by a separate network of dealers, the company made its higher-priced cars look special and avoided making its less expensive cars look less appealing by putting them together with superior products on the same showroom floors. Given Honda's success with this configuration, it is not surprising that Toyota and Nissan followed suit when they introduced their own luxury lines, Lexus and Infiniti, in 1989.

Product organizations also have several drawbacks. The most obvious of these is the loss of economies of scale stemming from the duplication of various departments within operating units. For example, if each unit carries out its own research and development functions, the need for costly equipment, facilities, and personnel may be multiplied. Another problem associated with product designs involves the organization's ability to attract and retain talented employees. Because each department within operating units is necessarily smaller than a single combined one would be, opportunities for advancement and career development may suffer. This, in turn, may pose a serious problem with respect to the long-term retention of talented employees. Finally, problems of coordination across product lines may arise. In fact, in extreme cases, actions taken by one operating division may have adverse effects on the outcomes of one or more others.

A clear example of such problems was provided by Hewlett-Packard, a major manufacturer of computers, printers, and scientific test equipment.[6] For most of its history, Hewlett-Packard adopted a product design. It consisted of scores of small, largely autonomous divisions, each concerned with producing and selling certain products. As it grew—merging with Compaq in 2002—the company found itself in an increasingly untenable situation in which sales representatives from different divisions sometimes attempted to sell different lines of equipment, often to be used for the same basic purposes, to the same customers! To deal with such problems, top management at Hewlett-Packard decided to restructure the company into four sectors—what they call "business groups"—based on the markets they serve: the Enterprise Systems Group (which provides information technology hardware for businesses), the Imaging and Printing Group (which focuses on printers for businesses and consumers), the Personal Systems Group (which focuses on personal computers for home and office use), and HP Services (which offers information technology services).[7] In short, driven by market considerations, Hewlett-Packard switched from a traditional product organization to an internal structure.

> Driven by market considerations, Hewlett-Packard switched from a traditional product organization to an internal structure.

Matrix Organizations: Departmentalization by Both Function and Product

When the aerospace industry was first developing, the U.S. government demanded that a single manager in each company be assigned to each of its projects so that it was immediately clear who was responsible for the progress of each project. In response to this requirement, TRW established a "project leader" for each project, someone who shared authority with the leaders of the existing functional departments. This temporary arrangement later evolved into what is called a matrix organization, the type of organization in which an employee is required to report to both a functional (or division) manager and the manager of a specific project (or product). In essence, they developed a complex type of organizational structure that combines both the function and product forms of departmentalization. To better understand matrix organizations, let's take a closer look at the organization chart shown in Figure 13.5.

Employees in matrix organizations have two bosses (or, more technically, they are under *dual authority*).[8] One line of authority, shown by the vertical axes on Figure 13.5, is *functional*, managed by vice presidents in charge of various functional areas. The other, shown by the horizontal axes, is *product* (or it may be a specific project or temporary business), managed by specific individuals in charge of certain products (or projects).

In matrix designs, there are three major roles. First, there is the *top leader*—the individual who has authority over both lines of authority (the one based on function and the one based on product or project). It is this individual's task to enhance coordination between functional and product managers and to maintain an appropriate balance of power between them. Second, there are the *matrix bosses*—people who head functional departments or specific projects. Because neither functional managers nor project managers have complete authority over subordinates, they must work together to assure that their efforts mesh rather than conflict. In addition, they must agree on issues such as promotions and raises for specific people working under their joint authority. Finally, there are *two-boss managers*—people who must

Figure 13.5   Structure of a Typical Matrix Organization

In a *matrix organization*, a product structure is superimposed on a functional structure. This results in a dual system of authority in which some managers report to two bosses—one for the specific product (or project) and one for the specific functional department involved.

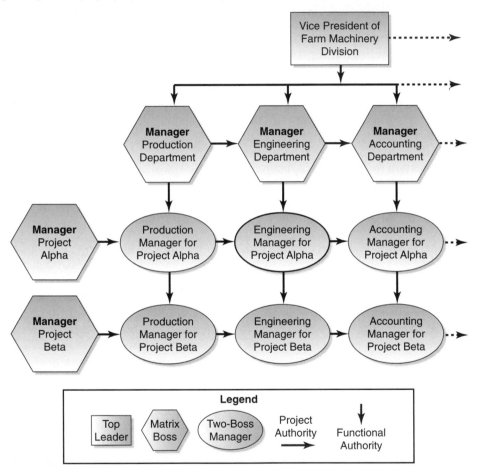

report to both product and functional managers and attempt to balance the demands of each. Because people working in this fashion have two bosses, they must have sufficient freedom to attain their objectives. As you might imagine, a fair amount of coordination, flexibility, openness, and trust is essential for such a program to work, suggesting that not everyone adapts well to such a system.

Organizations are most likely to adopt matrix designs when they confront certain conditions. These include a complex and uncertain environment (one with frequent changes) and the need for economies of scale in the use of internal resources. Specifically, a matrix approach is often adopted by medium-size organizations with several product lines that do not possess sufficient resources to establish fully self-contained operating units. Under such conditions, a matrix design provides a useful compromise. Some companies that have adopted matrix designs, at least for some parts of the organization, include TRW Systems Group, Liberty Mutual Insurance, and Citibank. If you think about these conditions, it's not surprising that matrix designs have become popular in psychiatric hospitals in recent years.[9] For a typical example, see Figure 13.6.

Companies that have adopted matrix designs, at least for some parts of the organization, include TRW Systems Group, Liberty Mutual Insurance, and Citibank.

Matrix designs offer several advantages. First, they permit flexible use of an organization's human resources. Individuals within functional departments can be assigned to specific products or projects as the need arises and then return to their regular duties when this task is completed. Second, matrix designs offer medium-size organizations an efficient means of responding quickly to a changing, unstable

Figure 13.6 Matrix Organization in a Psychiatric Hospital

Growing numbers of psychiatric hospitals have found it useful to structure themselves as *matrix organizations*. A typical matrix design for such an organization is shown here.

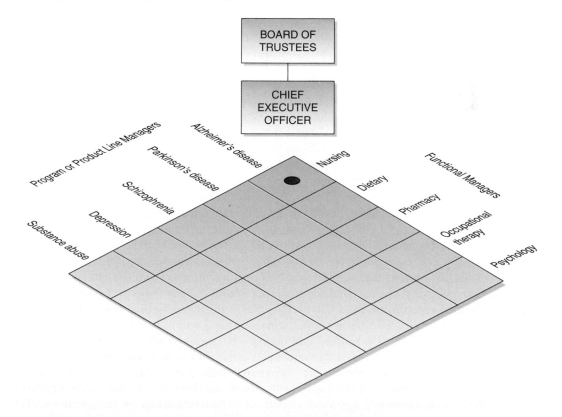

(Source: From Health Care Management, Organization Design & Behavior *4th edition by Shortell. © 2000. Reprinted with permission of Delmar Learning, a division of Thomson Learning: www.thomsonrights.com. Fax 800-730-2215.)*

environment. Third, such designs often enhance communication among managers; indeed, they literally force matrix bosses to discuss and agree on many matters. Unfortunately, matrix designs can create frustration and stress by having to report to two different supervisors. However, in situations in which organizations must stretch their financial and human resources to meet challenges from the external environment or to take advantage of new opportunities, matrix designs can be useful.

3
learning
objective

Traditional Organizational Designs

We began this chapter by likening the structure of an organization to the structure of a house. Now we are prepared to extend that analogy for purposes of introducing the concept of *organizational design*. Just as a house is designed in a particular fashion by combining its structural elements in various ways, so too can an organization be designed by combining its basic elements in certain ways. Accordingly, **organizational design** refers to the process of coordinating the structural elements of organizations in the most appropriate manner.[10]

Classical and Neoclassical Approaches: The Quest for the One Best Design

It is not difficult to realize that for organizations to function effectively, their designs must not be static but dynamic—changing in response to various conditions (e.g., governmental regulations, competition, and so on). As obvious as this may be to us today, the earliest theorists interested in organizational design paid little attention to the need for organizations to be flexible. Instead, they approached the task of designing organizations as a search for "the one best way," seeking to establish the ideal form for all organizations under all conditions—the universal design.

In Chapter 1, I described the efforts of organizational scholars such as Max Weber and Frederick Taylor. These theorists believed that effective organizations were ones that had a formal hierarchy, a clear set of rules, specialization of labor, highly routine tasks, and a highly impersonal working environment. You may recall that Weber referred to this organizational form as a *bureaucracy*. This **classical organizational theory** has fallen into disfavor because it is insensitive to human needs and is not suited to a changing environment. Unfortunately, the "ideal" form of an organization, according to Weber, did not take into account the realities of the world within which it operates. Apparently, what is ideal is not necessarily what is realistic.

In response to these conditions, and with inspiration from the Hawthorne studies, the classical approach to the bureaucratic model gave way to more of a human relations orientation (see Chapter 1). Several other organizational theorists attempted to improve upon the classical model—which is why their approach is labeled **neoclassical organizational theory**—by arguing that economic effectiveness is not the only goal of an industrial organization but that employee satisfaction is a goal as well. The key, they argued, was not rigidly controlling people's actions but actively promoting their feelings of self-worth and their importance to the organization. The neoclassical approach called for organizations to be designed with flat hierarchical structures (minimizing managerial control over subordinates) and a high degree of decentralization (encouraging employees to make their own decisions). Indeed, such design features may well serve the underlying neoclassical philosophy. (For a summary comparison between the classical and neoclassical designs, see Figure 13.7.)

Like the classical approach, the neoclassical approach also may be faulted on the grounds that it promoted a single best approach to organizational design. Although the benefits of flat, decentralized designs may be many, to claim that this represents the universal or ideal form for all organizations would be naive. In response to this criticism, more contemporary approaches to organizational design have given up on finding the one best way to design organizations in favor of finding different designs that are appropriate for the different circumstances and contexts within which organizations operate.

The Contingency Approach: Design Based on Environmental Conditions

learning objective

Today, it is widely believed that the best design for an organization depends on the nature of the environment (e.g., the economy, geography, labor markets) in which the organization is operating. This is known as the **contingency approach** to organizational design. Although many features of the environment may be taken into account when considering how an organization should be designed, a key determinant appears to be how stable (unchanging) or unstable (turbulent) the environment is.

If you've ever worked at a McDonald's, you probably know how highly standardized each step of the most basic operations must be. Boxes of fries are to be stored 2 inches from the wall in stacks 1 inch apart. Making those fries is another

Figure 13.7   Classical Versus Neoclassical Designs: A Summary

The classical approach to designing organizations assumed that managers needed to have close control over their subordinates. As such, it called for designing organizations with tall hierarchies and a narrow span of control. In contrast, the neoclassical approach to designing organizations assumed that managers did not have to carefully monitor their subordinates. As such, it called for designing organizations with flat hierarchies and a wide span of control.

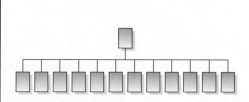

Classical Organizational Design

- Tall hierarchy
- Narrow span of control
- Close control over subordinates

Neoclassical Organizational Design

- Flat hierarchy
- Wide span of control
- Loose control over subordinates

matter—one that requires 19 distinct steps, each of which is clearly laid out in a training film shown to new employees. The process is the same, whether it's done in Moscow, Idaho, or Moscow, Russia. This is an example of a highly mechanistic task. Organizations can be highly mechanistic when conditions don't change. Although the fast-food industry has changed a great deal in recent years (with the introduction of healthier menu items and competitive pricing), making fries at McDonald's has not changed. The key to mechanization is lack of change. If the environment doesn't change, a highly **mechanistic form** of organization can be very efficient.

An environment is considered stable whenever there is little or no unexpected change in product, market demands, technology, and the like. Have you ever seen an old-fashioned-looking bottle of E. E. Dickinson's witch hazel (a topical astringent used to cleanse the skin in the area of a wound)? Since the company has been making the product following the same distillation process since 1866, it is certainly operating in a relatively stable manufacturing environment. Without change, people can easily specialize. When change is inevitable, specialization is impractical.

Mechanistic organizations can be characterized in several additional ways (for a summary, see Table 13.2). Not only do mechanistic organizations allow for a high degree of specialization, but they also impose many rules. Authority is vested in a few people located at the top of a hierarchy who give direct orders to their subordinates. Mechanistic organizational designs tend to be most effective under conditions in which the external environment is stable and unchanging.

Now, think about high-technology industries, such as those dedicated to computers, aerospace products, and biotechnology. Their environmental conditions are likely to be changing all the time. These industries are so prone to change that as soon as a new way of operating could be introduced into one of them, it would have to be altered. It isn't only technology, however, that makes an environment turbulent. Turbulence also can be high in industries in which adherence to rapidly changing regulations is essential. For example, times were turbulent in the hospital industry when new Medicaid legislation was passed, and times were turbulent in the nuclear power industry when governmental regulations dictated the introduction of many new standards that had to be followed. With the dominance of foreign automobiles in the United States, the once stable American auto industry has faced turbulent times.

Table 13.2	Mechanistic Versus Organic Designs	

Mechanistic designs and *organic designs* differ along several key dimensions identified here. These represent extremes; many organizations fall in between.

	Structure	
DIMENSION	**MECHANISTIC**	**ORGANIC**
Stability	Change unlikely	Change likely
Specialization	Many specialists	Many generalists
Formal rules	Rigid rules	Considerable flexibility
Authority	Centralized in a few top people	Decentralized, diffused throughout the organization

Unfortunately, in this case, the design of the auto companies could not rapidly accommodate the changes needed for more organic forms (since the American auto industry was traditionally highly mechanistic).

The pure **organic form** of organization may be characterized in several different ways (see Table 13.2). The degree of job specialization possible is very low; instead, a broad knowledge of many different jobs is required. Very little authority is exercised from the top. Rather, self-control is expected, and an emphasis is placed on coordination between peers. As a result, decisions tend to be made in a highly democratic, participative manner. Be aware that the mechanistic and organic types of organizational structure described here are ideal forms. The mechanistic–organic distinction should be thought of as opposite poles along a continuum rather than as completely distinct options for organization. Certainly, organizations can be relatively organic or relatively mechanistic compared with others but may not be located at either extreme. (Which particular form of organizational design do you prefer? The **Self-Assessment Exercise** on pages 452–453 will give you some insight into your individual preferences for mechanistic and organic organizations.)

Emerging Organizational Designs

Thus far, the organizational designs I have been describing have been around for a long time, and because they are so well known and often so effective, they are not likely to fade away anytime soon. However, during the past decade, several emerging forms of organizational design have come onto the scene. Given how popular and promising these seem to be, I will describe them here.

5
learning
objective

The Horizontal Organization: Designing with Process in Mind

If the experts are right, we are in store for a new way of structuring work in tomorrow's organizations—one that means more than just tinkering with the boxes on an organization chart. Enter the **horizontal organization**—an approach advocated by many organizational experts and touted by consultants from the firm McKinsey & Co. as "the first real, fundamentally different, robust alternative" to the functional organization.[11]

The essence of the idea is simple. Instead of organizing jobs in the traditional, vertical fashion by having a long chain of groups or individuals perform parts of a task (e.g., one group that sells the advertising job, another that plans the ad campaign, and yet another that produces the ads), horizontal organizations have flattened hierarchies. That is, they arrange autonomous work teams (see Chapter 9) in parallel, each performing many different steps in the process (e.g., members of an advertising team may bring different skills and expertise to a single team responsible for all aspects of advertising). Essentially, organizations are structured around *processes* instead of tasks. Performance objectives are based on customers' needs, such as lowered cost or improved service. Once the core processes that meet these needs (e.g., order generation, new product development) have been identified, they become the company's major components—instead of the traditional departments such as sales or manufacturing (for a summary, see Figure 13.8).

According to consultant Michael Hammer, "In the future, executive positions will not be defined in terms of collections of people, like head of the sales department, but in terms of processes, like senior-VP-of-getting-stuff-to-customers, which is sales, shipping, billing. You'll no longer have a box on an organization chart. You'll own part of a process map."[12] Envision it as a whole company lying on its side and organized by process. An ardent believer in this approach, Lawrence Bossidy, an award-winning executive at General Electric and Allied Signal, who came out of retirement to run Honeywell, says, "Every business has maybe six basic processes. We'll organize around them. The people who run them will be the leaders of the business."[13] In an industrial company, for example, these process might include new-product development, flow of materials, and the order-delivery-billing cycle. Individuals will constantly move into and out of various teams as needed, drawing from a directory of broadly skilled in-house corporate experts available to lend their expertise.

The horizontal organization is already a reality in at least parts of several of today's organizations—including AT&T (network systems division), Eastman Chemical (a division of Kodak), Hallmark Cards, and Xerox. Consider, for example, General Electric's factory in Bayamón, Puerto Rico. The 172 hourly workers, 15 salaried "advisers," plus a single manager manufacture "arresters" (surge protectors that guard power stations from lightning). That's the entire workforce; there are no support staff and no supervisors—only about half as many people as you'd find in a conventional factory. Bayamón employees are formed into separate teams of approximately 10 widely skilled members who "own" such parts of the work as shipping and receiving, assembly, and so on. The teams do whatever is needed to get the job done; the advisers get involved only when needed.

> General Electric's factory in Bayamón, Puerto Rico, has 172 hourly workers, 15 salaried "advisers," plus a single manager who manufacture "arresters." That's the entire workforce; there are no support staff and no supervisors.

Although carefully controlled studies have yet to assess the impact of this new approach, those who have used it are convinced of its effectiveness. One top McKinsey

Figure 13.8   The Horizontal Organization

In a *horizontal organization*, teams of employees with diverse skills are created to meet objectives relating to various core processes that must be performed.

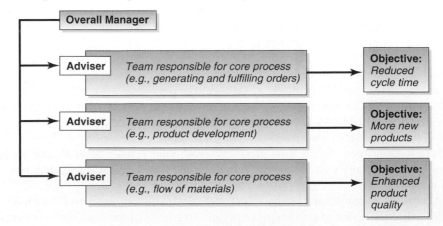

consultant, for example, claims that this new approach to organizational design can help companies cut their costs by at least one-third. Some of their clients, they boast, have done even better. Will the horizontal organization replace the traditional pyramid of the hierarchical organization? Only time will tell. Meanwhile, those who have turned to horizontal organizational structures appear to be glad they did.

The Boundaryless Organization: Business Without Barriers

You hear it all the time: Someone is asked to do something but responds defiantly, saying, "It's not my job." As uncooperative as this may seem, such a comment may make a great deal of sense when it comes to the traditional kind of organizational structures we've been describing—ones with layers of carefully connected boxes neatly stacked atop each other in hierarchical fashion. The advantage of these types of organizations is that they clearly define the roles of managers and employees. Everyone knows precisely what he or she is supposed to do. The problem with such arrangements, however, is that they are inflexible. As a result, they do not lend themselves to the rapidly changing conditions in which today's organizations operate.

Sensitive to this limitation, Jack Welch, the retired CEO of General Electric, proposed the **boundaryless organization**. This is an organization in which chains of command are eliminated, spans of control are unlimited, and rigid departments give way to empowered teams. Replacing rigid distinctions between people are fluid, intentionally ambiguous and ill-defined roles. Welch's vision was that GE would operate like a family grocery store (albeit a $60 billion one)—one in which the barriers within the company that separate employees from each other and that separate the company from its customers and suppliers would be eliminated.[14] Although GE has not yet become the completely boundaryless organization Welch envisioned, it has made significant strides toward breaking down boundaries, as have other organizations.[15]

For boundaryless organizations to function effectively, they must meet many of the same requirements as successful teams. For example, there must be high levels of trust between all parties concerned. Also, everyone involved must have such high levels of skill that they can operate without much, if any, managerial guidance. Insofar as the elimination of boundaries weakens traditional managerial power bases, some executives may find it difficult to give up their authority, leading to political behavior. However, to the extent that the elimination of boundaries leverages the talents of all employees, such limitations are worth striving to overcome.

> Although GE has not yet become the completely boundaryless organization Welch envisioned, it has made significant strides toward breaking down boundaries, as have other organizations.

The boundaryless organizations we have been describing involve breaking down both internal and external barriers. As a result, they are sometimes referred to as *barrier-free organizations*. However, there are variations of the boundaryless organization involving only the elimination of external boundaries.[16] These include the *modular organization* (in which secondary aspects of the company's operations are outsourced) and the *virtual organization* (in which organizations combine forces with others on a temporary basis to form new organizations, usually only briefly). I will describe these next. Meanwhile, for a summary of these three related organizational designs, see Figure 13.9.

Figure 13.9   The Boundaryless Organization, the Modular Organization, and the Virtual Organization

The true *boundaryless organization* is free of both internal barriers and external barriers. Variants, such as the *modular organization* and the *virtual organization*, eliminate only external barriers.

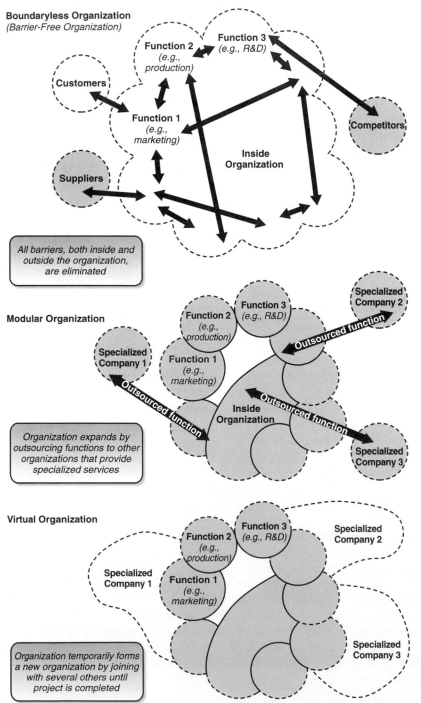

The Vertically Integrated Organization

Recall our discussion of the Commercial Metals Company in the case that opened this chapter. One thing that makes this company so special is the fact that it relies on its own companies for supplies and raw materials (e.g., its recycling companies provide scrap metals that are recycled into sellable products). Companies of this type, which own their own suppliers and/or their own customers who purchase their products, are said to be **vertically integrated**. Companies that only assemble products that they buy from suppliers and sell to customers, such as Dell, are not vertically integrated. For many years, Ford has been a good model of vertical integration because it has owned its own steel mills and its own financing arm for helping customers buy cars. This kind of efficiency associated with having built-in markets is a hallmark of vertically integrated companies, such as Ford and Commercial Metals Company. For a comparison between vertically integrated companies and companies that are not vertically integrated, see Figure 13.10.

Despite the benefits of vertical integration, companies organized in this fashion often face special challenges.[17] For one, they tend to find it difficult to balance their resources in the most effective manner, providing exactly enough resources to be used in manufacturing, and exactly the right number of finished products to be sold. A second drawback of vertical integration comes from the fact that because the company's suppliers are internal, they don't face competition to keep their prices down, potentially resulting in higher costs for the company. Third, because the various parts of the organization are so tightly interconnected, it is very difficult for the organization to respond to changes, such as developing new products. Because this would involve changes in supplies, manufacturing, and sales, the vertically integrated company faces more challenges than its nonvertically integrated counterpart when it comes to making such changes.

Modular Organizations

Many of today's organizations outsource noncore functions to other companies while retaining full strategic control over their core business. Such companies may be thought of as having a central hub surrounded by networks of outside specialists that can be added or subtracted as needed. As such, they are referred to as **modular organizations**.[18]

As a case in point, you surely recognize Nike and Reebok as major designers and marketers of athletic shoes. However, you probably didn't realize that Nike's production facilities are limited, and that Reebok doesn't even have any plants of its own. Both organizations contract all their manufacturing to companies in countries such as Taiwan and South Korea where labor costs are low. In so doing, not only can they avoid making major investments in facilities, but also they can concentrate on what they do best—tapping the changing tastes of their customers. While doing this, their suppliers can focus on rapidly retooling to make the new products.[19]

Smith Corona is another good example of a modular organization.[20] For 112 years, Smith Corona was a leader in the field of portable type-writers. Then, as word processing took hold, Smith

> Nike's production facilities are limited, and Reebok doesn't even have any plants of its own. Both organizations contract all their manufacturing to companies in countries such as Taiwan and South Korea. In so doing, they can concentrate on what they do best—tapping the changing tastes of their customers.

Figure 13.10   The Vertically Integrated Organization

A *vertically integrated organization*, like the one summarized on the right, owns the suppliers and/or the customers with whom it does business (the shaded portions of the diagram). Because it is involved only in the assembly business, the organization summarized on the left is not considered vertically integrated.

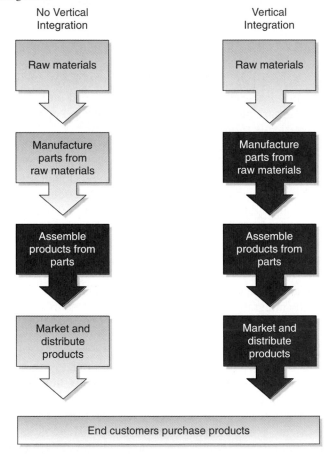

Corona was forced to sell all its plants and declare bankruptcy. However, because the brand name had value, the company reemerged to sell office products (such as fax machines and phones) that are made by others. The company clearly switched from one that specialized in the design and manufacture of products to one that deals only in selling under its name products made by others. Today's Smith Corona is a modular company insofar as it focuses on its core competency of marketing, relying on other companies to handle the manufacturing.

Unlike Smith Corona, which used to handle all aspects of the office machine business itself, some companies have existed only for purposes of assembling and/or selling products made by others. For example, Dell and Gateway buy computer components made by other companies and, performing only the final assembly themselves, put together systems ordered by customers. Online merchants operate in much the same way. Amazon.com, for example, specializes only in having a Web presence and an order fulfillment facility. Other than a few best-sellers, it doesn't inventory any books. It simply processes and fulfills orders. It is a modular company insofar as it combines its own expertise in order fulfillment with other companies' expertise in inventory handling and shipping to serve its customers.

Virtual Organizations

Another variation on the boundaryless organization is the **virtual organization**. Such an organization is composed of a continually evolving network of companies (e.g., suppliers and customers) that are linked together to share skills, costs, and access to markets. They form a partnership to capitalize on their existing skills, pursuing common objectives. In most cases, after these objectives have been met, the organizations disband.[21] Unlike modular organizations, which maintain close control over the companies with which they do outsourcing, virtual organizations give up some control and become part of a new organization, at least for a while.

Corning, the giant glass and ceramics manufacturer, is a good example of a company that builds on itself by developing partnerships with other companies (including Siemens, the German electronics firm, and Vitro, the largest glass manufacturer from Mexico). In fact, Corning officials see their company not as a single entity but as "a network of organizations."[22] The same can be said of NEC, the large Japanese computer and electronics company, and the software giant, Microsoft.[23] Both companies actively develop new organizations with which to network by providing venture capital funding for current research staff members to develop their own companies. These new companies are referred to as **affiliate networks**—satellite organizations that are affiliated with core companies that have helped them develop. The idea behind affiliate networks is that these new firms can work with, rather than compete against, their much larger parents on emerging technology.[24]

The underlying idea of a virtual organization is that each participating company contributes only its core competencies (i.e., its areas of greatest strength). By several companies mixing and matching the best of what they can offer, a joint product is created that is better than any single company could have created alone. Virtual corporations are not unusual in the entertainment industry. Indeed, Time Warner also has become part of several multimedia ventures. By sharing risks, costs, and expertise, many of today's companies are finding the virtual organization to be a highly appealing type of organizational structure. (For a discussion of the conditions under which an organization should "go virtual," see the accompanying **Winning Practices** section.)

Interorganizational Designs: Going Beyond the Single Organization

6
learning
objective

All the organizational designs we have examined thus far have concentrated on the arrangement of units *within* an organization—what may be termed *intraorganizational designs*. However, sometimes at least some parts of different organizations must operate jointly. To coordinate their efforts on such projects, organizations must create

Winning **Practices**
OB to the Rescue
When Should Companies Go Virtual?

More and more of today's companies are finding it useful to "go virtual," downscaling their hierarchies and networking with other companies on an ad hoc basis. Doing so allows them to move more quickly, standing a better chance of improving in a highly competitive environment. However, virtual organizations are far from perfect. Because people from different companies do not share common values, interpersonal conflicts are likely to occur, and coordination is often challenging. This raises an important question: When should companies organize in a virtual manner?

The answer depends on the how organizations fare with respect to two considerations: the type of capabilities organizations need and the type of change that will be made.[25] Specifically, organizational changes may be either *autonomous* or *systemic*. **Autonomous change** is one that is made independently of other changes. For an example, an auto company that develops a new type of upholstery may do so without revising the rest of the car. **Systemic change** is such that change in one part of an organization requires changes in another part of that same organization. For example, Polaroid's development of instant photography required changes in both film and camera technologies.

A second key distinction involves the capabilities needed to complete the project. In some cases, outside capabilities are required. For example, in the early 1980s, IBM was able to develop its first personal computer in only 15 months because it went outside the company for expertise (e.g., buying chips from Intel and an operating system from Microsoft). Other times, capability can be found inside the company. For example, Ford traditionally develops many of the components used in its cars, making it less dependent on other companies (although it does far less of this than it used to).[26]

By combining these factors, it becomes clear when companies should "go virtual" and when they should work exclusively within their own walls. *Virtual organizations work best for companies considering autonomous changes using technologies that exist only outside their walls.* For example, Motorola has developed virtual organizations with several battery manufacturers for its cell phones and pagers. In so doing, it can focus on its core business—the delivery of wireless communication—while ensuring it has the battery power to make such devices work.

In contrast, *companies should keep their focus inward when changes are systemic in nature and involve capabilities the company either already has or can create.* Under such conditions, relying on outside help may be far too risky—and unnecessary. For example, these days Intel is making extensive investments to enhance its current and future capacities.

Finally, for conditions that fall between these extremes (i.e., when systemic changes are being made using capabilities that come only from outside the company, and when autonomous changes are being made using capabilities that must be created), virtual alliances should be created with extreme caution. Clearly, the virtual organization has a key place in today's organizational world. The trick, however, lies in understanding precisely what that place is. These guiding principles represent useful guidance in that respect.

interorganizational designs, plans by which two or more organizations come together.[27] Two such designs are commonly found: *conglomerates* and *strategic alliances*.

Conglomerates: Diversified "Megacorporations"

When an organization diversifies by adding an entirely unrelated business or product to its organizational design, it may be said to have formed a **conglomerate**. Some of the world's largest conglomerates may be found in Asia. For example, in Korea, companies such as Samsung and Hyundai produce home electronics, automobiles, textiles, and chemicals in large, unified conglomerates known as *chaebols*.[28] These are all separate companies overseen by the same parent company leadership. In Japan, the same type of arrangement is known as a *keiretsu*.[29] A good example of a *keiretsu* is the Matsushita Group.[30] This enormous conglomerate consists of a bank (Asahi Bank), a consumer electronics company (Panasonic), and several insurance companies (e.g., Sumitomo Life, Nippon Life). These examples are not meant to suggest that conglomerates are unique to Asia. Indeed, many large U.S.-based corporations, such as IBM and Tenneco, are also conglomerates.

Companies form conglomerates for several reasons. First, as an independent business, the parent company can enjoy the benefits of diversification. Thus, as one industry languishes, another may excel, allowing for a stable economic outlook for the parent company. In addition, as in the case of vertically integrated organizations, conglomerates may provide built-in markets and access to supplies, since companies typically support other organizations within the conglomerate. For example, General Motors cars and trucks are fitted with Delco radios, and Ford cars and trucks have engines with Autolite spark plugs, separate companies that are owned by their respective parent companies. In this manner conglomerates can benefit by providing a network of organizations that are dependent on each other for products and services, thereby creating considerable advantages.

In recent years, however, many large conglomerates have been selling off parts of themselves in a move to concentrate on their core business.[31] For example, The Limited, the large women's clothing retailer, has closed or sold off some of its specialty stores in 1998 (e.g., Cacique and Abercrombie & Fitch) so that it could focus on its core business.

Strategic Alliances: Joining Forces for Mutual Benefit

A **strategic alliance** is a type of organizational design in which two or more separate firms join their competitive capabilities to operate a specific business. The goal of a strategic alliance is to provide benefits to each individual organization that could not be attained if they operated separately. They are low-risk ways of diversifying (adding new business operations) and entering new markets. Some companies, such as GE and Ford, have strategic alliances with many others. Although some alliances last only a short time, others have remained in existence for well over 30 years and are still going strong.[32]

A continuum of alliances. A study of 37 strategic alliances from throughout the world identified three types of cooperative arrangements between organizations.[33] These may be arranged along a continuum from those alliances that are weak and distant, at one end, to those that are strong and close, at the other end. As shown in Figure 13.11, at the weak end of the continuum are strategic alliances known as **mutual service consortia**.

Figure 13.11 Strategic Alliances: A Continuum of Interorganizational Relationships

The three types of *strategic alliances* identified here may be distinguished with respect to their location along a continuum ranging, at one end, from weak and distant, to strong and close at the other end.

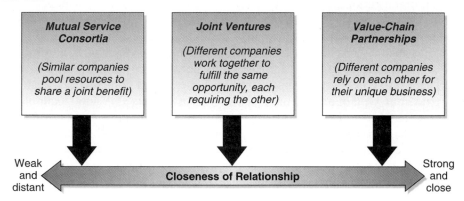

These are arrangements between two similar companies from the same or similar industries to pool their resources to receive a benefit that would be too difficult or expensive for either to obtain alone. Often the focus is some high-tech capacity, such as an expensive piece of diagnostic equipment that might be shared by two or more local hospitals (e.g., a magneto-resonance imaging or MRI unit).

At the opposite end of the scale are the strongest and closest type of collaborations, referred to as **value-chain partnerships**. These are alliances between companies in different industries that have complementary capabilities. Customer–supplier relationships are a prime example. In such arrangements one company buys necessary goods and services from another so that it can do business. Because each company greatly depends on the other, each party's commitment to their mutual relationship is high. As noted earlier, Toyota has a network of 230 suppliers with whom it regularly does business. The relationship between Toyota and these various companies represent value-chain partnerships.

Between these two extremes are **joint ventures**. These are arrangements in which companies work together to fulfill opportunities that require the capabilities of the other.[34] For example, two companies might enter into a joint venture if one has a valuable technology and the other has the marketing knowledge to help transform that technology into a viable commercial product.

In recent years, as information technology has flourished, many Internet-based organizations have developed **joint ventures** with newly forming companies (referred to as *start-ups*). Their mission: to facilitate the flow of knowledge and talent across companies in a manner that boosts their joint technical and marketing competence. This special kind of joint venture is known as a **networked incubator**.[35] These are partnerships between established companies (often Internet-based firms), which provide valued resources and experience, with start-ups, which are able to develop and market products quickly. When properly designed, networked incubators combine the best of both worlds—the scale and scope of large, established companies and the entrepreneurial spirit of small firms.

As an example, consider Hotbank, a company known as an **incubator** because it specializes in starting up new businesses. Hotbank is managed by another company, Softbank Venture Capital (SBVC), which leases the office space, funds the projects, and provides the basic services needed to run a business (recruiting, public relations, accounting, and so on). SBVC provides the services needed to develop business ideas identified by Hotbank. For example, Hotbank's first company was Model E, a firm specializing in build-to-order vehicles and a Web-based comprehensive service packet (e.g., registration, insurance, financing). It was able to get off the ground because of the business ingenuity of Hotbank and the resources of SBVC. Because networked incubators are a new form of business relationship, it is too soon to tell how successful they will prove to be. However, if early reports provide any indication, it looks like they will be quite successful.

An alternative to the joint venture.   Although forming joint ventures with other companies is a popular way for companies to grow in new directions, it is not the only way. An alternative that has been popular in many companies has been to create a **spinoff**—that is, an entirely new company that is separate from the original parent organization, one with its own identity, a new board of directors, and a different management team. The idea is that instead of looking around for a suitable partner, a rich and powerful company can create its own partner.

Consider, for example, the development of Expedia, Microsoft's online travel service. In 1996, Expedia was launched as just another Microsoft product.[36] As it became successful, Expedia was set up as a separate operating unit. Then, in November 1999, Expedia was "spun off" into a separate publicly traded company (i.e., it can be purchased by anyone on the stock market). This raised $84 million for Microsoft, and because the company retains 85 percent of Expedia's stock, it promises to make even more money in the future. Despite the highly competitive market within which it operates, Expedia has been flourishing, enjoying record profits in 2002. This is in large part because it was the offspring of a wealthy and successful parent (which gave Expedia a head start) and also because it was allowed to develop on its own as needed, without too much "parental supervision," so to speak. Further extending the parent–child metaphor, the spinoff company is forever associated with the parent company, providing services to it and getting help from it. However, it also is free to develop other business relationships that stand to strengthen it even further.

> In 1996, Expedia was launched as just another Microsoft product. As it became more successful, Expedia was set up as a separate operating unit. Then, in November 1999, Expedia was "spun off" into a separate publicly traded company

Strategic alliances in the global economy.   Strategic alliances with companies in nations with transforming economies (such as China and Eastern Europe) provide good opportunities for those nations' economies to develop. Given the rapid move toward globalization of the economy, we may expect to see many companies seeking strategic alliances in the future as a means for gaining or maintaining a competitive advantage. Frequently, companies form strategic alliances with foreign firms to gain entry into that country's market.[37] Such arrangements also may allow for an exchange of technology and manufacturing services. For example, Korea's Daewoo receives technical information and is paid to manufacture automobiles for companies with which it has entered into alliances, such as General Motors, as well as Germany's Opel and Japan's Isuzu and Nissan.[38] Some companies, such as the telecommunications giant MCI, are actively involved in several strategic alliances, including one in Canada and several in New Zealand.[39]

In addition to the financial incentives (circumventing trade and tariff restrictions) and marketing benefits (access to internal markets) associated with strategic alliances, direct managerial benefits also are associated with extending one company's organizational chart into another's. These benefits primarily come from improved technology and greater economies of scale (e.g., sharing functional operations across organizations). For these benefits to be derived, a high degree of coordination and fit must exist between the parties, each delivering on its promise to the other. Finally, it is noteworthy that strategic alliances with companies in nations with transforming economies provide good opportunities for those nations' economies to develop.[40] Given the rapid move toward globalization of the economy, we may expect to see many companies seeking strategic alliances in the future as a means for gaining or maintaining a competitive advantage.[41]

Strategic alliances can help minority-owned businesses.   Although members of minority groups represent about 28 percent of the U.S. population, they control only 12 percent of the nation's businesses. In an effort to bring parity to this situation by boosting the number of minority-owned businesses, the U.S. government requires companies to meet specified targets for conducting business with minority-owned companies. The underlying rationale is that this practice is good for business. Jethro Joseph, DaimlerChrysler's head of special supplier relations, offers a simple explanation: "If we buy from minority suppliers, they will hire minority employees, who will have the wherewithal to buy our products. We look at it as a never-ending wheel."[42] To get this wheel moving, many large companies are finding it useful to form alliances with minority-owned companies, creating relationships from which both parties can benefit. For a sample of some of these alliances, see Table 13.3.

> Jethro Joseph, DaimlerChrysler's head of special supplier relations, said, "If we buy from minority suppliers, they will hire minority employees, who will have the wherewithal to buy our products. We look at it as a never-ending wheel."

Are strategic alliances successful?   As our descriptions of the various types of alliances illustrate, there are clear benefits to be derived from forming alliances. These primarily come in the form of improved technology, widened markets, and greater economies of scale (e.g., sharing functional operations across organizations). However, as you might imagine, for these benefits to be realized, a high degree of coordination and fit must exist between the parties, each delivering on its promise to the other.

As you might imagine, not all strategic alliances are successful. For example, AT&T and Olivetti tried unsuccessfully to work together on manufacturing personal computers. Strong differences in management styles and organizational cul-

Table 13.3	Alliances Involving Minority-Owned Businesses

In recent years, many large companies have found it useful to enter into strategic alliances with small, minority-owned companies. Other companies have served as "matchmakers," bringing together firms with one or more minority group owners. Here are a few examples.

Large Company	*Involvement with Small, Minority-Owned Company*
Bank of America	Bank of America wanted to do business with R. J. Leeper, a black entrepreneur in the construction business. However, because he lacked experience, Bank of America helped him learn the business by getting him a job at a successful construction company and paying half his salary while he worked there. Leeper now has his own construction company, R. J. Leeper Construction, which is a supplier to Bank of America.
Procter & Gamble	Procter & Gamble purchases plastic bottles for Sunny Delight from a company that it helped create—a joint venture between Plastitec and minority-owned Madras Packaging.
DaimlerChrysler	DaimlerChrysler helped International Paper, one of its suppliers, form a joint venture with a black entrepreneur, Carlton Highsmith. His company, Specialized Packaging Group, now produces packaging for automotive parts made by Daimler Chrysler.
Ford Motor Company	Ford Motor Company officials wanted to buy conveyor systems from one of three minority-owned companies (Devon Contracting Services, Scion, and Gale & Associates), but they were too small. Ford helped these three firms merge, forming Tri-Tec, the larger and more stable company from which Ford now buys conveyor systems.
Johnson Controls	Johnson Controls purchases interior car parts from TKA Plastics. This company was the result of a partnership between two parties that Johnson Controls brought together: Del-Met, an injection molding company, and Michael Cherry, a black entrepreneur.

(Source: Based on Information in Weisul, 2001; see Note 42.)

ture were cited as causes (recall the discussion of culture clashes in Chapter 12). Similarly, a planned alliance between Raytheon and Lexitron, a small word processing company, failed because the of clashes between the rigid culture of the much larger Raytheon and the more entrepreneurial style of the smaller Lexitron. Clearly, for strategic alliances to work, the companies must not only be able to offer each other something important, but they also must be able to work together to make it happen.

You Be the Consultant

Designing a Rapidly Growing Company

The president of a small but rapidly growing software company asks you to consult with him about an important matter. As the company expands, several options for designing the company's operations are being considered, and your job is to help him make a decision about which route to take. Answer the following questions relevant to this situation based on the material in this chapter.

1. What would you recommend with respect to the following structural variables: hierarchy of authority (tall or flat), division of labor (specialized or not), span of control (wide or narrow), and degree of centralization (highly centralized or highly decentralized)? Explain the reasons behind your recommendations.

2. How do you think the company should be departmentalized — by task (functional), by output (product), both task and output (matrix), or process (horizontal)? What are the reasons for these conclusions?

3. If the company were thinking about entering into a strategic alliance with another, what factors would have to be considered? What kind of company would be an effective partner in an alliance with this software firm?

Self-Assessment Exercise

Which Do You Prefer—Mechanistic or Organic Organizations?

Because mechanistic and organic organizations are so different, it is reasonable to expect that people will tend to prefer one of these organizational forms over the other. This questionnaire is designed to help you identify your own preferences (and, in so doing, to help you learn about the different forms themselves).

Directions

Each of the following questions deals with your preferences for various conditions that may exist where you work. Answer each one by checking the one alternative that better describes your feelings.

1. When I have a job-related decision to make, I usually prefer to:
   _____ a. make the decision myself.
   _____ b. have my boss make it for me.

2. I usually find myself more interested in performing:
   _____ a. a highly narrow, specialized task.
   _____ b. many different types of tasks.

3. I prefer to work in places in which working conditions:
   _____ a. change a great deal.
   _____ b. generally remain the same.

4. When a lot of rules are imposed on me, I generally feel:
   _____ a. very comfortable.
   _____ b. very uncomfortable.

5. I believe that governmental regulation of industry is:
   _____ a. usually best for all.
   _____ b. rarely good for anyone.

Scoring

1. Give yourself one point each time you answered as follows: 1 = b; 2 = a; 3 = b; 4 = a; 5 = a. This score is your preference for *mechanistic organizations*.

2. Subtract this score from 5. This score is your preference for *organic organizations*.

3. Interpret your scores as follows: Higher scores (closer to 5) reflect stronger preferences and lower scores (closer to 0) reflect weaker preferences.

Discussion Questions

1. How did you score? That is, which organizational form do you prefer?

2. Think back over the jobs you've had. For the most part, have these been in organizations that were mechanistic or organic?

3. Do you think you were any more committed to organizations in which you worked whose designs matched your preferences as compared to those in which there was a mismatch?

Group Exercise

Comparing Span of Control in Organization Charts

One of the easiest things to determine about a company by looking at its organization chart is its span of control. This exercise will allow you to learn about and compare span of control within different companies.

Directions

1. Divide the class into four equal size groups.

2. Assign one of the following industry types to each group: (a) manufacturing companies, (b) financial institutions, (c) public utilities, and (d) charities.

3. Within the industry assigned to each group, identify one company per student. It helps to consider larger organizations inasmuch as these are more likely to have formal organization charts. For example, if there are five students in the "financial institutions" group, name five different banks or savings and loan institutions.

4. Each student should get a copy of the organization chart (or at least a portion of it) for the company assigned to him or her in step 3. You may be able to get this information from various companies' Web sites and/or by consulting their annual reports (which may be found in many libraries). If all else fails,

you may have to ask someone you know who works at a given company to show you its organization chart.

5. Meet as a group to discuss the spans of control of the organizations in your sample.

6. Gather as a class to compare the findings of the various groups.

Discussion Questions

1. Were you successful in being able to collect the organization charts, or were the organizations reluctant to share them?

2. Did you find that there were differences with respect to span of control?

3. Were spans of control different at different organizational levels or for different industry groups? In what ways were they similar and different?

Notes

Case Notes

Commercial Metal Company Web site: www.comercialmetals.com. *Commercial Metals Company 2002 Annual Report.* Dallas, TX: Commercial Metals Company.

Chapter Notes

[1] Daft, R. L. (2003). *Essentials of organization theory and design* (8th ed.). Cincinnati, OH: South-Western.

[2] Cameron, K. S. (1998). Strategic organizational downsizing: An extreme case. In B. M. Staw & L. L. Cummings (Eds.) *Research in organizational behavior* (Vol. 20, pp. 141–184). Greenwich, CT: JAI Press.

[3] Kaufman, L. H. (2000). Centralized or decentralized management. *Railway Age, 201*(8), 47–52.

[4] Schminke, M., Ambrose, M. L., & Cropanzano, R. S. (2000). The effect of organizational structure on perceptions of procedural fairness. *Journal of Applied Psychology, 85*, 294–304.

[5] Schminke, M., Cropanzano, R. S., & Rupp, D. E. (2002). Organizational structure and fairness perceptions: The moderating effects of organizational level. *Organizational Behavior and Human Decision Processes, 89*, 881–905.

[6] Anders, G. (2003). *Perfect enough: Carly Fiorina and the reinvention of Hewlett-Packard.* Middlesex, England: Portfolio.

[7] Hewlett Packard: About us. (2003). From the World Wide Web at www.hp.com/hpinfo/abouthp.

[8] Hymowitz, C. (2003, August 12). Managers suddenly have to answer to a crowd of bosses. *Wall Street Journal*, p. B1.

[9] Leatt, P., Shortell, S. M., & Kimberly, J. R. (2000). A matrix design for a psychiatric hospital. In S. M. Shortell & A. D. Kalunzy (Eds.), *Health care management: Organization design and behavior* (4th ed., pp. 280–301). Albany, NY: Delmar Publishers.

[10] Tushman, M. L., Nadler, N. B., & Nadler, D. A. (1997). *Competing by design: The power of organizational architecture.* New York: Oxford University Press.

[11] Stewart, T. A. (1992, May 18). The search for the organization of tomorrow. *Fortune*, pp. 93–98 (quote p. 93).

[12] Byrne, J. A. (1993, December 20). The horizontal corporation. *Business Week*, pp. 76–81 (quote p. 96).

[13] Bossidy, L., & Charan, R. (2002). *Execution: The discipline of getting things done.* New York: Crown (quote p. 44).

[14] GE: Just your average everyday $60 billion family grocery store. (1994, May 2). *Industry Week*, pp. 13–18.

[15] Ashkenas, R., Ulrich, D., Jick, T., & Kerr, S. (1998). *The boundaryless organization: Breaking the chains of organizational structure*. San Francisco: Jossey-Bass.

[16] Dees, G. D., Rasheed, A. M. A., McLaughlin, K. J., & Priem, R. L. (1995). The new corporate architecture. *Academy of Management Executive, 9*, 7–18.

[17] Harrigan, K. R. (2003). *Vertical integration, outsourcing, and corporate strategy*. Frederick, MD: Beard Group.

[18] See Note 13.

[19] Tully, S. (1993, February 3). The modular corporation. *Fortune*, pp. 106–108, 110.

[20] Werther, W. B., Jr. (1999, March–April). Structure-driven strategy and virtual organizational design. *Business Horizons*, pp. 13–18.

[21] Byrne, J. (1993, February 8). The virtual corporation. *Business Week*, pp. 99–103.

[22] Sherman, S. (1992, September 21). Are strategic alliances working? *Fortune*, pp. 77–78 (quote p. 78).

[23] Nathan, R. (1998, July–August). NEC organizing for creativity, nimbleness. *Research Technology Management*, pp. 4–6.

[24] Moore, J. F. (1998, Winter). The rise of a new corporate form. *Washington Quarterly*, pp. 167–181.

[25] Chesborough, H. W., & Teece, D. J. (1996, January–February). When is virtual virtuous? Organizing for innovation. *Harvard Business Review, 96*, 65–73.

[26] See Note 25.

[27] Nooteboom, B. (2004). *Inter-firm collaboration, networks and strategy: An integrated approach*. London: Routeledge

[28] Chang, S-J. (2003). *Financial crisis and transformation of Korean business groups: The rise and fall of chaebols*. London: Cambridge University Press.

[29] Lincoln, J. R., Gerlach, M., & Ahmadjian, C. (1998). Evolving patterns of keiretsu organization and action in Japan. In B. M. Staw & L. L. Cummings (Eds.) *Research in organizational behavior* (Vol. 20, pp. 303–345). Greenwich, CT: JAI Press.

[30] Miyashita, K., & Russell, D. (1995). *Keiretsu: Inside the Japanese conglomerates*. New York: McGraw Hill.

[31] Lubove, S. (1992, December 7). How to grow big yet stay small. *Forbes*, pp. 64–66.

[32] Kanter, R. M. (1994, July–August). Collaborative advantage: The art of alliances. *Harvard Business Review*, pp. 96–108.

[33] See Note 32.

[34] Harrigan, K. R. (2003). *Joint ventures, alliances, and corporate strategy*. Frederick, MD: Beard Group.

[35] Hansen, M. T., Chesbrough, H. W., Nohria, N., & Sull, D. N. (2000, September–October). Networked incubators: Hothouses of new economy. *Harvard Business Review*, pp. 74–84.

[36] Albrinck, J., Irwin, G., Neilson, G., & Sasina, D. (2000, third quarter). From bricks to clicks: The four stages of e-volution. *Strategy and Business*, pp. 63–66, 68–72.

[37] Fletcher, N. (1988, December 10). U.S., China form joint venture to manufacture helicopters. *Journal of Commerce*, p. 58.

[38] Bransi, B. (1987, January 3). South Korea's carmakers count their blessings. *The Economist* p. 45.

[39] Mason, J. C. (1993, May). Strategic alliances: Partnering for success. *Management Review*, pp. 10–15.

[40] Newman, W. H. (1992). Focused joint ventures in transforming economies. *The Executive, 6*, 67–75.

[41] Reuer, J. J. (2003). *Strategic alliances: Theory and evidence*. New York: Oxford University Press.

[42] Weisul, K. (2001, March 6). Minority mergers. *Business Week*, Frontier section, pp. F14–F19.

Chapter **Fourteen**

LEARNING OBJECTIVES

After reading this chapter, you will be able to:

1. **IDENTIFY** the major external forces responsible for organizational change.

2. **DESCRIBE** what is meant by strategic planning and **IDENTIFY** the steps in the process in the strategic planning process.

3. **DESCRIBE** why people are resistant to change in organizations and ways in which this resistance may be overcome.

4. **DEFINE** organizational development (OD) and **DESCRIBE** three OD techniques.

5. **DESCRIBE** the conditions under which organizational development techniques are most effective.

6. **DESCRIBE** how OD is affected by national culture and **EXPLAIN** the ethical concerns that have been voiced about using OD techniques.

Managing Organizational Change: Strategic Planning and Organizational Development

Can P&G Turn the Tide?

You wake up and brush your teeth with Crest toothpaste, bathe with Zest soap, wash your hair with Head & Shoulders shampoo, and apply your Cover Girl makeup. You then begin your household chores, washing clothes with Tide, putting fresh Luvs diapers on the baby, and cleaning the kitchen floor with your Swiffer dust mop. Taking a break, you sip your SunnyD as you pour yourself some Folgers coffee and munch on a few Pringles. If this sounds like you, then consider yourself a living advertisement for Procter & Gamble (P&G), the almost 170-year-old company whose products you've been using.

As you might imagine, a company that's been around this long has made more than a few changes in its day. Some have been in response to fundamental changes in society, such as in the 1920s, when the advent of electric lightbulbs pushed P&G out of the candle business. Other changes have been aimed at proactively improving business operations, such as in 1919, when the company sought to stabilize uneven

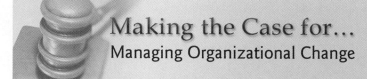

Making the Case for...
Managing Organizational Change

sales cycles by eliminating wholesalers and selling directly to retail stores, a move that would revolutionize the grocery business. Perhaps more than anything, P&G has always been responsive to the ever-changing demands of consumers. Parents seeking modern conveniences in the 1960s, for example, found P&G there with Pampers, the first disposable diaper.

Times may be different today, but P&G faces the same kinds of challenges to keep it at the top of the consumer products business. For example, although new products are the lifeblood of the company, P&G hasn't developed many successful new brands of its own recently (the Swiffer dust mop was the only one in the last 15 years!). Meeting the problem head on, CEO Alan G. "A. G." Lafley has been buying brands—Clairol in 2001 and Wella in 2003, among them. In 2002, P&G also entered into an agreement with Clorox to produce Glad food wraps and plastic food storage containers. In a move to save money while also allowing the company to do what it does best—market products—Lafley has decided to outsource some business functions, including the manufacturing of bar soap (including Ivory, the company's oldest surviving brand). Another change has come in the form of marketing P&G brands more creatively. No longer just a toothpaste, for example, the Crest name now also appears on the company's SpinBrush electric toothbrush.

Acknowledging that the culture at P&G has been resistant to adopting new ideas—"insular," some have complained—Lafley has gone out of his way to ensure that these fundamental changes will keep P&G vital for at least another 170 years. The key to his approach rests on building "understanding and commitment" among his personnel. With this in mind, he regularly spends Monday mornings in the office with a dozen other top corporate officers working on the week's game plan. To ensure that everyone gets the message, communication barriers—literally, walls on the eleventh floor of corporate headquarters—have been broken down and offices have been moved so that people now sit directly alongside those with whom they most often have to work. One of his colleagues refers to Lafley as "an excellent listener . . . a sponge." From what he hears, Lafley patiently reshapes everything the company does. And with profits rising a whopping 13 percent between 2002 and 2003 (a rocky period for most businesses), it's clear that Lafley already is making P&G "new and improved."

Managing Organizational Change

You should care about managing organizational change and development because:

1. The success—even the mere survival—of companies depends on their ability to adapt to change.

2. Overcoming people's resistance to change is a key determinant of organizational effectiveness.

3. Organizational development techniques can be effective tools for getting people to adapt to change.

There can be no doubt that Lafley has overseen a dramatic change in P&G operations—indeed, its basic business philosophy. Of course, it's not only P&G that has seen dramatic changes over the years. Just think about how the menus of fast-food restaurants have become more diversified, commerce over the Internet now occurs regularly, and banks are merging into "megafinancial institutions."

Although the impact of *organizational change* can be found everywhere, most people have difficulty accepting that they may have to alter their work methods. After all, if you're used to working a certain way, a sudden change can be very unsettling. Fortunately, social scientists have developed various methods, known collectively as *organizational development* techniques, which are designed to implement needed organizational change in a manner that both is acceptable to employees and enhances the effectiveness of the organizations involved.

I will review these techniques in this chapter. Before doing so, however, I will take a closer look at the organizational change process by chronicling different forces for change acting on organizations. Then I will explore some major issues involved in the organizational change process, such as what is changed, when change will occur, why people are resistant to change, and importantly, how this resistance can be overcome.

Today's First Rule of Business: Change or Disappear!

A century ago, advances in machine technology made farming so highly efficient that fewer hands were needed to plant and reap the harvest. The displaced laborers fled to nearby cities, seeking jobs in newly opened factories, opportunities created by some of the same technologies that sent them from the farm. The economy shifted from agrarian to manufacturing, and the *industrial revolution* was under way. With it came drastic shifts in where people lived, how they worked, how they spent their leisure time, how much money they made, and how they spent it. Today's business analysts claim that we are currently experiencing *another* industrial revolution—one driven by a new wave of economic and technological forces. As one observer put it, "This workplace revolution . . . may be remembered as a historic event, the Western equivalent of the collapse of communism."[1]

In recent years, just about all companies, large and small, have made adjustments in the ways they operate, some more pronounced than others. Citing just a few examples from the past decade, General Electric, Allied Signal, Ameritech, and Tenneco all have radically altered the way they operate: their culture, the technology they use, their structure, and the nature of their relations with employees. With so many companies making such drastic changes, the message is clear: *either adapt to changing conditions or shut your doors.* As technology and markets change, organizations face a formidable challenge to adapt. When they fail to do so, they are forced to close their doors forever.

> General Electric, Allied Signal, Ameritech, and Tenneco all have radically altered the way they operate: their culture, the technology they use, their structure, and the nature of their relations with employees.

learning
objective

External Forces for Organizational Change

What outside forces cause organizations to change? Although there are many different drivers of organizational change, five particular forces are sufficiently important to be described. These are the introduction of information technology, changing employee demographics, performance gaps, government regulation, and global economic competition.

Advances in technology.   Probably the most potent impetus for organizational change is the introduction of the computer. In offices, word processing systems have replaced typewriters; in factories, robots have replaced people performing dangerous and repetitive jobs; and in some recording studios, sophisticated synthesizer units housed in simple black boxes have replaced orchestras full of people. Although office personnel, factory workers, and musicians surely have not become extinct, computer technology has changed the way they are doing their jobs. For an overview of ways in which the introduction of high-tech devices in the workplace have helped people to perform and to better serve the needs of customers and society at large, see Table 14.1.

Table 14.1	How Has Computer Technology Changed the Way We Work?

Advances in computer technology have revolutionized many of the ways we work. Some key ways in which this has been occurring are summarized here.

Area of Change	*Old Way*	*New Technology Examples*
Use of machines	Materials were moved by hand, with the aid of mechanical devices (e.g., pulleys and chains).	**Automation** is prevalent—the process of using machines to perform tasks that might otherwise be done by people. For example, computer-controlled machines manipulate materials and perform complex functions, a process known as **industrial roboties (IR)**.
Work by employees with disabilities	People with various physical or mental disabilities either were relegated to the most simple jobs, or they didn't work at all.	**Assistive technology** is widespread—devices and other solutions that help individuals with physical or mental disabilities perform the various actions needed to do their jobs. For example, **telephone handset amplifiers** make it possible for people with hearing impediments to use the telephone and **voice recognition systems** read to people with visual impairments.
Monitoring employees	Supervisors used to physically enter the offices of employees at work and observe them from afar.	**Computerized performance monitoring** systems are in widespread use, which allow supervisors to access their subordinates' computers for purposes of assessing how well they are performing their jobs.
Customer service	Individual service providers did things to help employees, customizing goods and services as time and skill allowed.	**Personalized service** is likely to take the form of greeting visitors to one's Web page with information customized to match the goods and services in which they expressed interest in their last visit (e.g., Amazon.com does this).
Environmental friendliness	Products at the end of their lives were buried in landfills, often polluting the earth.	**Design for disassembly (DFD)** is the process of designing and building products so that their parts can be reused several times and then disposed of at the end of the product's life without harming the environment.

Although some jobs have been eliminated because of automation, technology generally has helped those who have become displaced find more interesting and personally fulfilling jobs. The widespread fear that many people had about "being replaced by robots" has proven to be unfounded. More typical is the situation in which people work side by side with robots. For example, although robots play a large part in the production of automobiles, such as General Motors' highly regarded Saturn, company officials acknowledge that the technology only works because of the people. Advanced technology alone won't build a successful car. In the words of the Japanese industrialist Jaruo Shimada, "Only people give wisdom to the machines."[2] The idea is that people and machines are complementary aspects of any organization.

Changing employee demographics.   There's no mistaking the fact that the composition of the workforce has changed in the past few years. As I noted in Chapter 5, the American workforce is now more racially and ethnically diverse than ever before. It also contains more women, more foreign nationals, and more elderly people.[3] To people concerned with the long-term operation of organizations, this is not simply a curious sociological trend but also a set of shifting conditions that force organization officials to make various adaptations. For example, human resources specialists need to know if there will be a drop in the number of qualified applicants (suggesting the need to import employees from other locations, or even to relocate the company), as well as the specific skills employees will be bringing to their jobs (suggesting the need to revise training programs) and their special needs (such as child care or flexible working arrangements). In the words of a high-ranking executive at General Electric, the changes in workforce demographics "will turn the professional human-resources world upside down."[4]

Performance gaps.   A product line that isn't moving, a vanishing profit margin, a level of sales that isn't up to corporate expectations—these are examples of **performance gaps**, discrepancies between real and expected levels of organizational performance. Few things force change more than sudden and unexpected information about poor performance. A good example is General Motors' decision of a few years ago to phase out its Oldsmobile brand. Although the Oldsmobile was produced for over 100 years, its failure to respond to changing demands (specifically, vehicles that were appealing to younger buyers) eventually led to its demise.[5] Organizations that are best prepared to mobilize change in response to downturns are best prepared to succeed. Indeed, General Motors officials are hoping that the decision to pull the plug on the Oldsmobile brand will help the company regain its prominence in the auto industry.[6]

> Although the Oldsmobile was produced for over 100 years, its failure to respond to changing demands (specifically, vehicles that were appealing to younger buyers) eventually led to its demise.

Government regulation.   One of the most commonly witnessed unplanned organizational changes results from government regulations. In recent years, restaurant owners in the United States had to alter the way they report the income of waiters and waitresses to the federal government for purposes of collecting income taxes. Moreover, the U.S. federal government has been involved in both imposing and eliminating regulations in industries such as commercial airlines (e.g., mandating inspection schedules but no longer controlling fares) and banking (e.g., restricting the amount of time checks can be held before clearing but no longer regulating interest rates). Such activities have greatly influenced the way business is conducted in these industries.

Global economic competition.   Competition from the marketplace is a key driver of organizational change. Any company that fails to keep up with the competition (with respect to price, services, or other key features) doesn't stand a chance of surviving. Although competition always has been crucial to organizational success, competition today comes from all over the world. As it has become increasingly less expensive to transport materials around the world, the industrialized nations have found themselves competing with each other for shares of the marketplace in nations all over the world. This extensive globalization of the economy presents a strong need to change and be innovative.[7]

For example, large American automobile manufacturers suffered in the 1970s and 1980s because they were unprepared to meet the world's growing demand for small, high-quality cars—products their Japanese competitors were only too glad to supply to an eager marketplace. As a result, the automobile business has become truly global in scope. Instead of domination by the traditional "Big Three" automakers (General Motors, Ford, and Chrysler), all based in the United States, today's auto market is dominated by the "Global Five" (General Motors, Ford, DaimlerChrysler, Toyota, and Volkswagen), only two of which are headquartered in the United States, and all of which have facilities throughout the world.[8]

Magnitude of Change: How Much Change Constitutes Change?

As you might imagine, not all organizational changes are equal in magnitude. Whereas some are minor and subtle, others are far more dramatic and far-reaching in scope and impact.

First-order change.   Change that is continuous in nature and that involves no major shifts in how an organization operates is known as **first-order change** (or **incremental change**). Changes of this type are apparent in the deliberate, incremental modifications Toyota has made in continuously improving the efficiency of its production process. Not surprisingly, employees are less threatened by incremental changes than by more monumental changes because they have time to adapt and to make appropriate adjustments.

Second-order change.   Other types of organizational changes are far more complex. **Second-order change** (or **quantum change**) refers to radical change, involving major shifts in different levels of the organization and different aspects of the business.[9] For example, many large companies, such as General Electric and Allied Signal, to name two, have radically altered the way they operate, their culture, the technology they use, their structure, and the nature of their relations with employees. Not surprisingly, quantum change often is quite jarring and highly traumatic to employees, and as such, getting them to accept such changes is often difficult.

Planning Strategic Change

Thus far, I have described unplanned organizational change. However, not all changes that are made in organizations fall into this category. Organizations also make changes that are carefully planned and deliberate. This is the idea of **strategic planning**, defined as the process of formulating, implementing, and evaluating organizational changes in ways that enable an organization to achieve its objectives.[10] In this section of the chapter, I will describe the strategic planning process.

Basic Assumptions About Strategic Planning

To understand the nature of strategic plans used in organizations today, it is important to identify three fundamental assumptions about them.[11]

1. *Strategic planning is deliberate.* When organizations make strategic plans, they make conscious decisions to change fundamental aspects of themselves. These changes tend to be radical and second-order changes (e.g., changes in the nature of the business) as opposed to minor, first-order changes (e.g., changes in the color of the office walls).

2. *Strategic planning occurs when current objectives no longer can be met.* Generally, when a company's present strategy is bringing about the desired results, change is unlikely. However, whenever it becomes clear that current objectives no longer can be met, new strategies are formulated to turn things around.

3. *New organizational objectives require new strategic plans.* Whenever a company takes steps to move in a completely new direction, it establishes new objectives, and it designs a strategic plan to meet them. Acknowledging that the various parts of an organization are interdependent, this new strategic plan is likely to involve all functions and levels of the organization.

To illustrate how these assumptions come to life, I now will describe some examples of strategic plans for change.

About What Do Companies Make Strategic Plans?

As you might imagine, organizations can make strategic plans to change just about anything. Most of the strategic planning today, however, involves changing either a company's products and services or its organizational structure.

Products and services.   Over the past few years, many well-known bricks-and-mortar retail establishments, such as Barnes & Noble, Toys "R" Us, and CompUSA, jumped on the e-commerce bandwagon after it became apparent that doing so would expand their customer base by extending their well-known names to the Web. They also made this strategic move as a hedge against losing business to companies such as Amazon.com, e-Toys, and Micro Warehouse, whose online-only presence made serious inroads into their respective markets. Some companies have even moved in the opposite direction. For example, Gateway made a strategic move from online presence to physical presence, with its Gateway Country stores. These are all examples of strategic changes in the delivery of services. Many companies also have made strategic changes in their product offerings. For example, Sony has added several new television sets to its product line, including tiny handheld units, and large, thin, widescreen plasma models in a strategic move to develop new segments of the market.

Often plans for strategic change create considerable challenges in organizations, as they struggle with the new technologies and skills required to succeed. For example, during the early 1990s, FedEx (which was Federal Express at the time) suffered dramatic growing pains as it sought to expand its market from North America to the rest of the world. Although service suffered at first under the strain of the added business, the company's international operations have proven successful. Still, outside North America, it is not FedEx but DHL that has the greatest presence in the parcel delivery market, suggesting that FedEx has a long way to go. However, with its recent acquisition of RPS, FedEx's strategic plan appears to focus more on chipping away at UPS's dominance in the North American market than on global expansion. As these examples illustrate, strategic plans in products and services can be quite complex.

> Sony has added several new television sets to its product line, including tiny handheld units, and large, thin, widescreen plasma models in a strategic move to develop new segments of the market.

Organizational structure.   In addition to making strategic plans about changes in products and services, companies also make strategic plans about their organizational structures (see Chapter 13). Consider, for example, PepsiCo's strategic decision to reorganize.[12] For many years, it had a separate international food service division, which included 62 foreign locations of its Pizza Hut and Taco Bell restaurants. Then, in 1990, because of the great profit potential from these foreign restaurants, PepsiCo officials decided to reorganize, putting these restaurants under direct control of the same executives responsible for the successful U.S. operations of Pizza Hut, Kentucky Fried Chicken, and Taco Bell. In 1997, however, PepsiCo made another strategic decision to get out of the restaurant business altogether. It spun off these three restaurants to form a separate company, TRICON Global Restaurants.

These days, many organizations have made strategic changes regarding the nature of the work they will do. In fact, they have completely eliminated units that focus on noncore sectors of their business and then have hired outside firms to perform these functions instead. This practice is known as outsourcing. For example, companies like ServiceMaster, which provides janitorial services, and ADP, which provides payroll-processing services, allow organizations to concentrate on the business functions most central to their missions, thereby freeing them from these peripheral support functions. Companies institute strategic plans to use outsourcing when the work they want to do is so highly critical and specialized that it requires outside assistance. For example, many manufacturing companies have found it more cost-effective to outsource their manufacturing operations to specialized companies than to build the expensive plants and find the trained workers required to build certain products. In fact, one industry analyst has estimated that 30 percent of the largest U.S. industrial firms outsource more than half their manufacturing.[13]

> Companies like ServiceMaster, which provides janitorial services, and ADP, which provides payroll-processing services, allow organizations to concentrate on the business functions most central to their missions, thereby freeing them from these peripheral support functions.

The Strategic Planning Process

The process of strategic planning typically follows 10 ordered steps, which I will now describe.[14] These steps are not immutable, and they are not always followed in prefect order. However, they do a reasonably good job of describing how companies plan change strategically. As I describe these steps, you may find it useful to examine the summary appearing in Figure 14.1.

1. *Define goals.* Strategic plans begin with clearly stated goals. Typically, these involve gaining a certain share of the market (e.g., market penetration of 40 percent) or achieving a certain financial standing (doubling the P/E ratio in five years). Organizational goals also can involve society (e.g., making $1 million in charitable donations) or organizational culture (e.g., making the workplace more pleasant for employees). It is important to note that overall organizational goals must be trans-

Figure 14.1   Strategic Planning: A 10-Step Process

Strategic planning—the process of formulating, implementing, and evaluating decisions that enable an organization to achieve its objectives—generally follows the 10 steps summarized here.

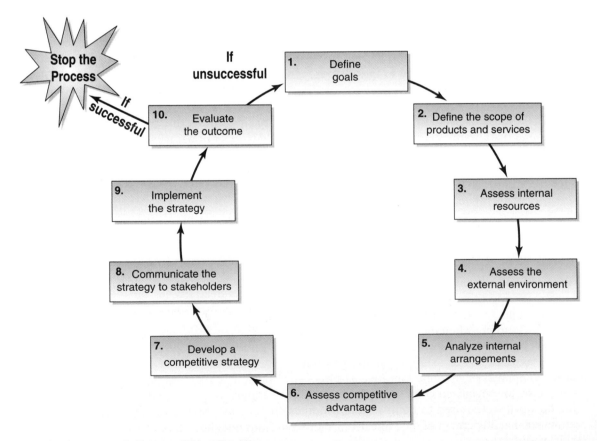

(Source: Based on suggestions by Christensen, 1994; see Note 14.)

lated into corresponding goals to be achieved by various individual units. For example, if a company has the goal of achieving 10 percent penetration into a market, it is important to establish clear goals for the marketing department (e.g., how to advertise to reach the right customers) and the production department (e.g., producing finished products at the appropriate rate to meet market demands).

2. *Define the scope of products or services.* For a strategic plan to be effective, company officials must define their organization's scope—that is, the businesses in which it already operates and the new businesses in which it aims to participate. If a company's scope is defined too broadly, it will dilute its effectiveness; if scope is defined too narrowly, it will overlook opportunities. Beech-Nut faced this issue when confronted with the fact that lowered birthrates shrunk the size of its market. In an effort to rebuild its business, Beech-Nut executives made the strategic decision to broaden its scope by developing products to feed elderly people with digestive problems.[15]

3. *Assess internal resources.* Organizations must ask themselves: What resources does the company have available to plan and to implement its strategy? The resources in question involve funds (e.g., cash to make purchases), physical assets (e.g., required space), and human assets (e.g., workers' knowledge and skills).

4. *Assess the external environment.* As I have noted throughout this book, organizations do not operate in a vacuum. Rather, they function within environments that influence their capacity to operate and to grow as desired. The extent to which the environment aids or hinders a company's growth—or even its existence—depends on several key factors. Specifically, a company has a competitive advantage over others when its resources cannot easily be imitated by others, its resources will not depreciate anytime soon, and competitors do not have better resources.[16]

5. *Analyze internal arrangements.* By "internal arrangements," I am referring to the nature of the organization itself. For example, are employees motivated to strive for corporate goals? (See Chapter 6.) Does the organizational culture encourage people to be innovative and make changes? (See Chapter 12.) Do people communicate with one another clearly enough to accomplish their goals? (See Chapter 8.) These and other basic questions about the organization must be answered to formulate an effective strategic plan. After all, unless the organization is operating properly, even the best strategic plans are doomed to fail.

6. *Assess the competitive advantage.* One company is said to have a competitive advantage over another to the extent that customers perceive its products or services as being superior (e.g., in quality, cost, or both) to those of other companies. Superiority may be assessed in terms of factors such as quality, price, breadth of product line, reliability of performance, styling, service, and company image.

7. *Develop a competitive strategy.* A competitive strategy is the means by which an organization achieves its goal. Based on careful assessment of the company's standing regarding the factors described earlier (e.g., available resources, competitive advantage, and so on), a decision is made about how to achieve its goal. Some possible strategies are described in Table 14.2.

8. *Communicate the strategy to stakeholders.* The term **stakeholder** refers to an individual or group in whose interest the organization is run. The most important stakeholders include employees at all levels, boards of directors, and stockholders. It is essential to communicate a firm's strategy to stakeholders so they may contribute to its success, whether actively (e.g., employees who pitch in to help meet the goals) or passively (e.g., investors who pour money into the company to help meet goals). Unless stakeholders

| Table 14.2 | Varieties of Competitive Strategies |

Some of the most popular competitive strategies used by today's organizations are summarized here.

Strategy	*Description*
Market-share increasing strategies	Developing a broader share of an existing market, such as by widening the range of products, or by forming a joint venture (see Chapter 13) with another company that already has a presence in the market of interest
Profit strategies	Attempting to derive more profit from existing businesses, such as by training employees to work more efficiently or salespeople to sell more effectively.
Market concentration strategies	Withdrawing from markets where the company is less effective and concentrating resources in markets where the company is likely to be more effective
Turnaround strategies	Attempting to reverse a decline in business by moving to a new product line or by radically restructuring operations
Exit strategies	Withdrawing from a market, such as by liquidating assets

fully understand and accept a firm's strategy, that firm is unlikely to receive the full support needed to meet its goals.

9. *Implement the strategy.* Once a strategy has been formulated and communicated, the time has come for it to be implemented. When this occurs, some fallout is inevitable as employees scramble to adjust to new ways of doing things. As I will explain later in this chapter, people generally resist change, but as I also will describe, several steps can be taken to ensure that the individuals making the required changes will come to embrace them.

10. *Evaluate the outcome.* Finally, after a strategy has been implemented, it is crucial to determine if the goals have been met. If so, new goals may be sought; if not, different goals may be defined or different strategies may be followed to achieve success next time.

If, after reading this, you are thinking that developing a strategic plan is very difficult and that carrying it out is even more challenging, you have reached the same conclusion as many top executives. For practice in creating your own strategic plan, see the **Self-Assessment Exercise** on page 483.

Readiness for Change: Accepting and Resisting Organizational Change

As you might imagine, there are times when organizations are likely to change and times during which change is less likely. In general, change is likely to occur when the people involved believe that the benefits associated with making a change outweigh the costs involved. The factors contributing to the benefits of making a change are as follows.

- the amount of dissatisfaction with current conditions
- the availability of a desirable alternative
- the existence of a plan for achieving that alternative

Theorists have claimed that these three factors combine multiplicatively to determine the benefits of making a change (see Figure 14.2). Thus, if any one of these factors is zero, the benefits of making a change and the likelihood of change itself will be zero. If you think about it, this makes sense. After all, people are unlikely to initiate change if they are not at all dissatisfied or if they don't have any desirable alternative in mind (or any way of attaining that alternative, if they do have one in mind). Of course, for change to occur, the expected benefits must outweigh the likely costs involved (e.g., disruption, uncertainties).

Why Is Organizational Change Resisted?

Although people may be unhappy with the current state of affairs confronting them in organizations, they may be afraid that any changes will be potentially disruptive and will only make things worse.[17] Indeed, fear of new conditions is quite real and it creates unwillingness to accept change. Organizational scientists have recognized that **resistance to change** stems from both individual and organizational variables.

3
learning
objective

Individual barriers to change.   Researchers have noted several key factors that are known to make people resistant to change in organizations.[18] These are as follows.

Figure 14.2   Organizational Change: When Will It Occur?

Whether or not an organizational change is made depends on people's beliefs regarding the relative benefits and costs of that change. The benefits are reflected by the three considerations reviewed here.

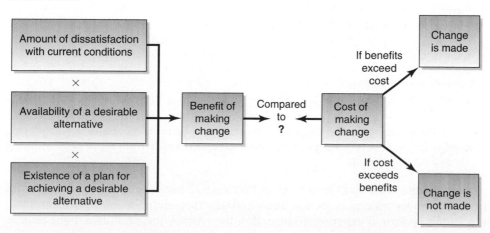

- *Economic insecurity.* Because any changes on the job have the potential to threaten one's livelihood—by either loss of job or reduced pay—some resistance to change is inevitable.

- *Fear of the unknown.* Employees derive a sense of security from doing things the same way, knowing whom their coworkers will be, and whom they're supposed to answer to from day to day. Disrupting these well-established, comfortable patterns creates unfamiliar conditions, a state of affairs that is often rejected.

- *Threats to social relationships.* As people continue to work within organizations, they form strong bonds with their coworkers. Many organizational changes (e.g., the reassignment of job responsibilities) threaten the integrity of friendship groups that provide valuable social rewards.

- *Habit.* Jobs that are well learned and become habitual are easy to perform. The prospect of changing the way jobs are done challenges people to develop new job skills. Doing this is clearly more difficult than continuing to perform the job as it was originally learned.

- *Failure to recognize need for change.* Unless employees can recognize and fully appreciate the need for changes in organizations, any vested interests they may have in keeping things the same may overpower their willingness to accept change.

Organizational barriers to change.   Resistance to organizational change also stems from conditions associated with organizations themselves.[19] Several such factors may be identified.

- *Structural inertia.* Organizations are designed to promote stability. To the extent that employees are carefully selected and trained to perform certain jobs and rewarded for doing them well, the forces acting on individuals to perform in certain ways are very powerfully determined—that is, jobs have *structural inertia.* Thus, because jobs are designed to have stability, it is often difficult to overcome the resistance created by the forces that create stability.

- *Work group inertia.* Inertia to continue performing jobs in a specified way comes not only from the jobs themselves but also from the social groups within which people work—*work group inertia.* Because of the development of strong social norms within groups (see Chapter 9), potent pressures exist to perform jobs in certain ways. Introducing change disrupts these established normative expectations, leading to formidable resistance.

- *Threats to the existing balance of power.* If changes are made with respect to who is in charge, a shift in the balance of power between individuals and organizational subunits is likely to occur. Those units that now control the resources, have the expertise, and wield the power may fear losing their advantageous positions resulting from any organizational change.

- *Previously unsuccessful change efforts.* Anyone who has lived through a past disaster understandably may be reluctant to endure another attempt at the same thing. Similarly, groups or entire organizations that have been unsuccessful in introducing change in the past may be cautious about accepting further attempts at introducing change into the system.

During the 1980s and 1990s, General Electric (GE) underwent a widespread series of changes in its basic strategy, organizational structure, and relationship with employees. In this process, it experienced several of the barriers just identified. For example,

GE managers had mastered a set of bureaucratic traditions that kept their habits strong and their inertia moving straight ahead. The prospect of doing things differently was scary for those who were so strongly entrenched in doing things the "GE way." In particular, the company's interest in globalizing triggered many fears of the unknown. Resistance to change at GM also was strong because it threatened to strip power from those

GE managers had mastered a set of bureaucratic traditions that kept their habits strong and their inertia moving straight ahead. The prospect of doing things differently was scary for those who were so strongly entrenched in doing things the "GE way."

units that traditionally possessed most of it (e.g., the Power Systems and Lighting division). Changes also were highly disruptive to GE's "social architecture"; friendship groups were broken up and scattered throughout the company. In all, GE has been a living example of many different barriers to change all rolled into a single company.

Factors Affecting Resistance to Change

To overcome resistance to change, it helps to discover the individual variables (e.g., personality) and aspects of the work setting to which such resistance is most closely linked. Doing this makes it possible to identify specific ways of changing people and/or changing situations so as to make them more accepting of organizational change.

This approach was taken in a study of officials who worked for a large governmental agency.[20] Using questionnaires that assessed a variety of different individual differences and situational factors, the researchers sought to identify the factors that were linked most closely to an important concept—openness to change (i.e., the extent to which someone is willing to accept changes in their organization). The researchers found that three variables in particular were most strongly linked to openness to change: resilience (i.e., the extent to which they are capable of bouncing back from adversity; recall the discussion of this variable in conjunction with the material on stress in Chapter 4), information about change (i.e., specific facts about how things will be different), and change self-efficacy (i.e., beliefs in one's ability to function effectively despite the demands of change). As summarized at the top of Figure 14.3, the relationship between each of these variables and openness to change was positive—in other words, greater amounts of these variables were associated with greater openness to change.

Of course, it's not only what people report on a questionnaire about their openness to change that matters but also how openness is related to key aspects of people's work attitudes and behavior. To learn about this, the researchers also assessed a number of variables in their questionnaire. What they found was interesting. Three particular variables were strongly associated with openness to change (see bottom portion of Figure 14.3). The first was job satisfaction (see Chapter 5). The more open to change employees were, the more satisfied they tended to be with their jobs. Furthermore, the more open the workers were to change, the less work-related irritation they showed (i.e., the less they tended to get angry or aggravated at work), and the less likely they were to quit their jobs. Thus, openness to change can make a big difference when it comes to these important aspects of the job. In view of this, it makes sense to make an effort to make people more resilient to change, to increase the amount of information they have available about how their organizations will change, and to boost their

Figure 14.3	Variables Linked to Openness to Change: Research Findings

As summarized at the top of this diagram, three factors—resilience, information about change, and change self-efficacy—are positively associated with openness to change. And, as shown at the bottom, openness to change is in turn related to job satisfaction, work-related irritation, and intention to quit.

Resilience, information about change, and change self-efficacy are associated with openness to change . . .

. . .and openness to change, in turn, is related to job satisfaction, work-related irritation, and intention to quit.

(Source: Based on findings reported by Wanberg and Banas, 2000; see Note 20.)

beliefs that they will be able to respond positively to new work situations. As you will see in the next section, several of these suggestions are incorporated into specific approaches to overcoming resistance to organizational change.

How Can Resistance to Organizational Change Be Overcome?

Because organizational change is inevitable, managers should be sensitive to the barriers to change so that resistance can be overcome. This, of course, is easier said than done. However, several useful approaches have been suggested, and the key ones are summarized here.[21]

Shape political dynamics. For change to be accepted, it is often useful (if not absolutely necessary) to win the support of the most powerful and influential individuals in the company. Doing so builds a critical internal mass of support for change. Demonstrating clearly that key organizational leaders endorse the change is an effective way to get others to go along with it—either because they share the leader's vision or because they fear the leader's retaliation. Either way, their support will facilitate acceptance of change.

Educate the workforce.   Sometimes people are reluctant to change because they fear what the future has in store for them. Fears about economic security, for example, may be put to rest by a few reassuring words from powerholders. As part of educating employees about what organizational changes may mean for them, top management must show a considerable amount of emotional sensitivity. Doing so makes it possible for the people affected by change to help make it work. Some companies have found that simply answering the question, "what's in it for me?" can help allay a lot of fears.

"Sell" the need for change.   For organizational change to occur, top management must accept the idea that change is required. And quite often, it's lower-level practicing managers, those who toil daily in the trenches, who offer the best ideas. For these ideas to be accepted and implemented, however, it's necessary for top officials to be convinced that the ideas are worthwhile. How, then, do managers "sell" their bosses on the need for change? A recent study has examined this question.[22] Scientists conducting this research interviewed managers from various departments in a large hospital, inquiring as to how they went about presenting their ideas for change to top management. Carefully analyzing the responses led them to identify the following three major approaches, known as "issue selling" techniques (for a summary, see Figure 14.4).

Figure 14.4   How Do Managers "Sell" Ideas About Change to Their Superiors?

Interviews with managers have revealed that to "sell" their superiors on ideas about organizational change, they rely on the three kinds of "moves" identified here.

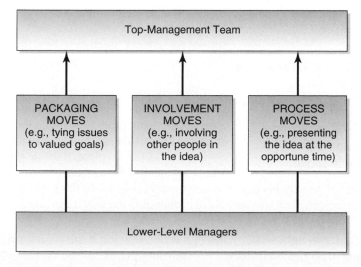

(Source: Based on suggestions by Dutton, Ashford, O'Neill, and Lawrence, 2001; see Note 22.)

- *Packaging moves.* This involves combining several ideas into a coherent whole. It includes such approaches as presenting one's ideas in the form of a clear business plan and "bundling" the idea together with other key organizational concerns, such as profitability.

- *Involvement moves.* This has to do with involving other people in the selling of the idea, such as other top-level personnel, others at the same level, or even others outside the organization.

- *Process moves.* This involves paying attention to matters of form and style, such as giving a thorough presentation with all the issues carefully thought out and presenting ideas at the most opportune time and in a persistent fashion.

Although one cannot guarantee that top leaders always will follow the advice of their lower level managers, for them to have any chance of doing so, they must be convinced of the merit of their ideas. And to increase the chances that managers' good ideas will come across, it help may well help to follow these moves.

Involve employees in the change efforts.   It is well established that people who participate in making a decision tend to be more committed to the outcomes of the decision than are those who are not involved. Accordingly, employees who are involved in responding to unplanned change, or who are made part of the team charged with planning a needed organizational change, may be expected to have very little resistance to change. Organizational changes that are "sprung" on the workforce with little or no warning might be expected to encounter resistance simply as a knee-jerk reaction until employees have a chance to assess how the change affects them. In contrast, employees who are involved in the change process are better able to understand the need for change and are, therefore, less likely to resist it. Says Duane Hartley, general manager of Hewlett-Packard's microwave instruments division, "I don't think people really enjoy change, but if they can participate in it and understand it, it can become a positive [experience] for them."[23]

It is important to emphasize that involving employees in change efforts means more than simply giving them a voice in determining the organization's operations. It also means actively engaging employees at all levels in the problems the organization faces. Here's an example. Officials from Shell Malaysia had long been unsuccessful in getting employees to work together to beat the competition. They were far too complacent, and the competition was rapidly gaining market share. In response to this, Shell officials called together all 260 managers for a $2 ½ -day session in which the problem of the rapidly encroaching competition was put before them. They emerged from this marathon session with a firm plan that was put into place. Back on the job, regular follow-up meetings were held to make sure the plan was implemented. Finally, because the employees bought into the problem and met the challenge themselves, Shell was successful in changing the way it operated.

> Shell officials called together all 260 managers for a 2 ½-day session in which the problem of the rapidly encroaching competition was put before them. They emerged from this marathon session with a firm plan that was put into place.

Reward constructive behaviors.   One rather obvious and quite successful mechanism for facilitating organizational change is rewarding people for behaving in the desired fashion. Changing organizational operations may necessitate changing the kinds of behaviors that need to be rewarded by the organization. This is especially critical when an organization is in the transition period of introducing the change. For example, employees who are required to learn to use new equipment should be praised for their successful efforts. Feedback on how well they are doing not only provides a great deal of useful assurance to uncertain employees but also helps shape the desired behavior.

Lead in a way that stresses the urgency of change.   It's not unusual for company officials to get in a rut, becoming lazy and complacent about the way they operate, even when it's necessary to take decisive action. This is *almost* what happened to Sears a few years ago. The retailing giant was losing customers rapidly as officers sat by merely lowering sales goals. That's when Sears' CEO Arthur Martinez lit a fire under everyone by stressing the importance of turning things around—or else! He generated a sense of urgency by setting very challenging goals (e.g., quadrupling market share, and increasing customer satisfaction by 15 percent). Although Martinez didn't have all the answers to Sears' problems, he provided something even more important—straightforward, honest talk about the company's problems, creating a sense of urgency that got everyone moving in the right direction.

> Sears' CEO Arthur Martinez lit a fire under everyone by stressing the importance of turning things around— or else! He generated a sense of urgency by setting very challenging goals (e.g., quadrupling market share, and increasing customer satisfaction by 15 percent).

Create relentless discomfort with the status quo.   Following military maneuvers, the U.S. Army thoroughly debriefs all participants in what is called an "after action review." In these sessions, careful feedback is given about what soldiers did well and where they need to improve. By focusing in a relentless, detailed manner on work that needs to be done, officers eventually get soldiers to internalize the need for excellence. Soldiers return to their home bases asking themselves how they can do something better (faster, cheaper, or more accurately) or if there is a new and better approach that could be taken. In short, the status quo is the enemy; current performance levels are never accepted. Things can always be better. Army brass liken this commitment to continuous improvement to painting a bridge: The job is never over.

Create a "learning organization."   Although all organizations change, whether they want to or not, some do so more effectively than others. Those organizations that have developed the capacity to adapt and change continuously are known as **learning organizations**.[24] In learning organizations, people set aside old ways of thinking, freely share ideas with others, form a vision of the organization, and work together on a plan for achieving that vision. Examples of learning organizations include Ford, General Electric, Motorola, Wal-Mart, and Xerox. As you might imagine, becoming a learning organization is no simple feat. In fact, it involves implementing many of the principles of organizational behavior described in this book. Specifically, for a firm to become a continual learner, management must take the three steps outlined in Table 14.3.

> Examples of learning organizations include Ford, General Electric, Motorola, Wal-Mart, and Xerox.

Table 14.3	Ways to Become a Learning Organization

Learning organizations are ones that are successful at acquiring, cultivating, and applying knowledge that can be used to help it adapt to change. To becomes an effective learning organization, managers must follow the rules outlined here.

Rule	Description
Establish a commitment to change	Unless all employees clearly see top management as being strongly committed to changing and to improving the organization, they will be unlikely to make the changes necessary to being about such improvements.
Adopt an informal organizational structure	Change is more readily accepted when organizational structures are flat (see Chapter 13), when cross-functional teams are created (see Chapter 9), and when formal boundaries between people are eliminated.
Develop an open organizational culture	As described in Chapter 12, managers play a key role in forming organizational culture. To adapt effectively to changes in their environments, organizations should have cultures that embrace risk taking, openness, and growth.

Although these five suggestions may be easier to state than to implement, efforts at following them will be well rewarded. Given the many forces that make employees resistant to change, managers should keep these guidelines in mind. (For a chance to think more about resistance to organizational change and ways to overcome it, see the **Group Exercise** on page 484.)

learning objective

Organizational Development Interventions: Implementing Planned Change

Now that you appreciate the basic issues surrounding organizational change, you are prepared to examine systematic ways of implementing it—tactics collectively known as techniques of **organizational development (OD)**. Formally, organizational development may be defined as a set of social science techniques designed to plan and implement change in work settings for purposes of enhancing the personal development of individuals and improving the effectiveness of organizational functioning. By planning organization-wide changes involving people, OD seeks to enhance organizational performance by improving the quality of the work environment and the attitudes and well-being of employees.[25]

Over the years, many different strategies for implementing planned organizational change (referred to as **OD interventions**) have been used by specialists attempting to improve organizational functioning (referred to as **OD practitioners** or **change agents**). These individuals, usually from outside the organization, coordinate and facilitate an organization's change efforts. All the major methods of organizational development attempt to produce some kind of change in individual employees, work groups, and/or entire organizations.[26] This is the goal of the three OD interventions I will review here.

Survey Feedback

For effective organizational change to occur, employees must understand the organization's current strengths and weaknesses. That's the underlying rationale behind the **survey feedback** method.[27] This technique follows the three steps summarized in Figure 14.5. First, data are collected that provide information about matters of general concern to employees, such as organizational climate, leadership style, and job satisfaction. This may take the form of intensive interviews, structured questionnaires, or both. Because it is important that this information be as unbiased as possible, employees providing feedback should be assured that their responses will be kept confidential. For this reason, this process is usually conducted by outside consultants.

The second step calls for reporting the information obtained back to the employees during small group meetings. Typically, this consists of summarizing the average scores on the attitudes assessed in the survey. Profiles are created of feelings about the organization, its leadership, the work done, and related topics. Discussions also focus on why the scores are as they are and what problems are revealed by the feedback. The final step involves analyzing problems dealing with communication, decision making, and other organizational processes to make plans for dealing with them. Such discussions are usually most effective when they are carefully documented and a specific plan of implementation is made with someone put in charge of carrying it out.

Survey feedback is a widely used organizational development technique. This is not surprising in view of the advantages it offers. It is efficient, allowing a great deal of information to be collected relatively quickly. Also, it is very flexible and can be tailored to the needs of different organizations facing a variety of problems. However, the technique can be no better than the quality of the questionnaire used—it must measure the things that really matter to employees. Of course, to derive the maximum benefit from survey feedback, it must have the support of top management. The plans developed by the small discussion groups must be capable of being implemented with

Figure 14.5   Survey Feedback: An Overview

The *survey feedback* technique of OD follows the three steps outlined here: collecting data, giving feedback, and developing action plans.

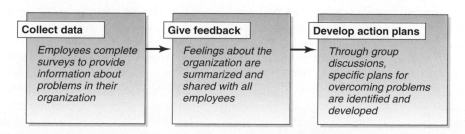

the full approval of the organization. When these conditions are met, survey feedback can be a very effective OD technique. (The basic idea behind survey feedback is that employees receive information that guides them through the process of making changes. However, another source of information that may be used for this purpose comes from finding out what competitors are doing. For a closer look at this practice, see the accompanying **Winning Practices** section.)

Winning **Practices**

Using Online Competitive Intelligence for Organizational Change

Only about 10 percent of American companies do it, and the other 90 percent probably should. What, you ask? The answer is **competitive intelligence (CI)**—the process of gathering information about competitors that can be used as the basis for planning organizational change. CI is a search for clues about what competitors are actually doing or considering doing and staying ahead of them by using this information as part of the strategic planning process. To stay competitive, some of the biggest companies—especially those in rapidly changing, high-tech fields, such as General Electric, Motorola, Microsoft, Hewlett-Packard, IBM, AT&T, and Intel—engage in CI all the time. In fact, Gary Costley, former president of Kellogg Co. North America, says that managers who don't engage in CI are "incompetent" insofar as it is "irresponsible to not understand your competitors."[28]

It's important not to dismiss CI on the grounds that it is unethical. CI is not industrial espionage (which involves illegally spying on competitors), and it is completely legal. CI efforts usually involve gathering readily available information, such as that contained in public records. In fact, it has been said that 90 percent of all the information a company needs to make critical decisions and to understand its market and its competitors is available in public data.[29] For example, companies are required to disclose information on their finances, inventories, and

compliance with various legal regulations. Documents containing this information are available to anyone online, and growing numbers of competitors are availing themselves of such information. One set of experts put it as such:

> By using the Internet, a company can monitor (manually or by using intelligent agents) the presence, posture, products, and pieces of other players in its industry. It can track the views of customers and seek out new ideas and expertise internationally. It can also draw upon files and databases from government agencies, foundations, universities, and research centers to broaden its thinking and help it be aware of the needs of the marketplace.[30]

So valuable is competitive intelligence from online sources that special software has been developed to mine that information.[31] Generally, CI information may be obtained online from a variety of sources. These include conference speakers, patent holders, former employees, technical recruiters, authors, and reporters. Companies also find it useful to post queries on bulletin boards and to join discussion groups.[32] Research has found that the more a company uses the Internet, the better quality competitive intelligence information it is able to collect. And, as the quality of competitive intelligence information improves, so

(continued)

too does a firm's capacity to make strategic decisions.[33] After all, companies that have competitive information not only recognize the need for change but also find it possible to make the kinds of changes that are necessary to succeed. Not surprisingly, companies that have advanced systems to monitor their competitors' activities are more profitable than those that do not have such systems in place.[34]

There's no mistaking the fact that competitive intelligence has become an important source of profit for many companies. As just one example, Robert Flynn, the former CEO of the NutraSweet division of Monsanto, has claimed that CI was worth some $50 million to his company (in terms of revenues gained and revenues not lost to competitors). With figures like these, it's easy to make the case that companies cannot afford to *not* make CI an important part of their strategic change plans.

Management by Objectives

In Chapter 6 we discussed the motivational benefits of setting specific goals. As you might imagine, not only individuals but also entire organizations stand to benefit from setting specific goals. For example, an organization may strive to "raise production" and "improve the quality" of its manufactured goods. These goals, well-intentioned though they may be, may not be as useful to an organization as more specific ones, such as "increase production of widgets by 15 percent" or "lower the failure rate of widgets by 25 percent." After all, as the old saying goes, "It's usually easier to get somewhere if you know where you're going." Peter Drucker, consulting for General Electric during the early 1950s, was well aware of this idea and is credited with promoting the benefits of specifying clear organizational goals—a technique known as **management by objectives (MBO)**.[35]

The MBO process, summarized in Figure 14.6, consists of three basic steps. First, goals are selected that employees will try to attain to best serve the needs of the organization. The goals should be selected by managers and their subordinates together. The goals must be set mutually by all those involved, not simply imposed. Furthermore, these goals should be directly measurable and have some time frame attached to them. Goals that cannot be measured (e.g., "make the company better") or that have no time limits are useless. It is also crucial that managers and their subordinates work together to plan ways of attaining the goals they have selected—developing what is known as an *action plan*.

Once goals are set and action plans have been developed, the second step calls for *implementation*—carrying out the plan and regularly assessing its progress. Is the plan working? Are the goals being approximated? Are there any problems being encountered in attempting to meet the goals? Such questions need to be considered while implementing an action plan. If the plan is failing, a midcourse correction may be in order—changing the plan, the way it's carried out, or even the goal itself. Finally, after monitoring progress toward the goal, the third step may be instituted: *evaluation*—assessing goal attainment. Were the organization's goals reached? If so,

Figure 14.6   Management by Objectives: Developing Organizations Through Goal Setting

The OD technique of *management by objectives* requires managers and subordinates to work together on setting and trying to achieve important organizational goals. The basic steps in the process are outlined here.

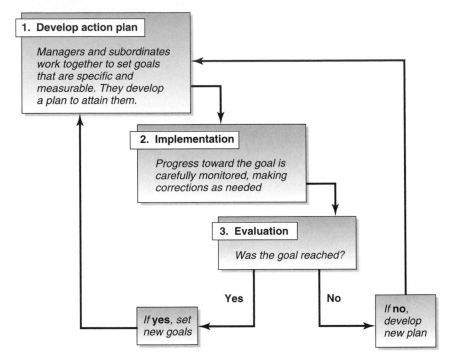

what new goals should be set to improve things still further? If not, what new plans can be initiated to help meet the goals? Because the ultimate assessment of the extent to which goals are met helps determine the selection of new goals, MBO is a continuous process.

MBO represents a potentially effective source of planning and implementing strategic change for organizations. Individual efforts designed to meet organizational goals get the individual employee and the organization itself working together toward common ends. Hence, system-wide change results.[36] Of course, for MBO to work, everyone involved has to buy into it. Because MBO programs typically require a great deal of participation by lower-level employees, top managers must be willing to accept and support the cooperation and involvement of all. Making MBO work also requires a great deal of time—anywhere from three to five years. Hence, MBO may be inappropriate in organizations that do not have the time to commit to making it work. Despite these considerations, MBO has become one of the most widely used techniques for affecting organizational change in recent years. It not only is used on an ad hoc basis by many organizations but also constitutes an ingrained element of the organizational culture in companies such as Hewlett-Packard and IBM.

Appreciative Inquiry

Although survey feedback and MBO are highly regarded OD techniques, they focus on deficiencies, such as negative feedback and unmet goals. A new approach to organizational development known as *appreciative inquiry* helps organizations break out of this focus on negative dynamics by emphasizing the positive and the possible.[37] Specifically, **appreciative inquiry** is an OD intervention that focuses attention away from an organization's shortcomings and toward its capabilities and its potential. It is based on the assumption that members of organizations already know the problems they face and that they stand to benefit more by focusing on what is possible.

As currently practiced, the process of appreciative inquiry follows four straightforward steps. These are as follows.[38]

1. *Discovery.* The discovery step involves identifying the positive aspects of the organization, the best of "what is." This frequently is accomplished by documenting the positive reactions of customers or people from other organizations.

2. *Dreaming.* Through the process of discovering the organization's strengths, it is possible to begin dreaming by envisioning "what might be." By discussing dreams for a theoretically ideal organization, employees are free to reveal their ideal hopes and dreams.

3. *Designing.* The designing stage involves having a dialogue in which participants discuss their ideas about "what should be." The underlying idea is that by listening to others in a highly receptive manner, it is possible to understand others' ideas and to come to a common understanding of what the future should look like.

4. *Delivering.* After having jointly discussed the ideal state of affairs, members of the organization are ready to begin instituting a plan for delivering their ideas. This involves establishing specific objectives and directions regarding "what will be."

Because appreciative inquiry is an emerging approach to OD, it has not been widely used. However, those organizations in which it has been used have been quite pleased with the results.[39]

Key Questions About Organizational Development

5
learning
objective

No discussion of organizational development would be complete without addressing three important questions—do the techniques work, are their effects culture dependent, and are they ethical?

The Effectiveness of Organizational Development: Does It Really Work?

Thus far, I have described some of the major techniques used by OD practitioners to improve organizational functioning. As is probably clear, carrying out these techniques requires a considerable amount of time, money, and effort. Accordingly, it is appropriate to ask if this investment is worthwhile. In other words, does OD really work? Given the popularity of OD in organizations, this question is very important.

The answer is generally yes: Research has shown that OD interventions tend to be beneficial when it comes to improving organizational functioning.[40] I hasten to add that any conclusions about the effectiveness of OD should be qualified in several important ways. Specifically:

- OD interventions generally are more effective among blue-collar employees than among white-collar employees.
- The beneficial effects of OD can be enhanced by using a combination of several techniques instead of any single one.
- To be effective, OD techniques must have the support of top management; the more strongly OD programs are supported from the top, the more successful they are.

Despite the importance of attempting to evaluate the effectiveness of OD interventions, a great many of them go unevaluated. Although there are undoubtedly many reasons for this, one key factor is the difficulty of assessing change. Because many factors can cause people to behave differently in organizations, and because such behaviors may be difficult to measure, many OD practitioners avoid the problem of measuring change altogether. In a related vein, political pressures to justify OD programs may discourage some OD professionals from honestly and accurately assessing their effectiveness. After all, in doing so, one runs the risk of scientifically demonstrating one's wasted time and money.

learning
objective

Is Organizational Development Dependent on National Culture?

For organizational development to be effective, people must be willing to share their ideas candidly with others, they must be willing to accept uncertainty, and they must be willing to show concern for others, especially members of their own teams. However, not all people are willing to do these things; this pattern better characterizes the people from some countries than others. For example, this profile perfectly describes people from Scandinavian countries, suggesting that OD may be most effective in such nations. However, people from Latin American nations are much the opposite, suggesting that OD interventions will be less successful when conducted there.[41] For a summary of the extent to which the basic assumptions of OD fit with the cultural styles of people from various nations, see Figure 14.7.

Although the predominant cultural values of people from the United States places it in the middle region of diagram in Figure 14.7, this is not to say that OD is doomed to be ineffective in American companies. Not all OD techniques are alike with respect to their underlying cultural values.[42] For example, MBO has become a very popular OD technique in the United States in large part because it promotes the American values of willingness to take risks and working aggressively at attaining high performance. However, because MBO also encourages superiors and subordinates to negotiate freely with each other, the technique has been generally unsuccessful in France, where others' higher levels of authority are well accepted.[43] Reasoning similarly, one may expect survey feedback to be unsuccessful in the Southeast Asian nation of Brunei, where the prevailing cultural value is such that problems are unlikely to be confronted openly.[44]

These examples illustrate a key point: The effectiveness of OD techniques will depend, in part, on the extent to which the values of the technique match the underlying values of the national culture in which it is employed. As such, OD practition-

Figure 14.7   Organizational Development: Its Fit with Cultural Values

Organizational development (OD) techniques tend to be more successful when the underlying values of the technique match the cultural values of the nation in which it is used. General OD values tend to conform more to the cultural values of some nations, shown on the right (where OD is more likely to be accepted) than to others, shown on the left (where OD is less likely to be accepted).

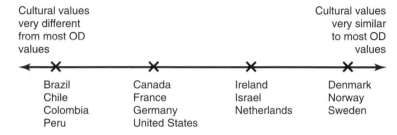

Cultural values very different from most OD values			Cultural values very similar to most OD values
Brazil	Canada	Ireland	Denmark
Chile	France	Israel	Norway
Colombia	Germany	Netherlands	Sweden
Peru	United States		

(Source: Based on suggestions by Jaeger, 1986; see Note 41.)

ers must fully appreciate the cultural norms of the nations in which they are operating. Failure to do so not only may make OD interventions unsuccessful, but also they may even have unintended negative consequences.

Is Organizational Development Inherently Unethical? A Debate

learning objective

By its very nature, OD applies powerful social science techniques in an attempt to change attitudes and behavior. From the perspective of a manager attempting to accomplish various goals, such tools are immediately recognized as very useful. However, if you think about it from the perspective of the individual being affected, several ethical issues arise.[45]

For example, it has been argued that OD techniques impose the values of the organization on the individual without taking the individual's own attitudes into account. OD is a very one-sided approach, reflecting the imposition of the more powerful organization on the less powerful individual. A related argument is that the OD process does not provide any free choice on the part of the employees. As a result, it may be seen as *coercive* and *manipulative*. When faced with a "do it, or else" situation, employees tend to have little free choice and are forced to allow themselves to be manipulated, a potentially degrading prospect.

Another issue is that the unequal power relationship between the organization and its employees makes it possible for the true intent of OD techniques to be misrepresented. As an example, imagine that an MBO technique is presented to employees as a means of allowing greater organizational participation, whereas in reality it is used as a means for holding individuals responsible for their poor performance and punishing them as a result. Although such an event might not happen, the potential for abuse of this type does exist, and the potential to misuse the technique—even if not originally intended—might later prove to be too great a temptation.

Despite these considerations, many professionals do *not* agree that OD is inherently unethical. Such a claim, it has been countered, is to say that the practice of management is itself unethical. After all, the very act of going to work for an organization requires one to submit to the organization's values and the overall values of society. One cannot help but face life situations in which others' values are imposed. This is not to say that organizations have the right to impose patently unethical values on people for making a profit (e.g., stealing from customers). Indeed, because they have the potential to abuse their power (such as in the MBO example), organizations have a special obligation to refrain from doing so.

Although abuses of organizational power sometimes occur, OD itself is not necessarily the culprit. Indeed, like any other tool (even a gun!), OD is not inherently good or evil. Instead, *whether the tool is used for good or evil will depend on the individual using it.* With this in mind, the ethical use of OD interventions will require that they be supervised by professionals in an organization that places a high value on ethics. To the extent that top management officials embrace ethical values and behave ethically themselves, norms for behaving ethically are likely to develop in organizations. When an organization has a strong ethical culture, it is unlikely that OD practitioners would even think of misusing their power to harm individuals. The need to develop such a culture has been recognized as a way for organizations to take not only moral leadership in their communities but financial leadership as well.

You Be the **Consultant**

Promoting Organizational Change

Things have been rough for the former employees at Small Town S&L ever since their institution was bought by First National Mega Bank. First National's procedures were more formal than those at Small Town. The CEO of First National is concerned about the employees' reacting negatively to the change and calls you for help. Answer the following questions relevant to this situation based on the material in this chapter.

1. Besides new operating procedures, what other planned and unplanned changes would you suspect are responsible for the employees' negative responses?

2. What barriers to change are likely to be encountered in this situation, and what steps would you propose to overcome them?

3. Do you think that an OD intervention would help in this case? If so, which one (or ones) do you propose, and why?

Self-Assessment Exercise

Developing a Strategic Plan

Developing a strategic plan is not easy. In fact, doing it right requires a great deal of information—and a great deal of practice. This exercise will give you a feel for some of the challenges involved in developing such a plan.

Directions

1. Suppose you are the president of a small software-development firm that for years has sold a utility that added functionality to the operating system used in most computers. Now, you suddenly face a serious problem: Microsoft has changed its operating system, and your product no longer serves any purpose.

2. Using the 10 steps outlined in Figure 14.1, develop a strategic plan to keep your company alive. Make any assumptions you need to develop your plan, but state these in the process of describing it.

Discussion Questions

1. How easy or difficult was it to develop this plan? What would have made the process easier?

2. What step do you imagine would be the easiest to implement? Which step do you think would be the most challenging?

3. What special challenges, if any, would the employees of your company face as they implemented this plan? How would you overcome these challenges?

Group Exercise

Recognizing Impediments to Change—and Overcoming Them

When it comes to confronting the reality of organizational change one of the most fundamental steps involves recognizing the barriers to change. Then, once these impediments have been identified, consideration can be given to ways of overcoming them. This exercise is designed to help you practice thinking along these lines while working in groups.

Directions

1. Divide the class into groups of approximately six and gather each group into a circle.

2. Each group should consider each of the following situations.

   - *Situation A:* A highly sophisticated e-mail system is being introduced at a large university. It will replace the practice of transmitting memos on paper.

   - *Situation B:* A very popular employee who's been with the company for many years is retiring. He will be replaced by a completely new employee from the outside.

3. For each situation, discuss three major impediments to change.

4. Identify a way of overcoming each of these impediments.

5. Someone from the group should record the answers and present them to the class for a discussion session.

Discussion Questions

1. For each of the situations, were the impediments to change similar or different?

2. For each of the situations, were the ways of overcoming the impediments similar or different?

3. How might the nature of the situation confronted dictate the types of change barriers confronted and the ease with which these may be overcome?

Notes

Case Notes

Berner, R. (2003, July 7). P&G: New and improved. *Business Week*, pp. 52–55, 58–59, 62–63. Procter & Gamble Web site: www.pg.com.

Chapter Notes

[1] Sherman, S. (1993, December 13). How will we live with the tumult? *Fortune*, pp. 123–125.

[2] Neff, R. (1987, April 20). Getting man and machine to live happily ever after. *Business Week*, pp. 61–63.

[3] Society for Human Resource Management. (2003). *2002 workplace demographic trends survey*. Alexandria, VA: Author.

[4] Stewart, T. A. (1993, December 13). Welcome to the revolution. *Fortune*, pp. 66–68, 70, 72, 76, 78.

[5] Kiley, D. (2000, December 13). GM waves goodbye to its Oldsmobile brand. *USA Today*, pp. 1B, 3B.

[6] Freeland, R. F. (2001). *The struggle for control of the modern corporation: Organizational change at General Motors*. New York: Cambridge University Press.

[7] Guillen, M. F. (2001). *The limits of convergence: Globalization and organizational change in Argentina, South Korea, and Spain*. Princeton, NJ: Princeton University Press.

[8] Howes, F. (1998, December 21). Future hinges on global teams. *Detroit News*, p. C1.

[9] Chaize, J. (2000). *Quantum leap: Tools for managing companies in the new economy*. New York: St. Martins Press.

[10] Pitts, A. C. (2003). *Strategic planning for sustainability and profit*. Burlington, MA: Butterworth-Heinemann. Dudik, E. M. (2000). *Strategic renaissance: New thinking and innovative tools to create great corporate strategies using insights from history and science*. New York: AMACOM.

[11] Meade, R. (1998). *International management* (2nd ed.). Malden, MA: Blackwell.

[12] McCarty, M. (1990, October 30). PepsiCo to consolidate its restaurants, combining U.S. and foreign operations. *Wall Street Journal*, p. A4.

[13] See Note 4.

[14] Christensen, H. K. (1994). Corporate strategy: Managing a set of businesses. In I. L. Flahey & R. M. Randall (Eds.), *The portable MBA in strategy* (pp. 53–83). New York: Wiley.

[15] Markides, C. (1997, Spring). Strategic innovation. *Sloan Management Review*, pp. 9–23.

[16] Collis, D. J., & Montgomery, C. A. (1995, July–August). Competing on resources: Strategy in the 1990s. *Harvard Business Review, 73*, 118–128.

[17] Marci, D. M., Tagliaventi, M. R., & Fabiola, B. (2002). A grounded theory for resistance to change in small organizations. *Journal of Organizational Change Management, 15*, 292–310. Duck, J. D. (2001). *The change monster: The human forces that fuel or foil corporate transformation and change*. New York: Crown.

[18] Nadler, D. A. (1987). The effective management of organizational change. In J. W. Lorsch (Ed.), *Handbook of organizational behavior* (pp. 358–369). Upper Saddle River, NJ: Prentice Hall.

[19] Katz, D., & Kahn, R. L. (1978). *The social psychology of organizations* (2nd ed.). New York: Wiley.

[20] Wanberg, C., & Banas, J. T. (2000). Predictors and outcomes of openness to change in a reorganizing workplace. *Journal of Applied Psychology, 85*, 132–142.

[21] Pascale, R., Millemann, M., & Gioja, L. (1997, November–December). Changing the way we change. *Harvard Business Review*, pp. 127–139. Nadler, D. A. (1987). The effective management of organizational change. In J. W. Lorsch (Ed.), *Handbook of organizational behavior* (pp. 358–369). Upper Saddle River, NJ: Prentice Hall.

[22] Dutton, J. E., Ashford, S. J., O'Neill, R. M., & Lawrence, K. A. (2001). Moves that matter: Issue selling and organizational change. *Academy of Management Journal, 44*, 716–736.

[23] Huey, J. (1993, April 5). Managing in the midst of chaos. *Fortune*, pp. 38–41, 44, 46, 48.

[24] Gard, G., Lindstroem, K., & Dallner, M. (2003). Towards a learning organization: The introduction of a client-centered team-based organization in administrative surveying work. *Applied Ergonomics, 34*, 97–105. Senge, P. M. (1990). *The fifth discipline*. New York: Doubleday.

[25] Austin, J. R., & Bartunek, J. M. (2003). Theories and practices of organizational development. In W. C. Borman, D. R. Ilgen, & R. J. Klimoski (Eds.), *Handbook of psychology: Industrial and organizational psychology* (Vol. 12, pp. 309–332). New York: John Wiley & Sons.

[26] Harigopal, K. (2001). *Management of organizational change: Leveraging transformation*. Newbury Park, CA: Sage.

[27] Joens, I. (2000). Supervisors as moderators of survey feedback and change processes in teams. In M. Vartiainen & F. Avallone (Eds.), *Innovative theories, tools, and practices in work and organizational psychology* (pp. 155–171). Cambridge, MA: Hogrefe & Huber.

[28] Ettorre, B. (1995, October). Managing competitive intelligence. *Management Review*, pp. 15–19.

[29] Teo, T. S. H., & Choo, W. Y. (2001). Assessing the impact of using the Internet for competitive intelligence. *Information & Management, 39*, 67–83.

[30] See Note 29 (quote, pp. 68–69).

[31] Chen, H., Chau, M., & Zeng, D. (2002). CI Spider: A tool for competitive intelligence on the Web. *Decision Support Systems, 34*(1), 1–17.

[32] Burwell, H., Ernst, C. R., & Sankey, M. (1999). *Online competitive intelligence*. Lanham, MD: Facts on Demand Press.

[33] See Note 29.

[34] Subramanian, R., & Ishak, S. T. (1998). Computer analysis practices of U.S. companies: An empirical investigation. *Management International Review, 38*, 7–24.

[35] Drucker, P. F. (1976). What results should you expect? A user's guide to MBO. *Public Administration Review, 36*, 12–19.

[36] Rodgers, R., & Hunter, J. E. (1991). Impact of management by objectives on organization productivity. *Journal of Applied Psychology, 76*, 322–336.

[37] Cooperrider, D. L., Stavros, J. M., & Whitney, D. K. (2003). *The appreciative inquiry handbook*. San Francisco: Berrett-Koehler. Watkins, J. M., & Mohr, B. J. (2001). *Appreciative inquiry: Change at the speed of imagination*. New York: John Wiley & Sons.

[38] Ludema, J. D., Whitney, D., Bohr, B. J., & Griffin, T. J. (2003). *The appreciative inquiry summit: A practitioner's guide for leading large-group change*. San Francisco: Berrett-Koehler. Whitney, D., & Sachau, C. (1998, Spring). Appreciative inquiry: An innovative process for organization change. *Employment Relations Today, 25*, pp. 11–21.

[39] Bushe, G. R., & Coetzer, G. (1995). Appreciative inquiry as a team-developed intervention: A controlled experiment. *Journal of Applied Behavioral Science, 31*, 13–30.

[40] Porras, J. I., & Robertson, P. J. (1992). Organization development: Theory, practice, and research. In M. D. Dunnette & L. Hough (Eds.), *Handbook of industrial and organizational psychology* (2nd ed., Vol. 3, pp. 719–822). Palo Alto, CA: Consulting Psychologists Press.

[41] Jaeger, A. M. (1986). Organizational development and national culture: Where's the fit? *Academy of Management Review, 11*, 178–190.

[42] Kedia, B. L., & Bhagat, R. S. (1998). Cultural constraints on transfer of technology across nations: Implications for research in international and comparative management. *Academy of Management Review, 13*, 559–571.

[43] Trepo, G. (1973, Autumn). Management style *a la française. European Business, 39,* 71–79.

[44] Blunt, P. (91988). Cultural consequences for organization change in a Southeast Asian state: Brunei. *Academy of Management Executive, 2,* 235–240.

[45] Patching, K. (2001). *Management and organization development: Beyond arrows, boxes and circles.* New York: Macmillan. White, L. P., & Wotten, K. C. (1983). Ethical dilemmas in various stages of organizational development. *Academy of Management Review, 8,* 690–697.

Integrative Case

The *Columbia* Space Shuttle Disaster

ORGANIZATIONAL BEHAVIOR AS A MATTER OF LIFE AND DEATH

February 1, 2003, was a tragic day in the annals of space exploration. Only 16 minutes from touchdown at the Kennedy Space Center in Florida, the U.S. Space Shuttle *Columbia* (NASA's mission STS-107) disintegrated upon reentering the earth's atmosphere. The otherwise successful 16-day scientific research mission ended in catastrophe. Lost was the entire seven-member crew: Commander Rick Husband, Pilot Willie McCool, Mission Specialists Michael Anderson, Dave Brown, Laurel Clark, and Kalpana Chawla, and Payload Specialist Ilan Ramon from Israel.

Within hours, the *Columbia* Accident Investigation Board (CAIB) was formed. Its chairman, retired Admiral Harold W. "Hal" Gehman Jr., headed a team of 13 committee members along with a staff of 120 administrative assistants and 400 NASA engineers to determine precisely what happened and why, and to recommend ways of avoiding a reoccurrence. Almost seven months later, on August 26, 2003, the board's findings were released in a highly detailed, seven-volume report. As one might expect given the nature of the investigation, the report contained copious technical details of engineering flaws that led to the shuttle's physical failure. The immediate cause of the accident was a breach in the thermal protection system resulting from a piece of insulating foam that separated from a fuel tank and hit part of the left wing shortly after launch.

But, according to the board, the stage for these technical troubles was set by a more fundamental cause—deeply rooted problems in the organizational management of NASA's Space Shuttle Program itself. One might not expect to find an OB focus in a government-initiated, postdisaster technical report, but it makes perfect sense. After all, people engineered the project, so any weaknesses in the way they

made decisions and communicated to one another were bound to make a difference. Tragically, they did. Add to this an organizational culture that condoned questionable compromises and the inefficient organizational design of NASA as a
whole, and you have the recipe for failure. Indeed, the board concluded that problems inherent in NASA's organizational management had as much to do with the
accident as the physical causes themselves. Until these were rectified, manned space
flights could not be resumed safely.

The board's analyses, which I will summarize here, illustrate key aspects of organizational behavior in action—specifically, the consequences of failing to follow
many of the important principles identified in this book. In this manner, the CAIB
report serves as a useful basis for integrating many of the major concepts from the
field of organizational behavior in dramatic fashion. If we can learn some valuable
lessons from this tragedy, then perhaps future lives will be saved and the seven
astronauts will not have died in vain. This integrative case is designed to showcase
those OB-related lessons. Specifically, this case will focus on three major organizational problems (each of which includes several specific subproblems) identified by
CAIB: (1) Time pressure eroded decision-making quality, (2) miscommunication
was rampant, and (3) a culture of overconfidence eclipsed attention to safety. To
provide insight into how these problems came into being, I begin by describing the
political environment within which NASA was operating.

Political Conditions Setting the Stage for Organizational Problems

Not operating in a vacuum, all organizations are responsive to external forces acting
on them (see Chapters 1 and 14). Specifically, because it is a government agency,
many of the forces NASA faces are political in nature. In the case of the *Columbia*
accident, these political pressures led to the creation of organizational conditions
that proved disastrous.

Ever since the Soviet Union launched its unmanned *Sputnik* satellite on
October 4, 1957, U.S. politicians pushed for dominance in space exploration. The
competitive zeal of "the space race" reached new heights when President Kennedy
pledged to send a man to the moon and bring him safely back to earth by the end of
the 1960s. Amassing the most sophisticated advances in technology and engineering
talent with unprecedented budgetary support, that goal was reached in July 1969,
unofficially declaring the United States the winner of the space race. Adding many
more successful missions to its record in the two decades that followed, NASA—its
Human Space Flight Program, in particular—became synonymous with cutting-
edge technological excellence.

Things changed in the late 1980s. The Cold War ended, and along with it was lost
the source of the strongest pressure to maintain dominance in space exploration—
the urgency of the historic struggle between the world's two superpowers. With no
equally strong political objective to replace it, Congress cut NASA's budget. And
within NASA, the Space Shuttle Program's budget was slashed by about 40 percent,
in the 1990s—repeatedly raided to compensate for overruns in the more glamorous
and high-profile International Space Station Program.

In response, the agency's options were clear. It either could adjust its ambitions to this new state of affairs by downscaling its plans or continue its ambitious agenda, requiring it to be more efficient than ever. Buoyed with optimism from its history of success and the self-image that it can overcome seemingly impossible challenges, NASA officials elected to push ahead with its programs although this now meant accomplishing more with less. "Faster, better, cheaper" became NASA's slogan in the post–Cold War era, but nobody at the agency was used to working that way. NASA's greatest successes came at a time when the funding required to support its projects in the safest possible manner essentially was there for the asking. Working efficiently was never stressed relative to safety. The new external realities reversed those priorities. This manifested itself in several key ways.

■ Between 1993 and 2002, the space shuttle workforce was downsized by 42 percent (see Chapter 14).

■ Key Space Shuttle Program responsibilities, including safety oversight, were out-sourced to private companies (see Chapter 14).

Along with the relentless pressure to increase the rate of space flights, the effects of these practices on managerial functioning were considerable. Increased time pressure coupled with reduced resources led to communication failures, both within NASA and between NASA and outside companies. As fewer people were expected to do more work than ever, the agency's emphasis on safety slipped. But, insofar as it had a stellar record of success—especially in the Apollo program, which repeatedly landed men on the moon—safety came to be taken for granted.

Although such complacency is understandable, it is hard to believe that few, if any, changes in management practice were made in the aftermath of the January 28, 1986, explosion of the shuttle *Challenger*. The immediate cause of that accident, which resulted in the death of seven astronauts, was judged to be the failure of a rubber O-ring that sealed two lower segments of the right solid rocket booster. This resulted in a 32-month delay and a $12 billion investment in new technology before returning the shuttle to flight. But, as in the case of the *Columbia* accident, the body investigating the *Challenger* accident—named the Rogers Commission, after President Regan's former secretary of state, who headed it—found that the physical cause of the accident had roots in the same fundamental management problems—miscommunication resulting from intense pressure and an efficient organizational structure. It is largely because the managerial lessons to be learned from the *Challenger* disaster were never heeded that the *Columbia* disaster occurred. And with this in mind, the CAIB has emphasized the role of managerial problems in the accident. I now will describe these.

Time Pressure Eroded Decision-Making Quality

As noted in Chapter 10, many factors contribute to the making of poor-quality decisions, including a commonly occurring one—time pressure. This was one of the most important problems that led to the *Columbia* disaster. In this case, the time pressure was caused by top NASA officials to ready *Columbia* for an impending project—the launch of STS-120 scheduled for February 19, 2004. This date was considered vital, "etched in stone," insofar as the *Columbia* was going to carry a major section of the

International Space Station called Node 2, completing the core of that vessel. Several workers interviewed by CAIB reported that management's focus on holding firm to that date led safety considerations to be compromised. Because delays in any one mission necessitated delays in future launch dates, workers had a sense of "being under the gun." With razor-thin margins in schedules, managers were unwilling to do anything that slowed things down. This took the form of several practices that compromised the quality of decisions.

Training Was Compromised

One of the key problems linked to efforts to meet severe time pressure came in the form of inadequate training (see Chapter 3) for flight controllers (these are the individuals you usually see on television stationed in front of massive displays at Mission Control). In fact, seven flight controllers used on STS-107 lacked proper certification. Five of these were scheduled to work on subsequent missions without completing the proper recertification process.

Not only were these vital specialists at Mission Control not properly trained, but also their managers were too busy to notice. One reason for this reported by the board is that many of NASA's managers were themselves not properly trained. According to its report, "NASA does not have a standard agency-wide career planning process to prepare its junior and mid-level managers for advanced roles" (p. 223). (Career planning is discussed in Chapter 4.)

Deviance Was Normalized

When the space shuttle was designed, it was specified that its external tank not shed debris and that the orbiter not be hit by debris. Both events occurred routinely, however. In fact, foam was shed and debris hit the orbiter on 113 missions. Yet, because no serious problems resulted, such occurrences came to be interpreted as routine. They were considered something to be addressed in the course of readying the craft for its next mission instead of an imminent hazard to the vehicle and crew. The CAIB report notes that shuttle program managers ignored their own rules by reinterpreting foam problems as posing what NASA referred to as an "acceptable risk" instead of a "safety-of-flight issue." According to the board, the key to this practice of "normalizing deviance" was the result of intense pressure to meet flight schedules. Because adhering to its own rules would have meant delaying scheduled launches, NASA managers found it convenient to ignore them in the name of expedience.

Life at NASA Was Highly Stressful

One of the most apparent ways in which time pressure can contribute adversely to job performance—especially the making of bad decisions—is by creating levels of stress with which people have difficulty coping (see Chapter 4). This appears to have been the case in the Space Shuttle Program. When NASA committed to maintain its projects despite Congress's reluctance to boost its budget, the agency was forced to find places to cut costs. One of the most obvious possibilities was to close one or more of its several human space flight centers located around the country. However, mere thoughts of doing so met with strong resistance from both contractors and the congressional delegations of the states in which those centers are located. With these "off limits," NASA's leaders were forced to cut drastically the size of the work-force as the primary means of lowering the shuttle's operating costs. This occurred steadily throughout the 1990s. The result was higher levels of stress among NASA employees, which stemmed from several sources.

- Workers were overburdened with higher workloads as they struggled to compensate for the reduction in the size of the workforce.
- Those who survived the layoffs were left feeling highly insecure about their futures with the agency.
- Because there were many changes being made in the nature of work being done (e.g., as workers were reassigned), workers felt considerable uncertainty about what they were expected to do.

By 2000, it had become clear to NASA that the workforce reductions had gone too far. As one official put it, "Five years of buyouts and downsizing have led to serious skill imbalances and an overtaxed core workforce. As more employees have departed, the workload and stress [on those] remaining have increased, with a corresponding increase in the potential for impacts to operational capacity and safety" (p. 110).

Miscommunication Was Rampant

The CAIB report revealed several sources of miscommunication among NASA officials that appear to have contributed to the shuttle's demise.

Opportunities to Voice Concern Were Limited and Stifled

To begin, it is clear that because members of the Mission Management Team were overconfident, they failed to meet on a daily basis as required. Doing so might have made it easier for concerns about the foam debris to be heard. However, the board reports unsettling evidence that even when the Mission Management Team did meet, leaders noticeably rushed the proceedings along, making it impossible to raise any safety-of-flight issues. Furthermore, they "created huge barriers against dissenting opinions by stating preconceived conclusions based on subjective knowledge and experience, rather than on solid data" (p. 192). The same applied to the operations of the mission's highly specialized debris assessment team. Here, the word of one particular high-ranking official was taken at face value even if he lacked the appropriate expertise or evidence. Among others in this group, "the requirement for data was stringent and inhibiting, which resulted in information that warned of danger not being passed up the chain" (p. 202). Engineers, who are supposed to have an easy job of bringing safety problems to managers' attention, faced obstacles to doing so. They "found themselves in the unusual position that the situation was *unsafe*—a reversal of the usual requirement to prove that a situation is *safe*" (p. 169).

Instead of encouraging dissenting ideas to be heard, which is usually considered a useful way to avoid groupthink in decision making (see Chapter 10), NASA officials stifled such efforts. Although NASA managers told the board confidently that "everyone was encouraged to speak up about safety issues and that the agency was responsive to those concerns" (p. 202), it found evidence to the contrary. In fact, some members of the Debris Assessment Team reported that raising contrary points about the safety of the shuttle would lead them to be singled out for ridicule by peers and managers. This lead the CAIB to conclude that "managers demonstrated little concern for mission safety" (p. 192).

Vital Information Was Ignored

Communication problems came not only in the form of discouraging dissenting information from being voiced but also by way of allowing information to get lost or ignored as it worked its way up NASA's organizational hierarchy (see the discussion of this communication problem in Chapter 8). For example, while *Columbia* was in flight, two engineers who were aware of *Columbia*'s debris strike developed alternative landing plans that could have been used had the risk been deemed sufficiently great. Unfortunately, their concerns never reached officials on the Mission Management Team, which had operational control over *Columbia*.

Repeatedly, efforts to communicate dangers associated with foam striking the thermal protection system were ignored as they were "rolled up" the hierarchy. As a result, shuttle program managers heard little about it in their daily briefings. This effectively desensitized them to the problem, resulting in missed opportunities to fix it. "In perhaps the ultimate example of engineering concerns not making their way upstream, *Challenger* astronauts were told that the cold temperature was not a problem, and *Columbia* astronauts were told that the foam strike was not a problem" (p. 202).

A further opportunity to base decisions on useful information was ignored by failing to use independent checks on the decision-making process as required. According to NASA guidelines, a flight readiness review is supposed to be conducted by an independent team based on their analysis of available data about the flight. In the case of STS-107, this process was characterized by the mission management team's chairperson as being "lousy" insofar as the rationale to fly was "rubber-stamped" by officials who missed signals of potential danger because they succumbed to time pressure.

The CAIB blames NASA's leaders for these problems directly. It states that they had a greater obligation than managers "to create visible routes for the engineering community to express their views and receive information" (p. 169). Because they failed to meet this duty, the report continues, leaders "not only blocked the flow of information to managers, but they also prevented the downstream flow of information from managers to engineers" (p. 169). To managers who claim that they did not hear the engineers' concerns, the board replies bluntly that were "not asking or listening" (p. 170). Unfortunately, this left members of the Debris Assessment Team without any basis for understanding the reasoning behind Mission Control's decisions, thereby weakening their acceptance of those decisions (as discussed in Chapter 10).

NASA's Organizational Structure Impeded Communication

The CAIB's report concludes that many of the communication problems that led to the *Columbia* accident were inherent in the organizational structure of NASA's Space Shuttle Program itself. An organization chart (see Chapter 13) showing how this unit was organized at the time of the accident is shown in Figure C.1.

Figure C.1   The Space Shuttle Program: An Organization Chart

The structural complexity of NASA's Space Shuttle Program is revealed by this organization chart. The multiple layers of hierarchy and complex lines of authority created conditions that contributed to the *Columbia* accident.

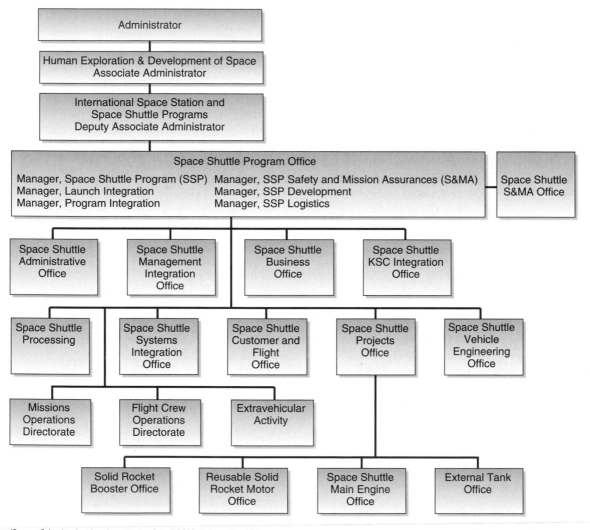

(Source: Columbia Accident Investigation Board, 2003; Volume 1, p. 17.)

NASA made many of the organizational changes recommended by the Rogers Commission report. Among these, the agency moved management of the Space Shuttle Program from the Johnson Space Center in Houston to NASA headquarters in Washington, DC. The intent of this move was to avoid many of the communication problems that were cited as responsible for the *Challenger* accident. Then, in 1996, this move was reversed by NASA Administrator Daniel S. Goldin, a self-proclaimed "agent of change" (p. 105). His rationale was that headquarters should concern itself only with strategic decisions (see Chapter 10) and that specific programs should be run from the agency's various field centers. This move resulted in conflict (see Chapter 7) insofar as it put the Marshall Space Center and the Kennedy Space Center under control of the Johnson Space Center, with which it previously operated at an equal level. This created a rivalry, as managers at Marshall and Kennedy did not readily accept the lead role of Johnson officials.

One of the key structural problems uncovered by the CAIB is that NASA is too complex to make efficient communication possible. As the agency developed over the years, requirements were put into place that made it unclear to many employees to exactly whom they were expected to report certain kinds of information. There was a serious lack of coordination with respect to safety—no centralized clearinghouse existed for information about safety and responsibility over it. The various units that shared these responsibilities at the time of the accident failed to coordinate their responsibilities in any organized fashion. The board referred to these roles as "uncoordinated," "conflicting," and "resulting in erroneous information" (p. 188). Its indictment of organizational structure is clear: "No one office or person in Program management is responsible for developing an integrated risk assessment. . . . The net effect is that many Shuttle Program safety, quality, and mission assurance roles are never clearly defined" (p. 188).

A Culture of Overconfidence Eclipsed Attention to Safety

From its inception, NASA's organizational culture (see Chapter 12) was characterized by "can-do" values and tenacity in the face of unprecedented challenges. After all, it was on an historic quest—not only to surpass the Soviet Union in the space race but also to reach the moon. On July 20, 1969, when Apollo 11 successfully landed on the moon, the dramatic success reinforced NASA's organizational culture. NASA employees believed they worked at "a perfect place," one that was viewed as "a highly successful organization capable of achieving seemingly impossible feats" and "the best organization that human beings could create to accomplish selected goals" (p. 102).

Culture Was Resistant to Change

Although there may have been a sound basis for these cultural beliefs in the 1960s, things changed quickly thereafter. With a secure victory in the space race, Congress felt less compelled to allocate generous budgets to NASA. At the same time, NASA moved from launching vehicles that were designed to be used only once to the Space Shuttle Program and launching vehicles that were reused to provide more routine access to space. The NASA of the 1970s was far more bureaucratic. The Appollo-era focus on designing new spacecraft at any expense was supplanted by new demands of flying a reusable vehicle repeatedly on an ever-tightening budget.

Despite these new realities, the culture at NASA did not adjust. "NASA personnel maintained a vision of their agency that was rooted in the glories of an earlier time, even as the world, and thus the context within which the space agency operated, changed around them" (p. 102). Because NASA's culture never fully adapted to the Space Shuttle Program, tension resulted. Employees continued to believe that the agency was still a "prefect place," leading them to resist change by rejecting evidence to the contrary (see Chapter 14). In the aftermath of the *Challenger* accident, however, this proved difficult. Yet, NASA's culture of success was so strong that it led managers to misperceive reality in order to make it conform to their beliefs (see Chapter 3). As managers strove to maintain their view of their organization, "they lost their ability to accept criticism, leading them to reject the recommendations of many boards and blue-ribbon panels, the Rogers Commission, among them" (p. 102). And, of course, by ignoring these recommendations, the agency insulated itself from corrective influences that were necessary to fix problems (this is the kind of thing that occurs in the course of groupthink; see Chapter 10). This led to "flawed decision making, self-deception, introversion and a diminished curiosity about the world outside the 'perfect place'" (p. 102). Experts within NASA even warned that such complacency "could lead to serious mishaps" (p. 108).

Safety Culture Was Broken

In its report the CAIB asks, "How could NASA have missed the signals the foam was sending?" (p. 184). The answer, it subsequently was determined, was "that detection of the dangers posed by foam was impeded by 'blind spots' in NASA's safety culture" (p. 124). Managers repeatedly told the board that the foam posed "no safety-of-flight issue" (p. 184), but its own investigation revealed otherwise. Specifically, "Shuttle Program management made erroneous assumptions about the robustness of a system based on prior success rather than on dependable engineering data and rigorous testing" (p. 104). Furthermore, "Shuttle Program safety personnel failed to adequately assess anomalies and frequently accepted critical risks without qualitative or quantitative support, even when the tools to provide more comprehensive assessments were available" (p. 177). Hence, NASA's safety culture was badly broken.

A key manifestation of this problem may be seen in the way in which Shuttle Program managers responded to requests for imagery from the Debris Assessment Team (the unit that was specifically in charge of assessing the impact of debris on the spacecraft). Instead of providing this information freely, as expected, managers made members of the Debris Assessment Team prove that there was a threat to safety involved before they would consent to doing so. According to the board, this is precisely the opposite of what would occur in a safety-conscious organizational culture. Typically, in organizations that deal routinely with matters of life and death, the burden of proof comes in the form of establishing that conditions are safe. In this case, however, NASA inverted this burden of proof.

Checks and Balances on Safety Were Absent

One particularly troublesome manifestation of NASA's deeply entrenched cultural belief in its own prowess and invulnerability was its willingness to eliminate the system of checks and balances on safety functions that was a hallmark of the Apollo program. Historically, two completely independent engineering teams cross-checked one another to prevent catastrophic errors. Although this practice was expensive, it was highly effective. Over time, however, NASA managers came to believe that the design of the space shuttle was sufficiently mature, making it "operational" rather than "developmental" and making the redundant procedures unnecessary. Based on the culture of success and supported by intense budgetary pressures, this cost-saving move was readily justified.

Despite this, many of NASA's top engineers protested. For example, in a letter to President Clinton on August 25, 1995, senior Kennedy Space Center engineer José Garcia claimed that eliminating this system of checks and balances constituted "the biggest threat to the safety of the crew since the *Challenger* disaster" (p. 108). Likewise, a report by the Shuttle Independent Assessment Team dated March 2000 cautioned against the "success-engendered safety optimism" that permeated the agency, cautioning the Space Shuttle Program to "rigorously guard against the tendency to accept risk solely because of prior success" and by "the desire to reduce costs" (p. 114).

Ultimately, NASA managers "won" this battle (if you can call it that). The engineers' concerns about risk and safety ultimately were defeated by management's belief that foam could not hurt the orbiter and by its zeal to keep on schedule. The rest, as they say, is history.

Conclusion

The *Columbia* Accident Investigation Board Report makes it clear that NASA's organizational problems contributed greatly to the shuttle's accident. No one single management mistake was responsible but rather it was the combined effect of many. "Each decision, taken by itself, seemed correct, routine, and indeed, insignificant and unremarkable. Yet, in retrospect, the cumulative effect was stunning" (p. 203). Indeed, it appears to be the case, as the board concludes, that "NASA has shown very little understanding of the inner workings of its own organization" (p. 202). With an eye toward the well-being of tomorrow's astronauts, and with the benefits of manned space exploration in mind, I hope that recommendations from the CAIB report are taken seriously. I also hope that readers of this book will heed the lessons learned from this case so as to avoid tragic misjudgments about key OB issues in their own organizations.

Case Note

Columbia Accident Investigation Board (2003, August). Volume 1. Washington, DC: U.S. Government Printing Office. All page references are for quotations from this report. Report also is available on the World Wide Web at www.caib.us.

Index

Page numbers in **bold** refer to figures